SLY AND ABLE

SLY AND ABLE

A Political Biography
of
James F. Byrnes

by

DAVID ROBERTSON

W·W·NORTON & COMPANY

New York   London

Copyright © 1994 by David Robertson
All rights reserved
Printed in the United States of America

First Edition

The text of this book is composed in Times Roman
with the display set in Benguiat
Composition by PennSet
Manufacturing by The Haddon Craftsmen, Inc.
Book design by Jacques Chazaud

Library of Congress Cataloging-in-Publication Data

Robertson, David, 1947 Aug. 11–
Sly and able : a political biography of James F. Byrnes / by David Robertson.
    p.   cm.
Includes bibliographical references and index.
1. Byrnes, James Francis, 1879–1972. 2. Legislators—United
States—Biography. 3. United States. Congress. Senate—Biography.
4. Cabinet officers—United States—Biography. 5. Governors—South
Carolina—Biography. I. Title.
E748.B975R63   1994
975.7′043′092 — dc20
[B]   93-19329

ISBN 0-393-03367-8

W. W. Norton & Company, Inc., 500 Fifth Avenue, New York, N.Y. 10110
W. W. Norton & Company Ltd., 10 Coptic Street, London WC1A 1PU

1 2 3 4 5 6 7 8 9 0

To S.L.M.,
for the beauty of her honesty

"Byrnes, whom enemies call the slyest, and friends call the ablest, member of the Senate, does not appear to have been born to wear the toga."

—JOSEPH ALSOP and ROBERT KINTNER
The Saturday Evening Post,
July 20, 1940

CONTENTS

PREFACE

Political power, not public fame, quickened the pulse of James F. "Jimmy" Byrnes. And as that pulse quickened for ninety years, Jimmy Byrnes—a former U.S. congressman, a former U.S. senator, a former associate justice of the U.S. Supreme Court, a former U.S. secretary of state, and a former state governor—continued to be influential on a national scale until only a few years before his death in 1972. Byrnes is arguably among the most experienced and least known of the "wise men" who exercised great political power just below the office of the president during the Roosevelt, Truman, Eisenhower, and Nixon administrations.

Nor did Jimmy Byrnes consider the office of the presidency itself to be beyond his abilities; and in attempting the possession of the Oval Office, Byrnes, who was known throughout the war years of the 1940s as the "assistant president," did not fail for lack of trying. Twice this intensely private and ambitious man from South Carolina was encouraged by Franklin Roosevelt to become his vice-presidential running mate, once in 1940 and again in 1944; and twice Roosevelt withdrew his political support for Byrnes' nomination at a critical moment during the party's national conventions after objections to Byrnes' nomination by the liberal wing of the

Democratic party and by organized labor and enfranchised black voters as his being "too southern."

Thus did Harry S. Truman accept his party's nomination to the vice presidency in 1944 with the speech folded inside his coat pocket that the Missouri senator only the day before had intended to deliver to the national convention, nominating Jimmy Byrnes to be Franklin Roosevelt's running mate. And thus did Truman, the day of FDR's death, call upon Jimmy Byrnes as the most politically experienced man Truman knew in Washington to become the U.S. secretary of state in 1945 and next in succession to the presidency, as the Constitution then provided.

By both instinct and preference, Byrnes avoided the limelight at the State Department that his successors George Marshall and Dean Acheson later found; but Byrnes' behind-the-scenes advice to the president in regard to the use of the atomic bomb and the United States' relations with the Soviet Union from 1945 to 1947 was so pervasive, and so carefully disguised, that one revisionist historian has described Jimmy Byrnes as the "forgotten man" in any discussion of the origins of the Cold War.

Following his retirement from the State Department, Byrnes began yet another career as his state's governor and as the obliquely powerful organizer of massive resistance to the social and economic policies of the Truman administration. Here again Byrnes' presence was of prime significance, but of little public memory. Together in the 1930s, Jimmy Byrnes and Franklin Roosevelt had consulted to create the largest public works program on the East Coast, the building of hydroelectric dams and flooding of the Santee River basin in South Carolina. Close to half a century later, this permanent flooding of rural roads in the Santee basin, isolating schools restricted to black children, led Thurgood Marshall to file the court suit in Clarendon County, South Carolina, that later was combined with other suits to become the historic *Brown* v. *Board of Education* decision by the Supreme Court in 1954.

Byrnes' political power underwent one more metamorphosis, as he succeeded in implementing the so-called southern strategy, which delivered his once Solid South to Richard Nixon and the Republican party in 1968. Here, as always, his political presence was profound, but seldom publicly seen. Also unseen were his countless private and political acts of liberality, which belied his identification throughout his lifetime with any ideology or racism. Byrnes was recognized by Walter White of the NAACP and by Sidney Hillman of the CIO as a foe to black voters and to organized labor, yet this most Bourbon of southern politicians contributed money to strike funds in his state and personally financed the higher education of many black citizens of South Carolina. A fiscal conservative, Byrnes frequently had provided Franklin Roosevelt with the necessary Senate votes that fundamentally changed the social and economic fabric of the United States and guaranteed the political success of the New Deal.

The complexity and the intuitive subtlety of Byrnes' motives make his political life a fascinating study of how a once obscure man possessed great political power, and how political power possesses a man, before leading once again to obscurity. It is this quality of the unknown and of the unknowable in the life of any greatly influential man or woman that both attracts and torments biographers and that leads such writers to try to construct what Walter Pater once called the "subjective immortality" of writing biographies. Not only Jimmy Byrnes but many of his once powerful political friends and enemies are now forgotten, although both domestically and internationally we live in the political world they created. To the degree that this book can with historical accuracy re-create the "subjective immortality" of the lives of Jimmy Byrnes and of such of his contemporaries as Sidney Hillman, Pitchfork Ben Tillman, and Walter White, it will have succeeded.

SLY AND ABLE

"Jimmy, You're Close to Me Personally."

Franklin Roosevelt and Jimmy Byrnes together sang a love song. Each man was proud of his voice, and each enjoyed singing sentimental ballads in the company of friends. Roosevelt was a full baritone, with all the subtle modulations of his patrician upbringing; Byrnes was an Irish tenor, and sang with a noticeable southern accent. At the time of their duet, the two men were at the height of their political powers, and they had known each other for more than thirty years. The song Roosevelt and Byrnes chose to sing together was a mutual favorite entitled "When I Grow Too Old to Dream, I'll Have You to Remember."

The occasion was the birthday party for Jimmy Byrnes held at the White House the evening of May 2, 1943. President Roosevelt was the party's host, and as his guests arrived outside the Oval Office, their gathering quickly became a lighthearted ending to a day of national crisis. That morning, a Sunday, Byrnes had gone to work in his office at the East Wing not knowing if by nightfall the United States would have enough coal supplies to continue fighting the world war. For weeks, wildcat strikes in coal mines across the country had threatened to shut down the nation's war industries, and shipments of military supplies to American forces overseas were in danger of being delayed for lack of fuel. At home, the miners' union and owners of the coal pits had been unable to agree on wages; and in response to the halt in production, Roosevelt on Saturday had nationalized the mines. Even though the federal government was now their new employer and though Roosevelt had promised an eventual pay raise, miners had continued in their refusal to work. There were rumors over the weekend that the president planned to arrest John L. Lewis, head of the United Mine Workers Union, or that he would call on the Army to mine coal. In issuing his executive order seizing the mines, Roosevelt had promised to address the nation about the coal situation in a "fireside chat" on Sunday evening.

Byrnes had worked throughout Sunday morning and afternoon, helping prepare the speech the president would read over the radio that night. No one knew what the miners would do. As the wartime director of economic stabilization, Byrnes was responsible for holding firm against any demands by the miners for increased wages; but he also had the job of staying in touch with negotiations being held that weekend between officials of the miners' union and the secretary of the interior. The government needed the miners back at work, and both sides knew it; troops were unskilled at digging out the coal and were badly needed elsewhere. To gain the miners' cooperation, Byrnes was willing to concede some pay raises, but he had to walk a fine line. He knew that too many concessions on his part could lead to angry walkouts by other labor groups that earlier had agreed to his "hold the line" policy on pay increases. Between the president's calls for revisions on his speech and the ringing telephones from Interior, Byrnes' small White House office became a hectic clearinghouse in the strike. Another man might have been overwhelmed, but in a political crisis Jimmy Byrnes seemed to thrive. Although he was physically small, Byrnes had the small man's trick of appearing to multiply himself in a fight, and he turned up everywhere, his darting gray-blue eyes scanning documents before he quickly gave directions to his staff. Talking over the telephone with negotiators, or taking into his confidence a visitor to his office, Byrnes alternated between threats and cajolery, both delivered in his persistent South Carolina accent. It was a masterful performance, which both his staff and much of official Washington had witnessed for years: the combination of Deep South charmer and Irish tough guy that was Jimmy Byrnes in political action.

One of the staff members had left a radio on, and the newscaster mentioned that this date, May 2, was Jimmy Byrnes' birthday. Byrnes laughed, and noted that the Sunday afternoon was more than that: it was also his wedding anniversary. With a petulant good humor characteristic of him, Byrnes remarked that "it was a devil of a way to spend a wedding anniversary and birthday, to say nothing of the Lord's Day!" His remark got back to the president. Franklin Roosevelt enjoyed expressing his affection for Jimmy Byrnes in acts of one-upmanship, and in the middle of a national labor crisis the president found time to arrange for a White House automobile to pick up Maude Byrnes later that night to join her husband at work. Jimmy Byrnes would have his birthday party after all, Roosevelt had declared; they would all celebrate in the Oval Office after the president's address to the nation that evening.

At ten o'clock that night Roosevelt went on the air. His radio speech had been partly written by Byrnes, but the performance was purely the president's. Speaking into the network microphones at his desk, Roosevelt announced his intention to use the Army, if necessary, to safeguard production at the mines. "Coal will be mined no matter what any individual thinks of it." But, once having stated his position in the strongest of political terms, Roosevelt now adopted a seemingly nonpolitical, intimately personal tone of voice. Tonight he was talking not only to the miners, he explained, but also "to their wives and children." Roosevelt described to a listening nation how the sons from those mining families "at this very minute—this split second—may be fighting in New Guinea or in the Aleutian Islands or Guadalcanal or Tunisia or China." The toughness of those miners' sons did not surprise him, Roosevelt said. "They come of fine, rugged stock." He ended his fireside chat by asking the miners, as he would ask a favor of a neighborhood family he had known for years, simply to come back to work. "Tomorrow the Stars and Stripes will fly over the coal mines," Roosevelt said. "I hope that every miner will be at work under that flag." It was a request astonishing both in its familiarity and in its arrogance: only Roosevelt could have brought it off.

But in a sense, the fix was in, and Roosevelt knew it. Minutes before the broadcast, Byrnes had hurried to the president with the news that John L. Lewis had agreed to a "truce" and was issuing a directive to the United Mine Workers calling off the strike. Either because he did not trust Lewis' personal word or because he trusted most in his own, almost magical powers of persuasion, Roosevelt had decided to go ahead with his speech. Afterward, with the miners headed back to work and Lewis upstaged at the last moment, Roosevelt was in a mood to celebrate. He pushed away from his desk and called his staff around him like a happy family. Then, looking up at Jimmy and Maude Byrnes, the president smiled and led his White House party in singing "Happy Birthday."

For a few hours these old friends forgot the war and the coal strike. Roosevelt had invited as his guests those members of his staff who had worked with him on his speech, and with whom he felt most comfortable. Besides Jimmy Byrnes and his wife, the others invited to his office that night were Grace Tully, the president's personal secretary; Steve Early, the White House press secretary; and Roosevelt's two longtime advisers Robert Sherwood and Harry Hopkins. On these occasions, Roosevelt usually insisted on himself mixing cocktails for the guests, in a manner that inevitably made Robert Sherwood think of a smiling and cheerfully inaccurate alchemist; and that evening, after drinks, Sherwood became the life of the party, dancing and imitating even the flapping of wings as he sang "When the Red, Red Robin Comes Bob, Bob, Bobbin' Along."

Roosevelt and Byrnes also exchanged lighthearted banter, as they had done for years. Byrnes on this birthday turned sixty-one, the same age as Franklin Roosevelt. Roosevelt knew that Jimmy Byrnes was an ambitious man, and throughout the coming year he would enjoy telling Byrnes that a man in his sixties was too old to run for any higher office. Jimmy Byrnes always gave as good as he got, even to the president of the United States. "That's a nice one," Byrnes would retort, his eyes flashing. "I worked ten hours a day around here doing your work." Byrnes always smiled at his boss when he made that remark, but President Roosevelt never denied the truth in Byrnes' statement.

That night, however, there had been work enough for everyone, including Roosevelt, and the president made certain that executive praise reached each person in the room. There were also rewards to be given out. Byrnes' toughness during the coal negotiations had impressed Roosevelt; by the end of May he had promoted Jimmy Byrnes from the Office of Economic Stabilization to a job newly created especially for Byrnes— director of war mobilization. With the exception of the presidency, the office of war mobilizer was to become the most powerful in government. Nor did this promotion necessarily show the limit of Franklin Roosevelt's generosity. For on that evening of May 2, 1943, as these two old friends sang their duet, another, unspoken birthday gift to Jimmy Byrnes was in the air: the gift of the vice-presidential nomination and, after Roosevelt's death, the gift of the presidency itself.

The fact was that President Roosevelt was dying. To the public, he was still the same, familiar FDR of a thousand newsreels: Americans instantly recognized the leonine head thrown back, the absolutely confident laugh from his wheelchair, the stylish cigarette holder clinched upward at a jaunty angle, the sure grasping of a stranger's hand while he pronounced the surprised recipient "my dear friend." But behind this public image was a private individual of declining health. His presiding over the nation's plunge into war had by 1943 begun to exacerbate a serious heart disease. The president's health always had been precarious since his earlier, incomplete recovery from polio, but by now his debilities no longer were concealable from his staff. The White House was unsettled further by Roosevelt's unannounced intention to run for a fourth term. Roosevelt was almost certain to be reelected in 1944 and destined, many believed, to die in office. The current vice president, Henry Wallace, was unpopular with the Democratic organization and was rumored by White House staffers who were friends of Byrnes, such as General Edwin "Pa" Watson, to be replaced on the next ticket. Whoever was chosen by Roosevelt as his new running mate was, therefore, likely to succeed to the executive office after the president's death. And in the year following that birthday party at the White House, the man whom Roosevelt was favoring as his likely successor was Jimmy Byrnes.

Roosevelt's appointment of Byrnes in 1943 as director of war mobilization marked a giant step in that direction. In effect, Roosevelt had simply split between the two of them the duties of being president. Roosevelt continued as commander in chief to concentrate on military and diplomatic responsibilities, but after mid-1943 the domestic business of the nation was left to be managed by Jimmy Byrnes. In his earlier position as director of economic stabilization, Byrnes had been responsible for controlling wartime wages and profits; now he was directly in charge of managing the nation's defense industries. This increase in powers was immense. Through his wartime directorate, Byrnes controlled the distribution within the United States of all military and civilian supplies; he determined rents; and he regulated the rationing of the nation's food, fuel, and clothing.

After 1943 considerable de facto powers were also added to Byrnes' job. With increasing frequency, Roosevelt was abroad in late 1943 and 1944, conferring with Allied leaders at sites that were often of dubious security. Byrnes usually was told by Roosevelt to be "in charge" during these absences. As an additional precaution, the president before traveling out of the country signed blank executive orders, which then were locked in Jimmy Byrnes' office safe at the East Wing. In an emergency, Byrnes was to unlock the safe and fill out the executive order, calling for whatever action he thought necessary.

Inevitably, newspapers had by 1944 begun referring to Byrnes as the "assistant president." The title was to Jimmy Byrnes' mind perfectly apt, but to Franklin Roosevelt it was annoying. The president recollected that there had been a temporary division of wartime responsibility, not of executive authority. Nevertheless, shortly before announcing for a fourth term, Roosevelt acknowledged in a memo to Byrnes that, between them, the two men controlled much of the presidency. The words were chosen, however, with that intriguing ambiguity that always had been as much a part of Roosevelt as his sunny smile. "You have been called 'The Assistant President,' " Roosevelt wrote Byrnes in June 1944, "and the appellation comes close to the truth."

If Byrnes became close to Roosevelt, it was because, like the president himself, he had matured as a politician from a background of both adversity and privilege. Byrnes did not share with Roosevelt the adversity of a physical handicap, but neither had he enjoyed Franklin Roosevelt's inherited money and family connections. Byrnes had worked hard for what he had gotten. Although a former Supreme Court justice, Byrnes had no formal education beyond the seventh grade, when he had dropped out of school to work full-time; and although he now occasionally enjoyed boasting of his friendship with Bernard Baruch, one of the nation's wealthiest men, Jimmy Byrnes had as a boy once sold pies on the streets of Charleston to help support his mother. The deficiencies in the backgrounds of both Roosevelt and Byrnes had made the men complementary to each other and, in many ways, had made them rivals as well. Roosevelt publicly outshone Byrnes at making friends; but behind the scenes Jimmy Byrnes was the better politician, and he knew it.

Byrnes' political primacy over Roosevelt went back years, to before his Supreme Court days, when Byrnes as a senator had managed many of the most important New Deal pieces of legislation. It was a truism among old-timers in the administration that President Roosevelt had never lost a bill that Senator Byrnes had supported, and the president had never been able to win passage of a bill that Byrnes had opposed. In the White House, Byrnes' base of political power in 1944 still was in the U.S. Senate, the result of friendships there with committee chairmen whom Byrnes had carefully nourished over a decade. Throughout the Capitol, Byrnes was fondly remembered as the host of "bullbat time"—after-hours drinking get-togethers held in Byrnes' office and named for the southern bird that appears at dusk. There, after a hard day's work tending to the nation's business, senators would relax in an atmosphere of friendly gossip, while Jimmy Byrnes generously poured the bourbon and led the group in singing old favorites, such as "Flow Gently, Sweet Afton."

But not everyone liked Jimmy Byrnes. Harry Hopkins, despite his past conflicts with Byrnes over fiscal and relief policies, had been the first to recommend in 1941 that President Roosevelt ask Byrnes voluntarily to leave the Supreme Court and become the director of economic stabilization. One day early in 1942, when Byrnes was arranging his East Wing office, Hopkins had dropped by to ask if he could be of any further assistance. "There's just one suggestion I want to make to you, Harry," Byrnes had said, smiling pleasantly. "Keep the hell out of my business." Now, two years later, Hopkins was chronically ill, and Byrnes had taken over many of his administrative duties. Convalescing at his Georgetown home, Hopkins regarded Byrnes from a wounded distance.

Byrnes' sudden rise to national power also had caused misgivings among organized labor and among Negro voters in the Democratic party. Union leaders knew Jimmy Byrnes as the enforcer of the administration's "hold the line" policy on wage increases, and after years of bitter confrontations, Byrnes and Sidney Hillman, political chairman of the Congress of Industrial Organizations, no longer bothered to conceal the rancorous dislike each man felt in the other's presence. Byrnes' relationships with blacks were more complex. In South Carolina individual black people usually spoke well of Jimmy Byrnes among themselves, and they recognized him as a white man with whom they could deal; but above the Mason-Dixon line Byrnes was profoundly distrusted by Negro political leaders. They were not impressed in the North by his private acts of friendship, and they wanted a public statement of support on civil rights and equal opportunity of hiring for defense jobs. Such a statement Byrnes would not give. Together these two opposition groups found an unexpected third ally among churchgoers. Byrnes had been born a Catholic, and although he later converted to Protestantism, in typical fashion he continued to enjoy a warm personal and political friendship with the Catholic archbishop of New York, Francis Cardinal Spellman. This arrangement, while it apparently satisfied Jimmy Byrnes' soul, satisfied practically no one else; and Democrats from both the rural, Protestant South and the urban, Catholic Northeast raised uneasy questions about Jimmy Byrnes' religious sincerity.

Byrnes was aware of these enmities, and together with his overwork as war mobilizer they had by 1944 begun to affect his previously unruffled personality. He was becoming high-strung, and quick to perceive a quarrel, a different person from the congenial southern administrator who had exercised great national power without ever quite appearing to do so. His defensive use of shorthand was an example of the change that had come over him. As a young man, Byrnes had learned shorthand at his mother's insistence, and lately he had acquired the disquieting habit of openly taking notes on his conversations with other politicians. He did so, Byrnes explained, so that there would be no misunderstandings later. What was more disturbing was that his notes were more a private language to himself than a record to be shared with others. Byrnes had altered the standard shorthand symbols into strange glyphs of hooks and slashes only he could read.

This secretive part of his nature was so distinct from his personality as a whole that to onlookers there appeared at times to be almost two separate individuals named Jimmy Byrnes. The first was the public Byrnes, whom everyone knew and most men liked: easygoing, courtly, always ready to assuage another politician's bruised ego with a helping of bourbon. Then, in an instant, Byrnes would become the other: snappish, wounded, self-protective.

How far these characteristics had prejudiced Franklin Roosevelt against him by the summer of 1944 was what Jimmy Byrnes had to find out in a hurry. The Democratic convention would open in Chicago in the third week of July, and by the middle of that month the president had not stated any preference for his new running mate; for reasons either of declining health or simply of guile, Roosevelt seemed inclined to let the convention select a vice president for him. Byrnes had not yet publicly declared his interest in the office, but if the president remained neutral, Byrnes knew he could count on support by more than seven hundred delegates who favored his candidacy. If, however, Roosevelt was not sincere in wanting an open convention, Byrnes knew, those seven hundred votes would vanish as soon as the presidential smile faded at the mention of Jimmy Byrnes' name. "You are the most qualified man in the whole outfit," Roosevelt had told Byrnes earlier that month, when they had talked about Byrnes' prospects to gain the vice presidency. Byrnes had expressed misgivings. "You must not get out of the race," Roosevelt had assured him. "If you stay in, you are sure to win."

Roosevelt was capable of both sincerity and honesty, but Byrnes knew that the president rarely practiced more than one virtue at a time. Accordingly, Byrnes met with Roosevelt on Thursday morning, July 13, 1944, six days before the convention was to open. At their Oval Office meeting, the president repeated his enthusiasm for having Byrnes on the ticket and his intention of not interfering with the convention's choice of a vice president. Roosevelt himself would not be at the convention, he told Byrnes; he was leaving that night for his home in Hyde Park, New York, and later would go on an extended tour of American military bases in the Pacific theater. But Roosevelt was taking action that would demonstrate to the delegates his faith in his war mobilizer as a future vice president. While Roosevelt was out of the country, he told Byrnes, he would make it clear that Jimmy Byrnes was "to be in charge." The meeting concluded to Byrnes' satisfaction, and he would have left the executive offices with a mind untroubled except for one particular. On his way out, walking along the white colonnade by the West Lawn, Byrnes passed Sidney Hillman of the CIO on his way to the Oval Office. Hillman also had an appointment with the president.

The next morning the *New York Times* headlined a story on Democratic contenders for the vice-presidential nomination "Byrnes Still High on 'Probable' List." That same Friday morning, the postmaster general, Frank Walker, asked Byrnes to join him for lunch. Walker usually acted as a functionary of the Democratic party, and also joining them, he told Byrnes, would be Bob Hannegan, the party's current national chairman. They would talk and eat at the apartment of a mutual friend. Byrnes may have had the worldly man's suspicion of being invited to lunch by the numerically superior side at their expense. If so, the suspicion was well founded. Over the food, Walker explained that he and Hannegan had been talking with the president; there had been a change, he told Byrnes, in Roosevelt's previous neutrality. If asked, the two party leaders now would have to say that Roosevelt did in fact have favorites among the vice-presidential contenders. The president had made clear his preferences, Walker said, and the men he had named were not in this room. As his vice president, Roosevelt now wanted either Supreme Court Justice William O. Douglas or the politically obscure Senator Harry S. Truman from Missouri.

Byrnes' face may have showed alarm at what he was told, but he was seldom taken aback. He quickly rejoined that on the preceding day the president had promised not to interfere with the convention's selection of the vice president, and that Roosevelt had emphasized that he would not state a preference. Walker and Hannegan seemed unimpressed. "I don't understand it," Hannegan said.

Jimmy Byrnes, however, immediately understood the situation. To his mind it had the classic characteristics of the Rooseveltian dismissal. The bad news would be delivered by a subordinate while the president, regrettably, would be out of town. If Byrnes was to have a chance at saving his vice-presidential nomination, he would have to move fast. Leaving the apartment, he returned to his office; placing a pad and pencil in front of himself for stenographic notes, he then asked the White House operator to connect him with the president at his home at Hyde Park, New York.

Over long-distance, Roosevelt's voice usually boomed so loudly through the telephone receiver that his words could be heard throughout the room. "Jimmy, that is all wrong," declared the confident voice from up the Hudson River. "That is not what I told them. That is what they told me." Byrnes then listened as Roosevelt explained his discussion with party leaders about possible vice-presidential candidates. The war mobilizer's fingers busily took down a stenographic record. "They all agreed that Truman would cost fewer votes than anybody, and probably Douglas second," Roosevelt said. "That was the agreement they reached and I had nothing to do with it. I was asking questions. I did not express myself. Objections to you came from labor people, both Federation and CIO."

Byrnes considered this new interpretation of Roosevelt's wishes. His cautious gray-blue eyes saw an opening. Roosevelt might be maneuvered into making a pro-Byrnes statement if the president thought it necessary to countermand any action by Hannegan or Walker. "If they make the statement that you expressed a preference for Truman or Douglas," Byrnes offered, "it would make it very difficult for me."

"We have to be damned careful about language," Roosevelt shot back. "They asked if I would object to Truman or Douglas and I said no. That is different from using the word 'prefer.' That is not expressing a preference"—here came Roosevelt's unspoken refusal of Byrnes' implicit request—"because you know I told you I would have no preference."

The finesse had failed. Roosevelt could not be trapped that easily. Still, the president hated to end a conversation with such an old friend without adding some encouraging words. "Will you go on and run?" Roosevelt asked. The almost irresistible Rooseveltian charm now came into play, and the president adopted his easy manner of talking about struggles for power as if they were the childhood pastimes of an idle hour. "After all, Jimmy, you're close to me personally," Roosevelt said. "I hardly know Truman. Douglas is a poker player. He is good in a poker game and he tells good stories."

Byrnes had heard enough. Roosevelt's transcribed statements would pass as sufficient proof to any wavering delegate that the president was neutral toward all vice-presidential contestants. Byrnes decided to declare his candidacy publicly. He ended his conversation with the president with small talk on both sides, but Byrnes could not resist a final jest at Roosevelt's expense. Roosevelt had told Byrnes in parting that the stories told by Supreme Court Justice William Douglas "are just as spicy as mine." Byrnes was in a position to judge, since he had served both with Douglas on the Supreme Court and with Roosevelt in the White House. Douglas' stories, he told Roosevelt, were better.

After putting down the telephone receiver with some satisfaction, Byrnes walked down the White House corridor and informed Harry Hopkins of his decision. Then he returned to his office. He had another important phone call to place.

Harry Truman was packing his bags at Independence, Missouri, that Friday morning. With his wife and daughter, he was traveling to the Democratic convention, and he liked to get an early start. Just as the Truman family was about to leave, the phone rang. Jimmy Byrnes was on the line with some unusual questions for Senator Truman. Byrnes asked if reports were true that Truman was uninterested in the vice presidency. At his end, Truman repeated that he was satisfied to remain where he was in the Senate. Byrnes then asked a question even more unexpected. At the convention, would Truman be willing to place Byrnes' name into nomination for the vice presidency? Truman understood Byrnes to say that he was seeking that office only because President Roosevelt wanted Byrnes on the ticket. Faced with this sudden request, the Missourian was both surprised and pleased. He was pleased that he could be of use at least indirectly to a president whom he admired; but he was surprised that such an experienced politician as Jimmy Byrnes would seek a junior senator such as himself to deliver the nomination speech. Only years afterward did Truman consider that by promising to make that speech, he might have eliminated himself from becoming the vice president. That morning he said yes.

At his desk in the White House, Jimmy Byrnes quietly thanked Harry Truman and replaced the telephone receiver. The man whom the nation called the assistant president had worked very hard for this moment. For years Byrnes always had taken care to pretend that the powers in his possession had come to him almost casually, just short of accidentally. As a consequence, Jimmy Byrnes had risen to the highest circles of government as an indispensable presence. Yet even men whom he most influenced had never been, to Byrnes' mind, fully aware of his own superiority. Such had been the conditions under which he had served Franklin Roosevelt for years, both in the executive offices during the coal strike and, earlier, on the Supreme Court and in the U.S. Senate. As of this moment, those days were over. Tomorrow he and Maude would leave Union Station on a train to Chicago. In a few days Roosevelt and Byrnes banners would have to be ordered. Then all that would remain for Jimmy Byrnes would be to go to the convention hall and claim his nomination.

Of course, he never made it. Byrnes did go to Chicago, but another man was chosen by Roosevelt to become his vice president and, ultimately, his successor. Franklin Roosevelt died within five months of his election to a fourth term, and two weeks before his death he spent a few moments rereading his letter accepting Jimmy Byrnes' resignation. Byrnes could never forgive what he considered to be the president's duplicity in choosing another man as his vice president, and he had resigned his position as war mobilizer. "It's a shame some people are so prima-donnish," Roosevelt had said.

Yet within a week after Roosevelt's death, Byrnes was back in government. His career was fated to take another turn, unanticipated by him or anyone else in 1944. Ahead of Byrnes was his appointment as secretary of state by President Truman, and the historic conferences and speeches —Stuttgart, Potsdam—that would inexorably link his name to the beginnings of the Cold War. For him there would be negotiations with Stalin and dinners with Churchill. There would also be inevitable disagreements with Harry Truman, and Byrnes' subsequent resignation from State.

After fame would come honors. Byrnes would return home to South Carolina to be elected, at age sixty-eight, the state's governor. As a respected elder statesman, he would be courted by national politicians, but Jimmy Byrnes would never again support the Democrat candidate in a presidential election. After receiving Byrnes' political endorsement, President Eisenhower would appoint the governor as a delegate to the United Nations. President Nixon later would seek out Jimmy Byrnes for his inveterate ability to change voters' minds, and in his advanced old age Byrnes would be the moving spirit for the Republican party's resurgence throughout the South. But neither party could give him the high office for which he had been so prepared, and Jimmy Byrnes would see the presidency pass time after time into hands less worthy, in his estimation, than his own.

After honors would come obscurity. Following his death in 1972, Byrnes would be quickly forgotten by a world where he had shaped many of the postwar realities. Even in his native South Carolina, he would be remembered by an aging generation more with a general affection than with a specific regard. A younger generation would remember Jimmy Byrnes practically not at all.

Jimmy Byrnes was the man who would be president. That he failed in this ambition was not due to any lack of ability on his part, much less of slyness; the political career of Jimmy Byrnes gives evidence that he possessed both these qualities to a remarkable degree. Rather, the career and personality of Byrnes were expressions of his strangely divided gifts, which finally proved, after many achievements and one profound disappointment, to have made him exceptional. Born a few weeks after the death of his father, into a home of near-poverty in Charleston, South Carolina, Jimmy Byrnes was given an emotional quickness that made older men feel protective of him; he was never rich, but he was given a personal charm that made rich people become his friends; and he was never president of the United States, but his rich political career brought him closer to the Oval Office than any other southerner of his generation.

PART ONE

POLITICAL FATHERS: LEARNING THE CRAFT

1882–1930

1

Can Anything Good Come Out of Charleston?

Even during the Depression, Jimmy Byrnes had remembered the carriage rides. He was in South Carolina in 1930, campaigning for the U.S. Senate, and by late spring he had felt victory coming closer. Everywhere the economic uncertainty of the past few years was raising new men to power, and as he saw the growing crowds of unemployed throughout his state and talked with them about their fears, he began to feel confident this was his year to become a senator. Not that he had done badly for himself in earlier years; despite the stock market crash of 1929, he was still a well-to-do attorney, and as he traveled across South Carolina in 1930 asking desperate men for their votes, he and his wife, Maude, still rode above the red clay or the hot pavement in his Reo Flying Cloud automobile. Good times or bad, Jimmy Byrnes always had looked out for the main chance, and he kept his eyes on the road.

In the middle of a busy campaign, however, Byrnes found his thoughts turning back to the carriage rides of his youth. There had been many such rides, beginning with his childhood at Charleston, South Carolina, where Jimmy Byrnes had received rides home in a horse-drawn carriage and other practical assistance from the first of two courtly judges who later greatly aided his career; and there had been the rides with Maude Busch, when he had courted this daughter of a prosperous Aiken hotel owner and merchant. Each carriage ride with another person always had moved Jimmy Byrnes a little farther along the road to worldly success, and it was with this significance in mind that Byrnes wrote his father-in-law at Aiken in late April 1930, with what he knew was a surprising request.

"I trust you will not conclude I have gone crazy," he began, "when I tell you that I want you to hire somebody to get the old carriage out of the carriage house for me."

As Jimmy Byrnes continued, he adopted the distinctive Irish charm that he applied, with his father-in-law as with everyone else, with a sure political hand. "I have no gray mare," Byrnes wrote, "but if the old thing can stand the trip and not be shaken to pieces, I want to give it to Maude."

The carriage was to be an anniversary present, but it revived other memories for Byrnes. It reminded him of the evening of his victory parade at Aiken in 1910, when he and Maude had celebrated his first election to Congress by riding at the head of the parade in a decorated carriage. Gathered around Byrnes on that night were all the people—his wife, his friends, the voters—who were important to him and whom he loved. And so years later, as he campaigned in 1930 for the place in the U.S. Senate that he hoped would give him a national prominence, his thoughts returned to the night of his first congressional victory and to that long-ago carriage ride: the night Jimmy Byrnes had it all.

James Francis Byrnes was born at Charleston, South Carolina, on May 2, 1882, seven weeks after his father died of tuberculosis. The father, also named James Francis Byrnes, had been a minor clerk with the city of Charleston and had hoped for something better. His branch of the Byrnes family had come to South Carolina from Ireland during the potato famine of 1846; by the time the first James F. Byrnes was born, in 1856, the Byrnes family had acquired land and was farming along the Yemassee River, in coastal South Carolina. There is no record of these Byrneses' taking an active part in secession or in the Confederacy; they were immigrants on their way up, not plantation owners on their way out. Years afterward it pleased Jimmy Byrnes the politician to have his family's antebellum holdings described as "extensive," and it is possible that in another generation or two the family might have worked its way up to the planter class, had the region's fortunes been undisturbed. But after the Civil War the first James Byrnes, like more aristocratic planters, was forced to seek salaried work away from the land. He moved to the city of Charleston, where he hoped to find a job and attend college. Instead, he met Elizabeth Mc-Sweeney, an attractive, dark-haired woman who was, like himself, from an Irish-Catholic family. They married, and rather than study law or finance, the elder Byrnes went to work as a city clerk. When he died unexpectedly at age twenty-six, he left his pregnant widow with a three-year-old daughter, two hundred dollars, and, soon afterward, an infant boy named James F. Byrnes.

Within a few months of burying her husband and of giving birth to her son, Elizabeth Byrnes went to work. Leaving the children with her mother, the young widowed Mrs. Byrnes, still in her midtwenties, traveled to New York City and spent several months studying dressmaking. Returning home to South Carolina, she gathered all the Byrneses and McSweeneys into her house on Calhoun Street, and there Elizabeth Byrnes began sewing dresses for the fine ladies of Charleston. In years to come, her hands were seldom free of the needle and thread. In addition to raising her daughter and son, Elizabeth Byrnes by her efforts over the next eighteen years supported her invalided mother, her sister's young son, and the sister herself, who also soon became a widow. All five of these dependents found a refuge under her roof; and for the rest of her life, the mother of Jimmy Byrnes proudly boasted that she had kept the house on Calhoun Street mortgage free.

That a widow with slender finances would have begun a dressmaking business in a society apparently impoverished by the Civil War is not so naive as it might appear. The fact is that by the 1880s South Carolina had become for white families like the Byrneses a comparatively prosperous place to be. With the end of Reconstruction in the 1870s, economic control of South Carolina had been returned to the hands of the conservative politicians who had guided the state's fortunes before the Civil War. This same class had lost no time in encouraging northern capitalists to reinvest in the state's railroads, textiles, and manufacturing companies. Regional differences were assuaged by the possibilities of mutual profits; and, specifically, the question of full civil liberties for blacks, so bitterly contested during Reconstruction, was now found to be an issue that a succession of Democratic governors and Republican presidents, from James Garfield to Benjamin Harrison, could profitably ignore. As a result of this new amity among investors, commerce throughout the South had begun to prosper by the 1880s.

This was the era both of the progressive southern newspaper editor Henry Grady's talks about "the New South" and of the sudden appearance in hundreds of courthouse towns across the region of statues honoring soldiers of "the Lost Cause," suitably idealized in uniforms of Carrara marble or, ironically, Vermont granite. The two phenomena were different expressions of the same prosperity, and South Carolina shared in its region's economic resurgence. "The industrial progress of South Carolina in the last ten years almost surpasses belief," declared the *New York Times* in an edition published a few months before Byrnes' birth in early 1882, and even the state's hard-pressed cotton farmers shared at least initially in this new prosperity, a fact of great economic significance to all those making their living in South Carolina.

The close of the Civil War had done nothing to diminish the world's market for cotton, nor had the American South lost its preeminence in supplying that staple: in 1880 South Carolina's output of cotton bales actually exceeded the record crop of 1860. To process these good postwar crops, textile mills had multiplied across the state, encouraged by a tax rate on industrial property that was low or nonexistent. And, as continued to be true until well into the twentieth century, the fortunes of practically everyone in the state would rise or fall depending on the market vagaries of cotton. Transmuted financially into silk evening dresses or new tea gowns for the wives of mill owners or their bankers, the good cotton of the early 1880s offered modest but steady income for Elizabeth Byrnes and her children.

The city of Charleston, where Elizabeth Byrnes began her household and her business, had long been accustomed to receiving the talents and wealth of all South Carolinians, just as surely as water runs downhill. Located on a narrow point of land surrounded by a natural harbor where the Ashley and Cooper rivers meet at the Atlantic, the city had been established in 1670 under a grant from the lords proprietor of the state. Later Charleston was home to South Carolina's ten royalist governors; and after the American Revolution and the removal of the state capital inland to Columbia, there was still many a backwoods patriot who claimed that Charleston continued to view the rest of South Carolina through royalist and proprietary eyes. "Can anything good come out of Charleston?" was a familiar upstate query throughout the nineteenth century. The city had a tradition of educating the sons of its leading families abroad, and Charlestonians had by 1800 acquired a culture distinct from that of the rest of South Carolina. "The small society of rice and cotton planters at Charleston," Henry Adams later wrote in his *History of the United States of America during the First Administration of Thomas Jefferson*, "with their cultivated tastes and hospitable habits, delighted in whatever reminded them of European civilization. They were travellers, readers, and scholars; the society of Charleston compared well in refinement with that of any city of its size in the world, and English visitors long thought it the most agreeable in America." Buoyed by the booming cotton markets of the early 1800s, these planters also spent their money agreeably. Charleston was home to excellent theaters, numerous grog houses, and several academies. The city boasted that its exports equaled in value those of almost the entire state of Massachusetts, and by midcentury Robert Mills and other architects of national repute had done for Charleston what Charles Bullfinch had earlier done for Boston—created a city of remarkable charm and beauty.

Underlying that charm and beauty was an absolute ruthlessness in the use of political power. Nationally, the city's interests had been aggressively protected through the first half of the nineteenth century by John C. Calhoun, who both as U.S. senator and as vice president had argued a state's right to nullification, or denial of federal authority, by force if need be. As a result of the political skills of Calhoun and other "fire-eating" senators, South Carolina enjoyed a political dominance greatly out of proportion to its area or population. When the U.S. Congress enraged cotton and rice planters in 1828 and again in 1832 by passing high tariffs on manufactured items—planters imported practically every item for use on their plantations, from toothbrushes to plowshares—Charlestonians and the state Democrats under Calhoun led in calling for a convention to "nullify" the national tariff laws. Congressional compromise resolved that issue peacefully, but it was just the preamble to the larger, impending crisis: South Carolina was the first state to secede, in late 1860, and many of these same planter families were among those that later cheered in the streets of Charleston when artillery in the city opened fire on Fort Sumter, plunging South Carolina and the rest of the nation into four years of civil war. For decades after their defeat, upstate South Carolinians, with considerable bitterness and some accuracy, still referred to the Civil War as "Charleston's war."

Even in Jimmy Byrnes' adulthood, the source both of this city's great wealth and of its great pride could be held, as before the Civil War, in the palm of one hand: the black seeds of the long-staple, Sea Island cotton. Prized for the luxuriance of the cloth that could be spun from it, the long fibers also are easily ginned, or separated, from the surrounding hulls and seeds, and Sea Island was the first variety of cotton to be grown commercially in the South. Much in demand during the late eighteenth and early nineteenth centuries, long-staple cotton could be cultivated in South Carolina only along the coastal low country, and this economic and agricultural fact of life early differentiated Charleston and the low country from the upstate. Hence, in the cultivation of their crops, these two regions had long before Jimmy Byrnes' birth parted company: the low country had committed itself to a plantation system based on extensive slave or tenant farm labor, while the up-country remained a largely undeveloped region of small sustenance farmers before the Civil War, becoming an increasingly industrialized area of cotton mill towns after the war.

By the time Elizabeth Byrnes had set up her household in the 1880s, Charleston epitomized this economic and political split. The city had come out of the Civil War largely intact—occupied by federal troops after a long siege in 1865, Charleston astonishingly was not deliberately set ablaze, as were several other major South Carolina cities, perhaps only because troops under the personal command of General William T. Sherman had already marched into North Carolina—but the low country's economic dominance and Charleston's great shipping affluence were now things of the past. After the Civil War the state's railroads, particularly the Atlanta and Charlotte Air Line, were directing commercial traffic along a north–south axis, rather than east toward Charleston and shipping by ocean. Capital investment in the new cotton mills also had followed the railroads inland to the upstate, changing such small cities along the route as Spartanburg and Greenville into significant commercial centers. But at the time of this prolific upstate growth, Charleston grew hardly at all. Between 1860 and 1880, this formerly great exporting city remained practically unchanged in population, increasing only from 40,519 to 49,984. By contrast, the port city of Boston more than doubled its size during the same twenty-year period, to more than 362,839. Still the most densely populated city in South Carolina, Charleston retained its political preeminence, the latter through a succession of state officials elected with political or social obligations to the city; but none of these leaders showed innovative leadership or economic daring. Known among themselves as Conservatives, these Charleston-based Democrats were known by the rest of the state as Bourbons, in reference to their experience in the Civil War and to Talleyrand's description of Bourbon French aristocracy after the Revolution: "They had forgotten nothing, and they had learned nothing."

But change is inevitable, even in Charleston. By 1880, two years before Byrnes' birth, the city had grown large enough to support two markets. The older and more fashionable market was downtown, near the row of elegant planters' mansions known as the Battery; the upper, newer market was located near the commercial docks close to the city's Fifth Ward, where many Irish families such as the Byrneses lived. Nor was the city inflexibly English Protestant in culture: many of Charleston's first families were of Huguenot, Sephardic Jewish, or Germanic origin, and the city was the diocese residence of the Catholic bishop of South Carolina. At the upper end of the city, in the Fourth and Fifth wards, newly arrived families were in the 1880s beginning to push into economic, if not social or political, competition with the families of the Battery, and many of Jimmy Byrnes' later skills as a political mediator emerged when he was growing up in this most worldly of South Carolina cities. Insofar as the terms "Old South" and "New South" can have specific meanings, they can apply to Jimmy Byrnes' future coming of age in the divided world of nineteenth-century Charleston.

For the present, however, the little boy helped his mother as much as he could, while she continued her sewing. When he was old enough to understand his importance to the family's finances, Jimmy Byrnes delivered dresses to his mother's customers, sold pies and newspapers in the neighborhood, and ran errands for a law firm in the city. And as his knowledge of Charleston's streets increased, so did his appreciation of what Elizabeth Byrnes had done for her children—for at the corner of Calhoun and Saint

Philip streets, which marked the end of the Fifth Ward and of his childhood's familiar territory, Jimmy Byrnes could see the five stories and attic of the Charleston Orphan House. Many of the children had been placed in the orphanage by single mothers who were unable to support their families. There was little doubt in Jimmy Byrnes' mind that, had Elizabeth Byrnes' spirit been less indomitable, or her needle less busy, he and his sister would have grown up in that building as wards of the state.

Jimmy Byrnes never forgot what his mother did. For the rest of his life, the sovereign image of his mother was of her sewing at the center of their house on Calhoun Street, earning the money to hold her family together. "All my childhood recollections of her were in the sewing room," Byrnes would write. "Later, when I had a job, I would find her still at work no matter when I returned home." One of Byrnes' first acts when he became a prosperous attorney was to provide her the means to retire from commercial sewing, but his memories of the precarious financial condition of his family during childhood never left him as an adult, and the details would surface at odd moments. Once, while secretary of state, Jimmy Byrnes passed the time during a tedious negotiation by writing absentmindedly and repeatedly in the corners of an official document: "Messrs. Morris, Brown & Co., Ltd., London." A reporter noticed the notes and asked Byrnes' secretary, who had known him for years, about their meaning. The name was a memory from Byrnes' childhood in Charleston, the reporter was told: "He bought boxes of merchandise from a concern by that name. The merchandise was resold by him—usually for a profit."

Throughout the 1880s and 1890s, then, Byrnes had a childhood that, while at times needy, was never deprived. Years afterward, Byrnes' older sister, Leonore, perhaps tiring of the emphasis on early poverty in her brother's political biographies, pointed out that their house in Charleston had a rose vine and garden in front and that, somehow, Elizabeth Byrnes had been able to afford a piano. Jimmy Byrnes' love of singing probably dates from those years on Calhoun Street, and he had sufficient free time between jobs to play sandlot baseball and to serve as an altar boy at St. Patrick's Catholic Church. By age ten, Byrnes had grown into a wiry, black-haired little boy with his mother's gray-blue eyes and a way of tilting his head back that was startlingly like Elizabeth's. A photograph of Jimmy Byrnes taken at that time shows a happy and laughing boy, his legs too long for his body, pleased with the attention of the grown-ups and with having his photograph taken: the spider's merry child.

Four years after this photograph was taken, fourteen-year-old Jimmy Byrnes entered the adult world of full-time work; more important for him, he entered the world of men. Earlier, Byrnes had quit parochial school. He had been a quick learner, and the nuns there had encouraged him to prepare for college in hopes of gaining a scholarship. But, "impelled by the ambition to help my mother," Byrnes later wrote, he left school for a full-time job. Despite the national depression of 1896, Byrnes got a place as an office boy with an old Charleston law firm: Mordecai, Gadsden, Rutledge, and Hagood, located downtown on Broad Street. His two-dollar-a-week salary added appreciably to the Byrnes family's income. Of greater significance to his rising fortunes was that in those Broad Street offices he came under the tutelage of a senior partner of the firm, Judge Benjamin H. Rutledge.

Judge Rutledge was the first of two courtly judges who acted as a father to Jimmy Byrnes. A descendant of a signer to the Declaration of Independence, and a member of one of Charleston's leading families, Benjamin Rutledge was a kindly and well-educated public man who was never known, even on the most sweltering of days, to have appeared on the palmetto-lined streets of Charleston without wearing his frockcoat. This formality of clothes reflected a formality of mind. To Judge Rutledge, the law was not, as it was to some judges, a pair of great equalizing scales, weighing all men's rights with a blind impartiality; rather, to him, justice was a series of delicately adjusted mental and social discriminations, so that the scales favored some men more, some men less. The courts themselves in his view were hierarchical and of varying quality; of Judge Rutledge it was reported that he "would have died rather than enter the rude precincts of the state courts." Here he was representative of his class and city, both in his firmness of mind and in its exclusiveness.

Still, aristocratic Charlestonians like Benjamin Rutledge practiced two cardinal virtues: they remembered social obligations, and they appreciated intelligence as a sign of good breeding. Judge Rutledge had slightly known Jimmy Byrnes' father, the city clerk; and he noticed the boy's quick mind. The judge now decided to interest himself in the education of his new office boy. He obtained a library card for Jimmy Byrnes—a not inconsiderable advantage in a century when most large libraries were private or charged reading fees—and he supervised a course of reading for him. *The Count of Monte Cristo* alternated with Edward Gibbon's *The Decline and Fall of the Roman Empire*. Between office duties, Jimmy Byrnes was given time with his books and questioned on what he had read by Judge Rutledge; and under the old man's supervision, the boy received an education in the 1890s that was in many ways a better preparation for the world than that which the sisters at a parochial school could ever have offered him.

This relationship with Benjamin Rutledge continued for four years, until after Byrnes' eighteenth birthday; its effects were long-lasting. For through his association with Judge Rutledge and his law firm, Byrnes was able to enter—at least as a spectator—into the society of patrician lawyers who gathered just a few blocks from the law office at the intersection of Meeting and Broad streets. Known as the Four Corners of Law, this was one of the most famous city intersections in the Southeast; the *Baedeker's*

Guide to the United States of 1896 recommended that no traveler leave Charleston without visiting it. Here at three of the street corners stood buildings representing each of the three civil authorities—the state courthouse, the Charleston city hall, the federal post office—while at the fourth corner ecclesiastical authority was represented by the stone archways and steeple of Saint Michael's Episcopal Church. Here at Meeting and Broad streets gathered lawyers and planters from throughout the South Carolina low country to deal, argue, gossip and talk politics, while from under the shade of public buildings elderly black women from the outlying sea islands sold flowers and baskets of woven palmetto leaves. Here, at the spot considered to be the omphalos of authority in nineteenth-century Charleston, the errand boy Jimmy Byrnes also could have heard discussion of the presidential election of 1896, when the Democrats under William Jennings Bryan and the new Populist party lost a three-way contest to Republicans under William McKinley.

For the time being, however, Jimmy Byrnes' mother had a more concrete view. She insisted that her son learn shorthand as a means to advancing in the world. Earlier in the 1890s she had paid for Byrnes to take lessons in the Gregg system at a local business college; now she held informal lessons at home, dictating a short passage for her son to note each evening before he went to bed. Her insistence that he have a skill and Judge Rutledge's wish that he have something better came together in 1900, when Jimmy Byrnes turned eighteen. A court reporter, or stenographer, was needed that year in the state's Second Judicial District, and the district judge was holding an open competition for all applicants at the upstate town of Spartanburg. Judge Rutledge had heard of the competition, and he encouraged his office boy to try for the job. Jimmy Byrnes borrowed a typewriter, traveled by train to the unfamiliar town of Spartanburg, and spent all day taking notes in competition. That night he returned to a hotel and began transcribing his notes into a finished text. Heavy drinkers in the next room interrupted the boyish-looking stenographer several times and urged him to join their party. But the gentle boy who was his mother's favorite turned the revelers away from his door and went back to his studies. The following morning he handed in his transcription, and the findings were announced: first place went to James F. Byrnes of Charleston. He was to appear in court at the next session in the upstate.

Byrnes' new job took him away from Charleston and his mother, and it marked his entry as an independent man among South Carolina's lawyers and politicians. It also began with a slight deception. Jimmy Byrnes was not old enough to work as a court stenographer. At that time court stenographers by custom, if not state law, were expected to be at least twenty-one, and Byrnes, despite his high score in the competition, was only eighteen. He solved this problem apparently by switching birth dates with his sister, Leonore, born in 1879; thereafter, Jimmy Byrnes always claimed to have turned twenty-one in 1900, the year he accepted the court stenographer's job. The deception is certainly forgivable, given his family's financial circumstances, and in itself is of no great significance; but it is noteworthy how carefully Byrnes kept his secret, for his substituting his sister's birth date for his own became known only years after his and Leonore's deaths. That Byrnes maintained this small deception decades after the circumstances that had made it necessary had been forgotten by everyone else except him says less about his veracity than about his prudence. In all important matters, Jimmy Byrnes was always honest; but in all matters, great or small, he also was always guarded.

At the time when Byrnes substituted the birth dates, Leonore may not have known and, if she did know, almost certainly would not have cared: remembering years later those Calhoun Street struggles by her mother, Leonore Byrnes emphasized, "In our family it was always 'tomorrow' that counted." Jimmy Byrnes' new salary would make a number of tomorrows more financially secure at the Calhoun Street house; and the three years of youth he signed away to help his mother may have compounded a homesickness he felt when, at eighteen, he said good-bye to his family and to Judge Rutledge and left Charleston for a new job and a new judge.

Jimmy Byrnes soon learned why a new stenographer was needed in the up-country district court: a Baptist preacher had shot and killed his predecessor. Such activity was not unusual in the state's Second Judicial District, a six-county area at the far end of South Carolina that in 1900 roughly paralleled the Savannah River as it rolled southward, swollen with mountain tributaries. The state of South Carolina has since colonial times been shaped by its river boundaries roughly like an arrowhead buried one hundred miles deep into the North American continent, the broad end of the arrowhead spread along the South Atlantic coast where European settlers had founded Charleston and other port cities and the point of the arrowhead embedded in the Appalachian Mountains and Piedmont, where Jimmy Byrnes now found himself. "The seriousness of Charleston society changed to severity in the mountains," Henry Adams had observed of the society of these southern Appalachians ninety years earlier. He described the population there in the early nineteenth century as "rude, ignorant, and in some of its habits half barbarous," and in the following century civilization still seemed largely to have passed by much of this region of the South. Here, one hundred miles inland from Charleston, was the South Carolina not of the planter but of the southeastern frontier: the majority of people always had been fiercely secessionist, but they were never large cultivators by low-country standards, and the conforming powers of organized capital and markets had had little effect here. It was a region of crossroads market towns and isolated farms; the geography varied from the sandy plains and pine barrens to the red-clay foothills of the southern Appalachians; and the inhabitants ranged from the agreeably urban to the dangerously feral. This judicial area accurately boasted of itself as being "the damnedest, gamecockingest, liquor-drinkingest, nigger-shootingest, sinfullest place in South Carolina." Politically the district was dominated by Edgefield County, a hotbed of anti-Charleston sentiment and the home of one of the state's most violent politicians, the populist senator Benjamin "Pitchfork Ben" Tillman. For the next twenty-six years Jimmy Byrnes called this district home, and for the next ten years he traveled its length, helping to bring its inhabitants under the rule of law. He was a long way from Broad Street.

But there was also a pleasant surprise for Byrnes. The office of the Second Judicial District was in Aiken, a town of a few thousand just over the Edgefield County line; and on moving there in 1900, Byrnes discovered a town in some ways more cosmopolitan than the port city he had left. Aiken had been spared the destruction of the Civil War, and in the years afterward the town had begun to solicit northern visitors as a winter resort. Railroad connections to the North were good, the region's weather was mild, and its spring waters were advertised to be therapeutic; and by the time Jimmy Byrnes arrived, there was established in Aiken a "Winter Colony" of prosperous northerners who traveled to the town each year for sophisticated pastimes such as polo playing, riding, and tennis. Byrnes had exchanged a stratified society for one promising an upward mobility. He could see the difference immediately upon his arrival. The streets of Charleston tended to be narrow, looking back to the eighteenth century, and were sometimes difficult to enter, even for horse-drawn vehicles; within the city near the Battery, many houses of Charlestonians were walled and shuttered, often concealing private gardens from public view. Aiken, on the other hand, was in 1900 a city of remarkably broad, tree-lined streets, looking forward confidently to the twentieth century and, ultimately, the automobile.

Many of the houses Byrnes saw in Aiken were recently built, their verandas generously situated to catch the evening breezes and the conversations of passersby. One of these fine houses belonged to Judge James H. Aldrich, Byrnes' new employer at Aiken. Aldrich, who enjoyed considerable local prominence as a district judge, was as sparse in build as Benjamin Rutledge was stout. The judge's father had died early, and as a boy younger than Jimmy Byrnes, James Aldrich at eighteen had served in a "cradle to grave" company of Confederate infantry when Union troops had passed nearby to Aiken. Now in a peaceful old age and sporting a handlebar mustache grown silver, Judge Aldrich began to take a paternal interest in his new stenographer. Like Judge Rutledge before him, Judge Aldrich gave Byrnes the means to move himself upward. The imposing judge possessed a fine library and a family pew at the local Episcopalian church, and he now saw to it that his new employee enjoyed the advantages of both. Shortly after settling in Aiken, Byrnes began to study law books in Judge Aldrich's library in hopes of passing the state's bar exam; and on Sundays the choir at St. Thaddeus Episcopal Church found itself enriched by the Irish tenor voice of this new arrival in town.

For six months each year, Byrnes left Aiken and traveled the district with Judge Aldrich, the old man and the boyish-looking stenographer making time as best they could, arriving by horse-drawn carriage or dog-legged railroad at the little courthouse towns of the Second District. Their arrival was an event of considerable local importance. Carrying his stenographer's pad and pencil, Byrnes would trail behind Judge Aldrich as the county sheriff cleared the streets with cries of "Oyez, oyez!" announcing to all malefactors that district court was now in session and that justice was to be done. Justice, as Byrnes discovered in these rough up-country towns, was apt to be like murder: quick and personal. For years afterward Byrnes enjoyed telling the story of a Second District magistrate who had interrupted a lawyer's pleading in his court to place a small note inside his desk drawer and to inform the lawyer that he was going home for lunch; however, the pleading attorney should not be concerned, the magistrate told him, and should he so desire he should continue with his argument. When the lawyer finished, he would find the magistrate's verdict written down on the note inside his desk.

After the disposition of such cases, usually heard by Judge Aldrich on appeal, both the judge and the lawyers for the opposing sides would adjourn to a hotel for further discussion and drinking. Here the young stenographer who had noted the words of men inside the courtroom took careful notice of their actions outside of it. It was in these drummer's hotels, punctuated by lawyerly tobacco spitting and judicious application of bourbon, that Jimmy Byrnes first learned the unspoken rules by which southern males at the turn of the century chose their leaders. He learned that it is an agreeable habit for a newcomer to tell mildly amusing stories about his own past, but that it is extremely dangerous even slightly to ridicule another southerner's family or misfortunes; that a salacious story at the end of the day could lighten a man's burden, but that only a fool speaks of such acts in the first person; and that the successful narrator of a racist joke must follow a formula as old as Attic comedy: that by the close of his story, no one is permanently injured, order is restored to the throne, and the gods laugh with the white men. For the years from 1900 to 1908, as he toured the district with Judge Aldrich, Jimmy Byrnes learned these lessons well. There was more. Byrnes also noticed the successful attorneys in the district, and he studied what made these men so successful in the courtroom: their easy familiarity with biblical allusions in argument, their propensity for a well-timed jest to please the galleries, and their constant presentation of what he termed "an affidavit face" toward the jury.

By 1908 Byrnes was ready. Earlier, he had passed the state bar examination and established a law practice at Aiken; but finding, in his words, that his "shingle attracted many agreeable callers but few paying clients," Byrnes had continued to work the district with Judge Aldrich. Now he saw his chance: in 1908 he declared his candidacy for the office of court solicitor, who in South Carolina is the district's prosecuting attorney. This elective post brought with it a comparatively high salary of $1,700 per year and considerable prestige. Writing as an old man, Byrnes was forthright about why he had wanted both: "I had become impressed by the importance of the Solicitor's role and I was vain enough to think I might do well in it."

He carried his vanity well. By 1908 Byrnes had matured into a trim, sharply dressed young southern blade; in political advertisements the promising candidate is described as "A Live Wire—He Is a Self Made Man." By this time Jimmy Byrnes had developed his preference for three-piece suits tailored to his frame of five feet, seven inches, and he had gained his life's maximum weight of about 140 pounds. His hair was the color of wet coal, parted in the middle after the current fashion, and he had picked up the habit, which would last a lifetime, of tilting his hat downward over one eye at a rakish angle. In later years, the appearance of Jimmy Byrnes in a newsreel would put the audience in mind of the entertainer James Cagney, as he danced and performed his way through roles ranging from gangsters to patriots. But to the citizens of Aiken in 1908 who saw Jimmy Byrnes coming down the street at a rapid clip, his distinctive gait—half a little man's strut and half a big man's promise—quite likely would have recalled the lighthearted music hall song "I'm Looking for the Bully of the Town."

It was during this campaign that Byrnes became known to the public as Jimmy. He was to keep this form of address as his political name for the rest of his life, and only his immediate family and a few intimates knew that he actually preferred to be called "Jim." Even as an elderly man, Byrnes would be greeted by the public with this diminutive of a name, sometimes by speakers many years his junior, and he was asked once if this public usage offended him. For a moment, the old familiar light came back into Byrnes' blue eyes, and he turned toward his questioner with a friendly but predatory smile. "Not at all," Jimmy Byrnes said pleasantly. "When a youngster calls me 'Jimmy,' I know I've got his daddy's vote."

Byrnes won easily. His majority was impressive—for every vote his opponents received, Jimmy Byrnes received two—and the ratio indicates a silent approval of his candidacy by the women of the area, who may have influenced the voting of husbands and brothers. Earlier Byrnes had moved his mother and grandmother to a house at Aiken, where his earnings had enabled Elizabeth Byrnes at last to give up her commercial sewing. In a small town, such filial devotion did not go unnoticed. In an additional step toward respectability, Byrnes had become a co-investor in—although not a writer for—the town's newspaper, the *Aiken Journal and Review*;

and Byrnes now attended the Episcopal church as an apparent convert and sang in its choir. A communicant there had caught his eye: she was Maude Busch, the daughter of a successful local hotel owner.

Not everyone in town approved of Jimmy Byrnes' sudden social rise. Resistance came from a surprising corner: not from Protestant, establishment Aiken, which always had been accepting of new arrivals; rather, the remonstrance came from Byrnes' natal church, in the person of the local Catholic priest, who dropped by the newspaper office one day to discuss with Jimmy Byrnes his attentions to young Miss Busch.

Even as an elderly man, Byrnes wrote of this visit from the Aiken priest with all the unhealed bitterness of an old family quarrel. By the close of his life, Byrnes knew that his childhood Catholicism had undeniably cost him election to the U.S. Senate once; it may also have helped deny him the presidency. Hence in his memoirs, Byrnes described this visit by the Aiken priest as the first of a series of intrusions into aspects of his life where the church had no business, and he shaped the incident for posterity as a political parable: the story of a priest who tried to outwit a politician.

According to Byrnes' version of the story, the priest, after some pleasantries, told Byrnes that "it was rumored that I was to be married and he thought he should present the position of the Church on 'mixed marriages.' " Here, Byrnes implied, the Catholic father made his first error. Only a political novice uses rumor as the reason for stating a position of any sort; if the rumor turns out to be false, the statement has only created unnecessary controversy. Byrnes listened for a while, then easily outmaneuvered his guest. He told the father that he "had no immediate plans to wed." In fact, Byrnes was not planning to wed Maude Busch immediately, but an eventual wedding had been planned. Byrnes implied that the priest should have been alert to such distinctions; but he was not, and the conversation then proceeded to an abstract discussion of "mixed" marriages in general. The priest left the newspaper office with no clear idea of what had been resolved, and shortly thereafter the twenty-four-year-old Jimmy Byrnes married Maude Busch on his birthday, May 2, 1906. The couple was wed in an Episcopal ceremony, and soon after the honeymoon, Byrnes formally converted to that denomination.

During the political career that followed, Jimmy Byrnes' religious affiliations moved over the entire theological landscape. When asked, he would usually describe his religion simply as "Episcopalian," without mentioning his earlier Catholicism; when the question of his conversion did come up, Byrnes would sometimes explain in press releases that "when he was about fourteen or fifteen years of age he decided to become a Protestant." And years later as senator and U.S. Supreme Court justice, Byrnes let pass uncorrected a biographical listing of himself as a Presbyterian. But whatever his political desires, the wholeheartedness of his marriage to Maude Busch cannot be questioned. Jimmy Byrnes was to be a devoted

and faithful husband, and, for her part, Maude Byrnes was quietly sup-
portive of her husband's career, although there is little record of her taking
an active interest in the details of his political life. There were always
spontaneous acts of affection between the two that onlookers—particularly
those who had known the couple for years—found quite touching. The
Byrnes' household would remain childless; like many couples who want to
have children and cannot, Jimmy and Maude Byrnes became deeply solicitous of each other's feelings: each sheltered the other from the disappointment both felt.

For the present, however, after their marriage and his conversion into
St. Thaddeus Episcopal Church, Jimmy and Maude Byrnes stepped easily
onto the rising circle of Aiken's young professional class. His victory for
the solicitor's office in 1908 was properly considered a promotion, and
Byrnes quickly began to make a name for himself as an aggressive and
popular state's attorney. He gained convictions in several well-publicized
murder trials; more praiseworthy, because he knew it would gain him no
votes and might cost him some, he succeeded in having Second District
courts accept the idea that assault by one Negro upon another was a
prosecutable offense, and that the testimony of Negroes could be accepted
as part of that court record. Winning agreement that black people were,
under some circumstances, legally human beings was no small accomplishment at that time and in that section of South Carolina.

However, the state's new prosecuting attorney was not so busy protecting injured Negroes that he forgot a lesson from his days with Judge
Aldrich: that a successful lawyer must provide drama for his rural courtroom audience. Byrnes was the first solicitor in the district to call in private
detectives, the Pinkerton Agency, to assist in prosecuting a murder case;
it was an act, he may have shrewdly guessed, that would appeal to the
upstate's peculiar sense of honor. *(Progressive? Why, man, we have murders here that'll beat anything you'll see up North. Things got so bad last
summer that Jimmy Byrnes had to call in the Pinkertons.)* By 1910 Byrnes
had become one of the best-known solicitors in his area of South Carolina.
That year he saw his chance.

In 1910 the Second District congressman, J. O. Patterson, was up for
reelection; the fifty-three-year-old Patterson had never been overly stren-
uous in providing services to his constituents, and for the past six years
most of the voting households around Aiken had received only free packets
of flower seeds mailed from Washington as concrete evidence of J. O.
Patterson's presence in the nation's capital. Now the congressman had
fallen ill and would apparently be unable to do even that. Patterson's poor
health would prevent him from campaigning actively that summer, and
Jimmy Byrnes announced that he was making a run for the congressman's
job.

Both by instinct and by upbringing, Jimmy Byrnes was an urban rather than an agrarian politician, and by beginning his first congressional campaign with promises of more efficient federal services, he instinctively aligned himself with the progressive faction of the Democratic party. Many Democratic progressives were southerners, but southerners more often from small towns and medium-size cities rather than from the farmlands, and these young politicians had little in common with the radical agrarians of an earlier generation who had started the Populist party and Farmers' Alliance in the 1880s and 1890s. The generation that "went progressive," in the phrase of the era, was the generation of men who, like Byrnes, had come of voting age at the turn of the century. By that time the Populist party of post–Civil War agrarians had ceased to exist on a national level. "But whereas Populism represented a kind of frantic threshing about by desperate farmers, Progressivism had more of a middle-class and urban tone," noted the historian T. Harry Williams. "Progressive leaders were likely to be lawyers, editors, even businessmen." It is significant that by the time Byrnes "went progressive," he fit all three of these categories.

The progressive promises of Byrnes' first campagin, better roads and lower tariffs, also were among the approved ideas then clustering around Woodrow Wilson, the reform candidate for governor of New Jersey and the acknowledged leader of the Democratic progressives. Byrnes had in 1910 not yet met Wilson, but the latter was becoming an increasingly well-known politician throughout the South. In October 1910 the *Atlanta Constitution* agreed to endorse Wilson for the 1912 presidential nomination, and Wilson-for-President clubs already had sprung up in Virginia and Texas. Wilson soon made several speaking trips to the Southeast, including an extended visit in 1911 to Columbia, South Carolina, and he generated a popular enthusiasm throughout the state for a progressive ticket in 1912.

At the moment, however, Jimmy Byrnes could not concern himself with the future of progressivism in 1912; first he had to win the local election of 1910. And in order to win that election, he had to win the support of a party organization that was in many ways a combination of Bourbon conservatism and rural populism. His earlier victory in the solicitor's race had demonstrated that Jimmy Byrnes could draw votes in the Second District outside his home precinct in Aiken, but that election could more properly be considered a vote of approval by the members of the state bar; the regular party organization had a broader composition and its own rules and customs.

The state Democratic party at that time dominated South Carolina politics so thoroughly that nomination to the party ticket was equivalent to winning office; the general elections in the fall were important only when there were runoffs between two Democratic candidates. Not only was South Carolina politics exclusively Democratic; in 1910 it also was almost exclusively white. Except in a few counties along the coast, there were practically no black or Republican voters in South Carolina, and the Republican party was historically identified as the party of black supremacy. As a result, Democratic insistence on party loyalty was total, and those who crossed party lines were ostracized as having endangered the purity of the white race (and they continued to be so treated until Jimmy Byrnes in 1960 publicly endorsed the Republican ticket). By the time of Byrnes' first entry into regular state politics, in 1910, the establishment of these two prerequisites to party membership—unswerving party loyalty and unquestioning acceptance of white superiority—had enabled the Democratic party of South Carolina to identify itself completely with the white ruling class. The same term was used by the party to refer to both a white man of voting age and a loyal Democrat: "member of the democracy."

The source of this Democratic strength was at the county level, where clubs were organized in each election precinct. Here Byrnes would appear to have been at a disadvantage. The precincts of Aiken would provide him some votes, but in order to win he would have to pick up support in the precinct clubs strung along the isolated townships of the six counties of the Second District. Byrnes was helped, however, by rules inherited from an earlier generation of agrarian radicals. Under the Bourbon rules, delegates had chosen their congressional candidates in closed conventions, where a newcomer like Jimmy Byrnes would have had little hope of upsetting an incumbent like Patterson; but under changes initiated years earlier by the agrarian radical senator Ben Tillman, the party now chose its candidates in districtwide primaries. Tillman also had added a characteristic twist: candidates were expected to appear together in debate at stump speeches to be held at each of the townships in their district, thus making physical endurance almost a requirement for holding public office in South Carolina. Here, on the "palmetto stump" of political touring, named after the subtropical tree that was the state emblem, Jimmy Byrnes' youth and quick wit could be displayed to best advantage.

Byrnes' candidacy also was given an unexpected boost that summer by the declining health not only of Representative Patterson but also of old Senator Tillman himself. Tillman, whose farm in Edgefield County was within the Second District, was recovering from a stroke and apparently chose to show no preference among the congressional candidates that year—provided, of course, that each remained politically acceptable to him and that each was a member in good standing "of the democracy." Given these small openings in a monolithic state party structure, Jimmy Byrnes soon created a break for himself. In spirit Byrnes might be a Wilsonian progressive, but on the hustling in 1910 he became a southern politician. And few southern politicians have ever campaigned with the natural animation, verve, and desire to win that Jimmy Byrnes showed.

Throughout that summer of 1910 Byrnes campaigned the length of the Second District, speaking against Patterson's inactivity at every opportunity. Joining him on the campaign was a third candidate, C. W. Garris,

whom Byrnes beat easily in that summer's primary. Garris then threw his
support to Byrnes in the September runoff between Byrnes and Patterson.
This support greatly aided Byrnes in picking up the swing votes, and it
was the first of many instances in which a defeated rival would work hard
for Byrnes' subsequent election. Jimmy Byrnes usually started very early
to lessen the sting of a later defeat. During that summer primary Byrnes
and Garris had shared a carriage in order to save traveling expenses while
campaigning, and during the long rides up and down the Second District,
the considerable charm of Jimmy Byrnes apparently won over his opponent. When the votes were cast at the end of the summer and Byrnes left
his traveling companion Garris behind, the defeated third man remained
a firm Byrnes supporter.

Now, in the September runoff, Patterson's ill health prevented him
from making speeches on the stump, and Jimmy Byrnes, in more than
forty-six public speeches, stepped up attacks on the "do-nothing" congressman. Gradually Byrnes began to pull ahead. Even for the younger
man, however, the campaign trail was becoming exhausting. Byrnes was
expected to visit each of the crossroads communities along the 150 miles
of the Second District, shake each extended hand with an animated enthusiasm, and consume each plate of offered barbecue without any apparent dyspepsia. Byrnes later confessed, "I wondered which would give
out first, my nerves, my money or my stomach."

All three held. On September 15, 1910, the ballots were cast, and after
a careful counting, Jimmy Byrnes was declared the winner by fifty-seven
votes. "Fifty-seven Is Enough," announced a banner stretched across the
street of Byrnes' adopted hometown. Six days after the election, Aiken
prepared to honor the new congressman with a torchlight parade, and
banners were strung along the route. "I love my wife, but oh, you Jimmie,"
read one. As the streets darkened, a brass band tuned up, and a horse-
drawn carriage was brought to carry the candidate in the parade; a crowd
of about two hundred well-wishers assembled. The band broke into "Has
Anyone Here Seen Kelly?" and the crowd laughed at this triumphant
reference to the successful candidate's Irish ancestry. Finally the candidate
himself appeared; riding with his wife and waving to his friends from the
carriage, an exhausted but exultant James F. Byrnes led his first political
parade.

The torchbearers had arrived at the town's post office, where a temporary
speaker's platform stood. Aiken's post office in 1910 was a substantial but
unornamented two-story, red-clay brick building; as a civic temple, it had
been erected by a citizenry of plain farmers to honor the most pedestrian
branch of their government. Its sole architectural distinction was a slightly
elevated dome above the second story, painted white and visible above

the leafy tops of the surrounding oak trees. Its presence that night, fitfully lit by the torches below, revealed that even here, in small-town South Carolina, there remained a memory of the neoclassical, Palladian style that Thomas Jefferson thought appropriate for public buildings.

Jimmy Byrnes quickly climbed up the temporary platform at the front of the building. He was expected to give the politician's traditional speech of thanks, and although his remarks were not recorded, they must have been deeply felt. Years later in his memoirs, when Byrnes recalled the townspeople of Aiken who had gathered around him that night, he emphasized what he had felt as a young politician: "They had indeed been good to me." Under the torchlight Byrnes could recognize many friends among the two hundred celebrants. Although his mother was not there—wishing to be in familiar surroundings in her old age, she had returned to Charleston—she knew of her son's honors, and she could reflect, along with him, on how far her family had advanced since those early Fifth Ward days and on how promising the future for her youngest child now was.

Jimmy Byrnes finished his speech. There were some further, quiet words of encouragement for the congressman-elect in the dark and some handshakes for remembrance's sake, and then the last of the flickering torches disappeared from Aiken's side streets. Byrnes was left with his victory, and with Maude. Soon they would move to Washington, and to whatever fate was awaiting him there. His future seemed limitless.

2

Pitchfork
Ben Tillman

Jimmy Byrnes' first entrance on the national stage was followed by something of an embarrassment: he caught the mumps. Shortly after delivering his maiden speech in 1911 to the House of Representatives—in which he pledged to join in the upcoming "battle of the ballots" to toss out Republican rule in 1912—a case of the childhood disease began making the rounds among congressional pages. Byrnes, who was self-conscious about his slight build and youthful appearance among the House's senior statesmen, felt himself becoming feverish; and to his discomfort, the self-proclaimed warrior was kept out of action for several weeks while he recovered from a pair of swollen glands. "Mr. Byrnes, of South Carolina," noted the *Congressional Record* with a nice diplomacy, "by unanimous consent, was granted a leave of two weeks on account of important business." Byrnes thereby was given time to recuperate—and what posterity didn't know, as far as he was concerned, probably wouldn't hurt it.

The leave also afforded Jimmy and Maude Byrnes more time to make themselves a home in Washington. They had already seen much in that city that was pleasingly familiar to two young people who had grown up in the South. The city of Washington in 1911 was only slightly more populous than Birmingham or Atlanta—and just as southern. Within the city's limits more than two hundred farms gave the nation's capital a distinctly rural look, and down the broad thoroughfares of Pennsylvania and Constitution avenues, lined with dusty trees, horse-drawn carts still delivered the town's milk or bakery goods at a slow, clip-clop pace. Jimmy and Maude Byrnes found their home across the street from the Capitol at the Congress Hall Hotel, where the registry of southern politicians made the building almost a small southern city in itself. Byrnes could here see the arrival of the longtime hotel guest Oscar W. Underwood, the Deep South majority leader of the House, driven in his wife's new electric car. Here also was the hero of southern agrarians, William Jennings Bryan, the orotund Great Commoner, who had stayed on for years and years. As Jimmy Byrnes crossed the hotel's lobby or entered the bar, he could spot a crowd gathering around the aging Thomas "Cotton Tom" Heflin, as a story in "true Alabama dialect was being told by the genial Senator," reported the *Christian Science Monitor*. Both inside the Congress Hall and out, there was much of the southern, small-town life in President Taft's Washington, and for white, middle-class couples like the Byrneses, life had a sweetness that characterized small towns in those prewar years. The hotel guests remembered for years afterward, for example, the Saturday-night dances staged by the Congress Hall Hotel management to bring together "the sons and daughters of the congressional family."

Life in the House of Representatives also promised to be sweet for southern Democrats, including Jimmy Byrnes. His success in the election of 1910 was part of a national sweep of congressional districts by the party, and the House had gone Democratic for the first time since 1892. Democratic control of the Senate and the presidency also appeared increasingly likely as the elections of 1912 neared, and for the presidential nomination many Democrats were favoring either Oscar Underwood, from Alabama, or the Virginia-born Woodrow Wilson. Either would bring to the White House the most southern administration of the twentieth century. To Jimmy Byrnes, who could count himself lucky to have gotten in at the beginning, the first term in Congress was a time to claim some power of his own and to cultivate the friendship of men who would be even more powerful later. He accomplished the first by gaining assignment in 1911 to the Sixty-second Congress' prestigious Committee on Banking and Currency. He moved toward the second by winning the favor of the cynical leader of the South Carolina delegation, George Legaré from Charleston.

Legaré was the first in a series of men, usually older, who acted as political fathers to Jimmy Byrnes, advancing Byrnes' public career and looking out for his private interests. This patrimony is a distinguished, even intimidating roll call of influence: it includes Woodrow Wilson, Bernard Baruch, and Franklin Roosevelt. Most, like George Legaré, were at least twelve years older than Byrnes; President Wilson and, later, Senator "Pitchfork Ben" Tillman were Byrnes' seniors by twenty-six and thirty-three years, respectively. But the filial thread common to all these disparate, powerful, and, at times, mutually antagonistic lives was an affection for their Jimmy. On each of these men Byrnes practiced, with varying degrees of success, what a contemporary of Byrnes called his "art of pushing ahead in the world pleasantly, the art of gaining power without seeming to realize it, without seeming to care for anything so much as enlivening the passing moments."

He enlivened the passing moments. All of the men Byrnes chose as political fathers possessed in addition to their power a sense of their own mortality and an awareness that each passing moment brought with it, minute by minute, a diminution of their power. Some were only a few years away from their deathbeds when they met Jimmy Byrnes, and knew it; some, like Baruch, were losing power when they met Byrnes, and they feared it. To both, the infirm and the afraid, Jimmy Byrnes gave an indispensable illusion. It was not simply that he courted these older men with respect, being always quick and able to do as they bid; that was their accustomed due, and most of these men, again like Baruch, had long expected all the respect that money and power could buy. But what Jimmy Byrnes gave, money couldn't buy. He gave not love but youth. While always attentively respectful, Byrnes dared to do what none of these men's paid courtiers dared; he treated these old men as though they were his own youthful contemporaries.

He enlivened the passing moment. Hence the pleasing illusion that time spent with Jimmy Byrnes was not time passing and that power given to him was not power lost. In fairness to and in understanding of Byrnes, whose father had died young, this illumination of a second life in older men may have had with Byrnes a necessity deeper than politics. But whatever its original psychology, this graceful art no doubt helped move Jimmy Byrnes along in the world. Few could withstand his charm. Throughout a long political career, the sole exception was Franklin Roosevelt, who, no matter how well pleased, refused even when dying to accept the tempting illusion of Byrnes' youthfulness. Roosevelt thus died without appointing Byrnes the successor to his power. In him Byrnes was to meet his match, perhaps because even while dying, Roosevelt was *the* supreme illusionist. But even during those frustrating years with Roosevelt, an intimate of Byrnes noted how well the South Carolinian "dissembles his ambitions behind a light and airy manner" and that "behind that smiling countenance is a shrewd and calculating mind." By then Byrnes had for many years practiced smiling. Since 1911 he had been developing his "art of pushing ahead in the world pleasantly." And not only was George Legaré the first of the political fathers on whom Jimmy Byrnes practiced his art; he was responsible as well for having taught him many of its finer points.

George Legaré was a successful city attorney in Charleston when Jimmy Byrnes, as a boy running errands to the Four Corners of Law, first heard his voice in courtroom debate. Years later, when they met in the House of Representatives, Legaré was even more of a worldly success; yet if Byrnes had looked closely at Legaré's elegant tailoring and urbane manners, he would have perceived that behind the smooth appearance of the Charlestonian lawyer lay more of Jimmy Byrnes' Calhoun Street world of poverty and push to get ahead than of a planter's moneyed privilege. Although his Huguenot family had been prominent in South Carolina politics for generations, George Legaré had been born "land poor" and, like the young Byrnes, had interrupted his education for salaried work. He was also, like Byrnes, small physically, and he shared with him the diminutive man's delight in triumphing by his wits. The Charlestonian's acerbic wit was a fearsome weapon among men, although his sharp tongue was somewhat softened by his droll little laugh and by his searching brown eyes, kindly and cynical. Men liked him and, in recognition of his abilities, were willing to move aside and accord him an aristocrat's place among other men. Even the state's notoriously ill-tempered Senator Pitchfork Ben Tillman, who normally had no use for Charleston's Bourbon aristocracy, declared himself a champion of George Legaré. "Men loved him in spite of themselves," Tillman exclaimed, "simply because they were obligated to."

Legaré had, in short, fashioned himself into an aristocrat. To Jimmy Byrnes, a self-made man with an eye on something better, the creation of this role offered the best of both worlds, patrician and political. The self-made man as aristocrat was a role Byrnes himself played for the rest of his life. Years after Legaré's death, there remained a shade of Legaré in Byrnes' voice when, as a senator or a Supreme Court justice, Byrnes would declare with an aristocrat's offhand attitude toward money that all he desired from public life was "two tailored suits a year, three meals a day, and a reasonable amount of good liquor." In fact, Byrnes desired a great deal more than that, but he had learned from George Legaré the art of combining his private desires with other people's pleasures.

Byrnes and Legaré saw each other frequently during the Sixty-second Congress, from 1911 to 1913. Byrnes came to know Legaré's little laugh, his soft Charlestonian accent, and his penchant for playing practical jokes. His new mentor's appearance also was remarkable. Legaré had a head that was very oval and pale; topped by a pair of smooth wings, which were his locks brushed backward, it gave his face the disconcerting look of an egg about to fly heavenward. His quiet laugh and his faint, almost mocking smile were often turned on Byrnes, and one day Legaré gave him a piece of political advice that very likely saved Byrnes' young political life.

Byrnes had become caught up in the work of the House Banking and Currency Committee, which had in 1911 begun a highly talked-about inquiry. Called the Pujo committee—after its chairman, Representative Ar-sène Pujo from Louisiana—this group of Democratic congressmen, including Byrnes, substantiated the existence of the so-called money trust, a near-monopoly of the nation's credit and finances in the house of Morgan. As promises of banking reform and a more flexible currency were gaining for the Democratic party a national popularity, Byrnes had hoped to share in the glory and to campaign for reelection in 1912 as an important national legislator. Here he almost overstepped himself. In his belief that he had been made for greater things, Byrnes neglected the political rise in his district of a local man named Calhoun; in a state that still revered the nineteenth century's John C. Calhoun, this South Carolina lawyer with the same last name had built up a following in the Second District and had declared his candidacy against Byrnes. It was George Legaré who pointed out to Jimmy Byrnes the folly of his ways.

Happening to meet with Legaré at the close of a summer afternoon session, Byrnes was eager to tell him about the publicity attending the financial investigation. The Charlestonian listened for a while. "Oh yes, Jimmy, I guess I did hear about that Pujo business," he at length replied. "Another thing I've heard with some regret was about that fellow Calhoun who's fixing to run against you." He paused and seemed to study Byrnes. "And let me tell you one thing." The quizzical brown eyes looked over Byrnes, and a faint smile began to play on Legaré's lips. "If you go home and talk to your folks about nothing but this money trust of yours, they'll listen for a while, and then they'll say, 'It's just too bad. He *was* such a *nice* little fellow!'"

Byrnes never forgot. Close to thirty years later he was still telling the story to journalists, laughing at his own innocence and quoting George Legaré with a deadly mimicry: "'It's just too bad. He *was* such a *nice* little fellow!'" But that was years after Byrnes had made his own congressional chair unassailable. On hearing Legaré's warning that summer day in 1911, Byrnes had no time to lose laughing. He set to work in earnest reminding the voters in South Carolina's Second District that they needed Congress-man Byrnes in Washington. Private bills, for instance, were a handy re-minder of a congressman's indispensability. Byrnes became a master of these acts of Congress for individual relief, covering, as he later explained, everything from recompensing "a contractor who had lost money building a post office, to replacing false teeth mislaid by a charwoman in the Federal Courts Building." A total of twenty-one bills for individual relief or pension increases were introduced by Byrnes during the three sessions of the Sixty-second Congress; by comparison, the other six members of the South Carolina delegation together introduced a total of only forty. If Jimmy Byrnes lost his place in Congress, it would not be because of the char-woman's false teeth.

In a more significant piece of legislation, Byrnes for the first time got the federal government into the business of maintaining state roads. Byrnes wrote one bill combining twenty-three earlier versions of road bills that had failed in the House for various reasons, and he prevailed upon the other lawmakers to back his version. His success involved a job of persuasion remarkable for a freshman congressman; and after the Senate passed the bill, federal funds for the first time were appropriated on an experimental basis to improve state roads used by rural mail carriers in, among other places, South Carolina's Second District. Saying that the spending of federal money was justified because of the presence of mail-carrying federal employees was an ingenious argument; and at a time when the federal government paid generously to have most mail carried by train, and railroad companies therefore had a vested interest in discouraging other experiments, passage of Byrnes' bill in the Senate was, once more, remarkable. Even the state's old Senator Tillman was impressed by this young man, although he doubted Byrnes' promise that the roads would thus be permanently improved. "No road can be made absolutely permanent," he wrote to Byrnes. Senator and Mrs. Tillman had recently taken the grand tour of Europe, and the senior senator wanted young Byrnes to have the benefit of his experience: "I passed from Sorrento to Amalfi on a road built by the Romans two thousand years ago and it was in fine condition," pronounced the senator. Unfortunately, times had changed, as the senator then informed the young congressman: "But these people were not building roads for the purpose of making money, and most of the work was done by slaves."

But Jimmy Byrnes' purpose in building roads was South Carolinian, not Roman. By the summer of 1912, Byrnes could present himself to the voters of the Second District as the "good roads" congressman, just as he had promised as a progressive candidate in 1910. Byrnes won an impressive victory in the primary and thus was able to return to Washington that autumn for what promised to be harvest time for southern Democrats.

By that fall the hopes of southern Democrats had been realized; in the upcoming Sixty-third Congress, southerners controled all important congressional committees and enjoyed large caucus majorities in both the House and the Senate, which that year also had gone Democratic. (Because of the large party majorities in both chambers, issues would be settled in caucus rather than on the floor in debate.) Most important, the presidency was now Democratic; Woodrow Wilson's victory that November over Republicans divided between Taft and Theodore Roosevelt guaranteed a Democratic administration in 1913 with the strongest southern representation since the Civil War.

Woodrow Wilson, born into a prominent Presbyterian minister's family in Virginia and raised at his father's manses in antebellum Georgia, had always regarded the South as having a special significance. Wilson grew up in Augusta, Georgia—separated from Aiken, South Carolina, and

Edgefield County only by the Savannah River—and there, as a four-year-old boy, experienced what was to become his first clear memory of childhood: standing at his father's gate, he heard men saying that Abraham Lincoln was elected and that there was to be a civil war; the young Wilson ran to his father and asked what it meant. Later, in the 1870s, Wilson's father had moved the family to Columbia, South Carolina, where the senior Wilson had attended the seminary, and it was in South Carolina that the teenage Woodrow Wilson, for whom religious duty would always be superior to all things, underwent a religious experience and enrolled as a member of a local Presbyterian church. "The only place in the world, the only place in the country," Wilson later wrote, "where nothing has to be explained to me is the South." The context of this sentiment was, significantly, Wilson's monograph *Robert E. Lee: An Interpretation.*

Astute observers of the president Wilson have noted, however, that his fondness for the South seemed to increase in proportion to the distance he was able to put between himself and the region, and Wilson himself could not have failed to notice that the distinctions of his careers as a scholar, college president, and reform governor came to him only after he left the South. (As a young man, Woodrow Wilson failed at establishing a law practice in Atlanta in 1882, at about the same time Elizabeth Byrnes was setting up her dressmaking business in Charleston.) Nevertheless, Wilson maintained his southern ties for political as well as sentimental reasons. Southern newspapers and party organizers in 1910 were among the first of his supporters in the campaign for the presidential nomination, and southern congressional leaders played an important part at the 1912 convention in turning aside a last-ditch attempt by supporters of Oscar Underwood of Alabama to wrest the nomination from Wilson. As a nonvoting delegate, Byrnes attended that Democratic convention at Baltimore beginning the sweltering week of June 23, and he and Maude shared a rented house there with another young couple sympathetic to progressive ideas, Franklin and Eleanor Roosevelt of New York. (The slender and then physically healthy Roosevelt also attended as a nonvoting delegate, and his participation at the convention was limited to organizing enthusiastic demonstrations for Wilson.) During Wilson's campaign that fall, his progressive platform calling for reduced tariffs and a more responsive national currency was favorably received in the South; in the agricultural regions there, lower tariffs on manufactured items were just as popular in the 1910s as they had been in the 1830s, and the promise of a new Federal Reserve banking system would make credit more accessible to southeastern urban businessmen. Consequently, the South, with its large block of electoral votes, went solidly for Wilson, and before assuming office the president-elect decided that he must cooperate with southern congressional leaders in both chambers in order to win passage of his progressive program. As a result, Byrnes got busy.

Byrnes obtained appointment to the newly created House Roads Committee in 1913 and once again made himself useful to the older generation in power. His patron George Legaré was now entitled by seniority to a place on the Appropriations Committee, the first of his state's delegation to hold majority membership there in the twentieth century. With an old friend like Legaré on Appropriations and his own membership on the Roads Committee, there seemed to be few limits to what Jimmy Byrnes could do for the Second District, or for himself. With the inauguration of President-elect Wilson just a few months away in March, the new year of 1913 appeared for Byrnes and other southern Democrats to be a time of renewed hopes.

But for George Legaré there was to be neither time nor hope. He had asked to be excused from the third session of the Sixty-second Congress, and had returned to his home in Charleston; his friends, including Byrnes, were told to expect him to return to Washington shortly. It was known that George Legaré was in frail health and in need of frequent rest; what was not known, and what Legaré had never mentioned, both out of political expediency and of good manners, was that he was dying. Legaré had tuberculosis. Earlier he had rested in the Appalachian Mountains of the South, hoping that the cooler air and moisture would heal his lungs; but although the droll little Charlestonian made many friends among the rougher mountain people, he could gain laughter but not more time. So he returned to his family's home at Charleston, and as he lay in bed on Friday evening, January 31, 1913, he died peacefully. Saturday morning Byrnes woke up in his Washington hotel and heard the news: the South Carolina delegation would leave that day by train for a funeral at Charleston.

After watching dapper little George Legaré be buried at Charleston's Magnolia Cemetery, Jimmy Byrnes returned to Washington: he did not intend to let any grass grow under his feet while he looked for a new political protector. He found such a figure in a man thirty-five years older than he, the senior U.S. senator from South Carolina, who, like Byrnes, had grown up fatherless. For this reason, and perhaps because with his new protector the passion for control was always strongest, the older man, Senator Benjamin "Pitchfork Ben" Tillman, may have chosen Jimmy Byrnes as much as Byrnes chose him. In political circles Tillman was known for "binding his friends to him as with hooks of steel," and for five years, from 1913 until the older man's death in 1918, those hooks drew Byrnes, ever willing, closer and closer. "There was hardly a day during the sessions of Congress when I did not either visit his office or speak to him over the telephone," Byrnes later recalled of his years with Tillman. "I came to love him, and in return he treated me as one of his sons."

This paternal treatment, both men knew, would do much to promote Byrnes into the Senate chamber; but that would be years ahead, after the old man died in office. For the present, the two men enjoyed each other's company as they daily discussed and dispensed political favors among the South Carolina delegation. Unlike George Legaré, Byrnes' new patron was not to be found at the barroom of the Congress Hall Hotel. Instead, Byrnes found him living with his wife the quiet life of a semi-invalid at the out-of-the-way Dewey Hotel, on L Street. There the couple was registered as Senator and Mrs. Benjamin Ryan Tillman of Edgefield County, South Carolina. Byrnes had chosen as his political protector a man who, though now frail in body, had dominated his state's politics for three decades by force of will or, if need be, by force of loaded guns.

"Mrs. Tillman and I miss your breezy visits to the hotel and office," the senator wrote Byrnes in 1913. When the hotel door opened, the face one saw did not encourage second visits. An empty eye socket above Tillman's left cheekbone immediately arrested attention; the features on that side of the senator's face had also been pulled downward by a stroke in 1910 into a permanent scowl. His single brown eye, a glint underneath a shock of black hair, and his still-bulky body and swarthy skin gave him the appearance of what Tillman himself cheerfully admitted was a murderous Catiline. The senator's rebarbative nature seemed confirmed by second impressions. "I am a rude man and don't care," Tillman often declared. In his frequent Senate debates he ignored parliamentary procedures, often refusing to yield the floor and jabbing the air toward his opponents' side of the aisle with a peculiarly violent motion of his arms. It was not simply his peculiarities, however, that packed the Senate galleries with spectators when Tillman had the floor; they came to hear as well as watch this strangely eloquent man who season after season wore the same rusty, black Prince Albert coat and creased plantation hat. Before addressing his audiences, Tillman would thank God for his peculiarities. "If I had none perhaps I would be an insignificant and unknown man." And then from the tongue of this one-eyed and rough-looking man in black there would come an eloquence unlike any other's. Everyone, friend or foe, who heard Tillman speak remembered it for years. His was "a far-reaching voice," remembered an unsympathetic journalist, "which, if harsh and stringent, had a sub-tone of appealing melody."

Ben Tillman was a good speaker in part because he was a good hater. His hatreds were to his mind direct and organizing: he hated Republicans and emancipated Negroes, big banking and big railroads, and any other forces he perceived as hostile toward southern farmers. Against all of them he fought—"sticking them with my pitchfork," as he liked to say. Byrnes knew his man; yet he had chosen neither a mere clowning provincial nor, worse, a railing preacher of hate. Had Tillman been simply that, Jimmy Byrnes, because of both his personality and his ambition, would never have hitched his wagon to such a baleful star. In choosing Tillman as his patron, Byrnes had his reasons. The senator appealed, by his defects and his strengths, to a national as well as a state constituency; and in him Byrnes had for the first time a protector for ambitions reaching beyond the Second District of South Carolina. For instance, Tillman's enmity toward Republicans and the black vote accurately represented the political realities of South Carolina that would extend throughout Byrnes' career to the last third of the twentieth century; Tillman's distrust of big business was the result less of his provinciality than of his participation in national Democratic agrarian politics; and his championing of financially pressed southern white farmers was a manifestation less of demagogism than of his instinctual alignment with the people he felt were most like himself.

It was in farming that this willful and sensuous man found a channel into which he could pour his passions. Byrnes often visited Tillman at his working farm at Edgefield, where in addition to raising cotton Tillman constantly experimented with new cash crops such as asparagus, pecans, and figs. Tillman almost never made money on these ventures; but as long as he cleared enough cash to plant another year, the season was to his mind no loss. For farming was to Ben Tillman more than just a politician's avocation; it was, as one astute observer of his character noted, "his window into reality." Even at the height of his national powers as a senator, his thoughts returned to the farm at Edgefield. On a spring day early in 1915, Tillman scribbled a note on stationery of the U.S. Senate Committee on Naval Affairs, of which he was chairman: "Peaches and Plum trees planted in orchard behind Aunt Kitty's, March 22, 1915." And then followed the names that were to his mind a delight, the farmer's poetry of the particular: "Crawford's late, Globe, Sharp Damson, Stonewall Jackson's Free."

Another of Tillman's delights, which Byrnes could see as he motored up to the Tillman veranda from the town of Aiken, was a profusion of flowers. Roses, lilies, narcissi, orchids, and seedlings borrowed liberally from the National Botanical Gardens enabled Ben Tillman to indulge a passion for horticulture that dated from his boyhood. "I have seen him walk among the flowers he had planted and speak of them as his children," Byrnes later recalled. Tillman took other surprising walks. While in Washington, Byrnes saw him occasionally strolling in literary discussion with the stalwart Republican senator from Massachusetts, George Hoar; the New Englander found in Tillman a companion deeply read in English poetry and novels. This and his friendship with Senator William Chandler, a Republican of New Hampshire, apparently filled a need in Tillman's character that superseded even his demands of party loyalty—a need for what another New Englander, Henry Cabot Lodge, shrewdly isolated as "affection and sympathy," which, Lodge added after Tillman's death, "I think he craved."

He might crave it, but he would never ask another man for it. He might look for it, and when another, younger man gave it, tacitly and with great deference, the way Jimmy Byrnes gave it, Tillman would love that man as though he were his son. But he would never ask. Asking would mean explaining, and as long as he lived, Ben Tillman felt that he never owed explanations. Only after his death would there be a fuller disclosure of what he had so wanted since before the Civil War. What Jimmy Byrnes had immediately sensed in 1912 was Ben Tillman's lifelong craving for love.

Seventeen-year-old Ben Tillman had volunteered for the Confederate Army in 1864 when a doctor decided to remove the boy's left eyeball and, with it, infectious flesh. His mother may secretly have been relieved that by a comparatively endurable sacrifice at least her Ben, her youngest and favorite son, might live beyond the war. Sophia Tillman had by 1864 already buried four sons: her eldest had been killed in the Mexican War, nine days after she had given birth to Ben; two sons had been murdered in private quarrels; a fourth had died of natural causes; and fifteen years earlier, her husband, also named Benjamin, had died of typhoid fever. Before his death the elder Ben Tillman had also killed a man.

There had always been the "desperate strain" among the male Tillmans of Edgefield County that, according to one historian of their generations, "flowered in numerous homicides in peace and a distinguished gallantry in war." Of Sophia Tillman's three sons who had survived peacetime, two, James and George, were in 1864 on active service with the Confederacy; it is not to be wondered, then, that she nurtured the hope that Ben, "the petted darling of his mother's heart," might be spared the opportunity of fatally demonstrating the family strain. Her fondness for her last born went beyond the fact that Ben's father had died when the boy was two or that the son was her dead husband's namesake; more deeply, the mother's fondness was based on the understanding between them, for throughout her twenty-seven-year widowhood, Ben of all her children seemed best to appreciate what she had done on land that was hers.

Sophia Tillman on her husband's death in 1849 had taken possession of 1,800 acres of Edgefield County and fifty slaves with which to work it. Edgefield is a thickety land, separated from Georgia by the Savannah River and crosscut by innumerable creeks. Yet cleared of its briars, slash pine, and scrub oak, Edgefield reveals its fundamental secret: a rich, alluvial soil, deposited deep over thousands of years by the Savannah on its way to the ocean, a loam crumbling easily between the fingers and varying in color from a reddish yellow to an unsullied white. For those who owned it and planted it in short-staple cotton that would grow in the upstate, that Edgefield loam was a source of wealth to rival that of the great low-country houses of Charleston. Sophia Tillman intended to work for her profit the 1,800 acres she was willed by her late husband, and she intended to work those acres as a farm matron, not a plantation mistress. Ben Tillman later told Byrnes that his mother had been her own overseer, meaning that she had worked side by side with the black slaves in the fields. Within a decade, this strong-willed woman had seen the results of her labor; she had increased her holdings to 3,500 acres and her slaves from fifty to eighty-six, and her household was considered among the wealthiest in Edgefield County. Not that Sophia Tillman ever forgot the value of a dollar: years after her death, her neighbors still told the story of having seen her slave, sent to market toward Augusta with a wagonload of cherries, stopped on the Savannah bridge and tossing the red fruit into the river. Such were Mrs. Tillman's instructions, the black man explained; she had set the fair price her produce was to bring and had made him promise that on the return trip he would toss the entire wagonload into the Savannah River rather than take a penny less. Sophia Tillman would rather that the chub and brim eat her cherries, she declared, than that her neighbors should enjoy the fruits of her labors by paying less than they were worth.

Many laughed, but only Ben Tillman seemed to understand; he alone of her children seemed completely to share her passion for never surrendering even the smallest part of the two possessions that mattered most: land and family. Ben Tillman had proved his fidelity to the first when, after improvident speculations by his older brothers, liens were placed against the Tillman property. Ben Tillman took a year off from school, and by selling butter and eggs at market and by calling personally on people with accounts receivable who had ignored his mother, he helped her clear the debts. His second loyalty, to family, he provided after a telegram came in September 1863 telling that his brother James had been shot in the left arm and was somewhere on the Chickamauga battlefield.

As an old man well into the twentieth century, Ben Tillman found his thoughts turning back to that long-ago journey with his mother to find his brother. In an autobiography unfinished at his death, Tillman told how mother and son immediately took a train toward the west Georgia battlefield where James Tillman lay, "to go to him and bring him home."

Arriving in Atlanta, they found that city swollen with the more than fourteen thousand Confederate wounded from the battlefield sixty miles away. Chickamauga was at that time (and later by historians) considered a great Confederate victory; if so, Ben Tillman may have wondered what a defeat would look like. "Every church and every building of any size had been turned into a hospital," he wrote; groaning, bloodied men seemed everywhere, and in the streets the boy who had scarcely traveled beyond a country market saw the terrible press of war: refugees, sutlers, prostitutes, journalists, and, above all, armed men in gray, frightened and angry. One of them had heard of an Edgefield man in a hospital nearer the battlefield; women were allowed no closer to the front than Atlanta, and leaving his mother in the city, Ben Tillman had traveled on alone.

After a night's ride atop a boxcar loaded with wounded, in the morning Tillman assisted a surgeon in changing the dressing of a man whose nose had been shot off—"the sight and scent of it made me deathly sick"—and got further directions to the hospital where his brother might be. There he found James, apparently rallying despite his bandaged elbow. The two brothers began to laugh, as though it were a rare joke to have been winged by a Yankee bullet. The jokes were premature; James Tillman eventually died of his wounds.

But not before Ben Tillman got him home. Sandy soil or living flesh, Ben Tillman understood that it was possession that mattered, and Sophia Tillman saw that it might be her youngest son, should he survive the war, who would keep and perhaps even add to what she had accomplished on the family farm. She returned Tillman to his studies at the local academy, where, despite meager rations—"Confederate money was plentiful but food was scarce," Tillman wrote in his autobiography—and increasing pain in his left eye, he read the whole of Horace and Virgil and was declared the class "brag scholar," or valedictorian. Sophia Tillman had hopes of sending Ben to South Carolina College after the war.

But in 1864 the Confederacy issued its "cradle to the grave" call for troops, whereby every white male from seventeen to fifty, Ben Tillman included, was liable for conscription. Despite increasing eye pain, Ben left school for home and wrote to an artillery company volunteering his services. He was awaiting a reply when, resting one fall day while his mother molded butter, he fell on the porch floor in convulsions. An army surgeon summoned by Sophia Tillman diagnosed a sore or tumor at the base of the eye and made his decision: operating by candlelight, he removed Ben Tillman's inflamed eye. In a way, the doctor may have done him a favor. By the time Ben had recovered in the spring of 1865, the war was over; before it had ended, there was many a seventeen-year-old boy, drafted in the fall of 1864 and dead by the spring of 1865, who might have wished he had Ben Tillman's luck. And throughout a long political life, Ben Tillman must have taken a grim satisfaction in knowing that there were many men, in both the North and the South, who wished that in his youth a bullet had stopped Ben Tillman.

The loss of his eye brought another benefit: Ben Tillman gained a wife. Before the war had ended, when Sherman's army invaded South Carolina, Sophia Tillman had sent her invalided son across the Savannah to comparative safety in Georgia. There at a cousin's house he had met fifteen-year-old Sallie Starke; three years later they married. It was to be a love match on both sides: as an old man, Tillman would still sing to himself the popular song of their courting, "Sallie Is the Gal for Me," and after Tillman's death, Jimmy Byrnes would recall how frequently he had witnessed Tillman quiet his volcanic anger, in Byrnes' description, "at a mere word from his wife, who called him 'Bennie.' " The young couple settled in 1868 on 430 acres given Tillman by his mother, and for the next eight years, until 1876, Tillman concentrated his energies on establishing his family and his farm, and continuing his education.

Almost every day in the 1870s and 1880s his wife would find Tillman at each midday's rest from his farm chores reclining on the porch floor and reading a book, the back of an overturned chair for a pillow, oblivious to his small children playing at his feet. He came by this study to know the British poets by heart, and in those early years he acquired his lifelong ability to quote Shakespeare and Robert Burns by the page. Partly his reading was a labor of love and partly an act of revenge. The Civil War had cut short Tillman's hopes as a scholar, and the war's short rations and other privations may have contributed, he believed, to the disease of his eye; by acquiring a literary education in spite of these circumstances, Ben Tillman not only fed his appetite for words, but those words became the means by which he could bend the war's personal defeats to his will.

In his married years after the Civil War, he fed other appetites as well: Ben Tillman ate as omnivorously as he read. Collards, pork ribs, turkey, fruitcakes, and pig's feet were among the favorites he consumed (when Byrnes first met Tillman, the senator was as large, though not as fat, as William H. Taft). Partly Tillman's gusto, like his reading, satisfied his childhood deprivations of wartime, when he had read Latin on an empty stomach; but food may have satisfied a deeper need in Tillman, an appetite for possession of the fields and the good things they gave. He brought to his work in his fields a passion men usually express in other carnal activities. A neighbor described Tillman thus: "He sowed oats broadcast, dipping his hands into the sack and letting fly the seeds; he shucked corn in the crib, covering his clothes with silks. . . . He saw to the milking of cows, and if necessary took a hand himself." In time, like his mother before him, Tillman became known as one of the hardest-working farmers in Edgefield County. For years it was his custom on market days to walk up and down the streets of the Edgefield market town, carrying a basket of eggs or butter proudly under his arm, followed by a Negro servant with a wagon full of Tillman harvest. Among men his "heavy agricultural strokes" were praised, and taking note of Tillman, the *Edgefield Chronicle* county newspaper declared, "it would be well if there were a hundred such pushing men as Ben Tillman within five miles of this place."

So long as pigs grew fat and butter churned sweet, Ben Tillman might never have troubled his soul overmuch, and he might have remained all his life simply what he was in the summer of 1876; a happy, hardworking South Carolina farmer. But inside he carried a seed different from that of the happy agriculturist—that "desperate strain" of his family's male line, which in the past had so often flowered into homicides. On a July night in 1876, the seed at last flowered into acts of murder; and when that night was over, both Ben Tillman and the politics of South Carolina even until the lifetime of Jimmy Byrnes had been together irrevocably changed.

South Carolina by July of 1876 was moving toward a second civil war that threatened to draw as much blood in the state as the first had spilled. This time the battle lines were racial. In the mid-1870s white farmers and former slaveholders such as the Tillman family still owned much of the real property in South Carolina, and they had begun to recover the material losses suffered by their class during the first Civil War; but the political power these whites had exercised before the war was now placed into black hands. Since 1865 South Carolina, the first state to secede, had been ruled first by military occupation and then by a succession of carpetbag governors, lately arrived from the North and controlling large majorities of black Republicans. White, usually Democratic voters were so outnumbered by black registration in their counties that they considered political participation hopeless. In 1872, in the state's general election, forty thousand eligible white voters chose simply not to cast ballots. It also disturbed these white landowners to see their former slaves preparing for a serious defense of their newly acquired civil rights. Under Republican governors blacks had begun to arm and drill themselves into the South Carolina National Guard, and across the state blacks occupied positions of local power such as those of town marshals and justices of the peace. More and more white men began to discuss armed intimidation of the black majority. A peacekeeping force of white federal troops had remained in South Carolina since 1865, but advocates of armed white revolt argued that these northern troops, at least tacitly, would support a white revolt by doing nothing. Advocates began to urge the organizing of secret military companies, or "rifle clubs," throughout South Carolina. Among white men this plan was discussed by various names: it was known as the Straightout, the Shotgun, or, most ominously, the Edgefield Policy.

The bad blood erupted on July 4, 1876. That day a troop of black militia was celebrating the national Independence Day by parading the streets of Hamburg, an Edgefield County market town on the Savannah River that lay within the congressional district that would one day be Jimmy Byrnes'. The parade blocked the passage of two white farmers in a buggy who had started up the main street just as the black militia company turned down it. Accounts differ: the blacks claimed that the two white men drew pistols and forced a passage through the troops; the whites maintained that the black advanced on their buggy with leveled bayonets. The two groups parted without violence, but each side swore out warrants against the other, and a trial date was set for the following Saturday, July 8. The afternoon of the trial, members of the various white rifle clubs began to ride into town. Among them was a one-eyed but strangely attractive member of the Edgefield County Sweetwater Saber Club: twenty-nine-year-old Ben Tillman.

What happened next is best described in the title of the congressional investigation that followed: the "Slaughter of American Citizens." Tillman himself later provided amplification. "It was our purpose to attend the trial, and if any opportunity offered, to provoke a row," he explained. And, he added, if no opportunity was offered to provoke a racial riot, "we were to make one." The Hamburg justice of the peace, apprised of this intent by the whites and of the large number of armed men in town, both black and white, postponed the trial. The rifle clubs then took the opportunity to make their row. About sundown they surrounded the black militia company and demanded the surrender of weapons. When its members refused, gunfire was exchanged. Some blacks broke and ran.

Among them was the Hamburg town marshal, a black man who, according to Tillman, "had clubbed a great number of white men" and who "was more hated by whites of the surrounding county than any other individual of the race." Fearing he would be killed if he was captured, the marshal made a desperate run for the Savannah River and possibly safety on the opposite shore. Thirty or forty pistols and rifles, including Ben Tillman's, fired at the running figure in the darkness, but astonishingly no bullet struck him, and the Negro had almost reached the water's edge. Suddenly a blast from a shotgun flipped the man nearly head over heels. Silence followed, and then voices in the night began to wonder whether the running silhouette was really the marshal and whether the blast had been fatal. Ben Tillman and a friend volunteered to go and make sure. About this time, Tillman later recalled, "after a period of intense darkness the moon rose and began to cast its lurid light over the strange and unaccustomed scene." At a South Carolina political gathering he addressed thirty-four years later, Tillman recalled walking down the street exposed to possible gunfire by the still-resisting blacks, kneeling by the crumpled figure, and taking a look. It was the marshal, and he was indeed dead; Tillman always remembered and later described to his after-dinner audience how the body had appeared in the horrible serenity of moonlight: "a large part of his face had been torn away by buckshot."

The slaughter had only begun. By this time the black militia members had been frightened into surrendering, and some thirty or forty of them were under guard, when word began to spread that a white man, McKie Meriwether, had been killed in the initial exchange of gunfire. Two Meriwether cousins approached where Ben Tillman was standing and asked whether the shooting of one fleeing Negro was sufficient reprisal for the death of their cousin. "It was agreed that we could not have a story like that go out as the record of the night's work," Tillman later told his audience. The Meriwether cousins and some others were allowed to take five black prisoners, one at a time, from the group of unarmed militia;

each black man was taken, in Tillman's words, "a little ways down the street and shot." Before the killing began, one of the executioners had run out of cartridges; Tillman, who after firing at the marshal still had five rounds in his pistol, lent the man a gun.

Before the fifth man was shot, there was a sudden recognition by Ben Tillman. When the last of the five black victims was pulled from the group of prisoners and taken down the street to die, Tillman "by a strange co-incidence" recognized a familiar face in his black features. In what now must have seemed another world, where a teenage Ben Tillman had read the Latin poets and hoped to become a scholar, this young Negro had been the errand boy at the Edgefield County academy where Tillman had studied and had "made our fires, brought wood, blackened shoes." This man too was taken a little way out of sight, and then there were pistol shots.

By now it was after midnight, and in Ben Tillman's words, "whether it was the white men were sick of their bloody work, or something else, I do not know," but the whites left off their killing of black prisoners; after firing a volley over the heads of the black militiamen, they allowed the rest to run away. The white men began to drift home, but Ben Tillman may have been reluctant to leave what he called the scene "of the battle." He was among the last to rein his horse away from the deserted village in the moonlight. Whether or not he had felt himself changed at the killings of Hamburg, and so was disinclined to return to his settled existence as an Edgefield farmer, is unknown; but there is no mistaking a change in the perception of Ben Tillman by his neighbors. By the close of the year, the Sweetwater Saber Club had elected Tillman its captain, and his white neighbors were beginning to speak of him as a developing political leader. For one fact had become plain to his fellow gunmen after that night's bloody work at Hamburg: Ben Tillman was not susceptible to the fears of ordinary men.

What perhaps he did fear most, and what ordinary men most eagerly accept, was a loss of control over his own fate. That would explain his determined reading after the loss of his eye, and his later fears of going into debt and losing his farm. But what other men most fear—death—apparently never moved Ben Tillman at all. So when the bullets of Hamburg began to worry the air, ordinary men grouped themselves around the bulky farmer from Edgefield and began to call him captain. For it was apparent that in a fight, even a fight to the death, Ben Tillman simply did not scare: he seemed to know that he would be the victor.

As he reined his horse away, Tillman became aware of a new feeling: he was very hungry. On his way home, he stopped at a neighbor's house, and ate heartily.

———

Despite a national outcry, no one was ever tried for the murder of the freed blacks at Hamburg. The Republican state government issued warrants for Ben Tillman, charging him and others present at the Hamburg massacre with acts of murder and conspiracy to commit murder, but the trials were delayed after a show of force by the white rifle clubs. These shows of force displayed clearly Ben Tillman's hand and his developing genius for political symbolism. The South Carolina rifle clubs had in northern newspapers been accused of futilely "waving the bloody shirt" of rebellion. Along with some other members, Tillman—who all his life was quick to ingest an insult and return it, not without some grotesque humor, larger than life—prevailed upon the wives and friends of the defendants to make for them shirts of blood-red flannel. The "red shirts" soon became a male fashion throughout South Carolina, and as each white man in the morning put on with his flannel shirt a tacit declaration of his willingness to fight the Civil War again, federal and state Republican officials soon felt themselves drowning in a red sea of Confederate pride. The Republican governor called on President Grant for help; the latter, perhaps apprised of the military strength of white anti-Reconstruction sentiment in the South and apparently unwilling to risk a new civil war in the last months of his administration for the sake of a few murdered Negroes in South Carolina, declined to get involved. A congressional investigation came to nothing. The Red Shirts continued their intimidation into the fall of 1876, when their armed presence at the polling places kept many black Republicans from voting in the general election of that year. White voters turned out in force, and although the election results remained bitterly contested into the next year, Republicans eventually were legally declared to be in the minority, and the state was "redeemed" from Reconstruction rule by the Democrats in 1877. The new state government was headed by Wade Hampton, a member of a prominent Bourbon Democratic family, and a former lieutenant general of cavalry under Robert E. Lee.

The fate of Ben Tillman and the other Red Shirts was also secured by negotiations held at Washington in 1877 with representatives of the Republican candidate for president, Rutherford B. Hayes. Neither Hayes nor his Democratic opponent, Samuel J. Tilden, had received a majority in the previous year's presidential election, and by the last month of the Grant administration in 1877, the nation still did not have a president-elect. Contested elections in three southern states—including South Carolina—could throw victory to either party in the electoral college, and Wade Hampton had sought favorable terms from the Republican party in return for releasing his state's electoral votes. The possibilities of this situation put a political gleam in the eyes of Rutherford Hayes when he looked southward. Hayes saw a chance not only to obtain the presidency for himself and his party for the next four years but also to achieve a major political realignment. His vision was of the same political will-o'-the-wisp that in the next century alighted on politicians as diverse as William Howard Taft, Richard Nixon—and Jimmy Byrnes: that is, the possibility that the Republican party, if it could only dissociate itself from an exclusive identification in the South with civil rights for black citizens, could then form a natural coalition with conservative Bourbon leaders, as happened in the case of Hampton and Hayes. Such a reconstituted GOP could indefinitely dominate the northern Democrats at the polls.

Rutherford Hayes and his advisers were the first to see these possibilities. For his part, Wade Hampton gave his personal assurances to Hayes that Negroes would not be maltreated under the return of Democratic Bourbon rule and that he and other conservative southern Democrats desired an end to radical Reconstruction solely in order to obtain northern capital to "revive our wasted industries."

The resulting Compromise of 1877, which made Rutherford Hayes the nineteenth president of the United States, was an elaborate deal that involved the electoral voters of many states other than South Carolina, and numerous issues between the Republican party and the South besides race. But the Red Shirts under indictment also were included in the final disposition. After taking office, President Hayes wrote to Governor Hampton that the federal government intended to bring to trial in South Carolina only three cases of indictment for racial violence, none of which involved the Hamburg murders. "The parties in all other cases," Hayes wrote Hampton, "need not prepare for trial." Thus, as the result of a complex political negotiation the terms of which he did not fully know and the conditions of which would extend far beyond his lifetime, Ben Tillman, the most passionate of Jimmy Byrnes' political fathers, was allowed to go free in 1877. In a way, it was good that Tillman was never brought to trial; otherwise South Carolina might not have been spared further racial violence. As Tillman himself recalled well into the twentieth century, reminiscing about his fellow Red Shirts and their Reconstructionist foes: "If they had attempted to put us in jail I am sure that we would have probably killed every obnoxious radical in the court room and town and gone on to Texas or some other hiding place."

After the nolle prosequi of the murder charges, which were not prosecuted for a supposed lack of credible evidence, Ben Tillman returned home to Edgefield County and there once more resumed his other life as a farmer. His mother had died in 1876, shortly after the success of his Red Shirt campaign; and as he entered the 1880s and increased his land holdings, Ben and Sallie Tillman shared between them five children born before the end of the decade. But by 1890—about the time eight-year-old Jimmy Byrnes was becoming aware of the world in Charleston outside his home —Ben Tillman had again left his farm and family for politics. Once more, Tillman's entry into the political world was marked by violence; and once more, his fury was directed at those who he perceived were intent on taking from him what the earth had justly given him. But whereas in 1876 the objects of his enmity had been principally Republicans and their agents, freed blacks, this time the target of his anger was the class he himself as a Red Shirt had helped restore: white Bourbon Democrats.

With the "redemption" of the state by the Democratic party and the election in 1876 of Wade Hampton as governor, political power in South Carolina had returned to the elite families, landed and usually highly educated, that had enjoyed power in the state before the Civil War. Between 1876 and 1890, a succession of prominent former Confederate officers, including seven generals, ruled South Carolina as the state's governors, senators, or congressmen. These same conservative Democrats were less than prompt in recognizing a political kinship with the smaller farmers, usually former private Confederate soldiers or, like Tillman, non-Confederates, who had helped return the conservatives to power. As a consequence, fiscally conservative state officials kept government services such as fertilizer inspection and the maintenance of farm-to-market roads inexpensive in order to pay off state debt incurred during Reconstruction and to encourage northern capital investment; the financially pressed smaller farmers were left to shift for themselves during the depressed markets of the late 1880s and early 1890s. The discontent increasingly heard at the county and precinct level about the state's lack of services to the small farmers was simply not acknowledged by these Bourbon administrations. Hence although both the small farmers and the Bourbons had been allies during the Reconstruction violence, their alliance had merely postponed for a few years the resolution of a conflict antedating the Civil War: between a populism centered in the upstate and a low-country Bourbon conservatism that was most fully represented by cultivated nineteenth-century Charlestonians—in Tillman's scornful description, "the most self-adulterous people in the world." This clash would play itself out in the political careers of both Ben Tillman and Jimmy Byrnes.

In 1890 Tillman made his major political move. An announcement stunned and outraged the political establishment in low-country South Carolina: a violent and unpredictable small farmer from the upcountry, Benjamin R. Tillman, announced his candidacy for the state's governorship. Once more, Ben Tillman was moving at the forefront of political forces he did not fully comprehend, but his genius had always been for the immediate, practical application of these forces to the circumstances he found at hand. In this instance, Tillman had foreseen the rise of a new political party, the People's or Populist party, in his call for an unprecedented government activism—as against Bourbon inactivity. The strength of the agricultural markets of the early 1880s had steadily diminished by the end of that decade, and throughout the 1890s the nation experienced the worst economic depression of its history. (In 1896 the boy Jimmy Byrnes was lucky to get a full-time job. Only two years earlier, thousands of unemployed men had marched to Washington under Populist banners as a self-declared "army," demanding government spending to create jobs. They were met by policemen with clubs.) Nowhere in the nation was the drop in income and need for credit felt more severely than in the agricultural South; farmers there, particularly in the cotton states, were being squeezed between low prices for their crops and high prices in transporting their goods to market.

In reaction, populism was spread throughout the South and West during the late 1880s by the organizations known collectively as the Southern Farmers' Alliance. Originating in Texas, where it established a cooperative buying and selling among cotton farmers, the alliance propounded an economic gospel of restructuring the national currency system to ease credit, a subtreasury plan to allow farmers to borrow on their crops, and government ownership of the railroads at innumerable meetings held at night around farmhouse kitchen tables and at rural schoolhouses. It rapidly became a potent political force; in 1889 the Southern Farmers' Alliance numbered over 20,000 members in 745 state and local organizations. Ben Tillman was equally quick to see that these local organizations could also become the basis of a personal and powerful political machine. Tillman had in 1889 set up county and precinct organizations modeled on the structure of the alliance, which in South Carolina he renamed the Farmers' Association. Representing his own Farmers' Association as the true organization for agrarian reform "within the democracy," Tillman succeeded in most precincts in placing his leaders into key positions of the local Democratic party. Conservative Democrats still held control of the state party at the state chairmanship level, but neither the state Bourbons nor the national agrarians seemed to realize that Tillman had in effect taken over both the state Democratic party and the movement for agrarian reform. These new men coming into power as Tillman's self-styled reformers shared another attribute, which they flaunted by the wearing of miniature silver pitchforks in their coat lapels: each was a "Tillmanite," and each was dedicated to the advancement of their political leader, Pitchfork Ben Tillman. "The symbolism of the pitchfork adopted by the farmer-politican was apt," noted the Tillman biographer Francis Butler Simkins. "To his agrarian disciples he was a simple but brave farmer using a favorite tool to attack the vipers that invested the road of civic advance; to his urban enemies he was wielding the favorite weapon of the devil to impale honest businessmen."

Never before had South Carolina seen a campaign like Ben Tillman's fight that summer of 1890 for the governorship, nor has it since. Several years earlier, Tillman had been behind a seemingly minor change in the rules by which the Democratic party ran its primaries. After the party previously had opened its nominating process from a closed caucus to an open primary, he had succeeded in further requiring all the party's candidates for state office in the primary to speak on the same date on the same platform at each county seat. Thus originated in Tillman's first campaign in 1890, the remarkable palmetto stump, the traveling political circus that continued to be a tradition in South Carolina politics well beyond the death of Ben Tillman. As a New Deal senator, Jimmy Byrnes would take his turn on the stump in 1936, debating Franklin Roosevelt's policies in hamlets throughout the state, as a direct heir of Ben Tillman's legacy.

Before he died, as an old man losing his powers, Ben Tillman explained to Jimmy Byrnes his reasons for having initiated the traveling debates. When Tillman began his political career, Byrnes later recalled, "he had the support of only one newspaper, and this a weekly. He had to reach 'the people,' and he told me that, since he could not provide them with a cockfight, he thought the voters of the rural areas would like to hear a debate between him and his opponents."

There was a second, unspoken reason in the air. "While Tillman described himself as the homeliest man in the state," Byrnes continued, "he was not unaware of his talent for extemporaneous speaking." Nor were the voters. Great crowds turned out at each stump on "speaking day" to see and hear Tillman debate the two other candidates for governor, each sponsored by a separate wing of conservative Democrats. Neither could rival the appearance in town of Ben Tillman. Often riding a farm wagon garlanded with corn tassels, pea vines, and other vegetable trophies, the hefty Tillman would wave to supporters as the wagon was pulled "by a hundred or more horny-handed sons of toil," as pro-Tillman publicists described them. Antic banners would wave over the heads of the crowds: "Bring Out the One-Eyed Plowboy" and "Hurrah for Tillman and Reform." When he took the stage at a crossroads town, his eloquence, practiced for so long at home that it had become one with his native tongue, never failed to help him on his feet. "I am left-handed and have written with my left paw," Tillman would confess, in reference to the hand that had penned such shocking political diatribes against the Bourbon rule published in county newspapers. "I am one-eyed," he continued, settling into a broadly comic catalog of his defects. "I'm simply a clod-hopper," said the former class valedictorian. For a long moment the man with the hard and sunburned face studied the eyes of each other voter in his audience. Then he smiled and said, "Like you are."

The crowd roared back its confirmation. It was about this time that Ben Tillman became well known for his nickname Pitchfork Ben; he was to wear it, like his creased and wide-brimmed planter's hat, the rest of his life. Tillman had earlier warned lawyers representing Bourbon interests that if they approached him, they would get from him "the pitchfork end every time." Now Tillman embellished his own metaphor, creating a story that he would hand down to Jimmy Byrnes. In turn, Byrnes would tell the story, with his own spontaneous delight, well into the 1950s. According to Byrnes, Tillman described "a farmer with a pitchfork in his hand walking by the side of a wagon loaded with hay. As he passed a neighbor's place a savage-looking bulldog attacked him and, just in the nick of time, the farmer stuck him with the pitchfork. The owner of the dog yelled, 'Why didn't you use the other end?' To which the farmer replied, 'Why didn't your dog use the other end?' "

After making Ben Tillman's story live again with his own laughter and gesticulations, Jimmy Byrnes would always pause and drive home the point of this little political homily. "The illustration," Byrnes would tell his audience, "delighted the farmers."

There were those whom the pitchfork did not delight. As the summer of 1890 wore on, both sides came dangerously close to violating the pledge of no violence in this political fight that Tillman at least initially had agreed to honor. As a Tillman landslide over his two Bourbon opponents for governor became imminent, Wade Hampton, now a U.S. senator, broke a white gentlemen's agreement among noncompeting Democrats and publicly declared himself uneasy with the style of Tillman's campaigning. Earlier, the *Charleston News and Courier*, a frequent voice of Bourbonism, had more directly attacked Tillman. The Edgefield farmer was the leader of those who, the newspaper claimed, were opposed to "the better classes, the people of education, intelligence, and civilized habits." Tillmanites, according to the *Courier*, were "people who carry pistols in their hip pockets, expectorate upon the floor, who have no toothbrushes, and comb their hair with their fingers." Tillman himself feigned a wronged innocence. "Why do Charlestonians hate me anyhow?" he asked, laughing—and would not stay for an answer.

In fact, Tillmanism was a combination of upstate rural toughs simply looking for a fight and a younger generation of responsible politicians who had grown impatient waiting for agrarian reform and personal advancement under the Charlestonian Bourbons. To both groups Tillman had the same appeal. "I want to tell you that the sun doesn't rise and set in Charleston," he declared.

As the summer of 1890 wore on, Tillman and his supporters redoubled their efforts, piling higher and higher the barbecued shoats and calves offered at each of his political gatherings, and making certain at each township that any farmer who desired it walked away from their rallies wiping from his lips a whiskey taste of what Tillman liked to call "the convivial dram." An ugly side of Tillmanism also began to manifest itself as the campaign intensified, with the adoption of the practice of "howling down" Tillman's opponents who attempted to speak from the shared platform. Hampton himself, in a scene that would have appeared incredible to those who remembered having closed ranks with the general in earlier battles, was "howled down." The site was Aiken, the future home of Jimmy

Byrnes. ("Good God!" exclaimed a shocked Hampton, who seemed to realize that for the first time Confederate military service was irrelevant to South Carolina politics. "Have the memories of '61, of '65, have they been obliterated?")

Tillman himself claimed that assassination was being plotted against him; he dramatized his possible danger by traveling to Charleston with several well-armed bodyguards. All in all, it was fortunate that the November election arrived before the passions fully ignited. And the results of the polling that day assured the largest inpouring of plain folk into Columbia the next year to see a governor inaugurated since the end of Reconstruction. For by a majority of almost four to one the voters had ended decades of Bourbon rule and chosen for their next governor the outspoken populist Ben Tillman.

Tillman's actions as a two-term governor, if not exactly qualifying him as "the first New Dealer," in Jimmy Byrnes' later words, nevertheless worked the greatest economic and social changes South Carolina was to see until the days of Franklin Roosevelt. As promised, Tillman began construction on an agricultural college for men and a separate college for women; the tax levy on individuals was slightly reduced and the tax rate on corporations somewhat increased; and for the first time in its history, South Carolina enacted a law limiting the hours of labor in the state's cotton mills. Yet the working of his will upon his state also brought out that "desperate strain" that Tillman carried in his male line. Under his governorship the state also executed a new constitution, which contained the first "Jim Crow" exclusionary clauses, denying full civil rights to Negroes. Prior to Tillman's ascendancy, Bourbon governors had kept Wade Hampton's personal promise to the national government in 1876 to allow black voters at least a limited access "to the democracy." Although there had been considerable de facto segregation of the races socially and in business during the Bourbon rule, the state Democratic party had openly asked for black support in elections and no post-Reconstruction governor had ever found it necessary to bar black voters by state law from casting their votes—until the time of Ben Tillman. Thus a state-mandated disenfranchisement of black citizens and the while-only Democratic primary became fixtures on the South Carolina political scene that lasted through Jimmy Byrnes' day, and thus the way was prepared in Tillman's administration for demagogues in the twentieth century who campaigned solely on racial hatreds.

Nor did Tillman forget about Wade Hampton personally. Still remembering Hampton's public disapproval of his style of campaigning (at Aiken, the site of his "howling down," Hampton had refused to ride in the same carriage with Tillman), the governor now put himself behind a move to unseat this most prominent of Bourbon politicians from the U.S. Senate and eventually to replace him himself. Some tried to intercede with the governor on Hampton's behalf, pointing out that in addition to having in common with Tillman an utter lack of fear of death, Hampton quite simply needed the money from his Senate salary. Despite extensive property, the Hampton family was "land poor," and it never recovered financially from the Civil War, when federal troops had deliberately burned the Hampton mansion outside Columbia while General Hampton was in Virginia. Despite these pleas, Tillman in effect turned a face of flint; perhaps most political conflicts are at base generational, and Tillman was aware that his victory that year represented the triumph not only of populism but also of a new generation of southern leaders with few or no personal ties to the Confederacy. In any case, in 1890 the seventy-two-year-old Hampton, who had been in poor health for years, was voted out of the U.S. Senate by the Tillmanite state legislature. Tillman was six years later elected by his hand-picked state legislature to Hampton's old seat. ("Life seems very closed to me, and I have nothing but duty to live for," Hampton had written his sister about the loss of his family's and his class's prestige. "It is very hard, but I try to say 'God's will be done.' ")

This was the apogee of Pitchfork Ben Tillman's political powers. The rise of Tillman as a state governor and a U.S. senator and of his Farmers' Association had coincided with the campaign by the national Farmers' Alliance and other groups to form a new People's or Populist party. Populist state candidates took more than a million votes in 1892; national Democrats knew that if they could achieve "fusion" with the Populists and other dissatisfied agrarians, their united party could prevail over Republicans in the presidential election of 1896. But the Democratic convention of 1896, after a fiery speech by Tillman, chose as its candidate the more pacific William Jennings Bryan of Nebraska, who despite a partial voting fusion with the Farmers' Alliance and the Populists, went down to defeat by William McKinley under a Republican platform of high tariffs and a strong gold standard. Ben Tillman was fated to remain where he was in the Senate, a minority of one within a minority party, as the Republicans McKinley, Theodore Roosevelt, and Taft retained control of the presidency and the Congress for the next sixteen years. Nor would populism itself ever again come as close as in the election of 1896 to gaining control; its failure meant that southern agrarians, particularly in Congress, would never regain the majority influence over northern industrialism and capitalism that agrarians had enjoyed before the Civil War.

By the late 1890s, Tillman's populism had become irrelevant to national politics, placing him outside both the capitalist-industrialist Republican majority and the rising young urban progressives—such as Byrnes—in the Democratic party. Even in his own state, Tillman had not succeeded in permanently loosening the Bourbon grip upon the concentration of land and capital; he had done little more than make lifetime political enemies for himself and at least place some of the "wool hat boys" in line for patronage previously reserved for the low-country elite. William Watts Ball, the patrician editor of the *Charleston News and Courier*, wrote with perhaps as much sympathy as his class was capable about Tillman's later career: "He was not a statesman. He was not even a first-rate politician. He was an artist, who drew pictures with words in bold, harsh lines and deep, and paling men, mistaking him for a deliverer, lost themselves in muddled and strained emotions and followed him."

Now he was increasingly an artist without an audience, and fewer South Carolinians were following their former leader. The years after 1896 brought physical as well as political defeats for Tillman. He suffered a stroke with a resulting partial paralysis in 1908, after a particularly heated argument over the policies of Theodore Roosevelt. He was further agitated when his eldest son, Benjamin Ryan, Jr., or "B.R.," chose to marry into one of the low-country's most socially prominent families. The couple separated, and when Senator Tillman learned that he would be denied custody of his two grandchildren, he again became apoplectic. On February 16, 1910, Tillman had a cerebral hemorrhage and fell down the Capitol steps. His recovery was slow and partial. At first he was left speechless and unable to move the right side of his body; his memory was confused. By the end of the year, though, his mind had cleared, and he was somewhat able to recover his powers of speech and locomotion. For the remainder of his years, however, Tillman would lean heavily on a walking stick to get about, and his oratory never quite regained the old fire. In a letter to a political intimate in 1911, Tillman complained of being unable to re-member recent events and of being strangely moved to tears by long-ago Edgefield County incidents. When he looked in the mirror, Tillman said, he felt as though he were watching an imposter of the old Pitchfork Ben Tillman. Perhaps he saw reflected there what the poet John Dryden had seen in the later life of the Roman senator Seneca: "a sort of shatter'd eloquence."

Age exacted another payment from his flesh. Tillman's seniority of seventeen years in the Senate would have entitled him, when the Democrats returned to majority rule, to claim the chairmanship of the important Senate Appropriations Committee; Tillman wanted the post and said so. But the Democratic caucus plainly told Tillman that his age and other infirmities precluded his appointment. As a conciliatory offering, his fellow Solons offered him the chairmanship of the Senate Committee on Naval Affairs—a pleasant sinecure in peacetime that provided its chairman with a handsome office with beveled mirrors and a chandelier.

To be passed over for Appropriations was a humiliation for Tillman. President-elect Woodrow Wilson had complained of "the crude and ig-norant minds of the members of the Farmers Alliance"—and, presumably, of members of Ben Tillman's Farmers' Association. Tillman still put in a full day's work, mainly answering correspondence, and his absolute leadership of the Democratic party in South Carolina was unchallenged; but the newspapers reported that Pitchfork Ben Tillman ("the broken pitchfork," some called him) now spent most of his days browsing in the secondhand bookstores around Washington—an old man in a black coat squinting with one eye at a page of poetry or of horticulture. It was at this time that Tillman first made the political acquaintance of the sprightly little man from Aiken, formerly of Charleston, who seemed to have sprung up unaided from the Second Congressional District, surrounding Edgefield. *"I came to love him,"* Jimmy Byrnes wrote, *"and in return he treated me as one of his sons."*

Jimmy Byrnes' first petition to Tillman in 1911 was not auspicious; the freshman congressman was worried that he had inadvertently offended his senior senator. Under the rules of patronage previously worked out by the South Carolina delegation, the state's U.S. senators had reserved to themselves all patronage appointments in South Carolina except the naming of postmasters; these statewide jobs were left to the House members to dispense in each member's district.

Accordingly, in his first congressional race of 1910, Jimmy Byrnes offered to a potential supporter the possible postmastership of Edgefield Courthouse, situated in the Second Congressional District. After all, if Byrnes won, postmastership endorsements would be his to dispense as he pleased. But after taking his place in Washington, Byrnes apparently was informed by the state delegation that, in regard to patronage in Edgefield, the exception to the rule was Benjamin R. Tillman. In his first letter to Senator Tillman, then in Edgefield, Jimmy Byrnes in 1911 told the old man about the promised postmastership the previous fall. "Since that time," Byrnes wrote, "I have learned, among many other things, that because of your residence in Edgefield County, it has been the custom to allow you to name the postmaster."

Byrnes in his letter then walked a fine line between not disappointing a constituent while not provoking the famous Tillman anger. "I, of course, would not think of endorsing any applicant nor would I attempt in any way to interfere with the appointment," Byrnes assured Tillman; "but if you do not intend to recommend the appointment of any applicant," he ventured, then he would prefer to keep his promise.

Tillman was mending from his stroke the previous year and, furthermore, was in the middle of a busy planting season in Edgefield; hence, to Jimmy Byrnes' almost certain relief, the senator's ursine anger was little aroused in his reply. "My dear Mr. Byrnes," Tillman began, verbally displaying all his teeth, "my attitude thus far has been one of impartiality as among all respectable applicants." Then, as if awakening fully to the danger of possible interference in his patronage by President Taft and the

GOP, Tillman began to bristle a little: "In all probability the scalawag republicans or some Negro will come into the game and until such a contingency I do not want to take sides for or against any man." Should the Republicans be so foolish as to press that contingency, Tillman had a suggestion: Jimmy Byrnes would make himself useful by carrying a message to the opposition. The senior senator from South Carolina might be willing to forgive his dear Mr. Byrnes for a little political trespassing; but, he told him, "it might be well for you" to inform high-ranking Republicans they were not to expect such forgiveness themselves. Tillman was aware, he told Byrnes, that some members of Congress questioned his patronage claim to the post office at the Edgefield County seat simply because Tillman lived six miles away at his farm in the country; such Republican sophistry did not change the facts, Tillman informed Byrnes. The post office was Tillman's, "and I consider it such. That has been recognized by McKinley and Roosevelt and I expect it to be recognized by Taft. So he would do the graceful thing to ask me to name the post master."

Tillman ended his letter to Byrnes with a political benediction. He would give him some free advice on how to impart this message to the Republican leader Joseph Cannon in a tactful manner, or at least in a manner that Ben Tillman considered tactful: "Of course you can do this in a way as not to give him a handle to work with. Say to him that no Republican need be appointed for he will never be confirmed while I live. Very sincerely . . ."

Byrnes' candidate got the job at the post office, and Jimmy Byrnes pressed his luck. Reelected in 1912, Congressman Byrnes again wrote to his senior senator, and again he asked him to bend the patronage rules to favor the representative from Aiken. An opening had come up in the Revenue Department to be filled by a South Carolinian; several members of the state's delegation, Byrnes among them, were preparing letters to the revenue commissioner endorsing various candidates for this political plum. But Jimmy Byrnes intended that his letter have an intensifier that his colleagues would lack: he wanted Senator Tillman also to write the commissioner, seconding Byrnes' choice for the job. To sway the old man, Byrnes pleaded homesickness on behalf of his candidate. Byrnes' friend, he told Tillman, was an Aiken native and a longtime admirer of the senator; the fellow worked as a clerk in Washington and could not afford to bring up his wife and children from South Carolina; and the worthy candidate sought a well-paying position in South Carolina solely, Byrnes assured Tillman, so "that he can be a visitor at his own home now and again."

Byrnes got his comeuppance within a week. "Dear Byrnes," began the senator, "Yours of October 23rd just received, and I have been thinking about your impudence. It was expressly understood, I thought, that if the senators gave the congressmen the appointments of all the postmasters in the state, we should have all the balance of the patronage. Now here you come and want me to give you my best places." Then, verbally, the hard-faced man began to smile. "But we are all selfish and you are not more so than the rest of us." And then came the concession. "I will write the letter you want me to."

But Ben Tillman wanted Jimmy Byrnes to learn that political generosity in this world always had its price: "if I should happen to have a poor stray Tillmanite somewhere down in your district who wants something in Washington," he warned, then Byrnes would have to reciprocate by finding Tillman's man a job. But, for the present, Senator Tillman would look after Jimmy Byrnes' friend. "I want to give him a good place because I like you so much. I can hardly refuse you anything."

Byrnes' response was prompt. "The better the Tillmanite, the better I will like him." Business now out of the way, the two politicians began a relaxed exchange of Palmetto State gossip. Tillman, with ill-disguised glee, described how "perhaps the stingiest" of his neighbors "had his pocket picked at the circus of forty five dollars. If you know how much he loves money, you will understand what his agony must have been." Byrnes himself had been "doing" the county fairs, as he expressed it, shaking hands and greeting constituents, and he reported back to Tillman in Washington that the South Carolina newspapers "said you did not look well." But, Byrnes added, "you certainly wrote letters like a well man."

In the letters that followed, the considerable charm of Jimmy Byrnes began to tell on the old man as their correspondence continued throughout 1913. In an earlier letter Byrnes had ended with his best wishes to "the official bottle opener," and in response Tillman admitted, "I have been amused at the way you sneaked off from that automobile party and left them high and dry." Apparently the conviviality of Jimmy Byrnes, to be immortalized during the 1930s as "bullbat time"—drinking get-togethers organized by Byrnes—had begun to attract Tillman. In early spring of 1913, Tillman invited Byrnes to his Edgefield farm; and, adding that "my flowers ought to be very beautiful," Tillman asked the young congressman to "bring Mrs. Byrnes along and let me show them to her." By the end of that year, Jimmy Byrnes was signing his letters with regards for Mrs. Tillman as well, and in response the senator wrote that Sallie Tillman "joins me in kind regards to you and Mrs. Byrnes, and we are both anxious for you and her to return."

As the two couples saw more of each other, the young Byrnes and his wife filled a need in the marriage of Senator and Mrs. Tillman; it is a need not uncommon in late middle age among those who have grown children, but who are not yet ready to consider themselves old: Jimmy and Maude Byrnes became the "young couple" in whom the Tillmans could see their own lives reflected, but this time with a charming modernity. In 1913, at age thirty-one, Jimmy Byrnes was younger and more vulnerable than Ben Tillman's eldest son; on the other hand, Byrnes had advanced his worldly career much further than had the fatherly Ben Tillman at the same age. Hence, either as peer or patron, Senator Tillman at his choosing could indulge himself in the affairs of Jimmy Byrnes.

The patronage of a senator, however, was a serious matter. Tillman's increasing affection for Jimmy Byrnes gave the latter access to federal jobs and funds usually kept out of the hands of a junior congressman. Of forty-eight letters in Tillman's files written by Byrnes between 1912 and 1917, twenty-three ask for Tillman's help in placing individuals into government jobs; eight request the senator's support of private bills for individual relief; sixteen deal largely with spendings for road improvements, river dredgings, and military construction in Byrnes' district; and one asks Senator Tillman to share a mailing list with Jimmy Byrnes.

Opportunities for patronage were greatly increased by the inauguration of Woodrow Wilson in 1913 as the first Democratic president in twenty years, and by the Democratic majorities in that year's Sixty-third Congress. Congressional Democrats had not enjoyed majority patronage in both houses since the Civil War, and in the first year of Wilson's administration the pent-up demand for jobs by the party faithful burst upon Washington in an unprecedented spectacle. The scene put Tillman in an apocalyptic frame of mind. In an allusion to the Democratic party's symbol, the senator quoted Scripture to the man from the *New York Times*: "The wild asses of the desert are athirst and hungry; they have broken into the green corn." No more than half in jest, Tillman added, "God only knows what the result will be."

One result was that Jimmy Byrnes came to act as Joseph to Ben Tillman's aging Pharaoh, distributing the corn of Democratic patronage to the faithful as Tillman became increasingly more preoccupied and ill. As early as 1915, in a patronage appointment of some delicacy, Byrnes had presumed to do what was unthinkable to any other member of his state's delegation: say no to Senator Tillman, and tell him how to act ("I therefore take the liberty of suggesting that you do not urge him anymore," Byrnes had written, declining to support Tillman's choice for the job). Throughout the remainder of Wilson's first term and into early 1917, as the presidential election of 1916 neared and America's preparation for entry into the world war became imminent, Jimmy Byrnes' political fortunes continued to rise as Ben Tillman's health and influence declined.

By the autumn of 1916, Byrnes and other Democratic members of the Sixty-third and Sixty-fourth Congresses could justly claim they had enacted all the major legislation requested by Woodrow Wilson in his New Freedom campaign of 1912. This legislation had sweepingly changed the nation's economy in the three years since William Taft left the presidency; and many of these changes directly benefited the southern agriculture and business constituency of Byrnes. The Underwood-Simmons Tariff Act put on the free list in 1913 most of the imported items used by farmers; the Federal

Reserve Act that same year created the mechanism for easier credit among small businessmen and farmers; and the Federal Highways Act of 1916 was written intentionally to benefit rural areas. Byrnes was particularly behind the passage of this last act. (His successful splitting of the Committee of Roads in 1913 into an independent committee, and no longer a branch of the House Committee on Agriculture, was an important first step; bills for the funding of roads now were the first priority of this new committee, and Byrnes was a dominant member among its new, smaller membership.) Wilson presented Byrnes with one of the two pens he used in signing the roads bill of 1916 into law a few months before the November elections. "In passing this bill we fulfill another platform pledge," Wilson told Byrnes.

When Byrnes returned home for the general elections that fall, there was an overall prosperity in the South as cotton prices remained high; after a flurry of uncertain prices at the start of the war in Europe, the market had gone up as government purchases for military uniforms and tents kept the demand for cotton high. Byrnes took an easy primary victory that summer in his district, and as he had no Republican opposition in the fall, he was invited by Democratic party leaders to campaign nationally for the Wilson ticket. Wilson managed a narrow win, despite losses in the eastern states, by combining majorities in the South and the West. After returning to the White House in mid-November 1916, Wilson in a letter to Byrnes acknowledged the congressman's contributions to his presidential victory, thanking him as "one with whom I have been associated in the great work of the last four years. Sincerely, Woodrow Wilson."

Jimmy Byrnes had reasons of his own to look forward to the next four years. Democrats had retained their majorities in both houses of the new Sixty-fifth Congress, and upon convening the first session in April 1917, House leaders appointed Byrnes to a place he had sought since 1911 when he came to Washington as a freshman congressman: Byrnes was now a member of the powerful House Appropriations Committee. The date of Byrnes' appointment, April 2, 1917, also was significant: that same day, Woodrow Wilson had sent to Congress a request for a declaration of war against Germany and other Central powers. Consequently, requests for military spending flowed through the Appropriations Committee at a rate unprecedented in the nation's history. Congressmen now approved military appropriations nearing the millions, not thousands, of dollars. Byrnes was one of three members selected to form the Subcommittee on Naval Appropriations, and he was able to direct some of that spending homeward for the construction of new shipyards in Port Royal, South Carolina, and in north Charleston.

In his subcommittee work, Byrnes also came to see on a regular basis one of the rising personalities of the Wilson administration: Franklin D. Roosevelt, who after sharing a house with Byrnes at the 1912 convention had secured a place for himself as assistant secretary of the navy. Roosevelt and Byrnes quickly developed a relationship of past familiarity and present trust, based primarily on their mutual dislike of paperwork. Byrnes was willing to pass favorably on Roosevelt's requests for naval spending even though, in some instances, the assistant secretary had not provided the subcommittee the necessary documentation to justify the request. It was mutually understood that, if the request was questioned by the full committee, Roosevelt would be responsible for filling the paper gap. This was heady and important business. Byrnes had obtained the influence over appropriations in the House that years before had been denied to Tillman in the Senate; in this new responsibility, Jimmy Byrnes took the initiative in looking after both his and Tillman's interests in obtaining patronage for South Carolina.

The month of May 1917 was bad for Tillman. He was troubled by a painful ulcer on his arm that would not heal, and he was unable to leave his Edgefield farm to attend his Washington office. Late in May, Byrnes telegraphed Tillman's son B.R., apparently because he did not wish to disturb the old man, and asked B.R. to apply pressure in his father's name: "Will you wire senator's name to [General Leonard] Wood at Charleston urging establishment of camp at Aiken?" The recipient of the telegram was Tillman's firstborn son, but in telling him what to do Jimmy Byrnes spoke with the confidence of an elder brother who knows he has the father's authority. Byrnes added to B.R.'s instructions a final imperative: "Make it strong."

Byrnes was aware that if he did not exercise authority in Tillman's name, nothing would get done. Also in May, Byrnes wrote to a constituent who earlier had hoped to get a job from Tillman but had been unable to meet with the senator. Byrnes himself would do what he could, the congressman wrote from Washington, but he cautioned there was little hope of obtaining anything directly from Tillman: "the old man was sick while he was here, and I did not talk business with him but once."

Byrnes was not so brusque with Tillman himself. In a letter that same month in which he advised Tillman which side to favor in a firing dispute with a Census Bureau employee, Byrnes shows prescient Irish charm: "It is strange that you should have written to me just as I had made up my mind to find out the condition of your arm." He closed, "We miss you very much up here, but I know that it is best for you to be at home, and I sincerely hope that your arm will soon be entirely well. With best love to you and Mrs. Tillman and all the family. . . ."

The old man had little more than a year to live and perhaps knew it; but he still showed a willingness to be pleased by his Jimmy: "Yours of May 11th received, and I was very much impressed at the post script. Like a woman, you always keep the good things you decide for a post script." Tillman then begins, with a suspicious zeal, to catalog his decline, somewhat like a Shakespearean actor rolling back his sleeve to show the scar from

Saint Crispian's day: "About my arm in which you appear interested—until two of [sic] three days ago I had made up my mind to go to some sanitarium and have the so-called specialist examine it with a microscope, and test the blood and all that sort of thing." But, he declares, "it seemed set to get well." Tillman then shows "the good part" to Byrnes: "the bottom of the sore has healed over and the trouble is about the rim now. For a long time the trouble was in the middle and the rim gave me no trouble. . . ." The letter continues in this vein for a lengthy paragraph, and as he stared at the page in his hand, Jimmy Byrnes may have seen more details about Ben Tillman's open sore than in truth he had desired.

But throughout South Carolina in 1917 there was increasing interest in all that aging flesh, as by the end of the year more and more state Democrats began to wonder whether Tillman's failing health would permit him another run at renomination in 1918. The deterioration of the senator's health was well known, and his mental powers had been a subject of speculation since his second stroke, in 1910; and if Tillman lived past 1917, he would already have enjoyed his Senate seat for almost a quarter of a century, longer even than had John C. Calhoun. Hence among state Democrats an open discussion broke out on the advisability of Tillman's retiring gracefully when his term ended in 1918 in favor of a younger, more vigorous candidate. At the end of 1917, though, Tillman found himself still alive and was in no mood to surrender his senatorial chair. Citing the extraordinary circumstances of the country's entry into the world war, Tillman publicly announced his intentions to offer himself for reelection again in 1918; so that there would be no misunderstanding, he reiterated his intention to leave the Senate in only one way: "feet first."

Tillman, by his forthrightness, may have hoped to discourage any competition in the primary and to have ended any discussion of his health as an issue; but neither would go away. A former Tillmanite, Cole L. Blease, began in 1917 to run against the old man openly, on a "reform" platform; and Tillman's friends counseled that the less said about his health, the better. Even Jimmy Byrnes, who in a reversal of roles now gave rather than received political advice, took a somewhat imperious tone in a letter to Tillman in 1917 telling him to not press his political luck. "You will make no further announcements about your senatorial business," Byrnes wrote in November, "as it is now in good shape and my judgement is that you had better let it remain so."

Tillman himself professed a Roman indifference as to whether the people returned him to the Senate; but back in Washington in early 1918, he worked behind the scenes to the limits of his health to make certain he would win his party's nomination. Tillman sent articles, anonymously, to South Carolina weeklies praising the virtues of the state's senior senator; he sought to preempt the nomination by having the state party endorse him officially, thereby eliminating the need for a primary race; and as the spring of 1918 approached, he wrote the president of the state's college for women, which Tillman had founded as governor, and asked for help in organizing the young ladies as Tillmanites in skirts. "It is entirely legitimate for these young women to fight my battles," he wrote the president of Winthrop College, "now that I am too old and weak to do it." But not so old and weak, Tillman might have added, that he was unable to shake hands and make a good impression. Writing his grown children from Washington, Tillman told them to prepare an automobile in Edgefield for his use. "I want to go home and have B.R. drive me over the state in the machine," he explained, "and show them I am strong enough to walk about and that I have not lost my mind."

Never very far from Tillman's mind as the primary of 1918 neared was the exasperation that, because of outside meddling, he now had to beat not one but two opponents. His first opposition had come from a former supporter in the statehouse, Cole Blease, a state senator who was campaigning on a platform of nativism and white supremacy extreme even by Tillmanite standards. Tillman's task was made easier by Blease's ill-advised attacks on America's entry into the world war, which in such a military-minded state as South Carolina had created a backlash against him. The delighted Tillman publicly stressed his Senate support of Woodrow Wilson's war policies. Victory seemed easy; but others were not so sure. Worried that Tillman's health might yet provide Blease a means to the nomination, and determined to present Wilson with an "anybody but Blease" chair in the Senate, progressive Democratic party members both within and outside South Carolina began to search for a more attractive candidate with whom to defeat Blease. The progressives settled upon a favorite who entered the primary as a third candidate late in spring 1918 and who seemed almost tailor-made to raise Ben Tillman's animus: the urbane and scholarly-looking Asbury Francis Lever.

The chairman of the House Committee on Agriculture, A. F. "Frank" Lever had long been one of Woodrow Wilson's favorite congressmen from South Carolina. Among that state's delegation, Lever—not Byrnes and not Tillman—had authored or sponsored the legislation that President Wilson considered most important for agriculture, including the Lever Food Control Act of 1917, which set guidelines for federal supervision of wartime food production. Lever, a youthful forty-three, was a Georgetown graduate and former schoolteacher, and he was an agricultural spokesman with whom Wilson was intellectually more compatible than with the flamboyant agrarian radicals of an earlier generation—men such as Pitchfork Ben Tillman. Indeed, there was little room in Wilson's New Freedom domestic program for the aggressive government action that had been proposed by these contemporaries of William Jennings Bryan. The agrarians had urged direct government intervention—such as nationalization of the railroads, in some cases—to favor farmers as a disadvantaged class;

the Wilsonian New Freedom, however, disavowed as a tenet of its faith any direct intervention by the federal government on behalf of any one special-interest group, advantaged or disadvantaged.

A case in point was the fight between President Wilson and the southern agrarian radicals over cotton price supports and the creation of the Federal Reserve banks. Collapsing cotton prices at the outbreak of the world war had led to a wave of farm bankruptcies throughout the South in 1914 and to the demand by some southern congressmen that the federal government support the price of cotton and make available cash for emergency borrowing by planters. This both the secretary of the treasury and Wilson himself refused to do. Some of these same congressmen also were among those who at this same time were blocking passage of the Federal Reserve Act, perhaps the most important piece of New Freedom legislation. These agrarians, infuriated by the lack of representation of farming interests on the Reserve Board of Directors and by the failure to provide for any sort of direct agricultural borrowing from the Reserve banks, almost succeeded in defeating Wilson's carefully planned bill in the Democratic caucus. As an attempt at compromise, Wilson had caused to be introduced a bill that would have federally regulated the receipt of goods in agricultural warehouses, thereby indirectly helping the cotton farmers by making it easier for them to borrow money on their crops. Southern radicals, however, were having none of it. They refused to let the compromise bill come to a vote, and they continued to oppose passage of the Federal Reserve Act, until only a personal appeal by William Jennings Bryan himself, who promised the radicals their interests would be considered at a later date, won the bill's approval by the caucus. Thus, by President Wilson's lights an important piece of national legislation had been unnecessarily endangered because of the narrow interests of a few sectionalists, and a compromise offering had been tossed aside simply because the southern radicals had wanted their cotton bill or none at all. The author of the attempted compromise was Frank Lever, and in the years that followed, as Lever made himself useful in other ways, Woodrow Wilson may have speculated that the time was right to encourage a new type of leader in the South.

Tillman knew that something was up. Before Lever had officially declared his candidacy, the senator had warned one of his Tillmanites in South Carolina that Lever might be "following his ambitions blindly" and was planning a run at Tillman's job. "Of course, if he runs his excuse will be that he was assured by those whom he consulted that I could not beat Blease and that he was compelled to come into the race to save the state's good name, etc." It was the etc. that bedeviled Tillman. Among South Carolina voters, even Tillman's popularity was eclipsed by Woodrow Wilson's, and if their wartime leader publicly showed a preference for Lever over Tillman in the Senate, then the latter was in trouble. Even Jimmy Byrnes, who in April made a quick trip down from Washington to Edgefield to see Tillman, apparently professed himself unable to say what Wilson was going to do ("Byrnes is writing this for me to sign," Tillman explained in a letter to his wife, indicating that the old man's arm still had not completely healed).

Lever declared his candidacy for Tillman's job on April 30, 1918. By early May, Tillman had turned to two other sources in Washington to determine whether the president planned to take sides. Tillman counted as his friends two men within Wilson's cabinet: both were southerners, and, like Tillman, both were men of discretion: Postmaster Albert Burleson, who, as the Texan arbiter of all Democratic patronage was nicknamed the Cardinal, and the Cardinal's equally worldly friend from North Carolina, Secretary of the Navy Josephus Daniels. Tillman may have felt himself between the devil and the deep blue sea, but his two friends told him what he wanted to hear. Hence, on May 9, when writing the president of Clemson Agricultural College, in South Carolina, asking for the use of an alumni mailing list, Tillman confidently remarked about Frank Lever: "At one time I felt probably he had been encouraged to become a candidate for the Senate by President Wilson and members of his Cabinet, but I have assurances from Burleson and Daniels that this is not true."

By this time Jimmy Byrnes knew better. Byrnes was back in Washington in early May to keep a special appointment, and as he walked up the steps to the White House, he may have reflected on his earlier visits there. He had met with President Wilson several times before on party matters, usually in the company of Senator Tillman; but on this Monday afternoon, May 6, the White House appointment book had simply called for a four-thirty appointment with "Rep. Byrnes, S.C." Byrnes later recalled that he went to the White House "wondering what it was about." But there was no reason to fear; unlike some of his colleagues who, as Byrnes put it, had found Woodrow Wilson to be a "cold, austere man," Jimmy Byrnes had soon discovered "that he had a very human side and often showed a warm desire to help those in public office whom he liked." Byrnes walked through the West Wing and into Wilson's ground-floor office.

"You must be a most unusual man!" The president who gave Byrnes this ebullient greeting still offered flashes of the lighthearted collegiate he had once promised to be. Wilson was then in the third year of a second marriage he considered a happy one; the stroke that would steal from him much of his intellectual powers was still more than a year away in the future. Wilson was an energetic and trim man, at 150 pounds about the same weight as Byrnes, and both men offered to the world the same blue-gray eyes. But the president spoke with the psychological advantage of being four inches taller than Byrnes, and he had another characteristic feature, disconcerting in a politician: Woodrow Wilson seldom praised without expecting the recipient to live up to the praise. For a long moment Wilson looked Byrnes in the eye. Then came the explanation.

"He had asked the Secretary of the Navy, Josephus Daniels, to find out from the Tillman family who was the best person to talk to about Senator Tillman," Byrnes later recalled being told. Wilson then repeated the answer he had been given: "Congressman Byrnes." There was more. "When he had asked the same question of his Postmaster General, Albert S. Burleson, who had served in Congress with Lever, my name had again been mentioned."

Byrnes said nothing as Wilson continued. "The President then told me that in view of Blease's attitude toward the prosecution of the war, the possibility of his coming to the Senate was disturbing." The president came to his point. "It has been suggested to me," he told Byrnes, "that I offer Tillman an appointment on some commission, like the Canadian Boundary Commission, which would require very little exertion and yet assure him security. Mr. Lever will then be free to make the race." Woodrow Wilson's strangely angular face looked at Byrnes. "How would Senator Tillman react to such a suggestion?"

So that was it. Jimmy Byrnes was to tell Ben Tillman he was too old to be a senator. And, if Byrnes declined this service, he might not be asked a second time to make himself useful to this president. In his recent remarks, the president had made perfectly clear his intentions toward southern intransigents.

On the other hand, Byrnes knew Ben Tillman well enough to be certain the old man would never forgive the White House for making this proposal; worse for Jimmy Byrnes, Tillman would never forgive the friend of the White House who had delivered this proposal. And if Tillman succeeded in hanging on, both to his life and to his senate chair, his former patron would have sufficient time and perhaps inclination to deal with a certain young congressman from Aiken. Five years earlier Jimmy Byrnes had gone to the funeral in Charleston of his first political mentor, George Legaré; but this spring afternoon, as the president waited for an answer, Byrnes still remembered George's droll laugh and the quizzical, pitying smile with which he had warned Jimmy Byrnes not to overreach himself, and thus be sent by the voters to an early political grave: "Oh yes, Jimmy. They'll listen for a while, and then they'll say, 'It's just too bad. He *was* such a *nice* little fellow.' "

Byrnes was nothing if not adept. He gave the president his answer, but while he did not tell Wilson yes, he did not tell him no either. According to Byrnes, he reminded the president that Ben Tillman was "a proud man." Wilson agreed that he also understood Tillman's oath to leave the Senate in only one way: "feet first." Nevertheless, Jimmy Byrnes would do for the White House what he could. Byrnes maneuvered so that Wilson's preference would be made clear to Tillman, but it would be Frank Lever, not Jimmy Byrnes, who would break the news to the old man. After leaving Wilson's office, Byrnes arranged a meeting between Tillman and Lever so that Lever could discuss his candidacy; if President Wilson and Byrnes had hoped that Tillman would take this meeting as a hint, and thus resign without being asked, the White House party was to be disappointed. According to Byrnes, Lever and Tillman met privately, and on his way out of the meeting, Lever was stopped by Byrnes and asked what Tillman had said. Lever laughed and repeated Tillman's reaction to his candidacy. "Go ahead and run against me," Tillman had said, "and I'll beat the hell out of you."

This was only partly an old man's bluff. Tillman's health was too poor now even for the planned automobile trip across South Carolina—for his son to drive "the machine" so that voters could look at Tillman and see that he had not lost his mind—but by the middle of May he had come up with another scheme. The state Democratic convention was to meet in Columbia, South Carolina, on May 15, and Tillman arranged to make a short speech to the delegates. The upcoming election would be Tillman's first run for office under the Seventeenth Amendment, which called for popular election of senators, and Tillman's appearance before the convention would give the party an important indication of his ability to wage an active campaign. His physical strength would support him for only a few moments on stage, and the powers of his oratory were now enfeebled; but it was the senator's entrance into the convention hall, rather than what he said there, that showed the old, sure Tillman touch for political melodrama. Tillman's younger son, Henry, had been commissioned a captain after the start of the world war, and as the Democrats convened at high noon, father and son entered the convention hall together. The sight of old Captain Tillman, who with his pistol had driven the last of the Yankees from South Carolina in 1876, now being tenderly supported on the arm of young Captain Tillman, who had volunteered to do his part overseas, stopped each delegate in his tracks: it was not just an aging senator who had entered the convention, but Southern History himself. For a moment the crowd's silence hung in the air, like a great wave before it crashes to the shore; then, according to newspapers, the convention hall burst with the sound of "ringing cheers." Ben Tillman had arrived. And once more, old as he was, he had demonstrated his ability to move the hearts of his fellow South Carolinians, if not their minds. Later, after Tillman was helped to the stage, it made little difference that the senator's speech was of slight substance or that it was quickly over. The old man managed to shout at the end, "To hell with German sympathizers, and thank God for Woodrow Wilson!"

Woodrow Wilson knew which war he had lost. Three weeks after the convention, one of the candidates received a letter on White House stationery: "My Dear Mr. Lever," began Woodrow Wilson, "I know that some time ago you submitted your name for the nomination in the Democratic primary election in South Carolina as senator from that State." Wilson went on to discuss the exigencies of wartime politics, and then came to his point. He asked Lever "whether you would not be willing to reconsider your decision and to remain in the House where you would continue to serve as chairman of the very important committee on agriculture." There was very little for Frank Lever to consider. A Tillman victory after the senator's appearance at the convention would be stopped only by a presidential endorsement; that endorsement plainly would not be forthcoming. "You are the Commander in Chief," Lever replied to the president, "and it is the duty of every man to be placed where he can best serve his nation." Lever withdrew, and Tillman returned to Washington in valetudinarian glory: six more years were all but promised to him, and his victory in the primary over Cole Blease seemed little more than a formality.

Frank Lever was not the only South Carolinian to receive a letter that summer from the White House, but the note to Jimmy Byrnes was of a different sort. With the rest of the state's House delegation, Byrnes had returned to South Carolina to campaign for reelection; he had not faced serious opposition in the Second Congressional District since 1912, and as he went about Woodrow Wilson's business in Washington in 1918, Byrnes may have expected another easy reelection that year from home. But by midsummer Jimmy Byrnes was in deep trouble. The prophecy of George Legaré seemed to have come true—that Jimmy Byrnes would become too busy with his national ambitions to notice the waning of his support back home. Byrnes returned to Aiken to find that two local lawyers had declared their candidacies against him; yet a third candidate, across the county line in Edgefield, also had filed against him. Each was potentially strong, and by mid-August most political observers agreed there was no certainty that Jimmy Byrnes would survive to a runoff after the primary that month.

A presidential endorsement would help, but Woodrow Wilson almost never involved himself at the primary level so long as each candidate supported the administration. Such was the case in Byrnes' district. Wilson's inflexibility regarding his own rules was one of his strongest traits, and he was not easily swayed by appeals to personal affection. Hence his reaction was all the more remarkable when he received a memorandum on August 22. Its author was a member of his cabinet, Albert S. Burleson—the Democratic "Cardinal"—and its subject was the young congressman who had made himself so helpful with the Tillman problem: "The Postmaster General wishes to remind the president to write a letter to Congressman James F. Byrnes, of South Carolina, somewhat as follows":

"My dear Mr. Byrnes," wrote Wilson from Burleson's draft. "I would be very much obliged to you if you would at some early time drop in to see me at the White House." Knowing that Byrnes would make public the letter, Wilson explained the reason for the visit in terms that brought credit to Byrnes: "You have always rendered such generous service to the administration and to the government as a member of the Committee on Appropriations that I am anxious to seek your service. Cordially and sincerely yours, Woodrow Wilson."

Byrnes with delight released the letter to newspapers, and since Wilson was then at the height of his wartime popularity in South Carolina, this presidential endorsement boosted the congressman's fortunes: Byrnes won handily in the primary at the end of the month and could take his place in Congress later that year without the need for a runoff. And as he celebrated his victory, Jimmy Byrnes enjoyed a greater good fortune than he knew: so strong had he become in his district that this August would be the last time he would have competition for a seat in the House.

There was to be no victory celebration that summer for Senator Ben Tillman. After his speech to the state convention in May, Tillman had returned to Washington and resumed full office duties. Perhaps he had hoped, as in the past, that a political fight would vivify his system. But the senator would not live to run another race. It was as if, after forcing a younger candidate from the field, after hearing once more the applause of South Carolina voters, after proving once more that Ben Tillman was not a man to be easily defeated, all that aging flesh had said, "Enough." On Friday, June 27, after dictating over fifty letters, Tillman complained of feeling ill and returned to his apartment; two days later he awoke unable to move his left arm and leg. The cerebral hemorrhage now began to spread paralysis over his entire body, and there would plainly be no recovery. Sallie Tillman and B.R. were at his bedside, and newspapers began setting his obituary into type: "Senator Tillman at Death's Door," announced a South Carolina daily. And unafraid to knock, Tillman might have added. He would not fear death. When he was younger, and had much more to lose, Tillman had not feared death: not when he had seen it at Chickamauga, nor when he had dealt it to other men at Hamburg, nor when he had sensed it in the air a hundred times at crossroad gatherings throughout South Carolina where his words and his appeals to racial and social hatreds had raised the passions of angry and dangerous men like a great howling animal. So he was not about to become afraid now, not when he was an old man in his seventy-first year dying in his bed. Tillman gave instructions for his funeral and asked that it be kept simple. Then the will seemed to let go of the body, and all that remained was a physical frame that was racked by nausea and that drifted in and out of consciousness. On July 1, perhaps to the relief of his family, Tillman became completely comatose.

Two days later Jimmy Byrnes and other members of the state delegation began to pack for a trip back home; Senator Tillman had died that morning, and Byrnes, along with other House members, was to accompany the senator's body on the train back to South Carolina.

Tillman today lies in earth where he found so much pleasure in life. His grave occupies a prominent corner of the Ebenezer Baptist Cemetery, less than two miles from the fields where he once farmed. From the churchyard stretching north are the white sandy plains of Edgefield County, shimmering in the hot air of summer. Peach trees extend in almost mirage-like straight lines across the fields, each green tree casting its individual shade against the sand. Hidden in the dark green at the field's edge, but occasionally heard with the sound of a far-off horn, freight trains of the Southern Railroad head north on their tracks toward Washington, or farther south, toward Aiken. Up these tracks, freight trains carried the produce of Tillman's farm northward to the big city markets—the bales of cotton, the boxes of asparagus, all the sweet fruits from the orchards that Ben Tillman each year hoped would make him a rich man, and which each year returned just enough for him to plant one more season. And down these tracks came the train carrying his body, south from Washington. Years before, in delivering a funeral elegy for George Legaré, Tillman had sounded almost shocking in his refusal to grieve. "The mystery is only solved by dying," he had declared to the Senate in 1913. Five years later, with Senate eulogies of his own, Tillman's body was returned to Edgefield for burial. The gravesite today is marked by a dominant, squared stone that on one side reads, simply, "Tillman." He lies there with his wife and son B.R.

Politicians may occasionally think of the dead, but their business is with the quick. After attending Tillman's funeral, Jimmy Byrnes returned to Washington; as the president had requested, he called at the White House. True to their word, Byrnes and Wilson did have some discussion on the upcoming appropriations bill. "But, in fact," Byrnes later declared, "we both had something else in mind!" The president quickly came to the true point of the meeting, and he stated his satisfaction at seeing a young progressive like Jimmy Byrnes reelected to Congress. Byrnes never forgot his pleasure at this moment; years afterward he recalled Wilson's words, noting that "the generosity of his congratulations was heartwarming." As he took his ease in the White House, basking in the praises of a powerful president, Jimmy Byrnes must have seemed to himself far different from that inexperienced congressman who had come to Washington seven years earlier: that young man had no powerful friends to help him and had promptly caught the mumps. And now, in many ways, Jimmy Byrnes *was* different. For as President Wilson smiled and extended his congratulations, one thought must have seemed obvious to both men: Jimmy Byrnes was on his way up.

3

Dear Mr. Baruch

Politically and privately, the years between 1918 to 1930 signified for Jimmy Byrnes a passage to disillusionment. Byrnes began the decade of the 1920s with his hopes inflated by the possibilities of his becoming the Democratic party's minority leader or his winning a seat for himself in the U.S. Senate; but by 1929 Jimmy Byrnes was to be neither a congressman nor a senator, having experienced in 1924 the first political defeat of his career, and in 1929 he recognized the first signs of an economic depression that affected both him and everyone else in the nation. Byrnes was always quick-witted in turning these events to his advantage, and he went out of the decade of the 1920s in better shape than he had entered it, becoming by 1930 both a prosperous attorney and a senator-elect; but, in between, there were years of frustration.

Byrnes began the decade by losing a powerful patron in Woodrow Wilson. The Democratic president, weakened by a stroke in 1919, was unable to seek a third term in 1920 and retired from politics to an invalid life in his Washington home. Wilson died there in 1924. Byrnes himself for the first time in his career became a member of a congressional minority party, as the Republicans gained control of both houses of Congress in the

1918 elections, and the GOP majority in the House continued throughout Byrnes' duration there. In addition, there was a rare lapse of control in his carefully pleasing public demeanor. Byrnes lost his temper over the issue of full civil liberties for blacks in 1919, and he lost it again in the early 1920s. Speaking from the floor of the U.S. House of Representatives, Byrnes delivered a series of bitterly racist and violently provocative speeches that continued for years afterward to cast Byrnes as a prime enemy of the political advancement of the Negro. At the same time, in an irony that must have seemed to Byrnes a mockery of his ambitions, the Ku Klux Klan in 1924 organized to defeat his attempt in South Carolina to succeed to Ben Tillman's chair in the U.S. Senate.

In his passage from optimism to disappointment, Byrnes' experiences of the political and economic events of the 1920s were no different from those of millions of other Americans; but Byrnes' difficulties were compounded by family troubles. Throughout the decade of the 1920s, as Jimmy and Maude Byrnes entered their late thirties, it became increasingly evident to the couple that they would be disappointed in their desire to have children. At this same time, Byrnes' elder sister, Leonore, was having troubles of her own with three children and a broken marriage. There had always been a close bond between Byrnes and his sister, as well as between them and Frank Hogan, their cousin of about the same age who had been raised with them at the Byrnes household in Charleston after Hogan's father also had died unexpectedly. Poverty, or near-poverty, is in early childhood a strong motivation later in adult life either to affirm one's family ties or to try to escape them; and to their credit, all three of these children raised by Elizabeth Byrnes continued as adults to remain close.

Frank Hogan and Leonore Byrnes both became prominent Washington attorneys, and both they and Jimmy Byrnes continued to aid one another in their careers. In 1913 Leonore Byrnes had obtained a federal job, presumably with some help from Congressman Byrnes, in the newly created Agricultural Extension Service. Jimmy Byrnes always insisted, "My sister had more sense in a minute than either Frank or I had in an hour," and Leonore Byrnes eventually put herself through George Washington Law School and became a New Deal attorney in the solicitor's office of the Department of Agriculture. But in 1913 she needed the salary from her new job for marital reasons. Leonore Byrnes had separated from her husband in 1911; their divorce became final in 1919. There were prolonged and bitter custody disputes over the couple's three children, who at the time of the divorce ranged in age from thirteen to eighteen years. Although Leonore Byrnes eventually won custody of all her children, her household continued to be a source of worry to Jimmy Byrnes.

Another concern to Byrnes in the 1920s was the declining health of his mother, who after a series of strokes plainly could not live many more years. With the strength of will that was characteristic of the Byrnes women,

Leonore Byrnes took her mother into her already strained household, and Leonore would continue to care for her mother throughout her decline. Jimmy Byrnes certainly provided some financial help during this time, but there must have been an anxiety unrelieved by giving money, and perhaps some guilt at his not being able to do more, when Byrnes received letters from Leonore such as this following one, undated from this period of their mother's illness:

> Friday.
> Good Friday at that.
>
> My dear Jim:
>
> Mother isn't much better—if any. She can sit up now for two hours a day—practically lying down in the chair, but getting a change of scene, but she hates to eat and every meal is a battle. However, we go ahead and make her eat. She likes oysters and they slide down, so I stop on my way home and get a half dozen every day. Hope she doesn't get tired of them. I see them opened, so they're fresh. . . . It takes a lot of pulling to get her back to normal—or, maybe it isn't normal for her to laugh and not worry. Her bum leg took a notion to move of its own accord, twice last night. It just flopped over the other leg. Her hand isn't very good. It just grabs at anything in sight and fastens on it, but she can't put it up to her head now. There isn't any real change but I'm afraid it's going to take a long time for her to pull out. . . . I'll write another bulletin pretty soon—and will attend to the flowers for mother. My love to you and Maude—I hope you'll have a happy Easter.
>
> Leo

Elizabeth Byrnes would die two days after Jimmy Byrnes won election as a delegate to the Democratic convention of 1932.

But however great the loss, there comes a certain knowledge as well. Despite terminations to his personal and professional happiness, these also would be the years of Byrnes' maturing. The end of the decade would bring to completion the political education of Jimmy Byrnes, and by 1930 he would be one of the acknowledged masters of Democratic politics and strategies. He would be among the earliest supporters of Franklin Roosevelt's campaign to win the 1932 Democratic nomination for president, and after the Democratic convention in Chicago that year, Byrnes would quickly be selected to join the "Brain Trust" of intimate advisers to candidate Roosevelt. And, most significant, Byrnes in 1930 would win the friendship of Bernard Baruch, one of the nation's wealthiest men and an independent financier to the Democratic party throughout the lean years of the 1920s and early 1930s. This relationship with Baruch would be the longest of Jimmy Byrnes' friendships and, emotionally, the most complex; money supplied by Baruch, and, equally important, what Baruch considered to be his special relationship with Byrnes, would go a long way in establishing Jimmy Byrnes as a politician with credentials deserving of the national party's attention. Byrnes himself eventually would become a contender for the presidency because of these early friendships with Roosevelt and Baruch, and the bases of these friendships were to be the events shared by all three men during the turbulent national Democratic politics of 1918 to 1932.

Following his reelection in 1918 and his congratulatory reception at the White House, the last year of the war continued to be promising for Jimmy Byrnes. In mid-October 1918 Byrnes was chosen as one of three House members to travel to France and evaluate the effectiveness of American logistics in delivering supplies to the front. It was Byrnes' first trip to Europe, and he paid his own way. After checking into the Hotel Meurice in Paris, the three congressmen—in addition to Byrnes the delegation consisted of Representative Richard Whaley of Charleston and, as senior member, Representative Carter Glass of Virginia—toured the military camps of the American Expeditionary Forces at Lille, Tours, and Verdun.

While in France, the group heard complaints from Rear Admiral William Sims that the U.S. Navy had been delayed by Washington's incompetence in supplying American troops for the 1918 offensive campaigns. Byrnes' firsthand inspection of military bases convinced him that the Navy had, in fact, done a good job in supplying U.S. troops in France, and his inspections later made Byrnes very valuable to Assistant Secretary of the Navy Franklin D. Roosevelt. Fifteen months after Byrnes returned home, Rear Admiral Sims went public with his charges that Secretary of the Navy Josephus Daniels, out of incompetence, had not provided enough U.S. destroyers to patrol against German U-boats in the North Atlantic, thereby prolonging the war by four months in the admiral's estimation and costing an additional 500,000 Allied lives on land and sea. The Republican-controlled Senate appointed a committee to hold public hearings on Sims' charges, as well as on other allegations of Democratic mismanagement of the war. These hearings threatened to put Franklin Roosevelt into an awkward position. The main target of the investigations, Josephus Daniels, was a well-liked Democratic loyalist and a close friend of Woodrow Wilson and had been a generous and kindly patron to his young assistant secretary. But as the Senate hearings might reveal, Roosevelt had been less than grateful to Secretary Daniels. In fact, throughout 1916–18, FDR had frequently complained in his letters to friends and in interoffice memos about what he had perceived as Daniels' incompetence. If called to testify, Roosevelt could be profoundly embarrassed—and along with him the Democratic party—by the presentation of these documents and by attempts to explain why, if Assistant Secretary Roosevelt had felt Daniels was endangering the war effort, he had not taken his concerns directly to Congress rather than simply complaining to his friends behind his superior's back.

Byrnes helped here by diverting the Senate away from Daniels and the Navy's home office. After returning to the United States, Byrnes appeared before the Senate committee to offer testimony on the Navy's efficiency in delivering supplies. Gratuitously, he also threw out a slur on Sims' character. During the war, he noted, Admiral Sims from his headquarters in England had faced "nothing more deadly than the dining tables of London," while Daniels was making the Navy "a fighting force of which every American was proud." Sims was born in Canada and was particularly sensitive to charges of favoring the British navy in managing the war. Byrnes' obvious willingness to engage in personal truculence with his dining-table remark, and the I-was-there authority on his trip to France, apparently persuaded the committee to drop the inquiry into the Sims charges. Although the Senate hearings on war mismanagement continued for some time, the committee's investigation moved on to topics other than the Navy, and Franklin Roosevelt was not called to testify. One month after the hearings finally ended, Roosevelt accepted his party's nomination for the vice presidency at the 1920 Democratic convention, and he received the congratulations of, among others, Josephus Daniels.

Aside from this on-site investigation of Admiral Sims' complaints, the remainder of Byrnes' tour of France was uneventful. News of the armistice on November 11, 1918, found the delegation at Edinburgh, Scotland, on its way home. A laughing Byrnes and Whaley celebrated the good news in a pub, holding two protesting and drunken English officers by their arms while Carter Glass took aim at the Allied officers for shots from a bottle of seltzer water. For Jimmy Byrnes, it had been a good war.

The next morning, Byrnes sailed for home while the two other congressmen chose to remain for a few more days. By arriving first back in the United States, Byrnes had precedence among the delegates in reporting personally to President Wilson on the results of the trip, and a few days later when Wilson's appointment secretary, Joe Tumulty, approved the meeting with the president, Byrnes used the occasion to advance both his career and that of his older friend Carter Glass. Byrnes had learned while he was aboard ship that Wilson's secretary of the treasury had resigned; he now urged Wilson to fill the Treasury position by appointing Glass, who in 1913 had managed the House bill establishing the Federal Reserve Bank. A few days later when Glass returned from Europe, Wilson's offer of the Treasury post was waiting for him. Later, both as a member of Wilson's cabinet and as a U.S. senator, Glass did not forget how Jimmy Byrnes had found the time to make political hay for him, and he returned the favor by guiding Byrnes' own career later in the Senate.

Wilson also listened to Byrnes' and others' urgings that the president personally attend the peace negotiations to be held in Versailles in order to accomplish the greatest of Wilson's postwar hopes, the creation of a congress, or League of Nations, with authority to stop future wars by the interposition of peacekeeping troops. After returning to Washington from France in the summer of 1919, Wilson presented the League treaty to the Republican-controlled Senate for a doubtful chance at ratification, and then, after what his White House doctor considered insufficient rest, he began on September 3 one of the most remarkable domestic speaking journeys ever undertaken by any chief executive in the nation's history. In twenty-two days Woodrow Wilson traveled over eight thousand miles across the country by rail, trying to maintain an average of ten rear-platform speeches a day, at every stop exhorting the crowds gathered around his seven-car express to show their popular support for Senate ratification of the League of Nations. The trip was certainly political; Wilson was determined to have the treaty ratified as originally presented to the Senate without any Republican amendments or limitations on the use of American troops. Furthermore, he was very willing to run for a third presidential term in 1920 on the single issue of League ratification. But to his mind the trip was also close to a holy campaign: he sincerely believed that in order to make the World War truly "the war to end wars," ratification of the League treaty was a moral as well as a political imperative.

Byrnes backed Wilson to the extent of his powers. In fact, one of the more attractive sides of Byrnes' character throughout the 1920s was the consistency of his support for Wilson's postwar program, long after Wilson had left office and after the League had been rejected by the Senate in March 1920. Although as a member of the House, Byrnes could not vote on the treaty, he repeatedly urged ratification of the League Covenant, and in speeches on the stump his personal admiration for Wilson was publicly expressed with a lack of self-interest and an absence of cynicism that was unusual in the 1920s. "America was not founded to make money," Woodrow Wilson had told Americans during his 1919 speaking tour, and although such altruism was no longer fashionable during the heyday of the Coolidge era, by the end of the decade Jimmy Byrnes was not apologetic for his having once been a Wilsonian idealist. "Some men may have forgotten Woodrow Wilson," Byrnes told his state's Democrats in 1930, "but they will be forgotten themselves when Woodrow Wilson's memory is fresh."

Wilson's decline, both physically and in the public's memory, began on this 1919 speaking tour. Fatigued by months of overwork, the president collapsed aboard his train near Wichita, Kansas, and in late September was returned to the White House, where doctors concluded that he had suffered a cerebral thrombosis. Wilson spent the next months in Washington at the White House secluded from most visitors, while he attempted to recover from a paralysis of his left side and a general disruption of his powers of speech and concentration. Byrnes, along with other members of Congress, was uninformed as to the extent of Wilson's disabilities, but the president's illness was reported in the newspapers, and the few details available were of sufficient seriousness to disqualify Wilson in 1920 from further consideration by the party for a third term. Byrnes went to the Democratic convention in San Francisco that year as a delegate pledged to Wilson's attorney general, A. Mitchell Palmer. Byrnes himself was safe politically, as he had no opposition that summer in the Second District.

Byrnes' preference for A. Mitchell Palmer for president regrettably links the South Carolina congressman's name with the infamous Palmer raids of 1919–20, when the attorney general ordered the arrests of thousands of politically suspect aliens and citizens. In the White House hiatus of leadership following Wilson's stroke, Palmer had ordered the arrests largely on his own perception of the public's demand for a greater policing of "un-American" groups after the war. Doubtless there was also Palmer's own desire to capitalize on public fears in order to win his party's nomination. But the sweep of Palmer's arrest orders—in a single night in January 1920, over four thousand alleged subversives were to be arrested in a Justice Department's coast-to-coast raid—and his apparent disregard for civil liberties were to make his actions repellent to many Wilsonian progressives. Given this background of political repression, Jimmy Byrnes' support for Mitchell Palmer as a presidential candidate in 1920 would appear to have been a mean-spirited political act at the beginning of a decade of mean-spirited politics.

But in fact neither Palmer nor any other Democrat was fated to become the president-elect in 1920. The Democratic convention that year was to become memorable only in its choice of a vice-presidential nominee, the photogenic and increasingly well-known assistant secretary of the navy, Franklin D. Roosevelt. Since failing health excluded Woodrow Wilson from a third term, progressives divided among themselves and finally nominated an undistinguished party regular, James Cox, the three-term governor of Ohio. To balance the ticket in the East, Roosevelt was proposed as a running mate. Byrnes was able to boost Roosevelt's abilities on the convention floor, where doubts were expressed about FDR's appeal to voters in the South. Byrnes had known Roosevelt from his frequent appearances before the Naval Appropriations Subcommittee. There was no cause to worry, Byrnes told the delegates; FDR was "a good salesman."

The ticket of Cox-Roosevelt went down in 1920 to what was then the worst defeat in the history of the party. For their presidential candidate the Republicans also nominated an undistinguished Ohio politician, Senator Warren G. Harding; the GOP vice-presidential nomination went to the taciturn governor of Massachusetts, Calvin Coolidge. Warren Gamaliel Harding possessed a head of an almost marbled handsomeness and, as he

later demonstrated as president, a mind of an almost breathtaking emp-
tiness. But the nation in 1920 was in the mood for normalcy, not competency. The ailing Woodrow Wilson's publicized insistence in 1920 that the
presidential election that year should be a "great and solemn referendum"
on League ratification proved to be a disastrous platform for Cox and
Roosevelt. The end of the war had brought a popular rise in isolationism,
and returning doughboys and their families were in no mood for talk of
another deployment of American troops overseas as part of the League's
peacekeeping force. Moreover, with President Wilson preoccupied with
League ratification and in poor health for much of 1919–20, the record of
his administration at reconversion to a peacetime economy could not be
presented even as consistently effective. The War Department's abrupt
cancellation of manufacturing contracts and the lack of any unified plan
for reemployment of veterans or redistribution of agricultural goods had
by 1920 caused an acute depression in some parts of the country. (In 1944
Byrnes remembered the political consequences of this slump while serving
as Franklin Roosevelt's director of war mobilization and reconversion.)

On the South during that presidential election, the price of
cotton—always a sure barometer to that region's political soul—had plum-
meted. With the bottom falling out of military contracts, cotton that on
the New Orleans market had sold for forty-two cents at the beginning of
1920 was by the time of the presidential election bringing little more than
fourteen cents. Harding, with a sure instinct for ambiguity, declared himself
"highly sympathetic to southern aspirations." The result was a debacle for
the Democrats, and Jimmy Byrnes could count himself very lucky that he
had no Republican opposition at the polls that fall in South Carolina's
Second District. Throughout the South, the Republican party did extremely
well in the elections of 1920. Harding carried Tennessee, and he received
40 percent of the vote in Arkansas, Georgia, Kentucky, and North Carolina. The old GOP political dream of a displacement of the Solid South
by a newly aligned Republican party had come the closest so far to reality
with the election of Warren G. Harding. Nationally the Republicans did
even better; the GOP carried 61 percent of the popular vote, and President-
elect Harding won thirty-seven out of forty-eight states. The message for
Democrats, including Byrnes, could not have been clearer: prosperity after
the war was now identified by the voters with the Republican party. Wilsonian progressivism, as a major political force, was on its way out.

On inauguration day Byrnes was back in the capital district. The morning of March 4, 1921, was sunny with a light breeze as President-elect
Harding arrived at the White House for a short ride to the Capitol together
with members of the congressional inauguration committee and outgoing
President Wilson. The contrast could not have been greater between the
halting, partly paralyzed, and embittered figure of Wilson who had to lean
on the arm of Harding in order to walk out of the door of the White House

and the vigorous, optimistic Wilson who had arrived there as president-elect himself in 1913. In 1913, after years of Democratic dormancy under the Republican-controlled Congress and the profoundly reactionary leadership of the GOP majority leader, Joseph "Uncle Joe" Cannon, Democrats had passed the acts that Wilson considered the milestones of New Freedom advancement—the Federal Reserve Act, the Underwood Tariff, the Federal Trade Commission. Now, on the last day of his second term, as he was lifted by Secret Servicemen and placed into the waiting automobile, it must have seemed to him that the nation was back to where it was before his administration: seated across from Woodrow Wilson in the automobile's jump seat, and barely concealing a look of triumph, was Uncle Joe Cannon, once again House majority leader.

Harding, who sat down beside Wilson, offered a further contrast in political fortunes. Wilson was a president of an inflexible personal morality, who considered public office to be literally a sacred trust. Warren G. Harding was in his personal life a smiling dissembler and a desperate adulterer; as president, he wished only to please his party's established bosses, to avoid his wife, whom he called Duchess, and to relax at the end of the day with a highball of whiskey bootlegged into the White House in violation of the Eighteenth Amendment. Harding's performance in public office, the scandals of those who worked under him, and the details of his private life later would make him a target of easy fun among historians; but it must be remembered that if Woodrow Wilson became president by practicing a few great virtues, Warren G. Harding became his successor by practicing a great many small ones. Not the least of Harding's better qualities was a solicitous regard for the feelings of others, and as the automobile arrived at the Capitol Building, Harding turned his attentions toward Wilson. Given his difficulty in walking, President Wilson plainly would be in danger of a fall if, even with assistance, he attempted to climb the numerous steps necessary to take him from inside the Capitol Building to the temporary inaugural platform outside the building's East Portico. Consequently, Harding politely told Wilson that he would consider it no discourtesy if the outgoing president chose not to join the others on the inaugural stand. It was important to him, Harding said, that President Wilson not overexert himself. "I guess I better not try it," Wilson agreed.

President and Mrs. Wilson returned by automobile to their private residence on S Street. A crowd of about two thousand was waiting for Wilson outside his house and reacted with applause as the car bearing the outgoing president drove up to the curb. It had been a long morning, and, once inside, Wilson met with few visitors and spoke very little; twice after cheers from the crowd outside, he waved from an upstairs window but each time drew back from the window as if to indicate he was too tired to make a speech. At about this time, a bulky figure was heading toward Wilson's front door. Josephus Daniels, the stout North Carolinian who was the outgoing secretary of the navy and the sometime friend of the late Senator Tillman, was making a farewell call on Woodrow Wilson. In Daniels' wake was a group of young southern congressmen: Carter Glass, Cordell Hull, Pat Harrison—and Jimmy Byrnes.

The front door of the Wilson house opened for this group. Byrnes always remembered his shock at seeing Wilson. Like most members of Congress, he had not met with Wilson since his stroke the preceding fall, and "after his months of illness and the severe strain of that morning, he was a pathetic figure," Byrnes later wrote. The congressmen, perhaps unwittingly, did what visitors usually do on certain other, similarly solemn occasions such as funerals: they stood about and admired the flowers that sympathizers had sent the family.

At that moment, an incident profoundly affected Jimmy Byrnes as he stood inside Woodrow Wilson's home, almost moving him to tears. Among the crowd outside, in a spontaneous act of farewell to Wilson—who had said that without his faith in God he would have gone mad when he learned of the Senate's rejection of the treaty for the League of Nations—a group of women began singing hymns. The singing was clearly heard through the windowpanes of the house, and at the first notes, everyone, including Jimmy Byrnes, recognized the hymn. It was the old evangelical standby "Onward Christian Soldiers."

Outside, in the wintry sunshine, Warren G. Harding was inaugurated president of the United States.

The years 1921–25 were the most frustrating of Byrnes' congressional career. On the one hand, his reputation continued to rise within the Democratic party; Jimmy Byrnes began to be talked about as a possible successor to the post of House minority leader, and in a widely circulated newspaper story two senior Democratic congressmen were quoted as agreeing—anonymously—that Byrnes was the best man for the post. "I think the best we could pick would be little Jimmy Byrnes of South Carolina," one was quoted as saying. "He is making headway in leadership faster than any other man in the House."

But there was little pleasure for Byrnes in becoming the diminutive leader of a diminutive party. Democrats had been a minority in the House since 1919, and their numbers decreased again after the elections of 1922; despite the unexpected death of Harding in 1923, and the indictment on criminal charges the following year of Secretary of the Interior Albert Fall in the Teapot Dome scandal, the GOP retained a strong popularity nationwide. Byrnes chose not to go after the minority post, although in floor debate he remained one of the most vocal Democratic critics of the domestic policies of the Harding and Coolidge administrations. Against GOP charges of Democratic mismanagement of the war, Byrnes defended the wartime deficits of the Wilson administration, and in his criticism of the Mellon Tax Act of 1921, which repealed the excess-profit tax of the war years and reduced other taxes for the upper-income brackets, he so assailed the bill's Republican sponsors that he almost provoked a fistfight on the floor of the House. His attacks on the GOP majority during those years earned Little Jimmy Byrnes another nickname in Congress: he began to be known as Battling Byrnes.

It was the issue of racial equality, however, that most brought out Byrnes' rancor. Prior to 1919 Jimmy Byrnes appeared moderate in his racial views, at least in comparison with Pitchfork Ben Tillman or, in his latter years, Senator Tom Watson of Georgia. Unlike these notable agrarians, Byrnes believed in some due process of law for Negro citizens, as evinced by his earlier actions as a county solicitor, when he successfully had prosecuted cases of assault by one Negro upon another. Of course, as a member "of the democracy," Byrnes never questioned the truth of white superiority or the necessity of a legal system of segregation. In defense of these values Byrnes, along with other southern congressmen, had spoken out against a national conscription act in 1917, arguing that white southern males should be allowed to serve in racially segregated units of the states' national guards. Byrnes' remarks on this occasion, though ill conceived, were not ill tempered, and his subsequent remarks on racial issues usually revealed nothing more than the fact that in order to be elected, Jimmy Byrnes, like many other southern politicians of the time, was capable of indulging in low clowning. ("Our 'Jimmy' on the Warpath," read a headline in a Second District newspaper during this period. "Too Many Negro [Mail] Clerks—Congressman Byrnes Wants to Know Why Five-sixths of Second District Clerks Are of a 'Real Dusky Hue.' "

After 1919, however, Byrnes became more choleric. The same terrible year that saw the Red scare and the Palmer raids, strikes in industry, a lethal flu epidemic, and a depressed economy, also brought some of the most violent racial riots in this nation's history. Nearly one hundred deaths resulted from fighting between whites and blacks in small towns across the country and in such major cities as Chicago, Knoxville, Washington, D.C., and Byrnes' own hometown of Charleston. There, after a fight between black and white youths on May 2, 1919, white sailors from the nearby Charleston Navy Yards overturned a shooting gallery at the state fairgrounds, armed themselves with rifles, and went on a rampage. Two blacks were killed, and seventeen other people of both races were injured before order was restored. In Jimmy Byrnes' opinion, black veterans recently discharged from France were squarely responsible for the riots in Charleston and other cities. Toward the end of that summer of racial turmoil, Byrnes took the floor of the House on a hot August afternoon and delivered one of the most inflammatory speeches on race ever read into the *Congressional Record*. Byrnes accused returning black servicemen in general and

W. E. B. Dubois in particular of attempting to turn the South into a "little Russia" through revolutionary violence. These accusations were strong stuff, but for a white southern congressman during the heyday of Mitchell Palmer they were also conventional stuff. Byrnes went beyond convention, though, in the bullying tone of his concluding remarks. If black citizens did not care for the realities of a postwar America, Byrnes said, then they could go elsewhere. In fact, he promised, such departures would soon be made involuntary if he had anything to do with it; Byrnes ended his speech by calling for a broader enforcement of the wartime Espionage Act to forcibly deport any black radicals who called for racial equality.

Byrnes' speech in 1919 marks a low point for civil rights in a year that is itself remembered as marking the nadir for civil liberties. This speech, and Byrnes' subsequent opposition to the Dyer antilynching bill of 1921, fixed his reputation for the next three decades as a racist politician. That Byrnes was an uncompromising segregationist, there can be no doubt; that, despite his violent rhetoric, he was uneasy with an armed intimidation of the black race is evinced by his own rejection of the Ku Klux Klan in 1924. The truth is that Jimmy Byrnes did no one any political good, including himself, by making these speeches. His blunders on race were further compounded when, in an unnecessarily mean-spirited speech as a lame-duck congressman in 1925, he opposed federal funding for predominantly black Howard University, in Washington, D.C. Byrnes always claimed later that he had made this speech as a favor to northern congressmen who were opposed to funding the university but who were unwilling to argue against the bill as unconstitutional because of large black constituencies in their districts. If this was true and if he in fact sold himself as the political carrier of water and hewer of wood for northern congressmen, then he made a bad bargain for himself; these speeches continued to cost him alliances with New Deal liberals for the rest of his career. Byrnes' racist posturing distressed the Bourbon editor of his hometown newspaper, William Watts Ball of the *Charleston News and Courier*, and in partial apology for his congressional demagogy, Byrnes wrote him a letter that unintentionally contained an observation on southern politics that would haunt him for the remainder of his long political career. "[I]t is certain," Byrnes wrote Ball in early 1920, "that if there were a fair registration they [black citizens] would have a slight majority in our state. We cannot idly brush these facts aside. *Unfortunate though it may be, our consideration of every question must include this consideration of the race question*" (emphasis added).

What is probably closer to the truth is that Jimmy Byrnes in the early 1920s did not care whether northern congressmen found his remarks on race to be offensive or whether they found them to be agreeable; he intended his speeches solely and exclusively for the white voters back home. Byrnes had to make himself less vulnerable to political charges by South

Carolina demagogues who were more successful than he at inciting racial hatreds on the campaign trail. In the succinct language of southern politicians, Byrnes had to make sure that nobody "outniggered" him. For in the summer of 1924, Jimmy Byrnes decided to give up the frustrations of a minority House seat for a place in the U.S. Senate; although the upper chamber was still controlled by Republicans, Byrnes could exercise considerably more power even as a junior senator than as a House member, and as one of two senators from South Carolina he would for the first time have statewide control over the dispensation of patronage jobs. Besides, Byrnes probably felt that he had been the most qualified candidate for the seat ever since the death of Ben Tillman and the withdrawal of Frank Lever in 1918.

By the summer of 1924 Byrnes was thus preparing himself to descend for the first time into the chthonic world of South Carolina's statewide Democratic primaries. His candidacy there would put him at odds with an opponent backed by the most racist elements of the old Tillman organization, and as a result of this campaign Byrnes eventually would be befriended by Bernard Baruch and other prominent national Democrats. First, however, Byrnes would experience the only electoral defeat of his career. His defeat in 1924 would come at the hands of a man whose demagogic statements on race and whose Ku Klux Klan support would continue to stalk his ambitions throughout the 1920s and 1930s—his opponent being a former state governor, a shadowy and irrepressible politician, Coley Blease.

Even in a state where a certain amount of flamboyance is expected from politicians as a matter of tradition, the career and personality of Coleman Livingston Blease strain credulity. Coley Blease, as he was universally known throughout South Carolina, consistently out-Heroded Herod, combining in one person the diverse roles of a charmer, a bully, a racist demagogue, and a comically inept pretender. He was more actor than politician, and given the staginess of his public behavior, no one in South Carolina should have believed in him more than a minute. But believe the voters did; during the decades before and after Jimmy Byrnes' campaign for the U.S. Senate in 1924, up would pop Blease with an astonishing regularity, running for Democratic party nominations to posts from senator to state governor. A tall, dark-haired, and impressively handsome man who was, unlike Byrnes, naturally inclined to demagogy, Blease was known by state Democrats to have an absolute control over about 40 percent of the old Tillmanite political machine, whose votes would go to him under any circumstance. Before running against Coley Blease for the Democratic nomination in 1924, Jimmy Byrnes doubtless had heard the story, reputed to be true, of the upstate farmer who in a transport of emotion at a Blease rally had shouted, "Coley, I'd vote for you tonight even if you was to steal my mule!"

The reason for Blease's phenomenal success at winning votes in South Carolina was simple: more than any other Deep South politician of his time, Blease identified himself with the cause of white supremacy. He collected around himself the most violently racist elements of the old Tillman organization. Throughout his career, Blease frequently sought—and received—endorsement by the state's Ku Klux Klan, and he once boasted that on election eve Negroes throughout South Carolina prayed for a Blease defeat. If indeed black people so prayed, their prayers were seldom answered. Beginning his political career in earnest during Ben Tillman's dying years, Blease quickly established a political constituency for himself statewide by appealing to the white textile workers whom the more agrarian-centered Tillman organization had ignored. On his campaigns he often barnstormed the little textile towns of the upstate, warning the inhabitants there of the dangers posed by the "baboons and apes" of the black race. He promised in a campaign for the state's governorship never to prosecute a case of Negro lynching; and when later reminded of the U.S. Constitution's guarantee of due process for black citizens, he declared, "To hell with the Constitution!"

Senator Tillman before his death had been furious over these actions —not because of the racism, which Tillman himself as governor had instituted in the state's Jim Crow laws, but because Blease was building a following for himself independent of Ben Tillman. Also, Tillman had promised at least *some* reform to his distressed white rural constituency of farmers; but throughout his long career, Blease said nothing to his mill workers about improving wages or working conditions in the state's cotton mills. Blease on the stump had only one sure promise: no matter how impoverished the white mill workers of South Carolina found themselves, they could always be certain that under his leadership the state's black citizens would be even more wretched. This simple message, combined with Blease's genius for dramatizing his ego, often resulted in electoral success. During the weeks preceding each primary election for the various jobs he sought in the 1920s, Blease frequently hired itinerant organ-grinders to tour the little textile mills of upstate South Carolina, endlessly braying out a campaign slogan on street corners, a slogan as catchy and mindless as a jingle for chewing gum: "Roll up yer sleeves and say whatcha please / The man for this office is Cole L. Blease."

If, after his two, two-year terms as governor from 1910 to 1914, the regular state Democratic party, including Byrnes, continued to ignore him, it was because Coley Blease was considered something of a political joke. During his tenure as governor, there was a persistent rumor that he enriched himself illegally with funds from the state treasury. Blease was never proved to be a thief, but more distressing was his documented attitude toward criminals already in the South Carolina penitentiary. Blease had an almost compulsive desire to set these people free. During his four years as governor, Blease granted executive clemency to an incredible 1,743 prisoners—still a South Carolina state record—often signing his name to the pardon in a flamboyant ink of Christmas-card red. Thieves, murderers, and sexual offenders were on the governor's pardon lists, but Blease was undisturbed. "I felt so good when I came downtown this morning that I decided to grant three pardons!" Blease once declared in a kind of political *agape*.

Even outsiders who are southern born have difficulty in appreciating the type of man Byrnes was facing as a primary opponent in 1924. In his magisterial study of the emergence of the New South, C. Vann Woodward mused why, "by some obscure rule of succession, Bleases tend to follow Tillmans," and thereby impede any true economic progress or rule of the law in the South. A generation later, Jefferson Frazier, a young southern undergraduate from Harvard University who had traveled to South Carolina to interview Jimmy Byrnes for his senior thesis, concluded simply that Blease "probably was a psychopath" who somehow had escaped involuntary hospitalization.

Yet even a madman might have his dreams of reason, and many of the political acts of Cole Blease, no matter how garish and irrational they appeared to the outside world, had the internal logic of the force of economic laws operating in his state. Blease's political cunning in identifying himself with the white cotton textile workers provided him with a constituency that was growing exponentially within his state. In 1880, South Carolina had still been an overwhelmingly rural state, with only 1,929 of its citizens working in cotton textile mills; by the summer of the Democratic primary of 1924, the number of textile workers was approaching 70,000. Although, unlike the state's black citizens, white textile operatives were allowed to vote in the primaries of the Democratic party as "members of the democracy," they knew they had been economically and socially disenfranchised by Bourbons, agrarians, and progressives alike. Particularly the last group, with which Jimmy Byrnes politically identified himself, viewed the textile workers as a barely educable, disease-ridden social problem rather than a legitimate political constituency.

In short, Cole Blease appealed to all those in South Carolina who could *not* afford to send their sons to Harvard; and like those of a later generation of southern politicians, such as Eugene "Bull" Connor and the early George C. Wallace, Blease's antics provided the poor white working class with a scapegoat, the black race, whom they could blame for their economic troubles. Thus if Blease was something of a political clown, he must be considered a clown with a loaded gun: he was capable of inflicting enormous damage to the political ambitions of those Bourbon or progressive politicians such as Jimmy Byrnes who attempted to oppose him.

Among those also running against Blease that summer of 1924 was the current incumbent U.S. senator, Nathaniel B. Dial. Politically inexperienced, Dial had been elected after Tillman's death by party regulars embarrassed by Blease's opposition to Woodrow Wilson in his unsuccessful race against Tillman, and in his six years as a senator, Dial had done little to create the forceful public personality so necessary to survival in South Carolina's one-party politics. Thus, with Ben Tillman now safely dead, Cole Blease saw his chance for an easy victory. All that stood in the way of his winning the Democratic party's state primary was the inexperienced Nathaniel Dial and the protégé of the late Senator Tillman's declining years, the youthful, even juvenile-appearing, Jimmy Byrnes.

The summer of the 1924 primary was unseasonably warm in South Carolina as in May, Byrnes, Dial, and Blease began their stump for the Democratic party's nomination, accompanied by yet another candidate, named John J. McMahan. This crowded field would fit Byrnes' usual campaign stratagem, which had worked well for him before: Jimmy Byrnes knew he might not be able to win first place over Blease in the primary, but he intended to win enough votes to keep the most formidable of his opponents from winning a clear majority. If he could secure second place, he would befriend the third- and fourth-place candidates and ask for their support in a subsequent runoff between himself and Blease. Byrnes therefore would have to obtain endorsements by both Dial and McMahan to have a chance at bettering his past claims to 40 percent of the electorate. But as the summer's primary wore on and tempers became more edgy, it grew increasingly apparent that neither Dial nor McMahan seemed inclined to participate in Jimmy Byrnes' long-term plans to become a U.S. senator.

The incumbent Senator Dial was particularly testy. He accused McMahan of being a "stalking horse for Byrnes," running solely at the instigation of Byrnes with instructions to embarrass Dial with questions about his integrity. Byrnes would then be free to take the high road, campaigning on economic issues. McMahan hotly denied Dial's charges, and while the two continued to quarrel, Byrnes tried vainly to make peace and come to some understanding with his competitors about the importance of defeating Blease in a runoff. Coley Blease meanwhile was content to joke with his audience and to increase his lead.

During his own turn on the stump, Byrnes seriously tried to stress to his audience the importance of economic issues to South Carolina. He did make some use of his speeches against funding for Howard University, telling his receptive white audience that if "they [northern blacks] leave Howard University, they are liable to drift down South and cause trouble." But to Byrnes' credit, his humanity kept breaking through. Alone among the Democratic senatorial candidates, Byrnes defended the federal government's planned payment of a bonus to black U.S. veterans of the First

World War. "We put them in the army," Byrnes reminded his southern audience; therefore black veterans must be treated "justly and rightly," he insisted on the stump. But Byrnes' attention was directed toward economics, not social justice. He promised that if elected to the Senate he would align himself with the "pocketbook alliance" of pro-agricultural representatives in the House and Senate. This bipartisan "farm bloc," as it was first called in the mid-1920s, acted as a check to the urban, probusiness bias of the Coolidge administration and already had obtained funding for new government loans to farmers. Byrnes wanted more of the same and after promising in his hometown of Aiken to use his influence for South Carolina if the voters sent him to the Senate, he was presented with bouquets of flowers from his local admirers. Senator Dial, speaking after Byrnes, acidly remarked, "That's right, give Mr. Byrnes the flowers."

Senator Dial's mood did not improve after the Aiken speech. On a hot day in late June, Dial and McMahan got into a fistfight over the Byrnes issue while sharing the same speaking platform in the rough little upstate milltown of Gaffney. Afterward there was no hope of reconciling the two men in a pro-Byrnes coalition. Although Byrnes picked up the endorsements of most of the major newspapers in South Carolina, Blease got a 16,000-vote plurality in the summer primary. Byrnes came in second. Byrnes and Blease were scheduled by the Democratic party for a runoff election later that September, but neither Dial nor McMahan was willing to endorse Byrnes or denounce Blease. However, in his second campaign that summer against Byrnes, the demagogic Blease was unable to resort to his usual tactics of race-baiting. Byrnes' own fiery speeches in favor of white supremacy on the floor of the House in 1919 and 1921 had taken care of that. Nevertheless, there was a certain issue on which Byrnes was vulnerable, which may have been suggested to Blease after the first primary by his friends in the state's Ku Klux Klan.

Byrnes already had been approached that year by the Klan. Shortly after declaring his candidacy for the senate, he received a visit in mid-1924 at his Washington office from Albert E. Hill, a Spartanburg lawyer whom Byrnes later identified as the grand kleagle, or leader, of the state's Ku Klux Klan. According to Byrnes' account of the meeting, Hill offered to administer to Byrnes the oath of membership in the Klan privately in Byrnes' congressional office. Byrnes could then tell his more liberal constituents that he was not a Klan member, and Hill could inform the Klan membership that Jimmy Byrnes was behind the Klansmen in principle. To give the grand kleagle his due, the argument was felicitously clever; it saved politicians like Byrnes any embarrassment, while it increased the "invisible empire" of the Ku Klux Klan, as no one could be sure whether or not a public figure was a Klansman. Hill had offered this invitation, he now assured Byrnes, to other candidates also in need of political help.

Without the support of the Ku Klux Klan of South Carolina, he added, Jimmy Byrnes had no chance of being elected to the U.S. Senate; this offer was being made by the Klan simply out of personal friendship.

Grand Kleagle Albert E. Hill probably was right. Without the help of the Ku Klux Klan, Jimmy Byrnes and many other southern politicians would in 1924 have had no chance at winning their state's elections. The Klan had not been a major factor in turn-of-the-century southern politics—in South Carolina, for example, Ben Tillman's Farmers' Association had so preempted the issue of racism that the Klan's presence there would have been superfluous. But after the rise of isolationism, the Red scares, and the race riots following 1919, Klan membership had spread across the South to the southwestern and midwestern states. Nationally the Klan had helped elect eleven state governors and sixteen U.S. senators by 1924. Within the eleven states of the old Confederacy, the Klan in the mid-1920s was an organization of the New South; its national headquarters on Peachtree Street in Atlanta produced a sophisticated marketing literature. The Klan broadened its appeal during the 1920s to include anti-Catholic and anti-Semitic invective in its literature and, under its prompting, signs began appearing in shopwindows from Florida to Kansas urging passersby to "TWK"—"Trade with Klansmen." By 1924 the national Ku Klux Klan had become so important politically that the Democratic National Convention that year refused to pass a resolution condemning the Klan for its acts of racial violence; that year an estimated two million white Americans had become declared or covert members of the KKK.

One who did not become a member that year was Jimmy Byrnes. He turned down the grand kleagle's offer. His refusal to join the Klan was a notable act of political courage, particularly considering the secrecy under which the offer had been made. (Other southern politicians of at least equal prominence with Byrnes had taken the Klan up on its offer. In Alabama, Hugo L. Black, who later served both in the Senate and on the Supreme Court with Byrnes, had become a KKK member in 1923, although this fact did not become public until 1937, when Roosevelt nominated Black to the Court. In 1924 Hugo Black also ran for the U.S. Senate and won.)

Byrnes' refusal to join the Klan indicates that, for all his tough talk on forcible deportations of blacks in 1919, he really had no stomach for the floggings, lynchings, and mutilations of Negroes that the KKK boastingly performed throughout the twenties. Also at work was a strong religious antipathy on Byrnes' part. The Ku Klux Klan of the 1920s was as much anti-Catholic as anti-Negro, and, particularly in the presidential elections of 1924 and 1928, the Klan campaigned nationally against politicians who were Catholic. By asking Byrnes to join the organization, the Klan was dropping a none-too-subtle hint that to obtain its support in his 1924 senatorial election, his earlier conversion to Protestantism was not enough.

He would have to renounce his former faith by joining an overtly anti-Catholic organization. This Byrnes flatly refused to do. Although he had been a Protestant for decades now, he remained in 1924, as he would for the rest of his life, Catholic in all his sympathies, and he would always be quick to defend the church in which his mother still was a communicant. So, if forced to choose between the Roman Catholic church and the Ku Klux Klan, Jimmy Byrnes was not about to take the side of the grand kleagle. The only question that must have nagged him as the September runoff with Blease approached was this: What would the Klan, whose friendly offer he had declined, do now that it was unfriendly?

Byrnes found out two days before the election. In the weeks preceding the September runoff, Byrnes vainly had tried to make inroads into Blease's upstate stronghold. But instead of Byrnes' appeals to regional economics, voters in the mill towns had been more interested in Blease's racial harangues and his sly jokes about Byrnes' obvious youth and ambition. Finally, two days before the election, there appeared in the *Charleston Evening Post* and other newspapers throughout the state an advertisement addressed to "The People of South Carolina." Byrnes must have sensed trouble as soon as he saw the advertisement. Although ostensibly an endorsement of Byrnes, the ad had been printed without his knowledge, and its intended effect was the direct opposite of helping his career. For decades afterward Byrnes and those closest to him continued to refer to this advertisement with bitterness as "the altar boy endorsement."

"We, the boyhood classmates at St. Patrick's Roman Catholic Church," the advertisement began, "classmates at St. Patrick's Sunday School, and boys who served on the altar with him, [and] also members of St. Patrick's parish, endorse the candidacy of James F. Byrnes for the United States Senate."

The endorsement went on to praise Byrnes' public career as an example that "a man can rise from the lowest to the loftiest station in spite of race, class, or creed prejudice." Following this statement of political piety were the names of twenty men who had been his schoolmates at Charleston while attending St. Patrick's Catholic School. Byrnes immediately recognized some as men who had business or social contacts with Blease.

The endorsement was a put-up job. Blease or his supporters, probably in collusion with the Klan, had coerced or duped Byrnes' former classmates into providing their names and reminding voters of Jimmy Byrnes' earlier Catholicism. In a state so overwhelmingly Protestant and fundamentalist as South Carolina, this identification would be fatal at the polls. Additionally, the advertised praise of Jimmy Byrnes as the senatorial candidate superior to "race, class, or creed prejudice" was not so winsome as it sounded. In any other state, these words might have passed for high praise. But South Carolina was not any other state. It was, for instance, not Massachusetts; it was not even North Carolina. That is, ever since colonial times, South Carolinians had *prided* themselves on valuing precisely those prejudices of race, class, or creed that other states at least officially deplored. To be identified with such liberal sentiments in South Carolina was Byrnes' undoing. The oldest political trick in the book, the kiss-of-death endorsement, had caught a star pupil of politics unawares. Byrnes' old political mentor Benjamin Tillman had been in his grave for six years now, but had Senator Tillman been alive that morning and seen the state's newspapers, he would have grinned at Byrnes' discomfort. There was no time now to write a rebuttal or to place it in the state's newspapers. If Jimmy Byrnes was to continue to run for national office from South Carolina, he would have to run as an altar boy.

Byrnes lost the runoff by about two thousand votes. In Byrnes' hometown of Spartanburg, the local newspaper until the late 1930s broadcast primary-night election results to the town's citizens by collecting the precinct results by telephone and then, through a cinema projector, showing the numbers in large figures upon a bed sheet hung outside the windows of a drummers' hotel across the town square from the newspaper building. Thus Byrnes was able to see the galling results of the altar boy endorsement cast hugely upon the traditional robes of the Ku Klux Klan. The senatorial race of 1924 was the only election Jimmy Byrnes ever lost, and this defeat, as Byrnes well knew, came at the hands not of a better politician but simply of an unscrupulous one. Cole Blease's campaign combined religious bigotry, racial hatred, low cunning, and a shameless buffoonery. It worked: the jingle-master won. Earlier Byrnes had resigned a safe seat in the House for a position of greater responsibility in the Senate, campaigning on economic issues he deemed important to his region. Now he was neither a congressman nor a senator; as Jimmy Byrnes considered what to do next in order to earn a living, the supporters of the future senator Blease celebrated his nomination throughout the state in a song of the candidate's own devising, which Jimmy Byrnes had doubtless heard many times before: *"Roll up your sleeves and say whatcha please / The man for this office is Cole L. Blease."*

Fate delivered a postscript to Byrnes' involuntary retirement from politics. In March of 1925 Byrnes was back in Washington, clearing out his desk and preparing for what he believed might be a permanent move back to South Carolina to practice law. Washington had changed considerably in the last few years. In 1924 Woodrow Wilson, the president who believed that America was not founded in order to make a profit, had died; Byrnes was among the thousands who had attended Wilson's funeral at the National Cathedral. Also in 1924 Calvin Coolidge, who had succeeded to the presidency after Warren G. Harding's death, had won his own first full term. The largest scandal of the Harding administration—the Teapot

Dome affair—had continued into 1925 with allegations that Edward L. Doheny of the Pan-American Petroleum Company had successfully bribed Interior Secretary Albert Fall for favorable consideration of oil-lease rights at the Teapot Dome reservoir. Both Fall and Doheny were under criminal indictments when Jimmy Byrnes happened one day in 1925 to meet a cousin and old childhood friend from Charleston, Frank Hogan, on a Washington street.

For a poor boy from South Carolina, Frank Hogan had done very well for himself. Hogan had become one of Washington's most prominent attorneys; eventually he would become president of the American Bar Association. On that day in early 1925, Frank Hogan was a smiling, full-chested man who presented a robust and toothy appearance to the world. He was a hail-fellow-well-met, and his rounded black spectacles gave his otherwise benevolent face an oddly pugnacious look: the attorney who carefully puts on his glasses in order to hit you. Hogan had a reputation as a lawyer who could win, and his current clients had excited considerable interest. As all of congressional Washington, including Jimmy Byrnes, was aware, Hogan had been retained by both Fall and Doheny to defend them against charges of bribery and conspiracy to defraud the government. Doheny was reputed to have paid Hogan a fee of a million dollars.

Frank Hogan was to earn his million-dollar fee. His arguments on behalf of his client Doheny were so impressive as to make Hogan, even in this era of Clarence Darrow and William Jennings Bryan, one of the most memorable lawyers of the 1920s. In his arguments to the jury, Hogan sometimes broke down and weep at his own eloquence; he compared the persecution of Edward L. Doheny of the Pan-American Petroleum Company to the trials endured by Jesus Christ, and he declared that in the federal government's indicting Doheny, the world had not seen such an injustice since the crucifixion some nineteen hundred years before. If Hogan's rhetoric was memorable, so were the juries' decisions. Despite two separate trials over a period of nearly five years, the federal government never succeeded in proving its case that Doheny had bribed Fall; and although Fall went to jail in 1931, having been convicted of accepting a bribe, Doheny was found innocent of charges of having bribed Fall. Frank Hogan's successful defense—and the size of the client's fee that had prompted that defense—were to become the bywords of the 1920s. "You can't convict a million dollars" was a proverb of the jazz age, and that expression had its origin in the person of Frank Hogan, who now stood smiling in front of Jimmy Byrnes.

Hogan at this meeting gave rise to another memorable remark. Byrnes by his own admission had not seen much of his cousin in the years preceding the Teapot Dome scandal, and after some good-natured ribbing about Hogan's "poor client," these two ambitious and closely related southern public men took each other's measure. The contrast was inescapable. As a congressman, Byrnes had voted for a special investigation of Teapot Dome oil leases; now, less than a year later, Hogan was a millionaire as a result of defending his clients in the same scandal, while Byrnes was out of office and headed toward an unknown future practicing law in South Carolina. The two men exchanged pleasantries and then said good-bye. In parting, smiling Hogan decided to give his cousin some down-home advice: "Jim," he told him, "the best client for a lawyer to have is a rich man what am scared."

Byrnes became a successful attorney. Shortly after the inauguration of Calvin Coolidge on March 4, 1925, Jimmy and Maude Byrnes left Washington for a new home in Spartanburg, South Carolina. The couple still had many close friends in Aiken, but their choice of Spartanburg as a residence was made less for sentimental and more for practical reasons: Byrnes had been offered a lucrative partnership in the Spartanburg law firm of Samuel J. Nicholls and C. C. Wyche. Sam Nicholls had been a congressman with Byrnes during the Democratic majority, and Byrnes had known Wyche as a longtime secretary to the late Senator Tillman. The partnership of Nicholls, Wyche, and Byrnes soon became known as one of the best-connected law firms in the state. There doubtless was another reason besides his law practice why Byrnes moved to a larger city in the upstate. His close loss to Blease in 1924 showed that, despite his considerable strength as a vote-getter in the low country and midlands, he lacked sufficient following in the upstate to overturn Blease's popularity there. If Jimmy Byrnes was to have a future as a politician, he would have to become better known in the populous mill cities that were springing up along the South Carolina–North Carolina border.

Such a place was Spartanburg, a busy regional metropolis of about 25,000 in 1925. Having grown along the north–south axis of the Southern Railway—and, later, of the new federal highway system—it was becoming an important manufacturing and distributing center. Spartanburg was a businesman's town, not a planter's; it dealt in cotton only as a wholesale item, and its civic leaders were not the old agrarian chieftains but the owners of the new, redbrick textile mills, or the downtown brokers in stocks and cotton futures and the corporate attorneys who served these clients' interests. Spartanburg's middle class expressed its prosperity in the 1920s not in an architecture influenced by the agrarian antebellum Greek Revival style but in suburbs of well-kept lawns and newly built bungalows; and even in its enforcement of segregation laws Spartanburg was not particularly southern, but simply in conformity with the civic codes of most American cities of the time. In all important ways, Byrnes' new city of residence was as all-American as the fictional Zenith of the novels of Sinclair Lewis. Shortly after moving into town, Byrnes joined several civic fraternities, including the Odd Fellows; he and his wife became members of the Spartanburg Country Club; he purchased a Reo Flying Cloud automobile; he hired Cassandra Connor, who was to be his confidential secretary for the next forty years; and he wisely decided not to run for public office. These decisions paid off. By Christmas of 1925 his annual income totaled $20,000, more than two and one-half times the amount he had ever earned in one year as a congressman.

Byrnes skipped the 1928 Democratic National Convention, in Houston, just as he had resisted the temptation two years earlier to run for his state's second seat in the U.S. Senate, which had come up for grabs in the primary election of 1926. Byrnes had known that a loss in 1926, so soon after his defeat in 1924, would have marked him as a perennial loser in South Carolina politics, and nationally the Democratic party by 1928 was far into one of its recurrent bouts of decade-long self-destruction. The party that year nominated as its presidential candidate one of the most divisive choices in its history, Governor Alfred E. "Al" Smith of New York, who had been nominated by Franklin D. Roosevelt. Smith was an unapologetic Catholic, an outspoken opponent of Prohibition, a delightfully irreverent wit, and an urban realist; that is, he was everything many southern Democrats considered to be wrong with their party. After Smith's nomination in the summer of 1928, many Democrats in the South announced their intentions of either voting for the Republican nominee, Herbert Hoover, or "going fishing" on election day.

Byrnes did neither. Although he had forsaken politics for some years now, Byrnes campaigned actively for Smith in South Carolina and other southern states, an act the otherwise prudent Byrnes knew might cost him some law business and perhaps some future votes. In part, this was an act of courage; by publicly declaring himself a Smith man, Byrnes was refusing to allow himself to be intimidated by the Ku Klux Klan, which was organizing on a state and national level to defeat Al Smith. There was also a deeper reason: a recognition by Jimmy Byrnes that Al Smith, a man a few years older than Byrnes, was the politician Byrnes might have become without the accident of his southern birth. Each man mirrored the other. Both Byrnes and Smith were natty dressers, and both enjoyed a reputation as well-fixed men; but despite current prosperity, each had come up the hard way, Byrnes quitting parochial school to work for a law firm in Charleston and Smith dropping out of parochial school to work at the Fulton Fish Market in New York City. And just as Byrnes had risen in the South by accepting the conventional power structure of older agrarians, so Smith had begun his move upward by becoming a subpoena server for the Tammany Hall organization. In Al Smith's receiving the Democratic party's nomination for the presidency, Byrnes may have seen a validation of Irish Catholics like himself in the party.

Unfortunately for Byrnes and Smith, the electorate did not see Smith's candidacy the same way. Throughout the nation, and particularly in the South, Al Smith's efforts in 1928 were like Jimmy Byrnes' campaign of 1924 writ large: Smith's religion and his opposition to Prohibition mobilized both the Ku Klux Klan and the conservative Protestant clergy against him. Herbert Hoover won an impressive victory nationwide, and of the eleven states of the former Confederacy, the GOP won a record five. The morning after the election, Byrnes could take some small comfort in the fact that, partly as a result of his efforts, Al Smith at least carried South Carolina.

For the remainder of the 1920s, Democrats, including Byrnes, had little else to do but mend their political fences. Byrnes was quick to reestablish contact with Franklin Roosevelt in particular. To all his visitors throughout the mid-1920s, Roosevelt had given the happy appearance of having recovered from his 1921 attack of poliomyelitis, and his singular victory in November of 1928 in the race for the governorship of New York—Al Smith lost his own state—confirmed the expectations of many Democrats that FDR would be the party's presidential nominee in 1932. The week after Al Smith's debacle at the polls, Jimmy Byrnes wrote his congratulations to Roosevelt, who was then vacationing in Warm Springs, Georgia. "When Al Smith lost New York and the Democracy lost Virginia," Byrnes wrote, "I retired and only today have I sufficiently recovered to do that which I wanted to do for several days, namely congratulate you on your splendid victory. Your election is the only comfort which I received out of the voting on last Tuesday."

Byrnes then warmly recalled for FDR the latter's "splendid administration in the Navy Department," and as one former New Freedom supporter to another, Byrnes recalled how in 1920 "it gave me great pleasure in the San Francisco convention to urge your nomination for vice president, and I am now only anxious to have the opportunity to urge your nomination for the Presidency." Byrnes visited Governor Roosevelt in Albany, New York, several times between 1928 and 1932.

But the fates of Byrnes, Roosevelt, and millions of other Americans were to be determined not by any individual plans for success made during the 1920s but by a larger turn of events at the close of the decade: the six trading days on the New York Stock Exchange beginning Thursday, October 24, 1929. Byrnes that morning was at the state capital of Columbia, South Carolina, on his way to attend the Clemson College–South Carolina College football game. The game was a traditional rivalry in the state, and for years had been scheduled to coincide with the opening day of the South Carolina State Fair, which always came in late October on a Thursday. Big Thursday, as the fair-and-football contest was known, marked a political and social congregation of prime importance in the state. Spectators at the fairground and at the stadium dressed to be seen, and although October temperatures in South Carolina can soar to the subtropical, men and women sweated through the festivities in fashionable fur coats and heavy sports jackets. As Byrnes' party was leaving the stadium that Thursday, he bought an afternoon paper. The headlines startled him: while he was at the game, record selling that morning on the New York Exchange had produced a financial panic on Wall Street unknown since the great depressions of the 1890s. Prices of all stocks were falling precipitously as investors sought to get out of the market at any price, and a further drop that afternoon was expected. In fact, during the course of the next five business days, blue-chip stocks lost billions of dollars in trading value, and by the following Friday, the stock market did not open at all. Byrnes' investments were limited and his losses therefore comparatively small, but in the months following that Thursday in October his stocks in several state-chartered banks and in the Reo Flying Cloud automobile company became worthless. Big Thursday continued throughout the 1930s to mean a day in Byrnes' home state devoted to football, heavy drinking, fairgoing, and politics; but the national historians who later described the stock market crash of 1929 and the subsequent Great Depression of the 1930s, gave the date of Thursday, October 24, 1929, another name: Black Thursday.

The Depression that is usually dated as beginning after the financial crisis of October 1929 actually started several years earlier in the rural southern and midwestern states. Farmers did not share in the businessmen's prosperity of the Harding-Coolidge era. Efforts by farm bloc legislators—whose numbers Byrnes had futilely tried to join in the election of 1924—were unsuccessful in gaining price supports for farmers, who throughout the decade were burdened by large surpluses. President Coolidge twice had vetoed, as inflationary, farm bills guaranteeing the federal government's purchase of crop surpluses at a predetermined price, or crop "parity," as its supporters called it. The combination throughout the 1920s of a series of bumper crops, an oversupplied market, and high interest rates meant that the farmers' net income declined during the decade, while that of many urban dwellers increased. (Of course, the city resident was most directly aware of this agricultural distress only in that he noticed that foodstuffs and textiles cost less.) In addition, the passage with President Hoover's approval of the Hawley-Smoot Tariff Act of 1930 raised import duties on many manufactured items to record highs, without including compensatory relief for farmers; and throughout the South and West, voters who had switched parties to vote for Hoover in 1928 were by 1930 returning to their traditional Democratic party allegiances.

Coley Blease was plainly in over his head during the economic events of 1929. Despite the growing number of unemployed among South Carolina textile workers, however, Blease might have succeeded in hanging on to his own job in the U.S. Senate had the stock market panic of 1929 not deepened into a full depression by early fall of 1930—a depression that began to affect the textile owners as well as their workers. Orders fell off at mills throughout South Carolina as both domestic and international markets for cotton textiles dried up, the result of financial chaos at home or the retaliatory high tariffs abroad in response to Hawley-Smoot. Equally alarming to the state's capitalists was the unprecedented number of bank failures throughout the South and the West. In the eyes of the mill owners, Blease may have been useful in diverting the racial passions of mill employees during a time of universal prosperity; but in these uncertain times Blease had outlived his usefulness. Byrnes later recollected, "Some businessmen who did not admire Senator Blease, and many others who had opposed him for years, began to urge me to be a candidate for the Senate in 1930."

Byrnes was easily persuaded. Cole L. Blease had dealt Jimmy Byrnes the only defeat of his political career, and the situation in 1930 presented Byrnes an opportunity to even the score. Unemployed mill workers might now be willing to listen to a campaigner who talked about economic issues; and although Blease retained his stronghold of support in the upstate, for the last six years Byrnes had lived and made valuable political connections in the upstate center of Spartanburg. Byrnes declared his candidacy in early May 1930.

This time, as he prepared his campaign and got ready to go on the stump, Byrnes was careful not to overestimate his own virtues—or to underestimate what he perceived as Coley Blease's vices. To forestall any attempt by Blease's supporters to raise again the question of his childhood Catholicism, Byrnes early in 1930 obtained a written statement by his Episcopal minister in Aiken affirming that Byrnes was a communicant of the Protestant faith. On a more secular note, Byrnes also wrote to an old friend from his House days, Joe Robinson of Arkansas. A thick-set and combative man, Robinson was now the Democratic minority leader in the Senate, having run for the vice presidency on the ticket with Al Smith. Byrnes secured a pledge from Robinson not to endorse Blease or any other opponent running against Byrnes in the primary (a move Byrnes knew might also reduce Blease's access to national campaign funds from the party). Back home in South Carolina, Byrnes established in Columbia a state headquarters for his campaign; and he took notes in his private shorthand on all influential people he met along campaign stops, and later wrote a personal notes asking for their support in the primary. Not least, Byrnes called on his congressional friends of many decades to obtain mailing lists of all registered voters each of South Carolina's congressional districts.

Nevertheless, the possibility of a Blease victory in the primary that summer still worried Jimmy Byrnes. Byrnes' quiet manner of speaking on the stump was no match for the melodramatics of Coley Belase; and, as in 1924, Byrnes competed on the hustlings with a third candidate, a popular state solicitor named Leon Harris. Byrnes knew he very likely would have to eliminate Harris in the first primary that summer, forcing Blease into a September runoff. Thus once more Byrnes would be dependent upon the good will of a defeated adversary to help finish off Blease in the fall. That help, as Byrnes had learned the hard way in 1924, might or might not be forthcoming. The situation by the summer of 1930 was to his mind shaping up as distressingly similar to his losing effort of 1924.

To ensure success against Blease in 1930, Byrnes would need to find a financial backer, someone who could promote his candidacy in the South Carolina business establishment and who could buy the radio and newspaper advertisements necessary for him to overcome Blease's personal effectiveness on the stump. For Byrnes that someone would preferably be a southerner, without a political career of his own to compete with Byrnes'—but also someone with strong ties to the Democratic National Committee, in a position to move Byrnes' career further along once he had aided Byrnes in winning his senatorial nomination and election. That Byrnes succeeded in finding such a patron—a combination financial angel and alter ego—is evident from a letter that arrived at the financial offices at 120 Broadway, New York City, a few weeks before the August primary. The letter bore a South Carolina postmark, and it was from Jimmy Byrnes; it was addressed to the well-known stock speculator who was himself a South Carolina native—Bernard M. Baruch.

Baruch, who had a history of contributing generously to select Democratic party candidates, was said to have foreseen the 1929 stock market crash and was one of the few major contributors to the Democratic party who had entered the Depression decade with his fortune almost intact. Baruch had a reputation for understanding the alchemy of finance, and of politics; indeed, long before meeting Byrnes, Baruch had grasped a secret no alchemist had ever possessed. Bernard Baruch did not waste his time looking for any philosopher's stone with which to turn base metals into gold; he understood that gold *is* the philosopher's stone. Money—whether represented by gold, currency, or stock certificates, and Baruch had plenty of all three—could change anybody into anything. Enough money had transmuted Bernard Baruch, for example, from being just another sharp trader on Wall Street to being a respected elder statesman and counselor to presidents. It could also transmute Jimmy Byrnes into a U.S. senator, and this was an alchemy that Byrnes also could understand. "Dear Mr. Baruch," began Jimmy Byrnes' letter of July 21, 1930, "I am a candidate for the United States Senate opposing Cole L. Blease. . . ."

Byrnes and Baruch. For the next thirty-five years their two names would be permanently linked, in one of the Democratic party's most enduring partnerships. The tall, white-haired financier and the nimble, youthful-appearing Byrnes were to become a familiar sight on the streets of Washington beginning soon after their first correspondence, in 1930. Baruch was one of the wealthiest men in the Democratic party and Byrnes one of the most ambitious; shortly after making the acquaintance of Baruch, Jimmy Byrnes would win his election to the Senate, and in the Senate chamber as a member of the Finance Committee, Byrnes would become one of the most loyal adherents to the fiscal conservatism favored by Baruch.

His friendship with Tillman had produced a voluminous correspondence, but Byrnes would commit few of his exchanges with Baruch to writing, and the details of their relationship are contained mainly in the elliptical remarks and reminiscences of a few other people who knew or served these two men. But so well known was the partnership of mutual interests represented by Byrnes and Baruch that by the mid-1940s it had become a subject of public satire. A newspaper cartoon appearing in the Washington *Star* on June 11, 1943, showed the newly appointed head of the Office of War Mobilization, Jimmy Byrnes, kneeling at the feet of Bernard Baruch, who was pictured in front of the White House dressed as an oracle in a flowing robe and beribboned forehead. Byrnes, dressed in a business suit, petitioned the mysteriously smiling Baruch: "What say you, sire, to the riddle of price control?"

Money talks, said observers of this friendship, and over the years money was discussed very frequently between Bernard Baruch and Jimmy Byrnes. But it would be inaccurate to suggest that the relationship between the two was exclusively that of buyer to seller, or of lesser client to his more important patron. Money was an idiom through which they communicated their mutual love of power. After winning his first senatorial election, Jimmy Byrnes became independent of the need for large contributions from Bernard Baruch or anyone else; once South Carolina sent a "member of the democracy" to the U.S. Senate, it usually kept sending him there, and for the rest of his Senate career Byrnes was never in danger of losing his place for lack of campaign funds. What Bernard Baruch did personally for Jimmy Byrnes in 1930 was to help line up contributors for Byrnes' first, big win over Coley Blease. Thereafter he helped with financial advice so that Byrnes could recoup the income he voluntarily had given up by becoming a U.S. senator. (In 1925, his first full year in private practice, Byrnes had earned $20,000 as an attorney. In 1931, when he became a U.S. senator, his salary was set by law at $10,000.) But if Jimmy Byrnes did not need Bernard Baruch's money after 1930, he knew plenty of other politicians who did. It was this access to Baruch's money, and his control over spending it, that later made Jimmy Byrnes into such a powerful politician.

Baruch eventually relied exclusively on Jimmy Byrnes' advice for the amounts and recipients of his political contributions. This financial intimacy with one of the wealthiest men in the Democratic party put Byrnes into an enviable position unique among his Senate peers. "Not many members of the United States Senate or House of Representatives can control the destinies of more money than needed for their own campaigns," Alexander Heard, a historian of political contributions of the 1930s and 1940s, noted. An exception to this rule, the same writer added, was "James F. Byrnes, influential senator from South Carolina." Through his influence over Baruch's contributions, Jimmy Byrnes was able to control the destinies of a great many more dollars than he personally needed; and through the use of these dollars, Byrnes controlled the destinies of many other members of the Senate. Byrnes became known as what Heard termed a "contributor-oriented solicitor," that is, a fund-raiser outside the party's usual structure, "whose usefulness stems from the confidence in which he is held by potential contributors. He is an advisor to persons of wealth."

In practical terms, this distinction meant that at election time Jimmy Byrnes drew up lists for Bernard Baruch of Democratic senatorial candidates for whom Baruch might wish, in Byrnes' happy phrase in a letter to Baruch in the late 1930s, "to play Santa Claus." Byrnes also kept Baruch informed of those men running for office who most "would appreciate your help." Byrnes' fellow senators from the South were usually the most appreciative. In a circumstance peculiar to politics below the Mason-Dixon line, elections there were unaffected by the Corrupt Practices Act of 1925, which had set a limit of $5,000 on campaign contributions by any one person during the general elections. Money spent to win primary elections was not restricted by the law. As southern politicians rarely faced Republican opposition in the fall, they thus were free to seek whatever money was needed to win their state's primaries. Baruch could give them what they needed, and Jimmy Byrnes became known in the Senate as the man to see if any of Baruch's money was needed.

During the senatorial campaigns of the late 1930s, Byrnes eventually directed Baruch's contributions—often in cash and occasionally delivered personally by members of Byrnes' senatorial staff—to such diverse candidates as Millard Tydings of Maryland, Alben Barkley of Kentucky, Guy Gillette of Iowa, Pat Harrison of Mississippi, and Harry Truman of Missouri. Some of these same senators, all of whom were fiscal conservatives elected with the help of Baruch's campaign contributions, became known to insiders around Washington as Baruch's Old Masters. The Old Masters were not paintings, such as another rich man might have collected; they were the senators considered as "owned" by Baruch, masters at delaying legislation the financier found objectionable. And his chief adviser in assembling this collection—the connoisseur telling Baruch which campaign constituted a worthy investment of his money, and which senatorial candidate was a potential loser—was the influential senator from South Carolina, James F. Byrnes.

Thus once more Jimmy Byrnes succeeded in advancing his career by forming a friendship with an important older man. (Baruch, born in 1870, was eleven years older than Byrnes.) Baruch would work very hard behind the scenes promoting the career of his younger friend, lobbying to have Jimmy Byrnes appointed to the U.S. Supreme Court and eventually to be considered for his party's vice-presidential nomination. (Toward that end, Baruch would succeed in May of 1944 in having Franklin Roosevelt accept an invitation to take an extended vacation for his health at Hobcaw Barony, Baruch's vast estate of 17,000 acres on the coast of South Carolina. Back in Washington, Sidney Hillman of the CIO was worried. According to his biographer, Hillman was certain that "Mr. Baruch, an old hand at inside politics, used every opportunity while the President convalesced to urge the cause of his old political alter ego, James F. Byrnes.")

If Byrnes' friendship with Ben Tillman was his political apprentice piece, his friendship with Baruch over the coming years must be considered the masterpiece of his career. Of course, like patronage under Tillman, friendship with Baruch could be difficult. Bernard Baruch had a reputation for vanity, he could become querulous, and he always was autocratic. Strain was inevitable in dealing with such a man, particularly since Jimmy Byrnes himself shared many of these same shortcomings. But a quality that Byrnes and Baruch also had in common, and which impressed friend and foe alike, was a capacity for beautiful manners in their personal relationships and for a certain circumspection in dealing with the needs of others. Baruch, for example, was very concerned with money, but he was equally capable of acting as if money were not his concern, often pressing small emergency loans on his employees and friends, with no apparent thought of repayment or personal advantage. Similarly, power was always very important to Jimmy Byrnes; but he was capable of acting as if power were not his object.

Baruch remained steadfast in his appreciation of Byrnes. "Isn't Jimmy Byrnes a delightful person!" he exclaimed to his official biographer in the 1950s during his retirement at Hobcaw Barony. Even as an old man, however, Bernard M. Baruch knew he had never been played as anyone's fool. Baruch was warned as early as the 1930s about his new friend by those who did not like Byrnes, and he was told by his advisers that Byrnes was taking advantage of the friendship with Baruch simply to increase the value of Byrnes' own stock portfolio on the basis of tips overheard from Baruch. But these objections would have seemed irrelevant to the stock speculator, particularly in his old age. As Baruch impatiently would have explained to these advisers, rich people do not want to have poor people for their friends: they want to have other rich people. And if Bernard M. Baruch in 1930 had chosen for his new friend a young man in need of some money, then Bernard M. Baruch was capable, within reason, of helping his younger friend become rich. It never distressed Baruch at any age to be told he was liked because of his money. Baruch considered his wealth to be an admirable part of himself, indistinguishable from his body or his personality at large: being rich was what made him Bernard M. Baruch, a fact which he accepted with as much certainty as the facts that Bernard M. Baruch was blue-eyed, or taller than most men, or smarter, or that he had been born Jewish, or that he was blessed in his old age with a full head of silver hair.

From their first meeting onward, Jimmy Byrnes seemed to have grasped intuitively this concept that Baruch had of himself and his money, a concept Baruch later made very explicit in his talks with the noted photographer Yousuf Karsh. Baruch, then in his seventies, offered Karsh some unsolicited advice on how to take the financier's portrait. "As you get older," Baruch said, "you will realize that every princess and every wealthy man is charming. I am so much more charming than when I was a mere twenty."

Bernard Baruch was one month away from celebrating his sixtieth birthday when he received his first letter from Jimmy Byrnes in late July 1930. It is likely that before writing to Baruch, Byrnes had a fairly detailed knowledge about him. Baruch's holdings at Hobcaw Barony made him one of the state's largest landowners, and besides his national contributions, Baruch occasionally gave money to South Carolina politicians. In fact, he enjoyed flaunting his southernness—it gave the public the impression he was not the Wall Street, urban speculator that in fact he was. Baruch's father, a Jewish physician from Camden, South Carolina, had served the Confederacy as an army surgeon under Robert E. Lee in the Army of Northern Virginia, and Bernard Baruch, as the middle of three sons, was just old enough in 1876 to have witnessed the rioting of Ben Tillman's Red Shirts during the election campaigns at Camden. For the rest of his life, Bernard Baruch dined out on these stories: he regaled after-dinner guests with the descriptions of his standing guard as a seven-year-old boy with a shotgun almost taller than he, while Red Shirts and blacks battled in front of his family's home in Camden; and Baruch enjoyed telling long, tendentious stories about the loyalty of his family's Negro retainer, the black maid whom he knew throughout his childhood as Minerva.

But to Bernard Baruch's father the postbellum South had held little romance. Apparently deciding that the South Carolina of Ben Tillman and his Red Shirts was no place for a Jewish physician with a wife and three small children, Simon Baruch moved permanently with his family to New York City. There the younger Baruch studied economics at City College and grew up to become essentially the financial animal, just as surely as Jimmy Byrnes, hundreds of miles southward, was growing up to become the political one. Beginning his career in 1891 as a clerk at a Wall Street brokerage firm, Baruch in a few years became an associate partner. A profitable series of small investments enabled Baruch to purchase a seat on the New York Exchange; and by his thirtieth birthday, primarily thanks to his shrewd buying and selling of shares in the American Sugar Refining Company and Amalgamated Copper, Baruch had become a millionaire. "I have a talent for making money," he later observed laconically.

Baruch was never a believer in hiding underground his God-given talent for making money—already he was exhibiting that zeal for publicity and confidence in his own abilities that accompanied him throughout his career. During the first decade of the twentieth century, Baruch reinvested his wealth and tripled his personal worth to over three million dollars. With this new wealth he purchased the large estate that became known as Hobcaw Barony, choosing to revive the name originally given to this plantation by one of its Royalist proprietors. During Byrnes' early career in South Carolina, the newspapers of Charleston and New York City frequently reported the market exploits of Bernard M. Baruch, now operating as an independent financial speculator and dubbed by the popular press "the lone wolf of Wall Street."

By the time Byrnes arrived in Congress in 1911, the lone wolf had become smart enough to have joined the progressive fold: Baruch backed Wilson early, and his large contributions to the party in 1912 made him a figure on the periphery of power during the first Wilson administration. Baruch's experiences on Wall Street had convinced him that the incorporation of the American economy was inevitable—he would have dismissed as romantic nonsense the program of Democratic agrarians to undo the industrial revolution and the resulting concentration of capital. Given the incorporation of major industries and capital as a fact, Baruch believed that the American economy would be most efficiently served by the creation of noncompeting cartels under general government supervision. But belief even in such mild government activism placed Baruch well to the left of much of the Republican party, and consequently he was one of the few Wall Street supporters of Woodrow Wilson's platform of New Freedom.

Wilson kept his distance from Baruch, however, and the speculator's economic advice was not taken very seriously until the economic crisis of the First World War demanded an immediate mobilization. President Wilson, to the surprise of many of his closest advisers, then appointed Baruch in 1918 to the chairmanship of the War Industries Board (WIB), a position analogous in powers and responsibilities to Jimmy Byrnes' own later position in 1943 at the Office of War Mobilization. Bernard Baruch's mastery of the details of the production of raw materials and his personal contacts at corporate boards—both having been gained during his years as a Wall Street insider—made him a natural for the WIB chairmanship, and the job provided Baruch the opportunity to put into practice his theory of organizing the nation's economy around cartels for a predictable supply of war materials and an orderly growth of prices and wages. Despite his qualifications, however, many conservative Democrats continued to distrust Baruch because of both his nominal religion and his way of having made his fortune. As a stock speculator, Baruch often had sold short; that is, he had gotten out of the market on the basis of privileged information before prices fell, and he later had bought back the same shares at deflated prices from less fortunate investors. Resentment of Baruch was perhaps inevitable. To forestall this anticipated criticism, Baruch early in his government career had announced he was taking most of his money out of the stock market and putting it into war bonds; but Jimmy Byrnes could remember how as a member of Congress he had seen a special congressional committee compel Baruch's testimony under oath that he had not used his government contacts to profit from a sudden wartime increase in steel prices by companies in which Baruch had continued to hold stock.

Baruch's testimony that he had never discussed his stock holdings with others in government seemed to quiet his congressional critics, but the anti-Semitic bias among others was less appeasable. One of Wilson's closest advisers, Colonel House of Texas, wrote the president in fiery italics protesting Baruch's appointment as WIB chairman: "I do not think the country will take kindly to having a *Hebrew Wall Street speculator* given so much power." (In his adult life, Baruch professed no religion; like Byrnes, he had married a woman who was an Episcopalian.) Even Baruch's critics, however, found it hard to argue against his economic success. Baruch's cartelist organization of the nation's industries produced wartime materials at an unprecedented flow, which was the envy of both Germany and the Allied powers; this accomplishment, combined with Baruch's earlier success in amassing a personal fortune in the unregulated Wall Street of the 1890s, combined to give him a reputation for uncanny economic wisdom.

Wilson was delighted with his protégé's success. Although his appointment of Baruch doubtless was influenced by Baruch's gift of $35,000 to the president's 1916 reelection campaign—the largest gift by a single donor—the efficiency of WIB validated Wilson's promotion of Baruch, and the president later selected the speculator to accompany him to the Versailles peace conference as his personal adviser on economics. To Baruch, these experiences of 1918–19 were illuminating. Like Byrnes, he would always consider service under Wilson to have been the idealistic high point of his government career; and he found that he now was perceived differently by the public as a result of this New Freedom association. No longer was Baruch described in the popular press as the "lone wolf of Wall Street" who manipulated the market for his personal gain; instead, Bernard M. Baruch was now "Dr. Facts," as he had been affectionately nicknamed by Woodrow Wilson. He became in the public mind the benevolent and informed adviser on economics who had helped President Wilson win the war. Baruch hired a publicist—the first of many in his employ—to promote this image of himself as an unselfish adviser to presidents, and although he continued to trade actively in stocks for the rest of his life, he announced publicly that hereafter he was devoting most of his energy and time to promoting his theories of economic growth and government control. Privately, Baruch began comparing his political abilities to those of Benjamin Disraeli—and he enjoyed being told by his friends that he was more handsome than Disraeli.

In fact, Bernard Baruch *did* succeed politically where many others failed, and he was one of the few high-ranking members of the Wilson administration to have come out of the war year with his reputation for efficiency intact. The inept handling of other areas of the economy not under Baruch's direct control made his efficiency at WIB even more noticeable, and although the board was scheduled for disbandment after the war, Baruch had hopes of continuing his system of government-sponsored cartels under the directorship of someone perhaps quite similar to Bernard M. Baruch. For a short while, the White House was reciprocally interested in Baruch's ambitions. After several cabinet resignations late in his second administration, Wilson briefly considered Baruch for appointments at Treasury, Interior, or Commerce. Once again, the usual charges arose that Baruch gave advice only in the form of disguised self-interest, and some Democrats were against the appointment because they were anti-Jewish. But it fell to Josephus Daniels, the secretary of the navy and the patron of FDR and Jimmy Byrnes, to make the most telling remark against Baruch. In a conversation with President Wilson, Daniels, who had been a Methodist superintendent of Sunday schools in North Carolina, subtly reminded Wilson that Bernard Baruch was susceptible to charges of having committed more than one deadly sin. Avarice, most frequently mentioned, was but one of the seven. Daniels' objection was elsewhere. Baruch, he reminded Wilson, was "somewhat vain."

Bernard Baruch was not present at that meeting to defend himself against the remark, but vanity is the key to understanding Baruch, just as earlier Byrnes had known that loneliness was the key to understanding Tillman. Baruch's vanity expressed itself most superficially in a series of adulterous affairs. Baruch often boasted of his having been a ladies' man in his youth on Wall Street, and even as the financier's physical abilities waned, his wealth and his fame in Washington enabled him, at least in his own mind, to remain a sexual champion. In part, Baruch's self-concept was correct. The aphrodisiac effects of power have been remarked upon, and by the time of his WIB appointment, Baruch had matured, with his blue eyes and his silver hair, into vulpine good looks. He knew he was attractive to women; and despite an outwardly happy marriage, Baruch by the time of Daniels' remark had begun to indulge in a number of extramarital affairs, which led to his being the subject of bad jokes made around wartime Washington by people like Alice Roosevelt Longworth.

But Baruch's vanity, like Byrnes', existed at a deeper level, and it motivated many of his political acts. In Baruch's case, it was the vanity of a man who wants to be considered indispensable—not simply to a woman, or to a few other men, but to his country at large. He had been able to consider himself in this role once before, when Woodrow Wilson placed him in charge of the nation's economy during the First World War. But Wilson declined further opportunities, having decided after talking with

Daniels and others not to offer Baruch any cabinet posts; and the succession of Republican presidents throughout the 1920s meant a return to laissez-faire economics and the removal of Bernard Baruch, for all his wealth and his ambitions, to the fringes of political power. Baruch had no desire to become president himself; he knew his Jewish birth was a practical disqualification, and he had little patience for the administrative details that come with the post. But for the rest of his life—and he lived until 1965— Bernard Baruch sought through his political contributions to make his economic advice indispensable to whatever Democratic president was in power. It probably was this political expression of Baruch's personal vanity, rather than any specific disagreements over policy, that later caused Franklin Roosevelt to so distrust Baruch. (After all, there can be only *one* indispensable man.) And it probably was the recognition by Baruch that his wealth was so indispensable to Jimmy Byrnes' own presidential ambitions that enabled the two to become such fast friends. Theirs was a relationship of mutual need, and the two discussed it from the beginning with a mutual frankness. ("You and I know that elevated human sentiment is not a sound basis on which to conduct human affairs," Baruch wrote to Byrnes in his old age.)

Thus the power of vanity, which many considered to be Baruch's greatest weakness, was to the financier's own eyes the source of his greatest strengths. Vanity, Baruch might have answered Secretary Daniels, is what makes the world turn. The vanity of riches, for example, had made Bernard M. Baruch a wealthy man beyond the dreams of a Josephus Daniels. Vanity is what had propelled Baruch, as it later would propel Jimmy Byrnes, out of the provincially southern state into which they both had been born; and it was vanity that would lead Baruch and Byrnes to pursue the great national offices to which they both felt their visions entitled them.

After his loss of his preferment in the Wilson administrations, Baruch began his drive to regain power in the Democratic party by making his South Carolina estate at Hobcaw Barony throughout the 1920s into an important center for national party finances. His efforts started soon after the Democrats had lost the presidential election of 1924 and Jimmy Byrnes had lost his first primary race with Coley Blease. During the dry years following the defeat of the national ticket and the subsequent loss of patronage positions, Baruch kept the Democratic party financially afloat with his contributions. Baruch gave $46,500 to the Democratic Senatorial Fund in 1926, for instance, and he followed that gift with a check for $40,000 for the party's senatorial elections in 1930.

Naturally, in exchange for this generosity Baruch expected that party leaders give at least *some* consideration to his special financial interests, and he expected that they pay at least a degree of respect to his considerable abilities as a host at his South Carolina estate. Hobcaw (rhyming with the crow's call and taking its name from an Indian word meaning "between the waters") was at the time of Baruch's possession a fallow plantation on the southern end of Waccamaw Point, a peninsula bounded on one side by the Waccamaw River and on the other by the Atlantic Ocean. Democratic hopefuls were expected to travel to see *him* at Hobcaw Barony. "I met frequently with party leaders to map strategy and discuss issues," Baruch later wrote of his political activity in this period of the late 1920s. "My home in South Carolina became the scene of many political get-togethers, which were lightened by the pleasures of duck-shooting and good conversation, for which Hobcaw was famous."

The pleasures of Hobcaw were particularly available during the 1920s to Democratic senatorial incumbents and aspirants. By 1924, Baruch had discovered in anticipation of the Corrupt Practices Act that U.S. senators from the one-party South were a good bargain. Baruch had noticed that southern senators, once elected, tended to stay in power—and stay grateful; on the other hand, the favors of a president, as Baruch himself had experienced during the administrations of Woodrow Wilson, tended to come and go. Joseph Robinson of Arkansas, Pat Harrison of Mississippi, and Alben Barkley of Kentucky were all men with whom Byrnes had served in his youth in the U.S. House of Representatives, and by 1930 all of these men had preceded him into the U.S. Senate. They were the first of the Old Masters to visit Hobcaw Barony.

But if such men first traveled to Hobcaw Barony out of political expediency, they returned to Hobcaw out of friendship. The considerable personal charm of Bernard M. Baruch added much to the conviviality of their political gatherings. Hobcaw was the personal southern residence where, in the words of one biographer, "Mr. Baruch became Bernie."

More important, as F. Scott Fitzgerald wrote about another fabulously rich man and his house during the 1920s, Baruch knew when to stop. It would have struck Bernard Baruch as crass to have asked his houseguests for a political favor in exchange for his money or his hospitality, and Baruch never did so; all he asked was that visiting Democratic politicians seriously consider his philosophy and his investments. As Baruch himself wrote in 1924 to the financial director of the national Democratic party, in turning down the latter's request for more money, he did not believe "in a system of barter and sale, of contributions and resulting recognition." Of course, to those Democratic senators who after duck hunting and conversations at Hobcaw could give him some recognition, Baruch was in a position to give back; an example was Joe Robinson of Arkansas, who had become a favorite hunting companion of Baruch's and who admired the economic theories of his financier host. In addition to the $40,000 that he contributed to the Democratic senatorial elections of 1930, Baruch also wrote an individual check in 1929 for $1,000 payable to the election expenses of

Robinson, who by then had become the Democratic minority leader in the Senate.

Baruch's house at Hobcaw encouraged such easy accommodations. Baruch had constructed a two-story, neo-Georgian brick mansion on a gentle hill overlooking the seacoast. For many years the house was accessible only by ferry or private yacht, and guests arriving at the estate's small dock at the foot of the hill found a short, winding path bordered with crushed oystershell that led up to the Baruch house under a canopy of live oak trees, pink and red azaleas, and green resurrection ferns. Inside the mansion were ten bedrooms, each with its private bathroom (occasioning at least once the waggish remark that Baruch had installed more indoor plumbing at Hobcaw Barony than existed in the rest of that area of low-country South Carolina combined). The furnishings of the new house also reflected Baruch's restrained, expensive tastes: in addition, the first-floor library offered a handsome selection of books and contained a concealed and excellently stocked liquor cabinet. Few politicians could withstand such comforts. As one of his biographers noted, Baruch at Hobcaw Barony "effectively bought for himself a powerful audience for his monologues on the American political economy."

Others of Baruch's contemporaries in South Carolina also thought the financier had bought himself an audience. Baruch's political entertaining at Hobcaw was increasingly noticeable to state officials, and in 1927–28 Baruch was forced into an expensive litigation with the state game warden after a dispute over registering Hobcaw Barony as a commercial club. Baruch was outraged at the implicit insult of labeling the Baruch family's private hospitality as commercial entertaining. In addition, Baruch was not universally admired by some of his poorest low-country neighbors, whom he regularly jailed for poaching on Hobcaw's 17,000 acres.

But it fell to U.S. Senator Coleman L. Blease to insult Baruch most publicly during the 1920s. The occasion was the debate on the floor of the Senate on April 18, 1928, concerning minor amendments to an otherwise unremarkable bill setting federal limits to the hunting of migratory waterfowl. Senator Blease, as expected, spoke against the bill on the grounds that he opposed any reduction of a state's authority, even in regard to migratory waterfowl. But at the close of his remarks, Blease unexpectedly digressed. In passionately chosen words, South Carolina's senator now attacked the bill as socially and economically unjust; and in a manner that could only be interpreted to be as gratuitously insulting as it was intended, Blease introduced into the pages of the *Congressional Record* the example of Bernard M. Baruch as an instance of economic arrogance.

"This bill does not apply to the rich man who comes into South Carolina and buys a big reservation, like Barney Baruch," Blease declared. "They come here and they have these large estates. They bring their friends. They have whatever they want. . . . They go out and hunt deer; they shoot quail;

they go fishing Sunday, Monday, or any other time they please and not a word is said. They are the mighty. They have the money."

Coley Blease then continued his homily. "But if some man who works in a cotton mill or works in a railroad shop from bright and early Monday morning until Saturday night at 12 o'clock [the traditional quitting time on weekends for the state's cotton mill workers] goes home, takes his little bath, gets a little fishing line or a little shotgun and goes out to fish or shoot a bird, why along comes your law and says, 'We will put you in jail.' 'Why?' 'Because you are a poor man, and you do not own a big tract of land.' "

Baruch was furious, particularly on reading the implied slur that he was religiously insensitive by allowing Sunday hunting parties at Hobcaw. As Baruch wrote to his attorney in considering a slander suit against Blease, since the lifetime of his father the Baruch family in South Carolina had forbidden the shooting of any hunting gun on their property on Sundays out of respect for the Sabbath of their gentile neighbors. Nor was the *Congressional Record* attack the last time Baruch felt himself personally harassed by a member of the Blease family. For years Baruch prided himself on his willingness to invest in South Carolina's economy, and after the assault in the *Congressional Record* Baruch also found himself threatened with a legal suit by a team of lawyers attempting to hold him personally and totally responsible for all debts of a failed South Carolina bank in which Baruch indirectly had bought stock. Byrnes, then safely in his second term in the U.S. Senate, went to extraordinary lengths to limit his friend's liability, and perhaps his vulnerability. Baruch was alarmed that the Georgetown suit was turning into an ugly episode of soak-the-Jew, in which neither Baruch's attorneys nor the opposing lawyers appeared interested in negotiating a settlement or limiting Baruch's legal bills. Baruch complained to Byrnes; and in response the junior senator wrote to Baruch that, without mentioning his patron's name, he had sought an advisory opinion on the possibility of deducting Baruch's legal losses from his taxes. Byrnes also later directed Donald Russell, a partner at Nicholls and Byrnes, to review the legal work done in the case by Baruch's attorneys. Further, Byrnes wrote to Christie Benet, the Bourbon senior partner of the law firm that Baruch had retained to protect him from the suit. Byrnes did not believe, he wrote Benet, "that the attorneys you employed are prima-donnas." And just in case Benet did not understand the occasion of this letter from his U.S. senator, Byrnes pointedly added, "You know how I feel about Baruch." The two sets of lawyers soon afterward came to terms; and for years afterward, both Byrnes and Baruch remembered that among the attorneys who had attempted to sue Baruch was a politically well-connected lawyer who was a former justice of the South Carolina supreme court. He was Eugene Blease, brother to Cole.

These, then, were the circumstances consequent to Bernard Baruch's receiving his first recorded letter from Jimmy Byrnes. "Dear Mr. Baruch . . ."

While Jimmy Byrnes in July 1930 was writing to his potential new financial angel, Coley Blease had not gone away. He was walking to and fro, appearing on improvised stages in front of dozens of courthouses throughout rural South Carolina, as he toured the state in his palmetto stump. The years had been kind to Blease; since winning his first term to the U.S. Senate in 1924, he had become a silver-haired, distinguished-looking legislator who now affected a scholarly pince-nez, which, together with his towering height, combined to give him a positively avuncular look. Blease in 1930 was a hale sixty-two years of age; by comparison, his main opponent in the primary, Jimmy Byrnes, had an almost juvenile appearance belying his forty-eight years. If Byrnes was to succeed with his plan to win second place in that summer's primary, and then to combine forces with the third-place finisher to defeat Blease in the fall runoff, then he would have to do some fancy catch-up campaigning. And as the candidates traveled the state together during that first primary in 1930, Cole Blease lost no opportunities in damning his younger opponent as inexperienced and too liberal.

Blease had chosen to run what he frankly admitted was a "nigger and liquor" campaign in 1930. He attacked such former New Freedom legislators as Jimmy Byrnes for allowing passage of the Eighteenth Amendment, which, according to Blease, had insultingly denied to white southern males their traditional free use of liquor. Thus, in the first year of the nation's worst economic crisis since the founding of the Republic, Cole Blease had unequivocally declared himself the people's champion for the right to get drunk. The "poor devil with half a pint of whisky" became the rallying cry of Blease's campaign. And, as always, the state's most populist senator also race-baited: Cole L. Blease assured South Carolina voters on the stump that only he could protect his state from a sure racial miscegenation brought on by liberals of the Woodrow Wilson stamp.

Byrnes hotly defended his tradition of Wilsonian liberalism and, ignoring Blease's obfuscations on race, instead campaigned almost exclusively on economic issues. In part, Byrnes could disregard racist tactics in the 1930 campaign because his own white supremacist speeches in the House from 1919 to 1925 had removed any doubts by South Carolina voters that Jimmy Byrnes was "a member of the democracy." Byrnes wisely let Cole Blease and the third candidate in this primary, Leon W. Harris, exchange bitter attacks throughout the campaign on each other's disloyalty to the white race. But if Jimmy Byrnes chose to talk almost exclusively about economics during the summer months of 1930, it was because at that time no clear-eyed observer could have talked about anything else: South Carolina was in terrible shape economically.

As Jimmy and Maude Byrnes rode all over the state in his Reo Flying Cloud automobile that summer of 1930, they witnessed the wreckage of an economy that had depended disastrously on the one cash crop of cotton. Drought had spread throughout the upper Mississippi valley and southeastern states during that first, cruel year following the 1929 stock market crash, and what little cotton was left growing in the sunbaked fields of South Carolina—either in the hardscrabble red clay of the upstate or along the vast alluvial fields of the low country—soon would not be worth the picking. Cotton that before the crash had sold for fifteen or sixteen cents per pound now brought a farmer only about nine cents—if indeed a buyer could be found. National orders for finished cotton goods had collapsed as the rest of the country also tried to deal with farm foreclosures, falling prices, closed factories, and rising unemployment. In the summer of 1930, for example, Byrnes in his travels could find only three cotton mills operating full-time across his state. Both in South Carolina and across the rest of the nation, there was a growing recognition that the financial chaos of 1929 might not be simply a temporary aberration; it might in fact be the beginning of a prolonged and pervasive national depression.

In his senatorial campaign in 1924, Jimmy Byrnes had talked economics, urging government activism for farm parity and a tariff favorable to agricultural procedures. At that time not enough voters had listened. Now, in the increasingly desperate conditions of summer and early fall of 1930, Jimmy Byrnes was beginning to attract more and more listeners to his stump speeches across the low country and in the mill villages. The poor economy provided Byrnes his opportunity. Fearing for their textile jobs and for their family farms, and uncertain of how Cole Blease could protect their interests with his theatrics in the U.S. Senate, the state's voters gave Jimmy Byrnes a strong second-place showing in the summer primary of 1930.

When the votes were tallied after election day on August 26, Byrnes had received 94,242 votes and Blease 111,989. The third candidate, Harris, had received 39,512. Thus, Byrnes had so far succeeded in his campaign strategy of forcing Blease into a runoff for his Senate chair; and this time the third-place loser, Harris, announced his endorsement of Jimmy Byrnes and asked his supporters to vote for Byrnes over Blease in the September runoff.

But although Jimmy Byrnes in 1930 was becoming the favored son of South Carolina voters, he was not yet out of the woods. There remained the large body of Coley Blease supporters to be dealt with—about 40 percent of the electorate—who would vote for Blease under any circumstances. ("Coley, I'd vote for you tonight even if you was to steal my mule!") To overcome Blease's greater effectiveness at gathering crowds at the stump, and to ensure that by the September run-off at least 60 percent of the electorate would have had the opportunity to listen to his economic message without interruptions, Byrnes needed more money to purchase large amounts of time on regional radio stations and to buy full-page advertisements in the state's newspapers. And it was to ask for that money that Jimmy Byrnes in July 1930 wrote to Bernard Baruch.

Byrnes' first letter, dated July 21, 1930, identifying himself to Baruch as "a candidate for the United States Senate opposing Cole L. Blease" had asked if Baruch was willing to send a written endorsement of Jimmy Byrnes' candidacy to Baruch's brother-in-law in South Carolina, a local banker interested in state politics. But more than Baruch's South Carolina connections was on Byrnes' mind. Baruch might also be willing, Byrnes carefully suggested in the sentences that followed, to provide a copy of that endorsement to any others of Baruch's acquaintances "to whom you would feel at liberty to write." Of course, Bernard Baruch was a man of extensive financial holdings, whose friendship was of great expediency to numerous other wealthy men; and Byrnes knew he was greatly increasing his chances of receiving political contributions from those recipients when, after receiving a letter from Baruch, they subsequently would be asked for money by Byrnes' supporters.

This request for a written endorsement was presuming a great deal on Bernard Baruch's loyalty to the Democratic party, particularly toward an ex–New Freedom congressman whom Baruch knew only by reputation. But perhaps what most intrigued Baruch on reading the letter *was* its presumption. Like Baruch, Jimmy Byrnes never asked for anything unless he could ask for everything. Unstated but implied throughout Byrnes' request was an invitation for Bernard Baruch to interest himself personally in Jimmy Byrnes' career by sending some of Baruch's own money. Byrnes knew that he was calling attention to himself by making this request for an endorsement, but he was also implying that his was a career in which Bernard Baruch—always an investor in politicians on the rise—ought to be interested. "The situation is very encouraging and I feel I have an excellent chance to win," Byrnes concluded his letter. "Therefore should you see your way clear to comply with my request, I hope you will do so at the earliest opportunity."

Baruch's answer to Byrnes' letter was not kept in the correspondence files of either man. But the fact stands out that in the two weeks between the end of the first primary in late August and the runoff election on September 9, 1930, Jimmy Byrnes obtained the money to buy radio time for his campaign speeches on a scale unprecedented in South Carolina politics. Byrnes was on the air in nearly half a dozen broadcasts during the last fourteen days of the campaign, on stations ranging from Charleston, on the coast, to Spartanburg, at the edge of the upcountry. As FCC regulations required an advance payment in full for each of these broadcasts, the financial backing available to Byrnes must have been considerable. Furthermore, in choosing how to spend this available money, the selection of radio had been astute. This medium was to become Byrnes' best campaign friend. Byrnes would never be an orator in the old-fashioned southern sense of the term, but he was to be one of the first national politicians to recognize that radio does not necessarily demand an old-fashioned oratory. Byrnes knew in 1930 what Franklin Roosevelt later knew with his use of fireside chats in 1933, or what Wendell Willkie also knew in the Republican campaign broadcasts of 1940: that radio creates an illusion of intimacy, as though the speaker were addressing the individual voters one by one. Its required speaking style was particularly suited to the soft-spoken, persistent voice of Byrnes, and he would return to the technique of radio broadcasts during crises throughout his future senatorial career. Freed from the mannerism of an agrarian oratory meant to be delivered by a man such as Tillman or Blease on the public stump, Byrnes in his campaign spoke into the microphone at downtown radio stations throughout the state as the friendly, urbane, well-connected attorney that he was. And in that uncertain autumn of 1930, frightened South Carolinians found his sotto voce advice on economics to be soothing.

Coley Blease during the runoff was probably unaware of Byrnes' written overtures to Baruch, or he almost certainly would have made public use of Byrnes' sponsorship by the New York–based, Jewish-born financier. But throughout the two-week campaign Blease complained regularly about what he called "outside money pouring into the state" to help elect Jimmy Byrnes. By the accounts of some politicians not in either camp, Byrnes that summer received $15,000 from the national AFL to defeat Blease, in addition to the financial help Baruch was providing. And Byrnes also received help from his state's organized labor in more confrontational ways. At that time, the strongest union was organized among South Carolina's printers and skilled laborers in newspaper back shops. Byrnes arranged for Earle Britton, a tough printer at the Columbia *State* newspaper and president of the South Carolina Federation of Labor, to take some of his journeyman printer associates on raids into Blease strongholds. There this physically intimidating group of unionists heckled Blease at his rallies and made clear their willingness to defend Byrnes' progressivism with their fists.

In response Blease quickened his pace of visiting courthouse squares and making rousing speeches, but he did not seem to realize, as Byrnes did, that by 1930 the statewide stump had become an anachronism: Byrnes could with one speech over the radio reach more South Carolinians in a single night than personally attended all Blease rallies during the two weeks of the runoff campaign.

Byrnes' election eve broadcast to the state, on September 8, was a case in point. In order to find a station powerful enough to broadcast throughout South Carolina on that evening, Byrnes had to travel across the state line to the comparative metropolis of Charlotte, North Carolina, where radio station WBT dominated the radio band across the Upper South. Usually the programming from the North Carolina station was a regionally pleasing mixture of news, country music, and big-band music, but this September night Byrnes bought a prime-time hour of broadcasting for an appeal to voters throughout South Carolina. Quietly, persistently, Byrnes in his broadcast reminded the voters of his home state that the runoff election there should be determined on economic issues, not on race or liquor. "Candidates for the United States Senate waste much sympathy on the so-called 'poor devil with a half pint of whisky,' " Byrnes told his radio audience. "I am more interested in the 'poor devil with a half bale of cotton.' If the price of cotton continues to go down, the price of a half bale of cotton will not buy much more than a half pint of whisky."

Byrnes then listed his stands in favor of protective tariffs for finished cotton textiles, for the production of lumber, and for other agricultural goods; he called for the federal government's construction of a veterans hospital in South Carolina to create local jobs; and he pointed out to the voters the likelihood that the depressed economic conditions would continue and that the state would need experienced national legislators. Finally, in what was a surprise appeal for votes, given the conservatism of South Carolina politics and society, Jimmy Byrnes declared that he was "proud" to have received labor's endorsement by the state AFL, and he announced at the end of his broadcast that he was hoping to receive the votes of the women of South Carolina. Jimmy Byrnes knew that the following day he would need every vote he could get, whether cast for him out of duty, labor, or love.

The next day Byrnes won by about 2,500 votes. After some hesitation, Coley Blease conceded defeat. The closeness of Byrnes' victory emphasized the importance of his last-minute radio broadcasts—and of the money that had made them possible. The runoff election of 1930 also marked the last time Jimmy Byrnes would run against Coley Blease as his main opponent. After this defeat by Byrnes, Blease would try again for the Senate against a new opponent in 1932, and again he would be beaten; and although Blease would remain a perennial figure in the background of South Carolina politics—he did not die until 1942—he would always find the considerable powers of the state's new U.S. senator aligned against him and would never again be able to hold a major office. Both in his 1930 campaign and in his attempted 1932 comeback, Blease was convinced that Jimmy Byrnes had been able through his friendships in Charleston to have ballots there marked for Blease "counted out" or changed to show a vote for Byrnes, and it was a fact that Jimmy Byrnes had won the Charleston precincts in 1930 by an astonishing 10-to-3 ratio of votes against Blease. "The only way you can convince me that I wasn't counted out in 1930 in Charleston," Blease later declared, "would be for God Almighty and his son Jesus Christ to come down and tell me so." That enlightenment was unlikely, because ballots in question were burned by the state Democratic party shortly after the 1930 primary election at the request of a party official who was never identified.

In defeating Blease's campaign, Byrnes effectively banished the last major survivor of the old Tillmanite organization, whose figure had cast such a shadow across Byrnes' own ambitions. As he went to his downtown campaign headquarters in Columbia the night of September 9, 1930, to receive the congratulations of his supporters, Jimmy Byrnes—the future selector of Bernard Baruch's collection of Old Masters in the U.S. Senate—was himself well on his way to becoming the most adept of all the Old Masters.

Byrnes' friendship with Baruch and his money in 1930 may have the determining factor in rescuing the younger man's political career from political obscurity; if so, Jimmy Byrnes never mentioned publicly that he felt an obligation. But soon after becoming a U.S. senator, Byrnes began to repay Baruch with the performance of many political favors, large and small. In 1932, for example, Bernard Baruch turned up at the Democratic convention at Chicago, where he spent the week entertaining his current mistress, Clare Boothe, and backing the wrong man, Newton Baker, for president. After Franklin Roosevelt had secured his party's nomination for the presidency over Baker and other rivals, Senator Byrnes personally walked Baruch over to Roosevelt's campaign headquarters and insisted on introducing Baruch to Louis Howe and other members of the Brain Trust who were then forming the inner circle of FDR's advisers; and throughout Roosevelt's first term in office, Byrnes would do what he could to promote Baruch's influence among the top policymakers.

Throughout the 1930s Jimmy Byrnes and Bernard Baruch would continue to act in other kind ways toward each other. To other politicians, they must have appeared at times to have been simply a pair of hard-boiled and amoral southern operatives interested only in their own careers; but the fact is that as a result of their shared experiences in politics—Bernard Baruch as a Jewish outsider, and Jimmy Byrnes as a Catholic outsider—both men by 1930 had come to have an almost Calvinist view of politics. Byrnes and Baruch both believed in a political world so hopelessly depraved that it could be redeemed only by the infusions of large amounts of cash.

A few years after winning the fall election, Senator Byrnes received an invitation from Baruch, then vacationing at Hobcaw Barony, to join him there in enjoying the pleasures of his retreat on the South Carolina coast. "My dear Jimmy," Baruch wrote, "there is plenty of bourbon and water. The river flows slowly by. The sun is bright and the breezes gentle. The azaleas, jasmine, dogwood, wisteria and honeysuckle are all in bloom. Every prospect pleases, and only human nature is vile. Bernie."

PART TWO

THE INHERITANCE: THE SENATE AND BEYOND

1931–1941

4

Fixer
from the
Palmetto State

Franklin Delano Roosevelt, throughout the stormy years of 1933–37, had one sure and steadfast indicator of political loyalty. During his first presidential term, whenever a visitor to the Oval Office expressed doubts about the political reliability of a congressman or a senator, Roosevelt's reaction was invariable. The muscular shoulders would twist in his chair, the handsome, oversized head would turn toward the visitor, and the president would display his famous smile and ask, "Was he with us B.C.?" B.C.—"Before Chicago"—was Roosevelt's personal abbreviation for any date prior to the Democratic National Convention in Chicago that nominated him for the presidency the week of June 27, 1932. By this test of political loyalty, Jimmy Byrnes was irreproachably "B.C."

Byrnes' friendship with Roosevelt antedated even the Wilson administrations. The two men and their wives had shared a rented house while attending the Democratic convention at Baltimore the summer of 1912; and eight years later, Congressman Byrnes campaigned loyally for the presidential ticket of Cox-Roosevelt. When after the November 1928 elections Franklin Roosevelt emerged as one of the few winners within his party, Byrnes wrote that same month to the governor-elect in New York urging him to run for the White House in 1932. And during the months preceding the 1932 convention, as Roosevelt looked for support in the South and the West for his candidacy, Byrnes turned up again as a strong Roosevelt supporter. "I'm very anxious to talk things over with you," Roosevelt wrote the new South Carolina senator in January 1932, "and if there is any chance of your coming over to Albany, I will be only too glad to have you stay overnight at the Mansion, and if Mrs. Byrnes would like to come, I would be delighted to have you both."

Apparently Byrnes' reputation for political circumspection had preceded him, for at the end of his letter Roosevelt added, "If for any reason you would prefer to have your visit remain unknown to the press if it can be arranged, as by agreement with the newspaper men, my guests at the Mansion are not subjects of query. Sincerely yours. . . ."

Byrnes recalled in his memoirs that he visited Roosevelt at the Executive Mansion late that same January, but apparently he took Roosevelt up on his offer of confidentiality. Neither the *Knickerbocker News* nor any of the other Albany newspapers recorded Byrnes' arrival, and there is no official record of his visit in any of the governor's appointment books. And Byrnes was even more cautious than Roosevelt knew: before taking the train north from Washington to confer with Roosevelt, he had first checked with the secretary to the Senate Democrats to confirm that supporters of Al Smith did not intend to announce his candidacy that month, and therefore they would not interpret this visit to Roosevelt as a betrayal of Byrnes' neutrality in the anticipated struggle between Roosevelt and Smith for their party's nomination at the Chicago convention.

Politically speaking, Jimmy Byrnes liked Al Smith; and in 1932 Byrnes had much more in common with this former governor of New York than with the patrician incumbent, Franklin Roosevelt. Byrnes and Smith both had suffered the discomfitures of having been raised as urban Catholics in a Democratic party that still centered much of its power in rural courthouses in the South and West. And unlike many southern Democrats, Byrnes had not bolted the party after Smith's nomination for the presidency in 1928. In fact, when Byrnes won his runoff election to the Senate in 1930 and Al Smith was still considered a possible presidential candidate, the *New York Times* announced the results with the page one headline "Byrnes, Pro-Smith, Is Victor over Senator in South Carolina Run-off."

But by the time of Byrnes' arrival at the Executive Mansion in Albany, both the pro- and anti-Smith factions in the Democratic party had agreed to bury the hatchet—"in Al Smith's neck," as one contemporary observer of the party remarked. The huge electoral losses in 1928 and the defections of voters in traditionally safe states across the South—the so-called Hoovercrats—made undeniable the divisions in the Democratic party over such issues as the prohibition of liquor, equity in tariffs for industry and agriculture, and the influence of New York City's Tammany Hall organization. Smith still harbored ambitions of receiving another presidential nomination and his diehard supporters controlled powerful political machines in Chicago, New York City, and Jersey City. But by 1932 Franklin Roosevelt had emerged as the candidate least objectionable to all geographic segments of the party. Roosevelt's careful endorsement as New York governor of the states' right to a local option on liquor control made him acceptable to all but the most "bone-dry" of the party's conservatives, and in late January he was preparing a national speech attacking the Hawley-Smoot tariffs, which would be soothing to the ears of farmers in the West and South. But despite the excellence of Roosevelt's chances, there remained an obstacle in early 1932 to his gaining the party's nomination. It was an obstacle that had existed in the Democratic party for a hundred years and that Roosevelt and his advisers knew could be overcome only with the assistance of friendly southerners such as Jimmy Byrnes— the so-called two-thirds rule.

Since the administration of Andrew Jackson, the Democratic party had required for its presidential nomination the votes not simply of a majority of delegates at the convention but of two-thirds of the delegates. Such an arrangement had, in effect, given the southern delegates a veto over the party's choice of a nominee. In 1932, as Franklin Roosevelt knew, it also gave Al Smith a possible indirect veto over Roosevelt's nomination. Roosevelt and his campaign manager, James Farley, hoped to arrive at the convention in Chicago with a majority of delegates officially instructed, or bound by their party's agreements, to vote for him; but if Smith succeeded in dividing southern support for Roosevelt, then the convention would deadlock, with neither Roosevelt nor any other announced candidate receiving the necessary two-thirds majority. In the event of such a deadlocked convention, Al Smith's friendship with the wealthy national Democratic chairman, John J. Raskob, and his control over the northeastern and midwestern urban voting blocs could once more make the Happy Warrior, as Roosevelt had once generously christened Smith in nominating him for the presidency in 1928, a presidential candidate in 1932. Or, at the least, a deadlocked convention might deny the nomination to Roosevelt, toward whom Smith had expressed an increasing bitterness since his defeat in 1928. Smith did not care to whom the southern delegates committed themselves, so long as all of them did not commit to Roosevelt, and so long as the two-thirds rule remained in effect.

But even without Al Smith's encouragement there were plenty of other contenders in early 1932 for the southern and western delegates. They included Representative John N. "Jack" Garner of Texas, who had become the Speaker of the House in 1931 and whose presidential candidacy was being boosted on newsstands and the airwaves by the powerful Hearst communication chain; there was also the favorite son candidacy of Senator

Joseph Robinson of Arkansas, who had run for the vice presidency in 1928 and proven to be much more popular than Smith; and, among eastern conservatives, Bernard Baruch was promoting the presidential ambitions of Governor Albert Ritchie of Maryland.

These dangers to the Roosevelt candidacy were real. Roosevelt and Byrnes, both good Democrats, knew that the two-thirds rule had denied the presidential nomination at the 1912 convention to one of the party's strongest contenders that year, Champ Clark of Missouri. Although Clark received a majority vote of the delegates on the first ballot—as Roosevelt hoped to do at Chicago—he had failed to gain a two-thirds majority, and the nomination consequently went to Woodrow Wilson. And twelve years later, a convention deadlocked because of the two-thirds rule between the supporters of William C. McAdoo and Al Smith after 102 ballotings denied the presidential nomination to McAdoo, who as Woodrow Wilson's son-in-law had been considered the favored Democratic nominee. Roosevelt had no intention of letting his political fate become that of the son-in-law. Therefore it was essential to Roosevelt's presidential ambitions in early 1932 that he maintain good relations with the southern conservatives, at least until the two-thirds rule could be abolished. (Since the rule itself could be revoked by a simple majority vote of the delegates, Roosevelt's advisers hoped to eliminate the rule at the convention before the day for presidential balloting.)

Or, failing the removal of the two-thirds rule, it was equally essential that Roosevelt's delegates from the western and southern states be formally instructed to vote for him regardless of a deadlock, so that the chairman of individual state delegations could not negotiate away any votes for Roosevelt in separate deals with Smith, Garner, or Ritchie. In pursuit of this strategy, Jimmy Byrnes for the next six months after their meeting together in Albany in January 1932 kept Roosevelt informed about the activities of these other candidates among the southern conservatives. Byrnes was well positioned to provide this information. In fact, many of these conservative Democrats whose support Franklin Roosevelt wanted so badly in his campaign for the 1932 Democratic nomination were the same powerful men in the Senate whose political favors Jimmy Byrnes had been cultivating since his arrival back in Washington as a freshman senator in late winter of 1931.

Police armed with automatic shotguns and tear gas bombs had surrounded the U.S. Capitol when Jimmy Byrnes walked to the front of the chamber, raised his right hand, and swore to the oath administered by Charles Curtis, Herbert Hoover's vice president. The time was early afternoon December 7, 1931. Outside at the foot of the Capitol steps a crowd of Communist party self-described "hunger marchers" estimated by the *Washington Post* at about sixteen hundred had assembled, singing the "Internationale" and demanding to present to the senators and congressmen of the newly convened seventy-second Congress the party's demands for federally guaranteed employment at a minimum wage and for national unemployment insurance. The marchers were turned away from the Capitol Building by District of Columbia police with no recorded arrests or injuries, but the years 1931–33 were to be filled with many such scenes of angry, threatening men witnessed by Byrnes, as national unemployment soared from over seven million people in 1931 to over twelve million in 1933.

Nor could the marchers always be dismissed as extremists. In the summer of 1932 a crowd of about 22,000 war veterans and their families crowded into Washington demanding immediate payment of a promised bonus for military service, and this time the federal government responded not with civilian police but with the military. Infantry companies of the U.S. Army along with cavalry and six armored tanks chased the veterans and their families from their temporary camps in suburban Washington and set fire to their shelters and belongings. There were at least two civilian deaths and numerous casualties from bayonet wounds and tear gas. And six months later, in January 1933, Jimmy Byrnes and other dignitaries were chased back inside a brownstone house in east Manhattan belonging to the mother of President-elect Franklin Roosevelt after an angry crowd, later described by *Time* magazine as Communists, broke up a congressional photograph-taking session on the front steps by shaking their fists at Byrnes and the other startled senators, and yelling, "When do we eat? We want action!"

But angry mobs of unemployed men and the radicalization of American politics were for the moment absent from Jimmy Byrnes' mind that afternoon in the Senate chamber on December 7, 1931. In his memoirs Byrnes did not mention the extraordinary circumstances at the Capitol Building on his first day as a senator, but the memoirs do record that a remarkable number of senior and influential members of the upper chamber went out of their way to seek out the junior senator from South Carolina and to shake his hand in welcome. They included Joseph Robinson of Arkansas, then the minority leader and as the chairman of the Democratic Steering Committee the final determinator of all the party's committee assignments; Pat Harrison of Mississippi, the ranking Democrat on the Finance Committee; and Carter Glass of Virginia, the ranking Democrat on Appropriations. These men were then the chieftains of Democratic power in the Senate, and by obtaining their public blessing, Jimmy Byrnes was well on his way to beginning his meteoric rise as a senator. Indeed, his rapid rise within the hierarchy of the U.S. Senate would be astonishing even by Byrnes' own impatient standards of success. Arriving in Washington in 1931 as a freshman senator, Byrnes in quick order would be jumped ahead by the Steering Committee over several other senators preceding him in seniority in order to receive coveted assignments to the Appropriations and the Banking and Currency committees. And just in case anyone should fail to guess the intentions of the Senate leadership toward one of its newest members, Pat Harrison hosted a dinner for Jimmy Byrnes the evening of his swearing-in; at that dinner the incumbent senators, who normally expected a freshman senator to be deferential to them, were introduced to Byrnes as Harrison's guest of honor. Whatever their private feelings, the senators must have recognized in Jimmy Byrnes someone who had an inside track to the top; in fact, within ten years, after gaining a seat in 1941 on the Senate Foreign Relations Committee, Jimmy Byrnes became, in the words of the historian George Mowry, "the most influential southern member of Congress between John Calhoun and Lyndon Johnson."

Byrnes' accelerated rise during the 1930s is even more remarkable when one considers the comparatively short time he spent in the U.S. Senate. In a chamber where the accreditation of power on the great standing committees or inside the party caucus was usually inflexibly governed by the rules of seniority, and where men measured their progress toward domination of their fellow senators not in the number of years they had served but in the number of decades, Jimmy Byrnes spent less than ten years as a senator. His resignation from the Senate to accept a Supreme Court judgeship was submitted in early July 1941, more than a year before the expiration of only his second term. To rise so high—to become the most powerful legislator from his region between the lifetimes of John C. Calhoun and Lyndon B. Johnson—Jimmy Byrnes had to start early. And it was to give himself such an early start toward senatorial power that Jimmy Byrnes in 1931 looked to the patronage of such men as Pat Harrison, Carter Glass, and Joe Robinson.

When Jimmy Byrnes sat down to eat his first supper as a U.S. senator the evening of December 7, 1931, Byron "Pat" Harrison was easily the most kindly disposed man sharing the table with Byrnes. The two did more than break bread together; they also divided much of the responsibilities for tax and appropriations legislation in the Senate during the 1930s. A perfect foil for the sharper-tempered Byrnes, Pat Harrison was more a partner than a patron of the junior senator, and the two were frequently appointed whips, or enforcers of party discipline on important legislation, after the Democrats organized the Senate in 1933. A tall, balding, and round-shouldered man who was as careless in his choice of business suits as Byrnes was dapper, Harrison moved his large body with the same unhurried and loose-jointed ease that in his youth had made him a star baseball pitcher hurling strikeouts for Mississippi State College. After early careers in semi-professional baseball, teaching, and law, Harrison had found his true vocation in politics, eventually winning election to the U.S. Senate in 1918.

Harrison had a disarming way of talking with other men and a jocose manner that even his enemies found relaxing, and during thirteen years in the Senate as a member of Democratic majorities as well as minorities, he had made remarkably few enemies for himself. Turner Catledge, a journalist who was himself from Mississippi and who was then covering the Senate for the *New York Times*, recalled that he could never hear the voice of Senator Harrison telling a funny story in the corridors of the Capitol Building without thinking of the character of Andy in the then popular NBC radio program "Amos and Andy." In fact, there was much in the senator's public performances that suggested the antic: Pat Harrison was charming, loquacious, fond of golf and contract bridge, delightfully witty, and slightly lazy. But Catledge was not so naive a reporter in the early 1930s that he failed to recognize that Pat Harrison was foxily turning a regional stereotype to his advantage. Knowing both Harrison and Jimmy Byrnes, Catledge later wrote that both "were born manipulators, and between them they could con the pants off anyone in Washington."

The Mississippi senator probably found it expedient that inexperienced politicians in Washington tended to think of him simply as a mellifluous party hack from the South who had nothing to contribute. "Honey catches more flies than vinegar," Pat Harrison might have instructed them, but in fact he never did so. Instead, he kept his mouth sweetly shut and went on accumulating more seniority and political debts, until by the early 1930s he had surpassed many of his more clever colleagues and become one of the most powerful men in the U.S. Senate. Harrison knew that he held a political IOU in his pocket from liberal Democrats for his having persuaded southerners to accept the Smith nomination in 1928 and to not deadlock the convention that year by their use of the two-thirds rule; and after the resulting losses, Harrison made additional friends for himself in the party by cheerfully volunteering to rebuild coalitions between northern and southern Democrats. As the ranking Democrat on the Senate Finance Committee, and after the reorganization of the Senate following the elections of 1932 as the committee's chairman, Harrison exercised a direct control over all the tax legislation considered by the Senate that would make him indispensable both to President Roosevelt and to representatives of private, conservative financial interests such as Bernard Baruch. Indeed, only in his relations with the latter did Pat Harrison ever meet his match in guile; that is, having flowed so smoothly around most obstacles in his life, Harrison himself at last stuck by his dependence upon Baruch's money. The plain fact was that in 1931 Pat Harrison was nearly broke; during the late 1920s he had invested heavily in real estate around Gulfport, Mississippi, and although he had become on paper a millionaire, the reverses of the Depression brought Harrison close to declaring personal bankruptcy. Only the loans of Bernard Baruch kept him solvent, and Harrison's dependence upon Baruch's money in 1931–32 was an open secret in the Senate known by Byrnes and others. Despite these financial reversals—or perhaps because of the paradoxical security of his financial dependence—Harrison remained a gregarious and optimistic man throughout the difficult years of the early 1930s. Turner Catledge found that although he was closer to Byrnes personally, Pat Harrison was the more open man. Despite the informality of after-hour drinks of bourbon with Byrnes, Catledge felt in talking with Byrnes there was about him "a certain caginess."

Much closer to Byrnes in personality and appearance was Senator Carter Glass of Virginia, the second of Byrnes' powerful Senate patrons. Ever sharp-witted and combative even at age seventy-one in 1931, Carter Glass was little changed physically from the five-foot, four-inch congressman he had been in 1918, when he had taken charge of a congressional delegation, including Jimmy Byrnes, on a fact-finding trip to the American Expeditionary Forces stationed in France. The only dramatic change that Byrnes saw in his old friend in 1931 was that the shock of red hair that once had stood like a cockscomb atop Carter Glass's head was now a distinguished white; otherwise, the senior senator from Virginia was still testily tolerant of most men in general and very fond of the company of Jimmy Byrnes in particular. Byrnes had known Glass as "the father of the Federal Reserve system" when the older man had secured passage through the House of that act establishing national banks in 1913, and Glass had been appointed secretary of the treasury in 1919 by Woodrow Wilson after the president had heard Jimmy Byrnes urge the appointment. Conservative to the point of being reactionary as he grew older, Glass was noted both for his absolute integrity in political dealings and for an absolute inflexibility once he had determined the right and wrong of an issue. "No one can help but like the old rooster," his friend, Representative Jack Garner of Texas observed, "but once Glass gets a notion in his head, neither hell nor Woodrow Wilson could change him." Leaving the cabinet in 1920 to accept an appointment by Virginia's governor to an unfinished term in the U.S. Senate, Glass had earned a profound respect from both Democrats and Republicans there for his knowledge of national banking. As a founding member of the powerful Byrd machine in his state, Glass was reassured of reelection; and as the ranking Democrat on the Senate Appropriations Committee and its chairman after 1932, Glass became the most prominent spokesman in his party for the limited-government view of the southern Democrats. Along with Senator Josiah Bailey of North Carolina, Glass was frequently grouped among the "southern Tories," who opposed expanded powers for the federal government.

Byrnes was more liberal than Glass, but the personal affection between the two was obvious, and Glass was sincerely committed to seeing his protégé Jimmy Byrnes succeed him to great authority in the fiscal committees of the Senate. Perhaps their sense of kinship came out of a shared adversity, as both of these men of slight physical strength had overcome by hard work and voracious reading in their youths the disadvantage of their families' inability to send them to college. Both men also had begun their business careers by becoming small-town newspaper publishers, although Glass in 1931 was still actively involved in managing his newspaper in Lynchburg, Virginia. Soon after Byrnes' arrival in the Senate, Glass used his influence as the ranking Democrat on the Appropriations Committee to secure Jimmy Byrnes an assignment there, having earlier helped Byrnes obtain a committee assignment to Banking and Currency. This preference marked only the beginning of Glass's patronage. During the next years as Carter Glass's health declined, the senior Virginian turned much of the day-to-day business of chairing the Appropriations Committee over to Byrnes. Nor did the political significance of this renewed friendship in 1931 between the seventy-one-year-old Glass and the forty-nine-year-old Byrnes escape the observant eye of Professor Raymond Moley of Columbia University, who within the year became a major economic and political adviser to the candidate Roosevelt. Ray Moley had early noted the possibility of allaying the fiscal conservatism of Carter Glass through the influence of "Jimmy Byrnes, whom Glass regarded with the affection like that of a father to a son."

Joseph T. Robinson was the third great chieftain of Democratic power in the U.S. Senate, and perhaps the most difficult, even for Byrnes, to cultivate without offense. A short, heavily built man who had appointed himself to the Senate from the governorship of Arkansas in 1913, Robinson had a great capacity for strength and refused ever to give up a struggle. In a fight, Joe Robinson was, as rural folk said, "stout-hearted." In fact, it had taken considerable struggle to rise, as Robinson did, from being born in a log farmhouse at Lonoke, Arkansas, as the ninth of eleven children, to being the favored guest along with Jimmy Byrnes at hunting parties on the Hobcaw estate of Bernard M. Baruch. Having received scant formal education in his boyhood, Robinson nevertheless obtained a state teaching certificate by age seventeen in 1889 and afterward read law at a judge's office in Lonoke. Like so many other southern politicians before and after him—for example, Pat Harrison and Lyndon Johnson—Robinson used his acquaintances gained through school teaching to scramble upward in his state's politics, eventually reaching the U.S. Senate.

Had he been born a generation earlier, the isolation and roughness of Robinson's early life in rural Arkansas might have combined with his legal education and his love of political power to make him one of the Senate's great agrarian rebels. Instead, Robinson chose party preferment in the 1920s by becoming one of the most reliable spokesmen for the conservative business interests in the Democratic party. The rewards were considerable. Bernard Baruch early interested himself in Robinson's career and, by providing political contributions and financial advice, gave Robinson enviable economic security. Robinson was elected by his party's senators to the post of minority leadership in 1923, and he was his party's choice for the vice presidency in 1928. The Arkansas native was an indefatigable campaigner for Smith, and his continued hard work as minority leader after the election loss won him the respect of the party. But despite his adoption of the hail-fellow-well-met boosterism of the 1920s, there remained in Robinson a core of the brutality and the unforgiving grudges of the nineteenth-century southwestern frontier: Joe Robinson was not a good man to cross in a fight. He showed this other side most frequently in partisan debate on the Senate floor; more privately, it manifested itself inside the shooting blinds on Hobcaw Barony. In the Senate, Robinson when angered often took political rebuttal as a personal insult, and in his debates he showed none of the eighteenth-century acerbic wit of a Carter Glass or the disarming guiles of a Pat Harrison. Instead, Robinson was blunt in his insults, sarcastic in his imputation of motives to his opposition, and apparently eager to engage in physical violence; when he was fully angered, his face would darken and he would turn toward the Republican side of the aisle with a scornful wave and the invitation "Come on," as if he wanted nothing so much as a fistfight. Nor was Robinson any less restrained in his killing on the South Carolina marshes. The minority leader apparently hunted with the same remorseless glee with which he tried to destroy his political opponents, and he consistently killed more birds than did any other of Baruch's regular guests at Hobcaw.

The violence offered an additional enjoyment: at least once, Robinson was heard to whisper to himself the name of a prominent Republican opponent as he sighted his shotgun on a bird and pulled the trigger, blowing off the animal's head. The incident scared the hunting guide who witnessed it, and amused Baruch when he was later told the story by the guide; but Bernard Baruch always had been a much more forgiving and much less violent man than Joseph Robinson, and Baruch may have seen humor in his friend's behavior when in fact none existed. Neither Baruch nor Jimmy Byrnes nor Pat Harrison nor Carter Glass ever had to face Joe Robinson's terrible partisan anger in the Senate, and their memories of him, both as the majority leader after 1933 and as their mutual hunting companion on trips to Hobcaw, were benign; but Turner Catledge also knew Robinson, and the journalist's memories were more disturbing. In his memoirs, Catledge remembered Joe Robinson as "a rough, tough man who brooked no interference. He would cut down his best friend to gain some political or legislative end." Catledge was writing in 1971, decades after Robinson's death of a heart attack in 1937, but even after those years there remained in the journalist's choice of words an almost physical fear of calling up in his mind the image of this heavy-handed man who once had so dominated the U.S. Senate. "I recall that he liked to go hunting and kill game until it became almost slaughter," Catledge wrote of Joseph Robinson. "The game laws were invented to stop men like him."

These were the men who in 1931 controlled much of the Democratic power in the U.S. Senate. None of them were by nature political liberals or experimenters. They did perceive the extraordinary seriousness of the nation's economic crisis that winter of 1931, and they were not indifferent, particularly Byrnes, to the human suffering it engendered. But they were not prepared to deal with the emergency of 1931–32 with any political means other than those used to deal with the other great national crisis of their careers some fourteen years earlier, during the Wilson administrations. Then, as younger members of the sixty-fifth Congress, in 1917–19, Byrnes and these other leaders had voted for temporarily increased powers to the federal government only for the duration of America's presence in the First World War. Now, in what promised to be a crisis even more severe, none of these senators were willing to consider any solution more radical than a temporary deviation from the principles of a balanced federal budget and an encouragement of private savings—or what Bernard Baruch, when invited in 1931 by Pat Harrison to testify before the Senate Finance Committee on the causes of the Depression, liked to call "restoring business confidence." (In fairness, in 1931 the unannounced candidate Franklin D. Roosevelt also had not decided on a permanent restructuring of the national economy in a new deal, a term not suggested to him by a speech writer until the week of the 1932 convention. Rexford Tugwell, a Columbia University colleague of Raymond Moley and also an economic adviser to Roosevelt, later recalled his frustration in not being able to persuade Roosevelt to give up what Tugwell considered too close an adherence to Woodrow Wilson's New Freedom and to consider the need for the permanent economic planning represented in Theodore Roosevelt's New Nationalism.)

Byrnes and Roosevelt both were to become quick learners, but for his first two years in the Senate, Jimmy Byrnes continued to see the events of 1931–32 only in terms of 1917–19, as evinced by his vote helping to defeat a liberal amendment to the Reconstruction Finance Corporation (RFC) act on January 11, 1932. Proposed to Congress by President Hoover in late 1931, the RFC was the Republican administration's major legislative attempt to stop the rising number of bank failures—2,560 closings since January 1930—and it was the type of emergency legislation of which conservative Democrats such as Byrnes could approve. Modeled after the 1918 act establishing the War Finance Corporation, the RFC would once more make the federal government a temporary source of capital during an emergency by providing government loans to banks and the businesses in which banks heavily invested, such as large insurance companies and railroads. Limited in its intrusion into the marketplace and precedented by a New Freedom act, the RFC bill was reported on favorably by Senator Byrnes and other members of the Banking and Currency Committee. But when the bill reached the Senate floor for debate, Senator Robert Wagner of New York and other senators from urban states supported an amendment authorizing the RFC also to make loans directly to municipal governments.

Byrnes knew firsthand that by January 1932 the nation's cities were in bad shape. In Byrnes' own hometown of Charleston, the city government that same month announced it simply did not have the money to meet its payroll, and paid its employees in scrip, a somewhat dignified IOU. Not since the Civil War had Charleston faced such a crisis. Actually, those having to "make do," as Charlestonians phrased it, with the city's scrip were the lucky ones—at least they had jobs. Unemployment in Charleston in January 1932 was reported as one in five, or 20 percent of the city's work force. The amendment supported by the urban Democrats such as Robert Wagner marked an attempt to deal directly with such human suffering in cities like Charleston, and it presumed an activism between the federal government and the states unenvisioned by the New Freedom. (Direct federal aid to municipalities later became a New Deal staple with the creation of the Public Works Administration in 1934 and a much expanded RFC.) In 1932, however, Hoover was opposed to this change in his administration's bill, and the vote on the RFC amendment thus split along party lines, most Democrats joining with Senator Wagner and the urbanites to vote for it. However, joining with Hoover's floor leaders on the Republican side of the aisle to defeat the amendment was Senator James F. Byrnes—along with Carter Glass, Pat Harrison, and Joseph Robinson. The RFC act itself did pass the Senate, with Byrnes' vote of approval, that same afternoon; but in their adherence to a strict fiscal conservatism and a limited federal activism, none of these senators showed a disposition to construct a Democratic party liberal ideology beyond what had sufficed during the lifetime of Woodrow Wilson.

But Jimmy Byrnes' concerns in early 1932 were not ideological. That is, despite the 2,560 bank closings, despite the armed guards at the U.S. Capitol, despite the inability of the largest city in his state to pay its bills, despite the seven million workers nationwide unemployed, Jimmy Byrnes knew that politically speaking the Depression was a Republican problem —and would continue to be so until the date of the next presidential inauguration, March 4, 1933. Until then, since the Democratic party had declined at the opening of the seventy-second Congress to organize the Senate (where Republicans in 1931 had held a one-vote majority with the handicap of numerous independents in their ranks) and since the majority of congressional Democrats offered no alternative to the Hoover administration's programs, Byrnes thought the wisest course for both himself and his party was to vote the Republican agenda, to hand Herbert Hoover sufficient rope to hang himself with politically, and simply to wait until twelve o'clock noon on March 4, 1933, for the beginnings of a Democratic presidency.

Byrnes had proposed this strategy in early November 1931, shortly after he agreed to work for Roosevelt. Joe Robinson in a confidential letter to Byrnes asked South Carolina's new senator for suggestions on how the Democrats in the Senate should respond to the Depression. In reply, Jimmy Byrnes told Robinson to go easy. To develop a Democratic agenda for economic relief, Byrnes warned Robinson, would succeed only in diverting attention from the responsibility of the Republican party. "Having no power, we should not assume responsibility," Byrnes wrote. Byrnes advised Robinson that "we should, if possible, let responsibility rest where it belongs, with the Republican administration."

But the confidence of Byrnes and other congressional Democrats that they merely had to wait until the November election and that 1932 would be a Democratic presidential year was not good enough for Franklin D. Roosevelt. Roosevelt had to make sure that 1932 was *his* presidential year. Always anxious about the South's loyalty to securing Roosevelt's nomination, the governor and his campaign manager, James A. Farley, throughout the first three months of 1932 grew increasingly uneasy with Jimmy Byrnes' behind-the-scenes strategy as they watched the majority of newspapers in South Carolina either endorse other candidates or remain neutral to Roosevelt's candidacy.

The Palmetto State was but one source of unease to Roosevelt and Farley, as throughout southern states in early 1932 the foregone choice of the state Democratic parties was by no means Roosevelt. From the historical perspective of his subsequent four presidential terms, it now is difficult to imagine that Roosevelt's chances for the Democratic nomination in 1932 were ever in doubt. But in early 1932 FDR was not president; he was not even FDR. That is, Franklin D. Roosevelt was, in Walter Lippmann's nearly lethal phrasing, "a pleasant man who, without any important qualifications for the office, would very much like to be President." The countryside in early 1932 was filled with equally pleasant men, some of whom also had southern delegates pledged to them. Maryland, as expected, had instructed its delegates to vote for their favored son candidacy of Governor Albert Ritchie. In Arkansas, the party faithful Joe Robinson withdrew his candidacy in order to help Roosevelt's chances, but the state's delegation remained officially uninstructed, and it required all of Robinson's force of will to keep the delegation in line for Roosevelt. The situation was even more unstable in Mississippi, where that state's delegation, officially uninstructed, favored Roosevelt by a margin of one vote. As the Mississippi delegation would vote as a unit for one candidate at the national convention depending upon a majority vote within its caucus, Pat Harrison would have his hands full in keeping his state from bolting from the Roosevelt camp. Texas and California were solidly for Jack Garner for president. Harry F. Byrd, governor of Virginia, was considered merely a favorite son candidate by everyone except the Virginians themselves, who were serious in their pursuit of the nomination, and it was consequently very difficult to negotiate with members of the Byrd political machine. And, in addition to the candidacy of Ritchie, Newton Baker, the secretary of war during the Wilson administrations, had powerful adherents among the big contributors to the Democratic party, including Bernard M. Baruch, who was reported to be hedging his support of Ritchie by also boosting the candidacy of Newton Baker. Thus the possibility of a dead-locked convention, and Governor Roosevelt's becoming simply another also-ran candidate for the nomination who failed to get a two-thirds majority past the southerners, had become apparent by March and early April 1932.

Roosevelt's concern became acute after reading newspaper reports in Albany of Governor Ritchie's receiving an enthusiastic reception on March 4 by the state Democratic party in Columbia, South Carolina. Within a week, Roosevelt had written to Byrnes, who Roosevelt knew just had returned to Washington from South Carolina. In his need to obtain up-to-date information on the activities of his competitors for the nomination, Roosevelt repeated a sentiment in his letter that sounded almost plaintive. "I wish much that you would write me confidentially what the reaction was and how things stand," he told Byrnes. Roosevelt usually kept himself informed personally on political developments throughout the South by his use of strategically planned trips to the therapeutic center in Warm Springs, Georgia, but Roosevelt unfortunately would be politically im-mobilized for the month of March, as he wrote Byrnes, while he stayed in Albany and attended to the state's legislature. Hence he repeated his desire to communicate with Byrnes. "I wish much that I might see you some day soon," Roosevelt wrote. "On Saturdays and Sundays I expect to be at Hyde Park and it would be fine if you could run up and spend the night with us." Having people come at *his* request always gave Roosevelt a sense of physically controlling a situation, and his insistence that he "wished much" that Jimmy Byrnes travel to New York State showed that he was worried about a situation in South Carolina that seemed to him to be slipping out of his grasp.

Byrnes' reply by return mail was that both he and Roosevelt in effect should sit tight. Byrnes conceded that Ritchie had "made quite a favorable impression and won some political support." However, Byrnes knew that the enthusiastic reception for Ritchie in his state was less the result of that candidate's personal appeal and more a demonstration of the power of Bernard M. Baruch. Baruch had emerged as one of the most formidable of the stop-Roosevelt Democrats, who distrusted the New York governor's lack of business experience and his political independence, and the financier had backed the prorepeal Ritchie, among other reasons, to undercut Roo-sevelt's support in the South among the moderately "wet" members of the party there. Repeal sentiment was particularly strong in Byrnes' hometown of Charleston, and what Roosevelt may not have known when he wrote to Byrnes was that Baruch also had asked Jimmy Byrnes to support Ritchie. Byrnes had turned the financier down, but he knew there were many state Democrats who could not afford such independence. Thus the impressive turnout in Columbia was simply the result of Bernard Baruch's calling due on the political favors owed to him. Or, as Byrnes more circumspectly informed Roosevelt, "I am confident that the invitation extended to him [Ritchie] was due primarily to an outside influence which is very friendly to him." Nor was Byrnes worried about the lack of newspaper endorsements for Roosevelt in his state. Public opinion counted for little in South Carolina's choice of delegates to the national convention, for the populism of Ben Tillman had not extended to the creation of a state Democratic primary to express a presidential preference. The state Democrats in 1932 selected their delegates through a complex sequence of precinct, county, and state conventions, and Byrnes was confident that through the intermediary of his friend Claude Sapp, executive chairman of the South Carolina Democrats, a majority of the delegates selected at the final state convention would be Roosevelt men.

What worried Byrnes more was Roosevelt's and Farley's insistence that the state party formally instruct its delegation to vote for Roosevelt. Byrnes feared that such instructions would offend the notorious touchy independence of the South Carolinians and result in a backlash at the convention in favor of Ritchie or Newton Baker. "There is a strong disposition not to instruct our delegates," Byrnes wrote Roosevelt, and he told the same to Farley when Roosevelt's campaign manager traveled to South Carolina later that March. Byrnes' plan was to have the state convention in Columbia in May adopt a resolution stating an unbinding "preference" for Roosevelt (which Byrnes would write) and then immediately to adopt the unit rule, binding all the state's delegates to the national convention to vote for the candidate supported by the majority of delegates. Roosevelt and Farley both reluctantly agreed, and the strategy went into effect at the state convention as planned; but such circumvention by Jimmy Byrnes in a southern state supposedly friendly to Roosevelt must have seemed to James A. Farley, a seasoned state party chairman, like the politics not of party but of egoism.

Farley was right. The eighteen votes South Carolina would cast at the national convention for the party's presidential nomination were controlled by thirty-two individuals to whom, Byrnes exempted, personal and family alliances were far more important than party organization. The lack of any significant Republican opposition in the state for decades prior to 1932 meant that the state Democratic party there had not found it necessary to build up the machinery to support candidates at the precinct or county level; as a consequence, aspirant politicians had built up their voting bases among those who lived nearby them or who were related to them. The importance of what the political scientist V. O. Key called the "friends and neighbors" factor in the one-party state politics of the South greatly complicated Byrnes' task in delivering the delegation to Franklin Roosevelt. South Carolina's delegates might switch at the last moment to Ritchie or Baker not on the basis of ideology or economic self-interest but simply to please a kinsman; and since an extended family can be an aggravation just as well as an alliance, Byrnes was afraid that the entire issue of instructing the delegation for Roosevelt might break down at any moment into a bitter internecine argument over which cousin tells which other cousin what to do. Additionally, Byrnes had to separate the traditionally feuding interests of the upstate and low-country delegates, who in this instance were quarreling over Prohibition.

And, finally, Byrnes had to be on the lookout for the early development of potential rivals to himself in the delegation. Because each delegate had survived the intense politicking of the three-tiered system of precinct, county, and state conventions in order to claim his seat at Chicago, it stood to reason that in the South Carolina delegation Byrnes would find at least one man almost as politically guileful and skillful as himself. (A possible example was a thirty-one-year old lawyer from Edgefield County in Byrnes' old Second Congressional District, J. Strom Thurmond. Thurmond was attending his first national convention as a delegate in 1932, and the young attorney watched Byrnes carefully and usually voted with him on issues in the delegation caucus. As a five-year-old boy at the beginning of the twentieth century in Edgefield County, Thurmond had been sent by his father to walk up to a speaker's platform and, terrified, to shake hands with a laughing Pitchfork Ben Tillman. This apostolic laying-on of hands apparently had worked. Thurmond would precede Jimmy Byrnes as the state's governor, and in 1948 he would be a national presidential candidate on a states' rights platform. In 1954 Strom Thurmond would follow Byrnes to the U.S. Senate, and by 1993 he had served there for thirty-eight continuous years.) However, in June 1932 Jimmy Byrnes was the man firmly in charge of his state's delegation. The contentious and individualistic delegates continued to quarrel among themselves over the repeal of the Eighteenth Amendment and the abolition of the two-thirds rule even while their luggage was being carried on the train to Chicago. But so well had Byrnes and Claude Sapp done their job by the third week of June that shortly after the "Carolina Special" left the Columbia train station carrying the delegates to Chicago in 100-degree heat, the *New York Times* reported that anti-Roosevelt delegates in the South Carolina delegation were expected "to have little say at the convention."

Byrnes continued his usefulness to Roosevelt and Farley after his arrival in Chicago by his behind-the-scenes maneuvering to forestall the influence of Al Smith and also to persuade Byrnes' fellow southerners to accept the revocation of the two-thirds rule. Byrnes' first task, eliminating the influence of Smith and his campaign manager, the national party chairman, John J. Raskob, proved to be the easier of the two tasks. On its opening day, Monday, June 27, the convention heard nominations for the position of permanent convention chairman, who would preside over the convention hall for the remainder of the week. Smith and Raskob proposed Jouett Shouse, a firmly anti-Roosevelt member of the national committee. Byrnes, as previously arranged with Roosevelt and Farley, rose to oppose the selection of Shouse and instead to place in nomination the name of Senator Thomas Walsh of Montana, known as a skillful parliamentarian and a safe Roosevelt man. Speaking to the convention for a quarter of an hour, Byrnes praised as "effective and efficient" Shouse's previous work in fund-raising for the national committee—that is, Byrnes was "burying the hatchet"— but he then concluded his speech by declaring that the convention chairman should be chosen not by members of the national committee but by a majority of the delegates themselves—that is, "burying the hatchet in Al Smith's neck." The South Carolinian's remarks were joined by a speech to the convention in favor of Walsh given by Senator Clarence Dill of Washington State, in order to demonstrate to the uncommitted delegates, as Farley planned, the breadth of Roosevelt's support from the West to the South. This southern and western coalition with the New York forces held, and in the first important test of Franklin Roosevelt's strength at the convention, his choice of Thomas Walsh as chairman was accepted by a majority of 626 to 528.

But a majority is not two-thirds, a mathematically irrefutable fact that became increasingly troublesome to James Farley, Jimmy Byrnes, and Franklin Roosevelt as the days drew on toward Thursday, June 30, and the moment for presidential nominations. The trouble had actually begun the week before the convention, on Thursday, June 23, when at the first meeting at Chicago of the pro-Roosevelt floor leaders, Farley allowed Senator Huey P. Long, the Louisiana "Kingfish" to make a premature motion that the Roosevelt forces petition the convention on the opening day to abolish the two-thirds rule. The reaction from most of the other southern delegations was predictably volcanic. Former U.S. Senator John Sharp Williams from Mississippi made public his declaration in a telegram to his state's delegation that "it would be idiotic on the part of southern delegates to give up a rule that has been a tower of strength in the South for 100 years." Pat Harrison was in full agreement in opposing any change in the rule, and the Mississippi delegation declared itself unanimously, 20 to 0, against any abolition. The *New York Times* noted that former Senator Sharp's influence was "reflected in the Carolinas," and over the weekend preceding the convention Farley saw his carefully constructed coalition for Roosevelt dissolving in front of his eyes over the issue of abolishing the two-thirds rule. Virginia, Texas, and North Carolina joined Mississippi for a total of 106 delegate votes opposing liberals on any rule change.

Byrnes personally was opposed to abolition, but he was able to hold his state for Roosevelt on the issue. The *New York Times* reported that South Carolina's was one of the few southern delegations willing to vote with Roosevelt on abolition, and over the weekend and during the first days of the convention the Palmetto State delegation was variously reported as being 18 to 0 and 15 to 3 in favor of abolishing the two-thirds rule.

Roosevelt and Farley knew, however, that with the exception of a few enthusiasts like Huey Long and professionals like Jimmy Byrnes, their cause for revoking the rule was lost among the southerners; and rather than risk further antagonizing his supporters from that region, Roosevelt, then at Hyde Park, sent word to the convention on its opening day that he was withdrawing support from any further efforts by Long or anyone else to change the nominating rules. After telephone consultations with Roosevelt, Farley also was dispatched to meet with opponents of the rule change. Governor Roosevelt, Farley assured them, was "1000 percent" opposed to any rule change at this convention. (The two-thirds rule would be revoked by Roosevelt's orders at the 1936 Democratic convention.)

Roosevelt's defeat on this issue took the shine off his initial success in determining his choice for the convention's chairman; it also greatly increased the odds of a deadlocked convention and the nomination of one of the numerous dark-horse candidates. After the motion to abolish the two-thirds rule had been withdrawn, the *New York Times*, in Roosevelt's home state, declared that Tuesday in a page-one headline that the choice of Newton D. Baker was likely as "A Compromise Candidate in a Deadlock." An accompanying story noted in its headline that with this early defeat of Roosevelt, "Ritchie's Chances Also Gain." As the day for nominations approached, Byrnes feared a repetition of what he termed the "disastrous" deadlocked convention of 1924.

Like all the worst of fears, this one took shape for Jimmy Byrnes shortly after five o'clock in the morning. The date was Friday, July 1, 1932, when after seemingly interminable nominating speeches for most of the preceding evening, there came just before daybreak the first of the roll call votes for the presidential nomination. Roosevelt came up short; with 666 votes he had a clear majority but was still 104 votes shy of two-thirds. Smith and Garner, respectively, took second and third places. Even though the exhausted delegates, including Byrnes, had been in a crowded convention hall with no air-conditioning for nearly twenty hours, another roll call began almost immediately; apparently both Farley and the managers for all other candidates hoped to pick up defections. On this second ballot, Roosevelt did gain eleven new votes, primarily from a shift in Missouri, but that slight gain was hardly the national groundswell that Farley had been hoping for. It was now obvious that the candidacy of Governor Roosevelt could not overcome the barrier of the two-thirds rule unless Farley could gain some time for negotiations with other candidates for an offer of the vice presidency in exchange for votes for Roosevelt. In addition, Farley, who had become so physically spent that he was directing operations while lying on a cot in the Roosevelt section of the auditorium's galleys, was worried that a third unsuccessful roll call vote could lead to an early-morning crumbling of enthusiasm for FDR and erode his candidate's previous totals. Accordingly, Roosevelt's floor managers moved that the convention adjourn that morning to convene for voting on nominations later that evening.

"No!" cried an angry apparent majority of Smith and Garner supporters. They obviously believed that Jim Farley was running out of votes for his candidate. For their part, the Roosevelt supporters were uncertain whether they could pass their motion to adjourn, and they withdrew their request. Thus, a third tedious roll call began early that morning, just as Jimmy Byrnes' worst fears were being realized. Sitting directly in front of the Mississippi delegation, Byrnes overhead a delegate there declare in the caucus before the state's voting that he could no longer support Roosevelt. Since Mississippi voted all of its twenty delegates as a unit depending upon a majority vote within its caucus, and since Roosevelt was favored within the state delegation by only one vote, Byrnes knew that a change of one delegate's mind could shift the whole state for Ritchie or Garner. The loss of twenty votes from Mississippi on the third ballot would wipe out Roosevelt's slight gain on the second balloting, and the defection of a supposedly safe Deep South state, dramatically occurring halfway through the roll call of states, might begin a nervous stampede of voters away from Roosevelt. This was just the situation Smith or Ritchie had been looking for. Byrnes in the early-morning crisis sought in the crowded caucus to find Pat Harrison, who was responsible for keeping his state under control.

But incredible as it must have appeared to Jimmy Byrnes, Pat Harrison was asleep back at his hotel room. Told that Farley planned to move for adjournment after the second balloting, Harrison had left the convention hall for his hotel unaware that the motion had been withdrawn. Byrnes was quickly invited to speak to the Mississippi caucus by some of Harrison's colleagues, and the South Carolinian was joined there by the irrepressible and pro-Roosevelt senator Huey P. Long of Louisiana, who had invited himself. Surrounded on one side by the Louisiana Kingfish and on the other by Jimmy Byrnes, the wavering Mississippi delegate, after what threats and cajolery can only be imagined, agreed to vote for Roosevelt only one more time, until a further state caucus later that day. The roll call was completed with Mississippi holding firm and with slight gains in other states shown by Roosevelt and Garner but with no two-thirds winner. Farley quickly supported a second motion for adjournment—this time carried successfully by a voice vote—and then rushed by taxi to Pat Harrison's hotel room, where he was joined by Jimmy Byrnes in dragging

Harrison, half dressed and still groggy, to meet with the Mississippi caucus. Byrnes, too tired to care much further, tumbled into bed in Harrison's room.

Farley was worried. He and Raymond Moley had discussed their concern before the convention that support for Franklin Roosevelt was "skin deep" among the southerners, and already that morning the example of Mississippi had demonstrated that, having failed three times to secure his nomination, Roosevelt delegates in the southern states were willing to switch their support to one of their regional dark-horse candidates to avoid a deadlocked convention. Farley knew he would have to deal, and he knew he would have to deal quickly, while all the pro-Roosevelt delegates were still considered his to deal. A rapprochement with Smith was unthinkable. And by Farley's count the delegates favoring Newton Baker, Ritchie, or Byrd alone were insufficient to gain a two-thirds majority for Roosevelt. That left Jack Garner and the Texans.

Taking advantage of that morning's adjournment, Farley conferred with Roosevelt's secretary and personal representative at Chicago, Louis M. Howe. Later that afternoon, Pat Harrison, who had voiced to Farley and Byrnes his despair of holding the Mississippi delegation any longer for Roosevelt, called Garner's campaign manager, Sam Rayburn, and asked for a meeting with Farley at Harrison's hotel room. There the offer of the vice presidency for Jack Garner was tendered for Rayburn to pass on to Garner, who had remained at Washington. In exchange, Farley asked for votes from the Texas and California delegations to give Roosevelt a two-thirds majority. Sam Rayburn, poker-faced, was noncommittal; but Farley was confident his offer would be accepted.

Later that Friday, after the convention reconvened, Chairman Thomas Walsh at 10:32 P.M. announced the results of the night's first roll call: a grand total of 945 votes for Roosevelt, including a majority of votes in the Texas and California delegations, and more than the two-thirds needed for nomination. After Walsh's announcement, most of the party's factions joined in a mutually relieved celebration of the fact that the Democratic party, after a comparatively short contest of four ballotings, had produced Franklin D. Roosevelt as its nominee. Excluded from the good feelings were a majority of delegates still loyal to Al Smith, who either booed loudly from the galleries or sullenly left the convention hall: the diehards died hard. On the floor Byrnes was among the ones who urged on noisy demonstrations for Roosevelt, while an amplified organist, in an attempt to drown out all opposition, at Louis Howe's request repeatedly played "Happy Days Are Here Again."

But the greatest service Byrnes provided to the Roosevelt organization came the morning after the celebrations, when he handed over for the New York governor's use the money of Byrnes' good friend Bernard M. Baruch. Baruch's suite at Chicago's Blackstone Hotel had been the unofficial headquarters of the stop-Roosevelt forces the previous week. On the Sunday before the convention, Baruch had arranged a conciliatory meeting in his rooms between Al Smith and William C. McAdoo of the California delegation in hopes of arranging for Baruch's favored candidates Ritchie or Baker just such a two-thirds coalition between the East and West as Jim Farley later was able to obtain for his candidate. Hence among the more astonished at Roosevelt's Chicago headquarters at the Congress Hotel on the Saturday morning after the balloting was Roosevelt's close adviser Rexford Tugwell, who remembered looking up and seeing in front of him the ebullient Jimmy Byrnes and, accompanying Byrnes, "the tall, lean figure of Bernard Mannes Baruch."

The speculator had come to see Louis Howe, who was preparing drafts of Roosevelt's acceptance speech. Roosevelt was expected to arrive at Chicago later that day by airplane from New York to deliver his speech to the convention that night, and the extent of Baruch's welcome at the busy headquarters was represented, in Tugwell's recollection, by the "sickly smile that Louis conjured up." Jimmy Byrnes perceived Baruch's visit as being much more collegial, and so he described it to Roosevelt in a letter written soon after the presidential candidate had traveled to Chicago and returned to Hyde Park. Byrnes explained to Roosevelt the significance of Baruch's visit. "The morning after your nomination he [Baruch] telephoned me at your headquarters," Byrnes wrote Roosevelt. "After talking of other matters, I urged him to come to headquarters, assuring him that your friends gathered there would be delighted to see him. I met him and the Roosevelt political family welcomed him most cordially." After hiding the truth behind this pleasant lie, Byrnes got down to cases: "He wanted to make a suggestion or two as to your speech and I took him up to Howe's room. I knew that Howe was busy and would want to destroy me for interrupting him but I thought it exceedingly important that we should get Baruch interested in your campaign."

Jimmy Byrnes did not mention that Baruch also had been accompanied at the Congress Hotel headquarters by the financier's current employee and former military associate at the War Industries Board, General Hugh S. Johnson. Johnson also requested a look at Roosevelt's acceptance speech, and by the end of July the probusiness general would be accepted as a major speech writer among the Brain Trust of intimate advisers to Roosevelt. Johnson—a short, bombastic man who loved publicity—had been "delegated to us by Baruch and accepted by Roosevelt," as Tugwell later complained. But as the election campaign of 1932 began in earnest, there was evidence of why it was "exceedingly important" to Jimmy Byrnes that Bernard Baruch become interested in the success of Roosevelt and that the financier have Hugh Johnson as his personal representative among the candidate's advisers. By the end of that summer, Tugwell was told confidentially "that Baruch now had become the most generous angel the party had." The financier's largesse to the Roosevelt campaign continued throughout the fall, and Baruch took a justified pride in its outcome in November. On the night of the presidential election, as Roosevelt's victory became apparent and was being celebrated, Ray Moley recalled that Baruch drew closer to him and whispered like a silver-haired godfather at a family christening, "I gave two hundred thousand."

Rexford Tugwell deplored the influence on the Roosevelt campaign of Baruch and his protégés Hugh Johnson and, later, George N. Peek; and Tugwell equally deplored Senator James F. Byrnes of South Carolina as the man who had brought all these terrible people aboard. Byrnes himself became a full-time member of the Brain Trust, at Ray Moley's invitation, after the senator had met with Roosevelt again at Hyde Park after the convention; and in mid-October, Byrnes joined Roosevelt's campaign train as a speech writer for the last two weeks of the campaign. There was considerable disagreement over the value of Byrnes' speeches among the original Brain Trusters, as represented on the right wing by Ray Moley and on the left wing by Rexford Tugwell and Adolf Berle. Moley liked what he called Jimmy Byrnes' "sharp mentality," and he considered Byrnes' wide acquaintances among congressional Democrats a political necessity of the campaign. Tugwell, however, never distinguished between political necessity and political expediency. The presence during the campaign of Jimmy Byrnes—with his insider-than-thou attitude, his "race" jokes, his consumption of Hankey Bannister bourbon, and his ready piano playing of "Carolina Moon" and "When Irish Eyes Are Smiling"—represented everything in Tugwell's experience that was politically and distastefully expedient. Tugwell's dislike of Byrnes was partly aesthetic; Rexford Tugwell simply did not like most politicians who came recognizably out of the culture of the South or West, as evinced by his dismissal of Huey P. Long at the convention as a "pudgy, overdressed loudmouth," rather than seeing Long correctly, as Franklin Roosevelt did, as potentially Roosevelt's most lethal opponent within the Democratic party.

But partly Tugwell's objection to Jimmy Byrnes was ideological. Senator Byrnes in his eyes was a representative of the group in the Democratic party that Tugwell had termed, with considerable accuracy, "the elders." The elders were former New Freedom congressmen and administrators who in Tugwell's opinion would commit Roosevelt after a presidential victory to the traditionally conservative Democratic policies of lower tariffs and reduced government expenditures. In opposition, Tugwell was arguing with Roosevelt for a plan of centralized and unprecedented government planning of agriculture and industry. The influence on the campaign of such elders as Jimmy Byrnes, Carter Glass, Josephus Daniels, and Senator Cordell Hull of Tennessee inhibited proposing new issues, Tugwell thought, and in his opinion their rhetoric obscured any substantial discussion of the issues. An example was Roosevelt's celebrated "Four Horsemen" speech, which he delivered to a wildly enthusiastic crowd in Baltimore on October 25. The speech had been written the same day on the campaign train by Byrnes, Jack Garner, and Senator Key Pittman of Nevada, and it ridiculed the "Four Horsemen" of Herbert Hoover's administration as "Destruction, Delay, Deceit, and Despair." (The literary inspiration of these men probably was not biblical but rather a 1924 newspaper column by the sportswriter Grantland Rice, in which he employed the image of the horsemen of the Book of Revelation to describe the players at the Notre Dame–Army football game.) The speech was one of the most aggressively partisan addresses Roosevelt gave during the 1932 campaign, and FDR was personally delighted with it; he autographed a copy for each of the authors. But more than thirty years later Tugwell was still angry about that speech, and in his memoirs he called the speech co-written by Byrnes as one of the worst of Roosevelt's first presidential campaign.

Byrnes' value as a political adviser with practical experience was more appreciated by Ray Moley, and Byrnes spent the remaining months of the 1932 campaign working with Moley over tariff issues and staying in a spare bedroom at the professor's residence. After celebrating the election victory of Franklin Roosevelt on November 8, 1932, with Baruch, Moley, and other campaign workers at the candidate's New York City headquarters, Byrnes returned home to Spartanburg. Three weeks later he traveled farther south to spend the Thanksgiving holidays with Roosevelt in Warm Springs, where he continued to give advice both ideological and grittily practical, as witnessed by an incredulous Henry A. Wallace.

Wallace also had been invited down to Warm Springs for the holiday, and the Iowa farm editor arrived early one morning during Thanksgiving week expecting to discuss agricultural policy with Roosevelt. However, the president-elect was still asleep, and Wallace instead found himself confronted with Jimmy Byrnes and Ray Moley. The idealistic geneticist from the corn belt who later became Roosevelt's first secretary of agriculture listened in astonishment as Byrnes tried to console Moley for Moley's having insulted a drunken lady in a railroad car the night before. The lady was Eleanor "Cissy" Patterson, publisher of the *Washington Times-Herald* newspaper. The two had visited Miss Patterson the preceding evening in her private railroad car, which was parked on a siding near Warm Springs. Byrnes and Moley arrived just as Miss Patterson, who in Moley's opinion was intoxicated, was berating one of her employees as "a cheap newspaperman." Moley, who may have had a drink or two himself, was incensed. "You're the one who's cheap!" he countered, and despite Jimmy Byrnes' attempting to make the peace, the president's senior economic adviser and the publisher of one of the nation's largest newspapers began an exchange of mutual invectives ending with Miss Patterson's shouting at Moley "to get the hell out" of her railroad car.

Now, the morning after, Moley was disconsolate. The *Times-Herald* was part of the national Hearst chain, and given Miss Patterson's reputation in the nation's capital for being personally vindictive, Moley was certain he had made a powerful enemy for Roosevelt. Henry Wallace stared as Jimmy Byrnes helped Moley try to compose an apology suitably diplomatic for Miss Patterson. But in the middle of their labors shortly before ten o'clock in the morning, a sunny Franklin Roosevelt, on awakening and being told of the incident, began to laugh. He had known Eleanor Patterson since they were both children, Roosevelt said; and he told Moley to send her a telegram telling her again that she was cheap. With a victory over Herbert Hoover only three weeks earlier by a majority of 472 electoral votes to 59, a happy Franklin D. Roosevelt plainly felt himself safely beyond the caprices of a William Randolph Hearst or a Cissy Patterson.

Similarly for Jimmy Byrnes, the months after November 1932 marked the happy time of political harvest. Byrnes had demonstrated his loyalty to Roosevelt both before and after the Chicago convention, and the senator was rewarded after the election with increasing access to the president-elect and opportunities to contribute to the future administration's policy during the four-month interregnum before Roosevelt's inauguration on March 4, 1933. Byrnes sat beside Roosevelt during the president-elect's first two news conferences at Washington in early December, helping to answer questions; and Byrnes was one of five senators invited on January 5, 1933, to the Roosevelt family's brownstone house in New York City to discuss future economic policy. (This was the same meeting at which the congressional delegation was chased from the brownstone's steps by Communist demonstrators shouting, "When do we eat? We want action!")

Byrnes' contributions to economic policy during these early planning stages of the New Deal were significant. Rexford Tugwell's misgivings to the contrary, Jimmy Byrnes was not completely identified politically with the "elder" southern internationalists who believed that the cures for the economic depression were a worldwide lowering of tariffs, less federal activism domestically, and an international agreement to stabilize major currencies. Byrnes instead was a member of what Professor Ray Moley, with some attempt at humor, called the "Look Homeward, Angel" school of economic thought. This group, including Moley and Tugwell, held that the causes of the United States' economic depression were primarily domestic in origin, and must be addressed by national planning before any major international cooperation could be attempted. Byrnes was fiscally among the most conservative of believers in "Look Homeward, Angel"; but unlike many southerners, the South Carolina senator also was willing to accept a protective tariff behind which, at least for the duration of the economic emergency, agriculture and business could adjust prices and wages under the direction of New Deal planning agencies. And as the Senate politician most likely, with his personal connections and committee assignments, to win passage of legislation for economic planning, Jimmy

Byrnes was increasingly heard as a counselor and adviser among the inner circle of the future Roosevelt administration.

Byrnes personally obtained the appointment in February 1933 of his conservative friend Lewis W. Douglas of Arizona as the administration's designate for budget director; the senator's approval also was sought before the naming of Daniel Calhoun Roper of South Carolina—one of the party's leading "elders"—as Roosevelt's secretary of commerce; and Byrnes was directly involved in drafting with Douglas one of the major pieces of legislation that Roosevelt had promised to introduce in the early months of his administration, the Economy Act of 1933. "The relation between the lively senator from South Carolina and the smiling man in the White House bears all the marks of being intimate and personal," *Collier's* magazine reported three months after Roosevelt's inauguration in March. Byrnes a month earlier also had been singled out by Arthur Krock in a *New York Times* article as the new administration's man to watch on Capitol Hill; Jimmy Byrnes, wrote Krock, was to be Franklin Roosevelt's "economic champion in Congress."

Byrnes had come into his inheritance. The political power that Jimmy Byrnes had sought from his older patrons beginning decades earlier when as a young man he had caught the attention of Woodrow Wilson now was in his hands. Only two years a senator, Byrnes through his friendships with senior, powerful men in the upper chamber had been selected for choice committee assignments on Appropriations and on Banking and Finance; now, as a result of these committee assignments and his fortunate association with Franklin Roosevelt, Byrnes came into possession of powers that singled him out from among the other ninety-five members of the Senate. In an informal poll taken among capital correspondents after the first six months of the new administration, the *Washington Post* reported that Byrnes was the correspondents' most likely choice among senators for a nomination to the next available cabinet opening; the reporters also selected Jimmy Byrnes as being one of the four "ablest Senate Democrats." (The others named were Carter Glass, Joe Robinson, and Robert Wagner of New York.)

Byrnes had waited patiently for this worldly success to be given him by his political elders, but less than a year before he finally received it, there also had occurred an event that had starkly reminded him that he himself was no longer a young man. In the summer of 1932, during Jimmy Byrnes' masterful behind-the-scenes control of the state Democratic convention, his mother, Elizabeth Byrnes died. Jimmy Byrnes left the state convention to go to her bedside after receiving word that she had suffered a final stroke, but she never regained consciousness before dying.

The pragmatic son of this selfless and inspirational seamstress now accepted the world for what it was in 1933, and he decided to enjoy his place in it. Although his black hair was flecked with gray, Byrnes retained his youthful habit of dressing impressively, and he favored trim, double-breasted dark suits, expensive Sulka silk ties, and the traditional southern accouterment of a sharply creased, dress gray Stetson. The photogravure section of the Washington newspapers on occasion illustrated the spring or fall change of men's fashions in 1933 by picturing the dapper Senator Jimmy Byrnes of South Carolina on the way to his office in the U.S. Capitol.

It was at this time that Byrnes made his celebrated remark that all he wanted from politics was "two tailored suits a year, three meals a day, and a reasonable amount of good liquor." A historian of diplomatic relations and an acute observer of Byrnes, Robert Messer, has noted the aptness of Byrnes' choice "of the new suit as the visible evidence of having lifted one's self from the drudgery of menial labor to respectable white collar prosperity." A new suit (along with marrying the boss's daughter) was the symbol in Horatio Alger's turn-of-the-century novels of the hero's successful rise from the laboring class to the capitalist class. Jimmy Byrnes always acutely remembered that only his hard work and his skills at shorthand learned from his mother had lifted him initially from the near-poverty of his Charleston youth. Byrnes' financial ability as a U.S. senator to purchase and wear business suits as well tailored as any of those worn by Bourbon gentlemen therefore may have been a validation to him of his success as a so-called Bourbon Horatio Alger.

Despite his political inheritance of power, money itself meant very little to Jimmy Byrnes during his senatorial career. Byrnes always was fond of repeating his maxim that a man could not make money honestly in politics, and if a man was dishonest, he did not belong in politics. The sincerity of Byrnes' maxim is shown in the personal financial details he offered in a letter written in March 1933 to a political acquaintance, turning down the latter's request to Byrnes for a small loan. Like thousands of other middle-class Americans in their banking accounts, Jimmy Byrnes had been caught in a financial squeeze when the Riggs National Bank of Washington had called in the repayment of his collateral loans used to buy stocks that were now selling at fractions of their pre-1929 value. "I owe $12,000 to banks," Jimmy Byrnes wrote in 1933 to his friend, explaining his reason for saying no to the loan, "and have borrowed every dollar I can on my life insurance." In addition to these bank debts, Byrnes added, he himself owed $2,000 "to a friend."

But if the financial possibilities of his political office meant little to Jimmy Byrnes, he valued the prestige and respect he knew money could buy. Like the new suit, these were the outward signs that this self-made man had, in fact, "made it." What he had made out of his political inheritance was a re-creation of himself as a successful Bourbon gentleman. Despite his unlikely background as a city boy who suffered from recurrent bouts of hay fever, Senator Byrnes in the 1930s began accepting invitations to the plantation open houses and deer hunts held in the low country by the aristocratic and Anglophilic property owners there. He also was delighted when Bernard Baruch made a present to him and Pat Harrison of lifetime paid memberships in the exclusive Jefferson Island Club, off the Maryland coast, where the Democratic elite met for politicking, drinking, and crabbing. And by the end of the decade he had become a member and a golf player—self-described as "the worst in the world"—at the equally exclusive Burning Tree Country Club, in suburban Washington.

The Bourbon political fathers, beginning with the late Judge Benjamin Rutledge in Charleston, had first given Jimmy Byrnes the opportunity to enjoy such social prestige, and as the contemporary journalist Joseph Alsop shrewdly observed, "in gratitude he imitated them." It is an irony, of course, that could not have escaped even Jimmy Byrnes' attention that the political inheritance that enabled him to re-create himself so successfully as a Bourbon gentleman had come during a period of unprecedented social and economic change of the New Deal, which Byrnes himself was advocating. But his public career and personal life always had been a combination of such contradictory impulses. Despite his later success in other branches of government and the comparative financial insecurity of his years as a senator, Byrnes at the close of his life declared this period of his public service to have been the happiest—the period of political inheritance in the U.S. Senate beginning with Franklin Roosevelt's 100-day special session of the seventy-third Congress.

Having advised inaction during the waning years of the Hoover administration, Jimmy Byrnes by mid-1933 was a changed man. Unemployment, bank failures, and depressed prices for manufactured goods and farm commodities were, as Byrnes knew, now the responsibilities of the Democratic administration. Consequently, Byrnes was of one mind with the president on the necessity for action. During the four months between March and June 1933, during the first session of the seventy-third Congress, President Roosevelt and his advisers released what could be described as a God's plenty of proposed legislation; and in the U.S. Senate, Jimmy Byrnes was the embodiment of that presidential energy. Byrnes assisted in drafting major New Deal legislation of the Hundred Days, including the Emergency Banking Act, authorizing the RFC to recapitalize the nation's banks by allowing government purchase of preferred bank stock; the Farm Credit Act and the Home Owners' Loan Act, providing federal financing of mortgages to distressed farmers or urban homeowners; and the Economy Act of 1933, which in the name of promoting greater efficiency gave Roosevelt unprecedented powers to reorganize the federal bureaucracy by executive order. Additionally, Byrnes during the special session acted as the administration's whip on the passage through the upper chamber of the bills creating the Civilian Conservation Corps (CCC), the Agricultural Adjustment Act (AAA), and the Federal Emergency Relief Administration. During this sustained activity, Byrnes was often described as the mercurial figure in a pin-striped suit working behind the scenes for the administration. The pro-Roosevelt *Today* magazine described Byrnes during the seventy-third Congress as most frequently "sitting at a forty-five degree angle in a senate chair, leaning toward the adjoining chair of some Democratic senator. . . . He has his fingers over his lips as he carries on a whispered conversation with the senator in the adjoining chair. Soon you will see him rise and slip over to a vacant chair beside another senator, lean over in the same position, and start another whispered conversation."

Jimmy Byrnes knew the angles. He became known in the Senate as the administration's "fixer," who could take control of a piece of legislation stalled by opposing viewpoints, improve the bill's chances for passage through compromise, and then quickly get the bill passed and off the legislative calendar. Cassandra Connor, personal secretary to Byrnes, later recalled how frequently Franklin Roosevelt telephoned the senator's office during the Hundred Days and subsequent legislative sessions. "I don't want to talk to him," the president sometimes told Miss Connor. "I just want to know what he's up to."

Most of these forty-five-degree approaches to other politicians took the form of unrecorded telephone calls or whispers in the Senate chamber, but the New Deal administrator Leon Keyserling left a record of his remarkable encounter with the South Carolinian. Keyserling in 1933 was a young lawyer newly recruited to Washington from Columbia University by Rexford Tugwell, and eventually he became an adviser on labor to Senator Robert Wagner and a federal housing administrator. Keyserling had learned his way around Capitol Hill, but nothing in his experiences had prepared him for dealing with Senator Jimmy Byrnes, whom he characterized as "a strange mixture." Keyserling later recalled:

> Byrnes called me up one day when I was in the housing agency. We were awarding contracts. We didn't have to award them to the lowest bidder if we thought he couldn't do the job. One builder in South Carolina had flopped miserably on his first job; he didn't have the means to do it. The second time around we awarded it to the second lowest bidder. Byrnes called me up and asked me to come see him.

"You've got to help me out," Byrnes told Keyserling. "This man [the lowest bidder] is my biggest enemy in Charleston, and if he doesn't get the project, everybody in Charleston will think that I stopped him because I'm his enemy or because he's my enemy, so you have to give him the project." Reflecting afterward that this builder might not have been such an "enemy" as Jimmy Byrnes claimed, Keyserling at least admired the senator's artistic indirection: "This was a new way of pleading for a project."

Not everyone appreciated such angular techniques. Senator Tom Connally of Texas had an ego at least as big as anyone else's, and Connally resented it that the junior senator from South Carolina was

> commonly regarded as a constant messenger from the White House. He was perfectly subservient to the president's will. Regardless of what he himself believed, he would urge senators to support the president's position. His function was to take an opposing senator into the cloakroom and make hints about patronage and other advantages that might accrue to that man should he support the president.

Patronage was in fact a skill mastered by Jimmy Byrnes during the Hundred Days, and it was also a sore spot among the other members of the South Carolina delegation, who were not as skillful as he in obtaining its use. Byrnes earlier had claimed the chairmanship of the Senate Audit and Control Committee, and despite his disparaging that committee in his memoirs as one of his "lesser" assignments, Byrnes privately boasted during his retirement that his control over that committee had given him what he described as a "virtual dictatorship of Senate patronage." Other committee chairmen from 1933 onward needed the approval of Jimmy Byrnes on Audit and Control in order to obtain operating funds for their own investigatory subcommittees, which can hold the public hearings on which national reputations are made. (This was a fact of political life learned by the comparatively unknown Senator Harry Truman in 1940. When Truman introduced a Senate resolution calling for a publicly held investigation of the defense industry, he was told to go see Jimmy Byrnes.) In exchange for operating funds, Byrnes therefore had the final say on Senate appointments to committee clerkships or the hiring of legal counsel to the committees.

Farther up the patronage tree of presidential nominations to federal attorneyships and judgeships, Byrnes also wasted no time. He quickly obtained from Roosevelt a nomination to a U.S. attorneyship for his former Spartanburg law partner Cecil Wyche; eventually a federal judgeship also went to Wyche. Nor did Byrnes slight the interests of the low country. Byrnes obtained a federal judgeship for the father-in-law of Burnet Rhett Maybank, the mayor of Charleston and a member of one of the low country's most patrician families. Perhaps most commendably, Jimmy Byrnes also remembered among his friends one of the most worthy and the least powerful: Asbury F. "Frank" Lever, who had been a distinguished congressman during the progressive era and who had been Byrnes' unsuccessful campaign manager in 1924, was out of office in 1933 and suffering from tuberculosis. Byrnes worked very hard during and after the Hundred Days to find a good place for Frank Lever, eventually obtaining for his friend a position as a state director of public relations for the Farm Commodities Commission.

Conspicuously left out of consultations for these patronage favors was the Democratic senior senator from South Carolina, Ellison Durant Smith. E. D. Smith had first come to the Senate in 1909 and became chairman of the Agriculture Committee when the party returned to power in the Senate in 1933. Smith was widely known by his nickname, Cotton Ed, but even without a populist nickname, Jimmy Byrnes was more influential. The Roosevelt administration repeatedly high-hatted Cotton Ed Smith, bypassing his claim to seniority and allowing the junior senator Byrnes to have the final say on most patronage positions. In part, Roosevelt's favoritism was simply the result of his close friendship with Jimmy Byrnes; but it also was an impersonal application of the law of "Before Chicago"—Senator Smith before Chicago had made the mistake of endorsing Newton Baker for the presidency. Roosevelt's decision in 1933 to award pride of place to Jimmy Byrnes in patronage matters eventually led Cotton Ed Smith to complain publicly that not even under the Republican presidents had he been treated in so niggardly a way in getting his share of government jobs. But the administration continued to favor Byrnes as too valuable an ally to lose in the Senate during the hectic days of the special session. "I seriously doubt that any man on Capitol Hill could have achieved the parliamentary victories realized by Byrnes," Ray Moley later wrote.

Byrnes' major victory for the Roosevelt administration during the last month of the Hundred Days was the senator's successful resistance to attempts at restoring the funds cut by the Economy Act of 1933. At this early point in his administration, Roosevelt was trying to steer an ideological course between those on on his left such as Tugwell who advocated centralized economic planning and the more conservative party elders on his right who believed that economic recovery would come as a result of balancing the federal budget and keeping both business and government small. From FDR's political tacking, a mixed three-part program for recovery emerged during the first months of 1933: first, centralized planning for agriculture and a system of price supports for crops as enacted in the AAA; second, a voluntary cartel agreement among industries for the stabilization of prices and wages as proposed in the National Industrial Recovery Act (NIRA); and, third, an immediate reduction in government pensions, salaries, and other expenditures as specified in the Economy Act.

Thus for the first congressional session of his administration, Franklin D. Roosevelt was at least one-third a fiscal conservative. In fact, reducing government expenses was such a high priority with Roosevelt that he intended the Economy Act of 1933 to be the first measure he proposed to

Congress during the Hundred Days; only the urgency of passing the Emergency Banking Bill on March 9 to deal with the bank holiday closings moved the Economy Act to the second place on the administration's agenda, where it obtained passage March 20.

In writing the administration's economy legislation that year, Jimmy Byrnes and Budget Director Lewis Douglas selected veterans' benefits as the likeliest source in the federal budget for forced reductions. Cutting veterans' pensions by 25 percent saved an estimated $383 million, thereby reducing by more than one-third the anticipated federal deficit of $1 billion for fiscal 1934. (In the same legislation Byrnes also included a section to cut some government salaries by 15 percent, lowering his and all other senators' salaries from $10,000 to $8,500 annually.) But by late in the Hundred Days session, as the Senate debated passage both of the NIRA and of the Byrnes-sponsored Independent Offices Appropriations Act during the first week of June 1933, veterans organized for a political counterattack to reclaim their lost payments by amending the Independent Offices Act.

Veterans, including such organized groups as the American Legion and the Disabled American Servicemen, composed the largest voter group in U.S. politics in 1933; they were more influential than voters in the farm bloc states, more numerous than members of any one urban political machine, more numerous even than the nativist Ku Klux Klan. The Senate responded to such electoral power, and during June 1933 several senators more fiscally liberal than Byrnes, including Tom Connally of Texas, offered amendments to the Independent Offices Appropriations Act reducing the veterans cuts from 25 percent to 15 percent. The situation was potentially ugly: President Roosevelt threatened to veto legislation that included the new amendments, almost certainly resulting in a vote in the Senate to override the veto and delaying action on the important recovery measure of the NIRA; at the same time, veterans' organizations were capable of organizing large demonstrations to protest the lost pension payments. Neither Byrnes nor anyone else in the Democratic party wanted a repeat of the preceding summer, when units from the Army and demonstrators from veterans' groups had battled in the streets of Washington over the issue of payment of the veterans' bonus, resulting in the loss of two civilian lives and irreparable political damage to President Hoover.

As the Senate haggled over the pensions in the summer heat, Byrnes was able to effect a compromise for his party a few days before the end of the special session. In an adroit exchange of amendments, Byrnes arranged for the pension cuts to remain at 25 percent in exchange for a Byrnes-sponsored amendment providing increased payments of fifteen dollars a month to Spanish-American War veterans. The legislative impasse thus was resolved, both the NIRA and the Independent Offices Appropriations Act became law on June 16, and some government economies toward balancing the federal budget were introduced. (In arranging this compromise, Byrnes surely had considered that, in the total population of veterans, the pensioners from the Spanish-American War were a small— and quickly decreasing—cohort.)

When an exhausted U.S. Senate finally adjourned the Hundred Days after midnight on the morning of June 15, 1933, Jimmy Byrnes had a legislative record, like the party's smiling leader in the White House, both experimental and conservative. Fifteen new laws redefining the practices of the nation's finance and commerce were passed by this special session of the Seventy-third Congress, and Byrnes was directly involved in writing six of them, including the Emergency Banking Act and the Economy Act. Reversing his earlier vote on the RFC during the Hoover administration, Byrnes also contributed to a fundamental restructuring of power and money between the federal government and the state government with his support for expanding lending activities to municipalities by the Reconstruction Finance Corporation. Additionally, his support for the AAA and the NIRA would bring a supervision by the federal government into the activities of private manufacturing and farming unprecedented even during his New Freedom days as a wartime congressman. And, for the first time, hundreds of thousands of citizens would be affected by the presence of federal dollars in their domestic lives through the activities of the Federal Emergency Relief Administration and the Home Owners' Loan Corporation.

But there were limits to Jimmy Byrnes' willingness to experiment with the economy. Despite his having grown up under the agrarian radicalism of Ben Tillman, Byrnes was a cautious progressive, not a populist. In 1933 he was suspicious of the "wild men" in the Senate, such as Huey Long of Louisiana, with their more radical cures for the nation's economic depression. Along with other southern Democrats of Bourbon inclinations, Byrnes had no use for Long's "Share the Wealth" program of heavily taxing the inheritances of the rich; and along with the banking and manufacturing interests of his region, Byrnes distrusted the inflationary plans of western agrarian senators to relieve farmers and other debtors by creating a cheap and plentiful supply of money. Hence Byrnes had become particularly alarmed earlier in the session when Senator Elmer Thomas of Oklahoma sponsored an inflationary amendment to the AAA, enthusiastically praised by Long, authorizing the president to devalue the gold exchange of the dollar by issuing greenbacks and resuming the free coinage of silver. Byrnes telephoned Ray Moley at home and advised that, since the inflationists had considerable popular support, the administration should get ahead of the movement with its own planned devaluation. Working with Moley at the White House's instructions, Senator Byrnes helped write a compromise version of the Thomas amendment, limiting the amount by which the president could devalue the dollar to no more than 50 percent its previous exchange value in gold. Byrnes succeeded in having his substitute amendment accepted into law before the end of the session, thereby providing some—but not unlimited—inflationary relief.

Thus just as Jimmy Byrnes had worked while a congressman in 1917–18 as an intermediary between the radical Tillmanite agrarians and the more urban progressives around Woodrow Wilson, so Jimmy Byrnes during the Hundred Days continued to be an intermediary between the economic radicals in the Senate and the more centralist liberals of the New Deal. This intermediary role sometimes put Byrnes into an uncomfortable position with his more unyielding conservative friends who liked the politics neither of Franklin Roosevelt nor of Huey Long. In the debate over the revised Thomas amendment, the old fiscal conservative Carter Glass begged the Senate with tears in his eyes not to lower the gold value of the dollar; and Bernard Baruch later wrote an angry letter to Jimmy Byrnes denouncing the new inflationary policy. (On reflection, Baruch decided not to mail the letter, probably deciding that it was wiser not to alienate one of his few personal friends inside the New Deal.) During the first congressional session, Byrnes' skillfull specialty as a fixer for the new administration emerged in his delivering compromise solutions, whether in cutting veterans' pensions or in increasing inflation. But his tasks became more difficult toward the end of the Hundred Days and afterward, as FDR remained pleasantly unmindful of the contradictions between his proposed relief measures and the fiscal conservatism of most congressional Democrats.

"You know, I'm a Democrat like you and Cordell Hull," Roosevelt liked to say to Byrnes, usually as his way of prefacing a discussion with him about some proposed new relief legislation. As Roosevelt's designated "economic champion" in the Senate, Byrnes came to dread that phrase. Jimmy Byrnes later recalled that whenever he heard Franklin Roosevelt blithely compare himself to Hull, he knew a "hot one" was coming.

Jimmy Byrnes handled the hot ones. A South Carolina journalist later privately described Jimmy Byrnes' tenure in the Senate with the image of a black female cook in the kitchen, sweating over a hot wood stove, while Franklin Roosevelt and his liberal friends sat in the dining room, laughing and calling out for more pie. This image has an element of truth. Whether in his service to Roosevelt's domestic agenda Jimmy Byrnes was, in fact, "perfectly subservient to the president's will," in Tom Connally's cruel phrase, or whether underneath the South Carolinian's pleasant exterior there was a growing dark resentment, or even plans to take the place of the smiling man who sat at the head table, Jimmy Byrnes never indicated. But it is evidence both of his personal loyalty to Roosevelt in 1933 and to his sincere belief in the need for economic reform that Jimmy Byrnes backed the early New Deal despite angry protests from his state's most conservative businessmen, many of whom had helped send him to the Senate in 1930.

"The R.F.C. money in South Carolina is being scandalously wasted," one millowner, perhaps representatively, wrote to Senator Jimmy Byrnes during the difficult winter of 1933. "Our people are not paupers and in the long run we would have been better off if this money had not been spent." Apparently not considering the benefits of finding heated indoor work for at least seventy otherwise unemployed workers, this correspondent continued, "Today thirty Negro women are being used in the Methodist church, and twenty in the Presbyterian church, and the same number in the Baptist church to wipe off pews. Squads of Negroes can be seen here picking up oak leaves."

Also critical of Byrnes' loyalty to New Deal liberalism was the widely circulated *Textile Bulletin*, the industry organ for cotton textile manufacturers published at Charlotte, North Carolina. The *Bulletin* noted, "In years past we were an admirer of Senator Jas. F. Byrnes of South Carolina. When he was a congressman he gave great assistance in opposing federal child care labor laws and he was an intense and ardent advocate of states' rights." But now, the *Bulletin* continued, "in his desire to appear as President Roosevelt's 'next friend' Senator Byrnes has completely reversed his former position and seems to be ready and willing to strip South Carolina and every other sovereign state of its reserved powers and to turn over to Congress every vestige of control over the internal affairs of the states." The *Bulletin* cautioned, "The people of South Carolina believe that they are capable of handling their own internal affairs and will not return to Washington any man whose chief objective seems to be the attainment of the position of 'Chief Gentleman in Waiting.' "

But if the Hundred Days legislation had cost Byrnes the votes of his region's most extreme laissez-faire capitalists, he had other fish to fry. Byrnes had made valuable political friends for himself among his state's bankers by speeding up the investments in early 1933 of RFC funds in South Carolina's financially distressed banks; an executive of one of the state's largest banks, South Carolina National, always remembered his gratitude to Jimmy Byrnes when the senator used his influence with the Comptroller of the Currency to override a federal bank examiner's recommendation in 1933 that South Carolina National be permanently closed and its assets liquidated. Byrnes got RFC refinancing, and the bank was back in business by the end of the summer of 1933. And among the needy multitudes of the state's population, the distribution of relief benefits also enhanced Jimmy Byrnes' rising political reputation. The Byrnes-backed Federal Emergency Relief Administration, under a program supervised nationally by Harry Hopkins, had by the end of June begun to distribute food, clothing, and work assignments to the state's unemployed; so efficient was the distribution and so urgent the state's need that in August 1933 it was estimated that fully one-fourth of South Carolina's population depended upon FERA for some sort of aid. And at least there were no more reports of children and elderly blacks starving to death.

Even the most potentially controversial program of the AAA, whereby the scholarly Secretary of Agriculture Henry Wallace, beginning in June 1933, urged South Carolina's cotton farmers to hitch their mules and plow under the 350,000 acres of planted cotton in exchange for promised government payments to keep the crop off the market, proved to be surprisingly popular. The cotton farmers had been discussing since 1932 the necessity for a "cotton holiday" of nonplanting when it had become evident there would be simply no buyers for the crop in 1933. They were delighted to receive payments of between seven and twenty dollars for each acre they took out of production. (The payments were financed by a processing tax paid by the owners of textile mills when they received a bale of cotton, which might have explained the enmity of the editor of the *Textile Bulletin* toward Byrnes) And, finally, even hard-to-please Charlestonians were accommodated by the repeal of Prohibition early in the Roosevelt administration, which meant that the port city's long-operating "blind tigers" and beer saloons were at least legal.

Jimmy Byrnes had done all that was within his political powers to relieve his state's economic suffering. After the adjournment for the summer of the Hundred Days session, Byrnes in late August vacationed at Sullivan's Island, north of Charleston, as much to recover his health as for recreation. (Such was the intensity of the drive for success by this self-made man that by late 1933 he had acquired both a vacation cottage by the sea and a case of colitis.) Jimmy and Maude Byrnes returned to Washington shortly after the New Year for the second session of the Seventy-third Congress on January 3, 1934, and Byrnes would continue his legislative leadership for the New Deal throughout the administration's second year in power. If by early 1934 the senator was beginning to have any doubts about the advisability of a continued economic innovation by the Roosevelt administration, he kept those doubts to himself. Besides, in an earlier speech to the New England Society of Charleston on December 22, 1933, shortly before he left for Washington, Byrnes in the "holy city" of secession told his audience that while he continued as a believer "in the rights of the sovereign states," he also thought the compact between the states and the national government during the 1930s "had to adjust to changing conditions." In short, Senator Byrnes was willing to suspend belief in a strict interpretation of the Constitution, at least for the duration of the New Deal's recovery policies. "Whether you believe these policies to be idealistic or revolutionary," Byrnes said to the Charlestonians in his soft, insistent tones, "you have the knowledge that most of them were authorized by Congress only for the period of the emergency. When the emergency passes they must pass."

But the spring and summer of 1934 brought not a lessening of the nation's economic emergencies but an increased fury as a result of a specific New Deal legislation. Ahead of the nation that year lay the largest and most violent industrial conflict of the 1930s, resulting from the attempted application of labor legislation of the Hundred Days. Beginning in Alabama and the Carolinas and spreading to twenty other states, the crisis eventually involved perhaps 500,000 workers and claimed at least sixteen lives. Despite Byrnes' calm Christmastime assurances to the New England Society of Charleston, by the time he spoke at the society's dinner a revolutionary change already had begun in his native state that could not be called back by words or revoked by congressional action. And like so many other violent struggles of national proportions originating in South Carolina, this conflict also had its roots in that state's wide cultivation of the dark green, low-growing shrub of the cotton plant, and in the labors of those people who processed its snowy white fibers.

In this instance, even though South Carolina's economy in early 1934 remained largely rural, the conflict was not occasioned by the allotment payments to cotton farmers introduced by the AAA; this New Deal program, although innovative, did not threaten the transfer of wealth from one class to another, as the state's largest planters usually benefited the most from the payments, and the black sharecroppers under the planters' control frequently were not paid any of the allotment. Rather, the unrest began among the urban, white laboring class of the approximately 80,000 textile workers at the hundreds of cotton mill villages scattered across South Carolina. Taking advantage of Section 7(a) of the National Industrial Recovery Act, a subsection thought at first to have little relevance for South Carolina's economy, the state's textile workers were demanding the rights they saw as guaranteed by the NIRA to form labor unions without interference by management and to negotiate with mill management for shorter hours and higher wages.

Previously dismissed as "lint heads," damned by Senator Tillman, and cheated by Coley Blease, the state's cotton mill workers as a result of the Hundred Days were demanding a participation in the economic restructuring promised by the New Deal. Eventually their demands spread nationally among textile workers in mills stretching from Alabama to Maine, and their movement brought the first major labor crisis of Franklin Roosevelt's recovery program. It also brought the first major defeat in political negotiations for Jimmy Byrnes. The struggles, political and violent, of all these people became known collectively as the General Textile Strike of 1934.

5

The General
Textile Strike
of 1934

Although the largest strike in the history of the United States, the General Textile Strike of 1934 has received surprisingly little attention. Most historians of the economic depression dispose of the textile strike in one or two sentences, before proceeding to fuller accounts of less extensive and less violent strikes in the automobile or steel industries later in the decade. Jimmy Byrnes himself, a major participant in efforts to resolve the textile strike peacefully, chose to make no mention at all of the conflict when he wrote his memoirs some two decades later. This omission by historians is due in part to the fact that the events of the textile strike, unlike labor conflicts in other industries in the 1930s, were not centered in one large urban area, such as Pittsburgh or Detroit, and thus do not lend themselves to easy retelling; there are as many histories of the textile strike as there were once mill villages stretching from Alabama to Maine, and each has its own localized history of the great events. Also, the textile industry has declined in importance for the U.S. economy since the years immediately preceding the 1934 strike, when it employed more American workers than either the steel or the automobile industry. Therefore, the economic issues of the strike, although at the time bitterly fought over, now appear of lesser importance for contemporary historians.

For the strike participants themselves, silence about the events of 1934 was not an omission but a deliberately chosen code of Appalachian conduct. Even today, many of the surviving strikers, now in their late seventies, stoically refuse to talk about what cannot be changed and what was, in the religious beliefs of some of them, preordained by God. Furthermore, within the closed community of the textile mill village, where the strike set armed neighbor against armed neighbor, the disputes of 1934 were considered to be private quarrels and not the business of an outsider. Whereas in the labor violence in larger cities the perpetrators fought like modern soldiers in anonymous crowds, each of the violent deaths in the small textile villages was followed by declarations by the friends and kinsmen of the dead that they "know who did it." Adhering to a code of earlier life in the Appalachian Mountains, these people did not seek redress from the law. Instead, the survivors dealt with those whom they considered to be responsible for violence against their kinsmen either by ostracizing their enemies in the village society or by later taking a more terrible, private retribution. Finally, among men of good will such as Jimmy Byrnes, a politic silence in later years about the events of 1934 was an understandable reaction, for despite the best efforts of Senator Byrnes and other politicians sympathetic to labor, the working and living conditions of cotton textile workers did not improve after the strike, and good will among men suffered an appalling defeat during the General Textile Strike of 1934.

The bitter feelings had been a long time coming. Even the conservative Bernard Baruch had advised a business friend in South Carolina in 1928 that the southern textile workers were underpaid and that in his opinion "it would be wise" for the state's millowners to increase wages in order to avoid unrest. Baruch's words were prophetic. Early in 1929, just over the state line at the major textile-manufacturing center of Gastonia, North Carolina, an organizing campaign by the Communist-led National Textile Workers Union resulted in over seventeen hundred workers at the giant, six-story Loray Mill in that city walking off their jobs over the issues of an extended work load and low wages. Before the strike ended in the fall of that year, the chief of the Gastonia city police had been shot dead in a confrontation with strikers, and two other policemen had been wounded. In apparent retaliation, a truck carrying strikers to a local labor rally later was forced off a rural highway by a crowd of armed men, and shots were fired at the fleeing occupants.

Killed by a bullet through the chest was Ella May Wiggins, a twenty-nine-year-old mother of five children, a Gaston County textile worker, and talented singer and composer of union ballads. Five "faithful employees" of the Loray Mill were indicted for Wiggins' murder, but in a later trial were acquitted of all charges. The unpunished murder of Ella May Wiggins marked the end of the Loray Mill strike, and the National Textile Workers Union was effectively run out of town after several of its members were charged with the death of the police chief and fled North Carolina after posting bond. But the strike at Gastonia was but one of several violent labor struggles at southern mills in 1929, including major strikes at Elizabethton, Tennessee, and Marion, North Carolina, as textile labor unrest that year crossed and recrossed the Blue Ridge, like fires seen at night across the mountain range. The outcome of all the 1929 southern strikes was the same: a complete failure at unionizing the textile work force; the restoration by management of the working conditions at the mills that had occasioned the strike in the first place; eviction from company-owned houses and exclusion from future employment of those workers suspected of union activity; and a willingness by both sides to use violence.

Conditions inside the mills did not improve after the first year of the Roosevelt administration. A sympathetic writer sent by Harry Hopkins in late 1934 to investigate conditions throughout the textile villages of New England and the Carolinas sent back reports of excessively long shifts, frequent malnutrition among children in mill villages, and poor sewage and health care at the company-owned towns. The lack of any improvement in the lives of the textile workers since the 1929 strike at Gastonia made that industrial city, in the opinion of the administrator's writer, his "idea of a place to acquire melancholia." The mill workers of South Carolina were described by Hopkins' correspondent as living in a condition of "feverish terror"—an economic fear of being laid off because of a lack of orders at the mill, or of not being able to keep up with the mill machinery during busy times, or of not being able to provide food or clothing for their children with the industry's low wages. The average weekly wage for many southern cotton textile workers during 1934 was twelve dollars or less for a fifty-five- or sixty-hour shift. By comparison, during that same fall of 1934 in South Carolina, children's shoes sold for over one dollar a pair; a girl's school frock cost between one dollar and three dollars, or one-fourth of a textile worker's weekly wage.

In fact, for the wage earner and the capitalist alike, the southern textile industry in the 1930s had become an example of Bernard Baruch's worst nightmares about the insecurities of a noncartelized industry. As a result of the vagaries of the cotton growing season and the boll weevil infestation, the millowner could never be certain, from one year to the next, of the price of cotton: those millowners who manufactured for the clothing trade also were subject to the demands of independent wholesale fabric brokers concentrated on Worth Street in New York City and in the "cutting trades" of the garment district of the Lower East Side. A sudden change in urban fashions, such as the shortening of women's skirts throughout the 1920s, could leave millowners with warehouses of unsold fabric. Compounding the problem, most of the one thousand cotton mills across the country in

1934 were small, locally owned, and lacking in what economists called a vertical integration of manufacturing function. That is, these independent mills competed among themselves for the numerous separate manufacturing tasks occurring after the splitting open of a bale of raw cotton at a mill's loading dock: the spinning, weaving, carding, bleaching, or coloring necessary to prepare the textile for the wholesale market. Each of these local mills added its own specialized manufacturing or transportation costs to the final price of the product. As a result, the relation between the high cost to the consumer in the 1930s of the finished textile—whether it was cotton cords inside automobile tires or a set of lady's fine bed sheets—and the profit of an individual mill was dangerously small. This fractional profit margin meant a constant price undercutting and intense competition throughout the cotton textile industry in the 1920s and 1930s. In 1934, for example, the largest firm in the industry controlled no more than 2 percent of the industry's total product.

Millowners responded to the increasing competition and shrinking profit during the Depression in the only way they saw as sensible in their labor-intensive industry: they speeded up the mill machinery and reduced their labor force. The introduction of high-speed Draper looms in 1929 enabled mill owners to increase the number of machines tended by one worker, thereby reducing the unit cost of the textile at a time when the fraction of a cent made the difference for the millowner between profit and loss. Despite the hard times, the reasoning went, so long as one cotton mill could outproduce at lower cost all other mills making the same product, the mill would stay in business. The millowners thus considered the extended work load a necessary response both to a new technology and to the changing business conditions of the Depression. But to the cotton mill operative, already working extremely long hours for low pay, the increase in work load in the late 1920s and early 1930s in some cases meant a change from operating twenty looms during a shift to operating over seventy looms a shift for the same pay. To management the change was toward a greater worker efficiency; but to the weavers and spinners, who felt their humanity was stretched beyond endurance by their operating so many machines at so fast a speed, this extension of the work force had another name: they called it, succinctly, "the stretch-out."

The "constant cry" was of the stretch-out, Hopkins' correspondent wrote in 1934 from the Carolinas. Men and women emerged from the mills at the end of their shifts shaking with fatigue. When asked how he was doing at the end of his shift, one stretched-out mill hand replied, "Tired, tired and weary, like all the others." In some instances, women who had worked their way up from their traditional jobs of spinners to become the better-paid weavers had to give up their jobs after the number of looms per weaver was increased; back inside the spinning rooms, the spindles at all mills in the South also had increased in speed for their female operators by the end of the 1920s. In fact, much of the bitterness and violence at the Loray strike was attributed to that mill's early introduction to the southern industry of the stretch-out system under a new mill superintendent from Connecticut. Shortly after his arrival, a group of Loray workers staged a mock funeral down the main street of Gastonia. They bore a coffin in which lay an effigy of the new mill superintendent. At intervals of about fifty yards the "dead" superintendent would sit up in his coffin and demand, "How many men are carrying this thing?"

"Eight," the crowd roared back.

"Lay off two," the effigy ordered. "Six can do this job."

The mordant humor was a mask for anger. Textile workers at southern mills under the stretch-out complained that they did not have time during their shifts to leave their looms for a drink of water; in the hot, lint-filled atmosphere of the weaving room, where windows frequently were closed to increase the humidity of the yarn for more efficient weaving, the lack of water was a serious privation. In the spinning room women workers also were humiliated by having to ask their male supervisors for a pass in order to leave their spindles and go to relieve themselves. Despite their popular reputation as shiftless and unenergetic employees, few American industrial workers had ever labored so hard and for so long under such unforgiving conditions as did the cotton textile workers in the 1930s.

Workers under the stretch-out also were hectored by the "second hands." These were the most experienced workers selected by overseers to guarantee production quotas in their section of the mill. Second hands were authorized to adjust the speed of the machinery and to give orders in the absence of a supervisor. Although there was considerable pressure on these men from their friends and relatives at the mill to lower the more unreasonable quotas of the stretch-out, a second hand who consistently "made production" knew he could expect to move onto a street of slightly larger mill-owned houses—"Second Hand Row"—and receive a larger paycheck. In that hard year of 1933–34, applying pressure on friends and relatives to make production quotas could mean the difference for a second hand whether he could afford to buy his daughter a school frock.

These conditions made impossible the traditional pride in the individual workmanship of a weaver or spinner—there is no individual craft in running seventy machines as fast as possible to meet a production quota—and for the first time, southern labor began to consider itself a distinct force in economic opposition to mill management. The idea of labor confrontation with management was new, and southern workers initially expressed their rising anger indirectly in the traditionally Appalachian form of songs and mockery: witness the mock funeral for the supervisor from Connecticut. In part, songs and humor always are the last refuge of the powerless. But, more ominously, this choice by southern workers was a continuation, however extenuated, of a tradition that had crossed the oceans with their

Scots-Irish ancestors who had settled in the Appalachians from the British Highlands; there, in a tradition that had puzzled and horrified even the Romans, Celts and Picts always had gone into battle singing and dancing, and there was a belief in ridiculing one's enemy in song before seeking him out and killing him.

It was no surprise, therefore, that textile workers at Winnsboro, South Carolina, expressed their anger with the stretch-out and their hatred of the perceived avarice of the mill supervisor Homer L. Sargent in a song widely popular among the workers, "The Winnsboro Cotton Mill Blues":

> Old Man Sargent, sittin' at the desk,
> The damned old fool won't give us no rest;
> He'd take the nickels off a dead man's eyes
> To buy a Coca Cola and an Eskimo Pie.

Women's songs of life under the stretch-out were less lighthearted. It was not just incidental that Ella May Wiggins, one of the leaders of the 1929 Loray Mill strike and among the most vocal opponents of the early imposition of the stretch-out, also was a mother of five children. As significant as the advent of high-speed technology in the textile industry was the percentage increase of married women and other women with children working in cotton mills. In 1907–8 married women working in the mills had accounted for 28.3 percent of the total female work force. In 1930 the percentage stood at 45.2, nearly half the total female work force. The category "Other"—meaning divorced, widowed, or, as in the case of Ella May Wiggins, women separated or abandoned by their husbands—totaled another 10 percent. Women made up slightly less than half of the total work force in the mills. Because women were expected in the textile village society to bear the major responsibilities for housekeeping and child care, the stretch-out during their shift added to the labor of women who in effect already had two jobs. Men could seek occasional relief from the stretch-out by attending a Coley Blease political rally, where they would be reminded that they were at least better off than the black man, or they could indulge in the "high lonesome" of a solitary drinking binge. But women textile workers could not so easily escape the responsibilities of tending to children or trying to balance the household budget. Southern women who were textile workers became significant organizers of resistance to the stretch-out, beginning with the ballads composed and sung by Ella May Wiggins.

A reporter for the *Nation* magazine sent from New York City to attend the Wiggins funeral in rural North Carolina transcribed one of her ballads, written in the traditional Appalachian stanza form and later sung at her gravesite. After noting the "startling red earth of this country" that was flung by shovels on Ella May Wiggins' coffin, the reporter took down the words to one of her union ballads, which a friend of hers sang:

We leave our home in the morning
We kiss our children goodbye,
While we slave for the bosses
Our children scream and cry.

And when we draw our money
Our grocery bills to pay,
Not a cent to spend for clothing
Not a cent to lay away.

How it grieves the heart of a mother,
You everyone must know,
But we can't buy for our children,
Our wages are too low.

Jimmy Byrnes had been attempting to eliminate the stretch-out since the passage of the National Industrial Recovery Act, in June 1933. Proponents of improved working conditions and of organized labor in the textile industry were encouraged by the inclusion in the act of Section 7(a), guaranteeing workers the right to bargain collectively. But the NIRA as originally drafted, under the influence of Bernard Baruch's former speech writer General Hugh S. Johnson, made no such broad concessions to labor as were later contained in that section; instead, concerned with the problems of how overproduction and cost cutting during the Depression had affected industrial profits, Johnson and the other authors of the bill wrote into the legislation a suspension of the nation's antitrust laws for two years. During that period, manufacturers in one industry would be free to form voluntary associations, or Baruch's longed-for cartels, to set industrywide codes of production, determine wages, and fix minimum prices. The codes were to be written by the manufacturers themselves; after approval at hearings before a National Recovery Administration (NRA), headed by Hugh Johnson, the codes would be enforced by district federal courts as law. The day-to-day administration of the codes would be performed by the manufacturers' associations, which became known as the code authorities.

But during early consideration of the NIRA legislation in Senator Wagner's labor committee, Leon Keyserling, the same attorney who found Senator Byrnes to be such a "strange mixture," objected. "You've got to have something about wages and working conditions and collective bargaining," he insisted. The code authorities retained the power of being exclusively manufacturers' associations with nonvoting government members: but Keyserling wrote into the bill the famous Section 7(a), stating that "employees shall have the right to organize and bargain collectively through representatives of their own choosing." The section also stipulated that workers be free from "interference, restraint, or coercion" in selecting their representatives. During consideration of the NIRA by the full Senate, Jimmy Byrnes also had tried to make the legislation more protective of employees. He amended the Senate version to require specific machine load limitations in industrial codes to be approved by the NRA. But in a conference with proponents of the House version of the bill, the Byrnes amendment was dropped.

Byrnes immediately protested the lack of protection from the stretch-out at the first NRA code approval hearing, in the last week of June 1933. As the cotton textile industry had suffered extensively from overproduction and cost cutting, General Johnson scheduled that industry for the first code hearing, held inside a crowded conference room at the Department of Commerce Building. George A. Sloan, the Vanderbilt-educated industrialist who represented the manufacturers' association of the Cotton Textile Institute, presented its proposals. Within a week they were signed by Franklin Roosevelt, with few changes, and became the NRA Code of Fair Competition Number One. Production was stabilized by agreeing to an industrywide limit of two shifts per week, each of forty hours; mills agreed not to sell below cost; wages for skilled workers in the South were not to drop below a payment of twelve dollars a weekly shift; and the principle of Section 7(a) was unchallenged. At Byrnes' insistence, General Johnson agreed to amend the code at a later date to include a national board to hear complaints about the stretch-out or "any other problem of working conditions."

As it was later constructed under Johnson's administration, the national board was composed of three members representing three distinct interest groups and was answerable to the director of the textile code authority. The chairman was Robert Bruere, a Columbia University professor of economics who represented the public; Bennette Geer, president of Furman University, in Greenville, South Carolina, and a former president of a cotton mill, represented the cotton mill manufacturers; and George Berry, national president of a printers' union within the American Federation of Labor, represented textile labor on the board. The Bruere Board, as it became known, was in turn to establish state boards to attempt a local mediation of labor problems. General Johnson, who was under intense political pressure from the White House to conclude this first code hearing successfully and quickly, accepted Byrnes' request for a future amendment for the national labor appeals board in exchange for a quick acceptance by labor representatives of the textile code. The general at the end of the hearings fulsomely praised the members of the Cotton Textile Institute for writing their own code of competition. "You men have done a very remarkable thing," he told them. "A very patriotic thing."

A reporter for the Associated Press traveling to the mill villages of the Carolinas in late July 1933 found a celebratory mood among workers the first week the NIRA-mandated code provisions of a weekly forty-hour shift went into effect. To persons accustomed to working sixty, and sometimes eighty, hours per week, the imposition of a forty-hour limit seemed to bring a sort of New Deal holiday. "The men want to fish, play baseball, do odd jobs around the house," the reporter wrote. "Most mothers say they want to spend more time 'tending the children.' " Over fifteen hundred textile workers in Greenwood, South Carolina, staged a spontaneous street dance in front of their mill office the Monday night after the first NRA-reduced shift had ended. "This had never been done before," the reporter noted with considerable understatement. "Most mills have high wire fences around them and watchmen to advise 'loafers' to 'move on.' But they were all 'loafing' because each had done his forty hours work. And they do say the watchmen attended the dance."

But, despite the apparent improvements of the NRA textile code, some of the celebrants at the dance quietly confided to the reporter that they "just can't help thinking that maybe there's a trick to it."

Jimmy Byrnes also saw no reason politically to jump for joy. As agreed, General Johnson amended the textile code to establish the national Bruere Board after Byrnes had held a series of public hearings in Spartanburg in the summer of 1933 detailing the problems of the stretch-out in the textile industry. But Byrnes was disturbed that General Johnson had not appointed a representative from the textile workers' labor organizations to the board. George Berry, president of the printing pressmen's union, who represented textile labor on the board, freely admitted that he knew little about conditions in cotton textile mills. In any case, the Bruere Board could take no action on its own, but had to submit reports of stretch-out abuses to the head of the code authority for its approval to obtain NRA sanctions against the offending mill. And as George Sloan of the Cotton Textile Institute had been designated the administrator of the textile code authority, which had no labor representatives, the manufacturers were in effect being asked by the NRA to judge their own alleged offenses.

This arrangement approved by Hugh Johnson was practically unique among the five hundred industrial codes written for the NRA. But even before these industry-biased state divisions of the Bruere Board were set up, Byrnes had begun to receive letters of complaint from workers that the mills had speeded up the machinery and returned to the stretch-out. Also, some workers who before the NRA code adoption had made over twelve dollars a week now found their paychecks reduced to that amount, as millowners sought to establish twelve dollars as the industry's maximum wage as well as its standard. Other experienced mill workers found themselves reclassified as "learners" under the NRA textile code and therefore not covered by the twelve-dollar standard. Finally, in General Johnson's haste to declare a first code victory for the NRA, there was little discussion at the Washington hearings of what Section 7(a) meant. This oversight seemed to indicate that NRA administrators had not given much thought to the consequences of that section for the cotton textile industry.

Two men who did see the consequences of Section 7(a) were Francis Gorman, international vice president of the United Textile Workers of America, and John Peel, that union's aggressive organizer for the South. Previously a small union within the American Federation of Labor, the UTWA had not been able to gain a substantial membership in the southern cotton industry in the 1920s and early 1930s. The union did not participate in the Gastonia strike of 1929, in order to avoid association in the mill-owners' minds with the violence and Communist leadership of the National Textile Workers Union. But southern mill management made no fine distinctions between the more radical organizers at Gastonia and the conservative leadership of the American Federation of Labor unions. Southern millowners fiercely resisted any attempts at UTWA organization, and with jobs scarce and management hostile to the point of firing workers suspected of union activity, southern textile workers declined to join. In 1933 the UTWA probably had no more than 7,000 members in cotton mills, and few of those worked in mills south of Virginia.

But taking advantage of the legal right to bargain collectively, which they now saw guaranteed to workers by the NRA code, Gorman and Peel in late 1933 and early 1934 began an ambitious recruitment of union membership across the South. It is an indication of both the accumulated bitterness over working conditions and a distrust of the permanence of the NRA-mandated improvements that southern workers signed up by the thousands. By early 1934 the UTWA could claim at least 80,000 members in the cotton mills, and at one time or another during that year perhaps as many as 350,000 workers in the cotton, wool, and silk industries were members of the union. In the South alone, the UTWA claimed to have three hundred locals spread among that region's cotton mills. For the first time in the history of southern industrialization, there was the possibility of a widely unionized, white working class. The southern paternal and Bourbon capitalism of the late nineteenth century was in danger of being replaced by the concept of representative, collective bargaining.

"Just can't help thinking that maybe there's a trick to it"—the trick, of course, was in the NRA's interpretation of Section 7(a). Backed with strong membership, the UTWA locals began demanding to represent workers in disputes with the local mill management or the state branches of the Bruere Board. In response, the code authority and Bennette Geer of the Bruere Board ruled that the right of workers "to bargain collectively through representatives of their own choosing" meant that only those actually employed at a particular mill were eligible to be representatives. Hence neither the code authority nor the millowners were obligated to recognize the UTWA unless that union represented *all* the workers at a mill. When the UTWA protested that its membership represented a majority of workers at many mills, Geer sought and obtained an advisory legal opinion from the NRA that the Bruere Board did not have to recognize the common-law precedent of majority rule in determining which organizations were chosen as bargaining representatives. Millowners thus sought to satisfy the collective bargaining requirements of the NRA code by organizing "Good Fellowship Clubs," or company unions, at their mills. In some cases, where physical force was deemed advisable to keep UTWA organizers out of a particular mill, or to intimidate union-sympathizing workers, second hands also were encouraged to organize "Picker Stick Clubs" at the mill. Picker sticks, used at cotton mills in weaving, were tapered wooden tools about half the dimensions of a regulation baseball bat, and usually made of the hardest hickory or laminated wood available. In the hands of a group of angry men, picker sticks were no joke: they could break a rib cage or fracture a skull.

Some of the worst offenders of the picker stick mentality were in Byrnes' home state of South Carolina. There a particularly bad example was in the tough little upstate town of Gaffney. (Twice in his senatorial campaigns Jimmy Byrnes nearly had become involved in fistfights at Gaffney.) The town had a reputation among labor organizers in the 1930s as being among the most dangerous places in the United States, second in labor violence only to Harlan County—"Bloody Harlan"—Kentucky. The major employers at Gaffney were Dr. Waite Hamrick and his two sons, owners of six mills in the area and members of a family prominent in the upstate's politics and Baptist religion. Supervisors at the Hamrick mills were quick to tell workers they were "yellow sons of bitches" if they did not assault union organizers. After the beatings, the Gaffney town police frequently claimed they "never seen nothing."

This reputation for the enforcement of "hard rules" apparently extended to the patriarch of the Hamricks, Dr. Waite Hamrick. "It is heart-rendering," a federal labor investigator later wrote about worker intimidation at the Gaffney mills in the 1930s, "to see one witness after another come to the witness chair, start to tell his story, catch Hamrick's eye, and then stutter his or her answers until courage returns." That same month of December 1933, when Jimmy Byrnes gave his Christmastime speech to the New England Society of Charleston on the necessity of adjusting to changing economic conditions, Waite Hamrick fired four workers at one of his mills for union organizing. When the state division of the Bruere Board, in a rare show of independence toward an owner, ruled that the four should be reemployed, the workers requested back pay for their lost time from work as a result of the illegal firings. Dr. Hamrick then closed down the entire mill, claiming a sudden falling off of orders, rather than readmitting the four workers with back pay.

"You are acquainted with the system of espionage, blacklist and oppression under which the mill operatives have worked and lived," John Peel of the South Carolina UTWA wrote in an angry letter to Jimmy Byrnes in November 1933. "I know you are honestly interested in the welfare of the textile workers," Peel continued. "If there is anything you can do to straighten the boards out, and get them functioning properly, instead of listening to manufacturers and their representatives, who are daily attempting to destroy all that is good in the N.I.R.A., we the textile workers will certainly appreciate it."

The situation was politically intolerable for Jimmy Byrnes. On the one hand, he had no desire to extend the hardships of the approximately eighty thousand full- and part-time cotton mill workers in South Carolina, who were an important constituency for him and for whom he had tried to amend the NIRA. On the other hand, Byrnes' general fiscal conservatism in the U.S. Senate had won him the support of many of even the most Bourbon of millowners, including Bennette Geer of the Bruere Board, who was a personal friend of Byrnes and a widely respected Protestant educator. But it also had become evident to Byrnes by early 1934 that Geer dominated the other members of the board, and just as George Sloan of the Cotton Textile Institute refused to recognize the UTWA, so the Bruere Board refused to recognize the existence of the stretch-out or worker intimidation as problems in the textile industry. Of the 3,920 complaints of NRA code violations that cotton textile workers lodged with the Bruere Board in 1933–34, including allegations of extended work load and unlawful discharge of workers, only 2 had by the summer of 1934 been handed over by the board and the code authorities to the Compliance Division of the NRA.

In his answering letters to Peel, Byrnes agreed that he had heard "in a general way" that Section 7(a) was being violated; but, given the power and the intransigence of George Sloan and Bennette Geer, the best the senator could advise was for Peel to be certain that workers filed copies of their complaints with their labor representatives on the state and national boards. Failing to get satisfactory action from that effort, Byrnes then advised Peel that the UTWA should consider appealing complaints of Section 7(a) violations not to the national NRA under the conservative General Hugh Johnson but to the federal district attorneys in the textile states. The fact that James F. Byrnes, by nature a cautious and conciliatory man, was advising a labor union to seek court action rather than negotiation indicates that by the spring and summer of 1934 Byrnes had lost confidence in the NRA's ability to mediate between owners and workers. This lack of confidence was expressed more forcibly by a crowd of pro-UTWA men in Anderson, South Carolina, who that same summer fought a rock and picker stick battle to close the mill there. With labor violence reported throughout the South in the spring and summer of 1934, the mood of the southern textile workers toward their NRA-regulated industry had changed within twelve months from desiring street dances in celebration to a willingness to engage in picker stick fights. All that was needed to set off a general strike across the nation was one intense spark of labor anger.

The spark occurred that summer in the state of Alabama as the result of a national NRA decision. General Hugh Johnson on May 22 approved a code authority request to reduce the weekly shift nationwide from forty hours to thirty hours in order to bring down unsold inventories. Workers' weekly salaries also were to be reduced by 25 percent. As a result of this code decision, many workers under the cutback no longer earned the industry standard of twelve dollars; some actually made less than they had a year earlier, before the NRA code had gone into effect. Gorman and the UTWA president, Thomas McMahon, immediately threatened a strike call. After negotiations that June with General Johnson, the UTWA officials agreed to accept the cutback in exchange for textile labor representation on the Bruere Board. The strike was canceled, although the union reserved the right to strike at a later time.

In the Alabama mills, however, the UTWA locals were spoiling for a fight. Ignoring the settlement by their national union leadership, textile workers at most mills in northern Alabama walked off their jobs by the end of June, and eventually over 23,000 workers in that state went out on strike that summer under UTWA local leadership, demanding a minimum wage of twelve dollars for the thirty-hour week, abolition of the stretch-out, rehiring of workers fired for union activity, and recognition of the UTWA as the workers' representative under Section 7(a). In addition to the Alabama strike, eight other independent strikes began in other southern states in 1934.

Gorman and McMahon called a special national convention in New York City of over five hundred UTWA locals for mid-August 1934 to discuss the union's dissatisfactions with the Bruere Board and the NRA code. McMahon and Gorman may have been attempting to seek a compromise among their members and so continue the UTWA national leadership's traditional reluctance to call for a strike action, but the national union was now dominated by the radical southern locals that attended the New York City convention in force. "Most determined among the strike forces at the convention were large groups of young men and women from the South as well as from northern mills," the *New York Times* reported. Many of these delegates, the newspaper continued, "had no money to cover their fare to convention and had 'hitch-hiked' all the way to New York." On the first day of the convention alone, southern locals presented over fifty resolutions for a general strike in the industry. South Carolina led among those eager to "go out."

Faced with such unexpected militancy, McMahon and Gorman had little choice but to acquiesce in the demands of the locals. A call for a general strike in the nation's cotton textile mills was announced at the last day of the general convention. Workers in the nation's wool, silk, and rayon industries were to be called out on a date to be determined after the cotton strike was in progress. The union leadership announced that the work stoppage was to be enforced no later than the beginning of the first working day after Labor Day, which was Tuesday, September 4. Francis Gorman would direct the strike from Washington, D.C., in order to be in easy traveling distance to the southern organizers. John Peel would be the UTWA's coordinator for the southern region, headquartered in Greenville, South Carolina. Since many mills in the Deep South did not observe Labor Day, the first attempt to shut down southern mills would therefore be on Monday, September 3. In calling for the walkout, in addition to the union's past requests of eliminating the stretch-out and Section 7(a) discrimination, the UTWA also set as a condition for recalling the strike order the establishment of an independent arbitration board for the textile industry, which would render decisions both final and legally binding. An uncharacteristically militant Thomas McMahon declared, "We will tell General Johnson we appreciate his efforts, but he is not big enough and has not enough authority to help us."

Jimmy Byrnes and Franklin Roosevelt both were on their summer vacation during the Labor Day weekend of the strike deadline. Roosevelt was at his "summer White House," at Hyde Park, New York, planning to travel to Newport, Rhode Island, for the final days of the America's Cup yachting competitions. Byrnes was getting his usual early fall relief from bouts of hay fever by staying at his beach cottage on Sullivan's Island, South Carolina. Both men, however, kept careful watch over the events by radio and telegram. The *New York Times* predicted the day before the strike that, if wool and other fabric workers joined in, perhaps one million workers nationwide would be on strike, making the projected work stoppage potentially the largest industrywide strike in the history of the United States.

A strike in the cotton textile industry had in fact become inevitable with the statement by George Sloan of the code authority in late August after the UTWA convention in New York City that the textile manufacturers would under no circumstance negotiate with the UTWA. Sloan persisted in maintaining that the UTWA was not a legally recognized representative of the industry's workers; hence the strike was, in Sloan's opinion, against the authority of the NRA rather than against the management of the individual textile mills. In response, Francis Gorman on the night before the strike sent out military-style "sealed orders" of plans of action by union organizers against mills that failed to honor the work stoppage. In the South, where three-quarters of the nation's textile workers

lived, John Peel asked workers in the eight states under his UTWA administration to consider using "passive resistance" in order to shut down the
mills.

Across the South that mild and pleasant evening preceding Labor Day,
millowners had to decide whether to shut down their factories in recognition
of the union's strike order or to open the mill gates at 6 A.M. on Monday
for the first shift and to brace for possible labor violence. The history of
labor, so frequently a part of the history of other regions of the United
States in the first third of the twentieth century, until now had largely
bypassed the South, leaving that region isolated in its agrarian-based economy, its concern with race, and its peculiar one-party political system. But
for Jimmy Byrnes and hundreds of thousands of other southerners that
September evening, history had arrived. The General Textile Strike of
1934 had begun.

The first day of the strike was an apparent success for labor, as most of
the southern mills chose not to open. (Those in Alabama already had been
closed down by the earlier wildcat strike there.) Across the Carolinas and
bordering states, about two hundred mills were reported closed that Monday, with at least 60,000 workers declared on strike in North Carolina
alone. Many of these textile workers there and in other states, free from
work on Labor Day for the first time in memory, attended Labor Day
rallies that, the *Washington Post* reported, the UTWA sponsored from
Alabama to Maine. In the southern Appalachians, prayer was frequent at
the opening of these rallies, and reporters both for national and for local
newspapers noticed the similarities between these southern Labor Day
gatherings and the emotional fervor and personal testimonies of religious
revivals.

This fervor should not have been surprising. Religion was more important than politics to most southern textile workers, and for at least one
generation they had brought down intact from their Appalachian mountain
homes to the mill villages a vision that saw the events of this world in the
stark terms of death, judgment, heaven, or hell. So it was natural that at
the moment of greatest personal and economic crisis for the southern cotton
textile worker, when the man or woman walking off the job was risking
both a loss of livelihood and possible eviction from a company-owned
house, that man or woman turned to the certainties of religion. And in
many cases this religion was not of the mainline Protestant denominations.
The Methodist, Presbyterian, or Lutheran churches in the mill villages
frequently were literally owned by the mill company, and the ministers
often were the salaried or retained employees of the mill; as a consequence,
many mill workers sought the greater personal freedom and expression of
free will by worshiping at one of the more Pentecostal denominations

outside of the mill sponsorship, such as the Assemblies of God, Church of the Nazarene, Free-Will Baptists, or the Wesleyan Holiness church. The prevalence of a generally believed, "final days" premillennial vocabulary and the active participation of women in labor leadership and violence set the General Textile Strike of 1934 apart from all the other conflicts of the 1930s.

"We fight for the Lord and our families," the UTWA's Roy Lawrence told workers in Charlotte, North Carolina, before the strike, in a combination of words that no one among them thought unusual. At the Labor Day rally held in Columbia, South Carolina, the striking textile worker George Brown opened the rally with a prayer: "We feel deeply in our hearts that we are asking for our rights. Grant that all we undertake to do will be done in a way Thou canst smile upon." A frequent simile of ministers speaking at these southern Labor Day rallies was the comparison of workers suffering under the stretch-out to the Hebrew slaves of the Old Testament whose Egyptian masters had commanded them to make bricks without straw. Even Byrnes' most hard-bitten ally in the labor movement, Earle R. Britton, the printing unionist who in 1930 had organized hecklers for Byrnes and threatened violence against Coley Blease supporters in the Horse Creek Valley, spoke words that combined Christian quietism and rock-throwing truculence. "Don't you believe it when they tell you you are going to fail," Britton told the men and women. "They said Christianity would fail, but it's still here. Our Christ always preached the same religion our labor leaders give us."

The calls for Christian forbearance did not last on either side throughout the first week. On the second, full day of the strike, more southern mills were forcibly shut down by UTWA workers, and the work stoppage spread to the New England states. By midweek, by a conservative estimate, 325,000 workers, or about 50 percent of the total subject to the strike call, had gone off their jobs; between 27,000 and 46,000 workers, depending upon whom one talked to, were out in South Carolina. Also, in that first week the deaths came. In the cotton mill town of Trion, Georgia, several "special deputies" sworn in to protect mill property were surrounded by a group of strike sympathizers. "Buddies, why don't you just give up your guns and join our side?" one of the strikers asked. In the ensuing pitched gun battle, one deputy and one striker were shot and killed, and twenty others on both sides were wounded.

During the first week, much of the early success—and the early violence—of the strike in the Deep South was the result of Francis Gorman's and John Peel's adoption of the tactic of the "flying squadron." Taking advantage of the isolation of many southern textile villages, which were often simply a series of factories on red-clay hills surrounded by company-owned houses with a single rural highway connecting one village to another, UTWA organizers collected workers on strike at one mill into caravans of sometimes over one hundred automobiles. The caravans, or "flying squadrons," would travel rapidly to another mill village selected at random, surround the factory, and demand that workers there stop production and join the strike. In the Gastonia area, where Ella May Wiggins had organized until her death, flying squadrons described as comprising between two hundred and a thousand people descended upon mills not abiding by the strike. Newspapers there reported "doors broken open at some mills, power shut off, and machines unbelted as workers were ordered from their frames."

To the Bourbon cotton mill owners, who were among the first industrialists to surround their factories with wire fences and hire "outside men," or security guards, the flying squadrons must have looked like their worst nightmares come to life. They were the mob, previously dismissed as Coley Blease's lint heads or Pitchfork Ben Tillman's populist wool-hat boys, and they were now at their gates in 1934 after the fifth year of the Depression, overwhelming in numbers and howlingly angry.

"Those cars and lines of cars were something new and strange, wicked and terrifying," Jonathan Daniels later wrote. "Or so the manufacturers thought." Daniels, the son of old Josephus Daniels and himself later an adviser to Franklin Roosevelt on southern politics, was in 1934 a young editor of his father's newspaper in Raleigh, North Carolina. Daniels was correct in seeing the General Textile Strike of 1934 in the South as one of the recurrent rebellions of the southern white "plain folk," as expressed forty years earlier in Ben Tillman's populist rebellion, or thirty years before that in the ferocious tenacity of Confederate infantry throughout 1861–65. (The rebellion of 1934 was exclusively a white economic rebellion in the South, as Negroes were not employed at southern cotton mills except as "sweepers," hired to clean the floor of lint and tobacco spittings. Sweepers had not been regarded by Johnson's administration as a category to be covered by NRA regulations.)

These "home-made Yankees" of the Bourbon southern millowners had good reason to be frightened, Daniels thought; despite southern labor's advertised reputation for docility, the local manufacturers knew better. "Many of these manufacturers came originally from the same red hills as those from which their workers come," Daniels wrote. "They know there is no dependable docility in their cousins at the looms. These cousins are the grandchildren of those who opined [in 1861] that it was a rich man's war but a poor man's fight and who fought like lank and indestructible devils just the same. Dig McClellan up and ask *him* if they were docile."

And despite his coming from a family that was a Raleigh model of southern gentility, the younger Daniels was not without some empathy for the lower-class occupants of these flying squadrons, many of whom in the fall of 1934 were his contemporaries, or even younger than he, in their late teens or early twenties. "It was good to be young then," Jonathan

Daniels later wrote of the flying squadrons of 1934. "Good to go in tumultuous crowd and shout at the fence of the Old Man's House, good to climb into Fords and rush across counties to join other familiar-unfamiliar young people in clamoring at the wire mesh of the mill gate."

In addition to the overall youth of the strikers, Daniels also noted the high number of single women in their late teens or early twenties riding the flying squadrons. Just as the first resistance to the stretch-out had been from married women and other working mothers, so the flying squadrons now brought out large numbers of single women working in the mills. Daniels thought he knew the reason why, and why the presence of these young women so added to the uninhibited actions of the flying squadrons. "Beauty is no advantage in the operation of a loom," he noted. "A girl knows that. And these girls, so long the mechanical adjuncts of spindle and loom, enjoyed the opportunity the strike gave them of holding excitement in their hands, of riding at night with their hair flying, of shouting at soldiers, of picnicking around night fires, and sometimes slipping off from the fires into the darkness with young men equally stirred in industrial war."

On Wednesday, September 5, a flying squadron of 105 automobiles and three trucks organized in Byrnes' home county of Spartanburg drove into the neighboring areas. "Women strikers clubbed workers at Greenville, South Carolina," the Associated Press wrote of the squadron's arrival at that city. "Hand-to-hand clashes were frequent." The squadron then drove to the afternoon change of shift at the Judson Mills, a factory complex formerly operated by Bennette Geer of the Bruere Board and now attempting to stay open during the strike. "Blows from oak clubs in the hands of two women pickets felled a woman worker in the blue uniform of the Judson Mills and left her bleeding," a reporter wrote. "She became unconscious a few seconds later."

Outraged millowners demanded and got from sympathetic state governments protection for their property and the nonstriking workers at their mills. The most common method in South Carolina was the naming of "special deputies," whereby the county sheriffs, frequently under the political control of the millowners, swore in as peace officers armed men who were willing to protect mill property as "constables without compensation." It was understood that the millowners would pay the men's daily wages. In Honea Path, South Carolina, for example, the owner of the local Chiquola Mill, who was also the town's mayor, authorized the hiring of 130 special deputies to protect his mill and its employees. The state militia, or National Guard, also was called out during the first week of the strike by the governors of Alabama, Georgia, North Carolina, and South Carolina to protect workers in those states from flying squadrons. The *New York Times* as well as the local newspapers throughout the South displayed large photographs of young men in these small towns, looking at the camera with bashful or stern expressions from behind their dark, trim militia uniforms and Stetson campaign hats, in between moments of setting up machine-gun emplacements overlooking mill gates and stacking their rifles at the ready.

The actions of the young women in the flying squadrons confronting these men in the state militia their own ages astonished Jonathan Daniels, who was raised to manhood in a region and a culture where the military was revered as an institution and women traditionally were deferential toward male authority. Daniels remembered for the rest of his life the sexual boldness in the fall of 1934 of these young women "taunting the soldiers and the high laughter."

On the third day of the strike, Wednesday, September 5, the same day that the flying squadron rolled out of Spartanburg County, possibly as many as 325,000 to 400,000 textile workers were off their jobs from the southern to the New England states. Fifty percent of the New England mills were reported to have closed down for the duration of the work stoppage. George Sloan of the code authority still maintained that the strike was an illegal action against the NRA authority to control production, and he continued to refuse to meet with officials of the UTWA. And the fatalities continued to rise: one of those wounded in the Georgia shoot-out later died.

Roosevelt had telephoned Jimmy Byrnes in South Carolina the day after Labor Day, September 4, for his advice on solving the strike. Byrnes mailed back a two-page letter to FDR the same day. Byrnes correctly defined for Roosevelt's attention the primary concerns of the striking workers as having nothing to do with the NRA's approval in May of lowering hours and wages.

"The two matters in which they are interested and as to which they look for relief are, first, the stretch-out system, and, second, discrimination against workers belonging to the unions," Byrnes wrote. As to the possibility of the Bruere Board's resolving the strike over these issues, Byrnes chose to answer that question by praising two members of the board. George Berry, representing textile labor on the board, was in Byrnes' phrasing "a splendid gentleman." Bennette Geer was "an exceedingly able man." But after these civilities, Byrnes got down to the hard case: "The employees assert that they have lost all confidence in the national board. I am responsible for its creation and I dislike to admit of its failure. However, I know that whenever a board of this kind loses the confidence of either side, its usefulness is at an end."

Byrnes then advised Roosevelt to abolish all the boards. He recommended that federal district attorneys be instructed to prosecute companies in cases of alleged illegal firings, without seeking explicit prior approval from Roosevelt's conservative attorney general, Homer Cummings. And finally, if the manufacturers persisted in refusing to meet with union representatives, Roosevelt should intervene personally to force the two sides to come together for arbitration. "If you are going to be forced to act sometime, it seems to me that you may as well act now," Byrnes wrote. "You will thus save Hopkins a decision upon the embarrassing question of relief to strikers."

The letter was the quintessential Jimmy Byrnes as the administration's fixer. Byrnes began by accurately analyzing for Roosevelt not what commentators said the textile workers wanted but what the workers really wanted; he made sure that everyone he knew personally on the Bruere Board got a share of the praise and none of the blame; he offered his advice to the president in the nonoffending, general words of an experienced and dispassionate government observer ("whenever a board of this kind . . ."); and finally, Jimmy Byrnes urged the adoption of his high-minded advice on the immediate grounds of political expediency, in this case saving Harry Hopkins from embarrassment. Hopkins, director of the Federal Emergency Relief Administration (FERA) and already a recognized favorite in the Roosevelt administration, had been harshly criticized in the national press for not stating outright that strikers were ineligible to receive food and other benefits; angry editorials that fall warned that Hopkins planned to violate the government's objectivity toward both labor and management in the textile dispute by having the FERA "feed the strike."

Byrnes knew of the failure of confidence in the NRA among textile workers before writing to Roosevelt because of the numerous letters he received from hourly employees in the mills asking him to use his influence to pass labor legislation superseding the NIRA. Typical both in its message and in its hard-won education among women mill workers was the letter Byrnes received from Minnie B. King, a textile worker at a mill near Slater, South Carolina. After writing a three-page, closely reasoned analysis of how the stretch-out system in all the nation's industries lowered workers' purchasing power more than it cheapened manufacturers' costs, Minnie King asked her senator to sponsor a national anti-stretch-out bill to which the NRA codes would have to conform.

"I believe that you could put over a national stretch-out bill if anyone could," she wrote Byrnes. "Will you try?" And then, in a reference to the Vanderbilt-educated George Sloan of the Textile Institute, Robert Bruere of Columbia University, and, possibly, Bernard Baruch, Minnie B. King added, "And once the confusion, caused by some 'Leading Industrialists' and others who know less about weaving than I know about the 'Einstein Theory' is cleared up, the general public will support it too. Really, I believe you could do it—won't you try?"

But the problem was that no matter how hard Jimmy Byrnes tried to apply a political fix to the textile crisis, Roosevelt did not want to intervene outside of the usual bureaucracy. The NIRA legislation itself was in the next six months coming up for congressional renewal, and in the face of mounting criticism of the NRA and its director, Hugh S. Johnson, Roosevelt was determined to prove that the agency could do its job of solving the textile strike without calling on the office of the president for direct intervention. Therefore, Roosevelt's response to the lack of talks between labor and management was to appoint on September 5 yet another advisory board. This board was to be headed by Governor John Winant of New Hampshire, and became known as the Winant Board. In his executive order creating the Winant Board, Roosevelt authorized it to gather information about the textile workers' complaints and "to suggest a plan for settlement" if both sides were willing to meet together. But the Winant Board could not compel arbitration, and it could only suggest, not mandate, any changes in the NRA-regulated textile industry. And while the Winant Board began its fact-finding task—Roosevelt had asked it to make its final recommendations to the secretary of labor no later than October 1—the violence in the South led to the inevitable new deaths.

The site was the Chiquola Mill in the little town of Honea Path, South Carolina. On Thursday, September 6, the day following Roosevelt's creation of the Winant Board, about three hundred workers were at the mill gates waiting for the morning change of shift when a flying squadron, backed by local unionists, tried to prevent the mill's opening. Anticipating the squadron's arrival, the millowner had distributed 130 of his armed special deputies throughout the mill building and on the company's grounds; nonunion or "loyal" workers already inside the mill building were given picker sticks to use against strikers who might try to force their way inside. The textile worker Mack Duncan was then a young man from a nonunion family employed at Chiquola Mill, and in his account of the events at Honea Path recorded forty years later, both the rawness of the violence and the personal nature of the killings were fresh in his memory. Duncan that morning in 1934 was in the mill office helping pass out picker sticks and sawed-off broom handles to other antiunion workers to use as clubs. "I would have left if my dad hadn't been there," he later explained. "He was a loom fixer at the time [the highest-paid labor position in the mill], and he had a gun; they'd deputized him." Picker stick battles and fistfights broke out in front of Mack Duncan's post at the mill office and outside at the gates as some of the morning-shift workers tried to get inside to their jobs. "Then all of a sudden you heard shooting. For about five minutes it was a regular din."

Duncan witnessed one of the shootings. "A fellow, Cox, he'd been an operator of the elevator in the mill. And he'd had a little run-in with a cloth doffer. The operator was a union man and he had an ice pick. But the cloth doffer was non-union, and he had a gun. And he shot the union man two or three times. I got sick myself from seeing so much blood, and I almost fainted."

The union man was, in the rhetoric of the time, Mack Duncan's class enemy: and many participants in the strike would have said that Duncan was justified politically, and in less physical danger, by ignoring the man lying wounded. "But I went to him. He got shot in the head. He was lying in a puddle of his own blood. I don't see how anybody could bleed that much. And his eyes looked like they had set back in his head like he was dying. I didn't think I'd ever see him alive again. And when it was over there was a lot of people hurt lying on the ground. They been shot and beat. And seven people were killed."

"Textile War Zone" was how the *Washington Post* the following day headlined its description of the strike in the Carolinas. Of the six men killed outright at Honea Path (one of the wounded died later), four were twenty-six years or younger; all the dead were unionists or union sympathizers. No one was ever convicted of the shootings. Once more, graves were dug in the "startling red earth" of the upstate, and once more biblical injunctions and violent threats were made in a community distantly overlooked by the serenity of the Blue Ridge Mountains. Over ten thousand people attended the funerals in Honea Path the following Sunday, September 9, for six of the strike victims.

A speaker at the funerals from the Federal Council of Churches told the assembled crowd, "They died for the rights of the hard-working man, who is close to God." A chorus assembled from the town's Protestant churches sang "In the Sweet Bye and Bye." And on the other side of town, South Carolina National Guardsmen patrolled the Chiquola Mill property, as an angry state director of the UTWA promised that "the automobiles will roll again" after the funerals in a return Monday of the flying squadrons to the state's mills. Moving between what were in effect two armed camps in Honea Path, a reporter for a South Carolina newspaper described finding one textile worker, a union man, recovering at his home with "his attractive brunette wife and the youngest of his three children. His right leg lies motionless, he explains, because a bullet hit it."

"It was a 32.20 Winchester bullet," the textile worker stoically told the reporter. "I know who fired it."

"Score of others profess to 'know who did it,'" the reporter wrote. "None of them is forgetting or expects to forget."

Will you try, Mr. Byrnes? Really, I believe you could do it—won't you try? Any attempt by Byrnes to lessen the hard feelings between labor and management became more difficult the second and third weeks of the strike. Millowners across the southern states announced in the week following the funerals in Honea Path that their mills were reopening for production, encouraged by the violent defeat of the flying squadron in Honea Path and by the presence of National Guard companies at other mills in southern states to protect nonstriking workers. In an attempt to prevent further killings, John Peel of the UTWA had countermanded the decision in South

Carolina to resume the flying squadrons, fearing more violent retaliation from the mill companies' deputies. But now striking textile workers in Byrnes' home state faced a new opponent: hunger.

With the mills open for reemployment, many county directors of the Federal Emergency Relief Administration in South Carolina, politically under the control of the state director in Columbia rather than under that of Harry Hopkins in Washington, began denying food and other relief supplies to strikers. Mills had been denying credit to striking families at the company-owned stores since the beginning of the strikes in late August, and of course those who were on still on strike were liable for eviction at any time from the company-owned mill houses. After several delegations of striking workers came to Byrnes' Spartanburg office in early September, giving examples of privation among mill families, Byrnes in the first week of the strike sent an unaccustomedly sharp-tempered telegram to Harry Hopkins.

"[The] people of textile community Spartanburg County beg that food be given them," Byrnes telegrammed, and he then instructed Hopkins to be certain that the South Carolina FERA administrator was abiding by national policy in being impartial toward strikers and nonstrikers. And Byrnes did more than simply send sharp-tempered notes to Harry Hopkins. In 1930, when Jimmy Byrnes wanted to be a U.S. senator, he had distributed five- and ten-dollar bills for "gasoline money" to aid in getting out the textile vote. Now, in 1934, when textile workers needed food, Senator Byrnes responded with one of the most charitable acts of his political career. By the end of the second week of the strike, Byrnes began mailing checks for ten dollars drawn on his personal account to UTWA relief committees to buy food for striking workers throughout his state. This generosity was never reported in the press.

As the labor conflict in the southern states developed into a mutual siege—striking workers were running low on food, and with the protection of 14,000 guardsmen on duty in the Carolinas, mills there reopened with "farmers, soda-jerks, and all sorts of people," according to John Peel's description to Byrnes—the violence spread to the New England states. By the second week of the strike, there were riots as strikers attempted to close mills in Saylesville and Woonsocket, Rhode Island; Danielson, Connecticut; Lawrence and Lowell, Massachusetts; and Lewiston, Maine. Guardsmen were posted in towns in Maine and Rhode Island, and the governor of Rhode Island declared parts of his state to be in a condition of Communist insurrection. Connecticut called out the state militia. Nationwide the total of dead in the strike had by September 13 risen to at least fifteen. Dozens of others were seriously injured, particularly by militia gunshot and tear gas bombs in Rhode Island. At this time perhaps over 500,000 textile workers were on strike, as the wool, silk, and rayon mills also had been closed by the strike.

Back in the South, Eugene Talmadge, the governor of Georgia, ordered the state militia there to forcibly round up about two hundred union organizers and sympathizers and to intern them for the duration of the strike at what the *New York Times* accurately described as "a barbed-wire concentration camp" on the grounds near Fort McPherson, outside Atlanta. Also, from mills in Georgia and South Carolina, Byrnes heard reports that owners there were paying the Bergoff agency of New York City to send "professional strike-breakers" to their mill villages. Ostensibly, the strike-breakers were imported to operate the plant machinery during the textile walkout: in reality, they were organized-crime gunsels, brought in to intimidate textile workers into going back to their jobs.

Will you try, Mr. Byrnes? Really, I believe you could do it—won't you try? Back from Sullivan's Island by the middle of the month and closer to the strike at his Spartanburg office, Byrnes wrote to U.S. Attorney General Homer Cummings on September 13 asking that federal district attorneys be instructed to act on complaints directly from textile workers who felt that their rights against illegal firings and intimidation under Section 7(a) were being violated. In response, Attorney General Cummings wrote to Byrnes on September 19 that he had read the senator's proposal "with a great deal of interest" but that he understood the NIRA legislation to mean that federal attorneys could be instructed to seek prosecution of alleged Section 7(a) violations only upon the specific recommendations of the National Labor Relations Board (NLRB). The NLRB had been created the year before as part of the NRA administration of Section 7(a). But like the Winant Board, the NLRB was purely advisory to the textile code authorities, and previous NRA rulings had determined that the Bruere Board's decisions on Section 7(a) took precedent over the rulings of the NLRB. Like the Winant Board, the NLRB could not compel action in the textile industry. In fact, the NLRB was the New Deal advisory board that had recommended the formation of the Winant Board.

The bureaucratic circle had closed, and it was impervious to the political fix. Jimmy Byrnes could not "do it." Thereafter, his role was reduced to that of an observer, waiting for the result of the Winant Board investigation.

On September 20, by which time the national death toll in the strike had risen to at least sixteen, the Winant Board released its report. Given the urgency of the situation, and the short time in which the board had to operate, the report was accurate as far as it went. The report criticized "the unique arrangement in textiles of management investigating management" that had been constructed by Baruch's handpicked man, Hugh Johnson, and it called for the abolition of the Bruere Board. In its place, the Winant report called for the formation of a new, independent board having authority to hear all Section 7(a) complaints. The existence of intolerable working conditions at many textile mills, the issue over which the UTWA had initially called for the strike, was substantiated by the report. Particularly in regard to the stretch-out, the Winant Board advised that machine loads and speeds not be increased for the remainder of the year.

But, on reflection, there was nothing new in the report's conclusions. Even the replacement of the Bruere Board by another presidentially appointed panel required no change in labor policy for the Roosevelt administration, and the issues of neither the stretch-out nor the low wages were specifically resolved by the report. Both simply were recommended as fit subjects for future "study" by the federal government for resolution at a later time. Most disheartening was the conclusion of the report, which though a vindication of the UTWA's description of the industry's poor labor conditions, conceded the primacy of George Sloan's no-recognition policy: "The board feels that under the circumstances of this situation an industry-wide collective agreement between the employers as a group and the UTWA is not at this time feasible."

Francis Gorman was between a rock and a hard place in regard to the report, particularly after Franklin Roosevelt the day after its issuance publicly called on labor and management to resume work under the recommendations of the Winant Board. On the one hand, although the report had declined to advise the recognition by management of the UTWA, it had substantiated the existence of conditions the union found objectionable, and Gorman was encouraged by the Winant Board's recommendation that employers not discriminate against strikers returning to work. On the other hand, the UTWA was losing strength incrementally in the South, where workers daily were being denied relief benefits and being evicted from company-owned houses. And events of the second and third week of the strike in New England indicated to him that this region could be just as bitter a battlefield as the Carolinas had been. Gorman also knew he could expect no sympathy in any settlement imposed on different terms later by the NRA's titular head, General Hugh Johnson.

The lack of objectivity by the industrial director of the NRA had become apparent in an astonishing speech Johnson made to a highly enthusiastic audience at Carnegie Hall the week before the Winant report came out. Speaking to the chairmen and other members of over four hundred industry code authorities, Johnson set aside his remarks on future NRA reorganization and instead launched into a verbal attack on the present textile strike. "When I think of George Sloan my heart weeps," the general told the capacity crowd of applauding industrialists. Johnson then attacked the UTWA leadership as being personally dishonest for having violated a "no-strike promise" to him in June, and he blamed the textile unrest on the presence of socialists at the UTWA convention. "The cotton textile industry is the very last place in the country where a strike should be ordered," the general declared, a sentiment that certainly would have surprised textile workers such as Minnie B. King. The national newspapers ran the full text of Hugh Johnson's remarks the next morning, and both organized labor and liberals in the Roosevelt administration were outraged by Johnson's ill-conceived words, which even his former employer Bernard Baruch might have found excessive. Baruch, however, had the good sense to remain quiet.

Being between a rock and a hard place, Francis Gorman of the UTWA chose the hard place. Choosing to see the Winant report as a vindication of his union's strike action, Gorman announced that he was declaring a victory and rescinding the strike call. "Return to work Monday morning as orderly as you walked out," he announced to the nation's locals, "conscious of having won your rights." He described the three-week textile strike by the UTWA not simply as a "triumph" but as "one of the greatest in labor history."

Southern locals, with their dead freshly buried and their wounded still bandaged, were outraged. They pointed out that none of the conditions announced at the beginning of the strike as necessary to be changed had in fact been changed. George Sloan of the Cotton Textile Institute had merely promised President Roosevelt that the manufacturers would give "serious consideration" to the Winant Board recommendations. More ominously, Sloan was reported as having "nothing to say" about whether millowners would rehire former strikers, as recommended in the Winant report. Nevertheless, within a week after September 22 the General Textile Strike was over. One former strike leader at a southern mill explained to a reporter from the *New York Times* why the local members were returning to work, in words that could have been used by a soldier in the Army of the Tennessee in 1865. They were not willingly surrendering, the strike leader told the reporter: they were leaving the picket lines only because "force and hunger" had driven them from the struggle.

In the following weeks, the pessimism of the southern locals was justified. "The workers 'accept' peace: their employers consider it," *Newsweek* magazine aptly summarized the end of the strike. The conditions under which the UTWA withdrew its strike call left George Sloan and the cotton manufacturers association sitting in what was then called the catbird seat, a position they had indeed been occupying since the first week of the strike. The need to dispose of an overstock of goods had occasioned the code authority's request in May for reduced hours even before the general strike, and during the work stoppage of the general strike the mills had used the opportunity to sell their surplus goods without incurring additional labor costs. Japanese imported textiles also had begun, in the months preceding the strike, to take a noticeable market share among such specialized products as hosiery, and the work stoppage gave domestic mills making those products, not having to meet a payroll, a chance to cut their prices. Now with the strike over and their inventories reduced, mills were not legally compelled to follow the recommendations of the Winant Board, and many of them returned to the stretch-out. And, encouraged by the success of their "no recognition / no negotiation" stance toward the UTWA during the strike, millowners took their traditional retribution against former strikers asking to return to work. In an optimistic letter written to Francis Gorman the first week after the strike had ended, Jimmy Byrnes complimented him on his "fine spirit" in offering a return to work in exchange for a settlement of Section 7(a) cases and the stretch-out by whatever presidential boards Roosevelt might appoint. "I hope that the manufacturers will in the same spirit comply with the request of the President," Byrnes wrote. But two and one-half months after he ended the strike, Francis Gorman complained that twenty-six mills in the South were still refusing to rehire strikers. Of those twenty-six, fifteen were in Byrnes' home state of South Carolina.

Blacklisted at the mills, or faced with a continuation of the stretch-out if a job was ordered, former strikers among the southern workers reacted with anger. Their anger was not directed at Jimmy Byrnes, who was recognized in South Carolina and elsewhere as an honest, if partly ineffective, broker between labor and management; rather, it was directed at Francis Gorman and the other national officers of the UTWA. Gorman had acted his part probably as well as any labor leader could have in his circumstances, particularly when the state military and police powers were so hostile in the areas he was trying to organize. Also, the inadequate relief funds in the national UTWA treasury (the AFL had been unable, or unwilling, to contribute to the UTWA strike fund), combined with the uncertainty of FERA benefits to strikers in many states, meant that Gorman really had little choice in calling off the strike by the third week in September. His decision also saved lives, if the events in the South were any indication of how the strike would have proceeded.

But particularly in the Deep South textile states of Alabama and South Carolina, Francis Gorman was scorned that autumn and for many years to come by textile workers who accused him of having "sold out" the UTWA locals and of not having had the stomach for the fight necessary to unionize the South. After the calling off of the strike by Gorman's order in September 1934, membership in the UTWA dropped off as precipitately as it once had risen, and for years afterward workers in the South were suspicious of any attempts to unionize mills by the AFL or the UTWA. As the South Carolina textile worker had told the man from the Associated Press at the street dance, "Just can't help thinking that maybe there's a trick to it."

Some good did eventually come to labor as a result of the textile strike. General Hugh S. Johnson, because of his increasingly erratic behavior and dependence upon alcohol, was removed at the end of September 1934 as the industrial director of the NRA. "Hugh Johnson was like McClellan to me," Arthur Krock of the *New York Times* later recalled. "He organized the NRA just as McClellan organized the Army of the Potomac, but once they had done that, both of them should have retired."

The obvious failure of the NRA to enforce the rights guaranteed by Section 7(a) also was a forceful argument for the passage by Congress of the Wagner Act of 1935, establishing the permanent National Labor Relations Board with authority to certify unions as legally binding bargaining agents and outlawing specific management tactics such as making membership in company-sponsored unions mandatory. Byrnes supported this legislation by Senator Robert Wagner, and he voted for it in the Senate. Byrnes also wrote and saw passed by Congress in 1935 a bill outlawing the interstate transportation of professional strikebreakers. And finally, the failure of the NRA and the defeat of the 1934 unionization drive in the textile industry brought into later national prominence the man who was to be one of the decade's most skillful advocates of organized labor, and the man who was perhaps Jimmy Byrnes' most skillful political enemy—Sidney Hillman.

Sidney Hillman was a turn-of-the-century immigrant from Lithuania who by hard work and a genius for organizing had risen from being an apprentice cloth cutter for Hart, Schaffner, and Marx to the union presidency of the 177,000-member Amalgamated Clothing Workers of America. Amalgamated, though initially denied membership by the American Federation of Labor, was one of the strongest urban unions in the early 1930s, and Hillman's earlier success marked him as a man with whom management would have to deal. When the Roosevelt administration, embarrassed by the performance of General Hugh Johnson, formed the National Industrial Recovery Board to run the NRA in 1934, after Johnson's forced retirement, Hillman was offered a place on the board. The intense, soft-spoken Hillman immediately saw the political possibilities of his appointment in forcing the conservative American Federation of Labor to take advantage of the collective-bargaining opportunities afforded by the New Deal. Hillman felt that the AFL's president, William Green, had been moving too slowly to unionize workers in the mass-production industries. Working with the coal mining unionist John L. Lewis, Hillman set up within the AFL structure the Committee for Industrial Organization (CIO) to aggressively pursue industrywide labor contracts under the protection of a newly strengthened NLRB. And when the CIO in 1937 decided to mount another organizing campaign in the cotton textile industry, Sidney Hillman directed the operation throughout the South.

Hillman's direction brought the southern textile labor movement as close to success as it has since come. Southern workers, disillusioned with the UTWA in the 1934 strike, responded to the promise of Hillman's committee not to collect union dues until a satisfactory contract was signed at a mill, and they liked the fact that new, politically well-placed national leaders had taken the organizing initiative away from Francis Gorman and Thomas McMahon. Although he did not succeed in organizing a majority of the region's textile workers, Hillman eventually obtained twenty-three enforceable contracts with southern cotton mills, affecting 17,000 workers. (In Gaffney, Dr. Waite Hamrick sponsored a religious revival to counteract the influence of the new labor campaign, during which it was claimed that CIO stood for "Christ Is Out.") Hillman's qualified but unprecedented organizing success in the South and his impatience with William Green of the AFL made his break with the AFL inevitable. In 1938, after fractious labor conventions marked by bitter infighting, Hillman and John Lewis led a number of unions out of the AFL to form the rival Congress of Industrial Organizations (CIO). Hillman took the southern locals out with him. Within a year after the formation of the CIO, Francis Gorman, who had succeeded McMahon to prominence in the UTWA, was ousted from his office, and the textile union was reorganized under CIO administration.

These were alarming developments to Jimmy Byrnes. William Green of the AFL had been a personal friend of his since the mid-1920s, and whatever the senator's occasional differences with Thomas McMahon and Francis Gorman, he had been safe in assuming that these two unionists were basically conservative men like himself always willing to find a conciliatory common ground. But now the largest union in his home state was united with a national labor organization that did not hesitate to use its legal rights or its influence independently of Byrnes in the Roosevelt administration to secure its aims. Just as the New Deal had in 1933 brought Jimmy Byrnes and the southern Democrats to power, so it was in 1934 bringing new people like Sidney Hillman to power.

Indeed, the rise of Sidney Hillman by 1934 as "the statesman of labor" showed many strange similarities to the earlier rise to power of Jimmy Byrnes. Both were physically diminutive men who converted others to their viewpoints by the force of their logic and the pleasantness of their natures. Even in the most partisan of fights, each man usually retained a certain sweetness of disposition, and a noticeable Old World or Charleston charm. Both men had in their youths, despite being physically unsuited for it, worked in the clothing trades, Sidney Hillman as an apprentice cutter for Hart, Schaffner, and Marx, and Jimmy Byrnes delivering dresses from his mother's sewing shop. Both men were pragmatists, who combined a passion for self-education with a restless ambition. And finally both were religious outsiders, Hillman having been born a Jew in Russian-ruled Lithuania and Byrnes a Roman Catholic in the Protestant Deep South. In that autumn of 1934, Sidney "Simcha" Hillman and James "Jimmy" Byrnes were curious mirror images of each other. Within the next ten years, by the time of Byrnes' serious attempt to achieve the U.S. presidency, each would come to loathe the other.

6

The Philadelphia Story

Lhe failure of the Roosevelt administration to intervene directly in the textile strike of 1934 did not hurt it that year at the polls. Jimmy Byrnes traveled from South Carolina to campaign for the administration's candidates in late October in congressional races in Ohio, Michigan, and other midwestern and northern states. Returning to South Carolina to vote in the November elections, Byrnes the morning after the polls closed saw a landslide victory nationwide for the Democrats, with his party winning a two-thirds majority in both chambers of Congress. "You are responsible for the glorious victory," Byrnes wired Roosevelt after the elections. "Every candidate from congressman to coroner declared your program was the issue. The result is a magnificent tribute to you."

Back in Washington for the opening of the Seventy-fourth Congress, in January 1935, Byrnes was appointed by Roosevelt to be the Senate floor manager of the most significant of the New Deal relief measures in 1935–36, the legislation establishing the Works Progress Administration (WPA). Earlier in 1933, as part of the National Industrial Recovery Act, the Roosevelt administration had created a program of federal construction projects termed the Public Works Administration (PWA), overseen by Secretary of the Interior Harold S. Ickes and funded by over $3 billion. But with nine million workers still unemployed in 1935, and mounting criticism to get the numbers of unemployed off the "dole" of the FERA, Roosevelt proposed this new public works program to provide more immediate, short-term employment than the long-term capital improvements of the PWA. Initial funding was budgeted at $4.8 billion, and Jimmy Byrnes was put in charge of the bill in the Senate, for the administration reasoned that only he could persuade Carter Glass on the Appropriations Committee to approve such a sum. Glass was unhappy with the amount, and introduced a motion in the committee to reduce it by $2 billion, but Jimmy Byrnes was able to defeat Glass' motion by one vote, and Franklin Roosevelt got his $4.8 billion. After a behind-the-scenes struggle between Ickes and Hopkins for control of this new agency, Harry Hopkins in the spring of 1935 was named the new director of the WPA.

Byrnes' participation in the creation of both the PWA and the WPA gave him an opportunity to establish statewide organizations for distributing the patronage of federal jobs. As the state director of the WPA programs in South Carolina, Byrnes obtained the appointment of Colonel Lawrence Pinckney, a loyal Byrnes supporter and a descendant of one of Charleston's first families. In an arrangement that displayed both Byrnes' love of noblesse oblige and his political cunning, Colonel Pinckney agreed to find employment for textile workers whom millowners had discharged as "personally objectionable" (that is, union organizers) on the WPA payrolls. Another member of the state board that recommended PWA projects was Byrnes' close acquaintance Burnet Maybank, the mayor of Charleston and a man whom Byrnes had determined to raise as his political protégé. And finally, to ensure close personal ties between the national administrators and their state agencies, Byrnes succeeded in the spring of 1935 in having the new director-designate of the WPA, Harry Hopkins, and his wife accept an invitation to join him and Burnet Maybank as their guests in late March for the annual azalea festival in Charleston.

There was more on Byrnes' mind than pink and white azaleas. His invitation was an example of his keen sense of political timing, as it coincided with the visit to another part of the state by Senator Huey P. Long of Louisiana. As the presidential election of 1936 approached, Huey Long emerged as the most formidable challenger to Roosevelt's candidacy from the left. Senator Long—the "Louisiana Kingfish"—had called for a radical redistribution of wealth that was anathema to both the New Deal and the Republican party. A moon-faced man with a penchant for clowning and wearing florid suits, Long nevertheless possessed a razor-sharp political mind, and it was likely that had he not held southern support in line for Roosevelt at the 1932 convention, FDR would not have received the nomination. Now, in early spring of 1935, Long was intent on claiming the next presidential nomination for himself. (Roosevelt had privately stated to Rexford Tugwell that he believed Huey Long to be one of the two most dangerous men in the country, second only to Douglas MacArthur on the right.)

In March 1935 Long was touring the southern states gathering support for his "Share the Wealth" program and publicity for his upcoming presidential bid. The week of the azalea festival in Charleston, Long swept into the state capital of Columbia, accompanied by his bodyguards and other members of his retinue, where he casually invited two hundred of his local supporters to join him at his hotel for lunch. The following day Long expected to address a large and enthusiastic crowd in front of the state capitol building. In the meanwhile, the Kingfish was characteristically free with his political judgments. He and Senator Byrnes were "personal friends," Long told the press, but he added, "I would like to see someone in the Senate from South Carolina who would vote differently or see Jimmy made to vote different from what he does."

The following day a personal friend of Long's in the U.S. Senate had prepared some surprises. Byrnes' invitation to Hopkins had given some four hundred public officials in Columbia, who otherwise would have been expected to greet Long, an excuse to travel to Charleston and meet the new WPA director. As a result, there was an embarrassingly small reception for Long at the state capitol—where the junior U.S. senator from South Carolina was, of course, noticeably absent. Byrnes also had paid a private stenographer to make a transcript of Long's remarks and telephone them immediately to Byrnes' office. Outside on the lawn in front of the state capitol, the crowd gathered for Long's speech was smaller than expected. Furthermore, during his introduction, Long was heckled. And someone had organized college students from the state college in downtown Columbia to unfurl huge banners just as Long began to speak, declaring "We Love Our President" and "Too Much Hooey."

Long's speech itself was vintage Kingfish. He denounced the "bloated fortunes" of "that South Carolina baron, Bernard Baruch," and he called for federal limits on private wealth. Addressing the few textile workers and farmers in the crowd, Long spoke in a demotic (and sincere) language Jimmy Byrnes never used: "You poor devils in the textile mills and in the cotton fields produce the wealth, not the Morgans and the Mellons," Long told them. "The Lord has invited us to a barbeque. It's all on the table before us. Shall the Morgans, Rockefellers, Mellons and Baruchs step up and take 90 percent of it?"

But the large banners made it difficult for those friendly to Long in the crowd to see or hear him; and when the students refused his requests to lower their banners, Long had to give up. "Your mothers ought to have taught you better manners," the Kingfish concluded. Meanwhile that same day, the newspapers in Charleston reported "perfect weather" for the events of the azalea festival, which included horse races, golf matches, classical music concerts, and floats with beauty queens, including Miss Gaffney, who was declared Azalea Queen. So while Jimmy Byrnes, Harry

Hopkins, and Burnet Maybank enjoyed the pleasantries at the azalea festival in Charleston, Huey Long was heckled by a sparse crowd in Columbia—at that time, a hot, flat, small city—and a stenographer paid by Byrnes took down the Kingfish's words in case of an embarrassing misstatement. The Kingfish's visit, of course, came to nothing, and Long picked up little support in South Carolina,

Jimmy Byrnes continued his control of political events and timing throughout the remainder of the Seventy-fourth Congress, as he prepared for reelection in 1936. Byrnes knew when it was necessary politically to break with the Roosevelt administration, and despite his earlier advocacy of domestic economy, Byrnes joined with Pat Harrison in overriding a presidential veto and in voting for payment of the veterans' bonus in the election year of 1936. Byrnes was also able through an adroit sequence of maneuvers and amendments to block Secretary of Agriculture Henry Wallace from reducing the twelve cents per pound subsidy paid to cotton farmers under the AAA. And in a carefully publicized congressional trip to eastern Pacific nations late in 1935, Byrnes lobbied the Philippine government to increase its import of southern-made textiles and to decrease purchases from the now troublingly competitive Japanese textile industry. By early spring of 1936 Byrnes knew he was in a strong position for reelection, although he was troubled by the possibility that racial demagoguery would again, as in 1924 and 1930, determine the character of his Senate campaign. And, of course, to mention race within South Carolina inevitably brought up a discussion of Coleman Livingston Blease.

"Signs point to my old friend Cole Blease entering the race," Byrnes wrote to Bernard Baruch the first week of June 1936. "This week he is making speeches declaring that the real issue in the campaign is whether we believe in social equality and from that I think that I will have to hear a lot of discussion this summer about Mrs. Roosevelt visiting Howard University and entertaining some persons of color at the White House." But Blease, having been beaten once by Byrnes, decided not to run for the Senate in 1936. By the middle of June only two minor candidates had declared against Byrnes for the Democratic nomination. Under the old rules of Tillman's palmetto stump, Byrnes was still obligated to tour the state giving speeches defending his New Deal record, but so confident was he of his renomination that he turned down an offer of financial support from Baruch, and he broke off his tour of the state to travel to Philadelphia a week after the primary began to attend meetings of the national platform committee of the Democratic party and prepare for the national convention there.

Byrnes went to Philadelphia confident not only of his renomination but also of Franklin Roosevelt's. The assassination of Huey Long as a result of a private quarrel in Baton Rouge had eliminated the only other major contender for the presidential nomination, and with the ticket of Roosevelt-Garner virtually assured, Byrnes anticipated running a state race based solely on economic issues. But, "unfortunate though it may be, our consideration of every question, must include the consideration of this race question"—the very words Byrnes himself had written to the newspaper editor William Watts Ball in Charleston in 1920 proved to be just as prophetic in 1936 as in 1924 or 1930. Despite the desire of Jimmy Byrnes to consider the issue of white supremacy in his state to be settled and to campaign solely on his economic record, he once again would be forced to run for the Senate in an election during which his loyalty to the state's system of white supremacy was an issue. Byrnes' attempt to sidestep these charges of disloyalty to the whites-only political system would be the last major crisis of his first senatorial term—and his most successful achievement as a political fixer. This time the dangers of racial demagoguery were raised not by his "old friend" Cole Blease but by the apparently malevolent antics in Philadelphia of the man whom Byrnes previously had dismissed as irrelevant to his political ambitions—South Carolina's senior U.S. senator, E. D. "Cotton Ed" Smith.

Senator E. D. Smith was seventy-two years old and feeling out of sorts in the summer of 1936. ("His name is Ellison Durant and he sure do," was Pat Harrison's oft-repeated jest.) A large, walrus-like man whose treble chins appeared to have been sculpted with runcible spoons, Smith had first come to the Senate in 1909, and he had been a faithful if uninspired supporter of Democratic Progressive Era legislation. Raised to the U.S. Senate by the Tillmanite organization, Cotton Ed Smith took the agrarian habit of claiming a nickname, and he never deviated from Tillman's twin precepts of agrarianism and white supremacy. "Cotton is king and white is supreme" was Cotton Ed Smith's constant campaign slogan, and it served him well enough in South Carolina to have provided him with reelection five times to the Senate by 1936.

In his attitudes toward black citizens, Smith was no worse, if no better, than many other white southerners in public life in the twentieth century who had been born before the Civil War. Like Carter Glass of Virginia, for example, Smith had made it clear throughout his senatorial career that he would "not be a party to the recognition of the 14th and 15th amendments." But unlike such southern populists as Tillman and Huey Long, E. D. Smith did not have the penetration of intellect to name and to seize control of the economic forces reshaping politics in his lifetime. The senator's repeated and simplistic advocacy of agrarian protectionism had become anachronistic in the controlled market economy and supported prices planned by Rexford Tugwell and Henry Wallace at the Department of Agriculture. "Senator Smith was getting quite old," a New Deal agriculture official later recalled about the early formation of the AAA and other agricultural programs. "He had reached the state that he didn't fully comprehend what we were trying to do." Seniority and the obituary column had made E. D. Smith chairman of the Agricultural Committee in 1933, a position he pointedly advertised to the administration by frequently wearing a cotton blossom in his coat lapel and fulsomely describing the happy lives of Negro sharecroppers on his cotton plantation in South Carolina. But the Roosevelt administration preferred to work around Smith and deal with the much more loyal Senator John Bankhead of Alabama as the New Deal's chosen "cotton senator."

Roosevelt certainly knew, perhaps from talking with Jimmy Byrnes, that Senator Smith, unlike Carter Glass, never had been known for his perspicacity. (Among Jimmy Byrnes' political intimates, E. D. Smith was referred to, on at least one occasion, as Cotton Head Smith.) Smith had further alienated himself from Roosevelt by embarrassingly delaying the nomination in 1934 of Rexford Tugwell as undersecretary of agriculture. The elderly, tobacco-chewing Smith saw in Tugwell, the macroeconomist and university professor, everything that the senator distrusted in the bureaucrats of the New Deal (Smith claimed, probably correctly, that Rexford Tugwell "would not know a cotton stalk from a jimson weed"), and it had taken all the influence of the president's friends, including Jimmy Byrnes, to force the Tugwell nomination out of the Agriculture Committee. Roosevelt had a long memory for such slights, and Smith's opportunities for major patronage effectively ended with that episode. Objecting more to Smith's obstructionism than to his pre–Civil War racism, Roosevelt attempted to "purge" Smith from the Democratic party in 1938. But the president's attempts were to be unsuccessful, largely because of the events of the 1936 convention in Philadelphia. There, in circumstances both tragic for racial equality and comic for Smith's personal dignity, E. D. Smith came face to face in the Democratic party with emancipated Negroes.

There is always a certain grim fun in recounting the indignities heaped upon any old curmudgeon, and Senator E. D. Smith's case is no exception. Smith arrived at the convention in Philadelphia a day late, having been delayed by attending the funeral of a colleague, and he missed the important opening-day speeches by James Farley and Joseph Robinson. Already irritated that he had not been assigned to any of the convention's governing committees, Smith was astonished when he was denied admission at the door of Philadelphia's Municipal Auditorium. Through an apparently unintentional mix-up in the South Carolina delegation, Smith's badge and floor pass had been given to an alternate delegate, and the convention's usher did not recognize the face of South Carolina's senior senator. There also did not seem to be a room reserved for the senator at the hotel of the South Carolina delegation. "I have represented my state in the Senate for twenty seven years," Smith exploded, "and when I come to the convention of my party I find no badge, no reservations, no nothing." Smith was mollified when Governor Olin Johnson of South Carolina finally was able to produce a badge for him, and the senator's hotel room was confirmed in time for Smith to attend the afternoon opening of the second day of the convention.

Just as Smith arrived on the floor that afternoon, however, the invocation was given by the Reverend Marshall Shepard of Philadelphia. The Reverend Shepard was a Negro, and this was an unprecedented appearance for a member of his race before a Democratic National Convention.

"By God, he's as black as melted midnight," Smith loudly exclaimed, and without waiting for the prayer to end, he immediately left his seat and walked toward the exit. Incredibly, before E. D. Smith reached the convention hall's doors, the band inside the municipal building began playing the song it had been instructed was to follow the Reverend Shepard's prayer. The song was "Dixie." The familiar tune began as Smith walked, and his progress toward the doors must have been impeded by the crowds of stamping, whistling, singing, and clapping delegates from the southern states around him, happily oblivious of Smith's struggles to reach the exit. By this time the condition of Smith's mind was approximately between thrombosis and apotheosis.

In fact, much of Cotton Ed Smith's indignation over events at the convention had probably been well calculated by the southern senator, just as the choice of the Reverend Shepard and the immediately subsequent playing of "Dixie" probably had been calculated in advance by a well-known gentleman farmer from Hyde Park, New York. Printed programs distributed throughout the Democratic convention in advance of the June 24 afternoon session clearly listed the opening prayer by Reverend Shepard of the prominent black church Mount Olivet Baptist Tabernacle in Philadelphia; these convention programs were readily available to E. D. Smith before his entry into the auditorium. And although he later described the delegates gathered in the municipal auditorium as a racial checkerboard —"a spot of white here, and a spot of black there"—the number of black delegates at the Democratic convention of 1936 was in fact minuscule.

Back in Washington, a laughing Franklin Roosevelt had told reporters at a press conference during the opening days of the convention that he had been "much too busy" to pay attention to the events at Philadelphia. As an indication that FDR had the southern faction under control, Roosevelt and Speaker of the House William Bankhead of Alabama had agreed that the Democratic party could be best served by Speaker Bankhead's not traveling to Philadelphia. Instead, this most important of southern congressmen had decided, Bankhead told reporters after his meeting with FDR, to return to his Alabama farm to milk his cows and "smell the clover." Subsequent historians have assumed that with this behind-the-scenes maneuvering "Roosevelt in 1936 chose a Negro minister to offer the convention invocation." There is some verifiable truth to this assertion. Before ministering at Mount Olivet, the Reverend Shepard had been a recorder of deeds in Washington, D.C., having been appointed to that position by Roosevelt. However, Roosevelt appears to have included no evidence of his personal decision to have the Reverend Shepard speak at Philadelphia, either in his own papers or in those of the Democratic

National Committee deposited at the Hyde Park presidential library.

Back in Philadelphia, Jimmy Byrnes and a majority of the South Carolina delegation did not join Smith in his walkout. (Burnet Maybank went with him at least as far as the door.) But reporters for national newspapers, eager for a salable story at a Democratic convention whose outcome was foregone, interviewed Smith at his hotel room that Wednesday afternoon. The senator told his press audience that he considered the Democratic party's appeals to Negro votes and its earlier abolition of the two-thirds rule at the 1936 convention to be "insults" to the South. Smith declared his intention to walk out of the convention again any time a black American speaker was at the podium. Smith's actions were certainly an insult to the Reverend Marshall Shepard, and although there is no question that the senator saw the inclusion of Negro participants in the Democratic party as tragic for his region, his actions were more accurately tragic for the chances of harmonious racial relations in the South. But it is unlikely that Cotton Ed Smith was aware of Karl Marx's observation that historical events that began as tragedy are repeated as farce, as evinced by the next day's events at the convention. On that following Thursday, Smith returned to the convention hall and—sure enough—arrived just as the black congressman Arthur Mitchell was addressing the convention. This time when Smith walked out, Burnet Maybank did not join him. There arose the ludicrous possibility of Smith's becoming a type of wandering outcast at the Democratic convention, forever damned to walking back and forth from his Philadelphia hotel room and seeing whenever he opened a convention hall door a free and proud black face. Smith himself put an end to this intriguing possibility by permanently quitting the convention. Newspapers across the country carried a Wirephoto of the exasperated senior senator from South Carolina tearing up his convention passes and throwing the pieces of paper high into the air. Smith was "mad as hell," he announced to the press. He was going back home to South Carolina and talk to the people.

Smith received something of a hero's welcome on his return to South Carolina. Although some newspapers there deplored his actions in Philadelphia, the *Charleston News and Courier*, the state's largest newspaper, applauded his "fearlessness" in walking out. At stump speeches beginning that summer of 1936 and extending throughout his campaign in 1938, E. D. Smith told and embellished his "Philadelphia Story." turning the respected Reverend Marshall Shepard into a nursery-room figure of Negrophobia. "Ed's masterpiece was The Philadelphia Story," the journalist Harry Ashmore later recalled. "So far as I know this was never set down verbatim at the time and the following rendition is based on my memory, and that of Turner Catledge, the managing editor of *The New York Times*, who heard it as a reporter and has always regarded it as a gem never surpassed even in his native Mississippi."

According to these two journalists, Smith's Philadelphia story went something like the following:

I told them about walking up to that great convention hall, and being stopped there at the outer door—outer door, mind you—by a stranger who demanded to see my credentials. "Young man," I said, "if we have reached a time when the senior senator from South Carolina has to have credentials to get into a Democratic convention, I don't want in." . . .

But when I came out on the floor of that great hall, bless God, it looked like a checkerboard—a spot of white here, and a spot of black there. But I kept going, down that long aisle, and finally I found the great standard of South Carolina—and, praise God, it was in a spot of white!

I had no sooner than taken my seat when a newspaperman came down the aisle and squatted down by me and said, "Senator, did you know a nigger is going to come out up yonder in a minute and offer the invocation?" I told him, I said, "Now don't be joking me, I'm upset enough the way it is." But then, bless God, out on that platform walked a slew-footed, blue-gummed, kinky-headed Senegambian!

And he started praying and I started walking. And as I pushed through those great doors, and walked across that vast rotunda, it seemed to me that old John Calhoun leaned down from his mansion in the sky and whispered in my ear, "You did right, Ed. . . ."

In his numerous and popular retellings of his story, Smith was touching, knowingly or not, upon one of the most potent myths in the minds of white southerners at that time. The same year that Smith walked out of the convention hall in Philadelphia, the North Carolina novelist Thomas Wolfe was composing his autobiographical novel *The Web and the Rock*, in which the grown protagonist, himself a writer in New York City, remembers a story heard throughout white barbershops and courthouses in the South of his boyhood. The story, Wolfe wrote, was sometimes about the adventures of "ole Jim" or "ole Bob," but never varied in its outline:

Some local hero—some village champion of the rights of white men and the maintenance of white supremacy—told the gory adventures of his one and only, his first and last, all-sufficient journey into the benighted and corrupted domains of the North.

The scene, Wolfe wrote, was in a restaurant of a northern city:

The plumed knight from below the Mason-Dixon line had gone in to get something to eat and had taken his seat at a table. He had progressed no further than his soup when, looking up, he found to his horror and indignation that "a big buck nigger" had come in and taken a seat opposite him and *at his own table*.

Wolfe's narrator then continues the story in the voice of the local raconteurs of his youth.

Well, ole Jim says he took one look at him and says, "You black son-of-a-bitch, what do you mean sitting at my table?" Well, the nigger begins to talk back to him, telling him he was in the North now, where a nigger was just as good as anyone. And ole Jim says, "You black bastard, you, you may be as good as a Yankee, but you're talking to a white man now!"—and with that, he says, he ups with a ketchup bottle and he just busts it wide open over that nigger's head. Jim says he reckoned he killed him, says he didn't wait to see, he just left him laying there and grabbed his hat and walked out. He says he caught the first train going South and he's never been North again since, and that he doesn't care if he never sees the God-damned place again.

"This story was usually greeted with roars of appreciation and admiring laughter," Wolfe wrote, "the sounds of thighs smitten with enthusiastic palms, gleeful exclamations of 'Odam! I'd 'a' given anything to've seen! Whew-w! I can just see ole Jim now as he lets him have it!" The story, Wolfe's narrator recalls, "in its various forms and with many modern innovations, was still current among returned wanderers from the Southland. . . ."

Cotton Ed Smith's walking out of the Philadelphia Municipal Auditorium in 1936 was simply another modern innovation of Thomas Wolfe's archetypal northern diner and lethal ketchup bottle. Smith himself apparently was made aware he was giving the people of South Carolina the fictive stuff they wanted, as he later explained to national journalists, by his constituency's refusal to hear any of his self-styled "highbrow" speeches in place of his recital of the "Philadelphia Story." (This title later was given to Smith's story by journalists in derisive reference to the Katharine Hepburn–Cary Grant romantic motion picture of the same name.) "It has been my custom to start out with the Magna Charta and trace the long history of the struggle for human rights," Smith told Ashmore and Catledge. "But the other night, up yonder in Pickens County [the county site of Clemson University, founded by Pitchfork Ben Tillman], I had started out with the fields of Runnymede and proceeded to the point where I had the boys in gray halfway up the hill at Gettysburg, when an old man in the front row spit out his tobacco cud and said, 'Hell, Ed, tell us about Phillydelphy!' "

Jimmy Byrnes, back in Philadelphia, was not amused. Smith's antics in that city and in South Carolina during the remaining days of the convention were animated by more than just the vanity of an old man who wanted public attention. The feelings of Cotton Ed Smith as he watched the younger Jimmy Byrnes be singled out for administrative preference while Smith himself was ignored can well be imagined; by walking out, Smith showed that, despite Jimmy Byrnes' comparative youth and talent, the state's senior senator still knew a few political tricks. And nothing is so malicious to talented youth as the tricks played in the name of vanity by an old man who thinks he has been neglected. By walking out, Smith placed those who did not join him in the seeming position of favoring social equality between the races, a position of sure death in the white-only politics of South Carolina.

"Where were Senator Byrnes and Governor Johnson, the other two most outstanding members of the South Carolina delegation?" asked the *Edgefield Advertiser* in Byrnes' old Second District. "Had the late Benjamin Ryan Tillman been United States senator or governor of the old Palmetto State, he would have stood shoulder-to-shoulder with Senator Smith with pitchfork drawn for a determined fight." Nor were these sentiments confined to the fierce counties of South Carolina's upstate. "The memory of Tillman and his ways are being spat upon," declared the *Charleston News and Courier.*

Byrnes did not immediately return to South Carolina after the adjournment in Philadelphia, but instead went to Washington, where he conferred at the White House with Roosevelt about national campaign strategy. The first week after the convention, however, a letter written by Frank Lever in South Carolina caught up with the senator. Lever warned Byrnes that the walkout as a campaign issue in the state's primary was not going away and that Smith was meeting with Byrnes' opponents to encourage them in its use. "Your opponents will undertake to use this Negro issue," Lever warned, "aiming it presumably against the president, but in fact against you as his representative, for all that it is worth."

In response, Byrnes that same first week after the convention succeeded in "planting" a story in the *New York Times* in which Byrnes, on seeing Carter Glass back in Washington after the convention supposedly "teased" the Virginian about having joined Cotton Ed Smith in the walkout. "I did nothing of the kind," the *Times* reported Glass as telling Jimmy Byrnes. "God knows I stand in need of prayer," Glass was quoted as saying. "I wish every Negro in the country would pray for me." The implication of the story, which Byrnes knew would be picked up by the South Carolina newspapers, was obvious: if the respected Carter Glass, whose views on race were no less reactionary than those of E. D. Smith, found the presence of a black minister unobjectionable, then the issue of Byrnes' not having joined the walkout was inconsequential.

South Carolina is not Virginia, however, and Carter Glass' eighteenth-century urbanities of manner would not satisfy Cotton Ed Smith's rough-looking farmer with his tobacco cud. Byrnes' opponents accused him of "hiding out" in Washington, afraid to face the people of South Carolina after his inaction in Philadelphia. Byrnes was forced to cut short his stay in Washington and return to South Carolina in July 1936 in order to defend himself in the primary. His position among the state's voters was compromised even further that summer by the rumor, which would have been considered unnoteworthy in most states outside the Deep South, that Senator Jimmy Byrnes had written a letter of recommendation requested by a black resident of his state seeking a federal job.

The rumor had persisted since the previous year, and Byrnes frankly admitted that it might be correct. The letter, a copy of which was supposedly stolen from Byrnes' correspondence files by a disgruntled clerk, had never surfaced during the 1936 primary, and Byrnes said that he had no memory of signing his name to it; but he also pointed out that his office was by mid-1935 receiving an average of three hundred letters a day requesting help in obtaining government jobs. Byrnes stated that unless the applicant was personally known to him, he had instructed his secretary, Cassandra Connor, to supply a form letter with his signature to the employing federal agency stating that if the South Carolina applicant had the necessary qualifications, the senator's office asked that the applicant from his state be given employment. "Under the circumstances," Byrnes wrote to a supporter who had questioned him about the supposed recommendation, "it is entirely possible that if a letter was received in my office from some person in South Carolina asking for a recommendation, that such a letter as you have indicated was written and my secretary would never know whether the writer was white, black, or blue." Byrnes then closed his letter with a paragraph that was extraordinary for a politician in South Carolina in the 1930s: "It would not bother me if this fellow has a letter of that character," he wrote, adding that he would "think more of a Negro hunting honest work" than of a clerk stealing from his office files.

But—"unfortunate as it may be, our consideration of every question must include the consideration of the race question." Byrnes' words in 1920 continued prophetically to vex him in the summer of 1936. The stronger of his two opponents in the senatorial primary, Thomas P. Stoney, a former mayor of Charleston, circulated photographs of the Reverend Shepard at stump speeches throughout the Palmetto State, and he fiercely denounced Byrnes for having promoted racial equality by not joining Smith in his walkout. E. D. Smith himself, although not up for reelection that year, nevertheless was glad to entertain visitors to his plantation home with his version of the "Philadelphia Story." And in July when Byrnes returned to South Carolina to rejoin the primary speaking tour, postcards were mailed throughout the state claiming, "A vote for Roosevelt and Byrnes will mean the day is coming closer when dirty, evil-smelling Negroes will be going to church with you, your sister, your wife, or your mother. Busses, trains, hotels, picture shows, bathing beaches will all see Negroes rubbing shoulders with you."

Back in Philadelphia, the Reverend Shepard had shown what could only be described as a Christian forbearance by publicly stating, "I feel sympathy and pray for Senator Smith, and pray to God that he may be emancipated from his prejudices." The Reverend Shepard then added, with slightly less forgiveness of tone, that if Smith was "looking for a party without Negroes, it looks like he will have to form his own party there in South Carolina." Smith heatedly responded, "I don't have to form my own party. The party already exists. It was born in the Red Shirt days of the Reconstruction period, when the gentlemen of South Carolina donned red shirts to rid our state of carpet baggers, scalawags, and Negroes."

Byrnes' personal appeal to his state's electorate that he had carefully constructed since 1930—an appeal in which white supremacy was silently ignored as a political given in order that economic questions might be discussed—was in danger of falling apart in July and August 1936. National newspapers and *Time* magazine sent correspondents down to South Carolina to follow Byrnes and Stoney on the palmetto stump, seeing this primary contest as an early indication of whether the South would leave the Democratic party over the issue of racial equality in the presidential election that fall. As Byrnes was repeatedly attacked by Stoney for his inaction in Philadelphia, a good friend and scholar, Frank Lever, assembled for Byrnes' use on the stump a compilation of historical quotes from past South Carolina leaders legitimizing a limited participation by Negroes in the Democratic party. "General Wade Hampton's last words were, 'God bless my people, both white and black,' " Lever wrote to Byrnes. Lever added scornfully; "The dying chieftain could ask God's blessing on the Negro, but no Negro could pray for E. D. Smith."

Byrnes' situation was distressingly similar to that of his primary contests in 1924 and 1930, when he had attempted to campaign on economic issues against an opponent running on racial supremacy. And Byrnes could not have failed to remember that General Wade Hampton, for all the reverence with which he was remembered by both black and white South Carolinians, and despite all the economic good he had brought to his state, was removed from his U.S. Senate office after a political campaign masterminded by one of South Carolina's most racist politicians, Benjamin Ryan Tillman. Jimmy Byrnes had bet his career on a combination of racial demagoguery and economic liberalism in 1924, and he had lost not because of the inaccuracies of his economic policies but because he had allowed his opponent Coley Blease to outdemagogue him. Might not 1936 be the year to bet on race again, when the racial issue through no fault of his own was so much more inflamed, and as a U.S. senator both he and the economic reformers in the Democratic party had so much more to lose?

To his credit, Byrnes refused to bet on race. He refused to get into an "out-niggering" contest with Stoney and instead concentrated on the stump exclusively in listing the economic benefits the New Deal had brought to South Carolina. In one of his finest expressions of his desire for racial tolerance and a comparatively high level of public debate, Byrnes announced in an opening stump speech in July in Charleston, "I shall appeal to your reason and intelligence and not to your prejudice." Byrnes then told his Charleston audience, "In your heart and mine there are certain prejudices. It is the duty of a good man to control and subdue these prejudices. I have no respect for the man who, for political gain, will seek to arouse the prejudices of the people. I believe the time has come . . . when a man can appeal to the best that is in us instead of the worst."

Byrnes practiced what he preached on the stump. He recounted for the farmers in the crowd the benefits of the cotton subsidy under the AAA; he pointed out the potential employment gains to the state through the PWA and the WPA; and he publicized to the state's textile workers his passage of the anti-strikebreakers bill and the endorsement of his candidacy by the national AFL. Any benefits to the state's Negroes from the New Deal programs, Byrnes claimed, simply were benefits to them that had "spilled over" as a result of increased prosperity for the state's population as a whole, and not the result of the Roosevelt administration's specifically favoring Negroes. And Byrnes took advantage of his prerogative as the incumbent Democrat on the stump in order to leave the speaking site as soon as he was finished, not staying to answer Stoney's charges about Philadelphia and presenting each time what was described as a "jeering rump" to his opponents.

In the nine weeks and forty-six campaign stops of the 1936 senatorial primary, these tactics began to have an effect. Byrnes, who may have been in serious electoral trouble in June, was by late July acknowledged to be far ahead of his two opponents. In mid-August, a week before the primary-election day, Carter Glass wrote down to Byrnes, "I am delighted to know that you are confident (to use the bad language you so often employ) of 'beating hell' out of your opponents." Jimmy Byrnes did indeed. When the polls closed on August 25, Senator Byrnes was the recipient of the largest majority in the history of his state's Democratic primaries. Byrnes won 87 percent of the vote and carried all his state's precincts but one. He received approximately ten votes for each one cast for Stoney. His overwhelming victory did not mean that race was no longer a factor in South Carolina's elections, as later campaigns, including E. D. Smith's, would indicate. But Byrnes did give proof that a Democratic candidate in the Deep South could successfully escape race-baiting and concentrate on a discussion of economic issues—if that candidate, like Byrnes, had established a public record as "a member of the democracy" of his region's whites-only party.

No one could seriously question Jimmy Byrnes' commitment to racial segregation and white political supremacy in 1936. But what was remarkable about such a cautious man as Jimmy Byrnes was that he was willing to take a risk in 1936 and "let the heathen rage," in one of his favorite phrases, offering himself to the state's voters as a spokesman for national economic issues while other candidates demagogued in favor of his region's peculiar institutions. Elevating the public debate in South Carolina above race-baiting was Jimmy Byrnes' most successful political fix in his first senatorial term. And as with any political fix, it was more expedient than just; in this case, it presumed a permanent disenfranchisement of his state's black citizens. But at least with Jimmy Byrnes in office, the state's black citizens would receive some economic benefits that would "spill over," and the state's most powerful senator was personally benign toward ambitious blacks in a segregated society, even to the point of writing them letters of recommendation. By these qualified standards of compassion, Byrnes was certainly an improvement over previous South Carolina senators such as Pitchfork Ben Tillman or Coley Blease; and he was also an improvement in 1936 over present U.S. southern senators, including Theodore "The Man" Bilbo from Mississippi and, of course, E. D. Smith of South Carolina.

In letting the heathen rage, Byrnes also had gained a reputation as a "national" southerner and a possible successor to Roosevelt after the re-elected FDR finished his second presidential term in 1941. Among the early backers of Byrnes' candidacy was the financier Joseph Kennedy, Sr. In the fall of 1936, after taking his usual autumn vacation on Sullivan's Island, Byrnes obliged his friend Kennedy by traveling up to Cambridge, Massachusetts, and addressing a Democratic club at Harvard University, presided over by Kennedy's oldest son, Joseph, Jr. In a "Dear Jim" letter, the elder Kennedy thanked the senator for "his going up to Harvard for young Joe. I realize that you had to stay over and that it was a nuisance for you, but it meant so much to him that I really was anxious to get you to go up."

Then, allowing his thoughts to pass to the executive office of more than a Harvard club, the elder Kennedy reviewed the coming political prospects for his children: "I expect my youngest—and by the way, he is four and I have another ten—will be presiding when Senator James F. Byrnes is Democratic candidate for president, if you want to wait that long."

It was a possibility. By the end of his first senatorial term, Byrnes was experienced in managing not only the successful passage of New Deal legislation through the Senate but also the social and racial consequences of that legislation. By an accurate accounting of his age, Byrnes would be no older than Franklin Roosevelt, an energetic fifty-eight, by the time of the Democratic convention of 1940. Even if, despite Joseph Kennedy's advice, Byrnes chose to wait longer, his reelection victory to the Senate gave him an enviable independence from the more liberal policies of the New Deal and enabled him to build alliances with conservative Democrats from the South and West without fearing retribution from the White House. After all, Jimmy Byrnes would not have to run for renomination to the Senate until the late summer of 1942. By that time Franklin Roosevelt would certainly have been out of the White House for more than a year.

7

A Vast Empire
Nearby

Harold LeClair Ickes never liked
Jimmy Byrnes. Partly this reaction was due to the insouciance that the
South Carolina senator wore like a high-tilted hat in his dealings with
Roosevelt's secretary of the interior. "Senator Byrnes was in my office this
afternoon," Secretary Ickes wrote in his diary in late December 1935. "He
has a very pleasant way of coming in at whatever time happens to suit him
and announcing [to Ickes' assistant] that he is going to stay until he sees
me. . . . Mad as it makes me, I haven't much recourse except to see him."
Ickes' attitude was also partly founded on the secretary's suspicions of
Jimmy Byrnes' commitment to the liberal policies of the second administration of the New Deal, despite Byrnes' earlier loyalty in Congress.
"Byrnes went along simply because he was up for re-election last year,"
Ickes confided in his diary in early 1937. "Now, with a term extending
beyond that of the president, he has jumped the traces and gone conservative." Temperamentally as well as politically, Byrnes and Ickes also had
been always at opposite poles. Jimmy Byrnes was a gregarious and usually
a generous-spirited man, inclined if possible to accommodate his beliefs
to the opinions of others. Harold L. Ickes, by contrast, was a powerfully

reserved individual of inflexible principles, whose apparent personal philosophy was that if the shoe pinches, wear it.

But the longest-lasting source of discord between these two men was the proposed construction of two giant hydroelectric dams in Byrnes' home state of South Carolina to be known as the Santee-Cooper project. The securing of what Jimmy Byrnes considered South Carolina's "fair share" of PWA funds from Ickes' office to guarantee the building of this project occupied a major portion of Byrnes' time throughout the 1930s—and, grudgingly, of Harold Ickes' time as well. "Of course, it was Santee-Cooper again," Ickes wrote with exasperation in his diary after one of Byrnes' unscheduled visits to Interior. Byrnes may have considered Ickes' time and the secretary's approval of PWA funds for Santee-Cooper to be due to the senator under the normal system of favors and awards in Washington. After all, Jimmy Byrnes had successfully worked to pass the first PWA appropriations for distribution by the Department of the Interior in 1933, and he had obtained additional funding in order for Ickes to extend the program in 1935.

But the Santee-Cooper project was no ordinary project, and Harold Ickes was no ordinary Washington administrator. To his dual role of interior secretary and national administrator of the PWA, Ickes brought a caution toward spending public money and a commitment to the conservation of natural resources that made him an ironic legend among his contemporaries. Concerned almost to the point of obsession that a scandal in his administering the $3.3 billion of PWA funds would discredit the New Deal, Ickes went over the budgets for proposed projects in worrisome detail, refusing to allocate funds unless significant public benefits could be shown by constructing the project. As a result of his exactitude, no major scandal has been determined to have occurred during Ickes' watch at Interior; but also as a result of Ickes' caution, the administration's publicly financed program proceeded so slowly that Democratic critics maintained that it did not fulfill its original purpose of providing employment and and new capital investment in the states' economies. "Honest Harold" and "Harold the Holy" were among the choicer names applied to Harold Ickes, not necessarily in admiration, by Democratic senators and congressmen who felt that Ickes' zeal for virtue was robbing them of once-in-a-lifetime opportunities for patronage. But "the man with the funny name," in Roosevelt's lighthearted description, enjoyed an unusually high and consistent level of political support from the White House. As a result, Secretary Ickes continued throughout the mid-1930s to look with suspicion on proposed PWA projects such as the Santee-Cooper dams in South Carolina as attempts at personal empire building and as ill-conceived engineering disruptions of the environment.

Honest Harold was right. The engineering project that Byrnes untiringly backed from 1935 to 1941 proposed an unprecedented diversion of the flow of one of the nation's longest system of rivers, the 538-mile Santee River, from its natural channel into the flow of a minor river 20 miles away, the Cooper River. The resulting flooding would create the largest man-made lake east of the Appalachian Mountains. The ecology of much of the 15,700 square miles of the drainage area of the Santee would be irrevocably altered, and at least 901 families would be forced to move from their homes as a result of the inundation of one of the most historically rich areas of the United States.

In response, Byrnes promised that perhaps ten thousand men would find jobs at the hydroelectric construction site, that a thriving channel of navigation would be opened from the port of Charleston to the inland capital of Columbia, and that an abundance of cheap, publicly financed electric power would transform the subtropical and underpopulated low-lands around Charleston into what one of the lawyers for the project called "a vast empire nearby." Byrnes persisted in obtaining PWA and other funding for the Santee-Cooper project even after the need for relieving unemployment in his state had ceased to be an acute problem, even after studies concluded that major shipping would never travel between Charleston and Columbia, and that a vast empire would never rise among the black gum trees and cypress stands of the low country. That he succeeded in getting the federal money—including the largest PWA grant for a construction project on the East Coast—and in seeing the Santee-Cooper project finally begin construction in 1939 indicates Byrnes' fierce determination to hold Franklin Roosevelt accountable to a promise made to Byrnes in 1935 to support the project. Once Jimmy Byrnes had concluded that approval of the Santee-Cooper project was justly his due, his pride would not allow him to see the project go unfunded. To satisfy that pride, Jimmy Byrnes successfully fought political battles over the Santee-Cooper project with Harold Ickes, the Army Corps of Engineers, Franklin D. Roosevelt and a member of his family, various environmental groups, and, finally, the U.S. Supreme Court.

In winning each of these fights, Jimmy Byrnes demonstrated that he was the most formidable national politician to have come out of South Carolina since the eighteenth century. A succession of earlier national southern leaders, including George Washington, had interested themselves in improvements on the Santee-Cooper basins; and many members of Charleston's first families, including one signer of the Declaration of Independence, had vainly invested their own money, and attempted to obtain the investments of others, in a scheme in the late eighteenth century to improve navigation on the Santee River, relieve unemployment among the state's slaves, and position Charleston as the prime city of a great empire. All these notables, including the celebrated low-country aristocrats Francis Marion and William Moultrie, had lost money and failed; only Jimmy Byrnes, born into an unfashionable neighborhood in Charleston and op-

River of the Carolinas:
THE SANTEE

erating as a political fixer in the midtwentieth century, succeeded. But if Jimmy Byrnes had intended to demonstrate to both the living and the dead that his pride could not be gainsaid and that a promise made to him, even by a president of the United States, must be kept, that demonstration on the Santee River came at a great public and private cost. For by November 1942, after an expenditure of $62 million, when the last spillways on the dams of the Santee-Cooper system were closed and the vast reservoirs began to fill, many of the homes and cemeteries that were flooded had once belonged to the aristocratic families named above—and a major portion of the low-country culture and aristocracy of which Jimmy Byrnes liked to consider himself an inheritor was forever buried under thousands of cubic feet of water.

Charlestonians long before Jimmy Byrnes had envied the geographic advantages of the Santee River, which flowed into the Atlantic some fifty miles north of the port city. The confluence of the Ashley and Cooper rivers, "flowing together at Charleston to make the Atlantic Ocean," in that proud city's not altogether ironic phrase, had provided the founders of Charleston with one of the finest natural harbors in the world; but although both rivers had been easily navigable to white planters and merchants since the seventeenth century, neither extended more than a few miles into the interior. The Santee, by contrast, represented the majestic climax of one of the Southeast's greatest river systems. Fed by its three great tributaries—the Broad, the Saluda, and the Catawba rivers—the Santee reached like three fingers of a giant hand into the richness of the frontier interior, extending more than five hundred miles back from the coastal marshes of the Atlantic to the mountain fastness of the headwaters of the Broad at Hickory Nut Grove, North Carolina. But this natural highway of the Santee emptied not into a usable harbor such as at Charleston but into treacherously shifting sandbars and unnavigable marshes. Hence, during the late eighteenth century, as the cultivation of cotton—and therefore the population and the wealth of the state—moved from the Carolina coast into the interior of the upstate, Charlestonians saw their port city as increasingly likely to be cut off as the major transporter of goods from the interior. Transportation probably would develop along the few southern rivers that run north–south, or along the new state turnpikes.

But in 1786 a group of prominent merchants and planters around Charleston thought they saw a way out, and also a chance to realize their personal fortunes. Noting that at one point the Cooper and the Santee rivers flow within only twenty miles of each other, the group obtained a state charter for the Santee Canal Company, issuing stock for $8,000 a share and authorized to construct a canal and charge tolls for passage of boats between the Cooper and the Santee rivers. Upon the stock company's completion of such a canal, the way would thus be open for Charleston to control by navigation the produce of the entire Carolinas, as no inland journey in the eighteenth century could ever hope to compete in speed with shipping by river down the Santee and through the proposed canal. The tolls, of course, could be adjusted upward as the canal company achieved a monopoly of trade, and the original stock would be reissued at immense profit to the original investors. Digging such a canal also would provide a welcome source of employment for the slaves on the numerous plantations along the Santee River. The termination of the Revolutionary War had brought an end to the protected market with Great Britain for the rice and indigo raised on these South Carolina plantations, and in those depressed times the large slaveowners along the Santee would be glad to rent out their slaves in exchange for cash from the canal company. The idea seemed plausible; and on the list of original subscribers to the stock company were many luminaries of late-eighteenth-century Charlestonian society, including the state's governor, William Moultrie. Also subscribing for stock were Edward Rutledge, a signer of the Declaration of Independence, and General Francis Marion, the famed "Swamp Fox" of Revolutionary War victories.

Moultrie wrote to General George Washington, not yet president, in the spring of 1786 asking for his assistance in getting the project under way. "I should be very happy if I could render any services to the company which are engaged in the laudable and important design of opening a cut between the rivers Cooper and Santee," Washington wrote back to Moultrie from his home at Mount Vernon, Virginia. General Washington promised to ask his "friend, the Marquis de Lafayette," which of the engineers in Europe was best suited to complete the South Carolina project. The man ultimately chosen to construct the project—Colonel John Christian Senf, an engineer who had served with both the British and the American armies during the Revolutionary War—probably was the best-qualified mechanical superintendent to attempt the canal. But in a character flaw that prefigured the twentieth-century creators of the Santee-Cooper project, Senf was remembered for years afterward by his eighteenth-century contemporaries in South Carolina as a man easily angered and "governed by an inordinate vanity, which would not brook the interference of a rival."

Such was Senf's vanity that he disregarded the previous surveys for the proposed canal, which had been planned to follow the numerous small creeks connecting the two rivers. Instead, he chose for his route a comparatively high, dry ridge at one of the farthest distances between the Santee and the Cooper rivers. (This route would later be along the site of major construction of the Santee-Cooper dams in the twentieth century.) In part, Senf's insistence on a new direction for the canal was the result of his not wanting to share the glory of the canal's ultimate completion with any of the earlier surveyors; and in part it was the result of company politics. Some of the directors of the Santee Canal Company did not want the canal crossing their plantation property, as they thought its construction a probable distraction (and possible escape route) for their slaves working in the fields. Other members of the company insisted that the route be altered so as to pass through their property, envisioning great cities developing along its banks and the value of their lands skyrocketing. One plantation owner went so far as to have surveyed the site of such a city on his property, which he intended to name for himself, and had its future streets carefully drawn and crosshatched in his plat book of imaginary riches.

The route chosen by Senf was not only dry; it also ran almost completely through virgin forests. Clearing a path through palmetto thickets, felling the trunks and extirpating the roots of great oaks, tulip poplars, and other trees, and hauling in all the needed tools and supplies overland added months and thousands of dollars to the completion of the construction project. Although nearby in air miles, the builders were isolated from the plantations on the Santee River as a source of supplies other than slaves, because that river had no harbor at its mouth. Consequently, supplies were brought in from Charleston, and the difficulty in reaching the eighteenth-century construction site can be inferred from the names given by area residents to the surrounding countryside, which between the Santee and Cooper rivers was almost completely swamps: Four Stump Swamp, Hell Hole Swamp, Tearcoat Swamp. This was the same region where Francis Marion and the few irregulars under his command had waged a savage guerrilla war against the British troops occupying Charleston, who on venturing from their city garrisons had found this river delta to be a green, lethal wilderness.

It was just as lethal a wilderness for Senf's workmen. The great killer was malarial fever, which continued to rage in the summer months along the low country until well into the twentieth century. During Senf's tenure, from the beginning of construction in 1793 to the completion of the canal in 1801, twenty-four white tradesmen and professionals died of fever at the canal site, including journeyman carpenters, brick masons, overseers of slaves, and two physicians and their assistants. No one apparently kept a record of the slaves who also died of malarial fever while working on the canal. A twentieth-century historian of the Erie Canal, begun a generation after the completion of the Santee Canal, has noted this omission: "Much has been written about the Irish 'bogtrotters' who built the Erie Canal—and deservedly so. But the conditions under which they toiled— muck up to their waists, hordes of mosquitos, malaria, poor food, the ground or a slab of wood for a bed—were no worse than what confronted the Negro builders of our southern canals, but no one has mentioned the hardships of these slaves." In regard to either the white laborers or the slaves at the Santee Canal site, Colonel Senf discovered what Harry Hopkins and Jimmy Byrnes discovered a century and a half later while trying to deal with a high labor turnover at the Santee-Cooper site: it was practically impossible for men to work in these South Carolina swamps during the summer, while the malaria raged and the temperatures soared.

There was also an unanticipated turnover rate among the forced labor of slaves working on the Santee Canal as a result of the increased cultivation of cotton throughout South Carolina after the introduction of the cotton gin in 1797. The slave masters realized that they could make more money by removing their black laborers from risky construction work and putting them to work in cotton fields. As occurred more than a century and a half later on the construction of the Santee-Cooper dams, these delays in construction because of the lack of skilled workmen and the large turnover among the unskilled workers greatly inflated the original cost of the Santee Canal. The estimated cost of construction by the investors in the company had been £55,000 sterling; by the time the canal was finished, the actual cost was closer to £220,000. In nineteenth-century dollars, the twenty-two miles of the Santee Canal were costing about $40,000 a mile.

But still John Christian Senf pushed on. The same "inordinate vanity" that made him so objectionable to his neighbors on the Santee plantations also made it impossible for him easily to admit defeat, even when confronted by malarial fevers and a seemingly illimitable wilderness. Senf took the place of his dead overseers, and in addition to his administrative duties he personally directed the work gangs of slaves, numbering eight hundred and sometimes one thousand black men and women yearly working on the canal. And, gradually, at great cost in money and human lives, the Santee Canal advanced the twenty-two miles toward its completion. When Senf finally completed the last mile, in 1801, he had achieved the greatest engineering feat yet attempted in the United States. The canal was indeed worthy of Senf's vanity: it was thirty-five feet in width, lined with excellently joined masonry, and carrying water to a depth of five and a half feet. The canal additionally contained ten locks to raise and lower boats traveling to and from the port of Charleston, because there was a sixty-nine-foot difference between the level of the Santee and the lower Cooper River. A ten-foot towpath was cleared along either side of the canal to allow boats to be pulled by teams of oxen or horses, although it was later found more economical to use slaves. Across each of the ten locks, Senf also had constructed a bridge for anticipated land traffic. Carried out with nothing more than picks, shovels, and drag pans, this excavation was probably the largest earth-moving operation in North America since the mysterious earth raising of the prehistoric Mound Builder Indians. The first boat traffic began to move through the Santee Canal from near Columbia in 1801, and the investors in Charleston at long last stood ready to receive their reward.

The canal did indeed do a steady business, not yet paying a return to its investors but encouraging their hopes, until the unusually dry years of

1817–19. Then, in the words of a nineteenth-century historian who had grown up on one of the plantations adjoining the canal, "there was manifested the error of Colonel Senf" in pridefully rejecting the recommendations of previous surveyors and deciding to build his canal along the high ridge route. The Santee Canal dried up. During the drought years of the second decade of the nineteenth century, the dusty roads leading into Charleston were choked with snowy wagons slowly carrying loads of cotton along the red-clay paths from upstate farms to the port of Charleston, while little boys from nearby plantations played in the canal's dry bed. Desperate to correct Colonel Senf's error, the canal company attempted to revive the usefulness of the canal by hauling into the swamps the latest in nineteenth-century technology, two huge steam engines. The plan was to lift water by steam power from the fallen levels of the rivers into the canal. One engine was placed by the Santee River and the other by the Cooper. The Santee engine operated at full speed, but drew barely enough water to replace the natural leakage from the canal. The Cooper engine ran for an hour, then stopped and never ran again.

"The scheme failed," a contemporary historian wrote of the melancholy end of the Santee Canal Company. "The great wealth did not come." As for their dreams of great cities rising along the banks of this South Carolina canal and of fortunes being realized among the aristocratic investors, "they were utterly deceived." Although the canal did recover its usefulness after the return of normal rainfall and river levels, the company never recovered from the financial loss and public embarrassment of its early failure, and the stock never paid a dividend, nor was it ever resold. By 1819 Colonel John Senf had moved elsewhere. The completion in 1840 of the South Carolina Railroad from Columbia to Charleston confirmed that commercial water transportation in the state already was an anachronism before mid-century. The canal was abandoned to nature, and in 1850 the company's charter was revoked by the state. The native trumpet creeper and the low country's sweetly poisonous oleander flowers grew around the locks that had been the pride of Colonel Senf; the green of the swamp began to encroach on the ten-foot-wide towpath, and deer shyly returned to graze where the feet of slaves had once trod; and copperhead snakes lived among the dry stones of the canal's bed.

With but one exception, the canal lay undisturbed for almost a century until the rise of Jimmy Byrnes to the U.S. Senate. In the early 1910s two South Carolina businessmen formed the Columbia Railway and Navigation Company in the hopes of once again persuading merchants and farmers to transport their goods down the Santee River rather than by railroad. The shipping company suffered in the depressed southern economy that preceded the national depression, and in the mid-1920s it was bought as a subsidiary of the International Paper Company. The international corporation acquired little more than a legal entity, because by the late 1920s the most noticeable asset of the Columbia Railway and Navigation Company was an old steamer, beached and rusting on the riverbank near Columbia. Newcomers to town invariably asked about that old boat abandoned by the river. That boat, they were told, was the pot of gold that the Columbia Railway and Navigation Company had found at the end of one of its rainbows.

Not quite. The company also acquired title to property including portions of the old Santee Canal, and in 1921 it obtained a preliminary license from the Federal Power Commission to link the two rivers with a new canal and to construct a hydroelectric dam at a site near the old canal. Taking advantage of the sixty-nine-foot difference between the channels of the Santee and Cooper rivers, which had occasioned Colonel Senf's careful construction of the original canal's ten locks, the Columbia Railway and Navigation Company determined that a dam built there could back up a sufficient head of water between the two rivers to generate perhaps 300,000 kilowatts of electrical energy. This power could then be sold, below the prevailing rates, to the city of Charleston and other coastal towns. Navigation also would be opened between the interior and Charleston.

Throughout the 1920s and the 1930s, the power license was amended and renewed several times as both the navigation company and its parent corporation, International Paper, tried unsuccessfully to raise private capital for the dam project. But in 1932, encouraged by Franklin Roosevelt's personal enthusiasm for publicly funded hydroelectric projects, Mayor Burnet Maybank of Charleston and a group of other influencial state politicians, including J. Strom Thurmond, determined to try for a federal appropriation for the project. They hoped to pass through Congress a funding bill for the Santee-Cooper similar to the legislation that had authorized the federal funding of the Tennessee Valley Authority. The Columbia Railway and Navigation Company, also sensing the possibility of new money, applied for both PWA and RFC funds to begin its long-delayed work under its power license. Elected officials and private entrepreneurs alike in South Carolina began in 1932–33 to see the same fata morgana of great empires and personal fortunes rising over the Santee swamps that had enchanted the gentlemen of Charleston a century and a half earlier. "A vision of an industrial empire in virgin land has taken over this state," the *Greenville News* later wrote in expansive praise of the project. Even the highly conservative editor of the *Charleston News and Courier*, William Watts Ball, who distrusted all grand schemes, fantasized in the early 1930s that perhaps two million new inhabitants could be added to the area around his city as a result of building the new hydroelectric dam.

In early 1934 some of these visionaries of empires, including Burnet Maybank, called on Jimmy Byrnes at his Washington office. They had expected advice from their senator on how to get a congressional appropriation for the Santee-Cooper project. Instead, what they got from him was an introduction to political realism. Byrnes told the delegation that "there was no chance on earth" for congressional funding of the Santee-Cooper project as a "little TVA." Unlike the Santee-Cooper project, he told them, the TVA crossed several state lines and thus had an entrenched congressional constituency; and whereas wilderness surrounded the Santee-Cooper site, the federal government had already made a substantial capital investment by building a nitrate plant at the main power station of the TVA and therefore could not afford to let the Tennessee project go unfunded. And, finally, completion of the TVA, unlike starting the Santee-Cooper, had been a Roosevelt campaign promise.

But the news was not all bad. Already by 1934 the New Deal had established its policy of funding only public institutions for relief purposes. Thus the chances were slight, in Byrnes' opinion, that the Columbia Railway and Navigation Company would obtain either PWA or RFC financing. Byrnes suggested to his state's delegation that they form a state public power authority, which could then apply to the PWA to assume the Columbia Railway and Navigation's loan application to build the project and which could buy the company's license from the Federal Power Commission authorizing the hydroelectric dam's construction. Payment from the state of South Carolina to the Columbia Railway and Navigation Company for its license and other equity could always be negotiated later.

The state's politicians took Byrnes' advice and in mid-1934 formed the South Carolina Public Service Authority, known also as the Santee-Cooper authority. The state authority succeeded in 1934 in assuming the Columbia navigation company's application for a $36 million loan from the PWA, and the authority also obtained the private company's power license. The agreement contained the provision that the authority would later pay the Columbia Railway and Navigation Company for its interests in Santee-Cooper at a price acceptable to the PWA. But as the power license exchanged hands, and the dimensions of the project authorized by the Federal Power Commission became public, the Santee-Cooper project from 1935 onward became the subject of a national controversy.

Since it first acquired its preliminary license from the Federal Power Authority in 1921, the Columbia Railway and Navigation Company had taken advantage of the depressed land prices and the possibility of low-interest federal financing to have its power license amended several times; so by the time of the last amendment in 1933, the Santee-Cooper project had increased by more than twice the area to be flooded. From an already large hydroelectric project that had originally entailed the submergence of 60,000 acres, the latest amended license authorized the flooding of over 130,000 acres. (Eventually more than 160,000 acres would be flooded.) Two mammoth lakes would be created by a diversion dam at the Santee

River and a hydroelectric dam at the Cooper River, forming the largest
bodies of inland water east of the Appalachians. The larger of the two
would be the upper basin, formed by an eight-mile-long dam across the
Santee River, which would hold back the flow of that river and permanently
flood a basin covering 155 square miles. By way of comparison, this man-
made body of water would be slightly larger than the naturally occurring
Lake George, in New York State, or about the same size as the Great Salt
Lake, in Utah.

A diversion canal eight miles long would connect the water in this upper
lake to the lower basin, to be formed by a hydroelectric dam at the Cooper
River, and creating a second man-made lake, of 95 square miles. The
powerhouse on the hydroelectric dam at this second lake was to be located
near one of the largest locks of the old Santee Canal in the little town of
Pinopolis. Once again, as in the eighteenth century when John Senf had
dreamed of great cities and navigation on the Santee River, the 1933 power
license called for a navigation lock to be built at Pinopolis. The twentieth-
century version was to be the largest single-lift lock in the eastern United
States, raising the expected river traffic seventy-five feet from the level of
the Cooper River into the waters of the lower reservoir. To accommodate
the future river traffic, the power license proposed that the upper Santee
River also be dredged from Charleston to Columbia, a distance of about
164 miles.

It was an economic curiosity why the Columbia Railway and Navigation
Company, which had not been able to obtain private financing for a much
smaller project in 1921, continued to amend and enlarge its power license
for the next twelve years. The company apparently figured that the cheap-
ness of the land to be flooded combined with the possibility of low-interest
federal financing offered an opportunity to increase the scale of construction or the resale worth of its Federal Power Commission license at no
additional cost to the company. When the state Santee-Cooper power
authority obtained ownership of the license to build the dams in 1934, all
that prevented the state from beginning work on this vast project was the
approval of its loan application with the PWA.

Conservationists, private power companies, and South Carolina residents in the proposed flood plain immediately sought to preclude approval
of that loan application at public hearings throughout 1934 and 1935. Engineers from the private Duke Power Company criticized the proposal as
likely to cost over $60 million at completion, rather than the $34.5 million
requested from the PWA. In fact, if the two dams were built to the specifications of the power license, the largest earth-moving operation on the
North American subcontinent would once again take place on the same
delta where Colonel Senf and the slaves under his direction had labored.
The private power companies also pointed out that if a market for the
potential 438,000 kilowatt hours estimated to be produced under the

amended license had ever existed in the low country, private power companies would have built hydroelectric dams there during the 1920s. Finally, opponents of the project attacked as ludicrous the idea of developing commercial river traffic along the Santee when railroads throughout the country in 1934 were in danger of going bankrupt from lack of freight to haul.

Residents of the Santee delta also were outraged that the proposed dams would flood many historic sites and force over one thousand people from their homes. At least six thousand graves, including that of Francis Marion, would have to be moved as well. Northhampton, the plantation home of the Revolutionary War hero William Moultrie, would be lost to the flooding, too, and scores of other houses dating from the eighteenth and early nineteenth centuries would be destroyed.

But conservationists and sportsmen, many of them from South Carolina, were the most vociferous in objecting to the Santee-Cooper project. At a hearing before a panel of Interior Department engineers in late 1935, officials from the Izaak Walton League expressed the fear that the permanent diversion of so much of the Santee River's flow into the two artificial lakes would cause what was left of the Santee's natural channel to the sea to become saline for miles upriver. The resulting change in water would kill the freshwater fish, the riverbank stands of trees, and ultimately the birds that roosted in them. The National Audubon Society held that this diversion would despoil the federal bird sanctuary at Cape Romaine, near the final estuary of the Santee River. Among the conservationists the most eloquent opponent to the Santee-Cooper project in South Carolina was Archibald Rutledge, a native resident of the low country who was poet laureate of South Carolina, a nationally known writer on ecology, and a sportsman along the Santee. In an article published in *Nature* magazine, Rutledge scorned the project as a selling-out of his state's birthright. "Thousands and thousands of acres of forest and swamp that are ideal refuges for wildlife will vanish," he wrote, "and in their place will be a muddy lake and a big powerhouse: a lake nobody who loves beauty could ever love, and a powerhouse that will stand as a monument to folly." Money from the PWA, Rutledge urged, could be spent in the Santee delta for more urgent needs, such as the improving of public health and education. (When the South Carolina state senate learned of Rutledge's article, it voted to revoke his honorary title of laureate.)

Despite this determined opposition by his state and nation's conservationists, businessmen, and sportsmen, Jimmy Byrnes persisted in trying to obtain approval of the Santee-Cooper authority's application for the PWA loan. What to Archibald Rutledge was a monument to folly was to Jimmy Byrnes a potential site of perhaps ten thousand jobs yearly. If the PWA loan was approved, the state Santee-Cooper authority would in turn contract the work for land clearing and for constructing the dams to private construction firms, thus putting new money into circulation throughout the state. This $37.5 million also would go a long way toward correcting what was, in Byrnes' opinion, the inequity of South Carolina's not receiving its "fair share" of federal relief benefits. Byrnes had always been quick to point out that although South Carolina residents were taxed at the same rate as the rest of the nation to support federal relief programs, the state received fewer dollars per capita than residents in urban, northeastern states. (He apparently and conveniently forgot that such programs as the AAA most benefited predominately agricultural states such as South Carolina.) Byrnes' stubborn advocacy of the Santee-Cooper project was therefore, at least in the first years of the fight, the result of what Jimmy Byrnes saw as his region's self-interests and not the result of his personal pride or ideology.

Ideology probably had the least to do with his stance. Unlike such New Deal liberals as Harold Ickes, Jimmy Byrnes was not ideologically committed to limiting the market share of private utility companies by building public power projects. Byrnes had always gotten along well with officials from the private (and politically significant) Duke Power Company, and in his pre-Senate years as a lawyer, Duke Power had retained the law firm of Nicholls, Wyche, and Byrnes to represent its interests in Spartanburg County. Moreover, the Duke Endowment, which obtained its income from investments in the private utility company, was during the Depression a major benefactor to Furman University, at Greenville, South Carolina, presided over by Bennette Geer, a longtime friend of Byrnes. As a senator, Byrnes also had broken with the administration in 1935 to help defeat the FDR-sponsored "death penalty" legislation, which would have required the permanent dissolution of utility holding companies under certain monopolistic conditions.

But if Jimmy Byrnes was not fully committed to the New Deal ideology of public ownership of electric power, neither was he strongly committed to the conservatism of an Archibald Rutledge. Even though that South Carolina conservationist was a close relative of Judge Benjamin H. Rutledge, the aristocratic Charlestonian jurist who had given Jimmy Byrnes his first job in a law office and on whose Bourbon demeanor Byrnes later modeled his own, there was no kinship of thought between Jimmy Byrnes and the Rutledge family on the proper use of land. To Archibald Rutledge, the undeveloped land along the Santee River was a "Santee Paradise," in the words of the title to one of his books, an antediluvian refuge from the excesses of twentieth-century urbanization, where a generous-spirited white aristocracy presided over a contented black peasantry. Jimmy Byrnes had no quarrel with the racial views of white property owners along the Santee River; but insofar as he was a representative of the "New South," he saw beyond the romanticism of an Archibald Rutledge to such facts as the yearly deaths of both blacks and whites in the delta from malaria, and rates of unemployment and poverty in the delta that were alarming even by South Carolina standards. If this was paradise, then Jimmy Byrnes, ever the pragmatist, sought to improve paradise with a couple of giant dams.

There was no denying that by the time of Jimmy Byrnes' rise to the U.S. Senate the Santee delta was in sore need of both public works and good works. A guidebook writer newly employed by the Federal Writers Project, established under Harry Hopkins as part of the WPA, spent a frustrating day in Hell Hole Swamp trying to find it. After driving for miles over the desolate South Carolina landscape and asking directions numerous times from residents, the WPA writer found that Hell Hole Swamp was never quite where one currently was, "its whereabouts always designated 'just a piece down the road.' " Residents of Hell Hole Swamp had good reasons to be circumspect in giving directions to strangers from an unknown federal agency; for decades during Prohibition, the primary employment among poor whites living in the swamp, other than occasional work at sawmills, was the distilling of illegal corn whiskey. Moonshiners proudly wrote "Hell Hole Swamp" on the fruit jars of contraband whiskey they produced at stills hidden in the swamp as the "brand name" known to drinkers throughout low-country South Carolina as the most potent of illegal alcohols; and when the WPA writer sought out the grave of an eighteenth-century notable in the area, the writer found that bricks had been removed from the gravesite's cairn, presumably for use in building an illegal distillery.

Moonshining was one of the few signs of industry in the area during the early 1930s. There were few paved roads in the Santee delta at that time, most routes simply being sandy trails along the high ground over swamps overhung on both sides with Spanish moss amid a preternatural stillness. In observation of a fact frequently cited by proponents of the Santee-Cooper project, the WPA writer noted on the tour of the area that few homes of white residents had electricity. None of the homes of black residents were wired for electric power. On passing the cabins of these black residents, many of them descendants of the slaves who had labored in digging the first Santee Canal, the WPA writer saw a life unchanged in its primitivism since the eighteenth century: "At dusk, open doors afford glimpses of the blaze that, never quenched winter or summer, furnished light, heat, and a means of cooking."

The once great houses of the plantation owners who in the 1930s so vociferously opposed the Santee-Cooper flooding were scarcely more enviable. At the height of the indigo, rice, and, later, cotton cultivation in the eighteenth and nineteenth centuries, the houses of these Huguenot planters along what was then called the French Santee had been architecturally among the richest in the United States. The Huguenots, who were early Protestant immigrants, did not build the usually imagined southern mansions with white, neo-Grecian masonry columns. Rather, they built with the native unpainted cypress wood and displayed their love of gables, fan-shaped windows, and elaborately carved mantelpieces and stairs. But with the collapse of rice production in this country and the move of cotton plantations farther into the southern interior, these old Huguenot parishes became economically remote and socially isolated even by South Carolina standards. By the mid-1930s many of these historic houses were in sad neglect and had simply been abandoned. In some instances no local heirs wanted the financial responsibility of the house; in other instances the property had been bought by northern hunting clubs, and the land and house on it had been deliberately allowed to fall fallow in order to return the property to primordial hunting grounds. In either case, the two- and three-story houses of the proud Huguenots were left to stand unoccupied above the surrounding swamps like great empty tombs of weathered cypress. The large rooms of one mansion, its Georgian paneling still intact, were used as a hay barn in the 1930s; and at the abandoned, once elegant nineteenth-century mansion known as Woodlawn, field mice ran across the bare floors, and above the mantelpiece of black-and-gold marble carved in the Empire style, vandals had scratched their messages into the wall plaster.

And of course there was the danger of death by malarial fever, just as in the days of Colonel Senf's work gangs. The five modern counties that in 1930 comprised the old Huguenot parishes were an "empty quarter" of South Carolina, containing only 8 percent of the state's population. But the counties also "emptied" the state's population in another, more lethal way, accounting during some years of the 1930s for more than one-third of South Carolina's total deaths from malaria. That state death toll was itself one of the highest in the United States; there were 264 deaths from malaria in 1937 alone. Even those whom the disease did not kill were left with debilitating fevers and chills recurring over a lifetime.

Jimmy Byrnes tried to emphasize the projected health benefits, improved flood control, and navigational improvements the Santee-Cooper project would bring to this impoverished area as the state authority's loan application made its way through the legal and financial reviews of the PWA. Toward that end, the senator in early December 1934 sent a telegram to the Army Chief of Engineers requesting that the Army hear testimony from him and other South Carolina representatives on the advisability of dredging the Santee River. In part this request was a clever attempt by Byrnes to charge some of the anticipated costs of the Santee-Cooper project to the federal budget for river improvements. But this request was also an attempt to rewrite an embarrassing report that Byrnes knew would be called to Franklin Roosevelt's attention by opponents of the project. Simply by bureaucratic coincidence, and with the worst possible timing for Byrnes' hopes for the Santee-Cooper project, the Army Corps of Engineers in 1933 had included in its periodic reports to Congress on the nation's rivers and harbors its survey of the Cooper and Santee rivers. The corps had found that "improvement by the federal government of the Santee River and tributaries for navigation, power development, or irrigation other than already provided for by existing projects, is not recommended."

Despite Byrnes' telegram and earlier letters asking that he and other South Carolinians be allowed to testify in favor of river improvements on the Santee, the general of the Army Corps of Engineers stuck by his guns and the earlier report. In his answer to Byrnes in early 1935, the general of engineers employed a flanking maneuver similar to the best of Jimmy Byrnes' political tactics. The general told the senator that the Army Corps of Engineers by regulations could not conduct another survey of the Santee River unless specifically requested to do so by the administrator of the PWA. Byrnes and the general both knew that such an action by Harold Ickes was unlikely until Ickes had obtained preliminary reports on the practicality of improving the Santee from his own engineers at Interior. Byrnes thus understood that he would be unable to prevent the unfavorable Army engineering report from being sent to Roosevelt's attention. In combination with the opposition to the Santee-Cooper project being voiced at public hearings on the project throughout 1934–35, Jimmy Byrnes knew that getting Franklin Roosevelt to declare himself personally in favor of the hydroelectric project was going to be a hard sell, despite FDR's love of building on a grand scale.

Byrnes also knew that by January 1935 Roosevelt had received written opposition to the proposed South Carolina project from a member of his own family. Nicholas Roosevelt, a Philadelphia cousin of the president and a plantation owner and sportsman along the Santee, had written a letter to both the president and Senator Byrnes urging a cancellation of the proposed project. "In viewing the situation from an unbiased standpoint," Nicholas Roosevelt wrote, "it seems that the damage which will be done to the local community will far outweigh any benefits to be derived from the development of this power, apart from the temporary advantage to be gained during the construction." Nicholas Roosevelt also questioned the investment of federal money in a project for which the past private owner, the International Paper Company, had never been able to obtain financing. "Any proposal whereby the government puts up thirty or fifty times the amount of money furnished by private ownership would appear to be open to the most severe criticism," he wrote pointedly to Byrnes.

The Santee-Cooper project also was opposed—as both Jimmy Byrnes and Franklin Roosevelt knew from the letters received at their offices— by the National Audubon Society, the Izaak Walton League, and the U.S. Biological Survey of the Agriculture Department. Even the Rural Electrification Administration, a division of the federal government upon which Roosevelt looked with particular favor, opposed the project. A former director of the rural electrification program eventually wrote to the president and warned him that the Santee-Cooper project was simply an attempt by South Carolina politicians to bail out the Columbia Railway and Navigation Company financially when it and its parent corporation, International Paper, were paid for their equity in the project by the PWA.

But such was the often cited "charm" of Jimmy Byrnes that Franklin Roosevelt was reluctant not to give Byrnes at least some qualified support and at least some money for the Santee-Cooper. Indeed, other politicians believed that Jimmy Byrnes' sponsorship of the Santee-Cooper project would more than offset the unfavorable engineering reports and the opposition by conservationists. In a bitter letter to Byrnes in May 1935, an executive of the private utility company Carolina Power and Light complained that he had heard the rumor that the Santee-Cooper project was going to receive funding for no better reason than "the fact that Senator Byrnes was in favor of it, and President Roosevelt will grant any request of his."

Byrnes immediately denied this rumor in his answering letter, but there was some truth in it. There was also the matter of what Harold Ickes considered the president's greatest weakness, his inability to tell his friends no. Thus when Jimmy Byrnes, Burnet Maybank, and other South Carolina politicians friendly to Roosevelt secured an appointment with him in late April 1935, in an attempt to speed up approval of the Santee-Cooper project by the PWA, Roosevelt avoided a firm commitment to his personally seeking funding for the project. But the president also avoided pointing out to such political realists as Byrnes and Maybank the preponderance of national opposition to the project in their state. Instead, FDR busied himself during the meeting by suggesting comparatively minor changes in the navigational features of the proposed shipping channel; and as the group left his office, the president made an indefinite promise that he himself would visit the site of the proposed dams in South Carolina and make up his own mind about the usefulness of the project. Franklin Roosevelt simply did not like to see his friends go away from him empty-handed.

Consequently, when Byrnes learned from a confidential source in the Interior Department in early July 1935 that the PWA financial review of the proposed Santee-Cooper loan was completed, and that the review was favorable, Byrnes immediately informed the president and asked him for a meeting to discuss the findings. Byrnes apparently feared that Harold Ickes, on also hearing that the financial report was favorable, would try to delay its transmittal to the president. Byrnes hoped, by meeting personally with FDR, not to go away from the president's office without first obtaining his specific endorsement of Santee-Cooper.

The Department of the Interior's financial review of the proposed Santee-Cooper dam construction had found plausible the state authority's plan for the PWA loan to be self-liquidating. The financial report estimated that the total cost of the South Carolina project under the amended power license would be $37.5 million. Of that amount, 45 percent of the total cost, or $16,875,000, was to be a direct PWA grant; the remainder of the money would be lent by the PWA and repaid by the power authority from sales of electricity generated from the Santee-Cooper dams over a thirty-year period.

But despite these favorable figures, Roosevelt still had misgivings about the economic necessity and environmental consequences of building the dams. When Byrnes pressed Roosevelt at their meeting for a written commitment to fund the project as outlined in the financial report, Roosevelt hesitated. Instead, as was usual with FDR when he did not want to refuse a friend, he became a kind of good-natured and laughing Rumpelstiltskin from Hyde Park. In this case, FDR told Byrnes at their meeting that he was willing to sign a letter written for him by the senator endorsing the usefulness of the Santee-Cooper project. But in exchange, Roosevelt said, he wanted Byrnes first to obtain an agreement in principle between Harry Hopkins and Harold Ickes to finance the Santee-Cooper construction and labor costs jointly. In particular, Roosevelt asked Byrnes to have Hopkins agree that about six million dollars of the project was to come from the budget of Hopkins' Works Progress Administration (WPA).

Jimmy Byrnes knew that Roosevelt was asking the politically near-impossible. The bitter rivalry between Hopkins and Ickes for preeminence in the control of the New Deal's relief policies was well known throughout Washington in mid-1935. Or, as Byrnes later chose to describe their relationship, "at that particular time [1935] the director of the PWA, Mr. Ickes, and the director of the WPA, Mr. Hopkins, were not very anxious to engage in partnership work." Even if these two rivals could be persuaded, or coerced, to work together in a partnership, Byrnes knew that the presence of two separately administered relief agencies would greatly complicate the future work at the Santee-Cooper construction site. Unlike the PWA, which contracted work to private companies, the WPA directly employed workers under its administration, paying them at a lower scale and employing them at different hours than the workers contracted through the PWA. Nevertheless, Roosevelt was smilingly insistent on this condition for his public endorsement of the Santee-Cooper project. As Jimmy Byrnes left the meeting, FDR laughed and told him that if he could succeed in getting Ickes and Hopkins to agree on the Santee-Cooper, or on anything else, Roosevelt would consider Byrnes for a high diplomatic post.

But the agreement was not so difficult for Byrnes to obtain as Roosevelt had perhaps wished. Hopkins sincerely thought that the PWA had moved too slowly in indirectly funding employment for those on relief, and he welcomed the opportunity to begin employing workers immediately on the Santee-Cooper project out of his WPA budget. Hopkins also saw that it was politically very much in his interest to have the agency he headed involved in what promised to be the biggest publicly financed construction project on the East Coast. Hopkins knew, too, that the dams were wanted very badly by Burnet Maybank. (A friendly deer-hunting politician of immense bonhomie, the Charleston mayor had become a close friend of Hopkins and had entertained him in South Carolina several times since the first visit to the azalea festival.) Having first obtained agreement from Hopkins, Byrnes therefore wisely decided not to tell Harold Ickes of the WPA involvement in the Santee-Cooper project until he had collected his promised letter from Roosevelt. Ickes could then be presented the signed letter from Roosevelt as a fait accompli.

Accordingly, having apparently assured Roosevelt that Ickes had agreed to the partnership, Jimmy Byrnes later dictated, and Franklin Roosevelt signed, a letter dated July 25, 1935. The letter was addressed to Senator Byrnes from President Roosevelt in regard to the proposed Santee-Cooper project. "I have determined to approve a loan and grant for the construction of the project," Byrnes ghostwrote for FDR. "The total cost of this project is estimated at $37,500,000." Roosevelt instructed Byrnes in the letter to confer with Ickes and Hopkins on the details of the financial allotments and then concluded, in Byrnes' enthusiastically chosen words, "From my study of the Santee-Cooper, I am convinced that its completion, which can be speedily underway, will not alone serve to overcome the distress caused by unemployment in this section, but will permanently contribute to the economic development of the Southeast. Very sincerely yours. . . ."

Jimmy Byrnes may have had a note signed by Franklin D. Roosevelt promising to pay $37,500,000, but the senator was not out of the woods yet. When reporters asked Harold Ickes in late July about Byrnes' public announcement that he had obtained presidential approval for financing Santee-Cooper, the interior secretary responded that Jimmy Byrnes was only "65 percent correct." Ickes plainly was implying that he had no intention of releasing the PWA money for the grant of not even 35 percent of the project's cost, although Byrnes might be successful in obtaining a federal loan for the remaining 65 percent. Ickes later reversed his position, saying that at the time he made this remark he was not aware of the existence of the letter signed by Roosevelt. But Ickes had no intention of allocating any significant amount of money for Santee-Cooper until he had received a final report on the project from the engineering division of the Interior Department.

Ickes knew that he stood on high bureaucratic ground here, as compared with Jimmy Byrnes and even Franklin Roosevelt. Byrnes admitted that it was "an unusual thing for the president to sign a letter of this character approving the project in the absence of a formal report from the administrator of the PWA." And as Roosevelt knew, from clearly established policy, Ickes had no authority to make a formal recommendation to the president on the project until he received the report from the Interior Department engineers. The engineering report, as Ickes was aware, might take until the end of 1935 to complete. The interior secretary hoped that by then, despite whatever letters the president might have written to Jimmy Byrnes, unfavorable publicity would have persuaded FDR to kill the project. In fact, Harold Ickes in 1935 was not in favor of building the South Carolina dams under any circumstances, and as he confided to his diary, he never had been. As early as 1934, rumors had begun to reach Ickes from Interior Department clerks in South Carolina that the Santee-Cooper project was a "wildcat scheme"—that is, proposed for PWA funding without sufficient geological or environmental research, and designed simply to inflate the political fortunes of Jimmy Byrnes and Burnet Maybank.

These rumors were given an increased circulation in the late summer of 1935, as Byrnes entered the last year of his senatorial term before his primary race for renomination to the Senate, and as Maybank, with Byrnes' backing, was preparing to run for the state's governorship. As these elections neared, Coley Blease was among those who claimed that the Santee-Cooper project was just a scheme to advance the popularity of Byrnes and Maybank; with considerable wit and some accuracy, Blease claimed that in the name of Santee-Cooper, a job was being promised "to every man in lower South Carolina and to quite a few in upper South Carolina." The vast scale of this project, combined with the uncertainty of its ever receiving Ickes' approval for PWA financing, added credence to Blease's claim that the dams and navigational canal promised by Byrnes and Maybank would never come into existence.

These rumors reached print with the publication on August 12, 1935, of a news story in the Charleston newspaper headlined "Santee Dam Plan Called Big Bluff, Byrnes' 'Politics.' " According to the story, company officials at the privately owned Carolina Power and Light Company had been told by a confidential source inside the Public Works Administration that the plans for the Santee-Cooper had been "pigeon-holed" indefinitely by Ickes. "On this basis," the story continued, "there was a tendency among some of the utilities officials to view the proposed development either as a myth or as a distant bridge to be crossed when reached and not before then."

The unnamed power executive quoted in the news story then made the cruelest charge against Byrnes. In this Depression year, the anonymous executive claimed, Jimmy Byrnes was soliciting campaign contributions from South Carolinians hoping to obtain a patronage job at the never-to-be-built Santee-Cooper site. "We certainly are not going into courts to fight against a campaign fund for Senator Jimmy Byrnes," he told the story's reporter. "And I believe that the Santee-Cooper is nothing but that. When he is re-elected, you won't hear any more about it."

Jimmy Byrnes was infuriated far more by this published half-truth than he would have been by a complete lie. Byrnes did not need major campaign contributions, as he showed by turning down in the next year offers of financial help in his senatorial campaign from Bernard Baruch and Joseph Kennedy, Sr. Nor was Byrnes actively soliciting contributions in 1935. But power, not money, was Jimmy Byrnes' treasure, and that was where the senator's heart was in regard to the Santee-Cooper. The construction project reflected, among other things, an attempt to build up an enormous reservoir of patronage jobs at Jimmy Byrnes' ultimate disposal. If the projections by the state power authority were correct in its application for the loan, about seven thousand workers would be employed annually at building the two dams and the navigational lock, and under Byrnes' agreement with Harry Hopkins at least $6 million would be used from WPA funds to select and pay many of these workers. Through the expected cooperation of Colonel Pinckney, his longtime friend who was head of the state office of the WPA, Jimmy Byrnes therefore would control one of the largest employing agencies in South Carolina. The South Carolina Public Service Authority itself, with projected PWA funding of $31.5 million to build the Santee-Cooper, also would be a powerful organization for patronage available to the senator's use. The state authority would be limited by PWA guidelines on awarding contracts to outside firms but would on its own be hiring engineers, land appraisers, attorneys, geologists, and stenographers. The present head of the authority was Byrnes' protégé Burnet Maybank. (In actual practice, neither Byrnes nor Maybank chose to be directly involved in selecting candidates for most of the lower-paying patronage jobs available when construction on the Santee-Cooper dams finally began. The two men delegated that daily task to Frank Lever, who worked very hard at distributing jobs fairly.)

So, contrary to the power company executives' casual dismissal of the chances of the Santee-Cooper project after Byrnes' reelection, the beginning of construction was essential to Byrnes' bringing both state and federal patronage under his control. And once having gained this control, Jimmy Byrnes was willing to use it to advance politically those subordinates who were loyal to him. ("Senator Byrnes wants an appointment preferably for Thursday to bring Mayor Maybank up with him to talk about Santee-Cooper," the presidential secretary Marvin McIntyre later wrote to FDR during Maybank's campaign for his state's governorship. "I think the real reason is to bring Maybank into the spotlight again," McIntyre added. "May I tell him OK?")

The executive from Carolina Power and Light was thus only half correct. Personal financial gain for Jimmy Byrnes had nothing to do with his backing of the Santee-Cooper project. But Byrnes did regard his controlling interest in patronage at the project in the same way that a Bourbon businessman born into a family of old money might regard his portfolio. For Jimmy

Byrnes, political patronage was like inherited money: it was always there, it always entered into his calculations with other people, but its public discussion he considered to be in bad taste. Byrnes therefore was deeply angered by the appearance of this news article in the *News and Courier*, discussing what he regarded as his private business.

Besides the article's imputation to him of the motive of personal gain, Jimmy Byrnes also was angered by its statement that the Santee-Cooper project had been "pigeon-holed" by Harold Ickes and that "you won't hear any more about it." It was this implication of political ineffectuality that bothered Byrnes the most. He seemed to feel that it was almost as bad having voters think he was dishonest as having them think he had lost influence with the Roosevelt administration. In private notes, written after the news story's appearance, in which he summarized his actions to secure financing for the project, Byrnes several times with evident strong feeling copied out the quotations from the story that the idea for Santee-Cooper was a "campaign fund" and "you will hear no more about it" next to his summaries of how he forced Roosevelt and Ickes to give the money for the project.

In fact, after this news story's appearance, Byrnes' efforts to obtain funding for the Santee-Cooper can no longer be dismissed simply as those of an energetic, personable senator trying to get his state's share of the New Deal pork barrel. Instead, the Santee-Cooper project became a symbol to Byrnes of his pride; and having obtained and publicized the letter from Franklin Roosevelt promising its completion, he was determined that never again could his political opponents claim that once Jimmy Byrnes spoke of a construction project, "you will hear no more of it again."

Byrnes therefore became particularly agitated when, by mid-1935, Secretary Ickes had alloted no more than $100,000 during the current fiscal year out of the budgeted $37.5 million to begin preliminary surveys on the Santee-Cooper. The senator's worries became specific alarms when the interior secretary informed him in late summer of 1935 that, although the PWA engineering division had reported favorably on the project, Ickes was appointing a special review board of outside engineers to determine the practicality of building the dams and canal. Byrnes hastily told Ickes that "it would never do to proceed in this way." Roosevelt had already endorsed the project, the senator told Ickes, and the presidents' letter on the Santee-Cooper was receiving wide publicity. Ickes, however, was unmoved. Byrnes then turned elsewhere for an ally, to Harry Hopkins. Hopkins had a vested interest in seeing the Santee-Cooper project get under way, and Byrnes knew that Hopkins had become a favored adviser to Roosevelt. "I want your help," Jimmy Byrnes wrote somewhat peremptorily to Harry Hopkins on September 18. "I know that the Santee-Cooper project is a PWA project. I know, however, that you may have an opportunity to talk with the Chief about it, and I want you to do so."

Hopkins apparently was unable to dissuade Roosevelt from allowing Ickes to have a final engineering review, and Byrnes took the project up with the president himself in a letter written on October 12. Byrnes pointed out to Roosevelt that despite what the president might have heard about the adverse effects of the Santee-Cooper project on the area's wildlife, these effects had been considered, with apparent public satisfaction, by the Federal Power Commission before it first granted the power license to the Columbia Railway and Navigation Company. The senator also argued that the engineering feasibility of the project had already been considered "not only by the engineers of the PWA, but also by distinguished engineers in private life and engineers of the United States Army." Byrnes earlier had sent the president a copy of the "Big Bluff" article, and he now again emphasized the politically embarrassing consequences to both of them in not proceeding with the project. "In view of your letter to me approving the project, which was given wide publicity," Jimmy Byrnes wrote the president, "our friends expect us to go through with the project."

But as with Harry Hopkins, his other favorite, Roosevelt refused this request from Jimmy Byrnes to override Ickes' decision for a special engineering review. FDR did send a copy of Byrnes' letter to Ickes, however, with a notation that he discuss the Santee-Cooper project with him at his earliest opportunity. Ickes remained outwardly cordial to Byrnes, saving his spite for his nightly entries in his diary. Byrnes' behind-the-scenes maneuvering to save the Santee-Cooper, Ickes wrote, had convinced him that the senator "isn't a strong man, but a sly and active one."

By the last month of 1935, Byrnes had received a warning from a political supporter that the delays occasioned by Harold Ickes in approving the Santee-Cooper were being used by Byrnes' opponents as evidence of inefficiency on the senator's part. Byrnes, who as a rule did not like to discuss the details of his work with those outside Washington, wrote back a letter betraying I've-been-working-my fingers-to-the-bone petulance:

> The president is for the project, [but] I do not know of anyone else in the administration who is for it. . . . Secretary Ickes is opposed to the project. The president can give him orders to go through with it, but you and I know what happens when a member of the Cabinet is ordered to do something which he is opposed to doing. The Director of the Rural Electrification Administration having no duty to perform in the matter, neglects his own duties to oppose the Santee-Cooper project. The head of the Biological Survey not only writes magazine articles, but delivers lectures to the newspaper men of the nation at the Press Club in opposition to it. The people interested in hunting estates employ publicity men to work up resolutions of Women's Clubs and Garden Clubs throughout the nation, and Ickes receives two or three hundred communications a

day opposing the project. The Army Corps of Engineers are opposed to it. . . .

After recounting his labors to defeat the above opposition, Byrnes stated
that he had heard the same rumors that the Santee-Cooper project was
simply a sham designed to promote Byrnes' political interests:

It is fair to say that the general belief in Washington is that the
project has no merit and that the president wrote a letter to me
approving it solely because of his friendship for me. That this is a
reflection upon the intelligence and character of the president, seemingly, does not occur to them.

Shortly after Byrnes wrote this letter, on December 17, 1935, Ickes
released to the public the report on the Santee-Cooper project he had
received on November 5, submitted by the final review board of engineers.
The board declared the project to be "feasible" from an engineering standpoint, but it declined to judge whether the hydroelectric project in low-
country South Carolina was economically justifiable. The report also
pointed out that the Santee River had never carried any commercial navigation of any consequence, and that therefore the engineers declined to
recommend that the river be dredged. The effect upon the environment
of the dams' flooding and the river's diversion would not be "sufficiently
grave," the report concluded, to delay proceeding with the project. Burnet
Maybank, hearing news of the report at Charleston, considered the engineers' qualified findings to be a vindication of the Santee-Cooper project,
and he left immediately for Washington to press Ickes and Roosevelt to
release allocations of money to begin construction. Ickes, however, saw
the engineers' qualifications as just the reverse, interpreting them as reasons to do nothing. As for Roosevelt, there was no telling: when asked at
a press conference about the Santee-Cooper project the same day the
engineering report was released, FDR nodded his head approvingly, but
said nothing.

    Jimmy Byrnes was out of the country, on his trip to the Philippines
promoting southern textiles, when the report was released, and when his
ship docked in Seattle he found waiting for him a number of telegrams
from Maybank and his own office advising him that they had been unable
to persuade Ickes to release any money to get the project under way.
Byrnes immediately wired the president, reminding him of his written
promise to Byrnes and of Byrnes' publicity for it; and by the time his train
had reached Chicago on his way back to the East Coast, there was a message
from FDR assuring him that the Santee-Cooper project "would be taken
care of." Nevertheless, as soon as Byrnes was back in Washington, he
went to the White House "bright and early" (as the newspapers put it)

the morning of December 19, 1935, to collect on his promise, or at the very least a few million dollars of it.

But though Byrnes appeared at the president's door early, Harold Ickes had been there before him. Ickes still had misgivings about the ecological effects of creating two giant lakes that would be too deep to support the marsh-dwelling migratory ducks and other waterfowl accustomed to finding sanctuary in the Santee delta. Such also was the concern raised in a letter-writing campaign by the National Audubon Society directed toward the Interior Department. "I told the president I didn't think we had an adequate report on the effects of the Santee-Cooper project on wildlife, especially migratory water fowl," Ickes noted in his diary. The president responded that the waterfowl, in a phrase frequently employed during the New Deal, would have to learn to adjust to changing conditions. And later that same day, Ickes returned to his office to find Jimmy Byrnes waiting for him, perfectly content "to stay until he sees me."

There was a reason for Byrnes' cheerful, unscheduled arrogance. He had in his hand a memorandum signed that morning by the president and directing the PWA to allot $5.5 million of the budgeted $37.5 million in order to begin work on the Santee-Cooper immediately after the start of the new year. The president's memorandum also directed Harry Hopkins to supply money from the WPA budget to pay for unskilled labor in clearing land for the dams' basins. Ickes' recommendation to Roosevelt earlier that morning to wait for further studies thus had been countermanded that same morning by Jimmy Byrnes' personal influence with the president. Like the migratory ducks, Harold Ickes apparently would also have to learn to adjust to changing conditions. All that remained possible for Ickes to do to demonstrate his disapproval of the project was for him to warn Byrnes that he intended to keep his eye on negotiations with the Columbia Railway and Navigation Company for its equity. Ickes recorded in his diary that he told Byrnes, "I would not pay excessive prices for the property and rights of the old company down there."

Although he had to accede to the president's written instructions, Ickes attempted bureaucratically to wash his hands even more thoroughly of Jimmy Byrnes' project. By late December 1935 Ickes had the PWA office send no more than a transmittal notice of the Santee-Cooper's $5.5 million funding to the president's office for Roosevelt's formal approval. Ickes did not include with this transmittal a letter stating his own recommendations of the Santee-Cooper project, which had been the standard procedure with all other PWA projects sent to the White House for FDR's signature. The day he received the transmittal, Roosevelt met with Ickes in the president's office, and as FDR signed the allocation to begin funding on the Santee-Cooper, he attempted to explain to Ickes why he had decided to back the project.

FDR's reasons for supporting the Santee-Cooper originated in the same elemental motive as those of Jimmy Byrnes: great pride. Jimmy Byrnes had been motivated, at least since Roosevelt's letter of July 1935, by his pride in his ability to hold a president to a promise and to demonstrate to his South Carolina enemies that when Jimmy Byrnes spoke of a construction project, it would be heard of again. Franklin Roosevelt's pride was more subtle, and more inverse. "He said that one thing that had made him so stubborn about the Santee-Cooper project was the fact that so many of his rich friends had urged him not to go ahead with it," Ickes wrote in his diary about his conversation with Roosevelt. There was indeed an economic truth that Roosevelt had recognized in Burnet Maybank's earlier public assertion that the sportsmen who were opponents of the Santee-Cooper construction wanted low-country South Carolina to remain a feudal reserve where game was more important than people. Ickes noted that Roosevelt during their meeting "spoke scornfully of rich men in the North buying fine old plantations in South Carolina and turning them into 'hunting lodges.' " Yet such was Roosevelt's pride that he did not consider how restoring these "fine old plantations in South Carolina" to their agricultural usefulness and their former architectural glory could best be accomplished by permanently flooding them under two lakes covering hundreds of square miles. Sufficient to Roosevelt was the demonstration to his rich friends of who was boss on the Santee-Cooper.

As for Jimmy Byrnes, on Christmas Eve 1935 he was traveling to a meeting in his state's capital called by Burnet Maybank and attended by other selected members of the South Carolina Public Service Authority. The weather that night was unusually snowy and icy for South Carolina, and Columbia was a long trip away from Aiken, to the south, where the senator and his wife customarily spent the Christmas holidays with Maude Byrnes' relatives. But both Byrnes and Maybank felt that the senator's presence at this meeting was essential. The state authority was meeting that night with representatives of the Columbia Railway and Navigation Company to settle a price for its interests in the Santee-Cooper site. Byrnes had made clear that he could handle only what he called "the Washington end" of negotiating a price with the navigation company; but since Harold Ickes had insisted that he would have the final approval of any settlement, and since Ickes had warned Byrnes that he would be looking closely at the price, it was advisable that Byrnes be present to vouch for the probity of the proceedings. The unusual Christmas Eve timing of the meeting was due in part to the urgency for Maybank and other members of the state power authority to meet a legal deadline of having completed the purchase of the private company's rights before the start of a new year. And, as must have occurred to Byrnes and Maybank, any delays in setting a price caused by interested citizens attending this open meeting on the Santee-Cooper project could surely be kept to a minimum by their meeting on Christmas Eve. Both politically and fiscally, Santee-Cooper must have appeared in the bag to Jimmy Byrnes that night. Southern newspapers published in states other than South Carolina had recently run stories in envious praise of "the big job that will pour millions into the state," the *Charlotte Observer* wrote, and for which Senator James F. Byrnes "has worked incessantly."

But waiting for Byrnes, Maybank, and other members of the authority at their meeting room in the state supreme court building that night were attorneys for the private utility companies operating in South Carolina. They intended a different sort of Christmas present for the Columbia Railway and Navigation Company and the advocates of the Santee-Cooper project. Having previously dismissed the publicly financed project as a "myth" and a "campaign fund," the private power companies now were taking seriously this attempt to compete for their business. Lawyers for the Carolina Power and Light Company announced to the state authority that they intended to challenge in federal court the constitutionality of the PWA's financing state agencies to produce and sell electric power.

Until the courts decided this suit, which everyone in the meeting room knew could take years, Carolina Power and Light also announced to those present that it was seeking a temporary injunction in the federal district court for Washington, D.C., barring Harry Hopkins of the WPA and Harold Ickes of the PWA from spending any of the money already allocated for Santee-Cooper. A lawyer for the Duke Power Company who attended the meeting stated the willingness of that politically powerful company to join in suits to stop the Santee-Cooper project. Burnet Maybank's comments were later described as unprintable, and the meeting adjourned within thirty minutes of this antagonistic turn of events. The question of what price the state authority should pay to the Columbia Railway and Navigation Company was left unanswered until there was a decisive resolution of the power companies' challenges in court. When Jimmy Byrnes stepped from the state supreme court building into the darkness of a cold Christmas Eve, he was coming away from the meeting empty-handed and not, as he had hoped less than an hour earlier, bringing home the biggest New Deal gift in the state's history.

But as so often in the career of Jimmy Byrnes, what seemed a setback actually worked to his advantage. Ahead was a three-year legal battle for the constitutionality of Santee-Cooper that was eventually appealed for a hearing before the U.S. Supreme Court. During this time Jimmy Byrnes voluntarily handled "the Washington end" of anticipating and influencing the decisions of federal judges at the district and appellate courts. So skillfully did he handle this end of the legal battle, in fact, that Franklin Roosevelt, always a keen appreciator of a jurist with a good political mind, began to consider that the U.S. Supreme Court itself might be just the place for Jimmy Byrnes after the final Santee-Cooper victory.

8

They Were
Utterly Deceived

T he three-year legal battle over the
constitutionality of the South Carolina Public Service Authority's receiving
PWA money to build the Santee-Cooper project set judicial records in the
state for the length of briefs filed, the amount of testimony given, and the
size of attorneys' fees later billed to the state authority. In addition to
challenging the constitutionality of the PWA's financing of public power,
the private utility companies sought a permanent injunction against the
project on the grounds that it was unrealistically budgeted and impractical
in its conception and that therefore Santee-Cooper was a subterfuge by
which the Roosevelt administration sought to control the rates set by private utilities. In support of this argument, engineers for the private companies testified that the actual cost of building a power project to the
dimensions of Santee-Cooper would be closer to $60 million than to the
budgeted $37.5 million. And the engineers denounced in court as "pre-
tensive, illusory, and inconsequential" the plans by the state authority to
promote a busy commercial trade up and down the Santee River.

In response, lawyers for the state authority argued that "the navigational features are primary" to the completion of the project and that the
flood control, health benefits, and recreational benefits of building the

Santee-Cooper would be "substantial." The estimate of the number of unemployed who would find work at the project yearly was increased from 7,000 to 10,000, and the hydroelectric dam at Pinopolis was presented in a court brief as "an abundant source of cheap electrical energy for the development of a vast empire nearby." The letters that George Washington and Franklin Roosevelt wrote in regard to the Santee-Cooper project were introduced into court as evidence over the centuries of the federal government's abiding interest in constructing improvements on the Santee River.

But the importance during this legal struggle of Jimmy Byrnes, who during his days as court solicitor had contributed his share of judicial rhetoric, was not in his presenting the constitutional issues in a well-written brief. Rather, it was in the sureness of his political instincts in planning the timing and circumstances of the Santee-Cooper arguments. Byrnes knew that two earlier challenges to the production of publicly financed power were being heard by federal courts in 1936, including an argument on the constitutionality of the TVA before the U.S. Supreme Court. Byrnes therefore advised seeking a postponement of the Santee-Cooper case until these two cases were decided. Unlike the Santee-Cooper, these cases offered better grounds in finding for the constitutionality of public power, as advocates for both of these other public utilities could provide favorable evidence by the Army Corps of Engineers on specific benefits for hydroelectric power or commercial navigation. Thus, it was possible, particularly if the Supreme Court found in favor of the TVA, that lawyers for the Santee-Cooper authority would get a summary dismissal of the suit in court, without having to go into a potentially embarrassing discussion of the Army Corps of Engineers' negative recommendations on the Santee-Cooper project.

Harold Ickes accordingly telephoned Burnet Maybank at Byrnes' suggestion and asked him for his assistance in getting the other members of the state power authority to agree to a continuance of the hearing for the suit against it. But the Charleston mayor had apparently taken a page from the negotiating book used by Jimmy Byrnes and Franklin Roosevelt. Maybank told Ickes that he would be willing to agree to a continuance of the suit if Ickes in turn would proceed with completing the paperwork and getting the signature of the president for the rest of the $25 million from the PWA budget to finish the project. Ickes, who by this time had had enough of Jimmy Byrnes, his friends in South Carolina, and the Santee-Cooper project in general, fell into what can only be described as a perfect snit. In Ickes' recollection, "there was a great deal of telephoning back and forth" between PWA lawyers and Maybank and other members of the power authority, and finally Ickes "got pretty short with them and told them they would either agree to the continuance or I would recommend to the president that he rescind the entire project." Jimmy Byrnes quickly placated Ickes and agreed that the secretary had been within his rights to resent the coercion. Maybank was brought into line with no further attempts to shake down the PWA for money before the case was heard. The power companies agreed to the continuance as well, and both sides settled down to see what the Supreme Court would do.

In early 1936 the Supreme Court found that the construction of hydroelectric dams in the Tennessee River valley with public funds was constitutional. Another similar public power project challenged by Duke Power also was upheld in favor of the government in federal district court. After these two rulings, which came more than a year after the Santee-Cooper authority was first served with notice of a suit, the power companies and the state authority went to court on March 8, 1937. Byrnes, however, was still worried that the arguments for the navigational and hydroelectric benefits of the Santee-Cooper project were not as convincing as those in the case of the TVA. Despite the precedents for public power just established, there was a good possibility that Carolina Power and Light could win the suit on the grounds of Santee-Cooper's impracticality or the unlikelihood of its receiving funding. Here Byrnes showed his sure prescience of what would affect a district trial judge politically. In the upcoming case of Santee-Cooper, it was in Byrnes' successful creation in court of the impression that the federal government was willing to put its money where its mouth was.

The administration had already shown a commitment to funding Santee-Cooper with Roosevelt's letter of July 15, 1935, which had instructed Harry Hopkins and Harold Ickes to provide at least ten million dollars for the start-up of the project. It was to prevent the spending of any of this money that the private power companies had obtained injunctions while the Santee-Cooper case was being heard in court. But Jimmy Byrnes knew that a further allotment of money, despite the project's being in litigation, would be a powerful inducement for a federal judge to take PWA lawyers at their word that the project would indeed improve the nation's rivers and provide flood control benefits. The problem was that neither Franklin Roosevelt nor Harold Ickes was willing to provide an additional allotment for the project while it was in a state of uncertain legality. To allot funds for Santee-Cooper or any other relief project meant that even though the money might not be spent in that fiscal year, the budget for the appropriate agency was charged that year for the amount of the allotment. Ickes argued, and Roosevelt agreed, that he should allot funds that could be used immediately to relieve unemployment, rather than be held in reserve until an injunction against Santee-Cooper might be removed at some uncertain time in the future.

But what Harold Ickes would not do in the Interior Department, Jimmy Byrnes could do in the Appropriations Committee Room of the U.S. Senate. Byrnes inserted in a supplemental appropriations bill for 1937 a provision that $132 million from general funds be reserved for four specific public works projects that had been "earmarked," in Byrnes' term, by the

PWA administrator, but "for which no formal allotments have been made." By prearrangement, Byrnes then had another member on the Appropriations Committee specify for the *Congressional Record* that the Santee-Cooper project was one of these four.

On September 2, 1937, after a bitter trial lasting more than eight weeks and producing testimony and documentation that both sides agreed was "voluminous," Judge J. Lyles Glenn of the eastern federal district court of South Carolina ruled that the creation of the South Carolina Public Service Authority was constitutional under the powers assigned to the PWA by the National Recovery Act. The judge therefore refused to issue a permanent injunction restraining the construction at the Santee-Cooper site. Judge Glenn noted that "one matter of legal importance has happened since the conclusion of the trial which this court should refer to in its opinion." He cited the fact that the U.S. Senate passed an amendment, which subsequently became law, in which "the sums of $16,650,000 as a grant and $14,850,000 as a loan were definitely earmarked for the Santee-Cooper project in South Carolina." This amendment, Judge Glenn observed in his decision favorable to the Santee-Cooper, "shows that Congress has intentions of completing this project."

Judge Glenn's decision was upheld in early 1938 by the federal appellate court in Richmond. Attorneys for Carolina Power and Light then gave notice, either in the small hope of a reversal on a procedural error or simply out of vindictiveness at being politically outmaneuvered by Senator Jimmy Byrnes, that they would appeal the decision to the U.S. Supreme Court. Given the Court's favorable decision on the TVA case, it seemed likely that this appeal would be denied. It was Jimmy Byrnes' job at "the Washington end" of the project to make certain that before the appeal was considered by the Court no politically embarrassing news became public about the Santee-Cooper that at the last minute might prejudice the justices against the project. Such an embarrassment had almost occurred before the first trial. A friendly journalist tipped Byrnes off to the fact that a report by the National Resources Board due soon to be made public expressed doubts about the market for the power to be produced by the Santee-Cooper project and recommended further study before proceeding with building the dams. Since Secretary Ickes was the chairman of the National Resources Board, publication of this report would put the Roosevelt administration in the logically interesting position of recommending the stoppage of a power project that it was arguing in court should be begun at once. Byrnes found that the report was on FDR's desk for his final review before being made public, and Byrnes' persuaded Ickes to delete this reference to the Santee-Cooper and therefore avoid a perhaps unintentional contradiction.

A potentially much more damaging report concerning the Santee-Cooper project almost became public record while the Supreme Court was considering hearing the power companies' appeal in the spring of 1938.

The justices' earlier decision confirming the constitutionality of the TVA had been largely determined by that project's demonstrable navigational and flood control benefits. Thus both Maybank and Byrnes had since the court's decision on the TVA chosen to emphasize the Santee-Cooper as a "three-in-one" project of electric power, navigation, and flood control in order to enhance its legality in federal court. But on March 19, 1938, while attorneys for the power companies were filing their appeal with the Supreme Court, the Army Chief of Engineers forwarded the most recent report on improving the Santee and Cooper rivers for flood control to President Roosevelt for his review. Floods along the Santee River had been recorded frequently since colonial years, but because most plantations in the delta in the twentieth century had allowed rice fields to become permanently flooded in order to encourage the settling of ducks for commercial hunting, the inundations were considered useful. Most homes and settlements also were protected by a series of levees built in the eighteenth century by the early Huguenot settlers. On the basis of these features and the residents' current use of the land, the Army concluded in its current report to Roosevelt that "the Chief of Engineers reports that improvements undertaken for flood control on the Congaree, Wateree, Santee and Cooper Rivers, South Carolina, are not justified at this time." (The Congaree and Wateree rivers combine near Columbia to form the Santee River.)

This was just the type of conclusion that could enable opponents of the Santee-Cooper project to distinguish between the uncertain usefulness of the South Carolina project and the TVA. Apparently it was now Jimmy Byrnes' turn to fall into a perfect snit, and he communicated his feelings to Roosevelt. Upon first acknowledging receipt of the Army's report, FDR noted with misgivings to its authors that he found it "at variance in some respects with the Santee-Cooper project, which has been approved in principle." Roosevelt then asked the War Department, before it released the report to the public, to check its conclusions with the prior recommendations for flood control along the Santee River made by the Department of the Interior, the National Resources Board, and the Federal Power Commission. He added, "And let me know whether substantial agreement can be reached before anything further is reported on." Apparently at Jimmy Byrnes' insistence, Roosevelt also pushed again for an alteration of the Army's report, sending a memorandum on April 25, 1938, to Harold Ickes: "Will you and [Acting Budget Director Daniel W.] Bell and Hopkins and [Chief Army Engineer] General Schley get together on this and know the exact status—because Senator Jimmy Byrnes fully expects us to go ahead with what he considers to be a promise. FDR."

By the second week of May 1938, with the Supreme Court's decision on whether to hear the power companies' appeal expected within the month, Roosevelt met at the White House with Ickes, Hopkins, and Bell. Together the four men were able to find a "substantial agreement" between the negative report by the Army engineers and the administration's previous approvals of flood control projects on the Santee River. With the understanding of the Army Chief of Engineers, the conclusions of the Army's report were construed to apply only to the upper reaches of the Santee River. Despite the report's explicit listing of the Santee River, along with its upper tributaries, as not in need of expenditures for flood control, and despite the published judgment by the Army in 1933 that no improvements on the Santee were justified, the latest report now interpreted the negative findings to pertain only to the upper Santee. The conclusions of the present Army report, in words that must have been difficult for Harold Ickes to accept, were determined as having "no connection to the Santee-Cooper project." A public commitment by the Roosevelt administration to the Santee-Cooper project thus was maintained in the face of the Supreme Court's impending review of the appeal, and a way was found to go ahead with what Jimmy Byrnes fully expected as a promise.

On Monday afternoon, May 23, 1938, Burnet Maybank and the senior attorney for the South Carolina Public Service Authority were at the U.S. Supreme Court Building waiting for the Court's decision on whether it would grant or deny the petition for appeal by the power companies. A reporter described the two as sitting "with glum faces and the air of persons waiting for loved ones to come from an operating room." But when news arrived from the justices' chambers that a single word—"denied"—had been written across the power companies' petition, Maybank's and the attorney's face were described by the same reporter as "lighted up as though it were raining pennies from heaven."

The two raced across the street to the U.S. Capitol Building to share the good news with Jimmy Byrnes. As it was now late in the afternoon, they found Byrnes enjoying his "bullbat time" of afternoon drinks of bourbon with Vice President Jack Garner of Texas. An impromptu party immediately took place, and Maybank and his wife later were the dinner guests of the Roosevelts at the White House in celebration of the Santee-Cooper's long-awaited legal victory. The Supreme Court's denial of the petition that day meant that money could be alloted and spent with no further legal challenges, and Maybank exultantly predicted that perhaps as many as ten thousand South Carolinians would be at work on the project by the fall of that year.

Actually, it was nearly another year, to the spring of 1939, before the first clearing for the two dams began. Before construction could get fully under way, the state authority needed in early 1939 to purchase the power license and other interests in the project from the Columbia Railway and Navigation Company. Also, the authority had to buy legal title to the more than 160,000 acres to be flooded and to oversee the removal of at least 901 families from these properties. And, most difficult, at least six thousand graves within the future dam basins had to be opened and the remains moved from the area of the flooding.

"Reports on 3,619 Graves Not Even a Good Start on the Census of the Dead," the *Charleston News and Courier* reported in early 1939 on the authority's efforts to locate and identify the hundreds of family cemeteries, of both black and white former residents, now forgotten and overgrown in this once populous delta cultivated since the early 1700s. Many of the graves would remain "lost" until the day that water from the two dams backed over the sites to obliterate them even more thoroughly, because in some instances parish books or family bibles had recorded a burial at a site where in the 1930s no stone or marker could be found. In other cases, local historians investigating an area cleared for the dams' basins found broken and now unlocatable headstones thrown by the Santee River bank by persons unknown. The remains of Francis Marion, a formidable fighter in the Revolutionary War, were removed from his plantation grave and reburied above the future waterline. The plantation itself was to be flooded. Other historic plantations, including the Springfield, Ophir, Somerton, and White Hall plantation houses, were to be lost to the waters.

Many other historic buildings, including churches with active black and white congregations in the 1930s, were to be destroyed by the flooding. The Department of the Interior attempted an inventory before the project fully began. In only once instance, that of a private house, did it recommend that government efforts be made to remove a building from the coming floods. In all other cases, the survey found, efforts to remove the buildings would not be worthwhile, as "only sentimental or historical associations" justified the buildings' preservation.

Most of the 901 families removed by the Santee-Cooper project were descendants of slaves freed from the neighboring plantations after the Civil War, and the black families that owned their own land benefited from the Santee-Cooper removal. Socially, the project brought the destruction of many small black rural communities and church congregations that had been stable for generations; but financially, it was a godsend, for it paid an average of over twelve dollars an acre for the land it acquired, at a time when farmland elsewhere in South Carolina was selling for less than two dollars an acre. The project also gave each resettled farmer one hundred chickens to restock the relocated farmers' homesteads, a not inconsiderable bonus in rural South Carolina during the 1930s, when poultry was a welcome addition to the usual diet of corn and pork, and selling eggs was one of the few sources of ready cash for farmers. The Santee-Cooper's improvement in the living conditions of property-owning black residents in the basins was an example of the New Deal's inadvertently "spilling over" benefits to southern blacks, as it had been characterized earlier by Jimmy Byrnes.

But the greatest beneficiaries of the state authority's purchase of land in 1939, at sometimes six times the state's average price, were the largest landowners within the projected flood basins, including the International Paper Company and its subsidiary the Columbia Railway and Navigation

Company. On that now distant snowy Christmas Eve in South Carolina in 1934, the Columbia company had opened negotiations for its interests in the Santee-Cooper project by negotiating its equity at $600,000. After the end of renewed negotiations, in April 1939, the company received from the state Santee-Cooper authority the sum of $470,543 in exchange for its 3,000 acres of land at the construction site and for its federal power license, blueprints, and surveys. At an average price of $12 an acre, this payment amounted to $444,543 for the company's non–real estate equity. (This figure also included interest for the private company's five-year wait on renewed negotiations while the state authority met the legal challenges to the project.)

Absentee plantation owners in the North, who had acquired land along the Santee River for hunting preserves, also benefited from the sale at these exceptionally high prices, even though many were unwilling sellers. The prices paid were so high because at most of these hunting preserves the land had deliberately been undeveloped and therefore had little appraised value. (Among the forced sellers of these northern-owned plantations to be destroyed by the Santee-Cooper was Nicholas Roosevelt, thereby demonstrating that with Franklin D. Roosevelt, at least in regard to politically important hydroelectric projects, water was thicker than blood.)

But many local residents in the basins of the planned flooding, despite the high prices offered by the authority, resisted with great bitterness the legally forced purchase of their property until the beginning of the final land clearing for the dams in late April 1939. In that same month Henry R. Dwight, a property owner near the proposed power station and navigational lock at Pinopolis, decried the Santee-Cooper project in a letter to the Columbia *State*, widely reprinted throughout South Carolina. Dwight wrote of the "desolation of plantations and farms, the destruction of homes, the ruin of churches, the desecration of cemeteries, and the exile of a whole people (over a thousand) white and Negro." According to this resident, "the whole Santee-Cooper project was conceived in sin and born in iniquity—the sin of reckless spending and the iniquity of ruthless destruction."

In fact, the Santee-Cooper project had been conceived in the twentieth century by Jimmy Byrnes and Burnet Maybank as only the latest of a series of schemes since the adventures of Colonel John Christian Senf in the late eighteenth century to win great personal fortunes and political fame by mastering this wilderness. And rather than being born in iniquity, the Santee-Cooper project was born in the South Carolina swamps as the result of the complex relationship of personal pride and political indebtedness between Franklin Roosevelt and Jimmy Byrnes. Despite the many voices of protest from local South Carolina residents such as Henry Dwight, there remained an unalterable law of politics in that state, which no one could undo: "Senator Byrnes is in favor of it, and President Roosevelt will grant any request of his." On April 18, 1939, clearing for the two giant dams began, and the largest earth-moving project in North America was once more under way.

The problems with money and labor began almost at once. As in the building of the eighteenth-century Santee Canal, delays in construction greatly inflated the costs of the twentieth-century Santee-Cooper project. In the four years since $37.5 million were first approved for the project in Franklin Roosevelt's letter to Jimmy Byrnes of July 1935, prices of construction material and of labor had risen while the amount of the grant and loan had remained the same, computed at 1933–34 prices. Eventually the original agreement was amended seven times as a result of unanticipated increases in costs. When the Santee-Cooper finally was declared substantially complete, in 1942, the state authority's indebtedness to the federal government for loans and the grant had risen far above the original $37.5 million, to $64,879,536.

Of that amount, $10 million had been spent for WPA labor in clearing land for the reservoirs. Like Colonel Senf before him, Harry Hopkins found it almost impossible to persuade men to work for long periods of time in the Santee delta. Unlike Colonel Senf, Hopkins was not dealing with a high turnover rate as the result of the laborers' fear of malarial fever. Before beginning extensive work at the project, the Santee-Cooper authority had brought to the site a malaria control adviser from the British Public Health Service in India, and so well had his team of mosquito exterminators done their jobs that by the fall of 1939 "no new cases" were reported among the workers at the Santee-Cooper.

Rather, the problems with the high labor turnover at Santee-Cooper site resulted from the work itself, the remote living conditions of the workers, and the fact, unforeseen by Jimmy Byrnes or anyone else in 1934, that the Santee-Cooper project would begin hiring large numbers of workers only in 1939. By that time, despite the recession of 1938, unemployment both nationally and in the state had declined significantly from the 1933–34 levels. Nationwide, employment and payrolls in manufacturing industries had climbed from 63.3 percent of the eligible work force in 1933 to 89.5 percent in 1939. Among workers in the construction trades in South Carolina, who would have been the most skilled men recruited for work at the Santee-Cooper site by the WPA, only 661 out of the state's total 22,047 construction workers were reported as out of work for the full twelve months of 1939 and eligible for WPA relief work. Defense hiring at the naval yard in Charleston also was returning more skilled and semiskilled men to private employment in 1939. As a consequence, many of the men eligible for work at Santee-Cooper either left the WPA work force within a few months for private employment or never turned up for work at the site at all.

This last group was the most troubling to the proponents of Santee-Cooper. Of the state's 18,389 unemployed workers assigned by the WPA to work at the Santee-Cooper site between 1939 and 1940, the public works project succeeded in these two years in retaining only 5,345 workers. Byrnes' friend and political ally Colonel Lawrence Pinckney came under constant criticism from the national office of the WPA, in Washington, for his failure to reduce the huge turnover at the Santee-Cooper site. In vain Colonel Pinckney wrote back numerous letters detailing the hardships of work at the site to Harry Hopkins' office, the colonel stating bluntly in one letter that the workers "live in camps where they are miles from town—in fact, located at the edge of swamps."

The swamps were only the beginning. Confronting these newcomers to the WPA work camps were the 160,000 acres covered with palmetto thickets, slash pines, oaks, or other hardwoods to be cleared for the dams' basins. The only previous clearings frequently were cemeteries where graves were scheduled to be moved. Otherwise, in this virgin forest, each of the standing trees had to be cut down, its stump grubbed out of the future lake basin, then piled onto a huge stack of other stumps and, amid the already hellish heat of the low country, set afire. The basins of the future Santee-Cooper lakes were lit with these bonfires, between which the men traveled and worked, their fires like giant versions of the blazes that had once been seen inside the cabins of the displaced Negro farmers, the fire "never quenched winter or summer."

There was also the problem with snakes. Clearing the land in the Santee delta reduced the habitat and concentrated the numbers of the venomous copperhead snake, which residents there considered to be almost commonplace. The copperhead is usually not aggressive, however, and its bites are seldom fatal unless the snakes are encountered in breeding or nesting swarms. Unfortunately, much more aggressive and potentially lethal are the two other species of poisonous snakes also found in large numbers in the Santee delta: the cottonmouth, or water moccasin, and the diamondback rattler. Even the gentle naturalist William Bartram, who traveled through the Santee delta in the early eighteenth century, found the water moccasin particularly horrific to encounter. Capable of dropping onto its victim's neck from trees or of biting a foot in brackish water, the water moccasin when aroused has a habit of dropping its lower jaw to display the deathly white interior of its mouth and, in Bartram's words, has its "crooked poisonous fangs directed right at you." Bartram wrote that he pitied those "who are compelled to labor in the swamps and lowlands" where the water moccasins are found.

But the poisonous snake that the workers at the Santee-Cooper site feared the most, and the largest and most territorially aggressive, was the diamondback rattlesnake. This snake had been named the Great King by the former Kiawah Indian inhabitants of the area, in honor of both its exceptional size and its fierce protection of its territory. The dry shaking of this snake's rattles, or its "bells," as the Indians had called them, brought a sure stop to men climbing over a brush pile or walking through close undergrowth. Diamondbacks can be more than six or seven feet long, weigh over twenty pounds, and, though thick as a grown man's forearm muscle, quickly strike and inject more than a tablespoon of amber-colored venom into a victim's arm or leg. For years the office headquarters at the Santee-Cooper construction site at Pinopolis displayed the skins of some of the largest diamondback rattlers killed in clearing the site, with what must have been a dubious effect on employee recruitment. On hearing the rattle of the diamondback while venturing inside the yard of an overgrown cemetery or an abandoned house, most men will repent of what they consider their sins and will wish themselves elsewhere.

But despite a turnover rate of more than two-thirds among the WPA work force, the work at Santee-Cooper progressed. Jimmy Byrnes was determined that his project be a success, and in 1941 he persuaded the members of the War Production Board to declare it "necessary for the national defense" so that the Santee-Cooper authority could claim priority on the delivery of construction machinery and supplies. This official declaration of the need to complete the project as soon as possible in the name of national security also justified the authority's decision to remove the WPA work force from the clearing of the upper basin, leaving that area to what the authority euphemistically called deferred clearing—that is, waiting until after the flooding caused by the dams to collect whatever trees and debris floated to the surface of the newly formed lake. The deferred-clearing policy also helped reduce the turnover and dissatisfaction among the WPA employees. To hurry the project along further, Frank Lever found a man to supervise the moving of the dead. And, in a twentieth-century innovation that John Christian Senf would have envied, floodlights and generators were brought into the swamps so that men could work twenty-four hours a day pouring concrete, hammering together forms, and moving earth for the foundations of the two great dams.

The Santee-Cooper project never reached its goal of providing 10,000 men with jobs, but at the peak of activity, before the start of the Second World War, about 7,300 men found work helping to build the dams. An eighteen-mile railroad was laid through the undeveloped wilderness to haul material to the site. Over 4,000,000 cubic yards of earth were moved for the project, 2,400,000 bags of cement were mixed, and 13,000,000 pounds of steel were used to reinforce buildings and dams. Gradually, the upper dam that was to divert the Santee River into the first of the two lakes took shape along its eight-mile-long front. The two-mile-long hydroelectric dam at Pinopolis also neared completion. And at Pinopolis, the concrete walls and steel doors of the seventy-five-foot navigational lock, the tallest single-lift lock on the East Coast, began to rise above the surrounding swamps, looking like the exterior of an office building misplaced from Charleston, thirty-six miles away.

The impoundment of water began on November 12, 1941. To document the success of the Santee-Cooper project, the Farm Security Administration had sent a young FSA photographer, Jack Delano, into the region to take for publicity purposes before-and-after photographs of the residents removed from the Santee-Cooper basins. Delano was glad to have the job, but in his letters to the FSA home office in Washington, the photographer wrote that he was appalled by what he found: "This seems like the most tortured, primitive, poverty-stricken (economically and socially) wasted area I have ever seen. Yet the potentialities are so great that one feels rather that the South must come out of it even though it has so many strikes against it." For all his misgivings, Delano and his wife stayed at the Santee-Cooper site, and, along with his fellow FSA photographers Walker Evans and Dorothea Lange in other parts of the state, Delano recorded the New Deal social changes in the lives of these South Carolina residents.

Delano took some required publicity shots, but his best photography also was motivated by a deep concern for the area's rural residents, black and white, who were facing the uncertainties of a government-mandated removal from their communities and homes. Nearly fifty years afterward, the Santee-Cooper basin was the only site of his FSA photographic work in the United States that Delano, after a distinguished photographic and cinema career in Puerto Rico, chose to revisit. Walking in 1990 over some of the ground remaining above water, he recalled his feelings for the people whose homes were now under the lakes. "I felt very sympathetic for these people who were facing this very serious problem," Delano said. "They were digging up graves in the cemeteries and moving them . . . and I felt that this was a very tragic moment in these people's lives."

"I suppose I've said this many times, but they reminded me of what William Styron said when asked the definition of drama," Delano said. " 'Drama is just people in trouble.' And these people were in trouble." The people who were particularly in trouble, in Delano's opinion, were the black residents along the Santee River, who were being moved into rural housing that he considered inadequate, or who were relocated to public housing projects in Charleston, where their employment skills as former farmers were marginal. "After having seen some of the awful shacks the Negroes have had to move into," Delano wrote in 1941 to his supervisor, "what can you tell an old Negro woman who says, 'I've lived on this land since I was a little chap—without shoes on my feet—without clothes on my back. Now it's my own and I got old getting it. Tell me, how they treating us folks in the other areas?' "

"Bit of South Is Doomed" was the unintentional answer in a *New York Times* headline before the last causeways were closed on the Santee-Cooper and the waters at last began to back up into the basins. Despite the concern of a few individuals like Jack Delano about the fates of the area's poor black residents, the focus of the *Times* story, like that of the rest of the nation, fell on the destruction of the white, pre–Civil War architecture and other historic sites in the Santee delta. "The tomb of [Francis] Marion at Belle Isle, formerly his brother's plantation, must be moved elsewhere," the *Times* noted. Also to be lost to the waters, the newspaper reported, were the plantation holdings of William Moultrie, another hero of the Revolutionary War and an investor in the eighteenth-century Santee Canal. The *Times* provided its readers with a vivid picture of the spreading river covering the once famous plantation houses of the delta: "Walnut Grove, the Oaks, and Belvedere will see the encroaching muddy waters of the Santee. Handhewn timbers, fastened with wooden pins, still as sound as when they were cut a century or more ago, must be salvaged or surrendered to the lake's waters."

Ceremonies for the completion of the Santee-Cooper power project and the filling of the 160,000 acres of reservoir space with water were broadcast live by the NBC radio network on November 12, 1942. Jimmy Byrnes was present and prominent among those credited with the project's success. The state authority, in honor of the two eighteenth-century patriots whose homes and graves the flooding had disturbed, decided to name the upper basin Lake Marion and the lower basin Lake Moultrie. Shortly after the dedicatory ceremonies, the five giant turbines inside the new power-house at Pinopolis began to turn as water from Lake Moultrie rushed over them. In the words of a press release from the Santee-Cooper authority, these turbines "began to spill out a golden flow of wealth."

More than just illusory wealth also began to spin through those turbines. Beginning in 1942, large deposits of black muck protruding above the water began to be spotted in Charleston Harbor. Heavy deposits of silt, or shoaling, had never been a major problem in the history of the harbor. But these new shoals, appearing so suddenly and mysteriously, now seriously impeded commercial shipping. When the Army Corps of Engineers attempted to remove the silt by dredging, the engineers found that shoals returned in a few days at the same locations. Since the shoaling occurred so soon after the start-up of the Santee-Cooper project, the engineers decided to look upriver. There they found the origin of the mysterious Charleston shoaling in the massive diversion of the Santee River, which the corps had, at Jimmy Byrnes' urging, approved for the Santee-Cooper project. The river's diversion from its original channel had eliminated that huge natural, wide estuary where the silt from its 15,000 square mile drainage area could settle. Instead, the Santee now was carrying sediment from its entire drainage area into the inadequate short channel of the Cooper River. Having no place else to settle, the silt was being deposited into Charleston Harbor.

"Here was manifested the error"—to repeat the historian's words regarding the consequences of Colonel John Senf's arrogance—of Jimmy Byrnes' and the state authority's disregarding previous surveys and recommendations on the Santee River. In the earlier instance the Santee Canal had run dry; this time the proponents of the Santee-Cooper had inadvertently created a phenomenon that was the exact opposite of what they had anticipated. One of the finest natural harbors in the world now was in danger of becoming an area of unnavigable shoals, and the costs of correcting this shoal damage threatened to far exceed the hoped-for revenue from increased navigation on the Santee-Cooper lakes. In 1943 the annual cost of dredging Charleston Harbor by the Army Corps of Engineers was $30,779. By 1944, after two years of operation by Santee-Cooper, the cost of dredging had risen to $302,897 annually. By 1965, the corps estimated, the total cost of dredging the harbor by the Army and the Navy from 1942 to 1965 as a direct result of the Santee-Cooper project upriver was $24 million. Dredging costs had thus accumulated by 1965 to almost two-thirds the amount of the original grant and loan for the Santee-Cooper construction authorized by Franklin Roosevelt in July 1935. "The great wealth did not come," the nineteenth-century historian had written of the end of the Santee Canal in words that could have prophesied the great building on the Santee River in the twentieth century. "They were utterly deceived."

The solution to the problem of shoaling at Charleston Harbor proposed by the Army Corps of Engineers, and which eventually received federal funding, was the building of yet another dam and canal, this time in order to redivert much of the Santee River into its original channel. Since such an action reduced the flow available from the reservoir to the power station at Pinopolis, the Santee-Cooper authority received permission to build additional power stations, fueled by oil or nuclear energy. And since the Army Corps of Engineers had approved the diversion of the Santee River, the corps agreed to assume the costs of constructing and maintaining the new dam for the river's rediversion and also to construct and maintain a generating station to supply additional power to the Santee-Cooper authority. The Army Corps of Engineers began operations at its new dam and power station in 1985. The construction costs that year were reported by the corps as $63.7 million.

Today the concrete dams and other structures of the original Santee-Cooper project rise above the surrounding lakes and subtropical coastal plains like white monuments to the ambitions of Franklin Roosevelt, the New Deal, and Jimmy Byrnes. By the time the project was declared completed, in 1942, the original loan and grant had been renegotiated seven times, to a final figure of $53 million (excluding the $11 million spent by the WPA in clearing the land for the reservoirs). Jimmy Byrnes got his state's "fair share" of relief spending, and with a vengeance: Santee-Cooper eventually received the largest amount of PWA funding of any project on the East Coast. Investigations into the cost overruns and the hiring irregularities at the Santee-Cooper site had become active issues in the administration of the PWA and in South Carolina politics by 1942. But by this time Jimmy Byrnes had left the U.S. Senate for the Supreme Court, and Justice Byrnes often stated publicly that he had had nothing further to do with the Santee-Cooper project after he had obtained the initial commitment for funding from FDR in July 1935. (In a cruel gibe to the childless Jimmy and Maude Byrnes, the *Charleston News and Courier*, which had become disenchanted with the project, published in 1941 an anonymous rhyme describing Santee-Cooper as an abandoned "baby" crying out for Senator Jimmy Byrnes to acknowledge his patrimony.) Burnet Maybank, however, always cheerfully acknowledged his connection to Santee-Cooper, and in this respect the observations of Coley Blease on the usefulness of the project to the political partnership of Byrnes and Maybank were correct: Maybank later ran successfully for the state's governorship, defeating Blease, among other candidates, in a race during which his skill at obtaining federal money and New Deal jobs at the Santee-Cooper site was widely promoted. In one important area the Santee-Cooper project did bring one of its promised benefits: deaths by malaria in South Carolina, numbering in the hundreds in the 1930s, were reduced to a total of four in 1950, primarily as a result of the mosquito control performed by the Santee-Cooper authority.

For Jimmy Byrnes, however, the Santee-Cooper project had already done its job in 1941 with his elevation to the Supreme Court, partly because of his demonstrated skills in the court fights with the private utility companies. But although it advanced the political ambitions of Byrnes and Maybank, the project was less successful in fulfilling the ambitions of its proponents to develop "a vast empire nearby." From 1945 to 1965 the predominant growth of jobs in the Santee-Cooper service area was in retail services rather than in manufacturing, and this growth was attributed mainly to the postwar national boom in tourism along such areas of the Carolina coast as Myrtle Beach. Since motels and restaurants do not require great amounts of electrical energy, and since this area already was served by private utilities, this economic growth cannot be directly attributed to the presence of Santee-Cooper. In fact, a 1965 economic survey at a state university determined that the Santee-Cooper project had an overall negative economic effect on the immediate region because of the amount of land under the lakes lost to timbering, farming, or the payment of private property taxes. In the five modern South Carolina counties that surround the two inland lakes and that make up what is left of the old Huguenot parishes, the U.S. Census reported in 1980, an average of 22.3 percent of the residents lived at or below the national poverty line.

In these old Huguenot parishes, the twenty-two work camps that once housed the thousands of WPA laborers have been dismantled, or else claimed by the waters of the two lakes. The big poisonous snakes are mostly gone. At the seventy-five-foot navigational lock at Pinopolis, standing incongruously above the surrounding palmetto thickets, there are no lines of commercial barges waiting to go upriver. The lock's greatest commercial activity occurred briefly in the 1960s during the construction of the interstate highway bridge across Lake Marion, when the lock transported the gravel for the interstate roadbed that made commercial river traffic even more of an anachronism. In the last decade of the twentieth century, the navigational lock is being used, incredibly, to raise minnows and other growing fish from the Cooper River into Lake Marion for the convenience of sportsmen.

It is a fisherman's paradise that Jimmy Byrnes inadvertently bequeathed as his best gift to his state as a result of his support for Santee-Cooper. The "big muddy lakes" that Archibald Rutledge claimed no one could love actually are usually an intense, cobalt blue color and have become among the most popular choices in the United States for sport fishermen. The huge, comparatively shallow impoundments of the warm waters of Lake Moultrie and Lake Marion are like enormous saucers for the nourishing of game fish, and each year hundreds of trophy-sized striped bass and truly enormous catfish are pulled from the waters. Residents of the surrounding counties can at least find employment some months of the years as fishing guides.

On an early summer morning in fishing season, after the red sun burns off the mist from the dark green of slash pines at the lakes' edges, the heat from the 250 square miles of water begins to stir in palpable waves. By midday, as if by mutual assent, both the fishermen in their boats and the fish they wish to hook tend to congregate within the narrow shadows of the bridge of Interstate 95 crossing Lake Marion. Under the guardrails of the I-95 bridge, the water catches in bright sunlight the reflections of automobiles of tourists speeding southward toward Florida, or of the heavily laden transport trucks rushing northward, the vehicles' reflections spreading over the lake's surface in distorted images of the late twentieth century. To the more than six thousand people whose graves were removed from below the waters, and to the hundreds more whose graves are still there, these images of traffic over the Santee-Cooper lakes would have seemed like the fragments of a grotesque dream that we can barely remember on rising, but from which we can recall a phrase we heard during our dreaming both familiar and puzzling:

"Senator Byrnes was in favor of it, and President Roosevelt will grant any request of his."

9

Jumping
the Traces

After receiving the nomination of his one-party state in 1936 and being assured of a seat in the Senate beyond Franklin Roosevelt's second term, Jimmy Byrnes indeed began to "jump the traces," in Harold Ickes' prophetic image of a nervous, headstrong horse escaping its restraints and going its own way. Before his return to the Senate in 1937, few southern elected officials had been publicly more in support of a liberal New Deal nationalism than had Jimmy Byrnes. For example, a week after the U.S. Supreme Court on May 27, 1935, declared the NIRA unconstitutional, Byrnes went back to South Carolina to make a speech criticizing the Court's decision. Probably as a favor to Franklin Roosevelt, to allow his administration to test public reaction to the idea, Byrnes proposed that the Constitution be amended so as to make legal the regulation of business by the NRA. Roosevelt eventually had other plans for the Supreme Court, and nothing more came of Byrnes' proposal, but it was extraordinary for Byrnes even to have suggested such a radical alteration of the Constitution in a state as conservative as South Carolina.

The exceptional loyalty of Senator Jimmy Byrnes to a New Deal economic nationalism under FDR during his first term in office can be matched only by the extraordinarily liberal career of that other South Carolinian master of national politics—John C. Calhoun. In his early-nineteenth-century career, Calhoun had anticipated Byrnes' love for an activist federal government constructing canals and promoting other internal improvements, such as the twentieth-century Santee-Cooper project so important to Byrnes. And much as Byrnes was FDR's designated "economic champion" in the U.S. Senate and voted against his region's traditional interest in a low tariff in order to protect the New Deal's experimental programs of the AAA and the NRA, so John C. Calhoun had voted for a protective tariff in 1816 and introduced in 1817 the bill for a revived economic nationalism with the charting of a National Bank of the United States.

Political commentators were speculating as early as 1937 that Jimmy Byrnes was on his way to becoming "the John C. Calhoun of the second Roosevelt administration." But in Byrnes' second term the comparison was not to the younger, liberal John Calhoun. Instead, Byrnes was compared to the older Calhoun, who had perceived economic threats to his native South in the national policies of Andrew Jackson and who had angrily resigned his vice presidency during the Jackson administration to spend the rest of his career blocking the interests of northern Democrats in the U.S. Senate.

During his career in the U.S. Senate, Jimmy Byrnes never broke formally with his party, and in late December 1937 he refused to join other southern Democrats in issuing with some Republican senators a bipartisan "Conservative Manifesto," protesting the New Deal's continued relief spending and unbalanced budgets. Without the support of powerful senators like Byrnes, the conservatives' manifesto went nowhere. But it was plain that by the end of the Seventy-fifth Congress, in mid-1938, Byrnes had in fact "jumped the traces" and withdrawn his support and considerable influence from many of Roosevelt's economic and social programs. Unlike that between Calhoun and Jackson, the friendship between Jimmy Byrnes and Franklin Roosevelt was never irrevocably torn, and the two men at times discussed their ideological differences over pleasant White House lunches. (On one occasion, Roosevelt greeted Byrnes with an impromptu singing of "Oh Where, Oh Where, Is My Wandering Boy?") Nevertheless, Jimmy Byrnes was identified by the *New York Times* in late December 1938 as one of three Democratic leaders of a "move to hold back the New Deal."

The other two leading opponents of the New Deal were identified by the newspaper as Vice-President Jack Garner and Senator Pat Harrison. Of the three, Jimmy Byrnes was the most aggressive in his attempts to withhold increased funding for such New Deal agencies as the WPA. As chairman of the appropriations subcommittee on relief spending, Senator Byrnes had attempted to block Roosevelt's request to Congress in April 1937 for $1.5 billion for WPA programs throughout fiscal 1938. In a nationally broadcast radio address on May 3, 1937, Byrnes argued that economic output for 1937 had exceeded that of 1928, the last year before the stock market crash, and that unemployment, although still heavy, had declined from the massive numbers of 1933–34. Byrnes apparently believed sincerely that the worst of the Depression was over and that what was holding back the recovery of private investment was primarily the disproportionate government spending on relief employment such as WPA projects. His statements that evening against the WPA appropriation can be interpreted as his declaration of independence from the second Roosevelt administration, or as his intention, long suspected by Ickes, of jumping the traces.

"As a member of the United States Senate, I voted for every recovery measure," Byrnes told his national audience. "If today the same conditions existed, I would vote vote for the same appropriations. *But the same conditions do not exist.* The recovery program of this administration has accomplished its purpose. The emergency has passed" (Byrnes' emphasis).

In the days after his speech, Byrnes tried unsuccessfully to cut $500 million from the administration's WPA request during his subcommittee's consideration of the relief bill. Although this effort failed, Byrnes succeeded in having the full committee agree to an amendment that would require local relief agencies to contribute 40 percent of the total costs of WPA projects. (The senator's favored project of Santee-Cooper was safely allotted and on the fiscal books prior to this amendment, and therefore not endangered by the 40 percent rule. Byrnes, who was determined to raise the political fortunes of his protégé Burnett Maybank, apparently put pragmatism above ideology when the record WPA spending in his state on the Santee-Cooper project could win votes for Maybank.) The president could waive this requirement if the local agency could document its inability to pay the 40 percent, a provision the press immediately termed the "pauper's oath." And, finally, the Byrnes amendment set a statutory limit of 3 percent of a project's total budget for administrative costs.

Roosevelt and Hopkins knew that together the requirement of a 40 percent payment by local agencies and the impossibly low ceiling of 3 percent for administrative costs would effectively kill the WPA. Having gotten the $1.5 billion relief request safely through the House with no such requirements, the president and Hopkins therefore were determined to defeat the Byrnes amendment in the Senate, so as not to have to accept any part of it in a later House-Senate conference committee. The summer of 1937 saw an acrimonious exchange of letters and words between Byrnes on one side and Hopkins on the other, as both sides lobbied to obtain the votes of senators in the middle. (At one point, during testimony before Byrnes' appropriations subcommittee, Byrnes asked Hopkins whether he could not "get by" for one more year with a reduced appropriation. Hopkins replied that he could, but he doubted the unemployed could.)

The Roosevelt administration was finally able to muster the votes to defeat the Byrnes amendment, as well as an amendment requiring a lesser local payment, offered as a compromise by Joe Robinson. And by the end of June 1937, the Senate passed the $1.5 billion appropriations for the WPA on the anonymity of a voice vote. But notice had been served to the administration that it could no longer count on Jimmy Byrnes, as it had during the Hundred Days, unquestioningly to approve relief legislation through the Appropriations Committee.

It was part of the growing troubles for the Roosevelt administration that Jimmy Byrnes was able to gather a significant core of like-minded Democrats who sided with him in voting for the reduced WPA appropriations. This core of dissatisfied Democrats became at times a coalition in 1937–38, when they were joined occasionally by Republican senators, usually from rural western or midwestern states, in attempts to cut relief spending, lower taxes, and balance the budget. By the end of 1937 this conservative coalition was strong enough to hand the New Deal its first significant defeat in relief-related legislation, by drastically cutting appropriations for a bill introduced by Senator Robert Wagner of New York to finance low-income urban housing. The conservative coalition headed by Byrnes from 1937 to 1939 varied in size and its membership was informal, as senators joined in and dropped out on the basis of the specific legislation being considered and the demands of their party caucus. And, despite Byrnes' growing independence from the New Deal, the senator himself, as noted earlier, was unwilling to sign the public manifesto of 1937 declaring a conservative agenda. Jimmy Byrnes had jumped the traces by 1937, but he was not quite ready to jump the Democratic party.

Conservatives on both sides of the party aisle in the Senate chamber were coming together, however, to oppose the introduction of New Deal policies in their southern and western home states, which a later generation would know as the Sunbelt. The concentration of conservative political power in this region and the realignment of party loyalties in the 1950s and 1960s from the Democratic to the Republican party throughout the South is usually dated for convenience's sake from the 1948 bolting of the national Democratic party by southern segregationists to form the Dixiecrat movement. In fact, this realignment had a much broader ideological base than race, and it had begun more than ten years earlier with the "hold back the New Deal movement" of Jimmy Byrnes in the U.S. Senate.

Byrnes was among the first of the southerners in 1937 to give political organization to the discontent that by 1938 had made even the inveterate Democratic loyalist Carter Glass wonder whether it would be better for the eleven states of the old Confederacy to forsake the Democratic party and the Compromise of 1877, whereby white southerners were left unchallenged in their social and economic superiority to southern blacks in exchange for an unswervingly loyal "Solid South" of white Democrats. It might be better to become a conservative Republican, Glass wrote angrily to a friend, than continue to be a Democrat and "face the new Reconstruction era that northern so-called Democrats are menacing us with." With the New Deal sponsoring domestic and economic legislation that many southerners like Glass felt was inimical to their region, it would no longer do for FDR blithely to excuse the differences by saying, as he had so many times to Jimmy Byrnes, that at heart he was a Democrat like Cordell Hull, meaning that he was an economic and social liberal only until the effects of the Depression were thoroughly eradicated.

Although Byrnes, unlike Glass, refrained from openly advocating a change in party registration while a senator, he would live to see the realignment against Roosevelt that he had once led with Republicans contribute to the transformation of the South by the mid-1960s into a largely conservative, GOP stronghold in presidential elections. And in 1968, still active in politics, Byrnes also would see, in the words of the historian George Mowry, a future "Republican president virtually accept the essence of Senator James F. Byrnes' 1938 'southern strategy.' "

What Jimmy Byrnes and Richard Nixon would plan as a southern strategy in 1968 was yet to come; what Senator Byrnes made of his southern strategy in 1938 was to combine votes with conservative rural Republicans to frustrate much of the New Deal's second-term legislation. Between 1936 and 1939 the conservative coalition was directly responsible for either defeating or substantially altering the child labor bill, the proposal to make permanent the Civilian Conservation Corps, the bill to extend the TVA to other regions of the nation, and a bill to establish national guidelines for wages and hours. Each of these measures was backed by the administration, and each was perceived by Byrnes and other members of the coalition either as an attempt to benefit exclusively the urban Northeast or to remove some economic advantage (such as lower wages in the South) to give the Northeast an economic parity. In resisting what he perceived as threats to his region, Byrnes succeeded in creating in the Senate in the late 1930s what John C. Calhoun had so frequently desired before the Civil War: a political system of what Calhoun called "concurrent majorities," by which geographic regions composing a voting minority can compel the national majority to compromise on issues between them. For much of the second term of the Roosevelt administration, primarily because of Jimmy Byrnes' activities, the spirit of John C. Calhoun's concurrent majorities reigned in the U.S. Senate.

But despite its intellectual antecedents in Calhoun and its leadership by Byrnes, the conservative coalition of the 1930s was not exclusively southern in its membership or orientation. A frequent participant was Senator Arthur Vandenberg, a Republican of Michigan. Others participating at one time or another were Senators Charles McNary of Oregon, Edward Burke of Nebraska, William King of Utah, and Alva Adams of

Colorado, the last three of whom were Democrats. Many of the Republican senators in this coalition were, unlike the southerners, in favor of passage of a federal antilynching bill and the enforcement of the Fourteenth and Fifteenth amendments to the Constitution. The emerging conservative coalition was formed along the economic and social divisions of urban and rural America, rather than on the North–South boundary or attitudes on race. All the members of the coalition—which usually averaged between twelve and fourteen Republican and between twenty-two and twenty-eight Democratic senators—opposed increased spending for housing and employment relief in big cities, particularly cities in the Northeast. All these senators thought that such expenditures inevitably resulted in increased taxes for small business men and reduced benefits for farmers; and all of them were distrustful of the apparent influence with Roosevelt after the presidential election of 1936 of such leaders of organized labor and urban intellectuals as Sidney Hillman and Harry Hopkins. Many of these coalition senators sincerely believed with Byrnes that by 1937 the worst of the Depression was over and that the emergency measures taken during the first term of the New Deal should be repealed or abolished. And, of course, the southern Democrats were positioning their party to have a much more conservative platform in 1940, when, it was assumed, Franklin Roosevelt would retire and the party would nominate a candidate who was not such a fervent New Dealer.

Yet it was no accident that the leaders of the conservative coalition in the U.S. Senate all were southerners. At the height of the coalition's activities, the *Washington Star* published Jay Franklin's column identifying Byrnes, Harrison, and other southern senators as among Bernard Baruch's Old Masters and claiming that Baruch was simply collecting back for his own conservative economic interests the Old Masters he had "loaned" the New Deal for the emergencies of the first term. Jimmy Byrnes, however, had never been so easily owned as Jay Franklin imagined, and he at least had never owed Baruch large amounts of money. To identify the southern region in the 1930s with economic royalism and political reaction is to overlook the fact that many senators who were also among the New Deal's most radical economic reformers came from the South—including Senators Huey Long, Hugo Black, and the racist but economically liberal Theodore Bilbo.

Race was more the sticking point. Southerners, including Byrnes, had become alarmed with efforts by New Deal agencies such as the Farm Security Administration and the New Deal–encouraged Southern Tenant Farmers Union to appoint black citizens to administrative posts or to increase government benefits to Negro farmers. During his estrangement from the New Deal, for example, Byrnes was surely aware that his friend Colonel Lawrence Pinckney had received orders from the WPA's Washington office, under Harry Hopkins' direction, to allot state money and labor to build housing for black tenants displaced from the Santee-Cooper basins who had not owned property and therefore not received any resettlement money. The South Carolina office objected to the housing project as an illegal spending of public money for private benefit, and the WPA-sponsored housing for the displaced black tenant farmers was never built.

But the final reason for the southerners' disenchantment with Franklin Roosevelt in the late 1930s was personal in a way that had nothing to do with either race or region. Turner Catledge, the Mississippi native who was then reporting on the Senate for the *New York Times*, characterized the difference between the president and his former supporters in the South as a degree of respect for the personal word. "The southerners were often old rascals," Catledge wrote of these senators in his autobiography. They were "not at all attractive in liberal terms. Yet you had to admire their honesty."

According to Catledge, the southern senators and congressmen of the 1930s "were men who lived by a code." It was a code, he wrote, that foremost "demanded that a man's word be his bond. If Sam Rayburn or Jimmy Byrnes gave me his word on something, I would have bet my life on it. This was a feeling that I never had about Franklin Roosevelt or many of his New Dealers."

It was this ambiguous use to which Franklin Roosevelt put his personal word that so often infuriated Jimmy Byrnes. Much of Senator Byrnes' obstructionism in the relief appropriation in 1937, for example, was due to the fact that Roosevelt had earlier promised Byrnes during a White House meeting that the administration would ask for no more than one billion dollars for the WPA; but after making that promise to Byrnes, Roosevelt met later with Harry Hopkins, who prevailed upon FDR to change his mind and ask for one and a half billion. Byrnes in 1962 still recalled this and other sharp disappointments in his appraisal of Franklin Roosevelt. "How could a man with so many fine qualities tell you one thing and so often do another?" Byrnes asked.

The rhetorical question is immediately a little suspect. Jimmy Byrnes himself had been no stranger during his political career to the intriguing ambiguities of truth. But even in 1962 there was enough sincere hurt in Jimmy Byrnes' rhetorical question to the then silent Roosevelt to reveal that this sense of frequent betrayal had been an important point in the 1930s in his political break with FDR. And for Byrnes and the other southerners, the sense of greatest betrayal came in 1937–38, between the death of Joe Robinson during the court-packing fight, the subsequent White House–engineered defeat of Pat Harrison as majority leader, and FDR's attempted purge of conservatives from the Democratic party in the primary elections of 1938.

———

Roosevelt's decision in early February 1937 to propose legislation to increase the number of justices on the U.S. Supreme Court is an example of what James Patterson, the best scholar of FDR's relations with conservatives in the Seventy-fifth Congress, called that president's "chief weakness in congressional relations: his love of surprising, dramatic action." Although Roosevelt had been turning over in his mind several plans to reduce the Court's authority since the "Black Monday" of 1935, when the Court invalidated the NIRA, he had discussed his thoughts with no one in Congress or in his cabinet except Attorney General Homer Cummings. Roosevelt and his attorney general apparently decided that proposing a constitutional amendment enlarging the interstate commerce clause to increase the powers of the presidency would take too long and be too vulnerable to defeat by local banking and commercial interests vested in the nation's forty-eight state houses. But the need for some sort of action must have seemed to Roosevelt to be acute, as a Supreme Court dominated by Republican-appointed justices continued to undo much of the New Deal in 1936. That year the Court found unconstitutional the AAA, the Guffey Coal Act of 1935, which nationally regulated the production of that fuel, and a New York State minimum-wage bill similar to one that Roosevelt hoped to propose nationally. Accordingly, with no further detailed explanations, Roosevelt on February 4, 1937, sent word to the chairmen of the congressional judiciary committees and other party leaders in the Senate and House that he wished to meet with them and members of his cabinet early the next morning at the White House.

Byrnes and Harrison, Roosevelt's two chief lieutenants in the Senate, were not invited to the White House meeting that morning, but within an hour of its adjournment, participants at the upstairs Cabinet Room meeting had described the details to them. After a cheerful good-morning, Roosevelt distributed down the long cabinet table copies of a bill to reorganize the federal judiciary—including the U.S. Supreme Court. The proposal gave Roosevelt the authority to nominate one new federal judge for each current judge who waited more than six months after his seventieth birthday to retire; as many as six new Supreme Court justices could thus be appointed. On the pretext that placing younger judges on the bench would promote efficiency in the judiciary, Roosevelt was actually proposing a breathtaking change in the constitutional checks and balances between the executive and the judiciary. Roosevelt frankly told the assembled Democratic leaders that the intention of his proposal was to "humble" the Supreme Court. A fifteen-justice Supreme Court, six to be New Deal appointees, would give Roosevelt all he needed to eliminate legal challenges to the New Deal.

The plan was so patently a scheme to pack the Supreme Court with New Deal sympathizers that this pejorative description stuck, and the bill became known, even on occasion among its proponents, as "the court-packing bill." The congressional delegation and cabinet members, with the exception of Cummings, sat in stunned silence. Joseph Robinson, who idealized the Supreme Court and was expected to secure passage of the bill through the Senate, was obviously disturbed. He was described during the silence after the president's remarks to have "flushed mahogany and stared down at the table top, as though his fate had been written in the wood for him to decipher." Roosevelt quickly broke off the meeting before any discussions could begin, saying that the press was waiting downstairs. He planned to announce his introduction of the court reorganization bill in a few minutes at a news conference. The congressional leaders would learn more about the bill when he sent down a message to Capitol Hill that day at noon, calling for its quick passage.

After the president had left the Cabinet Room, the meeting broke up into a confused, monosyllabic jumble. Inside Jack Garner's automobile carrying the congressional delegation back to the Hill, Hatton W. Sumners of Texas, the chairman of the House Judiciary Committee, broke the silence. "Boys," he said, "here's where I cash in my chips."

No other New Deal legislation so divided congressional Democrats and alienated public opinion from the administration. And on no other issue in 1937 did the conservation coalition usually led by Byrnes gain the overt or tacit support of so many moderate to liberal senators. Despite Roosevelt's confidence in early February that the court bill would quickly pass, opposed only by a few irreconcilable Jeffersonian Democrats and bitter-end Republicans, debate in the Senate continued until July. And the most partisan statements in debate over the bill came not in exchanges between Republicans and Democrats but in objections to the plan from members of the president's own party. As expected, the old conservative Carter Glass attacked the bill soon after Roosevelt's message to Congress, the Virginia senator rising from a sickbed in order to make a national radio speech against the measure. Glass, born within one generation of his fellow Virginian and former chief justice John Marshall, compared Roosevelt's bill to an attempt "to rape the Supreme Court." But senators and presidential advisers far to the left of Carter Glass also opposed Roosevelt's bill as an attempt to correct by subterfuge, and only halfway at that, what they perceived as the constitutional defect of unlimited review of congressional action by the Supreme Court. "If you're going to pack a court at all, you've got to really pack it," argued Roosevelt's assistant attorney general, Robert Jackson.

Jimmy Byrnes was one of the few members of the conservative coalition in the Senate and one of the few southerners to stick by the president and attempt to obtain passage of his court bill. Most of his friends in the Senate were either lukewarm toward the measure or actively hostile toward it. (Jack Garner, after hearing FDR's message read to the Senate calling for passage of the bill, left the vice president's podium and walked out of the chamber, holding his nose and making a Roman Colosseum gesture of thumbs-down as he walked by spectators.) Byrnes' longtime colleague Pat Harrison said he would support the measure, but then said and did nothing else publicly for it. Joe Robinson, although he admitted that the bill was a "pretty raw" deal for the Supreme Court, was obligated to work for its passage in the Senate out of his consideration of both his position as majority leader and his personal ambition to receive one of the Supreme Court appointments. Probably more out of personal loyalty to Joe Robinson, and the expectation that his friend Pat Harrison would become majority leader when Robinson moved to the Supreme Court, Byrnes went to work for the bill.

He did not work with his usual enthusiasm. After spending an hour with FDR discussing the proposal the second week of February, Byrnes told reporters outside the White House that he was at least "stronger for the plan than I was before"—quite different from his being stronger for it than *ever* before. Byrnes did agree to deliver the following week a national radio address arguing for the plan, a speech both he and FDR knew would help offset Carter Glass's speech. And although Roosevelt until the early summer of 1937 was unwilling to compromise, Byrnes from the beginning worked to find a way for some increased judicial appointments that both sides could accept as a compromise.

The trouble was that the heated feelings engendered on both sides by Roosevelt's self-described attempt to "humble" the Supreme Court did not go away as the Senate Judiciary Committee heard testimony, usually negative, on the bill during the following months. (Byrnes had agreed to the strategy that the court bill be introduced first in the Senate, because Representative Sumners' "cashing in his chips" remark had made it clear that the bill would never be approved by the House Judiciary Committee.) And as happened so frequently to Jimmy Byrnes when he took a political risk out of loyalty to the Roosevelt administration, the Ku Klux Klan began to rise up in opposition to him in South Carolina. A Supreme Court enlarged with six New Deal justices popularly was expected to render decisions more favorable to Negro plaintiffs in civil rights litigation. Editorials and news articles in both northern and southern newspapers interpreted Roosevelt's court plan as an attempt to gain Negro votes from the Republican party for a third-term presidential bid in 1940. As Byrnes continued to support the court plan through the spring and summer of 1937, a flier was anonymously distributed throughout South Carolina. "Warning!" was reproduced above a drawing of a watchful eye and the letters KKK. A picture of a hooded night rider carrying a torch was printed in red ink and below was the caption "Communism Must Be Destroyed. Hands Off the Supreme Court."

What made Byrnes' position even more vexing was Roosevelt's uncharacteristic refusal to compromise with him or other members of the

Senate on the court issue. Achieving a politically advantageous compromise between the more liberal policy advocates in the president's office and the conservative congressional Democratic bloc always had been Jimmy Byrnes' specialty. But for much of the legislative impasse on the court bill, Roosevelt refused to deal. Byrnes was very likely among the unnamed group of senators led by Jack Garner who the journalists Turner Catledge and Joseph Alsop reported had gone to see Roosevelt soon after the announcement of the court plan. When the senatorial group met with FDR, Catledge and Alsop recounted, "they asked to be empowered to fix the things up, probably on the basis of two or three [Supreme Court justices] instead of six additional justices, and they warned him that the issue was tearing at the vitals of the Democratic party in Congress. The President laughed in their faces, so loudly that a number of them were exceedingly annoyed and resolved there and then to offer no more advice unless it should be requested of them."

Catledge and Alsop reported that another senator, also opposed to the bill, had gone to the president and pleaded with him to ask for a smaller number of justices. The president, according to their report, disingenuously smiled and asked with mock indignation, "Why, Senator, would you *pack* the Court?"

After participating in such conferences, the usually genial Pat Harrison swore that it would be a "cold day" before he helped Franklin Roosevelt on the court bill. Byrnes, although more sharp tempered, stayed with the president on the issue. He needed Roosevelt just as he knew that Roosevelt needed him; among other issues of concern to the senator in 1937, Santee-Cooper was still in litigation and in need of Roosevelt's protection. Byrnes and Roosevelt were able to overlook their differences that spring and summer of 1937 in order to maintain a working partnership on the other issues of court reorganization and political patronage that each man wanted resolved. But the bad feelings just below the surface between congressional Democrats such as Senator Byrnes and the Roosevelt administration broke into the open in the final days of March, when the court bill was under consideration by the Senate Judiciary Committee. During this momentary pause before the fight on the floor over the bill, Jimmy Byrnes once again jumped the traces. In this case, the senator introduced an amendment declaring illegal the sit-down strikes of the Committee for Industrial Organization.

Since the first sit-down strike, in early January 1937, when workers occupied two General Motors plants in Dearborn, Michigan, the CIO, under the leadership of John Lewis and Sidney Hillman, had gained unprecedented membership and political strength. At least a million and a half workers had joined CIO unions by the first six months of that year. Hillman's and Lewis's success had been due partly to their aggressive use of the sit-down tactic, in which workers occupied the manufacturer's property and refused to leave or allow production until a contract had been negotiated. The sit-down strike contributed to organizing successes for labor in 1937 in the automobile and steel industries, and as an instrument both to express anger at management and to compel action, it seems to have captured the public imagination in 1937. That year there occurred widespread sit-down actions by workers seeking to unionize the sales staffs of department stores, utility companies, barbershops, and schools.

Although not greatly different from the flying squadron employed in the South in 1934, which also had interfered with the millowners' use of their property, the sit-down was viewed with particular abhorrence by southern Democrats as a new form of social disorder tolerated by the Roosevelt administration. The southern congressional delegations denounced the sit-down almost with unanimity as violation of the common-law sanctity of private property. Among southern senators usually favorable to organized labor, such as Byrnes, this resistance to the sit-down was directed against the CIO itself, which was rapidly taking membership away from the craft unions of the American Federation of Labor. (The AFL had denounced the CIO's use of sit-downs.) Ever since the CIO's unprecedented half-million-dollar contribution to Franklin Roosevelt's reelection campaign in 1936, congressional conservatives such as Byrnes had worried about the prominence in the party of men like Lewis and Hillman. The conservatives also noted that neither Roosevelt nor the Democratic governor of Michigan had called for the use of public police force to evict the sit-down strikers at General Motors. After returning from a visit among constituents in South Carolina in 1937, Byrnes wrote to Jack Garner that he had found among his state's Democrats "an even stronger sentiment against John L. Lewis and his methods" since his last visit. Byrnes then advised the vice president, in a certain reference to Roosevelt, that "one of these days, some of our friends are going to agree with us that the sit-down strikes and relief expenditures have not only injured the country, but also have seriously injured our party."

But in the case of Jack Garner, whom John L. Lewis characterized as "a whiskey-drinking, evil, old man," Jimmy Byrnes in effect was preaching to the church choir. Few men in Washington agreed more thoroughly with Byrnes than did Jack Garner that the Roosevelt administration's apparent condoning of sit-down strikes was a great mistake for the Democratic party. In a meeting with the president shortly before FDR left Washington in early March for a vacation in Warm Springs, Georgia, Garner pressed Roosevelt for a commitment that if sit-downs continued, he would take decisive action to end them.

Garner obtained what he considered a promise from FDR, but while the president was away in Georgia for the next few weeks gathering his strength for the upcoming court battle in the Senate, the sit-down strikes resumed and the White House took no action. Meanwhile, to Jimmy

Byrnes' alarm, the sit-downs and the CIO itself were turning southward. Hillman and Lewis met on March 4 in Washington in order to plan what was described as the "third major offensive in the nation's basic industries." This time, after organizing drives in the steel and automobile industries, the CIO's announced goal was to unionize the nation's textile mills and all other apparel workers. "This will be the greatest effort of the C.I.O.," Hillman announced on March 19, 1937. "This is going to be the best financed and best organized of the C.I.O. campaigns."

Within two weeks of his announcement, the CIO textile campaign headed nationally by Hillman opened a southern headquarters in Atlanta and began dispatching CIO organizers to eight southern states with a goal of gaining 350,000 new members in the region. The southern campaign met with initial success, particularly at the Marlboro Mills in Bennettsville, South Carolina, where over 1,000 workers signed CIO pledge cards. (There, in a scene that strangely foreshadowed the racial struggles in southern society in the 1960s, a group of white strikers blocked the shipment of a boxcar full of tire fabric made at the mills by standing as a massed group of protesters across the railroad tracks leading from the mill. Together they sang the hymn "We Shall Not Be Moved." A later generation knew the same tune by the words of "We Shall Overcome.") On March 31, 1937, Hillman was reported by the *New York Times* and Washington papers as having met with Franklin Roosevelt, now back at the White House, to discuss the labor situation. And on April 1, during a temporary lull in the court battle, Byrnes entered the Senate and by prearrangement with Jack Garner added an amendment to the Guffey coal bill of 1937, then under consideration. Byrnes' amendment read, simply, "It is the sense of Congress that the so-called sit-down strike is illegal and contrary to sound public policy."

As usual, Byrnes had picked the moment of his opponent's greatest vulnerability. Roosevelt needed an immediate passage of the coal bill in order to speed debate on his court reorganization bill, and if he chose to veto the bill because of the offending amendment, the resulting struggle to sustain or override his veto could tie up the Senate for weeks. But if FDR approved the Guffey bill with the Byrnes amendment intact, Roosevelt and his administration would be on record as considering the CIO's main organizational tactic as illegal.

All that day Byrnes refused attempts at compromise or to qualify the language of his amendment. The White House sent word to the Senate that Roosevelt considered a vote against the Byrnes amendment to be a test of party loyalty. Many conservative, anti-CIO senators thus were caught in the middle, as Byrnes had hoped they would be, between two irreconcilable positions. Among those caught was Joe Robinson, whose ambition to rise to the Supreme Court depended upon his successful management of the court bill and on his continued loyalty to the administration.

Robinson spoke frankly to his friend Jimmy Byrnes about the amendment: "I am for it, Jim, but I will have to oppose it." Byrnes had offered his amendment on a Friday; the Senate adjourned without taking action on it until Monday, when the Roosevelt administration hoped either to arrange a compromise or to have the votes to defeat the Byrnes amendment.

In the fond hope of arranging a compromise and of hurrying passage of the court reorganization bill, Joe Robinson accompanied Jack Garner to a meeting with Roosevelt at the White House. Garner, hard faced, came to the meeting in no mood to compromise on the illegality of the sit-downs. Neither was Franklin Roosevelt willing to make any concessions. As soon as the two men began to talk about the sit-down strikes, both Roosevelt and Garner lost their tempers. The president and the vice president of the United States began to abuse each other in such vile language that even Joe Robinson was shocked. He shouted at them to stop, and to both his horror and his relief, the meeting came to an end.

The mail Byrnes began to receive from his labor constituents soon after he introduced his amendment also showed how divisive the issue of the sit-down strike had become among Democrats. "We trusted you to be our friend," one UTWA organizer from Clifton, South Carolina, wrote to Byrnes within four days of the senator's introduction of his amendment. "But I am afraid your stand on this sit-down amendment will hurt you when you offer for another term in the U.S. Senate." Another letter written the same day to Byrnes from a UTWA organizer in Columbia was much more abusive. "We people here in South Carolina consider a man like you a Judas," wrote G. F. Wright, who worked at a Columbia mill carding cotton fibers. "You have hawked and spit in the face of labor, and if you keep that up, you may expect a defeat in the next election. We people had a lot of confidence in Cole Blease, until he crawfished on us so we sidetracked him into the Wilderness. And it is not impossible for us to do you the same way. . . ." (Byrnes was so angry over this letter that he did not answer it. Instead, he wrote to Colonel Lawrence Pinckney at the state WPA office and asked him to find out where Wright was employed.)

Back in Washington the Roosevelt administration had been able over the weekend to gather enough votes to defeat the Byrnes amendment the following Monday. But the damage this intraparty fight over the sit-downs had done to the chances for a successful passage of the court reorganization bill was immediately obvious to the journalists Catledge and Alsop. "Harrison, Byrnes, Garner, and Robinson had ruled the Senate together," they wrote. "Now the first three were in opposition on labor and spending, and therefore disinclined to give the President the help he would otherwise have had from them. . . ."

Byrnes and Harrison were even less inclined to support the court reorganization plan by the second week of April 1937. The Supreme Court, in an apparent reversal of judicial philosophy that month upheld the constitutionality of important New Deal legislation, including the Wagner Labor Relations Act and a minimum-wage law in Washington State. "A switch in time saves nine," was the happy byword among congressional Democrats. Byrnes cheerfully quipped to reporters, "I know not what effect the Wagner decision will have on the court plan, but it seems that the court plan already had some effect on the court." Then, on May 18, came two more good reasons in Byrnes' opinion for not continuing the court fight. The first was the announcement of Supreme Court Justice Willis Van Devanter's decision to retire at the end of the Court's current term. Justice Van Devanter had been one of the four justices most consistently finding against New Deal measures on constitutional grounds. His retirement and FDR's opportunity to appoint a more sympathetic successor, combined with the Court's recent swings in voting, meant that Roosevelt would probably have a safe 6-to-3 majority of pro–New Deal justices by the end of the year. And on the day of Justice Van Devanter's announcement, word also came to the president and members of the Senate that the Senate Judiciary Committee had voted in executive session not to recommend the court reorganization bill to the full Senate. This vote was even more embarrassing to the administration, given the majority of Democrats on the committee.

All these were good reasons for Byrnes to urge the president to give up the court fight. By Jimmy Byrnes' lights, all Franklin Roosevelt had to do was to accept with good grace what luck had granted him with the pending retirement of Justice Van Devanter, which would give FDR most of what he had wanted. And by the president's withdrawing the court bill from further reconsideration by the Senate, the Democratic party would also be spared the embarrassment of a public report by the Judiciary Committee.

Accordingly, two hours after Justice Van Devanter's resignation was announced on May 18, Jimmy Byrnes and Pat Harrison went to the White House and urged Roosevelt to give up the court fight. "Why run for a train," Byrnes asked Roosevelt, "after you've caught it?" The two senators also had come to lobby for the appointment to the Supreme Court of their old friend Joe Robinson of Arkansas. Robinson never had made any secret of his desire, expressed frequently in Senate cloakrooms, to cap off his public career with an appointment to the Court; and Byrnes and Harrison reminded Roosevelt that Robinson's appointment had been expected by party loyalists ever since the Democratic party returned to power in 1933 in recognition of Robinson's prior good service as minority leader and as running mate to Al Smith.

Although he remained outwardly cordial, Roosevelt was furious over this visit after Byrnes and Harrison had left. FDR resented what he considered an attempt by these two Senate conservatives to preempt his choice of Justice Van Deventer's successor. Roosevelt never had explicitly promised the next available Court vacancy to Robinson and Robinson never had been popular with the Democratic left. "Joe is too old (he is 65) and too conservative to be the president's first appointee to the court," the liberal *Nation* magazine editorialized after Justice Van Devanter's announcement. Roosevelt later met with Robinson in early June and told him that "there would be a bride, but there had to be bridesmaids"—meaning that Joe Robinson would get his Court nomination, but first he would have to obtain Senate passage of revised court bill that would allow Roosevelt to appoint at least two or three more new justices more liberal than Robinson. It was Byrnes' perception of this stubbornness on Franklin Roosevelt's part in insisting upon a ideological victory even after he had obtained the desired practical result—"running for a train after you've caught it"—that continued to alienate Jimmy Byrnes from FDR even as he worked throughout June and early July to help his friend Joe Robinson get his black justice's robes.

With the Senate headed for a showdown in early July on a modified court bill, Roosevelt decided to host a remarkable "harmony conference" in late June, in the form of a picnic on a grand scale at the Jefferson Islands Club, off the coast of Maryland. All the Democratic members of both the House and the Senate were brought over to the main island of the club at least once during the three-day period. There, in this enforced congeniality, Democratic conservatives and liberals alike mingled and made small talk in a well-publicized demonstration by the White House that differences over relief spending, sit-down strikes, and the court-packing plan were not destroying the party's unity. (Conspicuously absent during the three-day festivities was Vice President Jack Garner. After his argument with Roosevelt, Garner had earlier in June left Washington for an extended stay at his Texas farm. Garner frankly stated that his absence from Washington was the result of his disgust over FDR's seeming acceptance of sit-downs.) Byrnes and Harrison both received preferred first-day invitations to the picnic, and they were greeted on the island by a relaxed and charming Franklin Roosevelt, who was wearing an old pair of linen slacks and an open shirt with no necktie. For a while, chatting together while FDR sat in a chair under the shade of a big apple tree, Byrnes and Harrison almost felt that the happy days were there once again. Sunburned but happy, full of crabmeat and beer, Byrnes and the other senators returned to Washington for the final, self-destructive battle of the Democratic party in the summer of 1937.

Senate Majority Leader Joe Robinson had for months been under intense personal and political pressures to gain passage of the court bill prior to the opening of final Senate debate on the bill the first week of July. Now, handicapped by the absence of Garner and by Roosevelt's reluctance to follow fully the advice of Byrnes and Harrison, Robinson had seen the chances for the bill's passage and his own justiceship diminish as senators refused to vote for any modified version of the unpopular measure. Throughout the first two weeks of July, Robinson fought off opponents of the court bill in increasingly bitter debate on the Senate floor. Both sides promised "a fight to the death" over the measure, and contemporary observers in the press gallery above the Senate floor described Robinson during these final debates as a "huge, red-faced, heavy-bodied" man, alternately "bellowing his challenges and roaring threats to the the enemy."

On the stupefyingly hot afternoon of July 13, as the senior Democratic senator from North Carolina made a devastating speech against the court bill—indicating more votes lost by the administration—Joe Robinson suddenly sat down at a Senate desk next to Jimmy Byrnes. Robinson was not feeling well, he told Byrnes, and he was going back to his apartment at the downtown Methodist Building to rest. The following day, as the temperatures increased to a record summer high in the humid, unmoving air of Washington, Robinson told his friends and staff that he still felt too unwell to return to the Capitol. On the third day, Jimmy and Maude Byrnes received an early-morning telephone call from the management of the Methodist Building. The body of Joe Robinson had been found by the building's maid earlier that morning inside his hot, unair-conditioned apartment. The body lay dressed in pajamas on the floor next to the senator's bed. His reading glasses still were in place on his bed, and a copy of the *Congressional Record* was in his right hand. Apparently earlier the previous night Robinson had been resting in bed but unable to sleep, reading the prior debates on the court bill and looking for weaknesses in his opponents' arguments. For some reason, Robinson had gotten out of bed, and immediately fallen dead of a heart attack.

Joe Robinson's death effectively killed any hope that Roosevelt's court bill would ever pass the Senate. The necessary one or two senators might have voted for its passage out of loyalty to Robinson; but now even prior supporters of the bill believed, according to Catledge and Alsop, that Robinson "had worked himself to death fighting a lost cause for an ungrateful president." Bernard Baruch, who usually kept his temper in check when it was in his interests to do so, for once acted without calculation when he learned of Robinson's death. Baruch was boarding an ocean liner for his annual shooting vacation in Europe when he heard the news. Baruch immediately canceled his passage in order to attend Robinson's funeral in Little Rock, Arkansas, and then telephoned the White House. Baruch angrily told Roosevelt that he hoped FDR would now drop the court bill and "not kill any more senators."

In his lifetime Joe Robinson had been coarse, vulgar, unmerciful in a fight, and a difficult man to like—"not at all attractive in liberal terms," wrote Turner Catledge. Yet, along with Jimmy Byrnes and Bernard Baruch, many other men had liked Joe Robinson. Byrnes made preparations the day after Robinson's death to join practically all the other Democratic senators on a chartered train to Little Rock for Robinson's funeral. Senators such as Jimmy Byrnes had liked Robinson because, bad temper aside, Joe Robinson had been one of them: that is, Robinson had been frank in his ambition to rise in the world, willing to work very hard and put aside personal preferences for party loyalty ("I am for it, Jim, but I will have to oppose it"), and unembarrassed about claiming a large share of patronage for Arkansas in exchange for all his hard work and loyalty. The pressures on Robinson's party loyalty had been immense since his becoming majority leader in 1933, when this fiscally conservative friend of Baruch's had been given the prime responsibility for passing Roosevelt's liberal spending bills through the Senate. "You can't imagine the hell I have to go through," Robinson had once complained to Carter Glass. "In your case, Joe," Glass had replied unkindly, "the road to hell seems to be lined with post offices."

Now, after Robinson's death, Jimmy Byrnes was trying to send another good friend of his down that road lined with post offices. One of his reasons for joining the senatorial train to Little Rock was that he knew there would be intense politicking aboard that train for candidates to succeed Robinson to the post of majority leader. Pat Harrison wanted the job, and Byrnes was determined to get it for him. There were other candidates for the job, including the then assistant majority leader, Alben Barkley of Kentucky. (Byrnes turned down several requests from other senators that he run for the post himself. He wanted to retain his independence from the White House on relief spending and labor, Byrnes explained, and he also wanted to oblige his friend Harrison's ambitions.) The vacancy would be filled by a vote in the Democratic caucus held when the senators returned to Washington, and Byrnes agreed to manage Harrison's campaign among his fellow senators.

Byrnes had been correct in assuming that the lobbying for candidates to succeed Robinson would begin the moment the train carrying the floral wreaths and Joe Robinson's body in the rear car and live senators in the club car left Union Station. The senatorial politicking hushed only during the Methodist church service preceding Robinson's burial in Little Rock; it continued back aboard the train during the day-and-a-half return journey to Washington. Turner Catledge was on the train and reported in a dispatch to the *New York Times* that the funeral journey had become "a political convention on wheels." When the senators returned to Washington and read that description, Jimmy Byrnes and Pat Harrison summoned Catledge and two other reporters who had written similar stories to the Senate Office Building for a dressing-down.

"You newspaper boys should be ashamed of yourselves," declared the tall, birdlike, and balding Mississippi senator, who stood over the reporters like a scolding crane. "We've been to Little Rock to bury our good old friend, that distinguished American, Joe Robinson, and you are describing us as a bunch of callous politicians."

At this point, in Catledge's later recollection, "Senator Byrnes chimed in, pounding the table and shouting with outrage at our cynicism." Harrison continued his upbraiding. "Why, you say here in one place that we've been buttonholing Senators for their votes on the leadership contest." Catledge's recollection was that Pat Harrison then gave the longest of stage pauses, looked at Senator Byrnes, and, with a rising chuckle that he could no longer repress, asked with mock innocence:

"Jim, is there anyone we've overlooked?"

One man whose every possible move in the leadership contest Jimmy Byrnes thought he had not overlooked was Franklin D. Roosevelt. Roosevelt was known to be favoring Alben Barkley for the Senate post, both as a reward for Barkley's unqualified support of the court bill and because of what Roosevelt perceived as Harrison's unenthusiastic support of court reorganization as well as the New Deal's tax legislation. There was no direct evidence of Harrison's untrustworthiness. In fact, Harrison's adroit chairmanship of the Senate Finance Committee was the reason that Roosevelt had obtained passage of the Wealth Tax Act of 1935, raising corporate tax rates and increasing rates for private income at the higher levels. (Byrnes also had voted for the measure.) But despite Harrison's demonstrated loyalty, Roosevelt was convinced that, like Jimmy Byrnes, Pat Harrison was waiting for the opportunity to jump the New Deal traces. Roosevelt knew of Harrison's personal indebtedness to Bernard Baruch and believed that, like his patron, Harrison was at heart an economic royalist and would reduce rates if he could. Harrison also had announced that he intended to keep his chairmanship of the Finance Committee if he won the majority leadership post, a combination that Roosevelt knew would give the Mississippi senator the power to do what he chose on taxes independently of White House policy.

Byrnes was familiar with Roosevelt's thinking, and before the caucus vote he went to the White House and reminded Roosevelt of Harrison's past loyalties to the administration. He was not asking for a presidential endorsement of either Harrison or Barkley, Byrnes told FDR; all that he was asking was that the White House maintain the executive branch's traditional neutrality in the internal leadership decisions of the legislative branch. Roosevelt appeared agreeable; and before he left, Byrnes had obtained what he considered a promise from FDR not to intercede personally in the Democratic caucus election.

But the afternoon after his visit at the White House, Jimmy Byrnes read in the newspapers the text of a "Dear Alben" letter written by FDR to Barkley, and released to reporters. In his letter Roosevelt asked Barkley to continue the fight in the Senate for the court reorganization bill in consideration of his position as "acting Majority Leader of the Senate." Publication of this letter was persuasive evidence in the hands of Barkley supporters to convince wavering senators that the president was personally committed to their candidate for the majority leadership. Despite this setback to the supporters of Harrison and this seeming violation of Roosevelt's promise of neutrality, Byrnes was willing to concede that Roosevelt had written the letter before he had talked with Byrnes. And Byrnes was enough of a sharp trader himself to know that FDR had been under no obligation to mention the existence of this letter unless asked specifically by Byrnes.

But in a later subterfuge that fooled no one, including Jimmy Byrnes, Roosevelt did violate his promise of not intervening in the Senate race. Roosevelt simply got Harry Hopkins to do the job for him. Hopkins' authority to grant or to delay WPA funds enabled him to exert enormous lobbying pressure on senators thought to be leaning away from Barkley. Senators from states with established, urban political machines, which depended upon WPA funds to finance their patronage jobs, were particularly vulnerable to Hopkins' influence. But the Harrison organization, led by Jimmy Byrnes, also knew a thing or two about the use of urban political machines, especially those located in the former border states of the Civil War. Senator Harry Truman of Missouri later made much of his independence in resisting the political muscle of the Boss Pendergast machine and keeping his earlier promise to vote for Harrison, despite the requests of Pendergast to switch to Barkley. But in the days immediately preceding the Senate caucus vote, Catledge and Alsop witnessed Jimmy Byrnes and the other pro-Harrison men "laughing, more than maliciously, at the story of how a telegram ostentatiously sent to Truman by the Pendergasts' Kansas City organization [instructing him to vote for Barkley and sent at the request of Hopkins in the White House] had been preceded by a telephone call [from the Pendergast headquarters] telling him to pay no attention, to stick to Harrison."

At ten o'clock on the morning of July 21, 1937, the Senate Democrats met in the inappropriately dignified architecture of the Caucus Room of the Senate Office Building. There was considerable anger that morning, particularly among the southerners, at FDR's blatant violation of his promise to Byrnes. Even more-liberal senators who were no friends to Jimmy Byrnes resented this presidential intercession in the Senate leadership contest. "I heard that a carload of patronage jobs was being offered to anyone who would leave Pat for Barkley," scornfully observed Tom Connally of Texas, who continued to back Harrison out of personal friendship. Jimmy Byrnes had confidently told Pat Harrison that as his campaign manager he had collected at least two more votes than needed to secure Harrison his leadership job. Nevertheless, Byrnes proposed that morning that the voting be by secret ballot, reasoning that any wavering senator could therefore both collect his carload of patronage jobs and still vote for Harrison. Carter Glass volunteered his battered Panama hat, which he wore throughout the summer months, as the voting receptacle. Each senator dropped into the hat his vote written on a folded slip of paper. When the last of the ballots had been unfolded and announced to Byrnes, Harrison, and the other waiting senators in the room, the totals were 37 for Harrison and 38 for Barkley.

Pat Harrison was an old professional. Despite this unexpected disappointment, Harrison immediately made his way across the crowded room to congratulate Barkley and make an offer of unspecified support. But in the postmortem following the vote held at Byrnes' office, there was a continuation of the angry talk earlier that morning that the president "had double-crossed Pat." From a quick analysis of the vote, Byrnes deduced, for his own satisfaction and possible future retaliation, the identity of the senators who did not stick by their promises to Byrnes to vote for Harrison. In the opinion of those senators meeting in Byrnes' office, FDR had been "meddling in a family concern." And, in their opinion, the president by his meddling that morning had forfeited any future claims to party loyalty to be made either by himself or by Barkley. Not just Byrnes and Harrison now had jumped the traces but also many others of the thirty-seven voters for the Mississippi senator. Thereafter, many of them regarded Alben Barkley, in the cruel phrase of one of those present, simply as "an extended White House errand boy," to whom the senators owed no personal or party favors.

Thus the principals in the growing antagonism between the conservative, rural officeholders in the Democratic party and the White House's newly important constituencies of organized labor and urban poor had fought to an exhausted draw by the end of that hot summer of 1937. Roosevelt never got his extra Supreme Court justices. Jimmy Byrnes got his pride wounded, and Pat Harrison never got his job of increased responsibility. And the chair on the Supreme Court that would have belonged to Justice Joe Robinson went instead to Senator Hugo Black of Alabama, whose nomination in 1937 by FDR pleased neither many southerners nor northern liberals. (Black, a former member of the Ku Klux Klan, was far to the left of Byrnes economically, even more so of the late Joe Robinson. Nevertheless, Byrnes voted for the nomination out of both senatorial courtesy and regional obligation to see the seat go to a southerner.)

But Roosevelt was not finished with the conservatives yet. There would be one last fight between these two antagonistic factions within the Democratic party before the end of the decade that would also directly involve Jimmy Byrnes. And this conflict, too, would take place during the hot and quarrelsome days of late July and early August. The following summer, 1938, Roosevelt began in earnest his attempt to "purge" the Democratic party of selected conservative senators.

10

The Purge of 1938

As early as the "harmony confer-
ence" of June 1937, when Jimmy Byrnes and Pat Harrison sat under the
apple tree with Franklin Roosevelt at the Jefferson Islands Club, Harold
Ickes had speculated in his diary on the possible disintegration of the
Democratic party. "It may be that the Democratic Party may split," Ickes
wrote, "with the conservatives joining with the Republicans to form a new
party, leaving the Democratic Party as the progressive party of the
country." Harry Hopkins was thinking the same, and over the winter of
1937–38 Ickes and other like-minded advisers to Roosevelt met at Hopkins'
house in Georgetown to discuss how this seemingly inevitable split in the
Democratic party could be put to the advantage of the New Nationalism
liberals in the administration. The strategy that this group began to urge
upon FDR during the months following the court fight was for the White
House to strike first and "purge" the Democratic party of conservative
incumbents. Their plan was for Roosevelt to campaign for the defeat of
selected conservatives in the 1938 Democratic primaries.

The plan, like FDR's court bill, was certain to be called audacious. For
a president to back candidates to run against incumbents of his own party

was a White House involvement in congressional politics unheard of since the administrations of Andrew Jackson. But, like the court bill, the plan was certain to be called bold if it succeeded. The Democratic party then enjoyed its largest majority in the twentieth century, and Roosevelt, judging by his landslide 1936 victory, was then at the height of his personal popularity. By taking the opportunity at this moment of its greatest acceptance to purge it of disaffected conservatives, Roosevelt could personally turn his party into the liberal party of America.

It was an idea appealing to FDR. The broken promises and refusals to compromise that had so aggravated Jimmy Byrnes and other congressional conservatives during the Seventy-fifth Congress were not just examples of Roosevelt's being captious. FDR apparently believed sincerely that the conservative "elders" of his party were taking the Democrats down the wrong road. As Roosevelt would remark during his intervention in the 1938 primary in South Carolina, it was no longer sufficient for successful Democratic candidates to think of liberalism only in terms of the limited emergency measures of the Hundred Days. For the Democratic party to continue to prevail, Roosevelt would tell the members of the South Carolina democracy, it must be able to field a candidate who "thinks in terms of 1938, 1948, and 1958." Given his ideological commitment to remake the Democratic party and his immediate popularity in the last presidential election, the temptation to FDR must have been irresistible. After all, at his party's national convention in 1936, Roosevelt had been the first Democratic presidential candidate since Andrew Jackson to repeal the two-thirds rule of the conservatives.

Roosevelt had made up his mind a few days after the adjournment of the final session of the Seventy-fifth Congress, when, during a "fireside chat" on June 24, 1938, he reviewed for his national radio audience the accomplishments of the Congress just over. Roosevelt pronounced himself pleased, at least partly. Even the defeat of the court reorganization bill in 1937 had brought about a favorable change in the judicial attitude of the Supreme Court, Roosevelt claimed. "A lost battle which won a war" was Roosevelt's happy phrase describing that unhappy conflict. But less than one-third of the way through his radio chat, Roosevelt's appraisal of the past Congress suddenly turned harsh. After listing legislative defeats of the administration at the hands of the conservative coalition, Roosevelt declared that "never in our lifetime has such a concerted campaign of defeatism been thrown at the heads of the president and senators and congressmen as in the case of the 75th Congress."

Roosevelt then placed his criticism of the conservative coalition in a historical context for his national audience, and with his use of the pejorative political term "copperheads," revived from 1861–65 and meaning northerners who were southern sympathizers, Roosevelt revealed how even in late 1938 the divisions of the Civil War were affecting national voting patterns.

"Never before have we had so many copperheads," Roosevelt told his radio audience. "And you will remember that it was the copperheads who, in the days of the War Between the States, tried their best to make Lincoln and his congress give up the fight, let the nation split in two and return to peace—peace at any price."

Roosevelt went on to say that he did not presume as president to tell any member of either party how to vote in that summer's primaries. "Nor am I, as president, taking part in any Democratic primaries." But the part to be taken in his party's primaries by Franklin D. Roosevelt of Hyde Park, a private citizen and Democrat of some note, was another matter. As the elected head of the Democratic party, Roosevelt said, he was "charged with the responsibility of carrying out the definitely liberal declaration of principles set forth in the 1936 Democratic platform." And given the persistence of the copperhead conservatives claiming to be Roosevelt Democrats who opposed this national liberalism, Roosevelt said, "I have every right to speak in those few instances where there may be a clear issue between candidates for a Democratic nomination involving those principles, or involving a clear misuse of my name."

Jimmy Byrnes probably was feeling a little viperish himself when he heard Roosevelt's fireside chat. Byrnes immediately saw the potentially disruptive effects on the party of Roosevelt's becoming involved in a "few instances" in Democratic primaries. Byrnes knew that although the most unreconstructed Democratic opponent of the New Deal, Carter Glass of Virginia, was not up for reelection that year, Senator E. D. Smith of South Carolina was. Cotton Ed Smith was a likely candidate to be "purged" by Roosevelt during the summer's primaries. (That term was chosen by newspapers in sarcastic reference to the ideological "purges" of membership rolls then being undergone by the Soviet Union.)

Byrnes knew that, at the very least, as had happened so many other times when Roosevelt went hunting for liberal allies in the South, Cotton Ed Smith was likely to revive his "Philadelphia Story" and to make white supremacy a test of political loyalty. At the very worst, FDR's intervention in the southern primaries could drive the conservative state parties there into forming an independent, regional party. Not only would such a political bolting of the southern states mean an end to the "concurrent majorities" by which the national, liberal Democratic party had ruled in conjunction with the conservative Democrats, but an independent party would force professionals like Byrnes to make the hard choices of giving up their seniority in the Democratic party, joining the new regional party, or retiring from politics altogether. None of these alternatives was acceptable to Byrnes. Thus, like Roosevelt's, Jimmy Byrnes' motives during the upcoming Democratic purges of 1938 were a mixture of ideology and personal ambition. In the case of Byrnes, these activities translated into an effort to keep Democratic conservatives renominated and, at all costs, to keep Franklin Roosevelt out of South Carolina.

The conservatives had for months prior to Roosevelt's June fireside chat heard rumors that the president planned to campaign that summer against selected Democratic incumbents. "I think we ought to be mixing medicine about a lot of things," Bernard Baruch had written to Byrnes at the end of April 1938, in an invitation for some serious drinking and discussion of party politics. A few weeks before Roosevelt's radio address, Baruch in early May hosted an overnight meeting at his New York City town house for Jimmy Byrnes, Jack Garner, and other conservative members of Congress.

Shortly thereafter, Byrnes began acting as the dispenser of campaign funds from Baruch's bank account, advising the financier on which conservative candidates "most will appreciate your help." Senators Millard Tydings of Maryland and Guy Gillette of Iowa, both active Democratic members of the conservative coalition, had been targeted by the White House for replacement in that summer's primaries. Byrnes objectively appraised each of these men's chances and advised Baruch on the amount of money necessary for their primary races. Gillette and Tydings subsequently got contributions from Baruch for use in running against their administration-sponsored opponents in Iowa and Maryland. The political partnership of Byrnes and Baruch was probably never more active than during their behind-the-scenes maneuvers in the summer of 1938 to save some of Baruch's collection of Old Masters in the Senate.

Byrnes also had not given up trying to influence Roosevelt. Shortly after the White House purge activities were gotten under way by the president's staff and before Roosevelt himself made any appearances in state primaries, Byrnes met with FDR. Byrnes made it clear to the president that "it was folly to be tempted into using the power of his office to purge men who were independent thinkers, especially after the party had been shaken up by the mixed reaction to the Court plan." But where Jimmy Byrnes saw independent thinkers, Franklin Roosevelt saw only malicious obstructionists. Neither Roosevelt nor Byrnes was in a mood to compromise. The meeting between the two ended amiably enough, but in a clear statement of his intentions, Byrnes told Roosevelt "that I would do everything in my power to help my friends who were marked to fall under the ax."

In early August 1938 the first Democratic returns showed only a limited success for Roosevelt's attempts to liberalize the Democratic party with new candidates. Alben Barkley, for whom FDR had campaigned personally in Kentucky, was renominated, thereby almost certainly eliminating any future chance of Pat Harrison's ever becoming majority leader. And several liberal congressmen whom Roosevelt had endorsed in the Texas primary won their party's nominations, including a young Lyndon B. Johnson. But Senator Guy Gillette of Iowa, with the help of a thousand-dollar contribution from Baruch, won his state's primary. And the administration was unable to defeat Senator Alva Adams of Colorado one of the strongest opponents of the court reorganization bill. Three southern states—Georgia, South Carolina, and Maryland—held their senatorial primaries the last weeks of August or later in September. In each state a Roosevelt-sponsored candidate opposed the conservative Democratic incumbent, and Roosevelt therefore tried to save some of his purge attempt by campaigning personally in these three states.

The first week of August, Roosevelt completed a fishing vacation off the coast of Florida and began preparations for the return trip to Washington by railroad up the southern lines. Along the way FDR announced plans to make several stops in his "adopted" state of Georgia and there speak in favor of the Democratic candidate running in the state primary against the incumbent senator, Walter George. There were also rumors that Roosevelt's train would stop in South Carolina, where FDR would speak in support of the primary opponent of Cotton Ed Smith. The Georgia stops were bad enough, in Byrnes' opinion, since Walter George was a longtime family friend of Jimmy and Maude Byrnes. As for stops farther up the Southern Railway track, Jimmy Byrnes had no intention of letting FDR's train slow down in South Carolina.

Byrnes assumed this position not out of regard for Cotton Ed Smith's political future but out of regard for his own future, and that of his friend and protégé Burnet Maybank. Maybank, at Byrnes' prompting, was also a candidate in the state primary that summer, attempting to become the first Charlestonian since the Civil War to be nominated to the state's governorship. In his decision to act in 1938 as the political angel to Burnet Maybank's campaign, Jimmy Byrnes had revealed his usual faultless sense of political timing, his careful balancing of personal ambition against party seniority, and his nice sense of appropriate payback to an old political foe.

The sense of political timing had to do with the Santee-Cooper litigation, which was approaching its conclusion in 1938. Byrnes knew that the expectation of court approval of the project and the hopes of patronage jobs made this the best year for Maybank to make his run. Maybank's ambitions for even higher office also would be gratified if he won in the primary of 1938, as his probable reelection as governor in 1942 would leave him poised to succeed Cotton Ed Smith to the Senate in 1945, by which time Smith would almost certainly have retired or died. And as to Byrnes' sense of political payback, one of Maybank's main opponents in the 1938 primary for governor was Coleman L. Blease, who was attempting a comeback. To put the definitive end to Coley Blease's career through a defeat at the hands of his protégé was a pleasing prospect for Jimmy Byrnes. The skillfulness of Byrnes' moves and the importance to him of the 1938 state primary was perceived by *Time* magazine, which observed in August that if Jimmy Byrnes succeeded in his indirect plan to elevate his friends and eliminate his enemies, he would effectively own the state of South Carolina politically as "the senior partner of the team of Byrnes & Maybank."

But the prospect of a Cotton Ed Smith defeat was much less pleasing for Byrnes. The candidate whom the Roosevelt administration had encouraged to run against Smith was the state's populist governor, Olin D. Johnson. Johnson had announced his decision to run for South Carolina's Senate seat after a meeting with FDR when Johnson spoke literally at the steps of the White House. If Johnson should win, Byrnes knew, he himself would no longer be considered by the Roosevelt administration as the South Carolina senator more loyal to the New Deal. Byrnes also knew Roosevelt well enough to be certain that White House patronage could just as easily be shifted from Senator Byrnes to Senator Johnson in 1939 as it had been shifted from Senator Smith to Senator Byrnes in 1933. The claims of federal patronage also would be complicated because Byrnes and Johnson had the same hometown of Spartanburg. Low-country voters might feel shut out of consideration for federal appointments and express their unhappiness when Byrnes himself ran for renomination in 1942.

A victory by the young and energetic Olin Johnson in 1938 also would mean that Burnet Maybank would have a much more difficult campaign for the U.S. Senate in 1944—if the Charlestonian friend chose to wait that long. Byrnes knew from his own long, impatient apprenticeship under Senator Ben Tillman that Maybank might grow resentful of what he perceived as his career's being delayed by the seniority of Senator Jimmy Byrnes. Maybank might decide to run against his former patron Byrnes in the primary of 1942. Although he trusted and was very fond of Maybank, his friend's political betrayal would neither surprise nor disturb Byrnes. "That is human nature," Jimmy Byrnes wrote to Bernard Baruch in late April 1938, about Maybank's probable resentment if his ambitions were delayed, "and he [Maybank] is very, very human."

Therefore, although Byrnes did not particularly like E. D. Smith and had no particular quarrels with Governor Olin Johnson, he was doing all he could to secure the Democratic renomination of Smith. In a state where politics traditionally was conducted according to the dictates or whims of personal or family allegiances—the "friends and neighbors" phenomenon of South Carolina politics noted by the political scientist V. O. Key— Jimmy Byrnes showed himself to be a political professional. He could work with anybody, if it was in his interests and the interests of the state Democratic party for him to do so.

Into Jimmy Byrnes' carefully balanced political universe of the good and bad angels of human nature, Franklin D. Roosevelt in early August 1938 threatened to intrude, riding on a steam locomotive. Byrnes was worried that if Roosevelt's train did stop in South Carolina and FDR failed specifically to include Burnet Maybank and instead endorsed Olin Johnson, opponents of Maybank in the gubernatorial primary such as Coley Blease would use that omission to claim that Maybank did not have the support of the Roosevelt administration to deliver on Maybank's promise of more New Deal jobs. But Byrnes also knew that if Roosevelt stopped in the state and *did* endorse Maybank, Blease could organize all of white South Carolina's resentment of the New Deal to defeat Maybank in the primary. The issue of race had already come up with Cotton Ed Smith's revival of the "Philadelphia Story" in his primary race, and before the end of August, Smith also would make a campaign issue of the CIO's acceptance of black laborers in its organization. This kind of talk, in Byrnes' opinion, could do no good for anyone in South Carolina associated with Roosevelt. Byrnes therefore sent a long telegram to Harry Hopkins to give to the president when he and his fishing boat arrived at Pensacola, Florida. In the telegram Byrnes strongly argued against any presidential appearance in South Carolina.

Hopkins was an unexpected ally. Harry Hopkins and Burnet Maybank were close friends, and Hopkins was willing to forgo the attempt to purge E. D. Smith, in order not to endanger Maybank's candidacy. Roosevelt at first was willing to accede to both Byrnes' telegram and Hopkins' advice. FDR told reporters in Pensacola the first week of August that he had no plans to stop for political speeches in South Carolina. But in a later telephone call to Maybank, Hopkins warned his Charleston friend that Roosevelt was considering a brief campaign stop in South Carolina. Maybank later informed Byrnes that Hopkins had told him that Roosevelt changed his mind because "John L. Lewis was bringing pressure to bear on the president to interfere in the South Carolina fight."

Subsequently, it was announced that the president's train, after campaign stops for Roosevelt to speak out against Senator Walter George in Georgia, would stop briefly in Greenville, South Carolina, the night of August 11 for the president to make a few unspecified remarks. Governor Olin Johnson would have the honor of being the first South Carolina dignitary to board the president's train as it crossed the state line from Georgia. The state's other prominent Democrats, including Senators Jimmy Byrnes and E. D. Smith, would have the opportunity to speak briefly with Roosevelt when his train rolled into Greenville.

Approximately 25,000 people, among them a worried Jimmy Byrnes, were waiting at the railway station on the humid August night when the nine-car, air-conditioned presidential special arrived in Greenville two hours late. At earlier stops in Georgia, Roosevelt had made slashing verbal attacks on Senator Walter George and, in the incumbent senator's presence, called for his defeat and the election of the pro–New Deal candidate. Byrnes was now worried that Roosevelt planned to do the same in South

Carolina. Particularly dangerous in Byrnes' estimation was a remark made earlier by Senator Smith during Senate debates on the wage and hour bill, which Olin Johnson had subsequently used against the senator in their primary campaign and which Johnson may have passed on to Roosevelt for his use that night.

That bill, which would have prohibited the "southern differential" of industrial wages lower than those in the rest of the nation, had also been opposed by Jimmy Byrnes. But unlike Senator Byrnes, Senator Smith had made a foolish comparison on the floor of the Senate. "If, by way of comparison, a man can live on fifty cents a day in South Carolina and a dollar and a half in New England," Smith had said, then there was no need for the New Deal to legislate that employers in South Carolina must pay the dollar and a half. Fifty cents a day was a starvation wage even in South Carolina, and Governor Olin Johnson had seized on that remark to demonstrate that Cotton Ed Smith was an enemy to the state's workingman.

Now a prolonged cheer went up from the crowd as FDR's train, with a long whistle of steam brakes, came to a stop. While a Secret Service agent attached a public address and radio microphone to the platform of the rear car, Byrnes and Smith went aboard the train. Burnet Maybank, through the intercession of Harry Hopkins, also was brought aboard.

"There's the old pirate!" was Roosevelt's cheerful greeting to Smith. Laughing, looking tanned and relaxed, FDR exchanged pleasantries about his recent ocean travels with everyone in the railcar, including that presumed pirate—Cotton Ed Smith. When Byrnes asked Roosevelt what he intended to say in a few moments to the thousands outside, Roosevelt was nonchalant. "I'll tell them about fishing," FDR said, and smiled. "Wonderful," Byrnes replied. "We can all agree about fishing."

Another cheer went up from the crowd as Roosevelt appeared at the rear platform of the train, moved stiffly to the platform's railing, then waved a salute and smiled. "I got here," he cheerfully told the applauding thousands. Byrnes went outside the train and stood in the warm night air of the station alongside the railroad tracks while Roosevelt began his remarks, promising to be brief. So far, everything was going better than Byrnes had expected. Although Roosevelt chose to talk to the crowd about his recent speeches in Georgia against Senator Walter George, rather than tell his fishing stories, FDR had made no specific statement of preference for Olin Johnson in the Senate race.

In an apparent conclusion to his remarks—"Before I stop, and I believe the train is pulling out in a minute or two, I want to suggest two things to you"—Roosevelt first suggested simply that the Greenville crowd could expect to see the president visit South Carolina again soon. And then came the old FDR magic. "The other thing is, I don't believe any family or any man in South Carolina can live on fifty cents a day."

Why run for a train after you've caught it? All the anger toward FDR that Jimmy Byrnes had so carefully controlled since the Supreme Court fight of the previous year, when Roosevelt time after time had refused a compromise in order to insist upon an ideological victory, now burst into Byrnes' consciousness. Marvin McIntyre, a presidential assistant who was a friend of Byrnes, on hearing Roosevelt's remark immediately jumped back onto the train and pulled a bell cord, signaling the engineer to begin moving the train out of the station. The president's chief bodyguard, Mike Reilly, was startled by the train's sudden jolting forward and by the sight of Senator Jimmy Byrnes, who Reilly later remembered was "running alongside the tracks looking up at McIntyre's face. All the fighting Irish blood came to the fore, and you never heard such a thing in your life as he poured it on McIntyre."

Before Roosevelt could elaborate on his allusive remark about Smith, the extension cord of FDR's microphone on the rear car of the train connecting to the station's public address system was stretched to its limit, and then, with an amplified clang, the microphone fell from in front of the president down onto the steel rails and cinders below the moving rear car. The train picked up speed and quickly vanished into the humid Carolina night, carrying an enigmatic Franklin D. Roosevelt away from the turmoil he had created in Jimmy Byrnes' political world.

Smith quickly issued a statement the next morning claiming that Roosevelt had been "misinformed" about the fifty-cent remark by Olin Johnson, but in Byrnes' private opinion "the damage had been done." Not only had Roosevelt spoken out against Smith, probably provoking a backlash of white supremacy among the primary voters, but he also had failed specifically to endorse Burnet Maybank. Byrnes temporarily retired from public view to his vacation cottage on Sullivan's Island, but behind the scenes he worked very hard to undo the damage he perceived had been done by Roosevelt. Byrnes wrote to Baruch, advising him to wait and see what effect Roosevelt's remarks would have on Olin Johnson's strength before sending any money to Smith; but if Johnson forced E. D. Smith into a September runoff, Byrnes warned Baruch, to secure Smith's renomination "we will be called upon for substantial help after August 30th."

As to Maybank's chances, Byrnes earlier had requested that the Department of the Navy grant employees at the Charleston Navy Yards a day off with pay so that the workers could vote in the Democratic primary. Byrnes had argued that this policy was consistent with the day off with pay for government employees to vote in the general elections, because winning nomination in the Democratic primary was equal to winning the general election in the one-party state of South Carolina. (Byrnes knew that the navy yard workers would vote overwhelmingly for Maybank, the current mayor of Charleston and the man to whom many of them owed their jobs, thereby offsetting Coley Blease's expected majorities in the textile villages of the upstate. And, of course, to the state's textile workers, the primary election day would be just another workday, as no millowner was willing to pay workers for time off to vote.) Byrnes also spent out of his pockets in late August, hiring the services of a county sheriff, a U.S. marshal and "one or two other persons," as he told Baruch, to watch the state polls on election day for attempted fraud against either Smith or Maybank.

Byrnes' paid law enforcement officers were not the only ones watching the state's Democratic polling places that summer. Byrnes' fears that a Roosevelt visit would revive white supremacy as an issue that would harm any New Deal candidates had become a reality in South Carolina by late August 1938. By that time Smith was campaigning almost exclusively on his "Philadelphia Story" and the CIO's alleged race mixing, largely ignoring economic issues of importance to South Carolinians. But in an additional violent reaction to the U.S. presidency that no one in South Carolina had seen since the lifetime of Ben Tillman, the Red Shirts once again appeared at election time. Centered in the low-country town of Orangeburg, a group of Smith supporters had put on the red shirts and patrolled the area's polling places on the primary election night. To anyone with a knowledge of South Carolina's violent political history, the message was obvious. Just as the Red Shirts of 1876 had intimidated the state's black citizens in order to secure the return of a white supremacist government, so the Red Shirts in 1938 intended through intimidation to secure the renomination of South Carolina's most vocal opponent of racial equality and the domestic policies of the New Deal in general—Cotton Ed Smith. (The subjects of intimidation in the primary of 1938 were exclusively the state's white citizens who were in favor of the CIO or a stronger New Deal. The presence of black voters in the state's primary or general elections had, of course, been eliminated during the 1880s by that former Red Shirt governor, Pitchfork Ben Tillman.) Shortly before midnight on election eve, a contingent of the Red Shirts motored to the state capitol in Columbia, where they were greeted by Smith, and together they awaited the primary results underneath a statute of General Wade Hampton.

The South Carolina primary results of 1938 reflected a curious mixture of the revival of 1876 racial politics, the twentieth-century New Deal hydroelectric project at Santee-Cooper, and the behind-the-scenes organizing of Senator Jimmy Byrnes. Burnet Maybank, as a result of the personal magnetism and the potential for patronage jobs at Santee-Cooper, was able to overcome the backlash against the New Deal and easily defeat Coley Blease, by an almost two-to-one margin. And in what was widely interpreted as a rebuke to Franklin Roosevelt for having attempted to intervene in South Carolina's politics, Cotton Ed Smith received one of the largest majorities of his career, swamping the ardent New Dealer Olin Johnson by almost forty thousand votes.

A week before this primary election night, Franklin Roosevelt, back at Hyde Park after his truncated visit to South Carolina, had spoken to the people of that state in a national radio address during which he asked South Carolinians to forsake Smith and vote instead for a senatorial candidate such as Johnson who "thinks in terms of 1938, 1948, and 1958." But the events of the South Carolina primary that evening of August 30, 1938, revealed that Roosevelt's choice in his fireside chat earlier that summer of such Civil War terms as "copperhead" was more appropriate in understanding the state's politics in 1938. After meeting with his Red Shirt supporters at a torchlight rally at Wade Hampton's statue and receiving word of his primary victory, E. D. Smith himself had put on a red shirt and proudly posed for a photographer from *Time* magazine. To the frequent accompaniment of rebel yells (a convention of aged Confederate veterans also was meeting in Columbia that week) Smith gave an impassioned speech to match his martial outfit.

"We conquered in '76 and we conquered in '38," Smith declared, standing fast at the stone foot of Wade Hampton's horse. "We fought with bullets then, but today, thank God, we fought with ballots." Despite Franklin Roosevelt's best intentions—and the warnings of Jimmy Byrnes that FDR stay out his state's unpredictable politics—there were only cheers that night in South Carolina for the U.S. senator who was the champion of "Cotton Is King and White Is Supreme."

"Well, you beat me in that election down there" was Roosevelt's greeting to Byrnes when the two men first met again at the White House after the South Carolina primary. The administration's failure to purge E. D. Smith was but part of a larger, overwhelming defeat for the Roosevelt White House in its attempts to liberalize the Democratic party throughout the South that summer of 1938. Not only was Smith returned as his state party's nominee for the U.S. Senate, but in Georgia and Maryland voters also ignored the Roosevelt-backed candidates and returned Walter George and Millard Tydings, respectively, to the U.S. Senate by large majorities.

The failed purge of 1938 was an embarrassment for the Roosevelt administration that would not go away. Before the end of the year, Franklin D. Roosevelt would join one thousand other guests, including Senator Jimmy Byrnes, for a ghastly skit performed by the journalist members of the Gridiron Club at its annual banquet at Washington's Willard Hotel. After the food and drink had been enjoyed and the tables cleared, a curtain opened on a lit stage at one end of the hotel's banquet room. It revealed scenery purporting to be a South Carolina cotton field. (The New Deal's "Cotton-pickin' Project No. 37," according to the Gridiron dinner program.) Newspaper reporters costumed as Pat Harrison, Millard Tydings, Walter George, Cotton Ed Smith, and the senators' female admirers then visited the cotton patch to sing various ditties about the shortcomings of

the New Deal and the joys of white racial purity. The character of Cotton
Ed Smith was designed to be the showstopper. "Overcome by his zeal, he
ripped off his coat, revealing a red shirt," the *Washington Post* reported
the morning after. "Nor were the women impassive. They hiked up their
skirts in a jig of glee, revealing equally gleaming red petticoats."

Roosevelt's forced laughter may have joined that of the other guests
at the Gridiron Club dinner, but for the president to have considered some
revenge for the humiliation of his failed purge would mean only that he
was human. And, as Jimmy Byrnes remarked about a mutual friend, FDR
was very, very human. Jack Garner warned Byrnes in a confidential letter
written soon after the purge from the vice president's Texas farm, "One
of the newspaper boys wrote to me that he thought the 'Boss' would appoint
Governor [Olin] Johnson [to the position of a] federal judge, and intimated
it was because he wanted to spite you and 'Cotton Ed,' *etc.*" In his reply,
Jimmy Byrnes showed that he also was very, very human. Byrnes had been
angered by Garner's frequent and diplomatic "health trips" away from
Washington to visit his Texas farm during the divisive year of 1937–38.
The vice president used this device, Byrnes accurately guessed, to avoid
either publicly helping Roosevelt during the purge attempt or openly antagonizing Garner's conservative incumbent friends. Byrnes now wanted
to know why Garner had not chosen the conservative side. "Where were
you when little Sherman started marching through the South?"

The divisions among Democrats caused by differences over the court
fight, taxes and relief spending, the Senate leadership struggle, and the
attempted White House purge continued throughout the Seventy-sixth
Congress. Byrnes and Harrison, acting in conjunction with Bernard Baruch, Joseph Kennedy, Sr., and other probusiness power brokers in the
party, had already succeeded before the end of the Seventy-fifth Congress
in reducing the undistributed-profits tax on corporations, confirming Roosevelt's worst suspicions about the senators' reliability on his tax policies.
Byrnes and Harrison now took a sweet revenge on FDR's forced choice
of Alben Barkley as Senate majority leader, the two of them combining
enough votes soon after the Seventy-sixth Congress convened to defeat
Barkley's request for increased WPA spending for fiscal 1939. Harry Hopkins thus had to take a $150 million cut in the budget of his agency. (Byrnes
had publicly announced his plans to reduce WPA appropriations in the
upcoming Congress, during a speech to the Southern Society of New York
at the Waldorf-Astoria Hotel on December 7, 1938. On his way back to
South Carolina, Byrnes stopped the next day in Washington for a luncheon
meeting at the White House with Roosevelt. Roosevelt had read accounts
of Byrnes' speech in the morning papers, and it was at this meeting that
FDR greeted Jimmy Byrnes with an impromptu and good-natured singing
of "Oh Where, Oh Where, Is My Wandering Boy?")

Despite their ideological differences over taxes and relief spending, the friendship between Byrnes and the president was not irrevocably broken, as happened with that between Roosevelt and some of the other southern conservatives after the attempted purge of 1938. With the exception of his stand on these two important fiscal issues, Senator Byrnes once again became more of a "nationalist" southerner generally in favor of the New Deal's domestic and foreign policies throughout late 1938 and 1939. Byrnes and Roosevelt both were simply too skillful as politicians and too fond of one another personally not to work together on the issues where they were in agreement.

Roosevelt, furthermore, was characteristically reluctant to dwell for long on any personal defeats such as his attempted purge of the Democratic party, and he simply did not like to talk about bitter issues that separated him from people he considered his friends. When a visitor to the Oval Office brought up such topics, Roosevelt would frequently change the subject, or, if the visitor persisted, would pointedly say nothing, light a cigarette, and turn to look out his office window.

Despite his disappointment over the failure of the 1938 purge, Roosevelt therefore chose not to take any revenge or to hold a grudge against any of his old friends such as Byrnes who had blocked his attempts to liberalize the Democratic party. Jimmy Byrnes got his Santee-Cooper project, and Olin Johnson never got his federal judgeship. At their first meeting after that summer's primaries, when Jimmy Byrnes tried to discuss the details of the elections with Franklin Roosevelt, FDR cut him short. "We'll forget it!" he told Byrnes, and then, in Byrnes' later recollection, he "quickly went on to talk about a matter pending in the Senate in which he was interested." Only in talking in the White House with a visitor other than Jimmy Byrnes did FDR once express his disappointment in the results of the South Carolina primary, and even then the president couched his personal defeat in the most philosophical and seemingly disinterested of tones. "It takes a long, long time," FDR said, "to bring the past up to the present."

For Jimmy Byrnes the past had come up comfortably to the present in 1938–39. The twentieth-century improvement of the Santee-Cooper project that year passed its last court challenge; and, despite the political anachronism of Cotton Ed Smith's renomination, Byrnes continued to own his state politically as the senior member of "Byrnes & Maybank." Byrnes' mixture of a moderate New Deal liberalism and a progressive Bourbon conservatism appeared to have stabilized the forces that were threatening to tear South Carolina from the national Democratic party. Similarly, the return of conservative Democratic incumbents to the U.S. Senate from other states across the South and West that year appeared to signal a continuation of the "concurrent majorities" by which the national Democratic party ruled its divergent constituencies.

But, "unfortunate thought it may be, our consideration of every question must include the consideration of this race question." These unintentionally prophetic words written in a private letter to the Charleston newspaper editor W. W. Ball in 1920 continued to shape Jimmy Byrnes' political career nearly twenty years after he wrote them. The attempts by Roosevelt and others to liberalize the Democratic party in 1938 had revived the issue of white supremacy for southern politicians in a way that was far more divisive to the party than the simple theatrics of a Cotton Ed Smith. Smith had put on the red shirt in August 1938 as a matter of political survival in order to distract the voters of his state from his Senate record of opposition to the economic and social benefits the New Deal extended to South Carolina's white citizens. But the continuing efforts in 1938–39 by such New Deal liberals as Harry Hopkins and Senator Robert Wagner of New York State to extend these same benefits to the nation's nonwhite citizens threatened, in Byrnes' opinion, to undo the Compromise of 1877, which the Red Shirt rebellion had in part occasioned. And Jimmy Byrnes knew that if that sixty-year-old compromise fell apart in the 1930s, the rule of a one-party South and the dominance in the region of Democratic officeholders such as himself would end.

That compromise allowed the Democratic party of South Carolina and those of other southern states to remain the state parties of white political supremacy. In exchange for the national party's acceptance of the region's disenfranchisement of most of its nonwhite citizens, the South provided a solid bloc of white Democratic voters every two years in national elections. For white "members of the democracy" such as Jimmy Byrnes, the rewards in terms of seniority and job security were considerable.

In this arrangement Negroes simply did not exist as an important constituency for the Democratic party. In the southern states they were largely disenfranchised; in the northern states Negroes traditionally voted for the Republican party. And, as per the Compromise of 1877, whereby each national party was guaranteed its constituency of either white southerners or emancipated Negroes, the Republican and Democratic parties did not cooperate in Congress to extend by legislation the franchise or other civil rights to Negroes living in southern states.

Jimmy Byrnes' friend and fellow southerner Turner Catledge was the first publicly to speculate that the attempted purge of 1938 to liberalize the Democratic party was an initial sign that the Compromise of 1877 was off. Roosevelt in his personal appearances against such conservatives as Smith and Walter George stated his differences with these two senators exclusively in ideological terms, and if he also disagreed with them over the specific issue of the Democratic party's concern for Negro citizens, he chose not to state this disagreement openly during his visits to Georgia and South Carolina. But in a prescient article written in the *New York Times* late in the summer of 1938, Turner Catledge reported the anxiety of many white southern officeholders that the ideological differences were only the beginning.

"Constant reports from the North tell them of the wholesale transfer of Negro voters from the Republicans to the Democratic Party," Catledge wrote of the worried southern Democrats. "Quoted assertions of outstanding party leaders, including the president himself, are taken by them in many instances to mean that universal suffrage, including re-enfranchisement of the southern Negro, is part of the goal of those who have set out to modernize the Democratic Party."

Noting that Negro citizens, if enfranchised, would constitute a voting majority in many southern states, including South Carolina, Catledge foresaw an increased public emphasis on maintaining the political apparatus of white supremacy by the current Democratic officeholders in these states. If the state Democratic parties no longer were the guarantors of white supremacy in their region, Catledge wrote, the area's white voters would see little reason for maintaining a "Solid South" for Democratic candidates.

"The above is the reasoning not of demagogues alone," Catledge wrote, "but also of many thoughtful southerners who had hoped the day had come when candidates no longer could ride into office on the race issue."

Among those whom Catledge surely would have considered the "thoughtful southerners" was the journalist's friend and occasional drinking companion at "bullbat time"—James F. Byrnes. Byrnes always had preferred to ignore discussions of white supremacy as an unchallenged given in South Carolina and to concentrate instead on economic issues. At some risk to his own reelection, Byrnes had refused to campaign on "the race issue" in the summer primary of 1936, and he had been personally benign toward his state's Negro citizens so long as he had perceived no threats to the continuation of South Carolina's political system of whites-only Democratic party rule. But the past began uncomfortably to catch up to the present in 1938–39, despite the temporary defeat of the party's liberals in the failed purge attempt. Senator Jimmy Byrnes found he had to give more and more of his time to defending a political system and his own personal career based on the Compromise of 1877 against repeated attempts by Hopkins and other New Deal liberals to modernize the Democratic party.

Concern over race had been a motivation, along with a general belief in fiscal conservatism, in Byrnes' campaign throughout the late 1930s to reduce the expenditures for the WPA. WPA jobs as a possible source of patronage were a powerful inducement for northern Negroes to leave the Republican party and to vote the Democratic ticket in the upcoming election of 1940. Negroes also were the largest urban minority in many of the "doubtful" states for the Democratic party located in the Northeast and Midwest, and Byrnes reasoned that Harry Hopkins and other liberals in the New Deal would take advantage of this circumstance to increase the constituency of Negro voters in the party. Moreover, since the solidly Democratic Deep South states such as South Carolina were never "doubtful" for the national party in elections, Byrnes knew that there was less chance of obtaining an equal amount of WPA patronage for his state. Byrnes tried unsuccessfully throughout the late 1930s to pass legislation requiring the WPA to appropriate funds to each state on an equal per capita basis, and he did succeed beginning in 1939 in reducing funding for the WPA.

But the domestic racial issue during the last years of the second Roosevelt administration that most starkly separated the old Democratic party from the emerging new constituencies was the attempt by some of the party's liberals in the Senate and House to secure passage of a federal antilynching law. This effort throughout 1938–39 by Senator Robert Wagner and others was the clearest statement by the Democratic liberals that they considered the Compromise of 1877 at an end. No longer, in their intention, would the Democratic Solid South be allowed to withhold from southern Negro citizens civil liberties or due process of law without a federal intervention.

The reaction to the proposed antilynching laws in the Seventy-fifth and Seventy-sixth Congresses from southern Democratic officeholders, including Senator Byrnes, was predictable. One of Wagner's final efforts, called a bill "to punish the crime of lynching," was ridiculed by Byrnes in early 1938. "Its title should be," Byrnes told a bitterly divided Senate chamber, " 'a bill to arouse ill-feeling between the sections, inspire race hatred in the South, and destroy the Democratic Party.' " Senate debates over the Wagner–Van Nuys and Gavagan antilynching bills of 1938–39 in fact provoked Byrnes to make his angriest speech on race since his attacks in the House accusing the prominent Negro leader W. E. B. DuBois of sedition during the "Red menace" days of the 1920s. In the years since the 1920s, Byrnes had gained a deserved reputation as a southern politician with comparatively moderate views on race. But that reputation was lost in 1938–39 during the last struggles before the end of the decade for control of the Democratic party. Jimmy Byrnes made powerful enemies for himself as the result of his speeches against the antilynching bills. Such enemies included Walter White, a personal friend of Eleanor Roosevelt and the executive secretary of the National Association for the Advancement of Colored People (NAACP).

White had determined as a first priority of the NAACP to obtain passage of a federal antilynching bill before the end of Roosevelt's second term in office. White knew that the successor to FDR, who presumably would retire after two terms, might not be as interested as the current president and his wife in improving the civil liberties and economic conditions of the nation's Negroes and in including Negroes as an important constituency of the Democratic party. And for the first time since the establishment of the whites-only state governments in the South during the 1880s, there appeared to be a significant national revulsion in the late 1930s at the tolerance by these state governments of mob murders, or lynchings, of their Negro citizens. In the last year of the second Roosevelt administration, the *Washington Post* reported in a survey that 70 percent of the American people favored enactment of a federal antilynching law.

It was irrefutable that "Judge Lynch" had been tolerated by some state governments for years as a way to terrorize Negroes. In a report published in the *Congressional Record* in 1940, a total of 4,672 murders described as lynchings were listed as having occurred in the years 1882–1936. Negroes were overwhelmingly the victims of these crimes, with charges of rape, attempted rape, or "insults to white persons" being given as the reasons for the mob action. For these lynchings, a total of twelve convictions were secured by state governments between 1900 and 1930. In Byrnes' home state of South Carolina, where 158 lynchings were reported between 1882 and 1936, a total of two convictions for lynchings had been obtained in the first three decades of the twentieth century. There was no known imprisonment for the two found guilty. (South Carolina was by no means the worst offender. During this same period, Mississippi led the nation with 563 reported lynchings; Texas was close behind with 345. New York State also reported 2 lynchings in these years.)

Senator Robert Wagner, with the active support of White and the NAACP, had introduced antilynching bills since 1935. Wagner's measures would have attempted to stop the murders by holding state law enforcement officers liable to federal fines if they did not arrest and prosecute suspects within a specified time of a lynching. Byrnes always had publicly opposed lynchings. (He had been repelled by Coley Blease's jokey announcement while governor of South Carolina that state law enforcement officers should "tell me about it in the morning" if they knew that night of a plan to lynch a Negro.) But he joined with such Negrophobic senators as E. D. Smith on the Democratic side of the aisle in opposing the measures, in 1935 and again in 1938 when the Wagner–Van Nuys bill was reintroduced. Unlike Cotton Ed Smith, who spoke against the antilynching bills in terms of defending the virtues of southern white womanhood against rape-crazed Negroes, Byrnes took the comparative high ground among southern senators opposing the bills when he argued against them as unconstitutional intrusions of the federal government's law enforcement powers into a state's prosecution of the strictly local crime of murder.

Byrnes also recognized what he considered as northern liberal hypocrisy in the wording of the Wagner–Van Nuys antilynching bill. That bill specifically excluded law enforcement officers investigating murders committed by gangs of organized criminals from the penalties for slow prosecution. (Such crimes often were practically unprosecutable for lack of cooperating witnesses.) In Byrnes' opinion, rural and small-town racial violence by lynch mobs in the South was being singled out for federal prosecution in order to gain the Democratic party popularity in the "doubtful" states of the urban Northeast and Midwest, where rising gang violence by organized crime was being ignored. Byrnes and Senator Tom Connally of Texas, with the approval of Vice President Jack Garner, staged a question-and-answer exchange in 1938 to point out this discrepancy to the Senate chamber during debate on the Wagner antilynching bill. Given the 4,672 murders attributed to lynchings in the previous decades, their rehearsed exchange for the pages of the *Congressional Record* has a disturbing quality of a Mr.-Bones-and-Mr.-Jones vaudeville routine followed by a snare drumroll and a stage blackout:

"*Mr. Byrnes.* 'Mr. President, let me ask the senator from Texas if there is any difference between a mob and a gang other than a geographical difference?'

"*Mr. Connally.* 'Yes; there is a voting difference sometimes.' (*Laughter*)"

Byrnes joined with other southern senators of the conservative coalition in filibustering the Wagner antilynching bill to death for four weeks during the last session of Congress in 1938. Byrnes in his final speech against the measure during the filibuster doubtless was sincere in his description of the Wagner bill as "a bill to destroy the Democratic Party." The continuation of the one-party South—and of Democratic officeholders such as himself—depended in Byrnes' view upon the maintenance of the Compromise of 1877. "It undoubtedly is true," Byrnes said, "that the unity of the white people in the South in supporting the Democratic Party has been due to the belief that when problems affecting the Negro and the very soul of the South arose, they could depend upon the Democrats of the North to rally to their support."

It was this racial unity of the Democratic party that Byrnes in his filibuster speech accused Robert Wagner of New York State and other liberal Democrats of attempting to dismantle. "The senator from New York is prompted by . . . the hope of securing votes from the Negroes of New York City," he told the Senate.

In a remarkable personal attack, Byrnes then closed his 1938 filibuster remarks by turning from his desk on the floor to look toward the Senate gallery and point his finger at the seated figure of Walter White. The NAACP executive secretary had been attending the Senate sessions daily in hopes of seeing a motion succeed to cut off debate on the bill and bring the antilynching measure to a vote. White, a small, elegantly dressed Negro with blue eyes, very pale skin, and blond hair, must have been a disturbing doppelgänger for southern senators such as Jimmy Byrnes to have seen day after day looking down at them from the gallery.

"For years this man White has worked for this bill," shouted Byrnes, his voice rising in indignation. "Now that he has secured the balance of voting power in so many states, he can order its passage."

Byrnes then continued his attack on White and with perhaps unconscious irony described with complete accuracy the political agenda of the civil rights movement for the next thirty years:

What legislation will he next demand of the Congress of the United States? Will he demand that Congress enact legislation to punish the officials who fail to protect Negroes in the right to stop at hotels where white persons are entertained, following the law the Negroes recently had enacted in Pennsylvania? Will he demand the enactment of laws providing for the supervision of elections within the states? I do not know, but I know that he will make other demands, and that those who are willing to vote for this bill will acquiesce in his subsequent demands.

Pointing out and verbally attacking the person of Walter White in 1938 was extraordinary for this usually circumspect and courtly-mannered senator. Personal kindness toward individual Negroes had been a fact of the senator's life since his days as a court solicitor and private attorney at Aiken, when he had voluntarily and successfully defended a Negro who he believed had been unjustly charged with murder. Byrnes' subsequent actions as a justice on the the nation's highest court in reversing a lower court's criminal conviction of a Negro defendant also would show his scrupulous regard for correct judicial and police procedures regardless of the defendant's skin color. But that Jimmy Byrnes was animated in his 1938 speech by a personal hatred for Walter White as a man of color is undeniable as well. And it is also unquestionable that Byrnes, however kind he might be toward individual Negroes, had no intention of permitting the Democratic party to become the advocate of full rights for nonwhite citizens. The Democratic party had been "the house of our fathers," in a phrase popular both with white southern politicians and with historians in the early twentieth century, as the guarantor of white supremacy from the Bourbon fathers to the generation, including Jimmy Byrnes, born after the Civil War. To see Walter White actively following the deliberations on the Senate floor must have seemed to Byrnes an intolerable example of the kind of people the Roosevelt administration brought into "the house of our fathers."

At least partly as a result of Jimmy Byrnes' presenting Walter White of the NAACP to the senator's fellow Democrats as a specter of political ambition for the Negro race, a motion to invoke closure on the Senate filibuster failed, and the Wagner–Van Nuys antilynching bill effectively was dead for the Seventy-fifth Congress. Senator Wagner, vowing that "the battle must go on," in early January 1939 attempted to reintroduce the bill in the newly convened Seventy-sixth Congress, but his effort went nowhere. Franklin Roosevelt, apparently figuring that he still needed southern support in the Senate and that an attempt to override the expected filibuster was hopeless, did not instruct Majority Leader Alben Barkley to place the antilynching bill on the calendar for the Seventy-sixth Congress.

For the time being, the Democratic party was not going to split over the issue of racial equality. The coming of the Second World War also worked to delay the resolution of the ideological and racial disagreements that by the late 1930s seemed, in the opinion of Ickes and others, fated to tear the Democratic party apart. Despite Jimmy Byrnes' occasional anxieties, the Compromise of 1877 still was in force in 1939. Roosevelt had been right in his observation that it takes a long, long time to bring the past up to the present.

As for Walter White, he now rightly considered Senator Jimmy Byrnes to be a personal enemy who was primarily responsible for the refusal of the U.S. Senate to consider passage of an antilynching bill despite the public sentiment in favor of such a measure. (The enmity between Byrnes and Walter White was so great that White later found in his dislike of Byrnes a motivation for him to quit his three-pack-a-day cigarette habit. Judge Waties Waring, a white Charlestonian from a distinguished first family who had broken politically with Byrnes over the issue of political rights for Negroes, once was visiting at the Whites' home and witnessed White have a serious coughing fit after smoking a cigarette. Waring gave him a long look of Charlestonian appraisal. "Walter," the judge said, "whenever you light a cigarette you ought to say, 'Here's to you, Jimmy Byrnes. Here's to you, Strom Thurmond, . . . for let me tell you, that when you die, they're going to declare a national holiday. They'll be so glad to get you off their necks." According to his wife, White immediately crushed out his cigarette, and never lit another one.) Byrnes also continued in the late 1930s, as in the early 1930s, to use his control of the "minor" committee chairmanship of Audit and Control of Senate Expenses to deny investigatory funds for Senate hearings on reported lynching abuses.

But the dismay of White and other liberals over Byrnes' views on civil liberties for Negroes in the 1930s increased as the senator's second term approached its end. The cause for their dismay was not the certainty of Byrnes' receiving renomination in the South Carolina primary, for the events of 1938 had proven to the liberal Democrats that the removal of incumbents they considered ideologically objectionable was beyond their powers. Rather, it was that rumors became more and more frequent among all factions of the party in 1939–40 that Franklin Roosevelt was considering appointing his good friend Jimmy Byrnes a justice of the U.S. Supreme Court.

11

Justice Byrnes and the Coming of War

Even before the fight over additional justices for the U.S. Supreme Court began in early February 1937, rumors had reached Harold L. Ickes from inside the White House that one of the more conservative members of the court had expressed to Roosevelt a willingness to resign if the president would promise to appoint Jimmy Byrnes to the Court in his place. To the relief of Ickes and his friends, nothing more had come of the offer that year. Roosevelt apparently thought that he needed Byrnes to stay where he was, in the Senate working for passage of the court bill that would possibly gain FDR as many as six new Supreme Court justices. But as the chances for the administration's reorganization bill faded in 1937–38, and as Senator Byrnes continued to demonstrate his political mastery of the judicial system in preparing for hearings on the Santee-Cooper project, Jimmy Byrnes appeared very likely to be FDR's next pick for an available opening on the U.S. Supreme Court.

That likelihood seemed to grow when Justice Pierce Butler, one of the two remaining justices who had found most consistently against the New Deal in Court decisions of the mid-1930s, died in November 1939. Apparently the talk that Byrnes was to be nominated to Butler's chair was so great that Byrnes found it necessary to write to Bernard Baruch, then vacationing at Hobcaw Barony, and to caution him not to press their case. "Dear 'B.M.',," Byrnes wrote his friend in the first week of December. "Because you state you are going to see the president on Sunday, it occurred to me to suggest that you do not say anything to him further about the court appointment for me. I would not want him to think that we were bothering him about the appointment."

As a matter of fact, that Supreme Court nomination went to Frank Murphy, the former Democratic governor of Michigan, whose condoning of sit-down strikes in 1937 had been so objectionable to the southern congressional conservatives. That liberal choice by Roosevelt for the justiceship only increased the conviction of the congressional southerners that the nominee for the next opening should be selected from their ranks. Roosevelt's earlier appointment to the Court of Senator Hugo Black of Alabama did not in their opinion fulfill that southern obligation. The intellectual and solitary Senator Black never had been popular among the fraternity of congressional power brokers, and in the long memory of many senators, he was far too liberal to hold a seat on the Court that should have gone to Joe Robinson.

Carter Glass spoke up for other congressional southerners who felt this way. In private conversations with Roosevelt, Glass was joined by Pat Harrison in urging the president to appoint Jimmy Byrnes to the next available Court opening. Byrnes himself apparently wanted a justiceship, despite his frequently declaring himself happy to remain in the U.S. Senate. And, what seemed more surprising, Franklin Roosevelt also apparently wanted Jimmy Byrnes on the U.S. Supreme Court.

The continuing desire of the president to oblige Jimmy Byrnes' ambitions should have come as no surprise to those who knew both him and the senator. For all their past, occasionally bitter differences over such issues as financing the WPA and liberalizing the constituency of the Democratic party, FDR and Senator Byrnes had remained ideologically and personally close throughout the late 1930s. To less friendly associates such as Harold Ickes, Byrnes had irrevocably jumped the traces as early as 1937 and had long since "gone conservative." But a more balanced appraisal would be that Jimmy Byrnes remained in 1939–40 what he had been in 1933—a "strange mixture," in the words of one of the staff members of Senator Robert Wagner of New York.

On some domestic issues, especially those he perceived as threatening to the maintenance of his whites-only political system in South Carolina, Byrnes could be as reactionary as any other Bourbon politician born in the late nineteenth century in Charleston; but on other important issues of the late 1930s and early 1940s, particularly the administration's foreign policy toward Great Britain and Nazi Germany, the advocacy of an expanded navy and other armed forces for the United States, and FDR's desire for a highly centralized executive office, Byrnes could be as dependable an ally of the New Deal as any of Franklin Roosevelt's former Brain Trust advisers at Columbia University.

Such ideological loyalty demanded the rewards of higher office, including court appointments, as part of the rules of politics that both Jimmy Byrnes and Franklin Roosevelt always had observed. In fact, by FDR's reasoning a Supreme Court appointment would free Jimmy Byrnes from the constraints of South Carolina's elective politics based on race. The president's friend thus would be encouraged to develop further as a dependable New Deal liberal.

It would not have seemed implausible to Franklin Roosevelt that, in between the senator's filibustering antilynching bills and cutting Harry Hopkins' WPA budgets, Jimmy Byrnes was at heart a New Dealer. The proof was Byrnes' demonstrated loyalty in successfully managing the passage in 1939 of the executive government reorganization bill that FDR long had desired and in his hard work at the Chicago convention of 1940 to secure a third-term presidential nomination for Roosevelt.

Byrnes had succeeded to the chairmanship of the joint Senate and House committee on government reorganization following the death of its first chairman, Joe Robinson, in 1937. Roosevelt had long wanted this committee to provide him with a bill capable of passing both chambers and authorizing him to bring such offices as the Veterans' Administration and the Bureau of the Budget under the president's direct control. But the Senate upheavals caused by FDR's court reorganization fight and the attempted purge of 1938 had diverted Byrnes' attention and made it impossible for him to secure a consensus in the Senate and House on increased powers for Roosevelt's office. In early 1939, out of loyalty to Roosevelt, Byrnes tried again.

This time, despite outcries from some conservative Republican critics that the bill was creating a "dictatorship" in the presidential office, Jimmy Byrnes succeeded. The Administrative Reorganization Act of 1939 overseen by Byrnes in its passage through the Seventy-sixth Congress authorized for the first time the establishment of the Executive Office of the President. Dozens of agencies and bureaus from throughout the federal government were removed from congressional oversight or semiautonomous status and centralized within this new executive office. To those people living outside of Washington, D.C., who in 1939 were not directly employed by any of these reorganized federal agencies, interest in or even knowledge about the success of the Byrnes-managed bill probably was slight. But subsequent scholars of the office of the presidency have dated the beginning of the "modern" presidency—and the assumption of powers that were criticized during the Johnson and Nixon administrations as leading to the "imperial" presidency—to the passage of Jimmy Byrnes' reorganization bill in 1939. In seeing the political implications of the reorganization act and in accomplishing its passage when most other senators would have failed, Jimmy Byrnes also once more demonstrated to Roosevelt that he was the quintessential political fixer.

Roosevelt needed such a fixer working for him on the floor at the Chicago convention the summer of 1940. Roosevelt's decision earlier that year to accept renomination to an unprecedented third term if "drafted" by the convention had not been unanticipated, particularly by Byrnes. The senator silently withdrew his own presidential ambitions for the next four years. As early as February 1940, Byrnes had written confidentially to a South Carolina booster of the Byrnes-for-president movement, "Almost daily, I receive letters from men in northern states suggesting that in case the president is not a candidate, I should be considered for the nomination." Unfortunately for Byrnes' ambitions, Roosevelt by early July was an all-but-announced presidential candidate.

To a professional like Jimmy Byrnes, it was evident by summer of 1940 that among the Democrats only Franklin Roosevelt, liberal policies and all, stood a chance that year of defeating the Republicans, who had found an attractive candidate in Wendell Willkie, who, like Roosevelt, was able to give the appearance of a political centrist without losing support from either his party's right or its left wings. ("A simple, barefoot Wall Street lawyer" was how Harold Ickes zestfully described Willkie.) Nevertheless, FDR's decision to run for a third term left behind disappointed mainliners in the Democratic party, such as Jim Farley, the current party chairman, who had wanted the nomination for himself, and conservatives like Jack Garner, who had hoped to succeed Roosevelt as the next president in 1941 and to move the party away from the left. Byrnes agreed to go to Chicago to look after the president's interests and to comanage his renomination together with Harry Hopkins while Roosevelt remained at the White House. After all, Byrnes' presence would add some experience to his old friend's renomination efforts. This Democratic convention was to be Harry Hopkins' first. By contrast, it was to be the seventh in twenty-eight years that Jimmy Byrnes had attended.

Operating from separate Chicago hotels across the street from each other, Byrnes and Hopkins had managed by the third day of the convention to get Roosevelt most of what he wanted from the party's platform, including as strong a statement as possible on the likelihood of U.S. intervention in the European war, which had begun less than a year earlier, on September 1, 1939, after Germany's invasion of Poland. Since then international war clouds had darkened the primarily domestic and nationalistic economic concerns of the Democratic party. By the time the Democrats met in Chicago the third week of July 1940, France as well as most of the other European countries had fallen to Nazi armies. The air Battle of Britain also had begun, presumably in preparation for Hitler's invasion of England.

Roosevelt plainly favored U.S. military intervention in favor of Great Britain, but isolationists in the Democratic party initially insisted that the party platform declare that the Democratic administration would not intervene in the European war or, failing to avoid war, would not send U.S. military forces to fight outside of the Western Hemisphere. The best that Byrnes could do, as a member of the platform committee, was to suggest the qualification that U.S. troops would not be committed to European or Asian wars "except in case of attack" upon the United States. Even this qualification was at first unacceptable both to pro-British interventionists in the White House and to isolationists at the convention. Many Democratic delegates from the isolationist West and the Midwest threatened to walk out of the convention unless the platform remained unchanged. During a break in the platform committee hearings, Jimmy Byrnes took three of the leading isolationist senators for a caucus meeting inside an empty ladies restroom at the convention hall. Byrnes locked the door, and he refused to let anyone out of the restroom until the three senators agreed to add the "in case of attack" qualification to the platform. Under these circumstances, Roosevelt certainly could believe Byrnes when he later telephoned the White House to tell Roosevelt he had gotten the strongest interventionist platform possible.

Most important, Byrnes and Hopkins also gained on Wednesday evening a near-unanimous first ballot victory "drafting" FDR as the Democratic nominee for a third presidential term. To this point of FDR's nomination, the convention of 1940 under the guidance of Byrnes and Hopkins had been relatively harmonious, especially by Democratic party standards. Once more, as at the Philadelphia convention, a Negro religious leader had opened one day of the Democratic convention with prayer. But this time, when Bishop Ransom of the African Methodist Episcopal Church, the son of North Carolina former slaves, stood at the podium on Tuesday morning to deliver the opening prayer, no one had walked out. So thoroughly had the New Deal political firm of "Byrnes & Maybank" controlled the selection of South Carolina's convention delegates in 1940 that Senator E. D. Smith had even decided not to attend as a delegate and was not present at Chicago. (Cotton Ed Smith had remained at his plantation home "sitting on his veranda and hating F.D.R.," according to local newspapers.) But the Thursday morning after the presidential nomination, when Byrnes was selected by the national convention to officially notify Roosevelt of his party's decision, the domestic differences over ideology and race once more threatened to destroy the Democratic party's unity.

The conservatives and moderates at the convention were determined that if the New Deal were to continue beyond 1941 with Franklin Roosevelt at its head, then the vice presidency should go to a candidate from the party's ideological center or from its right. (Jack Garner, as a result of

both his bitter personal quarrel with Roosevelt over the issue of the sit-
down strikes and his ideological conviction that no president should serve
more than two terms, had declined to be renominated for the vice presidency.) Secretary of State Cordell Hull and Senator Jimmy Byrnes were
mentioned frequently by the conservatives and centrists as favorite candidates for the vice presidency, and Roosevelt talked with both Hull and
Byrnes before and during the convention about the possibility that one of
them would join him on the ticket. Hull, the leading ideological "elder"
of the Democratic party, would be sixty-nine by the time of the 1940
election, and Roosevelt apparently thought that his aging secretary of state
would make a pliable vice president. But Hull was determined to hold on
to his power at State should Roosevelt win in 1940, and he resisted FDR's
importuning to join the ticket; when Roosevelt even tried to kindly threaten
Hull into running by telling him that he (Roosevelt) would "have" to accept
Henry Wallace should Hull decline the nomination, the stiff-backed Ten-
nesseean simply deadpanned to the president, "That's all right with me."
Byrnes, who had already put aside his own presidential ambitions to ensure
a win by Roosevelt, sincerely believed that 1940 might not be his year.
Because his name had been mentioned more and more frequently since
the first day of the convention as a possible compromise vice-presidential
candidate, Byrnes knew from printed reports by a journalist friendly to
him that "other candidates for the post began circulating copies of a
Charleston newspaper carrying an editorial quoting from Byrnes' speech
against the anti-lynching bills. This was used in a number of delegations."
Now, when Byrnes telephoned Roosevelt at the White House at ten o'clock
Thursday morning to notify FDR of the nomination, Roosevelt had some
news of his own. He had been talking earlier with Harry Hopkins, FDR
told Byrnes, and Hopkins had advised Roosevelt that the issues of civil
liberties for Negroes and Byrnes' prior conversion from Catholicism precluded the South Carolinian from further consideration on the ticket. Hopkins had stated that both the CIO and the AFL had expressed a preference
for Henry Wallace as the vice-presidential candidate.

Such a choice was doubly disappointing to Byrnes. Not only was he
denied a spot on the ticket himself, but Secretary of Agriculture Henry
Wallace was the most prominent liberal administrator still active in the
New Deal since Rexford Tugwell's return several years earlier to Columbia
University. The conservatives were certain to object when Wallace's name
was brought before the convention. Nevertheless, as comanager of Roosevelt's nomination campaign, Byrnes told the president that he would "go
down the line" for FDR's choice for vice president. Later, when Roosevelt's preference for Henry Wallace was announced to the convention and
was greeted with loud jeering and boos by a majority of the delegates,
Jimmy Byrnes was as good as his word. Byrnes telephoned Roosevelt again
and got the president's permission to repeat to the angry delegates his

threat to give up the nomination for a third term if he was not allowed Henry Wallace as a running mate. "For God's sake, do you want a president or a vice president?" Byrnes shouted at the rebelling delegates.

As a direct result of Jimmy Byrnes' working the floor in such a fashion, an attempt by conservatives to vote House Speaker William Bankhead of Alabama onto the ticket as a compromise vice-presidential candidate was beaten back. The convention, although unenthusiastically, gave Roosevelt the running mate he wanted by nominating Wallace. Byrnes' successful performance at the 1940 convention was given approving attention at the White House by both Roosevelt and his personal counselor, the liberal jurist Samuel Rosenman. Rosenman earlier had characterized Byrnes dismissively as "an available candidate" for the vice-presidential spot on the 1940 ticket and "very anxious" to receive it. But after the convention Jimmy Byrnes at least had some of Rosenman's respect for the integrity of his personal word in "going down the line" for Henry Wallace.

"Harry Hopkins later told the president and me that Byrnes performed as he had promised," Rosenman subsequently wrote. "Although balked in his own ambitions, he went out among the delegates on the floor of the convention and used all the great force of persuasion and argument for which he was so well known in the Senate to help his successful rival. It was a fine display of political loyalty."

Such fine loyalty to New Deal liberalism deserved to be rewarded. Shortly after the convention ended, when the party chairman, Jim Farley, had resigned in disappointment over not receiving the presidential nomination, Roosevelt had offered the Democratic party national chairmanship to Jimmy Byrnes. Byrnes declined, citing the demands of his Senate work load, but he may also have had a larger reward in mind. Byrnes knew that he had greatly increased Roosevelt's political indebtedness to him. The senator had been disappointed in 1939 by being passed over for the Court when Justice Pierce Butler died, and Byrnes' political enemies had raised their usual objections to his Court nomination on the grounds of his former Catholicism and his presumed racism. Byrnes did not intend to be disappointed again, and he continued to work hard to put Roosevelt even more politically in his debt. Presidential favors due to Jimmy Byrnes after the convention multiplied to the point that, in addition to the certainty of the senator's renomination in his state primary, he could in 1941 reasonably expect a nomination to the next vacancy on the Supreme Court. Or, should Cordell Hull retire, there was the possibility for Byrnes to be nominated to become secretary of state.

Either for future repayment by appointment to the Supreme Court or to the cabinet, Jimmy Byrnes increased Roosevelt's indebtedness to him after the convention by his efforts in passing legislation that the Roosevelt administration considered essential to the survival of Great Britain. Byrnes had by 1941 become a leader of the congressionally significant and prowar

group of senators and congressmen who were termed the southern internationalists. Strongly pro-British, the southern internationalists gave
Franklin Roosevelt all the support he asked of Congress when, after gaining
a narrow victory over Wendell Willkie in the fall election of 1940, he
continued his policy of "all possible aid short of war" in aiding Great
Britain in its life-or-death battles with Nazi Germany. Some of the southern
internationalists did not want the Roosevelt administration to stop even
short of war. Senator Carter Glass publicly stated his regret that he was
too old to fire a first American shot against Nazi Germany. The alliance
of the administration with such southern internationalists as Jimmy Byrnes
and Carter Glass put Roosevelt doubly in Byrnes' debt. Not only was
Roosevelt able to obtain war aid to Britain and increased military spending
for the United States, but this agreement with southerners on foreign policy
enabled him by 1941 to break the powerful combination of the congressional conservative coalition.

To H. L. Mencken, the fact that southerners in the early 1940s were
willing to go to war to aid Great Britain out of memories of English aid
to their cause during the Civil War was simply another example of the
continued credulity of the white southerner. To Carter Glass and Jimmy
Byrnes, the fact that southerners were eager in the early 1940s to join the
fight with Great Britain against Hitler's armies and nazism was due, in
Glass's words, "both to superior character and to exceptional understanding of the problem involved" that they possessed. To Franklin Roosevelt,
the fact that the Democratic congressional conservatives were in agreement
on foreign policy with urban, interventionist liberals in his party offered
FDR a chance "to compose his ancient quarrel with Congress," in the
words of the contemporary journalists Joseph Alsop and Robert Kintner.
Former southern adversaries such as Glass and Byrnes who had opposed
much of the domestic policies of the second New Deal now took the lead
in promoting the administration's policies of preparing the United States
militarily for a world conflict. Along with Roosevelt, Byrnes expected the
United States' war against the fascist governments to begin in the North
Atlantic, and he used his position on the Appropriations Naval Subcommittee in the late 1930s and early 1940s to approve substantial increases
for warship production. Byrnes was indeed one of the few senators who
had seen Nazi military might firsthand, when during a tour of relief agencies
in Germany he had been an invited foreign guest to the Nazi party's 1938
Nuremberg congress and watched hundreds of planes fly overhead and
thousands of goose-stepping infantry pass in review. Byrnes was disturbed,
and probably a little frightened, by what he had seen. "No guy is going to
build this kind of war machine just to show it off," Byrnes later told Senator
Alva Adams. "Hitler wants to go places and see things."

At times, before FDR's election to a third presidential term, Byrnes
had even tried to push the administration into political confrontations with

the Third Reich, which Roosevelt appears not to have wanted. His friendship with Baruch and other southern Jews had made the senator exceptionally aware of the plight of European Jewry as nazism became more of a menace. Within a week after the infamous *Kristallnacht*, November 9–10, 1938, which saw the Nazi looting of Jewish synagogues and shops throughout Germany, Byrnes from his Spartanburg, South Carolina, home had sent an unaccustomedly sharp-tempered telegram to Roosevelt.

"Mere expressions of our sympathy, while encouraging to the Jews of this country, will offer no practical relief to the unfortunate Jews of Germany," Byrnes had wired. "I assume legislation is necessary to increase the quota of German citizens eligible for admission to this country and believe by inquiry you could be assured of the co-operation of the Congress. Certainly you will have my co-operation." (Roosevelt's response, in light of his administration's subsequent failure to ask Congress for increased immigration quotas favoring Jewish refugees from Germany, is chilling in its sunny and dismissing nature: "My dear Jim: Thank you for that grand telegram of November sixteenth. As you know, we are working on this problem which is certainly a difficult one. It is good to know that I can count on your co-operation and I do hope you will feel free to let me have any suggestions you may have on this subject. With all good wishes, very sincerely yours. . . .")

Roosevelt did call on Byrnes and place himself in his debt most deeply a few weeks before his third inauguration, in January 1941, when he asked Byrnes to be the floor manager in the Senate for the administration's most important prewar defense legislation, the Lend-Lease Act. This act, which authorized Roosevelt to "lend" navy destroyers and other armaments to Great Britain for use in combat against Germany and its Axis allies, was considered crucial by the administration in order to maintain the anti-Axis coalition and to gain time for the United States itself to build up armaments before ending its official neutrality and entering the war. Isolationists such as Senator Burton K. Wheeler opposed the bill, as did some politically powerful military planners, who feared that the transfer of equipment to Great Britain would reduce the armaments available to the U.S. Army and Navy. Nevertheless, returning to Washington in early January 1941, after spending Christmas at Spartanburg, Byrnes was confident that he had the votes to get Roosevelt his lend-lease bill passed through the Senate. And, as was usual when he felt he had the votes, Byrnes sent a telegram to Roosevelt with his cheerfully and frequently used phrase, telling FDR not to worry about the isolationist opposition and to "let the heathen rage."

Subsequent to a strategy meeting later that month with Byrnes, Pat Harrison, Alben Barkley, and Carter Glass at the White House over passage of lend-lease, Roosevelt asked the Democratic Senate Steering Committee to appoint both Byrnes and Glass to openings on the Senate Foreign Relations Committee in the newly convened Seventy-seventh Congress.

The presence of the two senators guaranteed a favorable report on the bill to the full chamber. For Byrnes, appointment to the Foreign Relations Committee in 1941 at the request of the president also represented the apogee of senatorial powers; the Foreign Relations Committee, like the Appropriations Committee, was one of the great standing committees of the U.S. Senate, and men usually devoted decades of their careers to obtaining appointment to it. Within the comparatively short period of less than ten years, Byrnes had gained membership on two such committees. The influence of Jimmy Byrnes in the U.S. Senate in regard to the lend-lease bill and the reliance of the Roosevelt administration upon him there are evident from the memorandum that the presidential assistant General Edwin Watson prepared for Roosevelt's reading on January 17, 1941. "Senator Jimmy Byrnes just phoned me that, in spite of all the howling going on now, the president will get 10 to 14 Republican votes on his 'lend aid' bill. We will not lose more than a dozen Democrats. This insures a two-thirds majority at any time for the president's measure. This is a better situation than there has been on any recent controversial bill in the Senate." (So accurately had Byrnes predicted the vote that he was within one senator of correctly numbering the split. Lend-lease passed the Senate on March 9, by a vote of 60 to 31.) "Senator Byrnes ended this phone message by saying, 'I am very well satisfied with the situation.' "

Characteristically, Jimmy Byrnes denied to the press that he had anything to do with the successful management of the lend-lease bill. But after Roosevelt signed the bill into law on March 11, the *Washington Star* declared in its analysis, "It is now established that the Lend-Lease came through the Senate as well as it did chiefly because of the able management of Byrnes. . . . It was Byrnes who made the [voting] checks, talked to the waverers, soothed the grumblers and shepherded the doubters into line."

Given the usefulness for the administration's interventionist foreign policy of Jimmy Byrnes' presence in the U.S. Senate, the question arises why Roosevelt continued to be so interested in appointing Byrnes to the Supreme Court throughout 1941. Roosevelt knew that his appointing Jimmy Byrnes to the Supreme Court not only would pay off all his political debts to Byrnes but also would effectively eliminate Byrnes from any further consideration as a vice-presidential candidate in 1944, regardless of who was at the head of the ticket. One potentially divisive contender would therefore be removed from the Democratic party, since no justice had yet resigned his lifetime "higher" office to seek such an elective post. (The vice-presidential ambitions in 1944 of Justice William Douglas, a Roosevelt appointee in 1939, were yet to be displayed.) Roosevelt also knew that Byrnes could scarcely decline the appointment, given both the senator's own ambitions for personal honors and his loyalty to the South in serving as a southern conservative on the Court. "Of course, I will appoint him," Roosevelt told Carter Glass, when Glass met with the president at the

White House in late January 1941. Justice James McReynolds, the last of the Court's four major conservatives of the mid-1930s, had just announced his retirement, and Glass came to lobby the president to appoint his friend Jimmy Byrnes to the vacancy. "He is just as much my friend as yours," Roosevelt continued. "I wanted him to be my running mate in 1940."

Appointing Byrnes to the Supreme Court also would allow Burnet Maybank to move up to the U.S. Senate, because as governor of South Carolina he could appoint a safe caretaker to serve the final year of Byrnes' term and then run for that office himself. Maybank was immensely liked by both Roosevelt and Hopkins and, in fact, was a more dependable New Dealer than Byrnes himself. And Roosevelt knew that if Maybank were to move to the Senate, the way would be clear for the man who was probably the most ideologically committed New Dealer in South Carolina, former Governor Olin Johnson, to run for the governorship again. Johnson, who had loyally tried to depose Cotton Ed Smith for the New Deal during the attempted purge of 1938, would have the opportunity if elected governor to build up a statewide organization for another try at unseating, "the old pirate" Smith in 1944.

Roosevelt knew that Byrnes would still be available to provide political counsel and influence for the administration's foreign policy even after moving to the Supreme Court. Byrnes made it clear that he shared with Justice Felix Frankfurter a lack of ethical difficulties with these "extracurricular" activities. And even if Byrnes should rule conservatively on domestic issues while sitting on the Court, no great harm would be done, in Roosevelt's opinion. The New Deal already had a safe majority of liberal justices, because Roosevelt's prior appointees—Black, Murphy, Frankfurter, and Douglas—had joined pro–New Deal justices already on the Court. Also in 1941 the elevation of Justice Harlan Stone to the position of the chief justice meant that Roosevelt could appoint another associate justice in addition to Byrnes. FDR selected a dependable liberal to accompany his nomination of Byrnes: his present attorney general, Robert Jackson.

However, the possibility of a Byrnes justiceship still was disturbing to Democratic liberals in such as Harold Ickes, Thomas Corcoran, David Lilienthal, and Walter White. White, on learning on March 16, 1941, that Roosevelt was determined to appoint Byrnes, sent a telegram to him. White's message arrived at the White House the morning after FDR had delivered a national radio address telling the nation that the first lend-lease shipments were under way and that Winston Churchill had assured the president that England was successfully bracing to resist a possible German invasion.

"Last night with magnificent eloquence you appealed to Americans to defend Democracy and to put aside all 'divisions of party or section or race or nationality or religion,' " the national secretary of the NAACP wrote in the telegram. "But today's newspapers report that you may to-morrow send to the Senate the name of James F. Byrnes of South Carolina as a member of the United States Supreme Court. We beg of you not to do so."

White continued, "If Senator Byrnes at any time in his long public career failed to take a position not inimical to the human and citizenship rights of thirteen million American Negro citizens, close scrutiny of his record fails to reveal it. We are sending to the White House a detailed record of Mr. Byrnes' opposition to educational, economic, and citizenship rights for Negroes as well as material on his savage attacks on legislation to stop lynching and mob violence." A four-page report accompanied White's telegram, containing excerpts from Byrnes' speeches, beginning with his remarks in the House against federal funding for Howard University in 1925 and including his filibuster speech against the antilynching bill of 1938.

White then ended his telegram to Roosevelt with an unsubstantiated fillip that Byrnes also was anti-Semitic: "Reports from credible sources of other racial and religious bigotry, particularly against Jews, manifested by Mr. Byrnes are still under investigation. We will shortly submit to you a supplemental memorandum on this."

But too many other people, in Franklin Roosevelt's opinion, would benefit from the nomination of Jimmy Byrnes to the Supreme Court for the president to change his mind now, regardless of the accuracy or inaccuracy of White's charges. Besides, in possible compensation, FDR had something else to offer the NAACP and other organized Negro groups in the spring of 1941 with the creation of the President's Committee on Fair Employment Practice. And any final doubts he might have had about a Court nomination for Byrnes dissipated when the Republican leadership in the Senate sent word to the White House that out of bipartisan respect for Byrnes' abilities and integrity as a senator, Republican senators were prepared to approve the nomination of Jimmy Byrnes to the Supreme Court by unanimous consent without the usual referral to the Judiciary Committee.

Within eight minutes of receiving formal notice of Roosevelt's nomination of Byrnes to a place on the high court, the U.S. Senate unanimously approved it during the morning session of June 12, 1941. (The nominations of Stone and Jackson were confirmed after hearings in committee.) In the absence of Senate Majority Leader Alben Barkley, who was recovering from a serious illness, Byrnes agreed at Roosevelt's request to remain as an active senator for another month following his Senate confirmation in order to manage the administration's continuing reorganization legislation. There was no strictly construed conflict of interest in this unusual arrangement by Senator Byrnes, as the next session of the Supreme Court would not begin until the following October and Byrnes had not yet resigned his

Senate office and taken his oath as a justice. But as a self-professed constitutional conservative, Byrnes later wrote that he was "terribly embarrassed" by FDR's request.

Over fifty persons crowded into the Oval Office at the White House to
watch Jimmy Byrnes take his judicial oath in front of Franklin Roosevelt
the morning of July 8, 1941. Byrnes was uncharacteristically reserved.
Roosevelt was characteristically ebullient. So many of Byrnes' friends from
the upper legislative chamber were present to see Byrnes take his oath
that Roosevelt laughed and "called the Senate to order." Among those
present was Byrnes' longtime friend and mentor Carter Glass, who in
photographs of the scene is looking on Jimmy Byrnes in a way that can
only be described as that of a proud father witnessing his son's long-
expected success. Bernard Baruch also was there, with plans to stay for
lunch after the ceremony and give the president his confidential advice on
the international situation. And Frank Hogan was there, the Republican
former president of the American Bar Association looking hale, hearty,
and very rich, a reminder to Byrnes that morning of how he and his cousin
Hogan had grown up together as poor boys at Elizabeth Byrnes' house in
Charleston and of how far by 1941 they both had come.

Byrnes had spoken his oath with his wife on one side of him and his
sister, Leonore Byrnes Fuller, at the other. Roosevelt beamed at all three
with the delighted look of a country squire who knew that he was being
generous in repaying a debt by awarding a piece of property to a tenant
rent-free for life.

As he spoke his oath to uphold his duties as the nation's newest justice,
Byrnes firmly placed his hand upon a Bible provided by his wife's family
and opened to the Eighty-second Psalm:

> *Give justice to the weak and the fatherless;*
> *Maintain the right of the afflicted and the destitute.*
> *Rescue the weak and the needy;*
> *Deliver them from the hand of the wicked.*
>
> *They have neither knowledge nor understanding,*
> *They walk about in darkness;*
> *All the foundations of the earth are shaken.*
>
> *I say, "You are gods, sons of the Most High, all of you;*
> *Nevertheless, you shall die like men,*
> *And fall like any prince."*

Roosevelt's exact words preceding the administration of the oath were not
recorded, but those present agreed that the president had said that, like
King Solomon, he wished he could "halve Jimmy Byrnes, keeping one half

in the Senate and the other half on the court. At that moment, he was losing the smoothest, most effective worker he had ever had in the Senate; at the same time, acquiring an unknown quantity for his court."

Jimmy Byrnes may not have been as successful a Supreme Court appointment as Franklin Roosevelt might have wished, but neither was he as great a failure as Walter White and others might have hoped. (Their bias against Byrnes still prevails. "Even Homer nods," was the wildly unfair judgment in 1977 of one historian of the judiciary in regard to FDR's appointment of Byrnes.) After taking his seat on the Court on October 6, 1941, Byrnes served as a justice less than twelve months, resigning shortly before the beginning of his second term on the Court, on October 3, 1942. Sitting for only one term, Byrnes did not accumulate a sufficient record of votes, written opinions, or dissents to make him one of the more substantive of the Court's justices. But contrary to the expectations of White, Ickes, Hopkins, and other administration liberals, Justice Byrnes did not isolate himself as a one-man member of the Court's extreme right wing; nor did Jimmy Byrnes, despite his continuing involvement in partisan politics and other "extracurricular activities" while on the Court, fatally embarrass the administration. Considered as a contributor to the nation's jurisprudence, Justice Byrnes was no Hugo Black. Yet when considered as one of the most "political" justices to sit on the Court, the independence of Byrnes' judicial decisions and his personal integrity improve by historical comparison. Jimmy Byrnes was no Abe Fortas.

Notable also when Byrnes first moved to the Court is the intriguing almost–brushing by in his chambers of one future president with one future almost-president. Justice Byrnes requested and was provided with a list and confidential appraisal of recent law school graduates as candidates to serve as his clerk. Among those considered were two Duke University graduates, one of whom was Richard M. Nixon. Byrnes' source of information wrote the justice that he had "asked cautiously" about both Nixon and the other Duke graduate "and confirmed my impression that they are good men; but no one used superlatives on them." Byrnes chose a graduate of another law school as his clerk, and Nixon, through the intercession of a Duke professor, eventually got a job in late 1941 as a staff attorney in the Office of Price Administration, an office that later reported administratively to Jimmy Byrnes as director of the Office of Economic Stabilization.

Byrnes proved surprisingly liberal in two majority opinions regarding civil rights that he wrote in the Court's 1941–42 term. In the case of *Edwards* v. *California*, Byrnes upheld the rights of individuals to travel freely from one state to another. During the Depression the state of California, in an effort to reduce its relief rolls, had prosecuted as a criminal offense attempts by its residents to bring unemployed relatives or acquaintances to live with them in California if the residents were unable to provide for the newcomers' upkeep. Despite his past advocacy of states' rights and his belief in fiscal conservatism in regard to relief spending, Byrnes wrote in his majority opinion that the California law exceeded the state police powers. Arguing that the interstate commerce clause of the Constitution also guaranteed the "commerce" of people moving freely from one state to another, Byrnes refused in writing the majority opinion to accept California's contention that, in his words, "a state might gain a momentary respite from the pressure of events by the simple expedient of shutting its gates to the outside world."

Byrnes further limited the police powers of the state by reversing the murder conviction of a black man who had been arrested for the death of a white man in the majority opinion Byrnes wrote for the Court in 1942 in the case of *Ward* v. *Texas*. Police in Texas had taken the accused black man, William Ward, from the church he was attending in the county where the murder had been committed. Handcuffing the defendant and moving him without a warrant, police carried Ward more than a total of one hundred miles to a series of county jails in Texas, where he was held over three days and nights, supposedly to protect him from pursuing lynch mobs. During that time the police continued interrogating Ward and depriving him of sleep until he confessed.

Ward later alleged that he also had been beaten and burned with cigarettes by the Texas policemen until he signed a confession. Justice Byrnes did not find the allegations of police brutality wholly convincing; nevertheless he failed to be convinced by the testimony of a Texas police officer in regard to Ward's confession: "Yes sir, we just sweet-talked it out of him." Byrnes led the Court in reversing the murder conviction on the grounds that moving "an ignorant Negro by night and day to strange towns and telling him of threats of mob violence and questioning him continuously" had resulted in an inadmissible confession. Byrnes continued, speaking for a majority of the Court, "The use of a confession under such circumstances is a denial of due process and the judgment of the conviction must be reversed."

One may object to Byrnes' patronizing characterization of "an ignorant Negro." But the import of Byrnes' written opinions on civil rights, and his concurring vote in 1942 Court decision finding an all-white grand jury to be prima facie evidence of racial discrimination against a black defendant, support Roosevelt's belief that, once on the Court and freed from South Carolina's elective politics based on race, Jimmy Byrnes would become more of a New Deal liberal. Byrnes was never predictably liberal on the Court, however. From the bench Justice Byrnes continued his conservative war against the CIO and its use of the sit-down strike, writing the majority opinion of a 5-to-4 decision that a sit-down strike by the union crew aboard a merchant ship stopping at a nonunion southern port was an illegal act at sea, and that the ship's owners were justified in firing the crew. Byrnes also voted with the majority in 1942 to uphold decisions by lower courts limiting organized labor's rights to picket, and he joined in a minority opinion approving a conviction during a labor trial for contempt of court against the West Coast director of the CIO.

If Byrnes as a justice belonged wholly to neither the liberal nor the conservative factions during his tenure on the Supreme Court, it was not because he was an original or iconoclastic thinker at law. Rather, it was because in his one year on the Court he found neither ideological nor personal friends among the other eight justices. Byrnes was a "misfit on the court," in the words chosen years later by Justice William O. Douglas, who served with him during the 1941–42 term. Byrnes "disliked the court work," Douglas remarked in his memoirs, and seemed to long to go back to his former work as a senator on Capitol Hill.

A comparison of Byrnes' dissents in his first year on the Supreme Court with Hugo Black's in his first year tends to confirm Douglas' thoughts about Byrnes' dislike of his court duties. Byrnes dissented from the majority opinions of the Court during 1941–42 on twelve occasions, always in concurrence with at least one other justice. He wrote no dissenting opinions, either for himself or for others. By contrast, during his first year on the Court, Hugo Black dissented sixteen times. On twelve of those occasions, Black was the sole dissenter. Justices Black and Byrnes both were self-educated men who had risen to the Court by hard work from their lower-middle class southern backgrounds. But the more numerous and frequently solitary dissents by Black—Hugo Black dissented alone as many times as Jimmy Byrnes dissented totally—reflect his attempt, working as a solitary intellect, to construct anew an interpretation of the nation's jurisprudence.

Byrnes' work for the Court, by contrast, reveals a mind that sought consensus rather than new constructions and that was fundamentally impatient with judicial procedures. Not only were his dissents less frequent, but on those many instances when Jimmy Byrnes did agree with the decision of a majority of justices and was not the author assigned by Chief Justice Stone to write the majority opinion, he usually added little to the draft of the opinion prepared by one of his peers. Justices reserve the right after conference to suggest changes in the form or phrasing of a majority opinion before it is released with their names; they argue for those changes with an accompanying circulating memorandum. If these changes are not adopted, a justice in agreement may file a separate, concurring opinion with the majority. Byrnes seldom exercised his rights to revision, and he never wrote a concurring opinion. If he agreed with the majority, Byrnes characteristically wrote "I approve" in a quick hand on the back of the circulating proof and simply passed it on to another justice.

Byrnes' reticence while the other justices joined in ideological debates was apparently a holdover from his Senate career, when he was more interested in the outcome of a vote than in the ideological speeches preceding it. This habit of mind made Byrnes the odd man out while on the Supreme Court. Beginning in its 1941 term, the new chief justice, Harlan Stone, encouraged full debate among justices during conferences. But in the conference notes of Byrnes' fellow FDR-appointee Justice Frank Murphy, there are no references to Byrnes' comments during discussions among justices on a number of major cases heard by the Court.

Nor did Justice Byrnes find with his fellow justices the happy, after-hours conviviality of "bullbat time" that he enjoyed in Congress, as when his ideological opponents there had put aside their differences in the 1930s for drinks of bourbon and the singing of hymns and other old favorites around Jimmy Byrnes' desk in the Senate Office Building. (Justices Black and Murphy, for example, were teetotalers.) Jimmy and Maude Byrnes did try to increase the sociability of the Court by hosting frequent dinners throughout 1941–42 for the other justices and their wives at the Byrnes apartment at the Shoreham Hotel. Justice William Douglas remembered that, in addition to his being charmed by the graciousness of Maude Byrnes, "the food was delicious and the drinks abundant. Jimmy had a strong tenor voice, and after dinner he led the justices and their wives in singing popular songs." As a result of these gatherings, Byrnes formed a strong social friendship—if not an intellectual or ideological friendship—with Justice Felix Frankfurter. But even in leading these forced judicial sing-alongs around a piano Jimmy Byrnes misplaced his energies, in Douglas' opinion. "The result was usually horrible, but Jimmy was undaunted."

He was undaunted, but he was very unhappy. Whereas Byrnes later declared that his Senate years were the most satisfying of his public career, it is incontrovertible that his one term on the Supreme Court was the unhappiest of his public life. Byrnes' being disconsolate as a justice probably was most surprising to Franklin Roosevelt. FDR had worked very hard in 1941 not only to get Jimmy Byrnes "off his neck," as the current phrase had it, but also to make him happy by giving him this promotion to the nation's highest court. There had been nothing to make FDR think that Jimmy Byrnes had not wanted a justiceship. Although Byrnes had never explicitly asked Roosevelt for an appointment to the Court, neither had he ever told him that he was not interested in becoming a justice. (Curiously, although Byrnes' patron Bernard Baruch had been urging Roosevelt for years to appoint Byrnes to the Court, there is no mention by Byrnes in any of his letters to Baruch of his ever wanting the job. The only instance of Byrnes' expressing any interest in the possibility of his being appointed to the Supreme Court is his cautioning Baruch in 1939 not to press their cause too vigorously with Roosevelt.) It was not that Jimmy Byrnes had set about to deceive Roosevelt or Baruch about his interest in serving on the Court. It simply was Jimmy Byrnes' nature not to refuse a promotion, whether he wanted the new job or not. And, at age fifty-nine, an appointment to the Court in 1941 had offered Byrnes the security of a lifelong job.

A reminder to Jimmy Byrnes that both his years and his personal advancement were limited had come to him in 1941, a few weeks before he took his oath as a justice. Pat Harrison, that genial wit and boon companion for decades to Byrnes, died an unexpected death of intestinal cancer on June 22 of that year. No longer would Byrnes enjoy the droll insider's gossip of his old Senate friend at "bullbat time," nor would Byrnes again see the tall and balding Mississippi senator eccentrically stripped to his long johns in the summer heat, playing golf on the fairways of Washington's exclusive Burning Tree Golf Club. The day after Harrison's death, Byrnes wrote to Mrs. Jack Garner, who had joined her husband in his retirement from the vice presidency at Texas, about the large number of men in the U.S. Senate whom Byrnes had known as his contemporaries and who were now ailing or dead. His thoughts then turned to his own upcoming move across the street to the Supreme Court Building. "After the excitement of life in the House and Senate, I do not know if whether I will be happy upon the court," Byrnes wrote Mrs. Garner. But, he continued, "I know that there comes a time when it is wise to pursue a more orderly life than I have led for the last ten or twelve years. I am confident that life [on the Court] will be longer, if not happier." Byrnes added, "From these statements you will rightly judge that I am depressed by Pat's death."

There were other losses. Also before Byrnes took his oath as a justice, Asbury Francis "Frank" Lever had died in 1940. Byrnes had always had a soft spot in his heart for Lever, who had represented much that was the best in southern progressiveness. Together they had been young and idealistic congressmen when Woodrow Wilson was president and the New Freedom was the Democratic catchword. Although Frank Lever had been unable to win an election for himself after 1918, Byrnes had continued to look after the practical interests of his scholarly friend, finding him government appointments in a number of New Deal agencies. Now Lever was dead, and it must have seemed to Jimmy Byrnes that one by one all the participants in his earlier political campaigns were passing from the scene in anticipation of his own passing. In early 1942 even Coley Blease died.

Byrnes continued in his efforts to live longer, if not more happily, while serving on the Supreme Court. After so many years of being addressed as Senator Byrnes, or simply as Jimmy, the title Justice Byrnes must have given him at least some pleasure, for it was coequal to the highest titles of the executive or the legislative branch. Byrnes in his robes did look the part of a Supreme Court justice. With his habitual quizzical and intelligent expression, he had the appearance of a well-draped owl. His yearly salary of $20,000 as an associate justice of the Court was larger than his salary as a senator, and he and Maude Byrnes settled into a comfortable life between their Shoreham Hotel apartment and their house at Spartanburg. Their Reo Flying Cloud automobile had long since been sold and replaced with a new Buick and, eventually, a Cadillac. Like so many other childless couples in late middle age, they also doted on a series of dogs, grieving when their canine family members were lost to old age or to the wheels of Washington traffic. Throughout much of the 1940s, Jimmy Byrnes' usual early-morning walking companion was a Scottish terrier named Whiskers. Outwardly, Byrnes had become one of the Bourbon judges he had so admired in his youth.

But this self-made man refused to find rest in his achievement of a justiceship. Byrnes had brought with him his congressional secretary, Cassandra Connor, to continue to be his assistant after he moved across the street to the Supreme Court Building, and he retained many of the energetic, restless habits of his Senate career. In his chambers or at his apartment, he daily read three or four of the nation's newspapers, quickly scanning the pages for political items. At his Shoreham apartment he listened to the radio until late at night, following the news of the war in Europe or of the defense buildup at home, allowing himself only a snatch of the big-band music or sentimental ballads of which he was so fond. In September 1941 he heard the announcement of Roosevelt's "shoot-on-sight" orders to the U.S. Navy patrolling the North Atlantic merchant sea lanes against German submarines or surface raiders. By early fall of that year, the Office of Production Management (OPM), one of the first war-planning agencies created by Roosevelt, also had announced its recommendations that gasoline be rationed on the East Coast and that the use of raw silk in civilian fabrics be eliminated in order to avoid dependence on Japanese imports and to save the material for possible use in military parachutes. Attaining prominence as one of the two cochairmen of the OPM was a man with whose career Byrnes was quite familiar. Sidney Hillman had been named by Roosevelt in early 1941 to that post, with particular responsibility for labor relations in the defense effort.

Justice Byrnes fretted. He talked to Roosevelt frequently about defense and political matters, but he now was simply another adviser on administration policies with no powers to execute those policies as head of an executive office, or to write them into law as a senator. Despite his frequent conferences with Roosevelt, Byrnes tended to be alone with his political thoughts in the evenings after his daytime work on the Court. As he had done so often while a senator, Jimmy Byrnes continued to take notes on his political conversations with Roosevelt and other government officials, written in the shorthand code only he could read. The newspapers read and discarded around him while the radio was playing softly in the background, the discontented Byrnes spent his nights solitarily reviewing the cryptic notes on his political thoughts.

At this time Byrnes drank too much Hankey Bannister bourbon, or at least what the new vice president, Henry Wallace, deemed as too much bourbon. (Byrnes once told Wallace that the habit of convivial drinking among justices had contributed to the effective functioning of the Supreme Court during his term there. "The great cure for discord in Jimmie's opinion is more free-hearted drinking," Wallace later noted disapprovingly in his diary.) Byrnes' single-minded and unhappy pursuit of domestic politics at this point in his life when he was so aware of his mortality was due in part to the fact that Byrnes had neither the distractions nor the consolations of children. In effect, his political thoughts *were* his children: they were his brood, and they came to him late at night in the winter of 1941–42. While alone, Justice Byrnes soothed their injuries, drank his bourbon, and planned retribution against those who had given his favorite thoughts any disappointments.

One day Byrnes had a visitor at his Supreme Court chambers. Turner Catledge, the Mississippi-born reporter for the *New York Times*, called on the justice. Catledge was one of the old gang, and he, Harrison, and Byrnes had once had a high time together at Byrnes's hotel suite at the 1940 Democratic convention. Catledge was simply making a social call on his friend, and he perhaps hesitated to stay too long and impose on the time Justice Byrnes allowed for reflection in his chambers. Byrnes, however, insisted that Catledge stay for a visit. "Come on in," he told him. "I get so damn lonely here."

PART THREE

LEAVING HIS FATHER'S HOUSE

1942–1972

12

The Assistant President

The Second World War rescued Jimmy Byrnes, just as war always rescues ambitious, restless men from civilian jobs they dislike. In Turner Catledge's later recollection, Byrnes "jumped at the chance" to leave the Supreme Court soon after the Sunday attack on Pearl Harbor, on December 7, 1941. The following Wednesday morning, Byrnes went to see Roosevelt at the president's request in his upstairs bedroom at the White House. The president was still in bed, studying incoming reports on the damage to the American fleet in the Pacific. War with Japan had already been declared by Congress before Byrnes' visit; declarations of war between the United States and the Axis powers of Germany and Italy would follow within a day. Byrnes was shocked at Roosevelt's appearance as he lay in bed, reviewing reports of American ships sunk and American lives lost at Pearl Harbor. Along with Roosevelt, Byrnes had expected the war with the fascist countries to begin in the North Atlantic, and to begin with more warning to American military forces. Byrnes later wrote that as Roosevelt told him "of developments since Sunday afternoon, he was more nervous than I had ever seen him."

Byrnes followed FDR as he wheeled himself into the bathroom and began to lather his face to shave. He needed Byrnes' help with upcoming war legislation, Roosevelt said. A successful prosecution of the war would require the office of the presidency to assume powers unheard of even in the emergency of the Depression, and Roosevelt needed Byrnes to persuade Congress to give the president that power now. If the United States and its Allies were to beat the Axis and Japanese armies, the entire U.S. economy, for instance, would have to be placed under government direction to set priorities for weapons production and to limit prices and wages so that the demands of the nation's civilian and military industries did not compete with one another. For Byrnes, despite the gloomy war news, it must have seemed like the happy times of the Hundred Days. Once again, Franklin Roosevelt was calling on his old friend Jimmy Byrnes to be his "economic champion" in political struggles with Congress at a time of national crisis. That morning while Roosevelt shaved, Justice Byrnes told FDR that he would help any way he could.

Byrnes, once he had determined to jump back into politics, jumped that December morning in 1941 with both feet. After their morning conversation, Byrnes returned to his judicial duties on the Supreme Court, but Roosevelt instructed his advisers that proposed war legislation and executive orders affecting the economy first be submitted to Justice Byrnes for his political approval. Attorney General Francis Biddle subsequently reported to Roosevelt that "all defense legislation is being cleared by the departments and then through Jimmy Byrnes, who takes care of it on the Hill."

What Byrnes took care of for Franklin Roosevelt on Capitol Hill was the behind-the-scenes sponsorship of the First and Second War Powers acts, both of which had passed through Congress by March 1942. As the nation's commander in chief, Roosevelt achieved unprecedented authority for the duration of the war with the passage of these acts, both written in part by Byrnes. Wartime activities ranging from the industrial production of tanks and artillery shells by private factories to the writing of press releases by the government's Office of War Information were brought under the direct control of Roosevelt's office by these acts. Byrnes was also among the first to urge Roosevelt to dismantle such prewar planning and procurement organizations as the Office of Production Management, of which Sidney Hillman was a cochairman. Byrnes argued for replacing the various and overlapping defense offices that Roosevelt had assembled in a haphazard manner since 1939 with one centralized authority. That authority in Byrnes' scheme, would be responsible for setting industrial priorities nationwide to win the war and would be headed by one man, responsible only to Roosevelt.

It was not that Jimmy Byrnes wanted this job for himself. As a matter of fact, in a memorandum on wartime mobilization that he wrote within five days of his early-morning meeting with Roosevelt at the White House, Byrnes directed his thoughts to the man who was Byrnes' greatest ideological opponent, the liberal presidential adviser Harry Hopkins. In a "Memorandum for Mr. Hopkins," Byrnes urged Hopkins to advise the president to "name a man—for convenience call him Hopkins—and charge him with the duty of supervising and expediting procurement." Byrnes continued, "If because of the deficiency in the supply of steel, there is a controversy between Army and Navy and civilian services as to the amount to be allotted to their respective needs, Hopkins should decide that controversy."

The important point to Jimmy Byrnes in his memorandum was that Franklin Roosevelt should see the need of immediately mobilizing the American economy for war under one man directly responsible to the president. Byrnes had not forgotten the sight of those hundreds of new military airplanes produced by German industry flying overhead for Hitler's proud display at the Nuremberg rally of 1938. The Third Reich had already gained a lethal head start in the production of such weapons by Hitler's having appointed a uniquely powerful minister of armaments, Fritz Todt, later to be succeeded by Albert Speer. Byrnes wanted the best administrator America could provide in a similar position of executive authority on this side of the Atlantic. "Pick the best man you have on the team," Byrnes wrote in his memorandum, "and let the heathen rage."

Byrnes' advice was sound, but Hopkins had not forgotten that the author of this memorandum had earned well his reputation as being *sly* as well as able. If the man named to this unspecified post were, for convenience sake, named Hopkins, then Harry Hopkins knew that Jimmy Byrnes would have succeeded in removing from the intimate circle of the president's advisers one of the South Carolinian's major competitors for Roosevelt's political attention. The individual charged with "supervising and expediting procurement" probably would, for example, no longer have the time or the staff to supervise personally the lend-lease program, a powerful position that Hopkins at the time of his receipt of Byrnes' memorandum enjoyed while he lived and worked upstairs at the White House. Furthermore, the appointment of a single individual, even if the choice were not to be a Harry Hopkins conveniently overworked, could be better controlled by such economic conservatives as Byrnes or Baruch than could a panel of several members. Hopkins therefore chose not to show Byrnes' memorandum to the president and instead urged Roosevelt to appoint a three-member committee to oversee the nation's war production. The three members could be chosen to represent equally small business and labor as well as the large capitalists and corporations favored by Baruch and Byrnes.

Accordingly, when Byrnes dropped by Hopkins' bedroom at the upstairs White House and learned that Hopkins had *not* shown the memorandum to the president, Byrnes asked to have back from Hopkins the copy of the memorandum. Byrnes then met with Roosevelt later that same day, January 12.

The president appeared to take Byrnes' advice. On January 16, 1942, Roosevelt created through executive order the War Production Board (WPB). His order gave the board's chairman "general authority" over the U.S. economy, and the board received powers to allocate to industries as it saw fit the supplies of scarce materials necessary for the nation's defense—as, in Byrnes' example to FDR in his memorandum, the power to resolve disputes between the Navy's wanting steel for the production of ships, the Army's wanting steel for the production of tanks, and the civilian industry's wanting the same steel for the production of automobiles to carry defense workers to their jobs at Navy or Army defense plants. To head this new wartime agency, Roosevelt chose Donald Nelson, a respected former executive with the Sears, Roebuck and Company, and certainly a conservative choice that gave Byrnes relief from the hypothetical Harry Hopkins. With the creation in 1942 of the WPB, the OPM by later executive order was abolished. Sidney Hillman was relegated to the position of labor adviser to the WPB, and his authority and that of organized labor appeared to be in eclipse under the latest reorganization.

There could be no doubt by now that Justice Jimmy Byrnes was back in business at the White House as a highly skilled politician and as a key adviser to Roosevelt on government reorganization and economy. When Byrnes accomplished the elimination of the OPM through the adoption of the arguments in his memorandum, he had been advising Roosevelt on war-related matters for less than a month since Pearl Harbor. Although he kept his position as a justice for the remainder of the Supreme Court's 1941–42 term, Byrnes spent most of his time making sure that war-related legislation was "cleared through Jimmy" by executive department heads. Chief Justice Harlan Stone informally agreed to excuse Byrnes from writing opinions for a short while in consideration of Byrnes' usefulness to the executive department during the war emergency. (Byrnes' patriotic as well as ambitious efforts in performing two full-time jobs at the same time account in part for his lack of concurring opinions and dissents during his only term on the bench.) But once in early 1942 Byrnes overstayed his White House duties while he discussed with Roosevelt the selection of Donald Nelson to head the WPB, and he was late in traveling down the length of Pennsylvania Avenue for that day's opening session at the Supreme Court Building. As the beginning of Byrnes' second term on the court approached, in October 1942, several mildly critical newspaper editorials appeared in regard to Roosevelt's "borrowing" Byrnes from the Supreme Court. Earlier, Attorney General Francis Biddle suggested to FDR that he should ask Byrnes formally to resign from the Court in order to serve as a presidential adviser. Roosevelt quickly dismissed the idea of

Byrnes' leaving the Court, however, in a way that made clear that the idea displeased him.

"Let's keep it open for Jimmy," Roosevelt always said, impatiently waving to Biddle the outlines in the air of an unseen future for Jimmy Byrnes and the other eight justices. "They can get along."

But as the October 1942 term of the Court neared, Chief Justice Stone asked Biddle to bring up again with Roosevelt the advisability of Jimmy Byrnes' retiring. The president again was reluctant to have Byrnes resign permanently from his lifetime appointment to the Supreme Court.

"Could we not appoint some 'old boy' for two or three years who would agree to retire when he reached seventy?" Francis Biddle remembered being asked by Roosevelt. The way would thus be open to "bring back" Jimmy Byrnes to the Supreme Court, in Roosevelt's words, after a three- or four-year stint by Byrnes working in the White House with FDR for the duration of the war. Biddle pointed out that such a scheme hardly conformed to Roosevelt's often announced intention to appoint more younger men to the Court.

There was a reason behind Roosevelt's reluctance to have Byrnes resign from the Court and join him at the White House offices. Franklin Roosevelt in 1942 was in the same political "jam" in regard to Jimmy Byrnes that had troubled him in 1938, 1939, 1940, and early 1941. As then, Roosevelt now needed Byrnes' political skills in 1942 to secure congressional coop- eration with the economic and reorganization policies that he considered essential. But bringing Byrnes permanently back into the White House's inner circle would once again require Roosevelt to accommodate Byrnes' conservatism and once again place him into Byrnes' political debt—a debt from the 1930s that Roosevelt had thought he had paid for a lifetime with his appointment of Jimmy Byrnes to the Supreme Court.

It was true that Byrnes was eager to come back to presidential and congressional politics, but Roosevelt knew his friend well enough to be certain that, however eagerly, Jimmy Byrnes would never come cheaply. Money was not to be Byrnes' price in returning to help the administration, Roosevelt knew, but the expenditure of power by the president. And if Roosevelt had been unwilling or unable in 1940 to expend the power necessary to make Jimmy Byrnes the next vice president or secretary of state, then to get Jimmy Byrnes back at his side in 1942 Roosevelt had to find a job with the power Byrnes would find acceptable payment for his giving up his place on the Supreme Court. Neither a vice presidency nor a cabinet post was available with which Roosevelt could pay for his old friend's return. Something else that Franklin Roosevelt could afford to give up in terms of his own presidential power had to be found for Jimmy Byrnes. Until he determined what that job and the price of giving it to Byrnes would be, FDR put off Biddle's requests.

Roosevelt found that something else for Jimmy Byrnes and a way out of his political jam in the fall of 1942. In the first eight months following the attack on Pearl Harbor, the need grew for FDR to appoint a largely independent administrator to direct the wages and prices of the U.S. domestic economy during wartime. The WPB under Donald Nelson, charged with the enormous bureaucratic task of allotting priorities among raw materials for defense production, was either unable or unwilling to deal with the issues of controlling inflation resulting from these military priorities and scarcities. It was all very well for the WPB, for example, with its twenty thousand employees in Washington, to enforce its ban on the use of iron and steel in the production of hundreds of common consumer products in order to save the metal for use in tanks and airplanes, as the WPB announced its intentions to do in May 1942. But Nelson's wartime board did not have the authority or the apparatus to control the consequent inflation as defense workers with large paychecks from overtime work chased the desired consumer goods remaining on the market before the WPB ban took effect, buying new automobile brake shoes, bathtubs, or typewriters, for example, at practically any asked-for price.

Inflationary consumer prices drove up the cost of the war effort across the economy. Farmers, for instance, fearing a future loss of their purchasing power, insisted on prices at least 115 percent above market level, or parity, in provisioning the military and civilian orders for food. And as long as prices for food and housing continued to rise, workers at defense plants and elsewhere insisted on cost-of-living increases beyond what management had budgeted for labor costs before the attack on Pearl Harbor had disrupted the expected business conditions of 1942.

The distortions to the domestic economy during World War Two were not only the result of the U.S. military's suddenly becoming in early 1942 the nation's largest consumer of steel, iron, rubber, gasoline, food, and men. Bizarre shortages and speculations occurred as the result of the war's sudden destruction and losses. The price of sugar, for instance, shot sky high as German U-boats made too dangerous the passage of the few available commercial ships to this country from Cuba, then the major supplier of cane sugar to the U.S. mainland. Additionally, the Japanese army's successful occupation of Indochina, Malaysia, and the Pacific islands by 1942 meant not only the loss to this country of Asian petroleum and much of the world's natural rubber but also a cutoff of tropical fats and oils then widely used in cooking. The futures market for these oils underwent wild price swings and made wartime fortunes for some U.S. speculators. (The frugal habit that persisted into the 1950s and 1960s in numerous otherwise prosperous households of saving rendered fat in an empty coffee can near a stove for future use in refrying is the result of many a wartime bride's memory of this sudden preciousness of lard in the 1940s.)

As a consequence of all these uncontrolled factors, in the four months between December 7, 1941, and the end of March 1942, food costs rose nearly 5 percent, and the prices of food and clothing overall were approximately 20 percent higher in March 1942 than a year earlier. The domestic economy was threatening to go out of control in 1942, just as control of the military situation was dangerously close to slipping from Roosevelt's grasp in 1942, following the greatest drive westward of the Japanese armies that year to the Aleutian Islands, off the coast of Alaska, and the bold attacks by German U-boats on American shipping off the Atlantic coast and in the Gulf of Mexico.

Commander in Chief Roosevelt knew that he had to stabilize wages, prices, and rents if the nation was in 1942 to manufacture without the interruptions of strikes or inflationary cost overruns the 45,000 airplanes, 45,000 tanks, and 500,000 machine guns FDR had determined were necessary that year for achieving an ultimate victory. Beyond the military victory he assumed American industrial strength would make inevitable within a few years, Roosevelt also faced serious political considerations regarding the economy. The lack of a stabilized economy and uniform price controls during the First World War had led to a period of wartime inflation and high profits in agriculture, followed immediately by a postwar deflation and depression. The result was that the Democratic party was voted out of the White House in the elections of 1920, despite the presence on the ticket of an attractive and ambitious candidate for the vice presidency, a young Franklin D. Roosevelt. FDR had no intention of letting Democratic party history repeat itself after the victory in *this* world war, particularly at this time he might expect again to be on his party's ticket. Accordingly, FDR pushed hard for economic stabilization. For help in this task he turned again to his friend Justice Byrnes. To achieve economic stabilization, Roosevelt for the sake of both his country and his presidency was willing to pay the price in power that he knew Jimmy Byrnes would ask.

In April 1942 after Byrnes had assisted in drafting the war powers acts and returned to his nominal duties on the Supreme Court, Roosevelt obtained congressional approval for the creation of the Office of Price Administration, with authority to place ceilings on rent in defense industry areas and to control the prices of some consumer goods. The same Congress, however, strongly controlled by farm bloc states, refused to place similar price controls on agricultural products, which were guaranteed by legislative act to sell 115 percent above parity. The price of food and the cost of living thus continued to rise. Some advisers, including Byrnes, urged the president to appoint an "economic czar" for the duration of the war, independent of the War Production Board and with final authority over both the Office of Price Control and the Congress to fix all prices, wages, and rents. Such an economic czar would have to be someone who was on friendly terms with the rural, conservative farm bloc of congressmen and senators and who would be skilled at getting concessions from them. The ideal candidate would himself be a former congressman or senator. "Pick the best man on your team," Byrnes some months earlier had advised the president in regard to choosing the head of the WPB. "For convenience call him Hopkins."

This time for convenience call him Byrnes. On the telephone in early September 1942, Byrnes told FDR that bringing food costs under control was of such importance in reducing inflation that Roosevelt should inform Congress that, unless it gave the executive office wartime power to fix all prices and wages, including agriculture products and labor, Roosevelt would create such a regulatory office himself by executive order. The legal authority for FDR's office to assume such sweeping powers over the economy and to ignore congressionally fixed agricultural prices could be found in an earlier legislative service that Byrnes had performed for Roosevelt, as Byrnes himself pointed out to FDR in their telephone conversation. The Reorganization Act of 1939, partly written and passed for FDR by then Senator Jimmy Byrnes, had reserved to the president the right to reorganize the executive branch with new agencies unless Congress specifically objected within sixty days of the proposed change. Thus, although Roosevelt was on shaky constitutional ground by simply ignoring an act of Congress that reserved for the congressmen the right to set wartime agricultural prices, Byrnes' plan provided at least a fig leaf's cover of constitutionality for FDR to claim these regulatory powers for his office.

Roosevelt liked the political cunning of Justice Byrnes' strategy, as he told his cabinet the day after their telephone conversation. Byrnes' plan to finesse the powerful farm bloc worked as FDR hoped. Congress, under Roosevelt's announced threat to act unilaterally by executive order under his government reorganization authority and the war power acts if no additional anti-inflation legislation was passed by the fall, sent to the White House for FDR's signature on October 2, the Stabilization Act of 1942. It directed the president to issue a "general order stabilizing prices, wages, and salaries affecting the cost of living." To enforce the order, the president was empowered to establish by executive order a director of the Office of Economic Stabilization (OES), with domestic economic powers that would eventually become second only to the president's. Roosevelt now had the legal authority for his economic czar. The question was which man would it be most convenient for Roosevelt to name as his economic second-in-command.

There was no question that Byrnes wanted the OES job for himself. The position of director of economic stabilization had the potential to become even more powerful than the chairmanship of the WPB. And, as so often when his ambitions were fully engaged in obtaining a coveted government position for himself, Jimmy Byrnes used the elegant figure of Bernard Baruch as his stalking horse. Baruch had earlier turned down the administration's offer of the post of economic stabilizer, as both Hopkins and Roosevelt had surely known he would. (Although Baruch's record as chairman of the War Industries Board during World War One was both praiseworthy and closely relevant to the current job of economic stabilizer, Baruch had made it clear that he wanted additional powers for the OES to set tax rates, which neither Roosevelt nor his secretary of the treasury was willing to give him. Baruch, moreover, in 1942 was seventy years old and in uncertain health.) A few days after Baruch's refusal, Hopkins paid a visit to Baruch's Washington apartment at the Carlton Hotel to ask the financier which other candidates he would suggest.

"As always," Baruch later wrote in his memoirs, "when an important and difficult job was to be done, I suggested James F. Byrnes."

At that very moment, in a bit of amateur theatrics that could have fooled no one, certainly not Harry Hopkins, James F. Byrnes happened by the Carlton Hotel and decided to call on his old friend Bernard M. Baruch. "I can still see him," Baruch years later said of Byrnes' entrance into the apartment, "his head cocked birdlike on one side in a characteristic Byrnes attitude."

In fact, this whole episode was a "Children's Hour," in FDR's phrase, of political intrigue among the president's friends, an activity in which Franklin Roosevelt always seemed to delight. Harry Hopkins and Roosevelt both may have known full well before Hopkins' visit that Baruch would suggest no one other than Jimmy Byrnes. In any case, Byrnes continued to play his part well in this little parlor drama of political seduction inside Baruch's apartment, which, as in any seduction, required the pretense that what is already decided is being given serious consideration. Baruch and Hopkins explained their conversation about the choice of an economic stabilizer to Byrnes, who presumably knew nothing of their discussion before he entered the room. Byrnes looked thoughtful. "If the Commander in Chief asks me, I'll accept," he said.

Byrnes lost no time in resigning from the Supreme Court, on October 3, 1942, after Franklin Roosevelt, in another midmorning bedroom conference at the White House, asked Byrnes that same day to accept the appointment as director of the Office of Economic Stabilization. Byrnes formally assumed the new office on October 15. The powers delegated to Byrnes in the language of Roosevelt's Executive Order 9250, creating the economic directorship, were sweeping and probably could not have been legally given up by any president to a nonelected official except under the exigencies of wartime. Byrnes was given blanket authority "relating to the control of civilian purchasing power, prices, rents, wages, salaries, profits, subsidies, and all related matters." The director of the OES was also designated as the final judge of any jurisdictional disputes among the various wartime agencies within the executive office on the implementation of economic policy. His decisions in these disputes were to be considered as final as the president's. In effect, Roosevelt by executive order turned

over to Byrnes the management of the civilian economy in order to allow
FDR to preside over the military and diplomatic management of the war.

"It is a task of housewifery on a continental scale," *Life* magazine later
noted in describing Byrnes' job, in an issue that featured a photograph of
him on the cover and a favorable story on him inside. "Should need arise,
decisions of the Economic Director will determine what each of us earns
and how we spend it; how much and what we eat; and where, how long,
and at what job we work." The domestic comparison by *Life* was apt. With
his resignation from the nation's highest court, Byrnes became Roosevelt's
steward in managing the estate of this nation for the duration of the war.
And as political examples stretching back to the Old Testament suggest,
the position of a trusted steward has traditionally enabled an outsider to
gain power in a household.

Like any good steward, Byrnes worked from inside his employer's
home. Apparently as part of the "price" Roosevelt had to pay for Byrnes'
services, the office of the director of economic stabilization was located in
the White House. A space was made for Byrnes' office in the new East
Wing, next to the offices of Roosevelt's principal military aide, Admiral
William D. Leahy. Byrnes and his staff moved into their renovated office
space so quickly that there was still uncovered lumber and wet paint around
them the first weeks of work, and working quarters were so cramped that
the only place in which the OES staff members could fit the wire services'
news ticker machine was the men's room. But despite the inconveniences
of working in the wartime White House—the OES could have found more
appropriate space inside the Treasury Building, literally a stone's throw
across the White House lawn—Jimmy Byrnes had made an important point
by locating his new office in the president's residence. In offering Byrnes
the position of economic stabilizer and in giving him authority to settle
jurisdictional disputes over economic policy, Roosevelt had declared,
"Your decision is my decision, and . . . there is no appeal. For all practical
purposes you will be assistant President." By insisting on exercising these
presidentially delegated powers from within the White House, Byrnes made
clear to his official visitors that he was taking seriously this commission to
act as the president's personal representative. To talk to Byrnes in the East
Wing about economic issues was to be tantamount to talking to Roosevelt
in the West Wing.

One other person who found out how seriously Byrnes was taking his
delegation of presidential authority was Harry Hopkins, who dropped by
the East Wing one day soon after Byrnes and his staff had moved into
their new quarters. Hopkins asked Byrnes if he could be of any help in
these first days of the OES's administration. The former Supreme Court
justice gave a long look at his political enemy in so many past ideological
struggles in Senate debate over the necessity of relief spending during the
late 1930s, and at the man who he felt had contributed to his failing to

receive the vice-presidential nomination at Chicago in 1940. "There's just one suggestion I want to make to you, Harry," Byrnes said pleasantly. "Keep the hell out of my business."

Jimmy Byrnes was back in action. He was soon as feisty and full of nervous energy as he had been when he arrived as the political fixer from South Carolina in 1931. While on the Supreme Court, Byrnes had complained to Turner Catledge and other journalist friends that as a justice he felt as if he were working inside a marble "mausoleum." Now, at the center of economic policy inside the White House, surrounded in his office by his new universe of fresh paint and raw lumber, Byrnes took on another lease on life. And, as was usual when he was fully engaged with the people and the political environment around him, Byrnes "enlivened the passing moment" of life in the wartime White House. FDR was greatly amused, for example, to learn that Byrnes, taking his wirehaired terrier Whiskers for evening walks, was in the habit of meeting the national Democratic secretary, George Allen, who was walking *his* wirehaired terrier, and the two men would wager which dog would urinate in the Washington parks more frequently during their strolls. Roosevelt laughed and told a member of the executive office, "You and I can make a lot of money out of that contest." Let the odds go high on Allen's dog, FDR said, and then bet on Whiskers. Roosevelt was certain that a fix could be put in so that Jimmy Byrnes' dog would win.

Not since his Senate years had Byrnes seemed to be so happy or so concentrated in his work. "Byrnes would just walk through the corridor there and see him [FDR] two or three times a day—usually every day," Marvin Jones later recalled. "He would get to this office at 8 o'clock in the morning and frequently worked until 8 o'clock at night, and he would eat lunch at his desk. I don't know how he stood it." Jimmy Byrnes had a reason to stand it. He was on his way to becoming indispensable to Roosevelt.

Becoming less indispensable to Roosevelt after Byrnes' autumn arrival at the White House was Donald Nelson of the WPB. Nelson had not even been notified in advance by the president's office of the appointment of Jimmy Byrnes on October 3, 1942. When Nelson read of his being named director of a new Office of Economic Stabilization on the news ticker machine in the WPB office, he assumed that he was being fired and that his replacement would be a man answerable to Jimmy Byrnes at the OES. Nothing of the kind was intended, the White House quickly moved to reassure Nelson, but one of Nelson's subordinates was skeptical. Bruce Catton, the future Civil War historian, was then serving as the director of public information for the WPB. Catton idealized Donald Nelson as a dedicated public servant who was determined to balance fairly the needs of the civilian and the military economies, but who was nevertheless fatally naive in his power struggles with such professionals as Jimmy Byrnes.

Catton, the future narrator of Lincoln's political struggles with his generals and of the intricacies of the Civil War presidential cabinet, saw immediately the "unmistakable sign from the White House" of the WPB's fall from favor with the appointment of Byrnes as the director of economic stabilization.

"The creation of this new office was a typical bit of Washington overlaying," Catton wrote three years after he left the WPB.

> For one reason or another the WPB setup had not worked out quite as expected. The remedy, therefore, was neither to serve notice on all and sundry that what the boss of the WPB said went, nor to put a new man in as head of the WPB with instructions to pull things together regardless of breakage, but to create a new agency overlapping everybody. Byrnes was designated as the super-umpire, a visibly embodied extension of the final power of the president. . . . There was now an agency to which the WPB's decisions could be appealed, conceivably an agency that would presently be deciding the issues WPB used to decide, possibly an agency that would take over the direction and operation of the WPB itself.

Catton's misgivings about the future existence of the WPB were justified. Although its chairman, Donald Nelson, was to have official relations with Byrnes that were outwardly cordial, he would have been mistaken in thinking that he had a good friend in either Byrnes or Baruch, both of whom mistrusted his ability to prosecute the war on the economic front. Within fifteen months of his White House appointment to head the OES, in October 1942, Jimmy Byrnes, his powers now augmented by his assuming the directorship of the Office of War Mobilization (OWM), sent a four-page letter to Roosevelt in January 1944 in which he urged that the WPB be merged with the OWM. Roosevelt did not allow Byrnes to absorb his last remaining bureaucratic competitor for administrative wartime power, as Jimmy Byrnes earlier had done with Sidney Hillman and the OPM; but perhaps in compensation, FDR in his written response to Byrnes' suggestion made explicit the division of power that had long been understood between them: "As you know," FDR wrote in turning down Byrnes' request to absorb the WPB, "you are indispensable on the handling and the actual settling of scores of problems which are constantly arising. You have been called 'The Assistant President' and the appellation comes close to the truth. Therefore, please put your mind to work to keep your work— or the better part of it—in that category."

By the time Byrnes received that intriguingly ambiguous response from Roosevelt in June 1944, he had been serving his country for over a year and a half as the "assistant president" in charge of economic stabilization and war mobilization. The attempt to obtain the War Production Board as part of the OWM, although unsuccessful, was just part of a larger ambition on the part of the indispensable Byrnes. Before the end of 1944, the "assistant president" was working very hard to obtain the office of the presidency itself.

Byrnes had begun to make himself indispensable to Roosevelt in 1942–43 by bringing the wartime cost of living under a centralized control. He did so by acting under the broadest possible interpretation of the executive order delegating presidential powers to him. Upon taking possession of his East Wing offices, Byrnes made clear by the size of his staff that he was in the presidential, rather than the bureaucratic, business. Byrnes brought with him as permanent staff members only a general office counsel, Ben Cohen, and two other assistants, Don Russell, an attorney who had come to Washington from Byrnes' former law firm at Spartanburg, and Sam Lubell, a writer and researcher who had worked for Baruch. It was plain by the comparatively small size of his staff that in the exercise of his newly delegated power, Jimmy Byrnes intended the OES to be a one-man show. The sole exception, and the one person in the OES to whom Byrnes possibly deferred as his equal, was Cassandra Connor. The small, fiercely proud Miss Connor willingly had moved with Jimmy Byrnes from his legal chambers at the Supreme Court Building to his new offices at the White House. Throughout the Second World War and beyond, the gray-eyed and devoted Cassandra Connor continued to act as a confidential secretary and political amanuensis to this ambitious man.

Byrnes first moved as economic stabilizer to control rising food prices. A proposed executive order written for Roosevelt's approval by Byrnes on October 19, 1942, called for the establishment of a food administrator to control the distribution and wartime consumer rationing of food, acting "under the general supervision of the Economic Stabilization Director." Roosevelt, probably unwilling to antagonize the Department of Agriculture and the War Production Board, both of which were then claiming final authority to control food, deleted the explicit reference to "general supervision" by the OES in issuing his final version of the executive order. But eventually Jimmy Byrnes had his way. He succeeded in obtaining the appointment of Judge Marvin Jones for the nation's food administrator. Jones, who had served as a representative from Texas in the House since 1917 and who had known Congressman Byrnes since the days of his patronage under Pitchfork Ben Tillman, was unquestionably loyal to the authority of the OES director, was also very popular with the southern congressmen who supported higher food prices, and was almost as canny a politician himself as Jimmy Byrnes.

Byrnes and Judge Marvin Jones had been friends since 1939 with another southern politician of the old school, Jesse Jones of the Reconstruction Finance Corporation, and together these three men cooperated on the use of vast amounts of RFC money to subsidize the production of food during the Second World War. Beginning with Byrnes' first directives as economic stabilizer, the RFC spent over $1.5 billion subsidizing the production of meats, flour, and butter before the end of the summer of 1945. Subsidies had the effect of keeping market prices low during the war, as farmers and other food producers could sell at market levels, or parity, having been guaranteed their profits up front with the payment of the federal subsidies. Many food items during the war were rationed by the directives of Judge Marvin Jones, later to be approved by Jimmy Byrnes, and these items could be bought only with hard-to-come-by rationing coupons. But for those civilians who had the required coupons, the desired food usually was there on the store shelves in rationed amounts and usually affordable on a wartime paycheck. Once again, Jimmy Byrnes' political skills as a compromiser triumphed.

The armed forces also liked the subsidy plan, because the military's huge orders for flour and meat were filled at prices not in excess of the market levels. And Byrnes and the Texas politicians were quick to point out that what the federal government spent with its left hand paying for food subsidies, it recovered with its right hand by paying out less money to feed the military. Byrnes' skills as a compromiser in stabilizing consumer food prices while at the same time also satisfying the military's budget for provisions brought envious praise from an anonymous official at the WPB, which itself had tried with much less success to balance the priorities of the civilian and military economies: "Suppose you and I have an argument in arithmetic," the unnamed WPB official once told Bruce Catton. "You claim that two and two makes four, while I claim that two and two makes six. We take it to Jimmy Byrnes for a decision. He's apt to get us both to agree that two and two makes five."

But one group that was not buying into Jimmy Byrnes' new math at the OES was organized labor, particularly the Congress of Industrial Organizations. Having stabilized food prices at mid-1942 levels, Byrnes next moved to persuade Roosevelt to establish wartime ceilings on all wages and prices, at whatever was their highest level up to September 1942, a policy violently objectionable to most labor groups. In the days after Pearl Harbor, organized labor in a burst of patriotic fervor had signed in late December 1941 a no-strike pledge for the duration of the war in exchange for guarantees by Roosevelt that a national mediation board would be established with representatives of both labor and the public who would arbitrate wage increases. Sidney Hillman personally had approved the names of all labor representatives to the board. But now, less than two years into the war, labor saw its right to wage mediation being taken away by the final authority of Jimmy Byrnes at the OES, and, despite the sacrifice being asked of labor to freeze wages at 1942 levels for the duration of the war, there was no evidence by the administration of any willingness to place 1942 ceilings upon the profits of the wartime employers.

On April 8, 1943, Roosevelt signed an executive order written by Byrnes and his staff requiring the civilian economy to "hold the line" by stabilizing wages and prices at their adjusted 1942 levels. The prices of some food items also were to be rolled back by the Office of Price Administration and the food administrator to levels of the previous year. The day after the order was released, the office of the White House appointments secretary was flooded with urgent calls from congressmen, manufacturers and labor leaders who wanted to see Roosevelt. All sought an exemption from the executive order for their special interests. Politically, that morning was among FDR's finest hours. He refused to see them, and his appointments secretary, General Edwin Watson, simply directed all the visitors down the hall toward the East Wing to see the "assistant president." Byrnes held firm. One of his visitors that morning was Philip Murray, president of the CIO. Enraged at what he considered to be a betrayal of labor's opportunity to earn increased wages until the war ended, Murray shouted in Byrnes' face and banged the desk between them with his fist. The following day Murray, at the insistence of Franklin Roosevelt, came by Byrnes' office and apologized. Byrnes was cordial, and far too pragmatic a man to hold a grudge over the abuse of government-issued furniture, but he also made clear to Murray his intentions: the economic stabilizer would approve no wartime wage exemptions for the CIO.

"The line was bent in many places," Byrnes later recalled of his enforcement of the anti-inflationary order, "but it held much better than I ever expected." He had reasons for his understated pride. Throughout the spring and autumn of 1943, he kept the inflationary pressures of demands for increased wages in critical industries to a politically acceptable minimum, holding down either by his skills at negotiation or by the threat of government takeover the initial demands for wage increases by workers in the nation's coal mines and railroads. (It was after the successful settlement of one of John L. Lewis' threatened strikes in the coalfields that Franklin Roosevelt held his White House birthday party for Jimmy Byrnes on May 2, 1943, at which they both sang "When I Grow Too Old to Dream (I'll Have You to Remember)".) By the end of Jimmy Byrnes' first year of economic stewardship, the tide of war, economically and militarily, had begun to turn in favor of the United States. Long lists of the names of American casualties were still being printed in single columns, usually up and down the second and third pages of regional newspapers, and consumer rationing and scarcities were to continue for two long years; but American forces in 1943 started to throw back the German armies in North Africa and the Japanese armies on the Pacific islands, and Jimmy Byrnes oversaw the greatest change from civilian to military employment in the history of the United States since the Civil War, with none of the inflation or profiteering that had characterized that war or the First World War. In short, neither Lincoln's cabinet nor Baruch's War Industries Board had done a better job.

Yet the ambition of Jimmy Byrnes was at least equal to that of these two men. Byrnes fretted about what he considered the underutilization of his talents in a politically thankless job at the OES. On May 14, 1943, he sent a letter to Roosevelt in which he unloaded his frustration: "I have presented to me daily by the departments and by members of Congress matters of far greater importance to you than the price of potatoes and beans." Additionally, Byrnes told Roosevelt that the president was being hurt politically by having as the head of the OES a man "so closely associated with you" in making unpopular decisions on wages and prices. Byrnes closed his letter by offering his resignation as director of economic stabilization: "If you wish me to serve in some other post where I can help you instead of hurting you, I shall be glad to serve."

Franklin Roosevelt was back in his political jam. To keep Byrnes happy, and to keep his highly regarded administrative skills working for him in the White House during the war, Roosevelt would have to invent another job for Byrnes at the cost of delegating additional presidential power. Fortunately, there was a need in 1943 for such a new, powerful presidential assistant. The WPB had continued since its inception to deal only hesitantly with the problems of allocating such scarce materials as synthetic rubber and high-octane gasoline among the competing needs of the Army and the Navy. Criticisms of Donald Nelson's administration were coming from the military with increasing frequency to FDR's attention, and in the Senate, the Special Committee to Investigate the National Defense Program—popularly known as the Truman committee, after its chairman, Harry S. Truman—called publicly for the creation of an armaments czar, just as Jimmy Byrnes earlier had been named the economic czar.

One of Franklin Roosevelt's greatest strengths was in making a public virtue out of government necessity and the tending of the egos of men. After receiving Byrnes' letter on a Friday, Roosevelt telephoned Byrnes and asked him to lunch with him the following Monday. Over their lunch trays in the Oval Office, Roosevelt told Byrnes he had no idea that Byrnes had been so unhappy with his OES responsibilities. The letter had spoiled his weekend, FDR said. Byrnes suggested the idea of his appointment to the post of a centralized war mobilizer, and Roosevelt told him to work with Samuel Rosenman and the Bureau of the Budget in preparing a draft executive order creating such an office. Two weeks after receiving Byrnes' letter, FDR announced that the war effort that day was "entering a new phrase," and issued on May 28, 1943, an executive order creating a superagency. The new agency, located in the White House, was to be known as the Office of War Mobilization (OWM), and its head was James F. Byrnes.

Its powers were vast. By the second full year of the war, Byrnes had succeeded in obtaining for himself authority over all civilian manpower related to war production—the authority to enforce settlement of priority disputes over war materials between all branches of the military and to control the procurement of military supplies in this country by Allied governments and the shipments of American food to Allied or liberated countries. (This latter power of the director of the OWM was greater than even Harry Hopkins' authority as the head of the lend-lease program.) "It appeared that Byrnes' authority was exceeded only by the president and equaled only by the joint chiefs of staff," the *Washington Post* noted in its news reports the day after the executive order was issued.

Bruce Catton's personal inferences that the rise of Jimmy Byrnes also meant the decline of the WPB proved correct. Byrnes received from FDR the additional authority to arbitrate without further presidential appeal any disputes arising among the numerous war production agencies and other civilian defense agencies headquartered in Washington (at least twenty-two major new agencies and offices had been opened there since 1942), the most prominent of which was the WPB. "This means the president has subordinated to Mr. Byrnes the other 'czars,' such as Mr. Nelson in the field of war production," the *New York Times* reported in explaining Roosevelt's order. Nelson had no comment when asked by reporters about the creation of the OWM, apparently planning "to follow a 'wait and see' policy to determine whether the new move were directed at him."

Byrnes interpreted his new authority at the OWM as reaching practically every Washington administrator, and in this move he was encouraged by Roosevelt, who was happy to be relieved of the political and logistical responsibilities of the home front and to be able to devote more time to the strategic ends of the war. Byrnes kept his offices at the East Wing, and the new director of economic stabilization, Fred Vinson, sensibly took up headquarters at the Federal Reserve Building. The direct line of presidential authority and personal access to FDR was thus kept open, by Jimmy Byrnes' decision, in that all-important corridor only a few steps from the East Wing to the Oval Office. And, like its predecessor office in the East Wing, the OWM was intended by Byrnes to be a one-man show. Byrnes retained most of his small staff of the original OES, adding as a full-time member only Walter Brown, a broadcasting executive from Spartanburg who handled Byrnes' public relations and some of his private investments in radio stations.

Now with increased presidential powers centralized in his East Wing office, Byrnes acted quickly in clearing work off FDR's desk. Throughout late 1943, while Roosevelt was away attending the Cairo conference, at which Far Eastern military operations were discussed with Churchill, and the Teheran conference, at which Stalin, Churchill, and FDR agreed to plans for an English Channel invasion of occupied Europe the following year, Byrnes relieved Roosevelt from attending personally to scores of tasks, ranging from war logistics to Democratic politics. A partial summary of some of Jimmy Byrnes' activities between his White House birthday party following settlement of the coal strike, in May 1943, and the month of May 1944, preceding the Democratic National Convention, reveals how broadly he interpreted his delegated powers and how he benefited Roosevelt.

Within this twelve-month period, Byrnes assisted in the development of the "Big Inch" oil pipeline being constructed overland between Texas and the East Coast to avoid the dangerous losses of American oil tankers to German U-boats operating in the Gulf of Mexico and the Atlantic. He advised Roosevelt on the need to placate Joseph Kennedy, Sr., who was unhappy with the combat decoration received by his eldest son (Byrnes wrote FDR in a background memo that the Kennedy father was advised that "little Joe was recommended to receive a certain medal. A board of officers on the staff of Admiral Halsey considered the recommendation and awarded a medal of less value than the one for which the boy was recommended. The father is greatly disappointed.") Additionally, Byrnes helped in the passage of the soldiers' voting act of 1944, which, despite congressional opposition by some southern conservatives such as Cotton Ed Smith, allowed the use of absentee ballots by members of the military, thereby making possible a large vote for Roosevelt in 1944 and the enfranchisement for the first time of many black soldiers ("This matter is of such very great importance that it may be wise to bring Jimmy Byrnes into the picture at this stage," Attorney General Francis Biddle wrote FDR about the bill in late 1943).

Byrnes in this period also tried to mediate a dispute in his OWM office between Vice President Henry Wallace and RFC Director Jesse Jones over responsibility for the wartime shortages of rubber and quinine—a dispute in which the two men had in newspaper interviews called each other liars (Byrnes broke up the meeting when he feared Jones would physically assault the vice president). Byrnes also supervised the production of naval escort vessels in order to be certain there were adequately balanced naval forces for the European invasion and for the Pacific theater; and he prepared executive orders to be approved in Roosevelt's absence authorizing the OWM to proceed with the government takeover of vital war industries in the event of strikes while FDR was in Teheran. It was small wonder, then, that by the late summer of 1943, newspapers reported Roosevelt telling a friend that, since appointing Jimmy Byrnes to OWM, he for the first time since the war began had the leisure "to sit down and think."

Conspicuously uninvolved in the performance of many of Byrnes' tasks in 1943–44 for the president was Donald Nelson at the WPB. Also uninvolved was Vice President Henry Wallace, except as a disputant in the embarrassing public episode with Jesse Jones that Byrnes had tried to quiet.

By the spring and summer of 1944, both Nelson and Wallace had fallen out of favor with Roosevelt. Wallace in particular was depicted by Democratic conservatives as a political liability, in conversations with FDR arranged by his appointments secretary, General Pa Watson, a good friend of Byrnes. Both administratively and politically, in preparing for the liberation of Europe or in telling dog-pissing jokes, Byrnes seemed to shine by comparison with either Nelson or Wallace. "I like Jimmy better than anyone else around here," Roosevelt told party leaders in a preconvention meeting at the White House in the summer of 1944.

In April 1944 Roosevelt dispatched Henry Wallace on an "urgent" fact-finding trip to Siberia and China, without indicating any particular urgency for Wallace to return until shortly before the Democratic convention. In July 1944 Nelson, too, was sent to China by FDR to act as the special military attaché to Chiang Kai-shek. Nelson would resign from the WPB shortly after his return. Having established China as the ultima Thule of his disfavor, Roosevelt in June 1944 invited Jimmy and Maude Byrnes to spend a few days with him at the presidential country retreat in the western Maryland mountains. In a pleasant contrast to the travel destinations of Wallace and Nelson, the camp was then known as Shangri-la. It was during this visit to Shangri-la that FDR first explicitly told Jimmy Byrnes that he wanted him to be his vice-presidential candidate in 1944.

"I have no political ambitions," Byrnes had written to Roosevelt in his May 1943 letter of offered resignation from the OES, just a few weeks before he became the second most powerful man politically in the United States. Now, after over a year of twelve-hour workdays in the East Wing of the White House solving the war's major production and political problems for Roosevelt, Jimmy Byrnes saw his opportunity to eventually become the most politically powerful man in the nation. Byrnes could be certain that the offer of a vice-presidential candidacy from Roosevelt in 1944 meant that he was in line to be the Democratic presidential nominee in 1948. Roosevelt had made clear his intention not be a presidential candidate again after the successful conclusion of the war, which Byrnes knew from his position at the OWM could not be more than a few years away. There were also the published reports, which Byrnes probably saw in the *New York Times* of May 1944, about the president's health not being able to withstand a full fourth term. As had happened so many times in his political career, Jimmy Byrnes might rise to power on the unexpected death of a patron.

There could be no doubt that Byrnes wanted the presidency itself. It had seemed tantalizingly close when FDR was still considered a two-term president. The ambition of Franklin Roosevelt for a third term in 1940, as well as what Byrnes could consider the enmity toward him of other men around FDR, had denied Senator Byrnes that nomination. But even Roosevelt's political ambitions had to have an end after the elections of 1944, and, once in the East Wing, Jimmy Byrnes through a combination of hard work and political cunning had methodically eliminated or reduced the White House influence of liberal rivals such as Ickes, Hopkins, Hillman, Nelson, Rosenman, and Wallace. And, as always, Bernard Baruch was acting as political angel to Byrnes' ambitions: before the president met with Jimmy Byrnes at Shangri-la in June 1944, he had spent the months of April and May on an extended vacation at Baruch's Hobcaw Barony. Byrnes had not been present for that visit, but he knew, and Sidney Hillman feared, that Baruch had used the opportunity to urge Roosevelt to put Jimmy Byrnes on the 1944 presidential ticket.

How many of these considerations went though his mind when Franklin Roosevelt made his offer at Shangri-la, Jimmy Byrnes never said. If he acted as usual, his gray-blue eyes betrayed no feelings, and even in the presence of the most intensely applied presidential charm at a country retreat, this subtle and ambitious man from Charleston kept his innermost thoughts to himself. Byrnes later did write after Roosevelt's offer to him of the nomination for the vice presidency, "I found myself beginning to think about it seriously."

But, "unfortunate as it may be, our consideration of every question must include the consideration of the race question." Byrnes' thoughts on race and politics written more than a quarter of a century before the weekend with Roosevelt at Shangri-la were once more to prove unknowingly prophetic in his own quest for higher office. The presidential election of 1944 was to be the first since the Compromise of 1877 in which the "invisible" black people of Jimmy Byrnes' earlier political career became politically visible nationwide. Negro voters were to emerge as the significant plurality for the Democratic party in a number of critical states in that election. This significance was due partly to the unprecedented migration in the late 1930s and early 1940s of black families northward above the Mason-Dixon line, where for the first time the franchise was available to them through urban political machines. The importance of the black vote was also partly the result of Franklin Roosevelt's efforts since at least 1938 to enlarge the constituencies of the Democratic party.

"It takes a long, long time to bring the past up to the present," FDR had remarked after the defeat of his party's faction in the attempted South Carolina purge of 1938; but by the summer of 1944 the present had begun to catch up to the past for the national Democratic party. As a sign that the voting patterns established after the Civil War no longer held in the elections of the twentieth century, large numbers of enfranchised blacks were beginning to leave the Republican party to vote for the Democratic ticket, and a critical factor in selecting the Democratic vice-presidential nominee in 1944 was his acceptability to black voters. In particular, a test of that acceptability was a potential vice-presidential candidate's willingness before the convention to support the continuation of the President's Committee on Fair Employment Practice, or, as that office for enforcement of nondiscriminatory employment had become known by 1944, the FEPC.

Not until it was almost too late did Jimmy Byrnes grasp the importance of the black vote in FDR's final determination at the convention of who would be the Democratic party's vice-presidential nominee. Politically speaking, black voters nationwide must have appeared "invisible" to Byrnes in his political considerations throughout much of the 1940s, just as they had been in his youth during Ben Tillman's lifetime, with Byrnes as a senator having contributed to filibustering out of existence any anti-lynching legislation in 1938 and having personally belittled Walter White from the floor of the U.S. Senate. Throughout the 1940s Byrnes had turned his attention toward what he considered more significant political rivals by reducing the influence with Roosevelt of such men as Harry Hopkins and Sidney Hillman. But despite Jimmy Byrnes' reputation as a "national" southerner more interested in economic issues than race, despite his significant findings in favor of Negro defendants as a Supreme Court justice, despite the pleasant invitations from Franklin Roosevelt to share in his executive powers at Shangri-la, and despite his own considerable political cunning in regard to the FEPC before the convention, the realities of race would determine why Jimmy Byrnes after 1944 remained only the assistant president.

13

The Convention of 1944

The coming of the Second World War had rescued not only the personal ambitions of Jimmy Byrnes but also those of the nation's almost thirteen million Negro citizens in 1941. Negro leaders, after years of frustration in the 1930s trying to secure passage of a federal antilynching law through a southern-dominated U.S. Senate and to end the whites-only primary in the South, saw an opportunity in the early 1940s to change tactics. The expansion of defense-related industries and the settling of large numbers of enfranchised Negroes in northern and border states promised to empower financially for the first time a politically important black working class and middle class there. And for the first time in the twentieth century, the Democratic party in its campaign platform of 1940 pledged to work for full civil liberties for black citizens.

Prior to the ascendancy of Franklin Roosevelt, those Negroes in the North who could vote usually had voted their best interests by voting the Republican ticket. In each party platform of a presidential election year since 1920, for example, the Republican party had consistently called for the speedy passage of a federal antilynching bill and for enforcement of the due process clauses of the Fourteenth and Fifteenth amendments to the Constitution. By contrast, the platforms of the Democratic party, except for a plank in 1904 attacking the GOP for encouraging "sectional and race agitation," had remained silent on the Negro. The platforms of 1932 and 1936 were no exceptions. But Franklin Roosevelt in the election of 1936 began to receive significant Negro majorities in urban districts, primarily because, in Jimmy Byrnes' earlier phrase, of the New Deal's "spilling over" of social benefits to black Americans. And in the election of 1940, FDR campaigned for a third term on a party platform, partly written and approved by Byrnes at the convention, that pledged "to uphold due process and the equal protection of the laws for every citizen, regardless of race, creed, or color."

The political and economic empowerment of the Negro population seemed to be developing in 1941 alongside the buildup of defense spending at the start of the third Roosevelt administration. Negro leaders were cheered by Sidney Hillman's public letter of April 11 in which the cochairman representing labor at the OPM urged private defense contractors with the federal government to "make ample provision for the full utilization of available and competent Negro workers." But leaders of black organizations soon noted that Hillman's cochairman at the OPM, William Knudsen, representing management, refused to sign the letter or to comment on his refusal to sign it; and in the same month of Hillman's letter, the number of black workers employed by government referral in twenty important defense industries actually declined to only 2.5 percent of the work force. To Negro leaders such as A. Philip Randolph, the charismatic union president of the Brotherhood of Sleeping Car Porters and Maids, the time had come for public protests and mass demonstrations against the Roosevelt administration's lack of support for defense employment for Negroes. Building on his political base of membership in the Negro union that he headed, Randolph organized in early 1941 the national March on Washington Committee, and the committee in May issued a formal call for at least ten thousand of the nation's Negroes to march on Washington on July 1.

In the midst of the lend-lease transfer of arms and the buildup of the nation's defense industries, the last thing Franklin Roosevelt wanted was the complication of ten thousand Negroes on the streets of Washington protesting the social inequities of his administration's defense program. Besides, as a result of his administrations' refusal to press for antilynching legislation in the 1930s and his nomination of Jimmy Byrnes in 1941 to the Supreme Court despite the near-unanimous objections of Negro groups, black Americans in the Democratic party were "due," in the baseball sense, and FDR knew it. On June 18, just six days after he had sent to the Senate the nomination of Byrnes as an associate justice of the Supreme Court, FDR met at the White House with A. Philip Randolph and Walter White in an effort to call off the march. Sidney Hillman and William Knudsen of the OPM also were present, along with Secretary of War Henry Stimson. White later recalled that during their conversation Roosevelt had turned to him and asked, "Walter, how many people will *really* march?"

Walter White never thought small. "I told him no less than one hundred thousand," he subsequently wrote. For a long time Roosevelt coolly looked at White without speaking, in an obvious attempt to determine whether the executive secretary of the NAACP was exaggerating or bluffing. White was given to flamboyance, but Roosevelt knew that Randolph had the organizational strength and the will to put on the streets of Washington the largest demonstration by Negroes in the nation's history. And, ever since witnessing the political disaster of Herbert Hoover's reaction to the Bonus March of 1932, Roosevelt had gone out of his way to avoid mass demonstrations in the capital district protesting economic conditions. According to White, Roosevelt after his long pause then asked the two leaders, "What is it you want me to do?"

Randolph told the president American blacks wanted an executive order declaring in unequivocal language the abolition of discriminatory hiring in defense industries having contracts with the federal government. In exchange for such an order, Randolph was willing to hold off the national march. Roosevelt agreed. On June 25, 1941, Roosevelt issued Executive Order 8802, requiring all defense contractors doing business with the U.S. government to include in their negotiated contracts a provision "obligating the contractor not to discriminate against any worker because of race, creed, color, or national origin." To investigate complaints of violations of this provision, the order established the presidentially appointed Committee on Fair Employment Practice. (Later the committee's name was rearranged to yield the acronym FEPC.) In late July, the same month Jimmy Byrnes took his oath in the Oval Office as Supreme Court justice, Roosevelt appointed the first members of the FEPC.

FDR's response to the calls to end racial discrimination was less than freely given; he simply ignored Randolph's request at the White House meeting also to racially integrate the armed forces. But the fact remained for thirteen million Negroes that FDR did respond. And perhaps in no other act of Roosevelt's four administrations was the president so politically in advance of the majority of his own party as in his creation of the FEPC. Succeeding generations of black and white Americans, reaching political maturity long after the FEPC was eliminated by a postwar Congress, have tended to assume that the national campaign for civil rights for blacks began approximately with the march on Washington led by Dr. Martin Luther King, Jr., in 1963, and that the federal government's policies of affirmative action to eliminate discrimination can be dated back to the creation of the Equal Employment Opportunity Commission by the Civil Rights Act of 1964. But both these events have their origins in that summer meeting at the White House more than twenty years earlier. A. Philip

Randolph had the political courage in 1941 to threaten to march; and Roosevelt had the political courage to create the Committee on Fair Employment Practice.

But if the creation of the FEPC in 1941 was an act of political courage, it was also the stepchild of the federal government, in the opinion of professional politicians like Byrnes; that is, the FEPC throughout the 1940s was the government entity no administrator or government office seemed to want. In a little over two years, the FEPC was located in three different wartime offices and had no fewer than four changes in national chairmen; and not until 1943 was a full-time chairman paid for his duties. Eventually the FEPC wound up in the executive office under the ultimate control of Jimmy Byrnes, who worked very hard to prove that, administratively speaking, it was no kin of his.

Roosevelt's executive order in 1941 located the FEPC in the Office of Production Management; after the OPM's dissolution, the committee was transferred to the War Production Board and then to yet another wartime organization, the War Manpower Commission. After complaints over jurisdictional authority from both the chairman of the FEPC and the War Manpower Commission, Roosevelt in March 1943 sought advice from Byrnes, still officially concerned only with economic stabilization, and from his special counsel Samuel Rosenman. After hearing their views, Roosevelt with a new executive order in May 1943 relocated the FEPC directly under his presidential protection as an independent part of the Office of Emergency Management, the general supervisory office for all defense and wartime organizations in the president's executive office.

Jimmy Byrnes in May 1943 could have claimed final authority over the FEPC if he had wanted it; the executive order signed by Roosevelt that month naming Byrnes as the director of war mobilization gave him explicit authority over all civilian manpower policy decisions related to the war. And as the director of the OWM, Byrnes in June 1943 was also named by FDR the liaison officer for the Office of Emergency Management, responsible for coordinating its wartime policies with all other government departments. But for once Jimmy Byrnes was not interested in bringing a part of the executive branch directly under his personal control inside his crowded offices at the East Wing; whenever complaints were brought to him by liberal congressmen or the CIO about instances of job discrimination—or complaints from private employers or southern congressmen about what they considered the overzealous activities of the FEPC—Byrnes denied his authority to intervene in the affairs of the FEPC. He smoothly directed his callers down the hall to the office of his fellow southerner Jonathan Daniels at the West Wing. Daniels, the liberal son of old Josephus Daniels and the former North Carolina reporter who had ridden with the "flying squadrons" of the textile strikers had by 1943 become an assistant to Roosevelt on racial matters, and Jimmy Byrnes was happy to have him there away from the OWM territory and with the problems of the FEPC on young Daniels' desk. For by mid-1943 the FEPC was shaping up to be perhaps the most controversial of all the wartime organizations, and by the end of that year Byrnes knew that the continuation of the FEPC was to be perhaps the major domestic issue of the 1944 presidential elections.

Jonathan Daniels early recognized that race and the issue of the FEPC would be of major significance in the 1944 election. "My feeling is that this question [of the activities of the FEPC] is becoming one of the sorest places in the whole business of the home front," Daniels wrote in a memorandum for Marvin McIntyre to bring to Franklin Roosevelt's attention in January 1943. "Involved in it are important aspects of both successful dealings with southern Democrats in the present Congress and the success of the war administration at the polls in 1944."

Daniels in that same memorandum then put his finger on what he perceived as Roosevelt's greatest political weakness—the ambiguity of his personal support for the FEPC: "At present, the president is being sharply criticized on this question by both white southerners who think he has gone too far, and by Negroes who feel that he is retreating from positions he has taken."

It was true that, in its efforts over the past two years to do social good, the FEPC had completely pleased no one, including Franklin Roosevelt. Despite inadequate financing and no more than thirteen professional staffers, the FEPC had succeeded by 1943 in holding public hearings in Los Angeles, Chicago, Birmingham, and New York City that documented widespread discrimination against Negroes, Jews, and Mexican-Americans in the hiring of employees in war-related industries. Reactions to the hearings from southern newspapers, which usually supported Roosevelt's domestic policies, were almost unanimously hostile, as editorials accused the FEPC of encouraging racial strife and promoting sedition. And early in 1943, while the FEPC still was part of the War Manpower Commission, it became involved in a highly publicized dispute with the manpower commissioner over the authority of the FEPC to investigate reports of widespread discrimination against Negroes in southern railroad companies. The FEPC planned to hold public hearings on the policies of southern railroads of systematically eliminating Negroes from consideration for jobs as firemen and engineers; but Paul McNutt, head of the War Manpower Commission, abruptly canceled the hearings on the grounds that taking the time for testimony would interfere with the railroads' necessary performance in wartime.

Civilian employment of blacks did not materially improve in other war industries by 1943, and A. Philip Randolph once again threatened the march on Washington and other mass protests if changes were not made in the FEPC. And in Congress, friends of the FEPC, after lobbying by

A confident and well-dressed Jimmy Byrnes at approximately age ten poses with a small dog at a photographer's studio in Charleston, South Carolina.

Elizaberth Byrnes, the mother of James F. Byrnes and Leonore Byrnes, circa 1900.

A young Jimmy Byrnes (*second from right*) has his cake and eats it too, at a party during Byrnes' years as a court reporter and solicitor in Aiken, South Carolina, circa 1910.

The most dangerous of all of Byrnes' political fathers, and the undisputed master of South Carolina politics from the late nineteenth to the early twentieth century, U.S. Senator Benjamin Ryan "Pitchfork" Ben Tillman.

"The Painless Statesman," Senator Jimmy Byrnes of South Carolina, was caricatured in *Collier's* magazine in the first year of the New Deal, when Byrnes emerged as Roosevelt's most energetic legislative ally during the Hundred Days.

U.S. Senator Jimmy Byrnes and some of the "bullbat boys" depart for a Jefferson Island outing in 1937. To Byrnes' left are Senator Robert J. Bulkley of Ohio and Senator Pat Harrison of Mississippi.

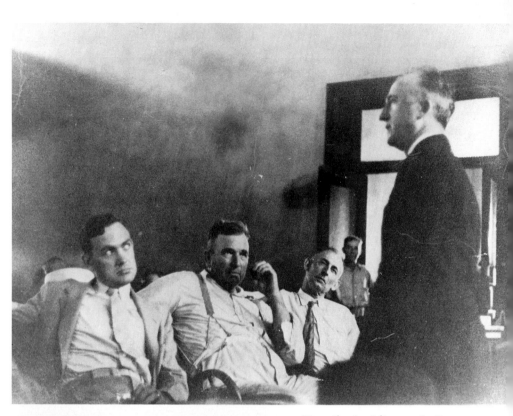

Skeptical whites-only "members of the democracy" listen to Senator Byrnes during the 1936 Democratic senatorial primary in South Carolina. Despite his opponents' appeals to the Ku Klux Klan during the primary, Byrnes refused to campaign on a racist platform.

"To hell with the Constitution!" frequently declared U.S. Senator Coleman L. Blease, who advocated lynching instead of due process for South Carolina's black citizens charged with crimes, and who was Jimmy Byrnes' most persistent political enemy.

pproximately four thousand graves were opened with the Santee
iver basin and the remains removed above the flood level in order
 accomplish Byrnes' and Roosevelt's most ambitious public works
roject in the eastern United States, the building of the Santee-
ooper hydroelectric dams. Here, in a Farm Security Administration
hotograph, the predominantly black crews work overtime to ac-
omplish their task before the rising waters cover the graveyards.

A small boy contemplates the government-ordered removal of his
family and their belongings from the area to be flooded in the
Santee-Cooper site.

The relief of having successfully paid off a political debt shows clearly on Franklin Roosevelt's face on a summer day in 1940 as he congratulates Jimmy Byrnes moments after Byrnes was sworn in as an associate justice of the U.S. Supreme Court in FDR's Oval Office. Standing behind the president are U.S. Senator Carter Glass of Virginia, a longtime patron of Byrnes, and Maude Byrnes.

Life pictured the "assistant president" at home with his dog Whiskers (the same dog that was the subject of Franklin Roosevelt's scatological teasing) on the cover of its January 4, 1943, issue.

Jimmy Byrnes in the mid-1940s kept close to the side of his last political patron, the financier Bernard M. Baruch.

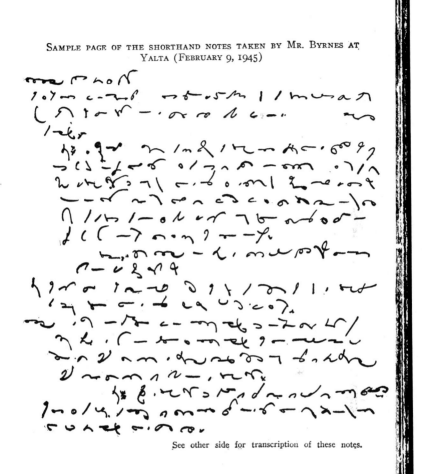

See other side for transcription of these notes.

A sample page of the shorthand notes taken by Byrnes at Yalta.

Only one week after Byrnes was appointed U.S. secretary of state, he and Truman were aboard the USS *Augusta* and plotting a political course toward the Soviet Union and the use of the atomic bomb en route to the Potsdam conference in July 1945.

Secretary of State Jimmy Byrnes keeps a firm grip on the arm of
Foreign Minister V. M. Molotov of the USSR (*standing*, next to
Byrnes, *at far right*) during the taking of this group portrait at the
last wartime meeting of the leaders of the Big Three, in Potsdam,
Germany, in August 1945. *Seated, from left to right:* Prime Minister
Clement Atlee of Britain, President Harry S. Truman, and Joseph
Stalin. *Standing, left to right:* Admiral William D. Leahy, Foreign
Minister Ernest Bevin of Britain, Byrnes, and Molotov.

A jaunty Secretary Byrnes keeps up a brave front in late December 1945, aboard a Coast Guard dingy en route to the presidential boat USS *Williamsburg* and a stormy confrontation with President Truman over Byrnes' diplomacy at the Moscow conference a few days earlier.

Officially "neutral" in the presidential election of 1952, Governor Jimmy Byrnes greets Dwight D. Eisenhower during the latter's visit to Columbia, South Carolina, in September of that year. Between the two men is Maude Byrnes.

Byrnes and his wife, front row, listen raptly to a young Billy Graham at a South Carolina religious revival. Byrnes also arranged for the North Carolina evangelist to deliver the opening prayer at Richard Nixon's campaign appearance in Columbia, South Carolina, in 1960.

"When they call me Jimmy, I know I've got their daddy's vote."
Byrnes, having resigned from the State Department in 1947 and
been elected South Carolina's governor running on a platform opposing Truman's domestic policies, picks a friendly face out of the
crowd during a triumphal February 1951 tour of his state.

Byrnes introduces Richard Nixon to South Carolina supporters during the 1968 presidential election. Byrnes, figuring his birthdate as 1882, is now 86 years old, but still going strong politically; note his characteristic hard grasp on his guest's right arm.

Randolph, introduced legislation to eliminate the temporary wartime committee, which was dependent on congressional funding from year to year out of the budget for the president's office. Randolph and his congressional allies instead sought to establish a permanent fair employment practices commission extending into peacetime and having authority to issue orders enforceable by courts to eliminate racial discrimination.

Congressional southerners also wanted the wartime FEPC eliminated for entirely different reasons, which is probably why Jimmy Byrnes after 1943 was so happy to tell them to go see Daniels from North Carolina down the hall. From the floor of the House of Representatives, John Rankin of Mississippi declared in 1943, "A bunch of crackpots down here in what they call the 'Fair Employment Practice Committee' seems to be doing everything they possibly can to drive the white people of the South out of the Democratic Party by trying to force them to accept Negroes on terms of social equality." If the FEPC was not soon eliminated, Rankin warned, the Democratic party in the South by the presidential election of 1944 "would be as dead as doornail."

In the next congressional session following Rankin's remarks, Representative Howard Smith of Virginia, a much more respected and powerful Democratic congressman than John Rankin, obtained funding for a "Select Committee to Investigate Acts of Executive Agencies beyond the Scope of Their Authority." One of the first executive agencies investigated by the Smith committee was the FEPC.

It was not surprising, therefore, that in March 1943, before deciding to save the Fair Employment Practice Committee by moving it into the executive office, Roosevelt had been tempted to wonder aloud to Jimmy Byrnes whether no man could rid the president of this troublesome FEPC. Roosevelt had sent to both Byrnes and Samuel Rosenman on March 11 a copy of an unsigned memorandum the president had received, suggesting the abolition of the FEPC and its replacement with a special unit in the Justice Department to investigate complaints of employment discrimination. "Let me know what you think," FDR asked his two advisers in an accompanying note.

Roosevelt frequently encouraged his advisers to argue opposing positions before making up his mind, and he certainly expected the liberal Rosenman to argue for a strengthened FEPC and Byrnes to argue for its abolition; the degree of Byrnes' opposition to the continuation of the FEPC also was probably desired by Roosevelt as an unguarded indication of how his ambitious adviser from South Carolina felt toward this emerging Democratic constituency of enfranchised Negroes. Jimmy Byrnes, however, despite his opposition to antilynching legislation and his obvious dislike of Walter White, had personally never been a racist southerner such as a John Rankin, or a Cotton Ed Smith, or a Pitchfork Ben Tillman; and by the time he received FDR's memorandum and note on the FEPC, Jimmy Byrnes also was far too wise and too experienced a political survivor to rise to such bait.

Byrnes wrote the president back by the end of the second week of March 1943 that he "believed it would be unwise to now abolish the Committee on Fair Employment Practice." Byrnes conceded that the FEPC "arouses serious opposition in the Congress" and that it "may only be a symbol." But, Byrnes argued, "the Negroes now want the committee. They regard it as the only tribunal before which they can present their various grievances." The FEPC was an economic "sounding board" for the nation's Negroes during the war, Byrnes wrote FDR, and Byrnes pointed out if the FEPC were to be removed, Franklin Roosevelt, and not Jimmy Byrnes, would receive the Negroes' blame: "I fear that if you abolished the committee they would still want the sounding board and would insist on seeing you. You would not have the time to see them. They would then urge that you had abolished the committee and refused even to listen to them."

Whatever his private feelings about the continuation of the FEPC, Byrnes made it clear in his answer to Roosevelt that he considered the committee only in terms of Franklin D. Roosevelt's best political interests. It was hard for FDR to argue with such logic. Within two months, by May 1943, the FEPC with a full-time chairman and increased enforcement powers was placed in the Office of Emergency Management, nominally under the final authority of Byrnes at the OWM. And as the nation's chief war mobilizer, and increasingly as Roosevelt's most trusted domestic adviser, Jimmy Byrnes remained in mid-1943 in his attitude toward black Americans as he had been for years: personally kind, legally scrupulous, and politically indifferent.

But to ambitious Democratic politicians such as Byrnes, it was becoming increasingly evident by the summer of 1943 that the forewarnings of Jonathan Daniels were true: that the issues of race, and particularly of the FEPC, were among the major home front concerns of black and white citizens. These concerns were sharpened by a series of racial riots, blamed by some conservative whites on the activities of the FEPC, occurring that wartime summer across the country, from California to New York State.

The most publicized racial violence broke out on May 24, at the shipyards of Mobile, Alabama, within a few weeks after the FEPC was reorganized in the Office of Emergency Management under Byrnes' final authority. The Alabama Dry Dock and Shipbuilding Company, a major government contractor with over thirty thousand employees at the shipyards, had earlier received an order from the FEPC to upgrade the jobs of some Negro workers to skilled welding positions. The FEPC now had the authority to force the promotions, and it did so. Although the work crews remained segregated, there was considerable hostility from the white laborers over the mandated promotions, and on the night shift of May 24, fights broke out between white and black crews at the shipyard. Over eighty workers were injured in the rioting, many of them seriously, before the governor of Alabama ordered the National Guard into the city in order to restore peace. (One of the worst beaten was a white laborer who had attempted to come to the aid of a black laborer being assaulted by two company guards.)

Before that summer was over, rioting had also broken out between whites and blacks in Beaumont, Texas, following rumors of a sexual attack by a black man upon a white woman, and in Los Angeles, where groups of white soldiers and sailors beat and stripped Negro and Mexican-American civilian men wearing "zoot suits." (The oversized coats and baggy pegged pants of the zoot suits did not meet wartime specifications by the Office of Price Administration for conservation of fabric, and were considered by the white population as a sign of slacking.) Similarly dressed Negro youths were beaten by groups of white civilians in Philadelphia, and in August race riots broke out in Harlem after false rumors spread that a white policeman had shot and killed a black soldier. But the worst racial rioting occurred in Detroit on Sunday, June 20, less than a month after the Mobile riot. The same week in June that Allied forces were fighting in Sicily and on the Pacific island of New Guinea, thirty-four people were killed in clashes between whites and blacks in Detroit, as whites rampaged through Negro neighborhoods and black snipers fired on them from apartment buildings.

Only Vice President Henry Wallace and the Reverend Francis J. Haas, the new full-time chairman of the FEPC, spoke out as members of the administration that the underlying causes of the Detroit riot were, in the words of Monsignor Haas, "inadequate housing, recreation, and public transportation." Back in California, Governor Earl Warren, chairman of a special committee to investigate the Los Angeles zoot suit riots, declared, "In undertaking to deal with the cause of these outbreaks, the existence of race prejudice should not be ignored."

But many conservative white Democrats blamed the FEPC itself for that summer's racial riots. That view had earlier been given credence by the published statement, which went unchallenged by the administration, by D. R. Dunlap, president of the Alabama Dry Dock and Shipbuilding Company, that the Mobile riot had been caused directly by the rulings of the FEPC. No public statements in the summer of 1943 or later about any other causes of these racial riots were forthcoming either from Roosevelt, speaking as the nation's president, or from Byrnes, speaking as the "assistant president" in charge of the full utilization of the nation's civilian manpower.

But before the end of the winter of 1943, Jimmy Byrnes' name was used, probably without his prior knowledge, in an attempt by conservatives to eliminate the enforcement power of the FEPC as an issue for the Democratic party before the elections of 1944. In a dispute with the federal government's war agencies in Kansas City, Missouri, the area telephone contractor, Southwestern Bell Telephone Company, had refused to sign a contract containing the antidiscriminatory clause required by the FEPC. Telephone service for the agencies in that area of the Midwest could be obtained only through Southwestern Bell. Hence in a written opinion authorizing the signing of a contract without the antidiscriminatory clause, the comptroller general of the United States, Lindsay C. Warren, decided that "no useful purpose" could be served by the government's insisting upon the FEPC restriction if the desired service could not be obtained elsewhere. The nondiscriminatory clause put forth in Roosevelt's executive order establishing the FEPC was, in Warren's wording, a "directive" of the president's wishes rather than a mandatory, legal requirement. Warren wrote his opinion in a public letter dated October 7, 1943, and addressed it for possible further comment to the nation's chief war mobilizer and liaison director of the Office of Emergency Management, James F. Byrnes.

Lindsay Warren in the 1930s had been a conservative Democratic congressman from North Carolina, and Jimmy Byrnes had known him well, as he knew practically everyone who had served in Congress since the administrations of Woodrow Wilson. The political friends of the FEPC immediately saw that this interpretation of the antidiscriminatory clause as a "directive" rather than as mandatory would effectively end the FEPC's enforcement powers over wartime contractors. They also suspected that in this public letter between Lindsay Warren and Byrnes there was prearranged attempt, in the editorial comment of the Negro newspaper *Chicago Defender*, at "a trial balloon to see what will be the reaction of the Negro and other liberal groups to the elimination of one more sore spot to the reactionaries."

It was also an immediate sore spot to the Roosevelt administration. The presidential press secretary, Stephen Early, a southerner and a good friend of Byrnes, quickly wrote to the *Pittsburgh Courier*, a newspaper nationally circulated among black communities, and denied that the letter had been requested by Byrnes or anyone else in the administration. Byrnes himself, despite being the obvious spokesperson as director of the OWM and as the one to whom the letter was addressed, had no initial public response, pro or con, to Warren's ruling. (Byrnes was not alone in trying publicly to appear neither hostile nor favorable toward the enforcement powers of the FEPC. Other ambitious Democrats apparently also were afraid that their hands would be stained with pitch politically if they took any side in this FEPC quarrel. Although the issue of the FEPC's enforcement of the nondiscriminatory clause with Southwestern Bell Telephone of Kansas City, Missouri, had arisen in a dispute with one of the largest employers and most powerful monopolies in his state, Senator Harry S. Truman made no public statements on the controversy that were recorded in the *Kansas City Star* or in any other newspapers. His senatorial files contain no correspondence with either side in this dispute.)

But in late October 1943 the comptroller general's ruling became even harder for the administration to ignore, despite the great happiness it had occasioned among conservative white Democrats. The national council of the CIO at the end of that month announced that it was calling on Roosevelt personally to overturn the decision. The ruling against the FEPC enforcement clause, if allowed to stand, would "gravely hinder production by eliminating employment of loyal, competent Negroes, Jewish, [and] foreign born workers," the CIO declared in a public telegram to the Roosevelt. The result of the comptroller general's decision, the CIO wrote, "aids Hitler propaganda and weakens American morale."

The Roosevelt administration was caught in this issue between two constituencies—the constituency of Democratics conservatives in the southern and border states whose votes FDR counted upon getting in the next year's elections, and the liberal constituency of organized labor and urban Negroes in the northern and midwestern states whose votes FDR had hopes of getting as well. Before the issue was decided, each group had called upon Jimmy Byrnes to intercede in its favor in the FEPC dispute. Lindsay Warren, who as a North Carolina congressman had repeatedly voted to exclude black citizens from a restaurant operated in the Capitol Building, had probably sent his letter to Byrnes in hopes of eliciting an approval from this southern director of the OWM. Franklin Roosevelt, who obviously inclined toward the FEPC since moving it into the executive office the previous spring, also asked Byrnes for help in resolving the Kansas City case politically. Roosevelt requested Byrnes to meet with him to discuss the FEPC case on November 4, 1943.

Byrnes contributed to the announcement of the administration's policy toward the FEPC's enforcement powers two days later, but it was Roosevelt, not Byrnes, who made that announcement. In making public that day a letter he was sending to Attorney General Francis Biddle, the nation's chief law enforcement official, in regard to government contracts, Roosevelt stated that there should be no misunderstanding about the inclusion of the nondiscriminatory clauses required by the FEPC. "These provisions are mandatory and should be incorporated in all government contracts," Roosevelt wrote in his letter to Biddle. In a comment after releasing the president's letter, Stephen Early, in an obvious reference to Roosevelt's critics among organized Negroes and labor, rather sourly remarked that he believed FDR's letter on the FEPC "clears it up once and for all."

Jimmy Byrnes' fellow southerner Stephen Early spoke more truth than he knew. Roosevelt's commitment to the FEPC made it clear to Democrats below the Mason-Dixon line and in the border states that the Compromise of 1877 was off. Following the publication late in 1943 of Roosevelt's letter on the FEPC, the administration had placed an anti–poll tax bill on the

Senate calendar, and in April of the following year, only three months before the Democratic convention, the U.S. Supreme Court, now almost totally dominated by FDR appointees, declared the whites-only Democratic state primary in Texas to be unconstitutional. (Had Jimmy Byrnes remained on the Court, his presence would have made no difference in the outcome of that decision. The Court agreed with the arguments of Thurgood Marshall of the NAACP by an 8-to-1 majority.) And once the Compromise of 1877 fell apart, the Democratic party would not be far behind. Since the summer of 1937 such a splintering of the Democratic party had been predicted by members as diverse as Harold Ickes and Carter Glass. But prior schisms in the Party, such as the activities of the conservatives in the 1930s, had not been over racial disagreements so much as ideological and economic differences over relief spending and the influence of organized labor. Professionals such as Jimmy Byrnes had usually been able to resolve these differences before a presidential election. But by the spring and summer of 1944, the Democratic party had begun to split over the issue of economic equality for blacks, and the southern white Democrats were in no mood to compromise. From Texas to Virginia they began to talk of leaving the party of Franklin Roosevelt.

Jimmy Byrnes' home state of South Carolina was one of the first in 1944 to threaten to secede from the national party. The political situation there was just as Byrnes had feared it might become in 1938, when he had urged Franklin Roosevelt to stay out of the Palmetto State and avoid splitting the white democracy over the issue of race. Despite his best efforts since then, the Democratic party in his state did split in a three-way controversy over race in 1944. In that year some black South Carolinians, barred by law from participating in the state Democratic party, formed the Progressive Democrats and planned to seek delegate credentials at the national convention. The established state party, although it did not allow black participation, was under the control of the loyal New Deal politicians senators Burnet Maybank and Olin Johnson, and it sought to be recognized by the national party as South Carolina's sole Democratic party. But other white supremacists led by the brother of the late Coley Blease formed yet another state party and planned to go to the convention in Chicago to insist on a platform affirming states' rights and the southern system of white supremacy. The Blease forces threatened to walk out of the convention and vote for independent presidential electors if any black Progressive Democrats were seated at the convention. And Cotton Ed Smith, who thrived on political confusion and who to the annoyance of certain individuals was *not* dead or retired by the spring of 1944, announced that as result of the administration's domestic policies, he could not support Franklin Roosevelt for a fourth term.

Similar revolts against Roosevelt personally and the racial policies of his administration were planned in 1944 by the conservative state parties of Virginia, Mississippi, Louisiana, Oklahoma, and, most ominously, Texas. This state with its large number of electoral college votes had been taken over by an anti-Roosevelt faction of the state Democratic party known as the Regulars, indirectly backed by the strongly segregationist governor Coke Stevenson and also, it was rumored, by Byrnes' old friend at the RFC Jesse Jones. The Regulars planned to go to the convention in Chicago in 1944 and demand no fourth term for Roosevelt. Other issues besides Negro civil rights contributed to the unhappiness of the Democratic conservatives with the Roosevelt administration. Vice President Henry Wallace, for example, was intensely disliked not only by the old eastern Wilsonian conservatives in the party such as Bernard Baruch but also by its wealthy "new men." These included oilmen who had risen to political prominence by amassing personal fortunes in the petroleum industry during the war, such as Sid Richardson of Texas and Edwin Pauley of California. But race was more to the sticking point, as Jimmy Byrnes reminded Roosevelt in a letter of June 1, 1944, a little over a month before the Democratic convention.

FDR was worried that, despite the best political maneuvers of Lyndon Johnson and Sam Rayburn, Texas remained in the hands of the Regulars. The state probably would send an anti-Roosevelt delegation to the Chicago convention. Roosevelt asked Jimmy Byrnes for his advice, including his comments on a proposal recently made to the president to raise the price ceilings on petroleum. Byrnes wrote back to FDR that "it is not necessary to increase the price of oil to carry Texas." Byrnes saw the issue differently: "The trouble in Texas is the Negro question, just as it is in South Carolina." Tactfully not including any possible names on the future presidential ticket, Byrnes then advised the president that in next month, if the Democratic platform did not contain a strong statement of commitment to Negro civil rights, "Texas and South Carolina will be overwhelmingly for the ticket. If the platform does contain commitments on these subjects antagonistic to the views of southern Democrats, there will be serious trouble in those states and in other southern states."

But the platform subject that Jimmy Byrnes knew would be most antagonistic to southern white Democrats, the continuation of the FEPC, remained very much in the news the early summer of 1944. The municipal government of Atlanta in May tried unsuccessfully to evict the FEPC from its regional offices in that city. And in the congressional debates in the session immediately preceding the national conventions, the FEPC continued as a political bone stuck in the throat of the southerners of the Democratic party. Only with the greatest of difficulty was the Roosevelt administration in June able to obtain a $500,000 appropriation through the House and Senate to continue the FEPC through fiscal 1945. The debate was widely publicized and rancorous. In the House, an Alabama congressman accused the FEPC of what a later generation would call "reverse discrimination" by favoring nonwhite employees at its field offices. Rankin of Mississippi also conflated the FEPC's activities with his worst suspicions of the CIO.

"Oh! This is the beginning of a communist dictatorship the like of which America never dreamed," Rankin told the House members when the FEPC appropriation bill came to the floor. "It is sponsored by the CIO Political Action Committee, headed by Sidney Hillman, a Russian-born racketeer whom the anti-communist American[s] of his own race despise, and who is raising money by the shakedown methods with which he is now trying to control our elections."

In the Senate, despite a determined and more dignified opposition to the FEPC led by Senator Richard Russell of Georgia, with some help from Senator Champ Clark of Missouri, the administration gathered enough votes from a Democratic membership depleted by summer absenteeism to approve the House-passed appropriation. (Harry S. Truman and other members of the Truman committee were not present during the FEPC debates, because the defense committee that spring was holding public hearings throughout the country. Unlike some absentee senators during the FEPC debate, Truman did not take advantage of his senatorial privilege of pairing his vote with another absent senator or allowing the Senate clerk to record how he would have voted had he been present.)

But no sooner, to the administration's relief, had the FEPC's annual appropriation passed in the third week of June, than Senator Robert Wagner of New York State and five other senators introduced a bill to create a permanent FEPC. Congress adjourned for the national conventions before taking action on the bill, but with the earlier formation of a National Council to Establish a Permanent FEPC, backed by more than a hundred other national organizations and cochaired by Senator Wagner and Senator Arthur Capper of Kansas, the movement for a permanent FEPC became a powerful lobbying force with the platform committees of the two parties. The Republicans, meeting in Chicago for their national convention the last week of June, were eager to recapture the black constituency the party had begun to lose in 1936. Thomas E. Dewey, who as governor had urged the New York state legislature to pass the first state civil rights legislation in the nation, accepted the Republican presidential nomination on June 28. He ran on a GOP party platform that stated unequivocally, "We pledge the establishment by federal legislation of a permanent Fair Employment Practice Commission."

Roosevelt could not be so forthright on the FEPC. It was not simply a matter of political embarrassment if the southerner delegations walked out of the Democratic convention over the platform of civil rights, as Jimmy Byrnes in his letter had warned him. It was also a matter of money. As early as the racial riots blamed in the South on the FEPC the previous summer, state Democratic parties in Georgia and Louisiana had announced that their executive committees would no longer contribute money to the Democratic National Committee until the national committee members "straighten out their policies in regard to the South." Southern contributions from such one-party states, including Texas, were an important source of campaign finances to the national Democratic party, since little of that money ever had to be returned to candidates in those states to finance campaigns against Republican opponents. For years the Democratic party had depended upon southern and southwestern money to finance candidates in the "doubtful" northern and midwestern states. If the southern delegations walked out of the convention at Chicago in protest of a strong pro-FEPC plank, Roosevelt knew, they would also be carrying their money with them.

Blacks did not have the money, but they did have the voters. It also could not have escaped Roosevelt's attention when several national newspapers in the summer of 1944 pointed out that in each of the four states that together made up one-fourth of the total electoral votes needed to win the presidential election—New York, Pennsylvania, Illinois, and Ohio—the percentage of the potential black vote in 1944 was larger than the percentage by which Roosevelt had carried each of these big states in 1940. Nor could Roosevelt count upon automatically receiving the black vote throughout the other eastern and midwestern states, despite his own popularity, and particularly that of Eleanor Roosevelt, among black voters. The last week of June a quarter-page advertisement—headlined "A Message to the Republican and Democratic Conventions from the Negroes of America!"—was published in the *New York Times*. Paid for by twenty-six national black organizations and declaring that "Negroes no longer belong to one political party," the advertisement cautioned both the Democratic and the Republican conventions that "no party or candidate for the presidency or Congress can expect the vote of Negroes without supporting legislation for a permanent federal committee on fair employment practice. . . ." Signatories to the advertisement included A. Philip Randolph, as well as Walter White and Thurgood Marshall of the NAACP.

Before the convention Roosevelt already had a vice president, Henry Wallace, who in 1944 probably was the most acceptable of any Republican or Democratic candidate to the black voters, and who probably would push the strongest at the convention to have the Democratic party platform match the GOP's commitment to a permanent FEPC. (Wallace later declared to the delegates in his speech seconding Roosevelt's nomination at the convention that "the future must bring equal wages for equal work regardless of sex or race.") But despite Wallace's appeal to the black vote and the endorsement of his second vice-presidential candidacy by the CIO-PAC, to Samuel Rosenman, Roosevelt had privately expressed his fear that if he insisted on Wallace for his running mate when the Democrats met in convention that July in Chicago, "it will split the party open, and it is already split enough between North and South."

Jimmy Byrnes had been a highly effective broker for FDR on economic differences separating the North and South during the New Deal years, and it must have occurred to Roosevelt that, if anyone could, Byrnes could broker the differences in the party over racial policies in 1944. On politically intimate terms with practically every southern and western conservative, Byrnes nevertheless had proved himself to Roosevelt as a credible backer of the FEPC. Byrnes had shown to FDR that as war mobilizer he was willing to stand his ground politically, as in the FEPC's dispute with the War Manpower Commission. Byrnes also had demonstrated that he understood the political advantages to Roosevelt in knowing when to say nothing, as in his avoidance of the attempted finesse of the OWM in the Kansas City case. And there was no question of Byrnes' high level of competency in his other administrative duties, as his performance as director of the OWM had demonstrated to Henry Wallace's disadvantage. Roosevelt could expect, too, that his ambitious friend the assistant president would accept and willingly run on a comparatively moderate civil rights platform in favor of the FEPC that would keep northern and midwestern blacks voting for the Democratic ticket. At the same time, Byrnes' presence as FDR's running mate would convince many of the southern delegations that the administration was not going to extremes on the issue of civil rights and that there was no need to bolt the party.

So it was that, in late June 1944, after three years of controversy over the activities of the FEPC and one year of the most violent racial rioting in the nation's cities until the decade of the 1990s, Roosevelt and Byrnes met for their weekend retreat at Shangri-la. Earlier that month FDR had sent Byrnes the "assistant president" memorandum. And there, among the bucolic splendors of the presidential cabins in the western Maryland mountains, Roosevelt and Byrnes came to their gentlemen's agreement: Jimmy Byrnes would be the next Democratic candidate for the vice presidency.

If the Democratic national convention had been held that June, James F. Byrnes would have been president of the United States in 1945. But the Democrats did not convene in Chicago until the third week of July, and in the intervening days, as the rumor of Roosevelt's intention to replace Wallace with Jimmy Byrnes spread among party officials, opponents to Byrnes' nomination used the available time to try to dissuade Roosevelt from his choice. The most powerful of the opponents was Ed "Boss" Flynn. Flynn was chairman of the Democratic party in the Bronx and controlled one of the most powerful political machines on the East Coast. He argued with the president that putting Byrnes on the ticket would cost the Democratic party at least 200,000 Negro votes in New York State alone. FDR would lose New York State, and probably the national election, Flynn told Roosevelt in a July 6 meeting at the White House, if Jimmy Byrnes was the president's running mate.

The thought of losing his home state in the election of 1944 to Thomas E. Dewey was to Franklin D. Roosevelt unacceptable; the thought of losing the national election itself went well beyond the unacceptable. In the intervening days, the arguments against Byrnes, as well as the arguments of those around Roosevelt who urged him to retain Wallace, began to have an effect on FDR. Several days after Flynn's visit to the White House, Anna Rosenberg, an adviser on economics and employment whose advice Roosevelt valued, came by the Oval Office on unrelated business. FDR suddenly asked her who she thought would be the best Democratic candidate for vice president. Byrnes, she answered without hesitation. But, as she subsequently informed Byrnes and his assistant Walter Brown at the East Wing, "the president said he would have to agree, but that the Negro question was acute. He said Byrnes would bring a lot of support to the ticket, but that his being on the ticket would cost heavily in those states with a large Negro population."

Roosevelt was still undecided about his choice for the vice presidency on July 11, only a week away from the opening of the convention and the same day that FDR made his long anticipated public announcement that "like a good soldier" he was running for a fourth term. In announcing his decision to run to a group of nearly one hundred reporters assembled at the White House, even Roosevelt was incapable of not inadvertently giving away some evidence to confirm the rumors of his physical deterioration, which the president's family and aides had worked so hard since early 1944 to deny or conceal. Four months earlier, after an undisclosed visit to Bethesda Naval Hospital, Roosevelt had been diagnosed as suffering from acute hypertension, bronchitis, and a damaged heart ventricle; that diagnosis, and Roosevelt's subsequent recuperative stay at Hobcaw Barony, in South Carolina, from April 8 to May 6, also had been undisclosed to the public. (Sidney Hillman was aware of Roosevelt's month-long stay as Baruch's guest, however, and according to one of Hillman's biographers, was deeply worried that Baruch "urged the cause of his old political alter ego, James F. Byrnes" upon the ailing president as a vice-presidential nominee.)

Now, the day after the July 11 news conference, the reporter from the *New York Times* wrote for his newspaper that even though Roosevelt appeared "gay and smiling," the president conducted the entire conference "with hands atremble." This palsy in Roosevelt's hands had become increasingly evident throughout the spring and summer of 1944, and at this July news conference a particularly politically embarrassing episode of it occurred. While the president gaily laughed and smiled with the reporters, he attempted to bring a lighted match to one of the minimum twenty-a-day Camel cigarettes he smoked. Despite all of his charm and distractions this day, it became evident to the reporters that for a painfully long period of time the president of the United States was unable to align his trembling hands holding the match to his cigarette holder. Finally, Stephen Early acted. A southerner who was Roosevelt's chief press secretary and whose personal loyalty to FDR was as fiercely protective as any bodyguard's (four years earlier in New York, Early had kneed in the groin and pushed to the pavement a Negro policeman who he thought was approaching too close to the president,) Early stepped forward. He bent toward the fumbling Roosevelt and gave him a light.

But despite his deteriorating health, Roosevelt had given no indication of his preference for a running mate. In fact, the day before Roosevelt made his announcement for a fourth term, he had met with Henry Wallace in the vice president's first visit to the White House since returning from China. FDR had promised then to issue a public letter of support for Wallace. Other, comparatively minor, names also were mentioned to the president by party officials eager to eliminate Wallace; the minor candidates included Fred Vinson, Paul McNutt, and Harry S. Truman. Roosevelt himself had suggested Justice William O. Douglas' name to members of his party, with a noticeable lack of enthusiastic response. And, of course, there was Roosevelt's offer in June to Byrnes at Shangri-la.

To help him decide, the president scheduled a White House dinner party for important Democratic officials on Tuesday evening, July 11. Those invited to the dinner in the private family quarters upstairs were Ed Flynn; George Allen, the party secretary; Robert Hannegan, the current national party chairman; Frank Walker, the postmaster general and a conservative who was friendly to Byrnes and who wanted Wallace off the ticket; Ed Kelly, the mayor and political boss of Chicago; and Edwin Pauley, the California oilman who was party treasurer. The president's son-in-law, John Boettiger, would join the group after the dinner for further discussions in the president's blue-painted oval study. The night of July 11 was sultry in Washington, but the Democratic party's bosses were dressed for serious business when they arrived at the White House, in identical dark business suits. To avoid notice from the press, the group had not arrived by the curving driveway that leads from Pennsylvania Avenue to the columned entrance at the North Portico. Instead, they took the White House's side street entrance at the East Wing. Jimmy Byrnes was waiting for them.

Byrnes, along with the other possible candidates under discussion, had not been invited to the dinner. But he was determined to get a message to Roosevelt through the agency of one of the guests and was standing by his OWM office to intercept the group. Walter Brown, who was standing with Byrnes at the East Wing entrance that night, recorded Byrnes' actions in a diary that Brown kept from Byrnes' knowledge for several years. According to Brown's diary, "Byrnes had been trying to talk with Walker. We flagged him, and he spent several minutes with Byrnes and he [Byrnes] gave him his views. He said if Mr. Douglas came out for the FEPC it would mean nothing but if he (Byrnes) came out it would mean something. He said if he came out for a constitutional amendment on the poll tax that would mean something."

It was an extraordinary gambit by Jimmy Byrnes. Walker and the other guests hurried upstairs for their meeting with Roosevelt, but Byrnes now knew that Roosevelt would receive the message. The place where Byrnes' word, presumably, would "mean something" was the U.S. Senate, where both the administration's permanent FEPC legislation and the anti–poll tax bill were certain to be stalled by filibuster in the next Congress. Byrnes had foreseen, almost as quickly as Roosevelt, that "the Negro question was acute" in the upcoming election. And always the political pragmatist, Byrnes in his message to FDR had offered both a reversal of much of his earlier positions on race and the possibility of legislative success for the Roosevelt administration's domestic policies promoting racial equality in the workplace. In return, all Jimmy Byrnes asked for was the vice presidency.

After the dinner and the meeting upstairs adjourned, Byrnes and Brown both heard details of the discussions, probably from Walker. Brown noted in his diary for that day and evening, "It was learned that at one time during the dinner, the Negro issue became so discussed that [Roosevelt's son-in-law] Boettiger attempted to call Congressman [William] Dawson, Negro congressman from Illinois, and get his opinion as to whether or not Byrnes would lose the Negro vote if he went on the ticket." Brown's elliptical diary notes continued, "All agreed at the dinner that JFB was the best man, but Kelly joined with Flynn on the Negro issue. FDR agreed Byrnes best man, but let guests do most of the talking, and he listened." It was apparent to Byrnes on learning of Roosevelt's lack of participation in the discussions that FDR had not yet made up his mind, or that the gambit on the FEPC had failed.

Or perhaps Roosevelt did not trust Byrnes' sincerity. The day after the upstairs dinner at the White House, Roosevelt met at the Oval Office with William Dawson, the congressman whom FDR's son-in-law had tried unsuccessfully to telephone the night before. Dawson was a combat veteran of World War One, a strong supporter of the FEPC in the House, and the only black member of either the House or the Senate in 1944. Dawson brought with him Mrs. Crystal Bird Faucett, a black member of the Democratic National Committee, also to talk with Roosevelt. "Special interest centered on this meeting," the *New York Times* wrote, "in view of recent reports of disagreement within Democratic ranks over whether the Democratic planks dealing with Negroes should be as specific as is the Republican platform on pledges for poll tax repeal, a permanent Fair Employment Practice Commission, and anti-lynching legislation." Neither FDR nor the guests were after the meeting willing to talk in specifics to the press about their conversation, but Dawson was known to be a committed Wallace supporter, and the congressman later told friends that he had expressed his misgivings about Jimmy Byrnes' being considered as a replacement for Henry Wallace.

Byrnes decided to speak for himself. On the day after Dawson's meeting, Byrnes was scheduled for a fifteen-minute appointment with Roosevelt to discuss OWM policies on civilian unemployment. He stayed nearly an hour with the president, talking politics. Walter Brown wrote down in his diary a word-for-word account later told to him by Byrnes of the conversation in the president's office. Byrnes began by asking Roosevelt if the president was still interested in having him on the ticket after the guests' discussion at the dinner. "All of us agreed you were the best qualified man and all of us would rather have you than anyone else," Roosevelt answered, "but they said they were afraid you would cost the ticket two or three hundred [thousand] Negro votes."

"Mr. President, all I have heard around this White House for the last week is Negro," Byrnes countered. "I wonder if anyone ever thinks about the white people.

"Did you ever stop to think who could do the most for the Negro? This is a serious problem, but it will have to be solved by the white people of the South. If Mr. Wallace or Mr. Douglas says he is against the poll tax that is not news and they cannot change the views of southerners. But if I say I am against the poll tax, that means something."

If Roosevelt looked out the windows of his Oval Office while Byrnes spoke, as he frequently did when someone was making an argument he did not want to face, he would have seen the last of the summer's rosebushes in full bloom in the garden outside his office. Rainless days had extended over Washington for the first two weeks of July, with afternoon temperatures in the high nineties. Roosevelt interrupted Byrnes to say that southerners who were considered friends of Byrnes that year had filibustered the anti–poll tax bill in the Senate.

"Well, did Mr. Henry Wallace stop the filibuster?" Byrnes asked in his scolding, Charlestonian accent. Byrnes then asked the question he knew would get FDR's full attention, for it dealt with the successful exercise of political power. "Do you think that I could have stopped the filibuster if I had been presiding officer of the Senate?"

Roosevelt quickly answered, "I believe you could have, Jimmy."

Roosevelt repeated to Byrnes that he considered him the best-qualified man for the vice presidency. "What we're trying to do is to find a candidate who will not cost the ticket votes," he told Byrnes. Roosevelt then said what his ambitious South Carolina friend wanted to hear. He still intended to release a letter supporting Wallace, FDR said, but he was giving Byrnes "the green light to run."

Byrnes left the meeting well satisfied. Apparently from that moment through the next week at the convention, Byrnes considered that he had convinced Roosevelt that his presence on the ticket as the vice-presidential candidate would benefit black voters. As for Roosevelt's promise to release a letter supporting Wallace, Byrnes knew from his own past experiences with FDR that it was like a dance card signed by a popular girl: by itself it meant nothing. More important to Byrnes' prospects was Roosevelt's statement that he was giving him "the green light to run." Repeated to wavering delegates uncertain about Byrnes' effect on the black constituency, the statement would vouch for Roosevelt's opinion that Byrnes would not harm the ticket in black precincts. With "the Negro issue" removed, Byrnes could expect to pick up support in the Ohio and Wisconsin delegations, where he had good friends among the party organizations and the leadership of the AFL, to add to his support in the southern and western states. And by no means were all of the party's urban bosses dead set against Byrnes. Frank "I Am the Law" Hague, boss of Jersey City and the undisputed dictator of New Jersey's state delegation votes at the convention, was a longtime booster of Byrnes for the vice presidency and had sent Roosevelt a telegram the day of the White House dinner, urging FDR to replace Wallace with Byrnes.

Byrnes had met with Roosevelt on July 13, a Thursday; with the Democratic convention scheduled to begin in Chicago the middle of the next week, Byrnes could now count on the possibility of 600 and possibly 700 delegate votes for his candidacy, well above the 589 votes needed for nomination. It appeared that Henry Wallace, in his race with Jimmy Byrnes for the vice presidency, never would hear the figurative starting gun. So pleased was Byrnes after his visit with FDR that he was not unduly worried even when he saw Sidney Hillman outside the president's office. Hillman was a firm Wallace supporter, and Byrnes knew Hillman had come to urge the president to retain Wallace.

How sincere Byrnes was in his promise to Roosevelt to push for Negro civil rights in exchange for FDR's presumed support at the convention, it is impossible to say; it can be said with accuracy that Jimmy Byrnes had never gone back on his personal word to the president in any prior political deal. In the remaining days before the convention, Byrnes moved to strengthen his position. He got a scare over lunch with Robert Hannegan the day following his visit to Roosevelt when Hannegan stated that FDR was now leaning toward Douglas or Truman. This comment by Hannegan was the first mention of Truman as a serious contender for the vice presidency. Byrnes immediately telephoned Roosevelt and transcribed their conversation in shorthand in order possibly to show it to wavering delegates. ("Jimmy, that is all wrong," Roosevelt said. "I hardly know Truman. Douglas is a good poker player.") And that same Friday, Byrnes telephoned Harry Truman and easily obtained his promise to make the nomination speech for Byrnes at the convention. Samuel Rosenman, who had never trusted Byrnes, later observed that, in addition to eliminating a potential rival, Byrnes also was shrewdly demonstrating that he was "a good liberal," in Rosenman's words, by obtaining Truman's endorsement. Despite his sidestepping of the FEPC issue in his state, Truman had forthrightly voted with Senator Robert Wagner and other liberals in attempting to end the southern filibuster of antilynching and poll tax legislation of the late 1930s. Byrnes was certainly always interested in eliminating potential rivals, but beyond that motivation, the desire to prove a liberal orthodoxy by having Truman nominate him probably had little value to Byrnes ("I hardly know Truman"). Possibly more important to Jimmy Byrnes in getting Truman's endorsement was the demonstration that, thanks to the friendly backing of Senators Truman and Champ Clark of Missouri, one more state with large black precincts, as in Kansas City and St. Louis, could be expected to fall into line for Byrnes.

Any lingering doubts Byrnes may have had about Roosevelt's acceptance of him as the vice-presidential candidate best able to broker both black and white voters were finally dispelled in an early Saturday morning telephone call Byrnes received from Mayor Kelly in Chicago. Kelly had been talking with Robert Hannegan, who was already in Chicago before the opening session of the convention on Wednesday, operating as the president's personal representative at the convention. (In describing Hannegan's role, the *New York Times* noted in early July 1944 that Hannegan thereby "will fill the places occupied at the 1940 convention by James F. Byrnes and Harry Hopkins.") Roosevelt himself would not be at the convention, because he was on his way across the country for a visit to Navy bases on the West Coast. Kelly had given some news to Hannegan, which he now relayed to Byrnes. Kelly earlier had talked with black political leaders in Illinois, and they had told him that blacks intended to vote for Roosevelt regardless of whoever else was on the ticket. Roosevelt's train was expected to make an unpublicized stop in Chicago for a last political consultation that morning before continuing on its way west, Kelly now told Byrnes, and both Kelly and Hannegan intended to inform Roosevelt that the dangers of Byrnes' antagonizing the black vote had been greatly exaggerated.

Within two hours Kelly telephoned Byrnes again. When he had heard the news, Kelly told Byrnes, FDR said the vice presidency was then "settled." Once again Roosevelt had told the party leaders that they had "the green light" to support Byrnes. Mayor Kelly asked Byrnes to come to the convention city as soon as possible, at Roosevelt's direct request. "He wants you in Chicago," Kelly said. The racial gambit appeared to have worked for Byrnes after all. Kelly's conversation with FDR inside his private car at the Chicago train switching tracks was conclusive evidence to Jimmy Byrnes that he had succeeded in adjusting his politics on race sufficiently to persuade Roosevelt to support him. And at the very time that Byrnes appeared to have supplanted Henry Wallace in Roosevelt's estimation, Byrnes also had been quite careful not to antagonize on the subject of race the southern and western Democratic conservatives who were his major supporters. Byrnes ended his conversation with Kelly by making arrangements to meet with him as soon as he arrived in the city the following day, a Sunday. Roosevelt had said that he wanted Byrnes in Chicago. Jimmy Byrnes had every intention of being there.

The Second World War was entering its third summer when the Democrats began to converge on Chicago the third week of July for their convention. On the European front, the Allied invasion of occupied France begun the previous month at Normandy was proceeding better than first anticipated. American and British armies now were moving eastward, eventually toward the Rhine River and Germany. In the United States the new B-29 "Superfortress" bomber came into full production and made the first round-trip bombing raids on the Japanese islands the month of July, 1944; the B-29s would be highly efficient the next year in the incendiary bombing of Tokyo, and the atomic bombs dropped on Hiroshima and Nagasaki would fall from B-29 airplanes. But also in July 1944 the Imperial Japanese Army in occupied Manchuria, at least three-quarters of a million men under arms, continued a successful offensive campaign against the Allied Chinese Army and captured a number of forward American airfields. And in the first week of July 1944 the total number of American casualties in the current war exceeded the total number of American casualties suffered in the First World War. Over 250,000 Americans had so far been killed, wounded, taken prisoners of war, or considered missing in action.

Lifesize cardboard cutout figures of thirty-eight U.S. "servicemen and servicewomen in grim battle poses, charging toward delegates' seats," had been placed around the walls of the Chicago Stadium on the orders of Edwin Pauley, the wealthy California oilman in charge of the physical arrangements for the convention hall. Pauley also had arranged for electrically wired displays of "Victory Vs" to be illuminated in fluorescent red, white, and blue colors when the national anthem was played inside the darkened hall. And at one of the highest corners of the girders supporting the Chicago Stadium's roof, workmen erected an eight-foot highly colored image of Franklin Roosevelt's face to overlook the convention floor below. It was the same giant image that had been used at the 1940 convention, according to one source working at the stadium, but the colors had been retouched. "It was a little pale."

Pauley himself also was busy in the days before the convention circulating among the arriving delegates as the foremost spokesman of the Anybody-but-Wallace movement. His motto before the convention to delegates had been "You're not nominating a vice president of the United States, you're nominating a president."

Jimmy and Maude Byrnes arrived in Chicago on Sunday accompanied by a South Carolina coterie of Donald Russell and Walter Brown. The Chicago fire chief was waiting at the train station in his impressive red automobile to take Byrnes directly to Mayor Kelly's apartment. The rest of the Byrnes party went to check in at the Skyliner Suite at the Stevens Hotel, arguably the best hotel rooms in Chicago at that time, for which the Office of War Mobilization had at the last minute been able to claim a priority, despite the angry objections of some other delegates who were under the impression they had previously reserved the suite. In what could be considered either a good or a bad omen for the Byrnes party, the spectacular views of the Chicago skyline from the hotel rooms had also been enjoyed from the same suite during the Republican convention by Thomas E. Dewey.

Across town Byrnes was enjoying a cheerful breakfast with Mayor Kelly and Hannegan. They gave him some further details of Roosevelt's reaction when FDR was told that the danger of losing the black vote with Byrnes had been exaggerated. "Well, you know Jimmy has been my choice from the very first," they quoted Roosevelt as having said to them. "Go ahead and name him." Hannegan did add that Roosevelt had requested that Byrnes' nomination first be discussed with the leadership of the CIO at the convention, but this request was in Hannegan's opinion simply a courtesy of prior notification. Later that same day, after Byrnes had left the breakfast, Mayor Kelly met with Alben Barkley, majority leader of the Senate, and the mayor told Barkley to pass the word that Roosevelt wanted Byrnes and that "it was in the bag for Jimmy."

Not quite. The same South Carolina delegation that next week was expected to place Byrnes' name into nomination for the vice presidency was itself being picketed on its arrival at the convention by the black Progressive Democrats protesting the whites-only membership of the state's established, pro-Byrnes party. And the same Sunday morning that Byrnes arrived in Chicago, the NAACP was convening for the last session of its wartime conference, which had met throughout the previous week in the city. Walter White made clear in his final speech to the NAACP audience that Sunday that at least some Negro leaders were not acquiescing in Roosevelt's apparent choice to replace Henry Wallace with Byrnes on the Democratic ticket.

Within a few hours of Jimmy Byrnes' breakfast with the mayor of Chicago, White began his speech by deriding what he called the "Southern revolutionists" and their plans if Wallace was not removed "to 'secede from the union,' and to do a host of other dire things not one of which they have the slightest intention of doing." White then cautioned his NAACP audience:

> But Wallace is only a pawn in the hardboiled game the southern revolutionists play with more than a fair chance of succeeding. Their real goal and purpose is to force the nomination as vice president on the Democratic ticket of a reactionary southerner. They count on the president not surviving another four years in the White House, or, more likely, his resigning when the war ends to head some sort of international peace commission and thereby turning over to the vice president the reins and power of office.

White concluded his remarks to an enthusiastically applauding crowd of at least twelve thousand NAACP delegates: "Let me solemnly warn the Democratic convention that if it nominates a southerner as vice president it can kiss the Negro vote goodbye." (In Illinois, the state in which White was then speaking, blacks had in 1940 made up 4.9 percent of the total state population over twenty-one. Roosevelt had won Illinois from the Republicans in the election of 1940 by a majority that was 4.8 percent of the total vote.)

Walter White was not the only problem. Most of the Democratic party members were well aware by 1944 that there was no love lost between Walter White and Jimmy Byrnes, and Byrnes could therefore dismiss White's remarks as expressions simply of a personal animosity. But given the closeness of the Illinois victory in the last presidential election, Democrats such as Kelly or Hannegan could not so easily dismiss the opinions of Negro leaders like William Dawson. Dawson not only controlled the black vote in his own district but could also swing the votes of southern Illinois, the "Egypt" area, as it had been known in slaveholding years, and an area heavily populated with blacks since Abraham Lincoln's lifetime.

So despite his earlier assurances to Roosevelt that Byrnes was not objectionable to his state's black political leaders, Kelly was still worried. The mayor obtained a promise from Byrnes before he left the breakfast that Byrnes would meet that very day with Dawson and once more get Dawson's approval, or at least his acceptance.

Although Byrnes later wrote a detailed account of his version of all the nomination activities at the convention, he made no reference to the three-hour meeting he held with Dawson that Sunday afternoon behind closed doors at the Democratic party headquarters suite at the Blackstone Hotel. Mayor Kelly was waiting when the doors opened and the two men emerged from their conference. Dawson, a balding, solidly built man who in his physical presence appeared not unlike a black Sam Rayburn, turned to look directly at Byrnes. "Mr. Justice, you cannot be my candidate," he said. Dawson then turned away from Jimmy Byrnes to face Mayor Kelly. "He cannot be my candidate," he told the mayor.

Dawson then walked away. Incredibly, the Byrnes camp even after this meeting continued to believe that the "Negro question" had been favorably resolved for its candidate. "This afternoon Byrnes saw Congressman Dawson as requested by Kelly, and he was OK," Brown wrote in his diary that Sunday. Brown's diary entries were his private opinions, which he kept separate from the press releases he issued for Byrnes, and there was no need for Brown to keep up a false front in his diary; that Brown stuck privately to his unfounded optimism that Byrnes "was OK" with Dawson and other Negro leaders does not indicate that Jimmy Byrnes had deceived Brown. Rather, it indicates that Byrnes and Brown had each deceived himself. Despite Byrnes' early recognition that Negro voters would be the critical constituency in the election of 1944, black people still remained largely "invisible" to him; that is, although racial inequities were a "serious problem," as he had told Roosevelt during their Oval Office meeting, Byrnes believed that it was a problem "to be solved by the white people of the South," as he had also told FDR in the same conversation. White people such as Byrnes would, in his opinion, determine the degree to which the racial problem would be addressed, such as a conditional acceptance by white leadership of the FEPC and the gradual elimination of the poll tax, with black leadership having no significant input on whether the extent of the change was enough. So long as white politicians like himself were willing to "give" on racial policies, Byrnes apparently thought he was "OK" with blacks.

The events of the next day encouraged Byrnes in this illusion. Southerners seemed to prevail that Monday in committee decisions regarding the disputed state delegations and the content of the party platform. Both the whites-only South Carolina delegation led by Governor Olin Johnson and the Texas delegation containing the Regulars were awarded full seating and voting credentials that day, since the national party apparently feared a floor fight if it contested the conservatives. The hearings on the platform statements on civil rights also indicated conservative victories, because the platform subcommittee members writing that plank studiously avoided specifics such as the GOP platform statement in favor of a permanent FEPC and an anti–poll tax bill. In its place were Democratic generalities acceptable to southerners that "Congress should exert its full constitutional powers" to protect "racial and religious minorities." The lack of specifics was correctly seen as a convenient political "out" by which the all-white delegations of the South could accept the platform.

Jimmy Byrnes that same Monday met with Harry Truman and had him recite for him the speech Truman was expected to give on Friday nominating Byrnes for the vice presidency. Byrnes also met that day with Philip Murray, president of the CIO. This meeting was in accordance with Roosevelt's expressed wish as reported by Robert Hannegan to "clear" the Byrnes nomination through Murray and Sidney Hillman, president of the CIO-PAC. (The choice of the words "Clear it with Sidney" was Hannegan's, not Roosevelt's.) Both the CIO leaders were present at the convention, but Byrnes had declined to met with Hillman; their mutual animosity had begun at least as early as 1937, when Byrnes had introduced his anti-sit-down amendment and Hillman was attempting to create a racially integrated unionized textile work force in the South. They had scarcely exchanged a civil word since. But in a conversation that Byrnes later characterized as "friendly," Murray had stated to Byrnes that if Wallace could not be nominated, then the union president would not oppose the selection of Byrnes. It was all Jimmy Byrnes needed to hear; and when he reported Murray's statement to Hannegan and Kelly, the three men agreed that it seemed satisfactory.

That same Monday the Wallace organization made public the promised letter that Roosevelt had written Wallace in support of his candidacy. But the support was lukewarm; FDR had simply stated in writing that, if he were a delegate to the convention, he would support Henry Wallace for the vice presidency. Byrnes was not worried; Wallace was not even at the convention yet, not being expected at Chicago until Wednesday, which was another sign of the Iowan's political inexperience. By the time Wallace arrived at Chicago, Jimmy Byrnes would already have had three days to clinch the 589 votes needed for the nomination. Byrnes planned to announce his own candidacy the following day, Tuesday. Hannegan had already had placards printed reading "Roosevelt and Byrnes."

But also on Monday, one Negro leader after another—including Walter White—had appeared before the platform subcommittee writing the plank on civil rights to claim that at least 6.5 million Negro votes would be lost to the Democratic party if its platform did not include specific pledges for a permanent FEPC and an anti–poll tax bill, as did the Republican platform written in Chicago a month earlier. The other Negro leaders appearing before the subcommittee included the Reverend Maynard Jackson of Dallas and Edgar G. Brown, director of the National Negro Council. These men came to the subcommittee's meeting for more than specific promises; they also came to eliminate Jimmy Byrnes from the ticket if possible. "In what was taken to be a veiled reference to James F. Byrnes, Director of the Office of War Mobilization, who is a possible vice presidential nominee," the *New York Times* reported, "Dr. Jackson told the sub-committee that either party which nominates for president or vice president a person with an anti-Negro record would be vigorously opposed by Negro voters."

And even more vigorous opposition arrived in town on Monday in the person of Ed "Boss" Flynn. Flynn had no sooner arrived in Chicago and entered a meeting of the Democratic National Committee already in progress Monday afternoon than Hannegan rushed him into a corner and said,

"It's all over. It's Byrnes." Flynn was a well-educated man who was rumored to enjoy reading books of history more than talking with other politicians, but no one becomes boss of the Bronx by displaying education and culture. According to those present in the corner scene, Flynn angered visibly and began to curse vilely. He loudly repeated his arguments that Byrnes would lose the Negro vote in New York State, and probably lose the election for Roosevelt. He was going to telephone the president, Flynn said; his telephone call to FDR's train at San Diego was followed by one that same afternoon from Hannegan, who also told the president about the CIO's unchanging first preference for Wallace as expressed to Hannegan earlier in the day in a visit by Hillman. Roosevelt and Hannegan agreed by telephone what to do, and later that Monday evening Hannegan met with Murray and Hillman. It was evident to them that neither Byrnes nor Wallace could be accepted as a candidate by all factions of the Democratic party. They settled upon a compromise candidate.

Jimmy Byrnes was at his Skyliner Suite that night, well satisfied with the day's earlier work with Truman and Philip Murray, when he had a visitor. It was Leo Crowley, a close friend of Byrnes, and the man chosen by Hannegan to deliver the bad news. Crowley informed Byrnes how Hannegan had relayed to the president earlier that night the unhappiness of the CIO and Flynn with his choice of Byrnes as vice president; Hannegan had been told by FDR, and now he asked Crowley to repeat to Byrnes, that the president had said Byrnes was a "political liability" and that "he should not run."

"His face flushed," later wrote Walter Brown, who was standing close to Jimmy Byrnes, "and it was apparent from this statement that the man he had served politically so faithfully had cut him to the quick."

But fate was not through with Jimmy Byrnes that night in the Skyliner Suite. After Crowley had left, and scarcely before Byrnes had time to recover from his shock, another visitor knocked at his hotel rooms. Harry S. Truman arrived. He had come to ask to be released from his promise to support Byrnes. Hannegan had informed him, Truman told Byrnes, that Roosevelt wanted Truman himself to run for the vice presidency. Despite his disappointment and his immediately past flush of anger, Byrnes was remarkably gracious. He "fully understood his position," he told Truman, and "of course" he was releasing Truman from his promise. Truman may have expressed some surprise; throughout this initial conversation he appeared to have been assuming that because of Roosevelt's request he would now be running against both Wallace and Byrnes. Byrnes then told Truman that he had not yet decided whether to withdraw, and he related what he had learned earlier in the night from Crowley. Byrnes did not blame Truman personally for the reversal of Roosevelt's favor, he said. But there were limits for Byrnes and Truman in regard to both graciousness and Democratic party loyalty in this aftermath of what both of them saw as embarrassing evidence of Roosevelt's betrayal. Whatever might be Byrnes' later decision regarding the vice-presidential nomination, Truman that night did not ask that Byrnes nominate him, should Byrnes withdraw, nor did Byrnes offer. After being released from his promise, the Missouri senator left.

Byrnes in his suite did not share his thoughts about Roosevelt later that night with anyone, with the possible exception of Maude Byrnes. There were certainly a number of memories and thoughts of Roosevelt for Jimmy Byrnes to consider: *"Jimmy, you're close to me personally." "You must not get out of the race. If you stay in, you are sure to win." "I'm giving you the green light to run."* And at last his own words: *"How can a man with so many fine qualities tell you one thing and so often do another?"*

Before making his decision on whether to withdraw his candidacy, Byrnes early on Tuesday morning had one more telephone conversation with Roosevelt while the president was at the West Coast. (Jonathan Daniels, whose respect for Byrnes seemed to diminish as Truman's star rose, wrote in 1950 that Byrnes attempted to telephone Roosevelt and that the call was refused. There is no other documentary evidence for this statement that Byrnes was thus humiliated.) According to a shorthand record later transcribed by Byrnes, the South Carolinian reached Roosevelt by telephone early on Tuesday, July 18, and asked about Hannegan's statement that Roosevelt considered Byrnes a "political liability." Roosevelt quickly denied having made that statement or having seen anyone to talk about Byrnes and the vice presidency.

"I have not seen anyone since I left home," Roosevelt was recorded by Byrnes as telling him. "The only thing I told Bob was to show you a letter I wrote to Bob on that assumption—it was in reply to a question from Bob; he wanted confirmation of the fact that I would be happy with Truman or Douglas. That was a week ago."

Byrnes then recorded Roosevelt as telling him, "I am thinking more in terms of the North than the South." Roosevelt continued, "I think we will carry the South anyway, but we have to think of the doubtful states." If Byrnes had any caustic remarks in reply to Roosevelt's blithely using the first-person plural "we" in this political conversation, Jimmy Byrnes left them unrecorded.

Also later the same day a cheerfully amoral Robert Hannegan explained to Byrnes what Roosevelt had meant about the existence of a letter that Roosevelt had wanted "Bob" to show Byrnes and that Hannegan had obtained from Roosevelt the evening of July 11, the night of the upstairs dinner party at the White House. In the signed letter, addressed to Hannegan and intended to be shown to delegates, FDR stated that he would gladly accept either Truman or Douglas as his running mate. Neither Byrnes' nor Wallace's name was mentioned: "Dear Bob: You have written me about Harry Truman and Bill Douglas. I should, of course, be very glad to run with either of them and believe that either one of them would bring real strength to the ticket. Always sincerely, Franklin Roosevelt."

The letter had been typed on White House stationery the day after the dinner party on July 11, but it had been postdated for Wednesday, July 19, the opening day of the full convention. Thus as early as that hot and rainless day in mid-July when Byrnes had met with FDR at the Oval Office and been given the "green light to run," Roosevelt already had picked Truman to be his running mate. Douglas' name had been added to the letter probably to avoid the appearance of FDR's dictating his choice to the convention, as he had done in 1940. After Hannegan had telephoned Roosevelt the previous Monday night to tell him of organized labor's and of Negro leaders' resistance to Byrnes' nomination, FDR had said that Hannegan was now "at liberty" to show Byrnes the letter. Walter Brown was not present then to observe whether Byrnes' face again flushed with anger at this news. When Byrnes told Hannegan about Roosevelt's denial of the "political liability" statement, according to Byrnes' transcript, "Hannegan with great earnestness said that if he never saw his children again he would have to say that it [Roosevelt's making the statement] was the exact truth."

The full extent of Roosevelt's double-cross was now clear to Byrnes. Roosevelt the previous week had only appeared to be wavering between Wallace or Byrnes. FDR from the first had been counting on the delegates for both men to cancel out one another by the first day of the convention, and thereby make it possible for Roosevelt to preserve through a series of compromises the old coalition of rural conservatives and urban liberals for one more win. The southern conservatives would be placated at the convention by the seating of their whites-only state delegations, by the adoption of an innocuous plank on civil rights not mentioning the FEPC, and by the elimination of the liberal Henry Wallace from the national ticket; the CIO and other strongly committed New Deal liberals in turn would be satisfied by the removal of Jimmy Byrnes as a vice-presidential contender, and the selection of a running mate more friendly to labor and Negro groups. For whatever it was worth, Hannegan now told Byrnes that he had considered throwing away the letter after talking with Roosevelt that Saturday morning in the president's railroad car, when FDR had been so enthusiastic about Byrnes as his running mate. He had kept the letter, Hannegan said, only after Roosevelt had told him to talk to CIO leaders in regard to Byrnes' nomination. Hannegan told Byrnes that the objections of Sidney Hillman later determined Roosevelt's and Hannegan's decision to proceed with their plans for a compromise candidate such as Truman.

Of his own bitter experiences with Franklin Roosevelt, Byrnes later wrote to Senator Burton Wheeler, "To him men were so many tools to be used for the accomplishment of what he believed to be a good purpose." Byrnes continued, "Certainly he [Roosevelt] played upon the ambitions

of men as an artist would play upon the strings of a musical instrument."
Presumably the good purpose could include winning one more election,
in 1944, by using the ambitions of Jimmy Byrnes to cancel out Henry
Wallace. But if Roosevelt was a professional in his use of men for what
he considered good political ends, so was Jimmy Byrnes. Like a professional, Byrnes attended to party business before he took his revenge. First
of all, he had a letter of his own to write that Tuesday morning, to Senator
Burnet Maybank, who was head of the South Carolina delegation. Maybank, the longtime Byrnes protégé who, as planned, had succeeded him
to the Senate, had intended to have the pleasure on Friday of placing his
patron's name in nomination for the vice presidency. Byrnes now had
Walter Brown draft a formal note to Maybank that "in deference to the
wishes of the president I ask that my name not be placed before the
convention."

Then to revenge. Byrnes could not politically strike directly at Roosevelt, given FDR's continuing popularity even with the southern conservatives after their early convention victories over the FEPC plank and the
seating of the whites-only delegations. But Roosevelt was vulnerable to
losing conservative votes through the publicizing of his dealings with Sidney
Hillman, and Byrnes considered Hillman the primary reason he had been
sacrificed as a candidate. Byrnes now intended to identify FDR as much
as possible with Hillman, and in this attempt he succeeded in defining the
convention in terms of "Clear it with Sidney" even for years afterward.

Byrnes through Turner Catledge, managed to plant a story in the *New
York Times* under Arthur Krock's byline and headlined "The Inflammatory Use of a Party Chairman," in which was detailed how, when Roosevelt
met with Hannegan at the rail yards before the convention, "the president
told the chairman to 'clear everything with Sidney'." Republicans by that
had July seized upon the statement "Clear it with Sidney" to characterize
the Democratic party as boss ridden and dominated by the special interest
of Sidney Hillman and the CIO-PAC. Buttons were printed sarcastically
urging the reader to "clear it with Sidney," and the Republican party's
campaign slogans, like the earlier House speeches by John Rankin on the
FEPC, conflated the activities of Hillman's CIO-PAC and those of the
president of the Communist party of America: "Sidney Hillman and Earl
Browder's Communists have registered. Have you?" asked the GOP.

Byrnes' analysis of the reasons for his rejection at the 1944 convention
and his use of Hillman as the means of his revenge were accurate as far
as they went. Hillman's political action committees were among the largest
contributors to the Democratic party, and his categorical refusal to accept
Byrnes as a vice-presidential candidate (as opposed to Philip Murray's
willingness not to oppose Byrnes) were among the reasons Roosevelt went
back on his promises. The CIO-PAC and its related committees, for example, raised $1.4 million of the $7.4 million contributed to the Democratic

party for the elections of 1944, and the CIO-PAC was instrumental in the Democratic party's carrying the state of Michigan that year. But Byrnes seems never to have considered that he was rejected because of the unacceptability of his candidacy to black Americans. In his mind, he had done enough, and perhaps he had; but Negro voters, unlike the CIO, had another party to go to in 1944, and by sacrificing Byrnes, Roosevelt was demonstrating to black voters that, despite his removal of Wallace, the Democratic party was still the party of social liberalism.

A letter written by Eleanor Roosevelt about Jimmy Byrnes to Walter White a few days after the convention adjourned seems to confirm that FDR's real intention in sacrificing Byrnes was to keep the black voters in the Democratic party. White earlier had sent a copy of his Chicago NAACP speech to Mrs. Roosevelt in time to arrive at the White House before the day of the vice-presidential nominations. In response, Eleanor Roosevelt wrote White in early August, "Both the president and I were as disturbed as you were by the reports which we received that Justice Byrnes was under consideration and showing considerable strength. I was very glad that he withdrew, but I was never quite sure that he was not being used just as a red herring to prevent Wallace from increasing his strength and to make Senator Truman the candidate."

Given Mrs. Roosevelt's analysis, White probably was substantially correct when he later was quoted in *Ebony* magazine that in regard to the 1944 convention "organized labor's coolness toward Byrnes did not help his cause. But the decisive factor in his rejection as running mate to President Roosevelt was the Negro."

It was perhaps a kindness that Jimmy Byrnes convinced himself, as he later convinced others, that he was rejected at the last moment because of the demands by Sidney Hillman and not because of the distrust of Byrnes by the nation's black citizens. Had he fully realized that he was not "OK" with black leaders, Byrnes probably would have felt an even greater sense of betrayal. More to Roosevelt's advantage than to his own, Byrnes had campaigned for racial moderation in South Carolina during his 1936 senatorial campaign and again during the court-packing controversy of 1937. Later, while on the Supreme Court and away from the "politics of color" of South Carolina, Byrnes also had demonstrated a scrupulous regard for the constitutional rights of Negroes in criminal cases; and there is reason to believe that had Jimmy Byrnes been directing the legislative agenda for civil rights in the last Roosevelt administration, he would have kept his word to FDR and secured passage of the civil rights bills, which Henry Wallace had failed to do. Byrnes was a segregationist, but he also was a man of his word; and having detected the demographic shifts of race within the Democratic party almost as soon as Roosevelt, Byrnes was above all else a political pragmatist.

Roosevelt was the supreme political pragmatist, however. He knew that Harry Truman had a record on Negro civil rights much more innocuous than Jimmy Byrnes', and that Truman had managed to say even less about the FEPC than had Byrnes. While these traits kept Truman on friendly terms with the Deep South conservatives, he also was personally liked and trusted by Sidney Hillman, and, unlike Byrnes, Truman had not insulted Walter White during the Senate debate on antilynching legislation. Truman "just dropped into the slot," as Ed Flynn later described the consensus at the White House dinner party when Roosevelt wrote his "Douglas or Truman" letter to Robert Hannegan. If Jimmy Byrnes later chose to think that he had no problems with the black constituency and that he had been denied the vice-presidential nomination because of the importunities of Sidney Hillman rather than the machinations of Franklin Roosevelt, then so much the better, FDR might have thought. Truman himself appears not to have been aware before the convention that Byrnes was being used by FDR as a "red herring" to promote Truman's candidacy. Truman had not seen the letter to Hannegan, and he was not certain until late in the convention that Byrnes indeed planned to withdraw from the race for the nomination. On Friday, July 21, when Harry S. Truman stood before thousands of cheering delegates at the Chicago Stadium and accepted his party's nomination for the vice presidency, he still had his copy of the speech nominating Byrnes inside his coat pocket.

Jimmy Byrnes by that time had left Chicago with his wife and friends. He had attended the convention through Thursday night, when the renomination of Franklin Roosevelt for a fourth term received a thunderous ovation from most of the delegates. Jonathan Daniels and his wife were seated that night in a box at the stadium next to Jimmy and Maude Byrnes' box. Daniels noticed that neither Byrnes nor his wife rose or joined in the applause. With an exquisitely malicious sense of the political payback, Byrnes had received from the White House that Thursday afternoon the message "Mr. Ed Pauley wants the Justice at a cocktail party for the California delegation Thursday afternoon at 5." On his arrival back in Washington, Byrnes left almost immediately for an inspection tour of the European theater of war, and he was away for most of the 1944 campaign.

Byrnes did return in time to make himself available for some campaign speeches during late October, and after Franklin Roosevelt personally asked Byrnes to give several speeches in a "Dear Jimmy" letter, Byrnes agreed to do so. Apparently the old affection between the two men that was "B.C."—before the Chicago convention of 1932—had survived even the disappointment of the Chicago convention of 1944. Despite his anger at the convention and his introduction of the "Clear it with Sidney" story in July in an attempt to cost Roosevelt votes, Byrnes in October spoke in a nationally broadcast program in favor of the Roosevelt-Truman ticket.

With Truman on the ticket and Byrnes on the stump, Roosevelt felt that his southern support was solid, and he continued to work to secure the constituency of urban Negroes with promises on the FEPC and other civil rights issues. Roosevelt met in October 1944 at the White House with Walter White and the other national Negro leaders Mary McLeod Bethune and Dr. Channing Tobias. Roosevelt assured them that, despite the absence in the Democratic platform of any plank that specifically mentioned Negro civil rights or a permanent FEPC, he intended after the war to integrate the armed services and to pursue immediately the passage of FEPC legislation in the upcoming Seventy-ninth Congress. When the Negro leaders asked Roosevelt whether he was unconditionally committed to passage of the permanent FEPC legislation, FDR replied, "Certainly, I invented the FEPC."

(Throughout early 1945, parliamentary maneuvers by congressional conservatives reduced the funding of the wartime FEPC to one-half its previous appropriation, and it ceased operation in the next year. After Roosevelt's death, a filibuster led by southern senators from states including Mississippi, South Carolina, and Texas also effectively killed any chance that the bill for a permanent FEPC would reach the Senate floor. The bill was never successfully reintroduced. "Do you think I could have stopped the filibuster if I had been presiding officer of the Senate?" Jimmy Byrnes had asked Roosevelt that hot summer day in the Oval Office.)

On November 7, 1944, Roosevelt won reelection to a fourth term, having managed to hold together the old Democratic coalition one more time. Roosevelt carried all of the Deep South and southwestern states, including even such conservative bastions as Mississippi, South Carolina, and Texas; and of the urban "big four" states with 135 electoral votes and significant black pluralities—New York State, Pennsylvania, Illinois, and Ohio—Roosevelt lost only Ohio to Thomas Dewey. The coalition thus held. Any day of reckoning in the Democratic party over the issue of race was postponed until at least 1948. It was an impressive political performance by FDR, even if it had come at the cost of disappointing one of Roosevelt's earliest and most affectionate friends, who had known the president from working with him inside the White House.

When Franklin Roosevelt returned to the White House from Hyde Park a few days after the election, a congratulatory telegram was waiting for him. It was addressed simply "to the president," and in its mixture of disappointment and affection, it also spoke to FDR with an almost domestic intimacy:

> November 8, 1944
> For a tired, quarrelsome, sick old man you sure can run.
> James F. Byrnes

14

Roosevelt's Last Gift

Don't be a sorehead, was the advice Jimmy Byrnes heard from his friend Marvin Jones, the Texas politician and national food administrator. Byrnes telephoned Jones soon after he had returned to Washington from the Chicago convention in late July 1944. "Byrnes was angry as he could be at Roosevelt," Jones later recalled. "He didn't say a word against Truman. He still thought Truman was above board on everything." But if Harry Truman was above board, then the man who was captain of the Democratic party's political ship was not, in Byrnes' opinion. "Roosevelt misled me," Jones recalled being told by Byrnes. The South Carolinian continued to speak about his hurt feelings at being refused the president's support at the convention. "I thought I had the assurance. It embarrasses me," he said. Then, considering his return that week to his desk at the OWM, Byrnes added, "I think I'm going to resign right at once this position."

"Jimmy, don't you do that," Jones cautioned the nation's war mobilizer and his old southern friend, speaking softly into the telephone receiver. "If you do that, they'll accuse you of being a sorehead. You continue on here for a while, anyway, and don't let them misjudge you." Marvin Jones never had heard such openly expressed anger and disappointment from the usually emotionally controlled and politically oblique Jimmy Byrnes. At all other times Byrnes had been so "smooth and worked everything out," in Jones' words.

Jones therefore continued trying to placate his friend over the telephone. The conversation of these two southern politicians began to sound remarkably like what Charlestonians of Jimmy Byrnes' generation would have called the talk of a pair of "old biddies," or aging unmarried ladies, one consoling the other over the vexations of an inattentive suitor. "You keep right on," Marvin Jones firmly told Byrnes. "I know the president still likes you. You have a fine record. Wait until you think this over before you do anything."

Jimmy Byrnes ended their conversation, saying primly, "Well, I'll study about that."

Byrnes did not resign that year. It was true that during the remaining months of the summer and early fall of 1944, Byrnes by his own account became less than fully attentive to his duties at the OWM, meaning probably that following his return from the Democratic convention he began to work at his White House office less than twelve hours a day. A personal note and a telegram, both received by Byrnes on July 27, 1944, when he returned to his Shoreham Hotel home at Washington, indicate that his anger at the outcome of the Democratic convention was cooling, or at least that his pain was being assuaged. The assuaging note was from Byrnes' closest former companion on the Supreme Court bench, Justice Felix Frankfurter. "No one appreciates better than you that it's the business of Supreme Court Justices *not* to be active in politics. But they are free to think," Frankfurter wrote Byrnes. "Jim, one of the strongest thoughts at the end of the week is that I have reason for more respect for you—and there wasn't room for much more! One other thought—what I wouldn't give for a talk over one of Maude's old-fashioneds." The other message was a telegram to Byrnes from Harry S. Truman, in response to a message sent Truman at the convention soon after Roosevelt's preference had become apparent to Byrnes. Strangely, Byrnes chose not to keep a copy of his original message to Truman, but the latter's response implies that Byrnes at the convention had at least chosen to congratulate Truman gracefully.

"Dear Jim," the new Democratic vice-presidential nominee cabled, "Your telegram of the 22nd was certainly appreciated by me. Everyone got a kick out of your manner of wording it.

"I will be in Washington next week, and you are the first person I want to see."

Truman ended this telegram with an almost naive self-identification that reveals that for the Missouri senator the possibility of his succession to the U.S. presidency had not quite sunk in and that this Democratic vice-presidential nominee still saw his primary duties after an anticipated November victory as returning to the U.S. Senate, where Jimmy Byrnes had accumulated a much more distinguished legislative record. Truman ended his wire modestly: "Sincerely yours, Harry S. Truman, U.S.S."

A few months after his return to the capital, Byrnes was asked by General George Marshall to confer with him and Generals Eisenhower and Patton in France on logistical problems then slowing the Allied advance on Germany. FDR put the *Sacred Cow*, his presidentially appointed airplane, at the disposal of the OWM director for this trip the first week of October. Byrnes thus was able to spend some time away from Roosevelt and further to work off some of his anger directed personally toward the president. Roosevelt himself remained what he always had been with Jimmy Byrnes, a marvelously manipulative and charming companion. A few days before the presidential election, FDR at a press conference was capable even of satirizing both his own public falling-out with Byrnes and his continued reliance upon Byrnes as a political problem solver and a valued source of domestic advice:

Q: "Mr. President, have you received any word that Senator (Carter) Glass (of Virginia) intends to support you for a fourth term?"
THE PRESIDENT: "I haven't, no. Better ask Jimmy Byrnes."
(Long pause here)
Q: "Thank you, Mr. President."
(Laughter)

"He *had* a way, the president did," Marvin Jones remarked to an interviewer years after Byrnes and Roosevelt had become reconciled.

In part, this political reconciliation between Byrnes and Roosevelt resulted from the fact that Byrnes was still highly ambitious and highly competent in government. The strong possibility remained that Roosevelt after the election would select him to succeed Cordell Hull as secretary of state. Hull, then in his late seventies and ill with throat cancer, was a former Tennessee politician who had known Byrnes while Hull was in the Senate and who had a personal regard for Jimmy Byrnes, it was reported in the *New York Times*, "amounting almost to hero worship." Roosevelt did nothing to discourage this hope on Jimmy Byrnes' part, at least not until after Byrnes had returned from France and made a national radio campaign speech for the administration in late October.

It is revealing both of Byrnes' hopes and of his ambitions that he chose to emphasize at the close of this October 30, 1944, radio speech the similarities between Woodrow Wilson's commitment to U.S. participation in a League of Nations after the First World War and Franklin Roosevelt's equally firm commitment to U.S. leadership in a postwar United Nations organization. There is no reason to doubt that Byrnes before this 1944 radio address always had been sincere in his public statements about the efficacy of organized international cooperation. If Hull regarded Byrnes almost to the point of hero worship, then so had Byrnes regarded Woodrow Wilson and his diplomacy as a personal ideal, and Byrnes had campaigned vigorously throughout the 1920s for U.S. membership in the League of Nations, both before and after Wilson's death. Byrnes was a "traditional southern internationalist," in the words of one historian of the 1970s not usually favorable to him. Jimmy Byrnes had been among the congressmen who had thought that Republican isolationists in the U.S. Senate after the 1920 elections contributed not only to the demise of the League of Nations and the eventual demise of world peace (and, incidentally, the closing of world markets to southern agricultural products and textiles) but also to the death of Woodrow Wilson.

"As a southerner," Byrnes told his radio audience in 1944, "I take particular pride in the strong support and active leadership which southern Democrats in the Congress have provided in matters involving international cooperation in war and in the peace." Byrnes reminded his listeners how in 1920, with the Republican victories in the presidential and congressional elections and with "the defeat of Cox and Roosevelt, who carried the torch for Woodrow Wilson, there was lost all hope of vindication of Woodrow Wilson's faith in international cooperation."

Byrnes told his national audience, "I pray history will not repeat itself." But he added, unless after the elections of 1944 there is a politically strong Democratic president (and, presumably, a physically healthy and politically well-connected secretary of state), "I do not think the Republican party under its present leadership can be relied upon to carry through effective peace plans for active participation in world affairs." Roosevelt telephoned Byrnes at the radio station immediately after the speech to congratulate him personally on his address.

But another reason why Byrnes stayed on with the Roosevelt administration as war mobilizer was his sincere belief that hard fighting lay ahead for the Allied armies. Despite recent U.S. naval victories on the Mariana and Philippine islands, an invasion of Japan might be necessary before the end of the Pacific war; and Byrnes was deeply troubled by what he had seen and been told by Generals Marshall, Eisenhower, and Patton during his October tour of the European battlefields. Unlike many civilians in the Roosevelt administration who optimistically expected a German surrender by the end of 1944, Byrnes knew from talking with these generals that U.S. forces in France were experiencing severe logistical difficulties in moving ammunition and gasoline to the frontline troops and that a successful German counteroffensive was a real possibility. By late autumn 1944, for example, an Allied division needed 700 tons of supplies daily to operate in the European theater, as opposed to 200 tons needed daily by a Wehrmacht division. Even if the Allied logistical problems were solved, however, the accumulation of supplies necessary to sustain an offensive campaign made the Allied forces still vulnerable to a blitzkrieg counterattack.

Thus after the defeat of the Republican ticket in the November elections and the return of Democratic majorities to Congress, Byrnes put aside his personal differences with FDR and acted quickly to consolidate before the end of 1944 a near-total mobilization of American resources and manpower for the last months of the war. Jimmy Byrnes always had been an advocate of waging what Joseph Stalin, in conversations with FDR and Churchill at the Teheran and Yalta conferences, liked to call a "hard" war: a war in which the civilian economy as well as the military forces of the Axis was to be overwhelmingly attacked, and in which the civilian economies of the Allied countries were to be greatly subordinated to military production. Eventually this commitment to a "hard war," as much as any other factor, led Byrnes to be the most active promoter in the Truman administration for a nonnegotiable surrender and the use of the atomic bomb upon Japan's cities.

Byrnes' advocacy at the OWM of a hard war beginning with a regimentation of the home front had been a long time coming. Soon after assuming the OWM post in 1943, Byrnes had clashed repeatedly with Treasury Secretary Henry Morgenthau over Byrnes' urging a program of compulsory savings to be deducted from workers' paychecks to help finance the war. Morgenthau had argued that such compulsory savings, in addition to being objectionable on civil libertarian grounds, would hurt the Treasury's drives for voluntary war bond purchases. (The compromise eventually proposed by Byrnes, to have federal income tax deducted in advance from paychecks, outlived World War Two.)

And as a continuing part of his campaign to prepare the home front for a "hard war," Byrnes had cautioned the American public in 1943 not to underestimate the willingness of the Japanese or German military to resist to the bitter end. Roosevelt and others in his administration had been greatly embarrassed for example, a few days before Christmas in 1943, when Byrnes anonymously leaked to reporters at a White House Yuletide party his speculation that the United States might suffer 400,000 casualties fighting German forces in the European theater within the next three months. Byrnes' holiday pessimism on the war had been anathema to many civilian economists in the War Production Board and labor unions, who already were planning the start-up of the nation's mass reconversion to civilian goods by late 1944.

But before the week of Christmas 1944, the great German counteroffensive that became known as the Battle of the Bulge began, and it justified Byrnes' predictions that there would be no easy end to the war. Eventually the German armies were pushed back, but not before 600,000 U.S.

troops—more than three times the number of American soldiers who had fought on both sides at Gettysburg—had been caught in the combat of this winter battle against German tanks and infantry from the Ardennes Forest spreading north into Belgium and south into Luxembourg and as far south as the Saar, near Switzerland.

The German counteroffensive gave Byrnes the perfect political occasion in late 1944 to put aside plans for civilian reconversion and to centralize more economic and social powers in the OWM. Within three months, beginning the weeks before the Battle of the Bulge in December 1944 and ending after his return abroad from the Yalta conference in February 1945, Jimmy Byrnes put into effect the most comprehensive program of military restrictions on civilian life known by American citizens before or after the Second World War. The nation's future "cold" warrior of postwar relations with the Soviet Union was first of all the nation's foremost domestic "hard" warrior in the final months of the U.S. military conflict with Germany and Japan.

On December 9, 1944, Byrnes, on his OWM executive authority to control the nation's civilian manpower, issued a "work or fight" order. Men in their late thirties who had previously been classified as ineligible for the military draft were required by Byrnes' order either to take jobs at industries deemed essential for the war effort or face induction into military labor battalions. Byrnes also arranged in late December that draft deferments be denied for college or professional athletes who continued playing their sport despite claims of injury making them ineligible for military service. And at the cabinet meeting of December 22, Byrnes successfully argued for the closing of the nation's racetracks for the duration of the war. Byrnes was taking this action, he subsequently told the public, in order to prevent absenteeism at war plants and to save gasoline for the military overseas that would otherwise have been used domestically for trips to the races. (Betting at horse racetracks had become a popular civilian diversion in the war years on both the East and the West Coast for war industry workers with large paychecks and few opportunities to buy rationed goods.)

Byrnes' "work or fight" order effectively signaled that he had no intention of releasing large numbers of civilian workers to produce consumer goods until the final U.S. military victory over the Axis powers. At the same time in early December that he promulgated this new policy, Byrnes asked Major General Lucius D. Clay, a West Point graduate and an expert in logistics, to become his deputy director. Byrnes' office in October had been renamed, optimistically, the Office of War Mobilization and Reconversion (OWMR), but General Clay's retention of his earlier responsibilities as the director of material for the Army made it clear that reconversion was going to wait. Back at the War Production Board, Bruce Catton saw the political handwriting on the wall, spelling out the demise of civilian planning for early reconversion as the result of Byrnes' appointment of General Clay. "If there ever had been any lingering doubt that WPB and all the other war agencies were going to do what the Army wanted," Catton later wrote about this selection of Clay in the winter of 1944, "it now vanished utterly."

Byrnes further acted in late 1944 to subordinate the consumer economy to the needs of the Army, even in ways disapproved of at the time by Secretary of War Henry Stimson. The mail-order firm of Montgomery Ward in Chicago had been maintaining since 1942 that it had no direct role in war production and that therefore it was exempt from the controls of the Roosevelt administration's wartime labor agencies. The government had briefly seized control of the company in early 1944, but had relinquished it six months before the presidential elections. The company still claimed that its right to private property exempted it from the labor regulations of the War Acts, however. Attorney General Francis Biddle did not intend to let such insubordination go unchallenged, and after the 1944 election he favored making an example of Montgomery Ward by taking over its operation for the duration of the war with the use of U.S. troops. Secretary Stimson profoundly disagreed, declaring to FDR that the company was "devoted entirely to storage, sale and distribution of civilian goods" and that U.S. soldiers even in wartime literally had no business running a Chicago mail-order company. Nevertheless, Byrnes shortly after a White House discussion with the president on December 26 provided the legal justification for U.S. troops to be sent to Chicago and take control of Montgomery Ward for the duration of the war. The policies of the previous civilian management, Byrnes later told a federal court in January when the owners sued, "seriously interfered with the successful prosecution of war."

Roosevelt fully backed these actions by Byrnes, as well as the subsequent order by the director of the OWMR on January 5, 1945, to cancel all civilian conventions bringing together fifty or more persons, as a means once more to save energy and to free passenger space on trains for troops. Byrnes followed up this order with a directive on January 10 requiring a wartime ban on outside electric illumination or neon lighting in some urban areas. (The darkened commercial districts or amusement parks of these cities in early 1945 were said by civilians, not necessarily in admiration of the frugal habits of the director of the OWMR, to have suffered a "Byrne out.")

And in a final tightening of government control upon private civilian behavior during wartime, Jimmy Byrnes on February 26 ordered all places of public amusement, including bars, movie theaters, dance halls, and nightclubs, to close at midnight. The aim at OWMR was, once again, to reduce worker absenteeism and to save energy. Freed by his rejection at the convention of 1944 from the political considerations of being FDR's vice president, this "assistant president" was waging economic war on the home front in 1945 with a vengeance.

Although the "work or fight" order of the OWMR had made the most drastic inroads on prior civil liberties (even a history of the OWMR written with its encouragement conceded that Byrnes' order created a de facto civilian draft), Byrnes' decision for a national midnight curfew proved to be the most unpopular of his wartime policies. Shortly after this decision became known, Byrnes received a telephone call at his OWMR office from an angry Mayor Fiorella La Guardia of New York City. La Guardia exclaimed that thousands of dollars would be lost by his city if the military could not patronize the city's nightclubs after midnight, and, in Byrnes' later recollection, he generally "talked as if New York City would secede from the Union if night clubs were forced to shut down so early." La Guardia pointedly reminded Byrnes that the OWMR had no police enforcement powers. The mayor intended, he told Byrnes, to keep his city's bars and cabarets open past the OWMR curfew.

The Little Flower did not know with whom he was picking a fight. Byrnes politely replied that, unfortunately, La Guardia was correct and the OWMR did not have police powers. The telephone conversation ended with Mayor La Guardia's apparent victory. Byrnes then promptly got in touch with General Marshall of the Army and Admiral Ernest King of the Navy and arranged to have military police of both services post as "off-limits" any New York City bar or nightclub that did not obey the national midnight closings, and to arrest any serviceman who entered them.

Byrnes enjoyed such bureaucratic victories, and they demonstrated that he was still a powerful and quintessential Washington insider. But there were critics both before and after the German counteroffensive of 1944 who believed that in ordering a greater regimentation of the American economy and society, Byrnes also was acting as an insider for Bernard Baruch and other conservative financial interests that had benefited from the government's tolerance of monopoly and concentration of capital during the war. The wartime efficiencies achieved by Byrnes at the OES and the OWM/OWMR unquestionably had come at the expense of U.S. small businesses and consumers. A "privileged one hundred companies," in the words of a postwar historian, were receiving 70 percent of all government war-related contracts by mid-March 1943; and after he became director of the OWM two months later, Byrnes and later General Clay did nothing to disturb that bias toward big business. Nor did Byrnes or anyone else at the OWMR apparently ever consider changing the procedure by which war material was ordered directly for the military by a military procurement officer, without any civilian board review of the effect that procurement would have on the needs of the home front consumer.

Byrnes and Clay likewise thwarted most efforts in 1943–44 by Donald Nelson at the OPM to begin moving civilian workers back into consumer industries as part of an "early" reconversion. The same week of Christmas 1943 that Byrnes had leaked to reporters his speculation that as many as 400,000 U.S. casualties might be suffered in the next few months, Henry Wallace described in his diary how there was "gradually shaping up an inner circle conflict" between those presidential advisers, including Donald Nelson and "Harry Hopkins' men," who wanted at least a partial reconversion to a civilian economy before the end of 1944, and those insiders, including "Baruch's men and Jimmy Byrnes," who opposed reconversion.

Byrnes characteristically left little paper trail of this thoughts, and what he himself planned for the postwar U.S. economy must be gauged by his public actions and his few public speeches. In a rare public appearance outside Washington, before the Academy of Political Science in New York City in May 1944, Byrnes had announced his support for a reconversion plan commissioned by the OWM and written with the counsel of Bernard Baruch and the Republican business executive John Hancock. Surprisingly, Byrnes chose to emphasize from the Baruch-Hancock report the suggestion that there should be a postwar federal subsidy of former war contractors, "particularly of small business, which has only limited working capital of its own." Byrnes also sketched an argument for a federally guaranteed minimum wage for war workers displaced after the peace by the cancellation of government contracts. "In an interdependent society the worker cannot make his own job, and the burden of unemployment must not be allowed to rest solely upon the worker," he declared. Neither the left wing of the Democratic party, including Donald Nelson and Harry Hopkins, nor Henry Wallace would have disagreed ideologically with such a sentiment, but Jimmy Byrnes probably was keeping an eye on the first postwar national elections rather than on ideology. Byrnes, unlike any of the above men, had held public office in 1918–19, and he remembered well as a former New Freedom congressman how the sudden cancellation of war contracts after the First World War had contributed significantly to high levels of unemployment and the defeat of the Democratic party at the next year's polls.

As the proceedings of the academy that night recorded, Byrnes ended his speech with a declaration sure to please practically everyone, from political scientists to the archetypal Rosie the Riveter. This former head of the OES asserted that, with the inevitable Allied victory and a continued fiscal discipline to control inflation, the advance deduction of federal income taxes from individual paychecks should be shelved (as, presumably, would be the excess-profits war taxes on large corporations): "Taxation which is best suited to the needs of a war economy is not at all suited for an expanding peace economy," Byrnes concluded. "With the end of the war there should be an end of the wartime system of taxation (Applause)."

But before the euphoria of a postwar prosperity could be enjoyed, Byrnes cautioned his audience of applauding political scientists, Americans had to recognize that "the roads to Berlin are not only long, but bloody." Byrnes observed that while he spoke, despite the military successes of the first six months of 1944, no Allied army was closer than 500 miles to Berlin or 1,800 miles to Tokyo; that the numbers of U.S. casualties that week totaled 173,239; and that at the site of the current Allied major offensive then under way in Italy, "no major European battlefield on which we might choose to fight can give the enemy the natural defenses that the Nazis have at Cassino."

Thus rather than representing "the coming together of the corporations and the military" into the "power elite" of the U.S. military-industrial complex of the 1950s and 1960s, as C. Wright Mills and other postwar historians later asserted, Byrnes' actions at the OWMR in the winter of 1944–45 support the statement by the officially sanctioned history of that office: Byrnes interpreted his duties as war mobilizer very narrowly. Byrnes saw his job, and General Clay's, as helping move munitions and material down what he perceived as that long and bloody road leading past Monte Cassino, the Ardennes Forest, Okinawa and the other Pacific islands, and, eventually, to Berlin and Tokyo. This job they did at the OWMR with a vengeance. A look at the U.S. Army's reappraisal of its spending needs after the German offensive of Christmas 1944, tells the story: Army spending for the first fiscal quarter of 1945 compared with the last fiscal quarter of 1944 was up 150 percent for .30-caliber armor-piercing bullets and up 237 percent for .30-caliber incendiary and other tracer bullets; and spending for artillery shells for 1945 was tentatively increased $3.6 billion from the total of $2.2 billion spent for all of 1944. By denying the release of civilian workers into industries other than war plants through such policies as the "work or fight" order, Byrnes and Clay kept those munitions moving along the road despite the objections of Nelson and others at the OPM.

But it would be well to recall the observation of a German officer after the Allied victory at and the German army's withdrawal from Monte Cassino that neither he nor the men under his command had been "defeated." In each of the three bloody battles to take the historic monastery town, the Allies had charged their American-made Sherman tanks toward the German positions, he said, driving directly into the line of fire of his 88-mm artillery. The German officer stated that he and his men simply had run out of shells before the Allies had run out of Sherman tanks. Byrnes and Clay never accepted the presumption, popularly believed but refuted by historians, that superior Allied technology and strategy made the defeat of the Axis powers inevitable. In fact, the Allied armies frequently were inferior to their German counterparts both in technology and in leadership. Rather, as Byrnes and Clay obviously assumed, the Allied victory was assured by an unrelenting and overwhelming flow of arms and material poured into the combat theaters by the giant industrial structures of both the United States and its wartime ally the USSR. That is, the war was to be won by what one historian has aptly termed "brute force"—firepower greatly disproportionate to the possible resistance.

For instance, it was exemplary of Byrnes at the OWM—or excessive, if one talked to Donald Nelson at the OPM—to have overseen in 1943–44 the production of 47,000 tanks, practically all of them the M4 Sherman model, while that same year the German industry was able to manufacture only 29,600 tanks and self-propelled guns. By the war's end the U.S. Sherman tank had become the most frequently used tank in the world, but this weapon produced in such vast numbers under the OWM/OWMR's supervision had only two virtues, maneuverability and ease of manufacture at U.S. automobile plants that a few years earlier had been turning out Cadillacs and Chryslers. Nicknamed by its crews "the Ronson" after the reliable, American-made cigarette lighter, the Sherman was spectacularly vulnerable to armor-piercing shells fired at its ammunition compartment, and in terms of the range of its gun, the thickness of its armor, and the survivability of its crew, the Sherman was dismally inferior to German frontline tanks. Indeed, by the U.S. Army's own admission of tactics during the Second World War, Shermans should attack the German panzers only if outnumbering them by five to one. Thus, even though Byrnes' office had assisted in the production of 47,000 tanks, the U.S. Army was still short, given the 5-to-1 ratio it deemed necessary for the U.S. tanks' survival, by about 200,000 additional Sherman tanks.

Similarly, a representative U.S. infantry division engaged in combat at the 1944 German offensive was ballistically and technologically inferior to a representative German division on the other side of the firing line. German divisions usually enjoyed a superiority of automatic and subautomatic weapons by a ratio as high as five to one, and in the availability of some weapons particularly horrific to ground troops—flamethrowers, for instance—their advantage was even greater. German infantry divisions usually carried twenty flamethrowers, while the U.S. infantry divisions usually had none. Given these facts of death, Byrnes and Clay seemed perfectly aware that an Allied victory was assured only so long as their governments continued to keep their economies on as full a war mobilization as possible. Byrnes' counterpart in administering the war supplies of the Third Reich, Armaments Minister Albert Speer, also noticed this commitment toward a full U.S. mobilization. "Paradoxically, from 1942 on," Speer wrote in his memoirs, "the developments in the warring countries moved in an opposite direction. The Americans, for example, found themselves compelled to introduce an authoritarian stiffening into their industrial structure, whereas we tried to loosen the regimented economic system."

Thus were Jimmy Byrnes, General Lucius Clay, Albert Speer, and all the other hundreds of thousands of perpetrators or casualties of the violence of the Second World War caught up by 1944–45 in a historical revisionism undreamed of by C. Wright Mills and other neo-Marxian academicians: a revisionist reduction of human individuality and significance, including the reduced significance of individual intelligence or heroism in combat. According to this revisionism, all that Jimmy Byrnes had to do after the defeat of the German offensive of 1944 was guarantee the mass production of U.S. weapons such as the Sherman tank at full speed, while all the U.S. military had to do was coerce the movement of weapons such as these "Ronsons," each carrying a crew of five young men, toward the German or Japanese lines until the other side ran out of shells.

Paul Fussell, later a noted literary and social critic, was at the time of Jimmy Byrnes' directorship of the OWMR a young infantry lieutenant serving in Europe. Fussell had been wounded once, but had been judged fit for continued duty at the firing lines and with the rest of his unit was expecting a transfer, should he survive the European theater, to the Pacific to participate in the invasion of Japan. Fussell has written eloquently of the cynicism of U.S. troops caught up in this new "revisionism" in the winter of 1944–45. The U.S. troops knew, Fussell writes, that

despite the advertising and publicity, where it counted their arms and equipment were worse than the Germans'. They knew their automatic rifles (World War One vintage) were slower and clumsier, and they knew the Germans had a much better light machine gun. They knew that despite official assertions to the contrary, the Germans had real smokeless power for their small arms and that they did not. They knew that their own tanks, both American and British, were ridiculously under-armed and under-armored, so that they were inevitably destroyed in an open encounter with an equal number of German Panzers. They knew that the anti-tank mines supplied them became unstable in sub-freezing weather, and that truckloads of them blew up in the winter of 1944–45. And they knew that the single greatest weapon of the war, the atomic bomb excepted, was the German 88-mm flat-trajectory gun, which brought down thousands of bombers and tens of thousands of soldiers. The Allies had nothing as good, despite one of them designating itself as the World's Greatest Industrial Power. The troops' disillusion and their ironic response, in song and satire and sullen contempt, came from their knowing that the home front then (and very likely historiography later) could be aware of these things.

Indeed, later historians could not or would not understand this tacit endorsement of Allied brute force by the administrators at the OWMR. "This was the winter of 1864–65 all over again," Bruce Catton angrily wrote of Byrnes' actions such as the "work or fight" directive, with Lee hopelessly pinned at Petersburg and Sherman starting up through the Carolinas and nothing in the cards anywhere to prevent the inevitable. What sort of figuring [at the OWMR] was going on anyway? What kind of logic was it, which said that it was precisely now that the heaviest load of the entire war should be imposed on the civilian economy—that it would take four-fifths as much war production to defeat crippled, isolated, navyless Japan as it took at the very peak of the war effort against both Japan and Germany?

Catton answered his own question: "Military logic to be sure." With this answer Jimmy Byrnes would certainly have agreed, had he not been so habitually tight-lipped, with a terse "Yes, of course." Byrnes, whatever compassion equal to Catton's he might have felt for soldiers on the firing line such as Fussell or for consumers at home, by his actions showed that he was willing to face and implement without public comment the ugly truth of the U.S. military's logic: that it was the quantity and not the quality of armor and arms, the application of massive firepower and not tactical brilliance, that was necessary in order for the Allies to defeat the Axis. It was, after all, the application of brute force by U.S. Grant at the battles of the Wilderness, Cold Harbor, and Seven Days, with consequently appalling casualties among his own conscription armies, that had brought Lee's army to be so hopelessly pinned to its static lines at Petersburg. Nor had Grant hesitated to continue pounding the enemy lines at Petersburg, on one occasion sending large numbers of black troops into an obviously lethal field of fire, until Lee was forced to back up his army into the pocket of Appomattox. "In static warfare, victory goes to the side which can fire the more ammunition," General Erwin Rommel observed of his own defeat by an Allied army some eighty years later, and even though the lines in Europe, at least, had become as static as those of the American Civil War in the Virginia of 1864–65, Byrnes was prepared to continue providing the U.S. Army with more ammunition to fire.

Actions speak louder than words. Byrnes' unspoken agenda to place increased industrial mobilization above all other domestic questions is most clearly seen in his attempt in mid-1944 to intervene with Roosevelt in the Du Pont and Imperial Chemical companies case. Attorney General Francis Biddle had targeted these two industries in early 1944 in an attempt by the Justice Department to revive the administration's prewar enforcement of antitrust laws, which at FDR's direction had since 1942 been ignored or suspended for the activities of the largest U.S. war contractors. Now, with the tide of the war apparently turning in the Allies' favor, Biddle notified the two companies that the Justice Department intended to file criminal charges against them and their chief executives personally, alleging that Du Pont and the British-based Imperial Chemical company had conspired to fix worldwide prices of chemicals and secretly agreed after the war to return to the German corporate members of their chemical cartel the markets they had previously enjoyed. Henry Stimson vociferously objected to the Justice Department's bringing criminal charges against one of its largest war contractors, and when FDR seemed to be inclining toward Biddle's argument for a resumption of antitrust enforcement, Byrnes at the behest of Stimson and Undersecretary of War Robert Patterson wrote to FDR on May 26, 1944, urging the president not to approve Biddle's pursuit of the charges. In the case of each company, Byrnes argued to Roosevelt, "lawyers would require the constant assistance of executives" in order to plan a corporate and personal defense, and production inevitably would be slowed at each of these two giant contractors.

But this spirited defense in his letter to the White House of corporate executives and their alleged monopolistic practices was not just a knee-jerk reaction by Jimmy Byrnes as an economic royalist, or as one of "Baruch's men," in the suspicious phrasing of Henry Wallace. Byrnes had a further argument to dissuade Roosevelt from approving the prosecution of Du Pont. "If Du Pont executives are engaged in the S-1 project in which you have invested so much money and in which you have so much hopes," Byrnes reminded Roosevelt, "I think it unwise to take the risk of diverting the attention of key men at this time to prepare an answer which can be prepared just as well when hostilities have ceased."

Prepared just as well when hostilities have ceased. Byrnes' argument implies not a covert agenda to advance a postwar, military-corporate "power elite" but an insistence upon placing the Allied military victory before all other questions. And in his reference to the atomic bomb research and development—known by the code name, among others, of "S-1 project"—Byrnes demonstrated at least a nominal familiarity with the ultrasecret Manhattan Project.

A skilled administrator who had shown a postelection loyalty to Roosevelt, who had a public history of a firm commitment to Roosevelt's ideal of the establishment of a permanent, international peace-making organization, and who had a working familiarity with the Roosevelt administration's most secret and most expensive weapons project—such a man must have seemed to Jimmy Byrnes in late 1944 to be inevitably advancing his name as Hull's successor as secretary of state.

Byrnes had told Roosevelt the previous fall, after returning from his tour of the European battlefields, that he had no intention of remaining at the OWMR after V-E Day. After the German counteroffensive collapsed in late December of 1944, the Allied victory in Europe even by Byrnes' expectations could not be any more than a few months away. As to the possibilities of any future work with the administration, Jimmy Byrnes had not been a sorehead, as Marvin Jones so wisely had advised, and the OWMR had performed what Roosevelt considered valuable services in the last few months; but Byrnes had by the late winter of 1944 received yet another disappointment from FDR that doubtless made him want to leave. After the ailing Cordell Hull had resigned in late November as secretary of state, Roosevelt, despite wide speculation in the press that he would appoint Jimmy Byrnes and Hull's own recommendation that Byrnes be his successor, had instead chosen Hull's much less experienced undersecretary, the pliable Edward R. Stettinius, Jr.

Even Stettinius had been puzzled by Roosevelt's choice of him over Byrnes. Roosevelt thoughtfully explained his reasons for the appointment to his new secretary of state the day after it was announced. "Jimmy had always been on his own in the Senate and elsewhere," FDR said to Stettinius. "I am not sure that he and I could act harmoniously as a team." Stettinius caught on quickly. "In other words, Jimmy might question who was boss," he said to the president. Roosevelt then responded with three short words that summed up the cooling of his political friendship with the independent-minded Jimmy Byrnes. "That's exactly it," FDR said.

Byrnes had wanted that job at State. Only a few weeks before Roosevelt chose Stettinius, Byrnes had turned down FDR's offer to appoint him to be the U.S. high commissioner to Germany after the war. Byrnes declined, because he did not speak German, he told FDR. (That job, and a brilliant postwar career, eventually went to Byrnes' OWMR assistant, General Lucius Clay.) But in turning down FDR's offer, Byrnes made clear that he would welcome other, larger postwar responsibilities. "One difficulty I anticipate is the ratification of a treaty providing machinery for the preservation of peace," Byrnes wrote, in an obvious reference to the expected duty of the new secretary of state to secure approval of the United Nations treaty in the Senate. "I was interested in that cause in 1919 and am still interested," Byrnes pointedly wrote to FDR.

But in late 1944 Franklin Roosevelt had been more interested in the Department of State's knowing who was boss than in Jimmy Byrnes' experiences a quarter of a century earlier as a supporter of Woodrow Wilson and the League of Nations. The youthful-appearing Edward R. Stettinius, Jr., who had suffered from the disability in wartime Washington of being known throughout the federal government as "Junior," got Cordell Hull's upstairs office in the wonderfully ornate State Department Building, across the street from the Oval Office.

It was probably at this time in late December or early January 1945 that Byrnes silently updated his resignation, determining not to wait until the formal declaration of V-E Day to leave the administration, but to give notice to Roosevelt as soon as the German armies appeared defeated. FDR knew that his chief assistant for the home front was disappointed; but he was not yet through with Jimmy Byrnes, either as a means to the president's political ends or as an object of his generosity. Roosevelt was planning in January 1945 to travel with other members of a U.S. delegation, including Secretary Stettinius, near to the Crimean town of Yalta, in the

Soviet Union, for a wartime conference with Stalin and Churchill. Byrnes was meeting with the president on an unrelated matter of shipping in late December 1944 when suddenly FDR said, "Jimmy, I want you to go with me on this trip to the Crimea."

The invitation was both unexpected by Byrnes and characteristic of Roosevelt. At the time it was extended, Byrnes already was planning to leave the administration, and he was "very, very upset about what he felt was unfairness or ingratitude to him," in the later description of Jonathan Daniels. From his office in the West Wing, Daniels was one of the few southerners still on good terms with both Byrnes and Roosevelt in late December of 1944. Daniels later remembered that Byrnes "was bitter then because he had wanted to be secretary of state" and that "there was much to be said for Byrnes' position." The rift caused by Roosevelt's view that Byrnes was too politically independent for State seemed to be permanent, but Daniels intuitively understood that this decision by FDR to take Byrnes along on the Yalta trip was an attempt to make their final parting more pleasant. "I have the feeling that Roosevelt carried him as part of the Roosevelt characteristic of protecting or trying to protect the face of people he was not willing to give all his confidence to," Daniels told an interviewer nearly twenty years later. The invitation to join the trip to Yalta was, in short, a good-bye gift by FDR in appreciation of Byrnes' past hard work.

Jimmy Byrnes by this time was accustomed to looking carefully into the mouth of any gift horse offered by Franklin D. Roosevelt, even one that promised to carry Byrnes to an important international conference. At this December meeting, Byrnes initially declined FDR's invitation, saying that his work load at the OWMR prohibited his leaving the country. Byrnes later was warned by two presidential aides, Steven Early and Edwin Watson, that Roosevelt planned to invite Ed Flynn of the Bronx to come on the Yalta trip as a reward for past political favors. Byrnes did not relish the prospect of traveling 5,700 miles to the Crimea in the company of the man who had cursed and raged at the prospect of his name being placed into nomination for the vice presidency, particularly since members of the presidential party for much of this overseas journey would be forced to share space in the below-decks quarters of the military cruiser USS *Quincy*.

But with a tone of "Oh come on" jocularity, Franklin Roosevelt in late January 1945 asked Byrnes for a second time to join the other delegates for the Yalta trip. This time Jimmy Byrnes agreed to go. Roosevelt had an additional political motive besides personal generosity in pressing these invitations upon Byrnes. FDR needed a messenger to Congress. On the agenda for the plenipotentiary sessions at Yalta were discussions of the preliminary agreements both for the United Nations treaty and for the Allies' policies for a postwar Europe. The acceptance by the U.S. Senate of whatever terms Roosevelt was able to negotiate on these issues at Yalta was by no means certain. Roosevelt had no intention of allowing Jimmy Byrnes to contribute substantially to these negotiations while he was at the conference, but looking beyond the Yalta conference, FDR apparently intended to use Byrnes' presence there to reduce isolationist criticism in Congress of the inevitable U.S. compromises made in those negotiations.

Jimmy Byrnes characteristically said very little then or later about his understanding of Roosevelt's motives. "Why the president insisted on my going I still do not know," Byrnes wrote more than ten years after his trip to Yalta. With keen understatement, Byrnes added, "Perhaps it was because I had a reputation with the Congress and the public for being more conservative than other members of our delegation, such as Stettinius and Hopkins." But despite his supposed puzzlement at FDR's motives, Byrnes did finally accept Roosevelt's offer. Byrnes apparently had his own plans for Yalta, intending as the price of his later help with Congress to participate in the conference more fully than the president intended.

As for Franklin Roosevelt, he characteristically talked about all the reasons he wanted Jimmy Byrnes to go with him on the Crimean trip except what was quite likely his main reason. In urging Byrnes to join him on the Yalta journey, Roosevelt in late January 1945 made the curiously humorous argument that their presence at the conference was needed on the grounds of health. "We are the only two well men in the crowd," he joked with Byrnes.

Sixty-one days after the adjournment of the Yalta conference, on February 11, 1945, Franklin Roosevelt was dead of a massive cerebral hemorrhage, suffered while he was resting in Warm Springs, Georgia. Once more, Jimmy Byrnes was to be the beneficiary of the timely death of a patron. Roosevelt's death could not give Byrnes the presidency, as so many in the Democratic party had feared, and some perhaps had hoped, at the convention less than a year earlier. But having been served so well during his lifetime by Jimmy Byrnes, FDR posthumously gave one last, best gift to his ambitious subordinate. Roosevelt unintentionally made Byrnes into a perceived expert on Yalta and other international affairs.

In insisting that Jimmy Byrnes accompany him to Yalta, Roosevelt had intended to use Byrnes as little more than a domestic political messenger with senators after the conference. But with FDR so soon gone, the new president, Harry Truman, saw Byrnes as the only credible participant who knew, in Truman's later words, "what went on at Yalta." Jimmy Byrnes did not contradict this opinion, and FDR was no longer there to gainsay this version of events. As a result, Jimmy Byrnes, who before Roosevelt's death could have hoped to influence Stettinius only as a private citizen after retirement, soon replaced him as secretary of state. Two months after Roosevelt's death, Byrnes once more stood near the Rose Garden to take an oath of office, this time an oath placing him next in succession to the presidency. Particularly after the death of a patron, Jimmy Byrnes always had made the most of what he was given.

Byrnes joined Roosevelt and other members of the presidential party in boarding the cruiser *Quincy* at Norfolk, Virginia, and departing for Yalta before the sun rose on the morning of January 23, 1945. Byrnes endured, along with all others on board, a storm-tossed, nine-day passage across the Atlantic. Characteristically, Byrnes was cordial toward Ed Flynn during the forced society of the voyage, and by the end of the Yalta conference Byrnes would be discussing the intricacies of domestic politics with Flynn as if no disputes over race had ever passed between them in Chicago. As for Roosevelt, he remained below deck in his cabin for most of the voyage, attempting to recover from a bad cold he had caught at his inaugural, and he usually joined the other passengers for a few hours only at lunch and dinner. Byrnes was seated next to Roosevelt for meals throughout the voyage, and occasionally the president rallied his spirits sufficiently to try to get a rise out of his old friend and new messmate. On the first Saturday out from land, FDR called for the table's attention, and with a facetious and pious face announced, "Father Flynn will say Mass tomorrow." Jimmy Byrnes laughed as well as any of them. Roosevelt was a merciless tease when he was feeling well, and he always seemed to enjoy selecting those who were closest to him for those kinds of jokes.

After the *Quincy*'s arrival in the Mediterranean Sea and the transfer of its passengers to U.S. military airplanes on the island of Malta, the delegation flew on to the Crimea, landing there on February 3. The American delegation was housed by its Russian hosts at a former summer palace of the czars known as the Livadia, near the town of Yalta. The fifty-room palace of very pale limestone and marble was approximately the color and the area of the White House, and Byrnes was assigned living quarters on the first floor of the three-story building close to FDR's own rooms. Not far from Byrnes' quarters was a former billiard parlor that had been converted into a private dining room for Roosevelt during his stay at the palace, and the president invited Byrnes to take his meals there with him.

But any hopes on Jimmy Byrnes' part that as a result of his physical proximity to FDR he was to be taken into the president's confidence at the Yalta conference came to an abrupt end the next afternoon, February 4. Roosevelt, Stalin, and Churchill gathered then shortly after five o'clock in the Livadia palace's ballroom for their first plenipotentiary, or Big Three, meeting to discuss the final military offensive against Germany. Byrnes joined the other U.S., British, and Russian advisers who were to accompany their respective leaders into this meeting. But the Soviet guard at the ballroom door did not find Byrnes' name on the list of those authorized by the United States for admittance. Embarrassed and angry, Byrnes walked away. Apparently neither the president nor his secretary of state had thought it sufficiently important for the United States' industrial war mobilizer to attend this first meeting. Byrnes heatedly swore to other members of the presidential party outside the ballroom, "I did not come along for the ride," and returned to his rooms.

Anna Boettiger, the president's daughter, who accompanied Roosevelt to the Crimea to oversee the care of FDR's health, later told Jonathan Daniels that Byrnes shortly thereafter "behaved dreadfully," in Daniels' words, and "made something approximating a scene with her father." Whatever the temper of their exchange, Byrnes must have made it clear to Roosevelt that, unlike Ed Flynn, he did not consider himself invited along just for the ride. If Roosevelt wanted the benefits of Byrnes' conservative reputation and of his personal word in obtaining congressional support of the Yalta accords, Jimmy Byrnes would have to be in the room when those accords were discussed. Roosevelt thereafter included Byrnes in the plenipotentiary meetings, seating him in a place of honor at the conference table in the Livadia ballroom, on the president's left and separated from him only by Roosevelt's translator of Russian, Charles Bohlen.

Roosevelt also made it a point to invite Byrnes to most of the purely social lunches and to the state dinners given each night after the plenipotentiary meetings, allowing Byrnes the opportunity to talk and drink informally with Winston Churchill, Joseph Stalin, and the other members of the foreign delegations. (The vodka consumed in mutual international toasts on these occasions—on one night more than forty such toasts were proposed and drunk—reminded Byrnes of "new corn," or unaged moonshine.) Byrnes and Churchill, who had met once before briefly, at the White House in 1943, got along at the Yalta conference particularly well; Churchill later said that although he saw Jimmy Byrnes too infrequently, he liked what he saw of him. V. M. Molotov, the Soviet foreign minister, would comment that he remembered Byrnes quite well from Yalta, after Molotov a few months later was told of Byrnes' appointment to State. As for Marshal Stalin, for the moment he kept any observations on Byrnes to himself; in Moscow, Stalin later said that Jimmy Byrnes was "the most honest-looking horse thief" he had ever met.

Jimmy Byrnes did no horse stealing or horse trading at this conference. Although he had gained admission to the plenipotentiary sessions, Byrnes was there as an observer. He did not participate in the discussions, nor did he attend the daily sessions of the Big Three foreign ministers held before each of the plenipotentiary meetings. It was at these sessions involving Stettinius and his Soviet and British counterparts that the specifics of the issues under negotiation at Yalta frequently were actually resolved. The reputation of Jimmy Byrnes in Washington after the conference as an expert on "what went on at Yalta" was not the result of anything Byrnes said while in the Crimea. It was the result of his recording what other people said. In a re-creation of his entry into domestic politics in South Carolina as a court reporter, Byrnes marked his entry into diplomacy by keeping a stenographic record of the comments at Yalta of Roosevelt, Churchill, Stalin, and their advisers.

Byrnes attended four of the six plenipotentiary meetings held between February 4 and February 9, and at each of them, sometimes writing with his hands and notebook concealed under the conference table while Stalin spoke, he took down a verbatim account of what he heard. He eventually filled forty-seven notebook pages with the McKee's New Standard system of shorthand characters he had learned in Charleston nearly half a century earlier. His transcribed notes do not vary substantially in content from the much more general statements of agreement publicly issued at the close of the Crimean conference. And others representing the U.S. State Department at the conference, including Roosevelt's translator, Charles "Chip" Bohlen, and Secretary Stettinius, also kept occasional personal notes on the conference as part of the expected routine. But the shorthand notes made independently by Byrnes provided an unprecedented word-for-word account of discussions among Roosevelt, Churchill, and Stalin on two of the Yalta agreements that later proved to be the most controversial in the United States.

These two decisions, after long discussion in plenipotentiary meetings, were the Western Allies' de facto recognition of the Soviet-dominated government already present in liberated Poland, as opposed to recognizing a non-Communist government operating in exile (supporting the "Lublin" Poles over the "London" Poles), and Roosevelt's and Churchill's agreement to grant three votes to the USSR as opposed to one vote for the United States in the proposed General Assembly as the price of Soviet support of the United Nations organization. Byrnes probably decided to transcribe the give-and-take on these agreements at the conference table as a service to Roosevelt. Byrnes was looking ahead to presenting evidence to conservative congressmen that FDR had not compromised any more than was necessary at the Yalta conference in order to keep the cooperation of the Soviets.

But the verbatim notes made by Jimmy Byrnes at Yalta very likely were more help than FDR actually wanted. Roosevelt had always been made very uneasy by knowing that audio transcriptions were being made of his private conversations. The use of a concealed microphone for tape-recording conversations in the Oval Office, installed in 1940 to prevent visitors from later misquoting the president, had been discontinued by Roosevelt after a few months. Nor had Roosevelt earlier in the war asked for or required transcriptions to be made of his conversations with Churchill at the Cairo conference or with Stalin and Churchill at the Teheran conference.

Roosevelt did not ask Byrnes to stop taking his shorthand notes at the Yalta conference, but he doubtless felt relief when Byrnes announced he was considering leaving the Crimea early on February 10, one day before the conference adjourned. Byrnes was troubled by reports he had been receiving from his congressional contacts in Washington. They described a growing domestic opposition to a bill Byrnes had drafted before leaving for Yalta to expand the "work or fight" order to include one million more civilian U.S. workers. The political coterie at the OWMR was urging Byrnes to return and lobby Congress personally for passage of this national service bill. Roosevelt himself encouraged Byrnes to take an early military flight out of the Crimea; FDR probably was delighted at the prospect of having Jimmy Byrnes back lobbying with Congress, where he felt Byrnes belonged, rather than taking notes at the plenipotentiary conferences. Additionally, the president asked Byrnes to give the first news conference to the U.S. media on the Yalta meeting as soon as he returned, and Byrnes agreed.

He was as good as his word. Arriving back in Washington by airplane on Tuesday, February 13, while Roosevelt continued his slower return aboard the *Quincy*, Byrnes immediately called a national press and radio conference. Speculation was intense among journalists and congressmen, as well as laypersons, over the agreements made at the Yalta conference, which journalists had been prohibited from attending or reporting on because of wartime censorship. Other than the official communiqué issued by the Allies at the close of the conference, Byrnes' version of events provided the first opportunity for journalists or the public to learn of the Yalta accords. Byrnes gave a masterly performance.

Byrnes had invited the overflow crowd of journalists to meet with him on his territory, at the East Wing inside a large room designated by Roosevelt in 1942 to be used as a movie theater by the White House residents and staff. As a result of wartime economies, the theater had been decorated with odds and ends left over from other White House construction, and it was painted in garish mismatches and hung with odd, orange-colored drapes. Byrnes began the news conference, according to the White House transcript, by thanking the "ladies and gentlemen" for coming on such short notice "to this funeral parlor with Hollywood parentage. (Laughter)." Thereafter, he continued by his adroit phrasing and his use of humor to hold in the palm of his hand what could have been a hostile group of questioners on Yalta. A reporter asked about a statement released that day by the London-based Polish government in exile, which denounced the Yalta agreement's recognition of the Lublin government as a betrayal of all non-Communist Poles. Byrnes turned the question aside and minimized the profound differences between the two groups in their plans for the government of postwar Poland. He joked that reporters could expect that there would be just as much difference in statements of facts issued by the London Poles and by the Stalinist Poles in Lublin as there were differences in statements of facts "made to the president by the Republican National Committee and the Democratic National Committee. (Laughter)."

Byrnes at this news conference, also at Roosevelt's prior request, did not discuss that the USSR had been allowed three votes in the proposed General Assembly of the UN, to the United States' one vote, telling the reporters only that the voting procedures for the United Nations organization had been "adopted as proposed" by FDR at the Yalta conference. Jimmy Byrnes finished his conference by giving the print and wire reporters assembled in the movie-viewing room at the East Wing what the writers termed "color," describing for them "the kind of uniform Stalin wore, and how he looked, the weather, and that sort of thing."

Byrnes' descriptions of the Yalta meeting and his words of confidence in its accords later were incorporated by journalists into the narratives they wrote to accompany newsreels on Yalta shown at movie theaters across the United States that week of February 13. Much of the initially favorable public reaction to the Yalta agreements and Byrnes' reputation as an expert on Yalta originated in this first, successful news conference.

Privately, Byrnes after his news conference lobbied with conservative senators such as Tom Connally and Arthur Vandenberg of the Foreign Relations Committee for support of the proposed United Nations treaty on much less optimistic grounds. Although, again at Roosevelt's request, Byrnes did not reveal the agreement on additional Soviet votes, Byrnes prepared the senators for the later disclosure of controversial Yalta details by arguing that Roosevelt at the conference had struck the best bargains possible, given the U.S. policy objective of keeping Soviet cooperation in the UN and the presence of large Soviet occupation armies throughout Eastern Europe. The comparative ease with which the UN treaty was later ratified by the Senate can be directly attributed to the fact that Jimmy Byrnes, known by senators to be a hard bargainer and also known to be by then politically independent of FDR, was nevertheless willing to vouch for the practicality of Roosevelt's dream of an international peace organization.

Roosevelt, back aboard the *Quincy* crossing the Atlantic, was being kept apprised by others in Washington of Jimmy Byrnes' behind-the-scenes work for the administration. "We are a day out and the trip has been excellent thus far," Roosevelt wrote in a dispatch received by Byrnes on February 26. "I think your press conferences have been grand." But FDR's fine words of praise no longer buttered any parsnips for Jimmy Byrnes. Within less than a month after receiving this message, Byrnes handed Roosevelt, then back in the capital, a typed letter of resignation from the OWMR. Byrnes noted in this March 24, 1945, letter that he had not initially planned to resign until after the final defeat of Germany; but now, Byrnes wrote FDR, "I do not think V-E Day is far off." Byrnes therefore wrote that his resignation would take effect in scarcely more than a week, on April 2.

Byrnes also informally told Roosevelt as he handed him the letter of resignation that, in Byrnes' words, he "was not mad at anybody" about the president's choice of a vice-presidential candidate at Chicago. There is every reason to believe Jimmy Byrnes. He had worked off the anger that had so startled Marvin Jones, and he had honorably repaid the president for the gift of the trip to Yalta by building a political consensus for the proposed new UN. Byrnes was disillusioned and tired, but he probably was no longer angry with FDR.

Roosevelt declared himself "knocked off my feet" by Byrnes' resignation, but he must have anticipated Byrnes' early departure since his choice of Stettinius as secretary of state the previous fall. Byrnes and his wife were to remain in Washington until April 7, awaiting the congressional confirmation of his successor at the OWMR. Thereafter, they planned to return to Spartanburg.

"I just hate to have you go," Roosevelt wrote in a personal note sent to Byrnes the day after receiving his letter of resignation. "I shall miss you and Maude more than I can tell you, but be sure before you take up anything else to get a bit of real rest." What, if anything, was meant by the "anything else" in terms of Byrnes' possible service later to the Roosevelt administration FDR did not specify. A letter written by Roosevelt for publication six days later formally accepting Byrnes' resignation seems to imply that FDR was considering calling on Byrnes for possible work in negotiating the postwar settlements or in the United Nations.

"It is not pleasant to contemplate the severance of a relationship which has been as delightful to me personally as it has been to the national interest which you have served with such singular devotion and fidelity," Roosevelt wrote in this letter of March 31, 1945. By that date FDR had preceded Jimmy and Maude Byrnes in traveling South, and FDR was himself in Warm Springs, Georgia, for a period of rest. "Although you go," this letter continued, "I shall like to think that at any time in the future I can avail myself of your wisdom, knowledge, and understanding. Always sincerely. . . ."

An aide in Warm Springs who brought the final copy of this letter for Roosevelt to sign late in the afternoon of March 31 remarked that Byrnes' retirement was a loss both to the justice and to the nation. "Yes," FDR replied, in a voice that seemed weary to the aide, and added, "It's a shame some people are so prima-donnish." Twelve days later, Jimmy Byrnes, then back in Spartanburg, heard on a local radio news bulletin that President Roosevelt had died.

———

"Can you find Jimmy Byrnes for me?" asked Harry Truman in a telephone call to Jonathan Daniels at the White House the evening of April 12, 1945, after Truman had taken his oath as president. Byrnes was located at the Spartanburg radio station of his business associate Walter Brown, and a military airplane was dispatched to South Carolina to pick up Byrnes and return him to Washington. Before boarding the airplane, Byrnes sent a "Dear Harry" telegram informing the new president that he would be at the OWMR office by the next morning.

But it was not to resume his prior work at the war mobilization office that Truman had called on Byrnes. Jimmy Byrnes rode with Truman on the train to Hyde Park for Roosevelt's burial services there on April 15, and after that necessary sacred business was finished, they attended to some necessary secular business. After the trip back Truman told Byrnes of his intention to ask for the resignation of Edward Stettinius, Jr., and to appoint Jimmy Byrnes as secretary of state. Byrnes repeated then to Truman only what he had said earlier to FDR, that he was interested in serving the cause the peace any way that he could; but there was also an unspoken understanding between these two men who had had such dissimilar fates at Chicago. The appointment to State would place Jimmy Byrnes next in succession to the presidency under the constitutional conditions then pertaining. The appointment would, in Truman's later explanation, "balance things up" for FDR's sudden withdrawal of public support for Byrnes at the 1944 convention. Truman's offer and Byrnes' acceptance of it that same day reveal that each man acted under a political code of values that went beyond the simple demands of personality or ambition. Jimmy Byrnes was no sorehead, and he did not hold a grudge against Truman. Similarly, Harry Truman was no welsher. He paid his political debts, even when they had been originally incurred by the man they had left behind at Hyde Park.

Stettinius actually had proved to be a highly effective secretary that April in preparing for the organizing assembly at San Francisco of the future United Nations, having assisted in obtaining Soviet agreement for the San Francisco assembly while at the Yalta conference. But a deal was a deal. Truman and Byrnes agreed that Byrnes would be named to Stettinius' position as soon as the current secretary ended his work at San Francisco and his resignation could be requested, probably by late June or early July. Typically respectful of others' feelings, as well as cagey, Jimmy Byrnes proposed that in order to spare Stettinius any personal or political embarrassment, he would return to Spartanburg and visit the White House only under circumstances allowing him to avoid publicity until his appointment was announced later that summer.

Byrnes' reputation as an insider at Yalta was a secondary reason for Truman's wanting to place the former OWMR director in charge at State as soon as possible, and was yet another instance of Roosevelt's posthumously advancing Byrnes' career in the first weeks of the Truman presidency. "He'd been to Yalta," Truman explained later when asked about his choice of Byrnes, "and he'd made a good many notes, and I wanted him to tell me what he remembered, and later to transcribe the notes he'd made, which he did."

Byrnes had sent fourteen pages of these notes, with impressive maroon-colored binding, to Truman by the second week of his presidency. Of course, Byrnes' shorthand notes were incomplete, because he did not attend all of the plenipotentiary sessions at Yalta and none of the foreign ministers meetings; more comprehensive documents on the Yalta conference were available to Truman at the time from the State Department under Stettinius. But Truman had made up his mind to follow the advice in foreign relations of this "hard hitting trader for the homefront," as he characterized Byrnes in his diary, rather than what he called "the smart boys in the State Department." Among the mistrusted smart boys, presumably, was Stettinius.

Byrnes did not possess as many secrets as he implied to Harry Truman during the new president's first weeks in office. As a result of Roosevelt's encouraging Byrnes to leave the Yalta conference a day early, for example, Byrnes had not been present for the seventh and last plenipotentiary session, at which Roosevelt had obtained the Soviet Union's promise to enter the war against Japan in exchange for Soviet occupation rights of the Kuril Islands and other rights in the Far East. But if Jimmy Byrnes in early 1945 did not possess knowledge of top-secret agreements made at Yalta for the defeat of Japan and for the Allied disposition of postwar Asia, he did know one big secret. This knowledge also was a gift from Roosevelt. Byrnes told Truman about the atomic bomb.

15

Politics
and the Bomb

"**D**ear Harry," Jimmy Byrnes in Spartanburg, South Carolina, began a telegram he sent to the nation's new president the evening of April 12, 1945. "I will be [at the] Office [of War] Mobilization tomorrow. If I can be of service, call on me." Byrnes found no inappropriateness in sending a telegram to the new thirty-third president of the United States familiarly addressed as "Harry." After all, less than nine months earlier, the junior senator Harry Truman had come to Byrnes' hotel suite and rehearsed for Byrnes the speech he had expected to deliver in Chicago nominating Byrnes for the vice presidency. And from another historical perspective, Jimmy Byrnes in the hectic hours after FDR's death on April 12, can perhaps be forgiven for writing to Harry S. Truman in a familiar, and possibly slightly patronizing, manner. On the afternoon that Franklin Roosevelt died, the former "assistant president" was in possession of a crucial fact that he knew was unknown to Truman: that the United States was manufacturing the world's first atomic bomb.

Truman first heard of the bomb's existence the same night that Byrnes sent his telegram to the White House, when Secretary of War Henry Stimson stayed behind after a brief meeting in the Cabinet Room following

Truman's taking of the presidential oath. "Stimson told me that he wanted me to know about an immense project that was under way—a project looking to the development of a new explosive of almost unbelievable destructive power," Truman later wrote in his memoirs. "That was all he felt free to say at the time, and his statement left me puzzled. It was the first bit of information that had come to me about the atomic bomb, but he gave me no details."

Jimmy Byrnes was the man who gave Truman a few details about the bomb early the next morning, when Byrnes met with him after arriving in Washington from his overnight flight from Spartanburg. Truman later wrote that Byrnes, "with great solemnity," told him "that we were perfecting an explosive great enough to destroy the whole world." Either then or during another of his frequent, unannounced visits to Washington before his becoming secretary of state, Byrnes on one occasion also told Truman what was more than simply a "detail" about the atomic bomb. Truman recorded that, in an early conversation, Byrnes stated to him the belief that, in Truman's words, "the bomb might well put us in a position to dictate our own terms at the end of the war."

Byrnes had known in general about the development of some sort of new weapon under the top-secret Manhattan Project since at least the autumn of 1943. But despite the impression Byrnes later made in telling Truman in the spring of 1945 about an explosive "great enough to destroy the whole world," Byrnes' concern with the Manhattan Project from the start of his knowledge about the project had had little to do with "solemnity" and a great deal with domestic politics.

This was a concern Byrnes carried with him to his membership on the Interim Committee, formed by Truman in late April to advise him on the future control of the bomb. On this committee, Jimmy Byrnes and his domestic political viewpoints prevailed; and four months later, in August 1945, at the end of a world war that seemed to have produced the most terrible ironies of the twentieth century, there came this one final irony: the atomic bomb was dropped on Japan not with the calculation that mankind now had an explosive powerful enough to destroy the entire world and that the concept of warfare and political conflict was therefore irrevocably changed. Nor was it used primarily because of any geopolitical strategy by Byrnes or Truman of "dictating our own terms at the end of the war." The bomb was used because Byrnes and Truman in August of 1945 were too good a pair of domestic politicians not to use it.

Byrnes as the director of the Office of War Mobilization had been quick in 1943 to detect the vast allocations of materials and funds to a Manhattan Project, the purpose of which was at first irritatingly unspecified to him. Byrnes had been equally quick to see the possible adverse political consequences to the administration if the project failed. On September 11, 1943, less than four months after FDR appointed him director of the OWM, Byrnes wrote to Secretary of War Henry Stimson to complain of "the secret Army construction which is comprised under the category of 'Manhattan'." Byrnes pointed out in this letter that the Manhattan Project alone was expected to cost more than one billion dollars by the end of that year and that it was receiving 20 percent more of the nation's carbon steel allocations than all other industrial and Army construction combined. Jimmy Byrnes wanted to know what all this steel, money, and other material was being used to build, and why he was not being told by Stimson or anyone else why there was such a high priority for this Manhattan Project.

"I know that the War Department may have some enterprise so important and so secret that it might be unwilling to divulge the purpose or details even to the Office of War Mobilization," Byrnes wrote to Stimson with a edge of sarcasm that was unusual for Byrnes. "However, you and I should assure ourselves that the projects included under 'Manhattan' are of such character and that zealous officials do not use the convenience of high priorities and secrecy attached to 'Manhattan' for the purpose of securing material for unrelated purposes. If not, then this project will sooner or later reach a point where such huge expenditures of public funds and use of such high priority material and labor will have to be justified."

Byrnes' files do not contain a written response from Stimson, but Byrnes must have been informed in greater detail orally, probably by him or later by General Leslie Groves, military director of the Manhattan Project, because Byrnes by mid-July 1994 had recommended to Roosevelt that antitrust charges against the Du Pont company be dropped for the "successful outcome of our project of highest priority, S-1." Groves had also met with Byrnes at the OWM's cramped quarters at the White House in mid-December 1944. The least politic of men, Groves had wanted Byrnes to use his well-known persuasive skills to persuade organized labor not to hold public hearings, as the unions were entitled to do under law, on the military's barring of union organizers from the Manhattan Project's power plant and industrial city in Oak Ridge, Tennessee. Groves that day explained enough about the Manhattan Project to Byrnes that the OWM director appreciated the need "to maintain a secrecy beyond that of any other project," in Byrnes' later words. Byrnes and Groves subsequently met at the OWM rooms with the leaders of the affected unions. Byrnes did most of the talking and, without telling them all that he knew, sufficiently impressed the union leaders with the need in the name of national security to keep the closed shops at Oak Ridge.

But not everyone would be persuaded so easily after the war, particularly if it could not be demonstrated to Congress that the bomb had been militarily practical or even needed to end the war. By the best OWM estimates, the cost for the Manhattan Project was expected to have doubled before the end of 1945. If the bomb proved undeliverable, Byrnes knew, even the presence by his side at future congressional hearings of an intimidating, bearlike general like Leslie Groves would not be sufficient to stop embarrassing questions in Congress about where all that money in the Manhattan Project had gone. In preparing for their meeting in late 1944 with the labor organizers in regard to Oak Ridge, Groves and Undersecretary of War Robert Patterson both had promised Byrnes that the physicists of the Manhattan Project would know by April 1, 1945, whether or not an atomic bomb could be built. But by early March the OWM had not received any word on whether the Manhattan Project would meet its deadline for the bomb, and Jimmy Byrnes was worried. This time he took his political concerns directly to the president, bypassing both General Groves and the War Department. Byrnes sent a memorandum to Roosevelt on March 3, 1945, warning him of political storm clouds ahead over the construction of the atomic bomb.

"I understand that the expenditures for the Manhattan Project are approaching two billion dollars with no definite assurance yet of production," Byrnes began his memorandum. "We have succeeded to date in obtaining the co-operation of congressional committees in secret hearings. Perhaps we can continue to do so while the war lasts."

Byrnes then conceded to FDR in the memorandum, "I know little of this project except that it is supported by eminent scientists." But with two billion dollars vanished into the thin air of the Manhattan Project by early 1945 and no confirmed delivery date of any results yet available to him, Jimmy Byrnes wanted FDR to know that he smelled political trouble. "Even eminent scientists may continue a project rather than concede its failure," Byrnes wrote FDR. "Also, it may be feasible to continue the experiment on a reduced basis."

The possibility of congressional investigations deeply worried Byrnes. Although he admitted to FDR at the beginning of the memorandum that he knew little about the Manhattan Project, Byrnes already was an old hand at the adversarial use of congressional postwar investigations. Byrnes could remember from his own terms in Congress how Republican charges of fiscal mismanagement of the First World War had contributed to the Democratic party's loss of control of Congress and of the presidency itself in the elections of 1920. The partisan charges had continued to surface as late as 1935, when Byrnes had found it necessary to testify before a Senate investigatory committee in defense of Bernard Baruch, who had been accused that year by Republican senators of personal financial dishonesty in his 1918–19 chairmanship of the War Industries Board. Byrnes could expect that he himself would be just as tempting a target after this war because of his own directorship at the OWM and of the much greater amounts of money Roosevelt had ordered put into the Manhattan Project.

Byrnes warned Roosevelt in his memorandum that if after the war the Manhattan Project was publicly disclosed to have been a failure, the two of them could expect to see "relentless investigation and criticism."

Byrnes then suggested in his memorandum that an independent review panel of qualified nuclear physicists not already working on the Manhattan Project be appointed by FDR to review the likelihood of the project's success. "Such a review might hurt the feelings of those now engaged in the project," Byrnes wrote. "Still, two billion dollars is enough money to risk such hurt." Byrnes' suggestion reveals the limits of his knowledge about the project, as all such qualified physicists in this country acceptable to Groves' security checks already were part of the Manhattan Project. But Byrnes' call for a review panel to issue such a finding, whether favorable or unfavorable, also reveals how large a problem was the issue of domestic political liability as perceived by Byrnes if the Manhattan Project failed. "A favorable finding would justify the continuance, regardless of future success or failure," Byrnes wrote to FDR about the advisability of a review panel. "An unfavorable finding would at least indicate the need for further justification by those who are responsible for the project.

"In any event," Byrnes concluded, "it would be clear that we were mindful of the tremendous expenditure of men and materials."

Roosevelt discussed Byrnes' memorandum on March 15, 1945, with Secretary of War Stimson, who told FDR that Byrnes' domestic political concerns were "jittery and nervous and rather silly." Stimson was certain that an atomic bomb could be produced and be ready for combat use within perhaps four or five months. The real issue, Stimson told Roosevelt, was whether the United States intended to attempt to maintain its monopoly on atomic weaponry after the war, or to attempt to set up some sort of international control and exchange of information on atomic weapons. The Danish nuclear physicist and Nobel laureate Niels Bohr had in a meeting the previous year with FDR had urged him to initiate such an international exchange of research between the United States and the two Allied countries next most likely to develop atomic weapons, Great Britain and the Soviet Union. Roosevelt at this meeting with Stimson indicated that he would decide between the postwar options of monopoly or international control in the next few months before the bomb was used.

But in less than thirty days after this March meeting, Stimson was talking about the Manhattan Project to a different U.S. president, a man who was much less informed and much less confident about atomic energy than Roosevelt had been. Truman, like Byrnes, was a product of the congressional hierarchy, and for at least the first year of his administration he shared Jimmy Byrnes' belief that in taking a new action there was nothing so safe politically as a prestigious review panel or a decision by committee. (The famous "The Buck Stops Here" sign was in April 1945 at least three years away from being placed on Truman's Oval Office desk.) At this same time, Stimson had been receiving advice in early spring of 1945 from his subordinates in the War Department on the political desirability of the president's forming an advisory civilian panel to discuss the use of the bomb and to make recommendations to Congress for the possible international control. When the war secretary in early May suggested the idea for such an advisory committee to the president, Truman readily agreed.

Stimson later also suggested that the president appoint one member expressly as Truman's personal representative on the committee. Stimson described this ideal candidate in a memorandum to Truman as a man "with whom the president has close personal relations" and "who was able to keep his mouth shut." Harry Truman had an immediate choice for this position, and Stimson agreed enthusiastically: James F. Byrnes.

So it happened that Jimmy Byrnes, who from the beginning of his limited knowledge about the Manhattan Project had been concerned almost exclusively with avoiding political scandal at the OWM, was chosen on May 3, 1945, as the president's personal representative on the Interim Committee. (The committee's name itself was selected with political sensitivity by Stimson, to indicate to members of Congress that after the war the executive branch had no permanent intentions of setting atomic policy without congressional participation.) Truman, from his conversation with Byrnes on his first full day of the presidency, may have mistakenly regarded Byrnes as something of an expert on the bomb; Secretary Stimson, who at times was inclining toward Niels Bohr's advocacy of international control of atomic weaponry, may have mistakenly believed that Byrnes' presence on the committee would increase the likelihood of congressional support for such control. Byrnes himself, although he quickly agreed to Truman's request that he serve on the advisory group, kept his own counsel about what he planned to do on the Interim Committee. Until his most opportune time, Jimmy Byrnes knew how to keep his mouth shut.

Events were moving quickly even before the Interim Committee's first meeting, on May 9. On May 8 the supreme Allied commander, Dwight D. Eisenhower, announced the achievement of V-E Day: Germany, having been racked throughout 1944–45 with night-and-day bombing attacks by Anglo-American air forces that had killed at least 600,000 of its civilians, unable to repel the American and other Allied armies at the Elbe River, and occupied by Soviet armies in Berlin, had accepted terms of unconditional surrender. The war in the European theater effectively was over. The Soviet Union, which previously had maintained a nonaggression pact with Japan, now was expected within a few months to start transferring troops and armored divisions to the Manchurian frontier in anticipation of a declaration of war on Japan, as had been agreed at the Yalta conference. Japan thus was fighting alone, with no credible evidence available to the Allies in May or June that its current government was willing to accept unconditional surrender, and this turn of events meant that Japan was the sole Axis country discussed by the Interim Committee as the target of an atomic bomb.

On the day Eisenhower announced Germany's surrender, Byrnes spent two hours with Stimson, the two of them talking alone at Stimson's office at the Pentagon. It was probably at this V-E Day meeting that Byrnes first was told in some detail by Stimson of the plans then being prepared by the Joint Chiefs of Staff to bring an end to the Pacific war by American invasions of the main Japanese islands. The tentative date for the first push by U.S. Marines and infantry onto the southernmost of the main Japanese islands, which the Pentagon code-named Operation Olympic, was November 1, 1945. The next invasion, aimed at landing U.S. troops on the populous Japanese island containing the Tokyo plain, code-named Operation Coronet, was tentatively set for March 1, 1946. The butcher's bill would be high for both military operations. The Japanese were expected by U.S. planners to resist this invasion of their homeland by fighting with all possible means, including not only kamikaze air attacks and the suicidal resistance of soldiers fighting from caves but also the arming of children and the elderly with sharpened bamboo stakes to fight the Americans. Casualties for the U.S. forces were estimated by General Douglas MacArthur at perhaps 31,800 for the first thirty days of fighting in November. As many as 500,000 to 1,000,000 American men might be dead, wounded, or missing before the combined Olympic/Coronet invasions could force the Japanese to surrender by the spring of 1946.

Byrnes subsequently mentioned discussing these anticipated invasion casualties with other members of the Interim Committee before the end of May, Byrnes never doubted the willingness of the Japanese soldiers and civilians to fight to their last old man or young boy. His certitude that the Japanese people would be more "fanatical" in their resistance unless shocked by the use of the atomic bomb was not racist, as a postwar generation of revisionist American historians would claim; contrary to the assumptions of some revisionists, Byrnes could better understand the motivation of Japanese resistance *because he was a southerner.*

It must be remembered that Jimmy Byrnes had been born at Charleston only seventeen years after the final battles of another total war when an invading U.S. army also insisting upon unconditional surrender had been met with die-hard resistance in 1864–65 by Confederate soldiers and civilians aged from sixty to sixteen years. The resisting teenage soldiers included the future senator Ben Tillman.) Byrnes knew firsthand from his upbringing in the South how fiercely a culturally and religiously insular people, with a traditional reverence for land and for military valor, would resist invaders they considered their inferiors. Herbert Feis, in 1945 the main economic adviser to the Department of State and later a leading nonrevisionist historian of the Second World War, knew Byrnes personally, and he emphasized in his histories how among other factors this historical awareness of "how the hopelessly beaten Confederate army had battled on" affected the decision makers in regard to using the atomic bomb against Japan.

After two hours talking alone with Stimson, Byrnes was joined in the secretary's office that afternoon by General Groves and by Stimson's special assistants at the War Department, George Harrison and Harvey Bundy. A second meeting was then held. "We all discussed the function of the proposed Interim Committee," Stimson later wrote in his diary. "During the meeting it became very evident what a tremendous help Byrnes would be as a member of the committee."

The following day, May 9, the Interim Committee met for the first time at Stimson's paneled office in the Pentagon. Byrnes was pointedly introduced by Stimson to the other members as the president's personal representative. The war secretary was to be the committee's chairman, with Harrison as alternate chairman, and apart from Byrnes there were five additional original members of the Interim Committee: Ralph Bard, an undersecretary of the navy; William Clayton, an assistant secretary at the State Department; Vannevar Bush, a former dean of engineering at the Massachusetts Institute of Technology and now director of the U.S. Office of Scientific Research and Development; James Conant, a distinguished chemist and president of Harvard University, who directed the Manhattan Project's fission work and who reported to Bush; and Karl Compton, a noted physicist and president of MIT. It was an impressive membership that could not have been equaled in either scientific accomplishments or political acumen. The latter was clearly important, as shown by the inclusion of Byrnes, Clayton from State, and Bard from the Navy, all of whom had to briefed by Stimson in order to bring their knowledge of the Manhattan Project up to that of Bush, Conant, and Compton. And as was shown clear by Stimson's introduction of Byrnes as the president's personal representative and later by Byrnes' own actions on this unequaled committee, Jimmy Byrnes intended to be first among the equals.

During its next three meetings, in May, the Interim Committee, before considering recommendations on the use of the atomic bomb, first discussed the issue of the postwar international exchange of atomic research and the inspection of civilian and military atomic facilities. Bohr had warned both Roosevelt and Churchill that the alternative to the presence of international control and inspection was a dangerous postwar arms race among all nations, including the Soviet Union, where Bohr expected an atomic bomb to be developed within a few years. Bush and Conant, in a memorandum sent to Stimson in September 1944, had urged that the United States initiate such a postwar agreement. But now, as the Interim Committee in the weeks after V-E Day considered the issue of the United States' sharing

atomic research with Great Britain and the Soviet Union, there was a new
voice to be heard. "Mr. Byrnes made short work of this line of argument,"
Conant was soon to write to Bush.

Vannevar Bush was absent from the Interim Committee's meeting on
May 18 at which this issue was discussed, and Conant filled in for Bush
the details of Jimmy Byrnes' chopping down the idea of international
cooperation. Sharing atomic research with the United States' closest ally,
Great Britain, let alone with the Soviet Union, could be politically untenable in Congress, Byrnes argued, as almost every major U.S. university
and major war contractor had contributed research to the Manhattan Project. "I can foresee a great deal of trouble on this front," Conant wrote in
regard to Byrnes' misgivings. Conant also warned Bush about the consequences of the committee's discussion on May 18 of an earlier agreement
at Quebec in 1944 between Roosevelt and Churchill for Anglo-American
sharing of atomic research. The agreement was shown to Byrnes at that
day's meeting, and he read it carefully, Conant informed Bush. "It was
interesting that Mr. Byrnes felt that Congress would be most curious about
this matter," Conant wrote.

Byrnes prevailed. Stimson, Bush, and Conant had all at various times
since 1944 expressed a qualified approval of the international inspection
and free exchange of atomic research among the Allies after the war's end.
Even the Army's chief of staff, General George Marshall, in an invited
appearance at the Interim Committee's next meeting, on May 31, speculated aloud that, in the version of his words recorded in the minutes of
the committee, "it might be desirable to invite two prominent Russian
scientists to witness the test" of the atomic weapon planned within a few
months at Alamogordo, New Mexico. Compton of MIT also spoke at that
meeting on the inevitability of the Soviet Union's scientists achieving an
atomic bomb within a few years and of the necessity of the United States'
establishing a process of international control and shared research. But
Byrnes' concerns about the domestic political culpability in giving away
two billion dollars' worth of research to the Soviet Union carried the day
in the committee's final decision taken on May 31.

Byrnes' comments on the political untenability in Congress of the
United States' sharing its atomic research were not specifically recorded
in that day's minutes of the committee's meeting, just as a decade earlier
Jimmy Byrnes' comments usually were not specifically recorded in the
Senate cloakrooms; but they must have been unusually forceful to have
turned the consensus of the Interim Committee away from the previous
statements by Marshall and Compton in favor of a mild attempt at international sharing of research. "*Mr. Byrnes* expressed a fear that if information were given to the Russians, even in general terms, Stalin would
ask to be brought into the partnership," the Interim Committee minutes

recorded in the day's summary. "He felt this to be particularly likely in view of our commitments and pledges of co-operation with the British."

Vannevar Bush apparently thought Byrnes was overstating the case, according to the minutes. "In this connection *Dr. Bush* pointed out that even the British do not have any of our blue prints on plants." Byrnes persisted, however; the Interim Committee minutes for the May 31 meeting record a final victory for him on the subject. "*Mr. Byrnes* expressed the view, *which was generally agreed to by all present*, that the most desirable program would to push ahead as fast as possible in production and research [of the atomic bomb] to make certain that we stay ahead and at the same time make every effort to better our political relations with Russia."

Even eminent scientists might be mistaken, Byrnes had written to FDR a few weeks before the president's death. Now, by his lights, Byrnes saved the Roosevelt and Truman administrations from a disastrous political mistake. He might be able to limit the political damage when the Quebec agreement on Anglo-American sharing of atomic research became known among isolationist Republicans in the Senate; but Jimmy Byrnes knew that no amount of his skill or cunning could have undone the domestic political disasters facing the Democratic party if it became known in Congress that the administration intended to share the fruits of the Manhattan Project's research with nuclear physicists in the Soviet Union. Byrnes must have listened with mounting incredulity as the academic members of the Interim Committee considered this plan with no regard for the limits of what was politically possible. Even a man whom Byrnes considered a realist, General Marshall, had briefly considered the idea before Byrnes could end such talk.

During the second part of the day-long meeting of the Interim Committee on May 31, Byrnes intended to save the Truman administration once more from a disastrous political mistake, which he knew was also being urged by some eminent scientists. Once again, by Byrnes' lights, they were recommending an act of irreparable folly: that the United States not use the atomic bomb on Japan or that it warn Japan before the bomb's use.

Byrnes knew that these recommendations were coming not from the Interim Committee's scientific membership but from a younger group of Manhattan Project scientists working at the University of Chicago. Their most active spokesman was Leo Szilard, an eccentric, droll, and brilliant Hungarian emigré physicist who with Albert Einstein had written Franklin Roosevelt a letter in 1939 that had persuaded FDR to begin government-sponsored research into atomic fission. Byrnes knew that Leo Szilard was the spokesman for this Chicago group urging a delayed use of the atomic bomb, because—in a tangled paper trail leading from Einstein's office at the Institute for Advanced Study, in Princeton, New Jersey, to the living room of Jimmy and Maude Byrnes' home in Spartanburg, South Carolina—Jimmy Byrnes had argued this point with Szilard in South Carolina three days before the Interim Committee's May 31 meeting.

Szilard and others working in fission research at the Metallurgical Laboratory at the University of Chicago had become troubled several months earlier about the necessity of using the atomic bomb on Japan as the military defeat of Germany and the Allied victory in all war theaters became more certain. In the same month of March 1945 that Jimmy Byrnes had expressed his political misgivings about the Manhattan Project to Franklin Roosevelt, Szilard had traveled to see Einstein in Princeton, New Jersey. He asked Einstein to write another letter to Roosevelt.

The purpose of this letter was to introduce Szilard to the president and to ask Roosevelt to read a memorandum on the atomic bomb prepared by Szilard. Einstein, who as a result of Groves' misgivings about his political and religious beliefs was not a major participant in the Manhattan Project, trusted Szilard's opinions; for security reasons Szilard could tell his friend Einstein "only that there was trouble ahead" regarding the use of the atomic bomb, which needed to be communicated directly to the president through nonmilitary and nonpolitical channels. Einstein wrote the letter to the president's office that Szilard requested, the two physicists hoping that Einstein's prestige would guarantee that Szilard's memorandum would reach Roosevelt.

It worked; the White House, after receiving the letter of introduction, set an appointment for Szilard to present his memorandum on May 8. Szilard was in his office at the University of Chicago on April 12, looking over a final revision of his views for Roosevelt's reading, when there was a knock at the office door. Another member of the Manhattan Project told Szilard that he had just heard on the radio that FDR had died.

Go and talk to Jimmy Byrnes at Spartanburg, South Carolina, was the advice Szilard next received from the new appointments secretary at the White House when he again tried to present a copy of Einstein's letter and asked to see President Truman. The request for Szilard to talk with Byrnes rather than Truman had come directly from the president himself, the appointments secretary told Szilard. Leo Szilard was puzzled, but replied that he would be happy to go anywhere that the president directed him. There was a reason for Szilard's puzzlement; Byrnes at this time, although traveling surreptitiously each week to Washington to confer with officials at State, was still maintaining the public fiction that he was simply a private citizen living in Spartanburg. Without enlightening Szilard, the White House appointments secretary then telephoned Byrnes in South Carolina and arranged for him to meet with Szilard at Byrnes' home on May 28. Szilard asked whether he could also invite Walter Bartky, a dean of the University of Chicago, and Harold Urey, who directed the Manhattan Project's research in gaseous diffusion at Columbia University, both of whom shared his misgivings about the use of the bomb on Japan. Szilard was free to bring anyone he chose, the White House told him.

This trio of scientists during the night of May 27 took the Southern Railway train out of Washington's Union Station for Spartanburg, South Carolina. The necessity of talking to Jimmy Byrnes there must have seemed inexplicably odd to the three, just as Szilard, with his East European accent and noticeable eccentricities, would have appeared odd to many of the other passengers on this southern-bound train. (Among the other passengers on the train that night closely observing Szilard was one of General Groves' undercover military intelligence agents, who had been following Szilard on his other trips and who was now at Groves' orders shadowing him on this trip to South Carolina. Groves was convinced, despite the lack of any evidence whatsoever, that Szilard because of his views on the bomb was spying for unspecified masters. Byrnes also had his own unfounded doubts about Szilard's loyalty.) Szilard, an abstracted-appearing bachelor who was very fond of theorizing on physics while soaking in a bathtub, did not appear to be preternaturally intelligent. Even a close colleague and an admirer of Szilard's scientific accomplishments, the French biologist Jacques Monod, once described Szilard simply as a "short, fat man." With his pear-shaped face and his habit at scientific conferences of closing his eyes and resting his hands over his potbelly, Szilard frequently gave the appearance of being sound asleep. "Yet from time to time he would wake up," Monod later said of Szilard at such a conference, "his eyes shining with intelligence and wit, to ask sharp, incisive, unexpected questions, which he would impatiently repeat when the answer did not immediately come straight and clear."

Szilard's incisiveness and his talent for asking the unexpected had led him along with Enrico Fermi to achieve a critical first accomplishment for the Manhattan Project, the world's first chain reaction of a plutonium pile at the project's Chicago laboratory in 1942. Now, as the crowded and darkened wartime train jolted southward in 1945, Szilard in his mind impatiently phrased and rephrased the question that was not clearly answered in his thoughts: why was Jimmy Byrnes so important to the Truman administration, and why was Truman insisting that Szilard see Byrnes rather than the president himself to discuss the use of the atomic bomb?

"Byrnes had occupied a high position in the government, but now was out of the government and living as a private citizen at Spartanburg," Szilard later recorded as his thoughts that night. "Clearly the President must have had in mind to appoint him to a government position, but to what position?" Szilard reviewed mentally what he and the others intended to discuss with Byrnes on their arrival the next day in Spartanburg. "We were concerned first about the role which the bomb would play in the world after the war. . . . We were also concerned about the future of atomic energy, and about the lack of planning of how this research might be continued after the war." How was the resolution of these concerns to be affected by Truman's insistence that the three scientists discuss them with Jimmy Byrnes? "Was he to be the man in charge of the uranium work after the war, or what?" Szilard thought. "We did not know." And so with Szilard impatiently wakeful in one of its compartments, the train rolled on into the night.

The weather on May 28, 1945, was mild in South Carolina, and Spartanburg appeared to be a city pleasantly provincial and far removed from an Asian war in which an atomic bomb would be used on human beings, when Leo Szilard and his two companions walked up the tree-shaded drive to Jimmy Byrnes' suburban home. The countryside surrounding the city of Spartanburg was then heavily planted in peach orchards, and the first of the summer's peaches were peacefully ripening pink and flame-colored in the fields with no violent storms predicted; one of the few visible signs in this small southern city of the war in Europe that had ended only that month was the notice in the previous day's local newspaper that 250 prisoners of war from Germany and Italy held in the United States were to be sent to Spartanburg County to help area peach farmers pick the expected bumper crop.

Jimmy Byrnes welcomed the three men into his house. He had previously received Einstein's letter, forwarded from the White House when it had rearranged Szilard's appointment, and Byrnes was now handed by Szilard a revised memorandum on the atomic bomb that he had prepared after FDR's death for Byrnes' inspection. Leo Szilard waited, the short man's faculties now as fully awake as when he asked incisive questions at scientific conferences, while Byrnes read the memorandum.

The document was an appeal for the same attempts at international control and sharing of atomic research that Byrnes had been working to defeat the previous weeks in the Interim Committee. Byrnes also must have felt impatience, although of a different sort from Szilard's, as he once again read these arguments, written by one more physicist with no practical political experience, in Byrnes' opinion. Szilard expressed the need for controls of atomic manufacturing "to extend to every territory on earth." Once more, the reasons given were the inevitability, in Szilard's view, of the Soviet Union's possessing an atomic bomb within a few years and the dangers of a resulting arms race. But the impatience Jimmy Byrnes felt on reading Szilard's fifteen-page memorandum must have turned to incredulity when he reached the final paragraphs. For there Szilard proposed that, in order to increase the world acceptance of controls, the U.S. forgo using the atomic bomb against Japan.

Szilard based this argument on the opinion, then beginning to be widely accepted, that, in his words, "Japan was essentially defeated and that we could win the war in another six months." Since the atomic bomb was not essential for the defeat of Japan, whether or not to use the bomb at the close of the war was not a military question, as Szilard understood the term; rather, it was a political question affecting the postwar relations among the other developing atomic powers. The likelihood of persuading the Soviet Union to accept controls could be increased, Szilard argued, if the United States were believed by the Soviets to have obtained an insurmountable lead in atomic research before the power of atomic weapons was demonstrated. "Such a demonstration may take place in the course of the war," Szilard wrote. "However, the psychological advantages of avoiding the use of atomic bombs against Japan, and, instead, of staging a demonstration of the atomic bomb at a time which appears most appropriate from the point of view of the effects on the governments concerned might be very great. Therefore the possibility seems to deserve serious consideration in deciding whether or not to use an atomic bomb against Japan."

Byrnes must have had trouble believing his eyes. His scientist visitor, whose good judgment was vouch for in a letter of introduction by Albert Einstein, was seriously proposing that the Truman administration ignore the domestic consequences of its actions and not drop the atomic bomb on Japan in order to pursue more perfect nuclear research. Byrnes may have agreed silently with Szilard's opinion that Japan by the summer of 1945 was essentially defeated, just as the German armies had been essentially defeated by the winter of 1944, and just as the Confederate armies had been essentially defeated by the summer of 1863; but getting the defeated armies themselves to accept that opinion had always been another matter. The image of half a million American casualties accumulating from Operations Olympic and Coronet while the atomic bomb went unused in the war administration's arsenal simply was politically unacceptable to Byrnes' mind.

Furthermore, his visitor was proposing that the power of the atomic bomb, in which the United States then held a world monopoly, not be demonstrated until a time in the postwar future when the Soviet Union was most in a mood to be impressed. Jimmy Byrnes decided to give his distinguished visitor a quick lesson in the rule that all politics, even geopolitics, is local. He looked up from the pages of the memorandum and sharply questioned Szilard. "How would you get Congress to appropriate money for atomic energy research if you do not show results for the money which has been spent already?"

Szilard had to admit that Congress would "expect results," in his words, for the two billion dollars spent on the Manhattan Project. Both men knew that the "results" presumably would be an atomic bombing of Japan. Byrnes had made his point, although he did not chose to contradict Szilard's assertion that the war with Japan would soon end without the use of the atomic bomb.

Jimmy Byrnes continued to appraise Szilard, who along with Bohr was widely respected among other nuclear physicists for his political opinions and who was clearly the leader of the scientific opposition to the use of the bomb. Leo Szilard at five feet six inches was shorter even than Byrnes, although his body was much more rotund; with his bright eyes and abstracted expression, a head topped by an abundance of curly hair, and an accent that was an amalgam of his scholarly life in Hungary, Germany, England, and the United States, Szilard would have had the appearance in the Byrnes family's living room of an animated and slightly disreputable Hummel figurine. Someone, probably General Groves, had briefed Byrnes on Szilard's East European background before the meeting. Byrnes now tried to persuade Szilard to give up his opposition to the bomb's use by appealing to the ethnic loyalties he assumed Szilard valued. If the United States demonstrated its military power by exploding an atomic bomb on Japan, Byrnes said, the Soviet Union should become "more manageable" in fulfilling its Yalta promises to hold free elections in Eastern Europe. "Well, you come from Hungary," Byrnes said to Szilard, turning from his other two visitors to directly face him. "You would not want Russia to stay in Hungary indefinitely."

Byrnes' statement deeply offended Szilard. The physicist made no effort to conceal his resentment at the remark, and not only because he took pride in being a naturalized American citizen. Of course he did not want Soviet occupation troops to stay in his native Hungary indefinitely, Szilard later recalled having impatiently answered Byrnes. But such a politically localized remark seemed to miss the point Szilard was trying to make— that, in his words, "by demonstrating the bomb and using it in the war against Japan, we might start an atomic arms race between America and Russia which might end with the destruction of both countries." It was to prevent such an international conflagration that Szilard at President Truman's request had caught a train to talk to Byrnes at Spartanburg; Szilard's purpose in making this journey was not for Jimmy Byrnes to talk to him as though he were just another congressional constituent susceptible to a special interest. "I was not disposed at this point to worry about what would happen to Hungary," Szilard later said of his hot response to Byrnes' statement.

It was after this remark that Szilard concluded that there was not "any way for me to communicate with Byrnes in this matter." As for Byrnes, he later wrote briefly and disparagingly in his memoirs about this meeting with "Dr. L. Szilard." Byrnes recounted simply that he received Einstein's letter from the White House after Roosevelt's death and met with the physicists to oblige the Truman administration. "As the Einstein letter had indicated that he would, Szilard complained that he and some of his associates did not know enough about the policy of the government with regard to the use of the bomb," Byrnes wrote, with some deliberate misconstruing of the content of Einstein's letter to FDR. Apparently the persistence of Szilard in asking impatient, incisive questions, which had so impressed the biologist Jacques Monod at scientific conferences, did not work in the nuclear physicist's favor when Byrnes wrote his final appraisal of Leo Szilard: "His general demeanor and his desire to participate in policy making made an unfavorable impression on me, but his associates were neither as aggressive nor apparently as dissatisfied."

Byrnes presumably was kinder in his later remarks toward professors Bartkey and Urey, because the two did not press the case for further deliberation on the use of the atomic bomb as urgently as did Szilard at this Spartanburg meeting. There was some final, inconsequential talk between the physicists and Byrnes on the U.S. program to acquire uranium ore, a subject in which Byrnes, to Szilard's surprise, showed little interest. Then the three scientists were shown to the door.

The short, fat man with intelligent eyes who had tried to stop the use of the atomic bomb on Japan walked out into the pleasant South Carolina sunshine. Szilard knew that his mission had failed completely. "I was rarely as depressed as when we left Byrnes' home and walked toward the station," he told an interviewer in 1960. In attempting to discuss the politics of using the atomic bomb, he and Byrnes had not even spoken the same language. To Szilard, the political question of using the bomb meant a consideration of the international relations that would be forever changed by its use. He foresaw the Soviet Union working independently to develop an atomic bomb within a few years of the war's end and a resulting postwar arms race. ("Joe One," the U.S. government's code name for the first Soviet atomic bomb, would be test exploded in 1949.)

But to Jimmy Byrnes, at least while he was serving on the Interim Committee, the language of atomic politics was domestic, not international, and it was spoken in the halls of Capitol Hill and not in the assembly chambers of the new United Nations then organizing at San Francisco. Byrnes did anticipate that detonating the atomic bomb over Japan would make postwar relations with the Soviet Union "more manageable," as he phrased it to Szilard, but he probably considered this effect as a secondary "bonus" of using the atomic bomb. Domestic political concerns were primary. Congress would "expect results" for the two billion dollars invested for the secret weapon of the Manhattan Project, and both the public and their representatives would be outraged if the Truman administration later were shown to have displayed any reluctance to win the war with Japan as quickly as possible by forgoing the use of this weapon. Byrnes knew that, put bluntly, internationalist-minded nuclear physicists did not vote in American elections in large numbers; people working on farms and in cotton textile mills in states such as South Carolina who had family members still fighting in the Pacific war theater did.

Szilard knew what Jimmy Byrnes was planning. "I thought to myself how much better off the world might be had I been born in America and become influential in American politics, and had Byrnes been born in Hungary and studied physics," Leo Szilard later remembered having silently deliberated during his melancholy walk to the Spartanburg train station. "In all probability there would then have been no atomic bomb and no danger of an arms race between America and Russia."

But there was an atomic bomb being assembled, and the short, wiry man who had been born in South Carolina to become a master of American politics wanted his country use it before the end of the war with Japan. Three days after meeting with Szilard, Byrnes was back in Washington for the critical two-day meeting of the Interim Committee on May 31–June 1. On the first day of this meeting, at which Byrnes disposed of the possibility of the committee's recommending any international control or sharing of atomic research, Byrnes and the other members also heard from the Interim Committee's advisory Scientific Panel. The panel had been convened from the civilian supervisors of the Manhattan Project's laboratories at Los Alamos, New Mexico, the University of California at Berkeley, and the University of Chicago. The supervisors were, respectively, Robert Oppenheimer; Ernest Lawrence; and Arthur Compton. Enrico Fermi, the coresearcher with Szilard into plutonium fission at Chicago, was the fourth member. Byrnes was keenly interested in the Scientific Panel's opinions on how long it would take the Soviet Union independently to develop an atomic bomb; apparently Szilard's memorandum was still worrisome to Byrnes, despite his casual dismissal of it while meeting with Szilard in Spartanburg. The panel's answers that day to Byrnes' question varied from Oppenheimer's scientifically forthright "I don't know" to an almost accurate low estimate of five years. General Groves, who also had been invited to the May 31 meeting, offered an opinion that topped the high side. Groves estimated that the Soviet Union would need at least seven or ten, and perhaps as many as twenty, years to produce its first atomic bomb.

The general told Byrnes what he wanted to hear; the president's personal representative on the Interim Committee chose to believe Groves, whose practical engineering experience with the construction and logistics of the Manhattan Project did in fact make him a more credible estimator than the physicists. After these assurances from Groves, the dire predictions in Szilard's memorandum of a dangerous postwar arms race immediately facing the next U.S. administrations lost their urgency for Byrnes. Even for a politician with as many professional lives as Jimmy Byrnes, twenty years is far beyond the normal span: neither Byrnes nor Truman would be expected to be in national office or responsible for atomic policy after twenty years. Mentally filing Szilard's fifteen-page memorandum away in a political never-never land, Byrnes then turned to what was for him the central, practical question for the Interim Committee to decide: how and when to use the atomic bomb on Japan.

The specific selection of Japanese cities, including possibly Hiroshima, Nagasaki, and Kyoto, to be bombed by atomic explosives was being determined simultaneously by a military Target Committee reporting to Stimson and independent of the civilian Interim Committee. But there was no question among the members of either the Interim or the Target Committee whether the atomic bomb was to be used. Civilian and military members alike assumed that if the atomic bomb was available for the defeat of Japan, it would be exploded on an enemy target. However, Byrnes was concerned that some members of the civilian committee, including once again the nuclear scientists whom Byrnes considered as politically naive, were not "hard" enough: specifically, that they were endangering the Truman administration by proposing that a warning be given Japan before the atomic bomb was dropped.

This proposal had been briefly mentioned at the May 31 morning session of the Interim Committee by a member of the Scientific Panel, Ernest Lawrence. When the committee that day broke for lunch shortly after 1:00 P.M. and gathered at two adjoining tables in the Pentagon dining room, Byrnes sat at Lawrence's table. Byrnes asked the Berkeley physicist to amplify his remark earlier that morning that a nonlethal demonstration of the atomic bomb, or at least an initial detonation over a target other than one of Japan's cities, would be sufficiently fearsome to cause the Japanese government to surrender. Stimson, who also was deeply troubled over the morality of the American military's bombing of Japanese cities with napalm explosives for the past year, was sitting at the other table. He joined in the discussion between Lawrence and Byrnes. Groves and Oppenheimer, and possibly other Interim Committee members, also spoke up as the issue of warning the Japanese was tossed between the members at the two tables for ten or fifteen minutes.

Jimmy Byrnes from his table appears to have dominated this brief discussion. If the Japanese were warned of the bomb's detonation at an area within their control, Byrnes later recalled having argued with members of the Interim Committee, "they might bring our boys who were prisoners of war to that area." Also, if observers from the Japanese government could be persuaded to travel to a neutral site to witness an atomic explosion and the new bomb proved to be a dud, Byrnes said, "certainly we would have given aid and comfort to the Japanese militarists. Thereafter, the Japanese people probably would not be impressed by any statement we might make in the hope of inducing them to surrender." Byrnes was perhaps unconsciously employing in his "aid and comfort" expression the same legal phrase frequently used in charges of sedition.

No one present at those Pentagon lunch tables was later remembered as having argued with Byrnes that prior warnings were even then being

given to the Japanese populace by the U.S. Army Air Corps before its
firebombing attacks. Beginning in early 1945 the Twenty-first U.S. Bomber
Command, based in the Pacific islands of the Marinas, had begun to carry
out a successful and highly publicized "hard" war against the Japanese
population and industry, dropping incendiary napalm bombs that in one
raid alone had killed 100,000 people in a deliberately set fire storm one
March night over the city of Tokyo. Thousands of leaflets were being
dropped from B-29s that May in preparation for the Twenty-first Bomber
Group's firebombing raids on ten other major Japanese cities. According
to intelligence received by General Curtis LeMay at the Marinas headquarters, the warnings were not causing the Japanese to bring either prisoners of war or increased antiaircraft guns into the targeted areas. In fact,
General LeMay personally contributed to writing the text of the leaflets.

"Civilians! Evacuate at Once!" the leaflets warned in large red and
black Japanese characters. The warnings continued in printed Japanese
text on the reverse side:

> These leaflets are being dropped to notify you that your city has
> been listed for destruction by our powerful air force. The bombing
> will begin within 72 hours. This advance notice will give your military
> authorities ample time to take necessary defensive measures to pro-
> tect you from our inevitable attack. Watch and see how powerless
> they are to protect you.
>
> Systematic destruction of city after city will continue as long as
> you blindly follow your military leaders whose blunders have placed
> you on the very brink of oblivion. It is your responsibility to over-
> throw the military government now and save what is left of your
> beautiful country.
>
> In the meanwhile, we urge all civilians to evacuate at once.

But now at lunch on May 31 no one persisted in arguing with Jimmy
Byrnes that a similarly worded warning to Japanese civilians about the
detonation of an atomic bomb was equally acceptable. Ernest Lawrence
later remembered hearing the remark, although he did not recall from
which of the two tables, that the "number of people that would be killed
[by the use of the atomic bomb] would not be greater in general magnitude
than the number of those already killed in the [firebombing] raids." This
remark indicates how waging a hard war in turn hardens men. The casualties of 100,000 dead after the Tokyo firebombing of March 9, which
had not been preceded by any of the warnings from the Twenty-first
Bomber Group, had become the norm, even for the civilian leaders on the
Interim Committee. Thus on the basis of this terrible arithmetic at two
lunch tables and of Jimmy Byrnes' unexamined arguments against a propaganda embarrassment or possibly endangering the lives of American pris-

oners of war, the Interim Committee decided that day not to recommend that Japan be warned before the use of the atomic bomb.

The committee regrouped after lunch at Stimson's office. For the remainder of its afternoon meeting, Byrnes' arguments at lunch apparently precluded any further discussion of a demonstration or of any other warning—just as at the committee's morning session Byrnes' arguments had precluded any further discussion of sharing research with the Soviet Union. The committee members spent the rest of that afternoon discussing the future of the Scientific Panel and the Chicago laboratory, where the research work was winding down as the bomb came closer to completion. General Groves was described in the minutes as saying he distrusted the loyalty of some of the scientists then in the Manhattan Project. Leo Szilard was not mentioned by name, but Byrnes in an off-the-record conversation had informed Groves of Szilard's visit to Spartanburg and of his memorandum recommending that the U.S. forgo the use of the atomic bomb. When Groves told Byrnes that he was already aware of this visit, thanks to the surveillance of Szilard, Byrnes was pleased. "The diligence of Groves impressed me then as it had done before," he later wrote.

Having thus preempted any discussion on the delayed use of the atomic bomb from what he considered the scientific left, Byrnes moved to determine the wording of the Interim Committee's report to the president. The next day, a Friday, June 1, the Scientific Panel was not present and Secretary Stimson was away on other duties when the Interim Committee met for its afternoon session. The War Department's special assistant George Harrison was nominally the Interim Committee's chairman in these circumstances, but Jimmy Byrnes had other plans. "While Stimson was away, Byrnes swiftly and decisively co-opted the committee," Richard Rhodes, a recent historian of the atomic bomb, has written. Byrnes knew that Stimson, like all other members of the Interim Committee, did not question whether the atomic bomb was to be used; but Byrnes wanted the committee's judgment on the use of the bomb to be on record as quickly as possible, and he wanted that record to be forceful, with none of the qualifications he had heard from Szilard or the Scientific Panel. A specific recommendation on the bomb's use was not on the agenda of the Interim Committee's meeting for that day, but Jimmy Byrnes had his way. As the president's personal representative on the committee, he insisted that it make explicit its decision. "*Mr. Byrnes recommended*," the minutes for that day's meeting concluded at the end of the afternoon, "and the Committee *agreed*, that the Secretary of War should be advised that, while recognizing that the final selection of the target was essentially a military decision, the present view of the Committee was that the bomb be used against Japan as soon as possible; that it be used on a war plant surrounded by workers' homes; and that it be used without prior warning."

Byrnes had won. Throughout most of the Interim Committee's meetings in May, he had kept his mouth shut. But he also had kept his eyes firmly upon the achievement of the unspoken agenda he had set for this advisory group, and on each of the two occasions, on May 31 and June 1, when the Interim Committee had in official minutes summarized its recommendations, the words chosen had been Jimmy Byrnes'. Clearly, Byrnes since his appointment on May 3 had had a three-part agenda for atomic power, and he had outmaneuvered the other members of the Interim Committee and the Scientific Panel on each of his objectives: that the committee recommend against the sharing of any atomic research with the Soviet Union; that it urge that the atomic bomb be used as quickly as possible in order to "show results"; and that the bomb be used without warning.

Byrnes' motivation in seeking each of these three recommendations was based on his perception of what was acceptable within the limits of domestic politics. The postwar decision of Congress after the explosions over Hiroshima and Nagasaki to continue full funding for the Manhattan Project and Truman's decision to abrogate the Quebec agreement for shared atomic research with Great Britain indicate that, at least politically speaking, Jimmy Byrnes acted correctly in obtaining his first two objectives. But the third recommendation that Byrnes pushed through the Interim Committee—that the atomic bomb be dropped on Japan with no warning—was not properly evaluated, even by the expediency of political standards.

Despite Byrnes' claim in his memoirs that during the meetings of the Interim Committee "we had carefully considered" the question of warning Japan before using the atomic bomb, the only discussion of such a warning had occurred for fifteen or twenty minutes during the committee's lunch break on May 31. Byrnes and probably also General Groves had kept these deliberations from going any further than lunch-table talk. The two men apparently felt that they had risked enough with a postwar Congress by identifying their careers with the Manhattan Project. "They had accepted the unavoidable risks of condemnation if the project on which vast sums had been spent turned out to be a mistaken venture," Herbert Feis later wrote. But even Feis, who as a historian usually was appreciative of Byrnes' and Groves' best motives in ending the war, noted that on this question of prior warning before using the atomic bomb, Byrnes and Groves "were not willing to widen the margin of exposure."

But on the afternoon that Byrnes pressed his recommendations through the Interim Committee, there was at least one member who dissented. Ralph Bard, the undersecretary of the navy, thought that because of "the position of the United States as a great humanitarian nation and the fair play attitude of our people" the decision to use the atomic bomb with no warning should have been given more consideration than Byrnes had allowed. Bard forwarded to Stimson a dissenting memorandum on June 27, 1945. In his memorandum Bard expressed the above "fair play" sentiments and recommended to the war secretary that an effort be made to contact the Japanese and "give them some information regarding the proposed use of atomic power." Bard argued that the usual calculations of domestic U.S. politics simply did apply in this unique case of determining whether the threat of atomic bombing and the Soviet Union's entry into the war would coerce Japan into accepting unconditional surrender. "I do not believe under present circumstances existing that there is anyone in this country whose evaluation of the chances the success of such a program is worth a great deal," he wrote to Stimson. "The only way to find out is to try it out."

Bard was not alone in his dissent. Leo Szilard returned the University of Chicago after his disappointing trip to Spartanburg, and by the first week of July he was circulating a petition eventually signed by sixty-eight of the Manhattan Project's scientists urging forbearance in the United States' use of the atomic bomb. This time Szilard sought to bypass Byrnes altogether: the Chicago petition was addressed to President Truman. The scientists asked that Truman exercise his "power as Commander-in-Chief to rule that the United States shall not resort to the use of atomic bombs in this war unless the terms which will be imposed upon Japan have been made public and Japan knowing these terms has refused to surrender." They also asked him before using the atomic bomb to consider "all the other moral responsibilities which are involved."

But these dissenters were a day late and a dollar short, in the parlance of Jimmy Byrnes. Timeliness and the value of access are all-important in determining whose information a president uses to make a decision. Byrnes had known these facts of political life long before the Interim Committee adjourned on the afternoon of June 1. Without waiting for the committee's recommendations to be typed from the minutes of that Friday's meeting and formally presented to the president later the next week by Secretary Stimson, Byrnes that same afternoon sped across the Potomac from the Pentagon building and went directly to the White House. As others of Byrnes' political opponents had discovered throughout the 1930s, Jimmy Byrnes had a way of getting to the president first.

"I told the president of the final decision of the committee," Byrnes subsequently wrote in his memoirs about his meeting late in the afternoon of June 1 with Truman. According to Byrnes' account, he and Truman then discussed the estimated casualties of Operations Olympic and Coronet, and the likelihood that the shock of an unannounced atomic attack would force Japan to surrender unconditionally without the necessity of the two invasions. It was the shadow of these estimated American casualties in the hundreds of thousands of dead and wounded that Jimmy Byrnes was trying to outrun in his motoring across town to see Truman. Convinced as a southerner that the Japanese people would fight a U.S. invasion to the bitter end, Byrnes apparently was certain that those urging a delay or a warning before using the atomic bomb were underestimating, or simply indifferent to, American casualties. Byrnes reminded Truman in their late-afternoon conversation of the fierceness of the fighting then being experienced by U.S. troops on the Pacific island of Okinawa. As he told the president, he was convinced that "the closer we got to Japan it was certain that an invasion force would be attacked with far greater fury and recklessness."

The contents of that day's newspapers argued for Byrnes' position and against any delayed use of the atomic bomb. The *Washington Post* for June 1 reported that official U.S. casualties in the four years since Pearl Harbor now totaled 1,200,887. The likelihood of the war administration's adding yet another 500,000 U.S. casualties to those figures by the planned invasions of Japan also loomed larger with that day's news reports of the fighting on Japanese-held Okinawa. Invaded in April as a preliminary to Operations Olympic and Coronet, Okinawa was then being defended by the Japanese ferociously. On an island less than half the size of Charleston County, where Jimmy Byrnes had grown to adulthood, nearly a quarter of a million American soldiers were being killed or wounded that June at a rate of greater than one in three. Offshore, although the U.S. Navy was unopposed by Japanese surface vessels, more U.S. sailors were being killed by kamikaze air attacks during the three-month Okinawa campaign than had been killed in the surprise attack on Pearl Harbor.

And ahead, of course, there was still Japan. The willingness then being demonstrated by the Japanese military to defend Okinawa suicidally made clear that any U.S. invasion and possession of the Japanese main islands themselves would have to be purchased by the American military with at least that same Okinawan 35 percent casualty rate. There were daily graphic reminders to Byrnes and Truman of these present and future American casualties. Inside the pages of the *Washington Post*, the *New York Times*, and the local newspapers for June 1, the names and one-column photographs of some of the 11,938 U.S. sailors, marines, and soldiers eventually killed at Okinawa continued to be published, as they had been for the last two months. The faces in the photographs usually appear impossibly young, the subjects having been photographed just after basic training, the similarities of their ages and dark dress uniforms giving all these young men the appearance in the June newspapers of being members of the same graduating senior class.

Politically it seemed unconscionable to Byrnes and Truman not to try to prevent further American combat deaths by using the atomic bomb on Japan before launching the planned invasions. "After we discussed it for a while," Byrnes later elliptically recalled in his version of this meeting with Truman, "he had to follow the advice of the Interim Committee." When he received Byrnes' informal report that afternoon, Truman had not yet given his approval as commander in chief to the plans by the Joint Chiefs of Staff for Operations Olympic and Coronet; but he was obviously determined as a result of this June 1 meeting with Jimmy Byrnes to use the atomic bomb before the date proposed for Olympic.

Byrnes and Truman may then have spent the remainder of the late afternoon talking about Truman's meeting with news reporters at the White House earlier that same day. Both in his conversation with the reporters and in a message that Friday to Congress, Truman had warned the American public that U.S. forces in the Pacific might have to be doubled by the addition of 3.5 million soldiers transferred from Germany before the defeat of Japan. In his meeting with the reporters, Truman, who himself was looking very photogenic and confident the first day of June in a light-colored, double-breasted suit and characteristic summer bow tie, also had emphasized that, despite rumors to the contrary, he had "no plans to name a new Secretary of State" after Edward Stettinius, Jr., returned from San Francisco.

Five days later, when Stimson kept a June 6 appointment with the president to formally present him with the Interim Committee's written recommendations, Truman told him that he already had been informed about the committee's decisions by Jimmy Byrnes. The war secretary later wrote in his diary that Byrnes, in Truman's description, "seemed to be highly pleased with what had been done." The military and political processes for the world's first combat use of an atomic bomb now were fully in motion, and sixty days after Truman told Stimson that because of Byrnes' visit the committee's recommendations were already known, on the morning of August 6, 1945, an atomic bomb exploded over Hiroshima.

Hence, Byrnes' comment to Truman that the United States' possession of the atomic weapon "might well put us in a position to dictate our terms at the end of the war," almost certainly was not intended, some revisionist historians later argued, as an invitation to Truman to join Byrnes in a diplomatic policy of atomic intimidation directed against the Soviet Union; rather, Byrnes' remark is more correctly interpreted as an argument to Truman that the combat use of the atomic bomb against Japan greatly decreased the risk, politically intolerable to both Truman and Byrnes, of accepting what appeared to be less than unconditional surrender. Although later historians such as Martin Sherwin concluded that "it is not clear whether Byrnes was referring on this occasion to Japan or the Soviet Union," the closest student of Byrnes' wartime service and diplomacy, Robert Messer, has argued that, "indeed, there is evidence to the contrary; that the bomb by providing a presumed breathing space of American superiority, allowed Byrnes for a time to contemplate an even more magnanimous policy toward the Soviet Union, than he otherwise might have pursued, had the United States possessed no atomic arsenal."

During these intervening sixty days of war and diplomacy, which saw Henry Stimson's final efforts, at the Potsdam conference, to persuade Truman's personal adviser on the atomic bomb to issue a warning to Japan, Jimmy Byrnes also enhanced his political power.

16

The Street to Hiroshima

Jimmy Byrnes was back at the Oval Office on the afternoon of July 3, 1945. This time he came to take his oath as U.S. secretary of state. Once more, the Senate the previous day had quickly and unanimously confirmed Byrnes' nomination to a high office, and Byrnes once more was to be accorded the honor of taking his oath at the White House. As evidence of Jimmy Byrnes' undiminished prestige in Washington despite his three months' official absence since leaving the Roosevelt administration, so many well-wishers had wanted to witness Byrnes' swearing-in ceremony that Truman and Byrnes were obliged to move the gathering from the Oval Office outside onto the steps leading from the Rose Garden into the presidential office. There, standing overlooking the same summer rosebushes that had been in bloom the previous July when FDR had deceived him about the vice-presidential nomination, Jimmy Byrnes took his oath as Harry Truman's new secretary of state.

Byrnes' swearing-in ceremony was only part of a busy first week of July for the war administration. The previous day, a Monday, the Senate in addition to confirming Byrnes' nomination had been formally presented with the United Nations Charter by President Truman, who had urged its speedy ratification. Byrnes and Truman were scheduled to leave the following Saturday aboard the cruiser USS *Augusta*, bound for a diplomatic conference in Potsdam, Germany. There the president and his new secretary of state were to confer with Churchill and Stalin on plans for a postwar Europe and for the issuance of an Allied statement on the prosecution of the war against Japan. Truman and Byrnes also were awaiting the results of the first test explosion of the atomic device at Alamogordo, New Mexico, which had been originally set for July 4.

Because of technical reversals, the Manhattan Project moved the test firing date back to July 16. The rescheduled explosion date would still allow Truman and Byrnes to know during their negotiations at Potsdam whether the atomic weapon was practical. But even after taking his oath of office and joining Truman aboard ship on July 6 to travel to Potsdam, Jimmy Byrnes continued to think about the use of the atomic bomb and the end of the war against Japan primarily in terms of the U.S. political consequences. Byrnes knew on sailing for Potsdam that he was leaving behind domestic political problems over ending the war that promised to be best solved for the Truman administration, like the problematic projected casualties of the Olympic and Coronet invasions, by the speedy detonation of an atomic bomb over Japan.

The partisan nature of concluding the war against Japan had begun in the Senate chamber the very day Jimmy Byrnes' nomination had been confirmed. At that July 2 session, Senator Wallace White of Maine, the Republican minority leader, followed up his successful motion for unanimous approval of Byrnes' nomination with a speech on the floor in which he then criticized Truman for possibly prolonging the Pacific war. The Democratic administration erred in failing to announce specifically to Japan what unconditional surrender would mean to it, Senator White said; if before the Potsdam conference convened, White said, the consequences of surrender were openly and quickly specified to Japan by Truman, then Japan might give up its fight.

Senator Homer Capehart, a Republican from Indiana, supported Minority Leader White's speech in a news conference with the *Washington Post* and the *New York Times* held the same day. "It isn't a matter of whether you hate the Japs or not," Capehart told the reporters. "I certainly hate them. But what's to be gained by continuing a war when it can be settled now on the same terms as two years from now?" Capehart then reiterated to the press his belief in the persistent rumor, previously denied by the State Department, that the Japanese government had within the last thirty days initiated "peace feelers" to U.S. officials. Senator Capehart said he had been told by an unnamed U.S. source that the Japanese had indicated a willingness to surrender if assurances were given that the Japanese emperor would be allowed to remain on the throne.

In fact, these peace feelers existed. The State Department by the first six months of 1945 had received scores of classified reports from its embassies and legations in neutral countries, ranging from Portugal to Sweden. Each told of contacts by individuals claiming to represent the peace faction in the Japanese government. The branch of U.S. military intelligence operated by the Joint Chiefs of Staff, the Office of Strategic Services (OSS), also passed on to State numerous reports of peace overtures from its own clandestine contacts with Japanese nationals or sympathizers, occurring chiefly in Switzerland. Byrnes was one day out from land aboard the *Augusta* when he received a telegram on July 7 classified "top secret" from Acting Secretary of State Joseph Grew describing the latest peace overture from the Japanese military attaché in Stockholm. In this report, as in all others the United States received from different sources around the world that year, the Japanese attaché offered to arrange a negotiated peace through the Swedish government if the United States would drop its insistence upon an unconditional surrender and guarantee the reign of the emperor.

Byrnes was not buying any of it. Although this latest Swedish proposal, like all of the prior peace feelers, offered to retain the emperor in return for peace, Byrnes did not believe that the worldwide contacts were part of a concerted effort by the Japanese government. It seemed highly likely that if any official contacts were to be made by Japan, the procedure would be the same one used by the State Department and the Japanese Foreign Office since 1942. Whenever each country had wanted to communicate with the other over such issues as the return of diplomats or the treatment of war prisoners, the U.S. secretary of state or the Japanese foreign minister had directly contacted the government of neutral Switzerland to pass on its communication. There had never been any resort to an intermediary fourth party, such as journalists, businessmen, or military attachés, to pass on the message as in the case of the latest feelers.

In the absence of this established diplomatic procedure, there was every reason for Byrnes to believe that all these peace feelers by late June 1945 were either acts of altruism by individuals unconnected directly with the makers of Japanese foreign policy or acts of attempted self-advancement by isolated fascists who clearly saw V-J Day rising over the horizon. It was certainly true that Byrnes could not have missed seeing the common condition of retaining the emperor in all these peace feelers; and it was equally true that if Byrnes himself were willing to act altruistically and ignore the political consequences in the United States of his actions, the Japanese government might accept his offer of such a negotiated peace. But what was most true of all was that Jimmy Byrnes, chosen as the "hard-hitting trader for the home front," always had prided himself on never being particularly susceptible either to appeals to altruism or to a hustle.

Byrnes therefore approved the actions of Grew when in a subsequent telegram to the *Augusta* the acting secretary described the department's efforts, while Byrnes and Truman were on their way to Potsdam, to put a stop to "the growing speculation in this country, as indicated in speeches, editorials, *et cetera*, as to whether the Japanese government had or had not made a bona fide peace offer."

Under Grew's directive, the department issued a statement to U.S. news services on July 10 that, while confirming Senator Capehart's assertions about the existence of Japanese peace feelers and contradicting the department's earlier denial, played down their importance. Without specifying the countries of incident, Grew's announcement confirmed that U.S. officials and other nationals at various embassies had been contacted by Japanese individuals or their sympathizers. Grew repeated the opinion held by both Byrnes at State and Allen Dulles at the Office of Strategic Services that in no case were these peace feelers made "by a person who could establish his authority to speak for the Japanese government." In his July 10 statement, Grew also repeated what so far had been Truman's sole definition of unconditional surrender. The term meant, Truman had said before leaving for Potsdam, "the termination of the influence of the military leaders who had brought Japan to the present brink of disaster" and "not prolonging the present agony and suffering of the Japanese in the vain hope of victory."

But whatever the effectiveness of this public denial by Undersecretary Grew, the assertions by Senators White and Capehart about the existence of Japanese peace feelers were political straws in the wind, and they continued to worry Jimmy Byrnes. Byrnes later angrily exclaimed to his South Carolina political confidant Walter Brown that Truman would be "crucified" if the he accepted anything less than an unconditional surrender by Japan. But as the *Augusta* and its presidential party sailed on to Europe and as Allied casualties in the Pacific war continued to mount, Byrnes also knew that the Truman administration might become equally vulnerable to Republican criticism after Japan's eventual surrender if the war administration appeared to have ignored any means to end the war more quickly by having refused to negotiate with Japan. The use of the atomic bomb thus became to Jimmy Byrnes' mind by mid-July 1945 a way to avoid not only the mass casualties of Operations Olympic and Coronet but also any postwar political "crucifixion" of his president—and, presumably, of President Truman's brand-new secretary of state.

Secretary of War Stimson was waiting for Byrnes and Truman upon their arrival at the outskirts of Potsdam on July 15. He met with them numerous times, probably to Byrnes' displeasure, before the opening plenary session of the Potsdam conference on July 17. Byrnes' angry outburst about the political naïveté of those in the United States willing to accept less than unconditional surrender from Japan very likely also included among its subjects Henry Stimson. Byrnes had not encouraged Truman to invite Stimson to attend the conference; in fact, Stimson had been obliged to invite himself to Potsdam, and he was not included among those assigned living quarters at the "Little White House," the three-story stucco villa that had been designated as Truman's and Byrnes' residence during the conference.

Jimmy Byrnes may have wanted to keep Henry Stimson at a distance in Potsdam simply because Byrnes did want to be preempted in the upcoming sessions by this elder Republican statesman who himself had been the secretary of state during the Hoover administration. Specifically Byrnes probably wanted to limit Stimson's access to the deliberations of the Potsdam conference because Byrnes knew that Stimson was among those proposing that the United States accept what Stimson had termed "the equivalent of unconditional surrender." In a memorandum sent to both Truman and Byrnes a few days before they had left Washington, Stimson had proposed issuing a declaration allowing the Japanese people to retain their emperor in exchange for an immediate surrender by their military.

Stimson had begun his argument by confirming his department's commitment to invasions of Japan as the military solution to ending the war. "The plans of operation up to and including the first landing have been authorized and preparations for the operation [Olympic] are now actually under way," Stimson had written to Truman and Byrnes on July 2. Stimson, like all other planners of Olympic and Coronet, anticipated high U.S. casualties. "The Japanese are highly patriotic and certainly susceptible to calls for fanatical resistance to repel an invasion," he again cautioned. Yet the secretary of war did not believe that Japan was "a nation composed wholly of mad fanatics of an entirely different mentality from ours." Stimson proposed to Truman and Byrnes that the Allies issue a proclamation to Japan during the course of the Potsdam conference offering "the equivalent of an unconditional surrender" by allowing the Japanese the possibility of continuing "a constitutional monarchy under the present dynasty," as one of the terms for an immediate surrender.

Before sailing for Germany, Jimmy Byrnes had sent a copy of Stimson's memorandum for review and possible comment to his fellow southerner and predecessor as secretary of state, Cordell Hull. Now waiting for Byrnes on his first full day at the Little White House on July 16 was Hull's urgently cabled reply. Hull knew little about the development of the atomic bomb and nothing about its scheduled test on July 16, but he warned Byrnes that if anything less than unconditional surrender was demanded of the Japanese in a Potsdam declaration, there was the possibility that "terrible political repercussions would follow in the U.S."

Jimmy Byrnes trusted Hull's political judgment implicitly, as only one secretary of state who had run successfully for elective office could trust another former secretary who also had spent time on the Democratic party stumps. (Stimson had never ran for a public office.) The day after receiving

Hull's cable, Byrnes wired a reply to the former secretary. "I agree that the issuance of statement should be delayed and, when made, should not contain commitment to which you refer," he assured Hull. There was an additional reason for Byrnes' persisting in his view of an unconditional surrender for Japan. On the evening that he read Hull's cable, July 16, Byrnes also received the awaited news of a different sort of "terrible repercussion," this one felt at Alamogordo, New Mexico. The atomic device tested there was exploded successfully, and the first report received by Byrnes at the Little White House indicated that the detonative power of an atomic bomb exceeded the expectations of the Manhattan Project's physicists.

Stimson at seven-thirty in the evening, Potsdam time, was the first to receive this cable describing the successful atomic explosion. "I took it at once to the president's house and showed it to Truman and Byrnes, who of course were greatly interested, although the information was still in very general terms," Stimson noted in his diary that evening. Truman's and Byrnes' interest in the cabled report apparently eclipsed any further attention these two men might have given another document also sent earlier that same day by Stimson. Once again, the war secretary was trying to persuade the administration, specifically Byrnes and Truman, to issue during the Potsdam conference an explicit proclamation to Japan on the Allied terms of surrender before either the use of the atomic bomb or the invasions became necessary.

These ideas were contained in a memorandum Stimson sent to the Little White House on July 16, one copy for Byrnes and an original for the secretary of state to give to Truman. In this latest memorandum the war secretary stated his case that "we are at the psychological moment to commence our warnings to Japan." Stimson enclosed with this July 16 memorandum another version of his July 2 draft proposal to the Japanese government, which offered some assurances of the emperor's continuation after surrender. Stimson urged that such a proposal be issued promptly "during the course of this conference rather than later." In reading this latest memorandum, Byrnes certainly realized the significant point that Stimson did not oppose the use of the atomic bomb or advocate a specific warning to the Japanese about the existence of the bomb before its use.

But when Stimson went to see Byrnes the morning after bringing him the cable on the successful Alamogordo explosion and his latest memorandum on Japan, he faced the same situation Leo Szilard, Ralph Bard, and he himself had faced when they had attempted to qualify Byrnes' use of the atomic bomb to effect an unconditional surrender: Jimmy Byrnes had gotten to the president first. "I went to the 'White House' for a conference with Byrnes early in the morning," Stimson recorded in his diary on July 17. "Byrnes was opposed to a prompt and early warning to Japan which I first suggested. He outlined a timetable on the subject [of] warning which apparently had been agreed to by the president, so I pressed it no further."

Up to this point, ever since his appointment to the Interim Committee, Byrnes had been the atomic politician. He had successfully outmaneuvered Stimson and all other critics of a "hard" war, and in his mind the domestic political reasons for using the atomic bomb against Japan had pulled together like a silken knot. But with the receipt on July 17 at the Little White House of a second cable further detailing the success of the atomic explosion and the arrival in Potsdam that day of Marshal Stalin to begin the first plenary session of the Big Three conference, Byrnes began to act more like the atomic *diplomat*. For the next eleven days of the Potsdam conference, Byrnes began to consider how the United States, sole possession of atomic weapons could be used to reduce Soviet postwar influence in the Far East. Or, as Byrnes said in an unguarded moment at "bullbat time" while at Potsdam with his confidant Walter Brown, he now believed that with the U.S. combat use of the atomic bomb "Japan will surrender and Russia will not get in so much on the kill."

Obtaining a Soviet declaration of war against Japan—getting Russia in on the kill, in Byrnes' frank manner of speaking—had been a U.S. diplomatic objective since at least the Yalta conference. The Joint Chiefs of Staff in a position paper prepared at Potsdam with their British military counterparts also had continued to urge this policy upon Truman. The Japanese armies in occupied Manchuria were at that time believed to number as many as 750,000 men under arms. It was to prevent the transfer of these troops across the Sea of Japan to fight against Americans in Operations Olympic and Coronet or to prevent their continued resistance after the eventual surrender of the Tokyo government that had made Roosevelt willing at Yalta to offer U.S. concessions to the Soviet Union. These included trade rights in China and Soviet occupation rights on the Kuril Islands after the surrender of Japan. In exchange, Roosevelt obtained a promise from Stalin to enter the war against Japanese troops in Manchuria as soon as possible after the defeat of Germany. Byrnes had supported this policy of allowing the Soviets their unobstructed Far East sphere of influence in exchange for their help in getting in on the Japanese kill— until he received news of the assured success of the atomic bomb.

Thereafter Jimmy Byrnes made an effort, to reverse U.S. diplomatic and military policy and to delay Soviet entry into the Asian theater until the war with Japan could be won with the atomic bomb. In making this decision, Byrnes appears to have acted independently of Truman and his military and other diplomatic advisers, who at least officially still favored Soviet entry. Byrnes, however, dominated discussions of foreign policy with Truman at Potsdam, in part because of the adroitness of the housing arrangements, which left Stimson and others who might oppose Byrnes' views shunted off to villas at a distance from the Little White House. Those who were politically outcast also included the current U.S. ambassador to Moscow, Averell Harriman. "Jimmy Byrnes played his cards pretty close to his vest," Harriman recalled of Byrnes' activities at Potsdam, "and I was not alone in being ignored. Stimson also had plenty of free time. So we sat in the sun together outside his villa talking about when and how the Japanese might be brought to surrender, and how to deal with the Russians after the war."

While those who were unfavored sat in the sun and discussed a peace they were not allowed to fashion, Byrnes quickly acted on his newfound atomic diplomacy. Byrnes apparently on his own sent a cable from Potsdam to the Chinese foreign minister asking him to travel to Moscow and to keep the Soviet government talking as long as possible about the details of the Soviet postwar concessions in China. A satisfactory conclusion to these negotiations between China and the Soviet Union had at Yalta been agreed to be a precondition of any Soviet declaration of war against Japan. This strategy of delay was appreciated immediately by Winston Churchill, who had been told of the success of the atomic explosion, and who later talked privately with Byrnes at Potsdam. No notes or records of this meeting appear to have been kept by Byrnes, but Churchill, in a note written to himself recorded the intent of their conversation. "Mr. Byrnes told me this morning that he had cabled to T.V. Soong advising him not to give way on any point to the Russians, but to return to Moscow and keep on negotiating pending further developments," the prime minister wrote. Churchill then concluded his short *aide-mémoire*: "It is quite clear that the United States do not at this present time desire Russian participation in the war against Japan."

But this time it was Stalin's turn to play the honest horse thief, taking away Byrnes' opportunity for atomic diplomacy. Stalin arrived in Potsdam about noon on July 17, and shortly afterward he and his entourage paid a courtesy call at Truman's and Byrnes' villa. After some initial bandying remarks by Byrnes that he was scheduling the opening time for the next day's plenary session to accommodate Stalin's known fondness for staying up all night and rising late, the Soviet marshal got down to business. Twice in this informal conversation before the official opening of the Potsdam conference, Stalin repeated to Byrnes and Truman that the Soviet Union would "keep its word," as given at Yalta, and declare war on Japan by mid-August. Molotov also later remarked that the Japanese could scarcely mistake the Soviets' intention, as the massing armored divisions of the Red Army had been visible at the Manchurian border for weeks.

Molotov's remark on the unmistakable Soviet military strength in Asia had an implication for the American delegation at Potsdam, and in case Byrnes missed the intent of the Soviet foreign minister's remark on July 17, Secretary of the Navy James Forrestal made the point explicit when he talked privately with Byrnes on July 28. At this meeting, five days after Byrnes had talked with Churchill, Forrestal brought a message from General Eisenhower that the general thought that Truman's main purpose at the conference should be to secure Soviet entry into the war. Byrnes disagreed, and stated that he thought Truman was beginning to disagree with that view also. Forrestal then said explicitly what Molotov had implied—that U.S. atomic bomb monopoly or no U.S. monopoly, "it would take a large army to keep the Soviet Union out of the Pacific war." Byrnes had to admit that militarily the Soviet Union was capable of entering Manchuria with or without prior Chinese approval, and there was little that the U.S. armies could do to change this situation. At the end of their conversation, Byrnes told Forrestal that he agreed with him.

Thus ended Jimmy Byrnes' brief flirtation with atomic diplomacy. His attitude toward the Soviets by the end of the Potsdam conference very likely was most honestly expressed in a conversation he had back in Washington with the conservative Republican senator Warren Austin on August 20, soon after Byrnes returned from the conference. Austin recorded in his diary that "Secretary Byrnes had hoped we could finish up with the Japanese *without* [Austin's emphasis] participation by the Russians, but [Byrnes said that] the atmosphere of the conference and the attitude of the Russians made it inevitable that Russia come in." Presumably, among the elements of "atmosphere" that made Byrnes accept the inevitability of Soviet participation were the twenty-five Soviet divisions Stalin had promised at Yalta to send across the Manchurian frontier as soon as the USSR declared war on Japan.

Stalin had brought other news to Potsdam as well. Both at his first, informal meeting with Truman and Byrnes at the Little White House, on July 17, and at the tenth formal plenary session, on July 28, Stalin told his allies of a new attempt by Japan to arrange a negotiated peace with the United States and Great Britain through the mediation of the then neutral Soviet Union. This latest proposal to the Soviets was significantly different from the earlier peace feelers in Switzerland or Sweden. This request, Stalin told Byrnes and Truman, had been relayed to the Soviet government from the Japanese emperor through the imperial ambassador to Moscow. Emperor Hirohito requested that the Soviet Union receive a peace mission dispatched by the emperor and headed by Prince Konoye, who was described by the Japanese ambassador to the Soviets as a recipient of "high trust in the Imperial Court" and as "prominent in Japanese political circles."

It was evident to all of the Allies that, unlike the previous peace feelers, the Konoye mission undeniably had been initiated at the highest level of the Japanese government. Whether Prince Konoye would have ultimately succeeded in Moscow is unknown. The Japanese minister of foreign affairs at Tokyo, Shigenori Togo, in preparation for securing Moscow's permission for Prince Konoye's mission, had cabled the ambassador to Moscow on July 21, instructing him to tell the Soviets that the Japanese government desired above all "to have the Soviets deal with the United States and Great Britain." In exchange, Togo instructed his country's ambassador to offer a promise from the Japanese government of "considering the Soviet demands in Asia." But Stalin was not about to lose the Soviets' guaranteed sphere of influence in the Far East by agreeing to receive this mission and mediate an end to the Japanese war before Soviet troops were ready to occupy Manchuria. "Our answer of course will be negative," he told Byrnes and Truman on July 28.

Stalin's disclosures actually were not surprising to either Byrnes or Truman. Thanks to the extraordinary feat of the U.S. intelligence in breaking the Japanese diplomatic cipher before the war, at least some of the diplomatic cables intercepted between Minister Togo and the ambassador to Moscow in regard to the Konoye mission had been decoded and made available to Stimson in Germany on July 16. After the arrival of Byrnes and Truman in Potsdam, Stimson had shown the two men what he had received by no later than July 17. Secretary of the Navy Forrestal also brought more intercepted and decoded cables with him to Potsdam and showed them to Byrnes when they talked on July 28.

Byrnes' knowledge of these Japanese cables later led some revisionist U.S. historians to theorize that while at Potsdam he practiced an atomic diplomacy much more sinister than his attempted China venture. In the mid-1960s, following the U.S. State Department's publication of some of these Japanese cables and the initial publication, in 1949, of Leo Szilard's memoirs, in which the nuclear physicist emphasized Byrnes' remark to him in 1945 that exploding the atomic bomb over Japan should make the Soviet Union "more manageable," a new theory of Byrnes' motivation for his diplomacy at Potsdam was proposed. According to this theory, the explosions of the atomic bombs over Hiroshima and Nagasaki were unnecessary, and Byrnes knew by the time of the Potsdam conference that their use was unnecessary. His motives were ulterior. Byrnes was intent upon a combat use of the atomic bomb less for military victory over Japan than for coercion of the Soviet Union in the postwar world.

According to this interpretation, Byrnes willfully ignored the possibility of a negotiated peace with Japan as evinced to him in the intercepted cables; and he suppressed the opinions of Allied military leaders that the entry of the Soviet Union into the Pacific war made the defeat of Japan inevitable in the near future and rendered the planned U.S. invasions unnecessary. As with his China diplomacy, Byrnes' motivation here was assumed by the revisionists to be an effort at limiting the Soviet sphere of influence in the Far East and at coercing the Soviets as a result of the atomic explosion to accept a greater U.S. influence in Eastern Europe. To achieve these ends, went the revisionist argument, Byrnes was willing to destroy the cities of Hiroshima and Nagasaki. This argument was pursued most aggressively among the revisionists by Gar Alperovitz in his 1965 book on the events at Potsdam preceding the Japanese surrender, *Atomic Diplomacy*. In his 1985 "Introduction" to the reissue of this work, Alperovitz reiterates, "As suggested by Leo Szilard's report on his conversations with Byrnes, at least some of the major figures seemed to know that the war was over but wanted to use the bomb anyway."

Jimmy Byrnes was to have after Potsdam a second career as a self-proclaimed elder statesman for more than a quarter of a century, and he lived long enough to have read some of the revisionist interpretations of his urging the use of the atomic bomb. In 1964, Jefferson Frazier, interviewing Byrnes for his honors paper at Harvard University, noted that, even at the age of eighty-two, Byrnes "parried questions with the ease of a professional." Neither in interviews nor in his two memoirs did Byrnes ever choose to answer the revisionists' questions.

By the time of Frazier's interview, Byrnes was in the habit of quoting to his interlocutors a classical passage from Livy's *History of Rome*, supplied to him by his friend George Curry of the University of South Carolina. Byrnes would cite the statement by a Roman consul "If . . . any one thinks himself qualified to give advice respecting the war which I am to conduct, . . . let him come with me into Macedonia." (The "come with me to Macedonia" tag may also have been a privately ironic reference by Byrnes to his successful diplomacy during the summer of 1946, when two U.S. aircraft were shot at and forced down over Yugoslavia. There were fervent calls to the U.S. press, including the *New York Times*, to send U.S. troops into Yugoslavia in response to this incident, described as the "curtain-raiser to World War Three." Despite tough public statements delivered by diplomatic note to the Yugoslav government and Byrnes' visit from Paris to view U.S. troops holding parades along the Yugoslav border, Byrnes spoke informally to the Soviet foreign officer to "get things straightened out" with Marshal Tito. The Yugoslav government paid indemnities to the families of the killed airmen, and the calls for U.S. military intervention subsided.)

But at the same time that the revisionists, in the face of Byrnes' silence, were reappraising his motives at Potsdam and questioning the veracity of his few public comments on the decision to use the atomic bomb, the revisionists themselves were subjected to remarkably ad hominem attacks by more establishmentarian academics. Principally, these attacks came from the historians (themselves no admirers of Byrnes) at universities situated around the archives of the Harry S. Truman Presidential Library, in Independence, Missouri. Representative of this midwestern group is Professor Robert Ferrell of Indiana University, who devoted much of a 1974 essay published under the sponsorship of the Truman Library not to a refutation of the revisionist arguments but to a discussion of the fact that

Gar Alperovitz had been born in 1937; therefore, Ferrell maintained, Alperovitz "could not have remembered much if anything about World War II, the beginning of the Cold War, and even the Korean War." Ferrell further emphasized that many of the revisionists were either in graduate school or at their first university teaching jobs in the early 1960s and therefore "came to manhood at a time when the draft calls for the U.S. Army were small." (Ferrell apparently did not consider the possibility of a revisionist historian who is female, and thus not subject to the U.S. draft in the 1960s, or who was not in graduate school in the 1960s, who "came to manhood" during the Vietnam War, and who *still* questioned the assumptions of the state after an honorable discharge from an involuntary service.)

But whether dismissed with a neo-Bourbon politeness in Columbia, South Carolina, or subjected to academic bullying at Bloomington, Indiana, the revisionist charges against Byrnes' diplomacy before, during, and after the Potsdam conference deserve a more serious hearing. For the benefit of the general reader with no ideological or professional ax to grind, the term "revisionist historian" might best be discarded. As the political scientist Michael Leigh argued in a thoughtful essay, also published in 1974, the term "revisionist" had come to mean by the middle of that decade any non-Soviet scholar who viewed "American foreign policy as dictated by other than purely altruistic motives." In an attempt to bring at least *some* reason into an otherwise intemperate debate among the first postwar generation of academic historians, Leigh proposed making a critical distinction between the revisionists and all other historians on the basis of whether or not a particular historian's account imputes in a primary way the motive of military considerations in the decision by U.S. officials such as Secretary Byrnes to use the atomic bomb against Japan. Leigh's distinction provides a useful Occam's razor in appraising Byrnes' actions at Potsdam as an atomic diplomat.

Some of the revisionists who became prominent in the 1960s and 1970s, such as Gabriel Kolko, *do* attribute military considerations among other motives in Byrnes' championing the use of the atomic bomb against Japan. Other prominent revisionists, such as Alperovitz, William Appleman Williams, and Lloyd Garner, deny that military considerations were ever foremost in Byrnes' mind when he urged the combat use of the atomic bomb. Those in the latter group, which includes what the scholars termed the "radical" revisionists, see a very different Jimmy Byrnes.

Alperovitz, in a subsection of his 1985 introduction to the reissued *Atomic Diplomacy* entitled "Special Problems in Connection with Byrnes," characterizes the new U.S. secretary of state at Potsdam as "an exceedingly complex, secretive, and devious politician." Later he describes him as among those U.S. public figures who attempted to make their nation's citizens "prisoners of officials who have an interest in withholding evidence." Alperovitz argues that Byrnes consistently considered the U.S. monopoly of the atomic bomb and its demonstrated willingness to use it against its enemies the guarantor of his success in postwar negotiations with the Soviets. Byrnes needed the atomic leverage, Alperovitz emphasizes, to continue to hold his domestic critics "prisoners" and to extricate himself from the Yalta accords with which Byrnes *"was personally and politically identified"* (Alperovitz's emphasis). Hence, even before Potsdam, Alperovitz argues, Byrnes had been engaging in an elaborate charade, meeting secretly with the Interim Committee not out of a desire to avoid undercutting the authority of Secretary of State Stettinius in negotiations in San Francisco; rather, Alperovitz maintains, Byrnes' charade of "resting" at Spartanburg, South Carolina, enabled him to publicly promote the continuation of the Grand Alliance while privately traveling to Washington and urging upon Truman and the military the combat use of a weapon so intimidating it would make the continuation of such an alliance with the Soviet Union unnecessary in the postwar world. "Considering what we know of Byrnes' general attitude," Alperovitz writes, "it is very difficult to believe that Truman did not have very clear (and tough) advice from him on strategy concerning the bomb and the Russians during the summer months" of 1945 preceding the Potsdam conference.

That by the end of that summer tens of thousands of Japanese civilians in Hiroshima and Nagasaki had died in blinding flashes of atomic energy was the perfection of Byrnes' elaborate charade, Alperovitz concludes. He notes that various Japanese representatives and citizens had unofficially been attempting to negotiate a peace with the Allies before the atomic attacks, and that both General Eisenhower and Admiral Leahy argued against the U.S. use of the atomic weapon; but, Alperovitz concludes, "it is simply a fact of history that neither President Truman nor Secretary Byrnes appears to have experienced the moral difficulties with killing large numbers of civilians that so disturbed men like Eisenhower and Leahy."

It is regrettable that the revisionists, themselves subjects of unfair personal attacks, have employed the same ad hominem brush on the historical reputation of Secretary Byrnes, frequently misstating the most easily verifiable facts of his life. Alperovitz, for example, repeats in his 1985 reissue the comparatively inconsequential mistake first printed two decades earlier that Byrnes had served as a southern governor *before* becoming a senator and a secretary of state. Much more disturbing is the flat assertion in Gabriel Kolko's 1968 book, *The Politics of War*, that "in 1948 Byrnes supported the Dixiecrat candidacy for the presidency." It is not simply that this misstatement could have been corrected by Kolko in a visit to the back stacks of periodicals available at any public library, and corroborated by the private correspondence available at the Byrnes archives (Byrnes publicly and privately disavowed any support of the Dixiecrats both in 1948 and afterward). But this misstatement, occurring in the chapter entitled

"The War with Japan and the Potsdam Conference," undeniably and inaccurately imputes to Byrnes a motive of racism in his urging the use of the atomic weapon against the Japanese. Either by scholarly carelessness or by intent, this false statement suggests a spirit of herrenvolk in Jimmy Byrnes as an atomic diplomat, later to be expressed domestically by his (mistakenly imputed) support of the white supremacist ticket of the Dixiecrats in 1948.

Gar Alperovitz, has never, either in print or in conversations with this author, imputed the motive of racism to Byrnes' championing the use of the atomic bomb against the Japanese. But Alperovitz demonstrates a similar disregard for the verifiable facts of chronology. He emphasizes, for example, Byrnes' hope, recorded by his PR assistant Walter Brown at Potsdam in his diary on July 24, 1945, that "Japan will surrender and Russia will not get in so much on the kill." Yet in the text of neither edition of *Atomic Diplomacy* does Alperovitz offer any specific mention or even a general discussion of Byrnes' comments recorded by Senator Warren A. Austin, Republican of Vermont, in his conversation with Byrnes at his Shoreham Hotel suite on *August 20, 1945*, eighteen days after the Potsdam conference. Austin that night recorded in *his* diary, "*Respecting the Russian Participation in the war against Japan*: Secretary Byrnes had hoped that we could finish up with the Japanese *without* participation by the Russians, but the atmosphere of the conference, and the attitude of the Russians made it inevitable that Russia come in" (Austin's emphasis).

In his haste to emphasize the importance and primary significance of Walter Brown's diary of conversations with Byrnes at Potsdam, Alperovitz also has disregarded the principle of independent corroboration. Brown's daily journal of conversations with Byrnes at Potsdam, maintained without the knowledge of the secretary, was first made available from Walter Brown's office safe to Robert Messer during his research for his 1975 dissertation on Byrnes. Messer judiciously describes this Potsdam source in the bibliography of his dissertation as "those candid revelations of Byrnes' private thinking [that] flowed forth with the bourbon and branch water at 'bull bat time'—the late afternoon at the end of their working day." Ten years later, Alperovitz in his 1985 introduction inflates this source to justify the assertion that "we are beginning to know Byrnes better each day." But the scholars, revisionist or otherwise, who examine Brown's subsequent use of his diary are apt to be disappointed. The privately printed, two-volume reminiscence of Secretary Byrnes published by Brown in 1992 is a pleasant account of his former employer, but offers no additional revelations from his diary of a secret agenda of atomic diplomacy directed by Byrnes toward the Soviet Union at the Potsdam conference. It must also be noted that Brown's factual objectivity as a Washington correspondent was seriously questioned by an editor of the largest newspaper subscribing to his syndicated political column in the 1940s. And many of the obvious misstatements of Byrnes' religious affiliations in press releases issued during his tenures as U.S. senator, Supreme Court justice, and secretary of state—first detected by Messer in researching his dissertation—were written by Walter Brown, not then officially in the employ of Byrnes, but apparently seeing no contradiction in his work as an independent journalist and his deliberate confusing of Byrnes' past in the preparation of news releases for use by newspapers and radio.

Alperovitz also is wrong in his flat assertion that during Byrnes' supposed pre-Potsdam charade of traveling secretly from Spartanburg, South Carolina, to meet with the Interim Committee "[n]ot even his closest associates, men who were usually kept abreast of his dealings, were informed of the work he had undertaken for Truman in connection with diplomatic matters, to say nothing of the atomic bomb."

On May 3, 1945, Byrnes, then at Spartanburg, wrote to Benjamin V. Cohen at Washington. After noting that he "told Walter [Brown] that he was wrong" in previously telling Cohen that Byrnes was unhappy to have left government office, Byrnes added, "The president has asked me to represent him on a committee appointed by the Secretary of War to make an investigation of a matter so secret he would not mention it over the telephone. I suspect that it has to do with some of Vannevar Bush's work. It will require me to take a trip with the Secretary of War the latter part of May."

Cohen was no "bullbat time" drinking companion. He had served as one of Roosevelt's closest advisers, had been the legal counsel at the OWMR, had attended the Bretton Woods conference confirming the decision to establish a permanent postwar United Nations organization, and would be Byrnes' choice to serve as counselor to the U.S. State Department. (In the acknowledgments to both his 1965 and his 1985 editions of *Atomic Diplomacy*, Alperovitz thanks Benjamin V. Cohen, among others, for "the provision of information.")

Despite this shading of chronological and factual evidence and incompleteness of research, Alperovitz commendably urges future historians researching Byrnes' championing the use of the A-bomb and his subsequent diplomacy toward the Soviet Union to "learn from investigative reporters, and the kind of argumentation one finds in good legal preparations at well-prepared trials when all the facts are not known." The question regarding Byrnes seems to be, as the scholar Gregg Herken observed, whether the same judgment could be applied to Secretary of State Byrnes that Senator Arthur Vandenberg applied to Dean Acheson: that Jimmy Byrnes was the kind of lawyer a client would like to have if one were guilty as hell.

Alperovitz's verdict is, of course, that Jimmy Byrnes and his client Harry Truman were guilty as hell: both of them guilty of disregarding Japanese peace feelers received during the summer of 1945, and Secretary Byrnes also of persisting until 1947 to pursue atomic diplomacy when it had become obvious that the Soviet Union was not intimidated militarily or diplomatically by the U.S. monopoly of atomic weapons.

"Byrnes left office complaining that the Russians 'don't scare,' " Alperovitz repeats three times in both editions of *Atomic Diplomacy*. Byrnes' culpability from Potsdam onward is particularly hellish, Alperovitz concludes, because "[b]y early summer [1945] the better part of the Imperial Navy had been sunk and the Imperial Air Force had been reduced to the impotence of sporadic kamikaze attacks." American leaders, including Secretary Byrnes, were by the time of Potsdam aware of the peace overtures that various Japanese individuals made to OSS officers and other U.S. officials in Switzerland and elsewhere; and because the Japanese diplomatic cipher had been broken four years earlier, Alperovitz argues, American officials, including Secretary Byrnes, deliberately disregarded the potential for peace represented by the Prince Konoye mission to Moscow. Hence, in his judgment, the U.S. officials" "decision to use the atomic bomb was made at a time when the best intelligence and military advice indicated there were other ways to end the war without an invasion."

Yet the obligation of a good legal defense for Secretary Byrnes, charged posthumously by Alperovitz and other radical revisionists with pursuing atomic diplomacy at Potsdam, demands that Byrnes' statement to Dulles that the Soviets are "stubborn, obstinate, and they don't scare," be noted as occurring not in 1947 when Byrnes "left office." As the James F. Byrnes transcript at the Dulles Oral History Project, in Princeton, New Jersey, makes explicitly clear, Byrnes made this statement to Dulles after returning from the conference of the Council of Foreign Ministers at London ending on *October 2, 1945*. Byrnes was to remain as U.S. secretary of state for more than a year afterward; was to attend five more conferences with the Soviet foreign minister; was to make several nationally broadcast radio addresses in which he attempted to persuade the U.S. public to accept a legitimate Soviet sphere of influence in the Balkans; and was to astonish the cabinet member Henry Wallace when, less than thirty days after making this remark to Dulles, Byrnes declared in late 1946 that the United States "should stand pat" in China and "not give Chiang Kai-shek anything whatsoever until he agreed to come to terms with the Chinese communists and give them some places in a combination cabinet." Thus, a good defense attorney could argue that Byrnes' remark to John Foster Dulles could judiciously be interpreted as a defensive effort to convince the fiercely anti-Soviet Dulles that the continuation of the postwar Grand Alliance with the USSR was both desirable and necessary; if there were any further attempts to intimidate the Soviets with the U.S. monopoly, as Byrnes seems to have considered at Potsdam in delaying a China-Soviet settlement, the Soviets, despite Hiroshima and Nagasaki, would not "scare."

As to Alperovitz's subjectively described "sporadic kamikaze attacks" of early summer 1945, it is well to recall that the U.S. Navy had suffered more casualties from kamikaze attacks during the Okinawa campaign than from the surprise, non-kamikaze bombing and strafing of U.S. naval forces at Pearl Harbor three and a half years earlier. And in a message to Congress on June 1, 1945, Truman had officially announced the U.S. government's intentions to "move three million troops out of Europe in a year and launch a larger overseas force against the Japs than ever fought the *Wehrmacht* and *Luftwaffe*." There would not be even a partial demobilization of U.S. Navy forces currently operating in the Atlantic and Mediterranean theaters, Truman cautioned; because of U.S. naval losses against Japan, all "but a handful" of the naval forces then in Europe would travel to the Pacific theater. These redeployed U.S. naval forces could continue to expect high losses in combat against the Imperial Air Force, Truman warned; he repeated estimates that the Japanese military held as many as 3,000 combat aircraft in reserve after Okinawa for protection of the mainland islands and that, despite the horrific napalm bombing of Japanese cities, Japan's industry still was capable of producing an estimated 1,250 to 1,500 airplanes per month.

However, as Alperovitz reminds his reader, a good investigative reporter will be wary of any U.S. official's estimates of the potential resistance of its wartime enemies. But a good investigative reporter will also remember that the existence of the early Japanese peace feelers had been published with the same front-page prominence in the *Washington Post* a month before Truman's congressional address; and five days *before* Truman's address to Congress and the public, the same newspaper had printed a broadcast from Tokyo—received and translated in London, patently issued by Japan's new government, in hopes of increasing the success of the Prince Konoye mission—stating that should the Allies desire peace with Japan, "it would be possible that proposals could be made through Russia." And, as it will also be noted later, within days of the V-J Day and atomic bombings of Hiroshima and Nagasaki, Secretary Byrnes called a press conference at the U.S. State Department Building to discuss publicly the U.S. government's prior knowledge of the Prince Konoye mission. Also immediately after the war, the U.S. Strategic Bombing Survey, frequently cited by revisionists to support the contention that U.S. strategic bombing and a naval blockade together could have ended the war, confirmed Truman's earlier publicized fear of Japanese airpower. According to the U.S. survey, Japan at the end of the war possessed approximately 2,675 kamikaze airplanes capable of tactical combat use, and about an equal number of conventionally equipped airplanes for other combat use. Many of these warplanes were concealed in "underground hangers," some of which were simply natural caves near cleared fields, which would have been impervious either to U.S. strategic bombing or to the U.S. Navy's offshore artillery strikes.

Thus, by the standards of both good investigative reporting and good legal pleading, the supposed attempt by Secretary Byrnes before and after Potsdam to keep the U.S. public, in Alperovitz's phrase, "prisoners of officials who have an interest in withholding evidence," was an abysmal failure. The size of the Japanese military's potential air resistance, as publicized by Truman, was confirmed by a postwar survey, which had a vested interest in finding that U.S. airpower alone could have ended the war by August 1945; and both the early Japanese peace feelers and the later Prince Konoye mission occurring during Potsdam had been publicized, the latter by Secretary Byrnes himself, on the front pages of the largest U.S. newspapers.

Byrnes at Potsdam placed the greatest emphasis on his reading of the intercepted Japanese cable dated July 21, 1945, shown to him in Potsdam on or before the day he talked with Stalin on July 28. This cable explicitly declared Japan's intention to fight on rather than accept an unconditional surrender. And to Byrnes' practiced political eye, the third paragraph of the July 21 cable implied that the "war" faction of the Japanese military still strongly dominated the Tokyo government.

This intercepted cable was from Minister Shigenori Togo in Tokyo to his ambassador in Moscow, and it contained instructions for the Moscow ambassador in preparing for the request to the Soviet government to receive the Konoye peace mission. Under no circumstances, Togo cautioned, should the Soviets be told that the Konoye mission was ready to discuss the possibility of an unconditional surrender. The message from Minister Togo reads, in the translation by the U.S. intelligence service handed to Byrnes for his inspection in Potsdam in the summer of 1945:

> With regard to unconditional surrender, we are unable to consent to it under any circumstances whatsoever. Even if the war drags on, it becomes clear that it will take more blood shed. So long as the enemy demands unconditional surrender, the whole country as one man will pit itself against the enemy in accordance with the Emperor's will.
>
> It is in order to avoid such a state of affairs that we are seeking a peace which is not a so-called unconditional surrender through the good offices of Russia. It is necessary that we assert ourselves so that this idea will be firmly driven home to the Americans and the English.
>
> Therefore, it is not only impossible for us to request the Russians to render their good offices in obtaining a peace without conditions, but it would also be impossible from the standpoint of foreign and domestic considerations to make an immediate declaration of specific terms.

His reading this July 21 cable in Potsdam, Byrnes later told Herbert Feis back in the United States, depressed him greatly. The sense of the cable, Byrnes elaborated, was that "if the Japanese continued to fight on, it would mean the use of the atomic bomb *and* probably the Soviet entry into the war" (italics added). The various influences and fears operating since May in Byrnes' mind—the political disasters attendant on the Democratic administration's accepting anything less than an unconditional surrender from Japan, the decision by the Joint Chiefs of Staff to launch an invasion if Japan did not surrender, the willingness of the Japanese government and military to resist ferociously, and the resultant hundreds of thousands of American lives to be lost—pulled together into a silken Gordian knot.

There is no reason to doubt that James F. Byrnes as a private individual was any less sincere in his statement of despair over the conundrum of ever obtaining an unconditional surrender from Japan than was Leo Szilard, in stating his depression in walking to the Spartanburg train station after failing to solve the riddle of communicating with Byrnes. But unlike Leo Szilard, Jimmy Byrnes, after reading Minister Togo's cable of July 21, was convinced that only United States' exploding the atomic bomb could sever the silken knot of the Japanese war.

On July 26, 1945, the heads of government of the United States, Great Britain, and China issued a declaration from Potsdam through worldwide radio broadcasts in various languages calling upon Japan to surrender its armies unconditionally. The Allies promised that a military occupation of Japan after its surrender would be brief, but they made no mention of their intention to retain the current emperor or the present Japanese dynasty. "There are no alternatives," the declaration read. "We shall brook no delay." The Japanese government officially responded to the Potsdam declaration by describing its intentions toward its terms with a Japanese phrase that can be variously translated into English as "to ignore" or as "to treat with silent contempt."

Prior to the issuance of the Potsdam proclamation, and after private consultations with Byrnes and Churchill, Truman had on July 24 also casually informed Stalin of the recent U.S. success in exploding an atomic device at Alamogordo. As part of an obviously prearranged strategy approved by Byrnes and Churchill, Truman informed Stalin in as offhand a way as possible, choosing for their conversation the crowded moments after the formal plenary session for that afternoon had ended, and while the members of the national delegations were packing up their briefcases and leaving the conference table. Byrnes later described the scene in his memoirs:

> At the close of the meeting of the Big Three on the afternoon of July 24, the President walked around the large circular table to

talk to Stalin. After a brief conversation the President rejoined me and we rode back together to the "Little White House" together. He said he had told Stalin that, after long experimentation, we had developed a new bomb far more destructive than any other known bomb, and that we planned to use it very soon unless Japan surrendered.

All the accounts recorded by those present at the scene, including that of Byrnes, agree that Truman used neither the words "atomic" nor "atomic energy" in his conversation with Stalin. Byrnes was exultant. He believed that the United States had skillfully precluded any later Soviet charges that it had deceived its wartime ally the USSR about atomic power while at the same time it had not revealed enough about the Manhattan Project to spur the Soviets into speeding up their own declaration of war upon Japan. Byrnes later gleefully told Warren Austin that he believed that Stalin had been caught "asleep" to the implications of Truman's remark to him at Potsdam.

Joseph Stalin may or may not have been unwittingly "asleep" at Potsdam, as Jimmy Byrnes phrased it. Soviet espionage rings then operating in the United States and Canada may have already informed the Soviet marshal about the success of the Manhattan Project prior to his hearing of the bomb's existence in such an oblique way from Truman at Potsdam. According to Byrnes' version of what Truman told him during their automobile ride back to the Little White House, all that Stalin had said after hearing Truman's remark was that "he was glad to hear of the bomb and he hoped we would use it."

Four days after the adjournment of the Potsdam conference, on the morning of August 6, 1945, an atomic bomb was dropped from a B-29 by parachute and exploded without warning over the port city of Hiroshima. It killed immediately at least 78,000 people. The terrible arithmetic discussed during lunch at the Pentagon dining tables two months earlier had proven accurate. Fewer had been killed outright by this atomic blast than had been burned to death in the March 9 firebombing attack on Tokyo. Among the fatalities of this first combat use of the atomic bomb were at least two of the twenty-three American prisoners of war then being held in Hiroshima.

On August 9 a single B-29 again dropped an atomic bomb without warning onto a Japanese city, killing immediately at least 25,000 people in Nagasaki. The attack on this second city proceeded despite a military intelligence caution sent from the headquarters of the U.S. strategic air forces in the Marinas to the War Department in Washington. The caution, also sent to Secretary Stimson personally, stated that a prisoner of war camp with 1,000 Allied and American occupants was reportedly being maintained by the Japanese military about one mile from the center of downtown Nagasaki.

Also on August 9, Soviet armies began to move with overwhelming force against the Japanese troops stationed in Manchuria and Korea. The previous day V. M. Molotov, the Soviet foreign minister, had summoned the Japanese ambassador to Moscow to a meeting at Molotov's office. The ambassador had hoped to be told by Molotov that his government approved the Prince Konoye peace mission; instead, Molotov handed the ambassador the Soviet declaration of war upon Japan, effective the following day.

Having by then arrived back in Washington along with Truman, Jimmy Byrnes on the morning of August 10 received a telephone call from the White House and was asked to come from across the street in the State Department Building as quickly as possible to the president's office. There at about nine o'clock Byrnes was shown a message from the Japanese government that had been brought earlier that morning from the chargé d'affaires of the Swiss legation in Washington. The Swiss government was passing on to the United States at Japan's request a statement from the Japanese ambassador in Bern that the Tokyo government was willing to accept the terms of the Potsdam declaration. There was a sole condition. This willingness to surrender was being made, in the wording of the Japanese message, "with the understanding that the said declaration does not comprise any demand that prejudices the prerogatives of His Majesty as Sovereign Ruler." Identical messages were being sent that morning at Japan's request to the other Allied governments, and a U.S. response was requested by Tokyo through the intermediary of the Foreign Office of Switzerland.

Admiral Leahy, the principal military adviser to both FDR and Truman, who was in the Oval Office with Truman when Byrnes arrived, had prepared a draft message accepting the proposed Japanese surrender. Stimson came into the office a few minutes following Byrnes' arrival and, after reading the message, also spoke out strongly for accepting the Japanese proposal as offered immediately. Byrnes protested angrily. He saw in the Japanese insistence upon the "prerogatives" of the emperor a refusal by the Japanese government to accept the unconditional surrender as specified by the Potsdam declaration. He reminded Truman that at Potsdam the two of the Big Three of the Allies then signing the declaration—the United States and Great Britain—had stated clearly that there was to be an unconditional surrender, with no alternatives to be accepted, and that this statement had been issued before the destructiveness of the atomic bombing of Japan had become apparent and before the Soviets had entered the war.

"I cannot understand why now we should go further [in accepting a conditional peace] than we were willing to go at Potsdam when we had no atomic bomb, and Russia was not in the war," Byrnes argued. Jimmy

Byrnes stood alone among the presidential advisers at the Oval Office that August morning in his insistence upon an unconditional surrender from Japan. Byrnes' digging in his heels on this issue indicates that, contrary to the interpretation of the revisionists, his earlier statement to Truman about the atomic bomb's enabling the United States "to dictate our own terms at the end of the war" was almost certainly intended by him to apply more to the surrender of Japan than to postwar relations with the Soviet Union.

Indeed, had Byrnes been advocating since May 1945 the dropping of atomic bombs on Japan primarily to keep the Soviets from gaining influence and territory in the Far East, as the revisionist historians later maintained, he would scarcely have argued so forcefully in August with Truman to prolong the war with Japan until an unconditional surrender could be obtained. As Byrnes and all others in the Oval Office that morning were aware, the Soviet armies by the second day of their Asian war had pushed nearly one hundred miles into Manchuria. Stalin plainly intended to make hay while the moon shone on his Asian war, and the longer the United States delayed accepting a surrender by Japan, as Byrnes was then advocating, the more days were available to the Red Army to move farther into China and the Korean peninsula.

As usual, Byrnes' primary motivation was domestic politics. Later that same afternoon, at "bullbat time" with his diary-keeping assistant Walter Brown, Jimmy Byrnes confided to Brown that if the United States had replied to Japan with Admiral Leahy's initial response, that message, in Byrnes' description, "would have led to the crucifixion of the president." Truman apparently agreed. After listening that morning to his aides debate the wisdom of accepting the Japanese proposal as first offered, Truman had put aside Leahy's first answer and directed his secretary of state to draft the reply to be sent to Japan.

The domestic political concerns behind the answer to Japan were also recorded that busy summer day by Henry Wallace. Wallace, who had been retained by the Truman administration as the secretary of commerce, described in his diary the scene at the White House later on August 10, as Truman and Byrnes arrived at the Cabinet Room for the usual Friday afternoon cabinet meeting.

"The President, who usually comes to cabinet not later than 2:05, came in about 2:25 saying that he was sorry to be late but that he and Jimmie had been busy working on a reply to Japanese proposals," Wallace wrote in his diary. "Byrnes then read very slowly the Japanese proposal just as it was printed in the press late in the afternoon. He then read the reply which Truman indicated had been worked out by Byrnes, assisted by Stimson, Leahy, and Forrestal that morning." Following this reading by Byrnes, Wallace noted in his diary a remark by Truman to his cabinet in apparent explanation of the reply written by Byrnes. Truman, a practicing Southern Baptist, employed an evangelical religious term for offerings given above the usually called-for tithe to describe what he and Byrnes regarded as the political consensus behind the insistence on unconditional terms for Japan: "Referring to hard and soft terms for Japan," Wallace wrote, "Truman referred to 170 telegrams precipitated by the peace rumor of August 9. 153 of the 170 were for hard terms—unconditional surrender. They were free-will telegrams—not inspired—and were mostly from parents of servicemen."

The reply that Byrnes along with his assistant Benjamin Cohen had written out that morning provided what Byrnes judged to be a politically acceptable compromise in the United States. It sought to satisfy both the domestic majority of those who wanted a strictly unconditional Japanese surrender and the minorities, represented by Stimson and Leahy in the administration and by Capehart and White in the Senate, who were eager to end the war immediately and willing to accept what Stimson had called the "equivalent of unconditional surrender."

Byrnes' reply did not explicitly reject the Japanese condition that after surrender the present ruling dynasty retain the "prerogatives of the Emperor," in the Japanese terms. "Our position is as follows," Byrnes wrote. "From the moment of surrender the authority of the Emperor and the Japanese government to rule the state shall be subject to the Supreme Commander of the Allied powers who will take such steps as he deems proper to effectuate surrender terms."

Byrnes' draft retained Leahy's and Stimson's willingness to accept the Japanese condition of the permanence of the ruling dynasty, while adding his own condition of the emperor's reduced authority. No one in the administration would be politically crucified if Jimmy Byrnes could help it. Byrnes "laid special emphasis" while explaining his draft reply to the cabinet on the point that the "top dog" over Hirohito must be an American, according to Wallace's diary account. Having preserved the appearance that the United States did not seek a conditional peace, which along with avoiding invasion casualties he considered to be his two domestic political necessities, Byrnes was now willing to accept a de facto conditional peace. The two atomic bombings thus had preserved for Byrnes and Truman the political necessities and had "shown results" in all the political senses of the term; and Byrnes thus was now able to accept a conditional surrender and call it unconditional.

After consultation with the other Allies, this U.S. reply, with some revisions approved by Byrnes, was relayed to the Japanese government on August 11 through the intermediary of the Swiss Foreign Office. The Japanese did not immediately acknowledge receipt of the reply.

Therefore, that same Saturday of August 11, Jimmy Byrnes requested through Secretary of War Stimson that another U.S. Army Air Force raid be made over Japan's cities. On August 13 and again on August 14, a number of B-29s flew over the selected cities, including what was left of downtown Tokyo. This time the American airplanes did not drop an atomic bomb or loads of napalm. Instead, they dropped canisters that exploded in midair and released thousands of leaflets printed in the Japanese language. These printed messages, which showered down upon the inhabitants of Japan's cities, were the texts of the Japanese offer of surrender on August 10 and of Byrnes' reply on August 11 on behalf of the United States.

Jimmy Byrnes had requested these missions because he had become concerned in the days preceding the leaflet raids that the Japanese government was withholding from its people the news of the surrender offer and of Byrnes' reply. Byrnes therefore had decided to use a long-practiced political means to help his diplomacy by "leaking" the story of surrender terms to the Japanese people and, he hoped, increasing the popular demand among the Japanese people for peace.

On the morning of August 13, a member of the royal court picked up one of the leaflets of Byrnes' reply in the courtyard of the imperial palace and showed it to Emperor Hirohito. On reading the leaflet, the emperor and the military faction in the parliamentary government knew that it was no longer possible to keep concealed from the Japanese people the fact that their government could end the war with the traditional dynasty intact. By this time the Japanese government also had been apprised by its military and scientific experts that the single, city-destroying bombs being dropped by the Americans were, in fact, atomic weapons. The next day, Emperor Hirohito announced his acceptance of the surrender terms spread by leaflets in a special radio broadcast to the Japanese people. In explaining his reasons for accepting the inevitability of Japan's defeat, the emperor described the American enemy's use of a "new and most cruel bomb, the power of which to do damage is indeed incalculable, taking the toll of many lives."

At about four o'clock in the afternoon, Washington time, Byrnes received a telephone message at his State Department office from the U.S. ambassador to Switzerland, informing Byrnes that the Japanese government through its ambassador to Bern had announced its acceptance of the condition of Byrnes' reply. A formal Japanese acceptance of the terms would be transmitted shortly through the intermediary of the Swiss legation. Jimmy Byrnes literally ran as fast as a sixty-three-year-old man could run across West Executive Avenue to President Truman's office to tell him the news.

Later that night of August 14, the crowds celebrating V-J Day in Times Square were estimated by the *New York Times* to number approximately 500,000 people—about the minimum number of the estimated U.S. dead and wounded that Jimmy Byrnes had been told to expect after Operations Olympic and Coronet. Byrnes joined in the celebrations at Washington,

but neither then nor later did he exult over what he considered the necessary use of incendiary bombs and atomic blasts over Japan's cities in
order to spare Americans future combat.

It is, of course, a post hoc fallacy to assume that because events occurred
a certain way, they must have occurred that way. But *given* the Allies'
decision to pursue a strategy of "brute force" against the Axis nations,
and *given* the domestic and political pressures on U.S. officials to accede
to this strategy and to preserve the appearance of an unconditional surrender, the combat use of the atomic bomb became an inevitability. "Having found the atomic bomb, we used it," President Harry S. Truman told
the U.S. public after the bombing of Hiroshima; and the significance of
James F. Byrnes by the president's side was that, having helped Truman
find the bomb, Byrnes urged its combat use more quickly than any other
individual as the U.S. secretary of state would have. Diplomatic consequences of the atomic bomb's detonations for postwar U.S.-USSR relations
were at best secondary.

Byrnes spoke of his wartime motivations at a news conference he held
in Washington on August 29, 1945, just two weeks and a day after the
acceptance of the Japanese surrender and shortly before he left to attend
the conference of the Council of Foreign Ministers meetings to begin planning the outlines of the postwar world. Contrary to the later assertions of
revisionist historians that U.S. officials sought to conceal the existence and
seriousness of the Prince Konoye peace mission, Byrnes at this mid-1945
news conference became the first U.S. official to disclose it publicly. His
remarks were published the following day on the front page of the *New
York Times*, under the heading "Japan Beaten before Atom Bomb, Byrnes
Says, Citing Peace Bids." At his news conference, Byrnes emphasized to
the reporters that "before the atomic bomb was heard of by Japan, they
[Japanese officials] were seeking peace and seeking to bring it about
through the Soviet Union."

Byrnes at this news conference then outlined the sequence of events
leading up to the rejection of the Prince Konoye overtures and stated
explicitly what he had never denied to Leo Szilard the previous May—
that Japan had essentially been defeated militarily before the United States
used the atomic bomb. "The U.S. Army, Navy, and Marines, with the
help of its British Allies, and the valiant Chinese forces which had been
at war, had won that war as the result of the shedding of blood we all
regret."

The public man who had spent his life trying to deal honestly with
political issues of moral ambiguity then spoke honestly to the ambiguity
of his choice in advocating the use of an atomic weapon to speed at least
the appearance of an unconditional surrender and prevent a futile Japanese

resistance to invasions. "Whenever we think of the effects of the bomb," Byrnes said, "we ought to recall that if it only facilitated the surrender, and it certainly did that, it saved the lives of hundreds of thousands of American boys." Byrnes called attention to "the lives of hundreds [of thousands] of Japanese boys and millions more of its people who would have perished."

Jimmy Byrnes, the politician turned diplomat, stood facing his pressroom audience. On that late August day in 1945, a little over three weeks after the explosions over Hiroshima and Nagasaki, Byrnes then summed up as honestly as he ever would the multiplicity of fears, ambitions, patriotism, and good intentions paving the way to the use of the atomic bomb. "It was not a one-way street," he said.

17

Rocking the Boat with Truman

On the evening of December 15, 1946, more than five hundred men and women dressed in their best evening clothes gathered at Washington's Statler Hotel to resume one of the capital's most well-publicized annual dinners and social events. The Gridiron Club, composed of members of the national press corps, had suspended its annual dinner and show of satiric skits in late 1941, to be resumed after the successful end of the Second World War. Now the first postwar Christmas neared, and with the Allied armies occupying the defeated Axis capitals of Berlin, Tokyo, and Rome, reporters and editors of the U.S. newspapers were in a mood for fun.

So apparently were Harry S. Truman and the other guests of the Gridiron Club. Dressed in a well-fitting tuxedo, the president appeared relaxed both during the dinner and during the skits after the food was cleared, as journalists impersonated members of Truman's cabinet and other important members of his administration. And in a break with tradition that not even the late, self-dramatizing and teasingly witty Franklin D. Roosevelt ever dared, Truman played himself in the after-dinner skits, reading his lines aloud while seated at the dais in the banquet room. However biting the satire or sophomoric the script, Harry Truman during the dinner kept up the persona by which many of the reporters present had known him since he first arrived in Washington as the junior senator from Missouri: the thirty-third president of the United States was a good-natured kibitzer in formal wear.

The climax of the evening's entertainment, however, was the Gridiron Club's final skit, in which the main character was a noted public figure other than Truman. As the stage orchestra, in honor of the newly confirmed Undersecretary of State Dean Acheson, struck up the chords of the popular railroad-traveling tune "The Atchison, the Topeka, and the Sante Fe," the reporter Lewis Wood of the *New York Times*, costumed as James F. Byrnes in a southern riverboat captain's outfit, waited offstage for his entrance cue along with two other reporters, one in blackface as a Negro deckhand. In the banquet hall, the lights dimmed and the master of ceremonies announced to the president and the other guests the grand entrance of "the showboat of American foreign policy—here comes James F. Byrnes and his brave new crew!"

The orchestra then struck up "Here Comes the Showboat!" as the *Times* reporter Wood strutted onto the stage with one of the other reporters and, according to the script's directions, began "wrassling the wheel" of a cardboard ship's bridge and imperiously giving commands. The Gridiron script continued:

BYRNES: "Full speed ahead!" (jangles bell) "Full speed astern!" (more bell) "Full speed amidships!" (Helluva lot of bell) "We're off!"
SAILOR: (resignedly) "Well, where are we going this time?"
DECKHAND: (enters pushing bale of cotton) "Whadda you mean where is we going? Where is we been?"
SAILOR: (doggedly) "I still want to know: which way are we going?"
BYRNES: "Let's compromise and go sideways!"
SAILOR: (persisting) "Upstream or downstream? Forward or back?"
BYRNES: "What difference does it make? At least we're going!"
DECKHAND: "Don't look that way to me, boss. We's aground." (he shoulders his bale and exits).

Jimmy Byrnes was not present at the president's table that night to join in the general laughter at the Gridiron's perceived vacillations of the new U.S. secretary of state. Three days earlier, Byrnes and a few of his most trusted advisers at the State Department had flown out of Washington aboard an Air Force C-54 transport airplane, en route to Moscow and negotiations with Stalin. But while Byrnes was away, there were plenty of others willing to take his place at the president's side, both at hotel banquet tables and at the White House offices, and to encourage in Truman's mind this perception of Byrnes as a hapless ideological trimmer. One such new addition to the White House personnel was a blond, photogenically handsome young naval reserve officer, recently arrived in Washington from a good family in St. Louis. He was identified in the alphabetical guest list of the Gridiron Dinner published the following day in the *Washington Post*: "Lieutenant Commander Clark Clifford, USNR."

Clifford was but one of the numerous new men who in the eights months since FDR's death had begun to fill the coveted federal offices on Pennsylvania Avenue and across West Executive Drive at the multistoried State Department Building. Edwin Pauley, to name one notable example, had been known prior to 1945 only as an aggressive, successful California oilman, a Democratic contributor with remarkably deep pockets, and an early supporter of Truman. Pauley was now the U.S. commissioner on wartime reparations from the defeated Axis governments. Also newly powerful in Washington was Donald Russell, who only a few years earlier had been a junior partner at the Spartanburg, South Carolina, law firm of Byrnes and Wyche. Russell was now an assistant secretary of state for administration. And there was also Byrnes' longtime "bullbat" companion Walter Brown, formerly a correspondent for many small-town South Carolina newspapers and a son-in-law of a prominent former U.S. senator from Georgia. Brown now handled public relations for the U.S. Department of State.

Across the short stretch of pavement separating the State Department Building from the White House, there was near the Rose Garden the office of General Harry Vaughan, for many years known only as a politically ambitious member of the Missouri National Guard. Vaughan was now a principal military adviser to the president of the United States. And, of course, there was the current occupant of the Oval Office, who had worked there for only a little more than nine months: Harry S. Truman.

Among the men who rose to power and stayed in office in the months following FDR's death, only Jimmy Byrnes could credibly claim to have a government record of great national distinction prior to 1945. Truman, for instance, upon succeeding to the presidency, had met neither Stalin nor Churchill; Byrnes, by contrast, had met Churchill twice and discussed wartime policy with him, and he had met with Stalin and the other members of the Soviet delegation at the Yalta conference. Byrnes' sole possible rival as the most authoritative man still active in government was Henry Stimson, as formerly notable Roosevelt aides such as General Edwin "Pa" Watson and Harry Hopkins had either died or resigned because of declining health by the end of 1945. Other major political figures still in office and in apparent good health and presidential favor, such as Henry Wallace and Harold Ickes, were to resign their posts early in the Truman administration. And even Secretary of War Stimson had left Truman's cabinet at the end of September 1945. Truman himself was keenly aware that Jimmy Byrnes had the reputation as the most knowledgeable man in his administration, and at least in the months preceding the Gridiron Dinner the president had openly acknowledged his political and administrative debts to Byrnes.

Donald Russell later recalled those early months of the first Truman administration and told how, when traveling with Truman and Byrnes aboard the *Augusta* to the Potsdam conference, he had witnessed Truman at a mealtime propose a fulsome toast to Byrnes. Truman had told those present at the ship's mess table how he had endured snide remarks from his fellow Solons as the "senator from Pendergast" when he first had come to the U.S. Senate from Kansas City in 1935. One gracious exception among the Senate leader still stood out in Truman's memory. Looking at Byrnes sitting beside him at the table and raising his glass in a toast, Truman said that in his lonely years as a freshman senator, only Senator Jimmy Byrnes "had treated me like a human being."

Harry Truman again recorded his high estimation of Byrnes' character and his willingness in the first months of his presidency to rely upon Byrnes' judgment during a solitary moment during the ocean passage to Potsdam. "Had a long talk with my able and conniving Secretary of State," Truman wrote in his diary. "My, but he has a keen mind! And he is an honest man."

Jimmy Byrnes would have agreed with Truman's estimation. Byrnes' return to Washington from Potsdam on August 7 had given him his first opportunity since taking his oath on July 3 to be present and to assume daily duties at his ornate upstairs office at the State Department Building. By the end of September 1945, Byrnes' administration and his changes of personnel at State had won him the near-unanimous confidence both of domestic politicians and of the diplomatic community. Jimmy Byrnes came to the State Department bringing with him his usual South Carolina coterie of Russell, Brown, and, of course, Cassandra Connor, his personal secretary. But he had also quickly recruited Benjamin Cohen, a New Deal liberal and a former aide to Byrnes at the OWMR, who was widely respected in Washington for his legal brilliance. Cohen become counselor of the State Department in September 1945.

And in another personnel choice that was well received throughout the U.S. diplomatic community, Byrnes at the end of September obtained the Senate confirmation of the courtly and experienced Dean G. Acheson as undersecretary of state, in charge of administering the department during Byrnes' absences from Washington. Byrnes also continued the orderly restructuring of the State Department's responsibilities and staff into the geographical "divisions" and "offices" that had been begun by his predecessor, Edward Stettinius, Jr. And in a head-rolling move that pleased conservative Democrats and Republicans alike in Congress, Byrnes quickly fired Nelson A. Rockefeller, for whom Byrnes probably felt a personal and political distaste, as the assistant secretary of state for Latin American affairs.

Jimmy Byrnes enjoyed being the U.S. secretary of state. His first post-war international conference was set for late September in London, where he would meet, as had been arranged at Potsdam, with the foreign ministers of the major Allied powers to begin drafting preliminary peace treaties with Italy and Finland, and with the minor Axis countries in the Balkans. Byrnes regarded this first conference of the Council of Foreign Ministers as but a quick preliminary to his major business of drafting the Allied peace treaties with Germany and Japan. Throughout his first year at State, Byrnes remained optimistic that he and his Allied counterparts would quickly dispose of what he called the "spade work" of the minor treaties. At press conferences Byrnes boldly predicted that the "spade work" would be completed for the final drafts of the treaties with Germany and Japan by the council and that newly independent governments would be established for those countries within "twelve to eighteen months." Byrnes added, "I don't mind saying that it [the drafting of the treaties] is not such an unreasonable hope"—which is to say, while Jimmy Byrnes could reasonably hope to be the secretary of state who would receive the credit for this accomplishment.

Byrnes' confidence both in himself and in the success of his impending diplomatic negotiations on the future of postwar Europe and Asia was well captured in an "appreciation of the personality of Mr. James F. Byrnes" prepared by Lord Halifax, the British ambassador to the United States, for reading by the British foreign minister in London before Byrnes arrived for postwar talks. "Small in stature with quick observant eyes and a lively face, he is richly endowed with characteristic Irish charm," Halifax wrote to his minister. Jimmy Byrnes was, in Halifax's estimation, "a born politician," who was well known in Washington for "his capacity for friendly relations with virtually everyone with whom he has ever come in contact, and his skill and smoothness as a negotiator on the behalf of the late Mr. Roosevelt to whom he was, until almost the end, very deeply devoted." Yet it would a mistake, Halifax cautioned his minister, to consider Byrnes simply another opportunistic member of the new American administration with an eye on the main chance. An important distinction in Jimmy Byrnes' own eyes, Halifax cautioned, was that he saw himself as the one public official in the Truman administration solely responsible for keeping his country's course smooth.

Byrnes "is said to pride himself on his capacity to act as a cautious mediator and conciliator in the most strained situations," Halifax wrote in his confidential communiqué; the new U.S. secretary of state perceived himself as the "careful, slow but indefatigably earnest peacemaker; as one who lays aside all personal predictions and prejudices in order to keep his country's course on an even keel in dangerous waters; the ideal pilot, the idealistic honest broker."

Whatever the accuracy of this self-estimation by Jimmy Byrnes as "the ideal pilot" of the Truman administration, Byrnes showed promise, Halifax wrote to London, of being a "tactful, friendly, reasonable, and accessible Secretary of State. . . . He has an eye for ability, and is not afraid of surrounding himself with clever young men in the best old New Deal tradition." The British ambassador drily added, "In this respect he differs markedly from Mr. Truman."

Yet Lord Halifax and others saw signs that Jimmy Byrnes' personality itself might be too stormy for him to become the administration's reliable "steersman." There was, for instance, Byrnes' persistence, even after Truman had been in his presidential office more than six months, in addressing the chief executive in front of others as "Harry," rather than as "Mr. President." Byrnes ignored the advice from Dean Acheson to show more deference in public toward the new president, and Truman appeared not to mind this familiarity; but to many of the new men who had been promoted or retained in the White House by President Truman, including Byrnes' fellow southerner Jonathan Daniels, this familiarity toward the new president seemed bred of contempt.

"I'm sure that he felt he was a more able man than President Truman," Daniels later recalled of Byrnes and his actions during his first months at State. Jimmy Byrnes "was running a race with John C. Calhoun," in Daniels' opinion, seeing himself as both the South's and the Truman administration's preeminent public man. As such, Byrnes did not have to bother to explain his diplomacy to the president, in Daniels' estimation. "Byrnes had decided he was going to run foreign policy and that he would casually tell the president about it."

Byrnes' conviction of his own superior diplomatic and executive ability displayed itself on occasion not only in disdain toward the president above him but also in sudden anger toward professionals who worked under him. "Mr. Byrnes is known to regard the State Department with a highly critical eye and to be irritated by the manner and outlook of the typical career man," Lord Halifax had noted. One career man at the State Department, Theodore Achilles, soon learned the accuracy of this when he first approached Secretary Byrnes about setting up procedures to inform Dean Acheson and others in Washington of the progress of the Council of Foreign Ministers meetings in London. Achilles, a respected administrator in the Office of European Affairs, then witnessed one of Jimmy Byrnes' sudden shifts from geniality to choler.

"Hell, I might tell the president sometime what happened," Byrnes snapped to the startled diplomat, "but I'm never going to tell those little bastards at the State Department anything about it." There is perhaps more to Byrnes' remark than just intemperance; as the British biographer of Henry Stimson, Godfrey Hodgson, has noted, there was a remarkable uniformity of background among the career employees of the U.S. State and War Departments of the 1930s and 1940s: Ivy League educated, suspicious of public opinion and populism, and largely Republican. Byrnes at least recognized his political enemies, but it did not seem to occur or to matter much to Jimmy Byrnes that Theodore Achilles might consider himself among those whom Byrnes had just maligned as "the little bastards." This story made its rounds among the professionals in the State Department.

Personalities aside, Jimmy Byrnes also had his ideological critics outside the State Department. Secretary of War Henry Stimson had distrusted Byrnes' policy of withholding all information on the atomic bomb from the Soviet government ever since Byrnes had argued so successfully for that policy during the summer meetings of the Interim Committee. (Stimson may also have held something of a personal grudge against Jimmy Byrnes for having made sure that Stimson and Averell Harriman had plenty of "free time," while others at Potsdam discussed the combat use of the atomic bomb and the terms of the Japanese surrender.) Eight days after Byrnes left Washington on September 4, 1945, to attend the first Council of Foreign Ministers meeting in London, Stimson handed to Truman a memorandum containing the war secretary's final thoughts on the effect of the atomic monopoly on the upcoming negotiations. Although not referring to Byrnes by name, Stimson's memorandum cautioned the president against those of his advisers who sought to enter the postwar negotiations "having this weapon rather ostentatiously on our hip."

Yet despite these warning signs and his reading of Stimson's memorandum, Truman for his own good reasons continued to express confidence in Byrnes at least until the end of his first six months in office. Among those good reasons was the fact that, until George Marshall or Dean Acheson could convince Truman otherwise, Jimmy Byrnes was the only choice for secretary of state the president felt he had. Unlike Franklin Roosevelt, Harry Truman did not enjoy acting as his own secretary of state. ("How I hate this trip!" Truman had written in his diary on the way to Potsdam, where he had deferred to Byrnes' guidance during much of that conference.) Byrnes had always exuded confidence in his own abilities to solve any negotiable problem, including those of foreign diplomacy; and despite Stimson's misgivings Byrnes gave every indication of attempting to continue Roosevelt's wartime policy of the "Grand Alliance" of cooperation with the USSR. Until Truman was ready to propose a different policy toward the Soviet government, Jimmy Byrnes seemed the man most likely to continue the old one successfully.

"I know how to deal with the Russians. It's just like the U.S. Senate," Jimmy Byrnes at this time was breezily explaining to the other members of the U.S. delegation traveling with him aboard the *Queen Elizabeth* to the London meeting. "You build a post office in their state, and they'll build a post office in our state." Indeed, rather than becoming Stimson's bellicose atomic diplomat intent upon intimidating the Soviet Union, Byrnes' diplomacy at his first postwar conference was based upon his willingness to offer the Soviets a quid pro quo of diplomatic recognition of the Soviet regimes in Asia, in Eastern Europe, and in the Balkans in exchange for Soviet cooperation in quickly finalizing the drafts of the preliminary peace treaties. When a Republican hard-line member of the U.S. delegation accompanying Byrnes to London, John Foster Dulles, objected to Byrnes about his apparent willingness to acknowledge the Soviet sphere of European influence, Jimmy Byrnes replied in terms he might have used in the cloakrooms of the Senate back in the old days when he was dealing for Roosevelt along with Pat Harrison. "We've pushed these babies [the Russians] about as far as they will go," Byrnes told a doubtless startled Dulles. "I think we better start thinking about compromise."

But despite Byrnes' confidence that he could resolve all the postwar difficulties among the great powers through the rules of senatorial compromise, the London conference of the Council of Foreign Ministers ended in failure and produced no signed treaties. V. M. Molotov did not want to play post office. In regard to an early discussion of the Balkans, the Soviet foreign minister categorically rejected even Byrnes' comparatively minor condition that Western journalists be allowed to travel in Bulgaria and Romania before the United States recognized the results of elections scheduled there by the occupying Soviets. As for Byrnes' hopes of quickly resolving the "spade work" of drafting treaties with these former Axis countries, they came to less than nothing. The Council of Foreign Ministers, in formal meetings in London lasting from September 11 to October 2, could not even agree on which of the Allied governments should sit together at the conference table to begin the drafting work.

Citing the lack of signed armistices by China or France with the Balkan states, Molotov persistently refused to recognize the rights of these countries to participate in the talks among the Big Three concerning Bulgaria and Romania. Byrnes and the British foreign minister, Ernest Bevin, fearful that endorsing such exclusion would foredoom any cooperation among these former Allies on future treaties, and also unwilling publicly to compromise the authority of France and China as members of the Security Council of the United Nations even before the first meeting of the UN, refused to proceed until this seating issue could be resolved.

Two days into this deadlocked conference, Byrnes approached Molotov at a social reception held at the House of Lords and, "in typical senatorial fashion," according to Walter Brown, who witnessed the episode, asked the Soviet foreign minister to "cut out all this stalling and let us get down to work." Neither at that reception nor later was Byrnes able to effect a compromise, however; and although he indicated a willingness to accept the exclusion of France and China, provided a face-saving arrangement could be arranged, he came under intense personal lobbying from Dulles to call off the conference rather than accept Molotov's preconditions. Dulles even followed Byrnes into the bathroom before the secretary left his quarters for an early-morning session of the ministers, and threatened to telephone Senator Arthur Vandenberg of the Senate Foreign Relations Committee and have him denounce Byrnes on the Senate floor if Byrnes did not call for the adjournment of the conference. Nevertheless, Byrnes left the bathroom and persevered to achieve some sort of middle ground in the negotiations, despite Dulles' threats and Molotov's intransigence.

As the arguments among the three national delegations continued into a third week with no sign of compromise on the Balkan issue, Byrnes was observed by a journalist to be absentmindedly and repeatedly writing in a corner of an official document, "Messrs. Morris, Brown & Co., Ltd., London." The words were the name of a nineteenth-century exporting firm that had been stamped on goods Byrnes as a boy had sold on the streets of Charleston. The tedium of the deadlocked negotiations at Lancaster House in London was now apparently after half a century recalling that early labor to his mind. Early on the evening of October 2, with no resolution of the Balkan controversy in sight, Byrnes arranged for the foreign minister from China to move that the London meeting of the Council of Foreign Ministers permanently adjourn. The Big Three were not even able to agree on the wording of a final communiqué.

Byrnes was back in Washington on October 4, and he met the next day with Truman, and, three days later, with members of the Senate Foreign Relations Committee. "It took considerable courage for Byrnes to end the London Foreign Ministers' meeting and perhaps incur the onus of breaking up the wartime association with the Soviet Union," Bohlen later wrote in admiration of the secretary. Byrnes had resisted the importuning of Dulles in order to hold four additional council meetings in an attempt to break the deadlock over participation by China and France and recognition of Bulgaria and Romania. "It was certainly not Byrnes's intention when he took the job as Secretary of State to engage in a series of confrontations with the Soviets," Bohlen added. But in a national radio address preceding his appearance before the Senate committee, Jimmy Byrnes himself had made it clear that he did not intend to assume any personal blame for the failure to maintain a postwar entente cordiale with the Soviet Union. "In the past I have been criticized and commended for being a compromiser," Byrnes told his national audience on the evening of October 5. "I confess that I believe that peace and political progress in international affairs, as in domestic affairs, depend upon intelligent compromise." But without directly criticizing Molotov, Byrnes added, "Compromise, however, does not mean surrender, and compromise, unlike surrender, requires the assent of more than one party."

Privately, among his cabinet peers and his associates in the State Department, Byrnes was more characteristically colloquial. He heatedly expressed his opinion to Edward Stettinius, Jr., that "the Russians are welshing on all the agreements reached at Yalta and Potsdam." And at a meeting with the secretaries of war and navy on October 23, Byrnes as a result of his London experience with Molotov's intransigence insisted upon continuing his policy of no shared atomic research with the Soviet Union. "Mr. Byrnes referred to a visit he had received from Dr. Oppenheimer who thought Stalin should have been approached with regard to the atomic bomb a month ago and that there should be no delay in discussions," according to the State Department notes of this October 23 meeting. "Mr. Byrnes agreed that the whole problem of cooperation is predicated upon free inspection at all times. He cited the fact that we cannot recognize the Rumanian and Bulgarian regimes because we cannot get information on conditions there and our representatives have difficulty getting around." Byrnes then told the war secretaries that he had replied to Oppenheimer that "if this is true in Rumania and Bulgaria it is considerably more true in Soviet Russia, and he [Byrnes] had asked Dr. Oppenheimer whether full inspections under conditions such as he had described could be had in the Soviet Union today. Dr. Oppenheimer, he said, finally admitted that this situation was pretty bad."

But despite the admission even by liberals in the Truman administration that U.S. relations with the Soviet Union in the late fall of 1945 were "pretty bad," Jimmy Byrnes was not yet ready to become the nation's first Cold Warrior.

Witnesses in the first Truman administration to Jimmy Byrnes' willingness to accommodate what the secretary perceived as the legitimate security needs of the Soviet Union were as politically disparate as James Forrestal and Henry Wallace. In the weeks immediately after the collapse of the London conference, Secretary of the Navy James Forrestal suggested to Truman that the president publicize Soviet-U.S. disagreements in order to enlist support for a slowed U.S. reconversion to a civilian economy and a continuation of a national service. Byrnes, despite his prior war record as an advocate of total civilian mobilization to military demands and his recent record of pressing Robert Oppenheimer to admit that relations with the Soviet Union were "pretty bad," nevertheless disagreed. In a documented instance that serves as a categorical rebuttal to those later historians who claim Byrnes hardened his attitudes toward the Soviets after the failure of the London conference, Forrestal recorded in his diary that Byrnes argued against such publicity, maintaining that the Soviets would only see such actions as a U.S. provocation. And the liberal secretary of commerce, Henry Wallace, no admirer of Byrnes, likewise recorded in his diary his surprise at Jimmy Byrnes' declaring a willingness to accede to Stalin's conditions for a postwar settlement in China as agreed upon at Yalta. In a cabinet meeting on November 27, 1945—six weeks after the London conference and two weeks before Byrnes tried again to achieve a rap-

prochement with the Soviet government at Moscow—Wallace recorded,
"Jimmie Byrnes outlined his policy as being one of using our armed forces
to disarm the Japs in China and Manchuria."

Wallace continued his record of Byrnes' statements, "At the conclusion
of getting the Japs out Jimmie Byrnes thought the United States should
stand pat and not give Chiang Kai-shek anything whatsoever until he agreed
to come to terms with the Chinese communists and give them some places
in a combination cabinet."

Thus, if there is present in these statements prior to the Moscow conference any of the atomic saber rattling toward the Soviet Union that later
revisionist historians claim to hear in Byrnes' diplomacy, it was inaudible
to Byrnes' contemporary critics. Indeed, even the later revisionist critic
Lloyd Gardner, never inclined to ascribe admirable motives to the secretary's public actions, concedes that "despite the failure of atomic diplomacy
at London—or *perhaps, as Byrnes now appeared to believe* [emphasis
added] the failure to *use* atomic diplomacy properly—he continued to think
that peace was just a matter of mixing various policies."

Such a description of Byrnes' diplomacy, despite its disparagement of
Byrnes' insight—that peace was "just a matter of mixing various
policies"—could just as well have been applied to Roosevelt's diplomacy
at the Teheran and Yalta conferences to continue the Grand Alliance
beyond the Second World War. And, like the late FDR, Byrnes presumed
that he could "get through" to almost any individual if only they could
meet personally. Hence within a month of his pessimistic report to the
cabinet secretaries, and with little advance notice of his new intentions
either to President Truman or to the British government, Byrnes on his
own initiative shortly after Thanksgiving Day called on Molotov to agree
to a second meeting of the Allied foreign ministers before the end of
December 1945.

This time Byrnes suggested that they meet in Moscow, where the U.S.
secretary could, if necessary, meet personally with Stalin. Byrnes had confided to Walter Brown before issuing this invitation that if Molotov's stubbornness threatened to endanger this second conference, Byrnes would be
able to go over Molotov's head and deal with Stalin directly. Byrnes apparently trusted that Stalin, who remembered Jimmy Byrnes from Yalta
as "the most honest-looking horse thief" the Soviet leader had ever met,
would be capable of a frank compromise and friendliness with the American
secretary when his functionary Molotov was not. On behalf of his government, Molotov promptly accepted Byrnes' offer; the British government,
after complaints from Halifax over a lack of time to prepare for the Moscow
conference, did so reluctantly.

Ready or not, with or without the considered assent to the conference
by the British government, Byrnes on December 12 departed from Washington by airplane with the clear intention of dealing with the Soviets and

beginning the "spade work" of drafting the first treaties. By inviting Molotov to host a conference in Moscow limited to the governments of the Big Three, Byrnes in effect had accepted Molotov's preconditions laid down at London of excluding France and China from the preliminary discussions of the Balkans; and this time John Foster Dulles was not invited to accompany the secretary. Byrnes traveled with just those professionals in the State Department whom he most trusted: these were primarily Ben Cohen; the Russian translator Charles "Chip" Bohlen (whom Byrnes had known since the Yalta conference); and H. Freeman Matthews, the director of the Office of European Affairs, whom Byrnes invariably called Doc.

Byrnes made no arrangements before leaving Washington to have dispatches sent from Moscow at regular intervals to Truman's vacation residences during the Christmas holidays in Independence or in Key West, Florida. The U.S. secretary of state plainly intended to make his own decisions while in the Soviet capital. Charles Bohlen noticed this lack of preparation and asked Secretary Byrnes why. "In sharp tones, he said that he knew when it was necessary to report to the president and when it was not," Bohlen later recalled being told. "I was put in my place and I stayed there."

Most crucially, Jimmy Byrnes did not arrive in Moscow wearing the atomic bomb "rather ostentatiously" on his hip; Byrnes instead put the bomb on the negotiation table. Although still maintaining his policy of no shared atomic research with the Soviets in the immediate future, Byrnes brought with him to Moscow one of his former associates on the Interim Committee, Dr. James Conant. Conant encouraged the Soviets to support a proposed UN commission empowered to inspect all nations' nuclear facilities, and Byrnes implied to the Soviets in the opening meetings of the conference that in exchange for their cooperation in forming this UN commission and in settling the Balkan matter, they could expect greater access to the U.S. atomic research.

Thus the building of political post offices had finally begun, at least in Byrnes' imagination. During the twelve-day December conference in Moscow, which included two personal talks with Stalin, Byrnes obtained an initial Soviet agreement to support the United Nations Atomic Development Authority, on the basis of procedures outlined by David Lilienthal of the TVA and Undersecretary Acheson. He also gained a Soviet promise, in exchange for a later Anglo-American recognition of Romania and Bulgaria, to see that at least two local opposition ministers were included in the Communist governments of each of these Balkan countries.

As for the drafting of the peace treaties with the former Axis satellites, Byrnes successfully offered to the Soviet and British foreign ministers the type of lawyerly distinction that in the past had proved so useful in arranging Senate cloakroom compromises. Byrnes proposed that a larger *conference* of advisory but nonvoting Allied foreign ministers convene with the Council of Foreign Ministers of the Big Three powers. China and France thus would be represented at Paris, but only "to review" and to make "recommendations" on the final texts of the peace treaties. Stalin endorsed this idea after a face-to-face meeting with Byrnes. After the U.S. secretary had complained at this and at a second meeting of his difficulties with Molotov in resolving the Balkan issue, Stalin had smiled good-naturedly and ironically joked "that this was unexpected news."

General Charles de Gaulle was reported to the American delegation to be incensed over this arrangement, but Byrnes' compromise held. This compromise regarding the number of Allied governments drafting the first peace treaties was agreed to in Moscow on December 24 and released to the press at Byrnes' direction the following day. "And so, on Christmas morning, 1945," Byrnes subsequently wrote, "people throughout the world learned that five months of negotiation had at last brought agreement on the holding of a conference to help restore 'peace on earth.' " The Moscow conference adjourned with cordiality among the Big Three on December 27 and with promises to meet again at Paris the following spring.

Byrnes was ebullient. He had reason to believe before leaving Moscow that he had "gotten through" to Stalin and that he had successfully continued the Soviet–U.S. entente cordiale into the postwar world. The arrangements had been confirmed for the first treaties with the minor Axis countries to be drafted at Paris within twelve months of V-E Day, and the prospects now looked good to Byrnes that once this "spade work" was accomplished, the United States and the Soviet Union could come to a reasonably quick agreement on the treaty with Germany. And less than a month away from the first convening of the UN General Assembly, scheduled for January 1946, Jimmy Byrnes had obtained from the Soviets an agreement in principle to support the United States on the establishment of the UN Atomic Energy Commission. Truman, when he learned of the adjournment at Moscow, praised Byrnes' efforts in general terms when speaking to the *New York Times* on December 28. Dean Acheson also wired his congratulations to his superior at the State Department, cheerfully referring to Byrnes as "St. Nicholas." Jimmy Byrnes was looking forward to returning home.

The arrival of Jimmy Byrnes' airplane at National Airport in Washington on December 29, 1945, should have marked the conclusion of what he then considered his greatest diplomatic triumph, preserving the Soviet alliance. Instead, it marked his emergence as the nation's first diplomatic Cold Warrior—and, the beginning of his ultimate downfall as Truman's first appointed U.S. secretary of state. The Acheson-Lilienthal report, the formal articulation of the offer of shared atomic research on which Byrnes pinned so many of his hopes at Moscow, would become a document of shambles by the summer of 1946. Conservatives both within and outside of the U.S. Senate that year insisted upon adding to this document, put forward by Byrnes and endorsed by Truman, the critical qualification that the proposed UN agency controlling atomic energy be exempt from the directives of the UN Security Council. The Soviet Union thus would be denied the power to veto any punitive measures to be imposed by the international policing body, and the U.S. military thus would be able to maintain a de facto monopoly over the accelerated production of atomic weapons. The obvious result was to be the Soviet Union's rejection of the proposal in UN debate and the its disavowal of the Christmas-time deal struck with Secretary Byrnes at Moscow in 1945. "The Soviets could not permit us to maintain that monopoly," Chip Bohlen later recalled. "This was an understandable position." Byrnes also was to be particularly galled by this defeat, because he had invited the conservative Bernard Baruch to review the text of the original Acheson-Lilienthal report, and Baruch had given the impetus for changing the report. With the prospects for international control and sharing of atomic research increasingly a dead issue at the UN, Byrnes confided to Dean Acheson that directly involving Baruch in the secretary's efforts to entice Soviet cooperation was "the worst mistake I ever made."

And contemporaneous with this failure was the apparently premeditated decision by Stalin and his factotum V. M. Molotov not to bargain in good faith at the Paris conference, whether or not Jimmy Byrnes delivered the promised atomic goods. Byrnes was, in fact, perhaps the only "honest broker" at the Paris conference. He sincerely believed that rational compromise was yet possible among the great powers in the tradition of Roosevelt's Grand Alliance and Woodrow Wilson's Fourteen Points. A cynical British observer of both diplomatic and literary duplicity, Harold Nicolson, who in a lifetime of disappointments had attended the Versailles conference in 1919 and the Paris conference in 1946, could not help noting that in contrast to the "aura of prestige" that had surrounded Wilson in 1919, there was a "haze of vague benevolence which enshrouded, and at times bemused, Mr. Byrnes." Georges Clemenceau in 1919 had observed that Woodrow Wilson at Versailles had talked like Jesus Christ but acted like the chauvinistic Lloyd George; a generation later, Secretary Byrnes on occasion might talk like Senator Arthur Vandenberg or John Foster Dulles, but he preferred to act like Franklin D. Roosevelt. The problem was that Joseph Stalin apparently considered the Grand Alliance to have died with FDR at Warm Springs, Georgia, and to have been thoroughly buried when tanks of the Red Army rolled into the Potsdam railroad station in Berlin, and when other Soviet armor and troops occupied Warsaw, Sofia, and Bucharest. Despite Byrnes' hopes of a reasonably humane sphere of USSR influence, the Soviets did not come to Eastern Europe to build post offices.

But more immediate to the cause of Byrnes' troubles upon his arriving home was that the secretary seemed unaware of, or indifferent to, the animosity he had left behind at the U.S. embassy in Moscow. This ill will was directed toward Byrnes primarily by the U.S. ambassador, Averell Harriman, and the chargé d'affaires at the embassy, George Kennan. Both men had felt slighted by Byrnes' ignoring their advice during his bout of "personal diplomacy" at the Moscow conference (Harriman's animus went back to his slight by Byrnes at the Potsdam conference), and both were ideologically opposed to Byrnes' efforts to continue the Soviet alliance.

George Kennan, in particular, was opposed to Byrnes' compromise on the Balkan issue by including opposition ministers in the governments there; he later wrote that he found it "absurd to suppose that anything essential was going to be changed by the inclusion of one or two non-Communist ministers in the cabinets of countries which already had a police system along the lines of the Soviet NKVD, entirely under Russian control." At the Moscow conference, Kennan sat directly behind Byrnes during one negotiation session, and he wrote in his diary on December 19, 1945, that the secretary's "main purpose is to achieve some sort of agreement, he doesn't much care what." To Kennan's mind, Byrnes' motivation at the conference was simple: "He wants an agreement for its political effect at home."

However, despite these open and concealed expressions of discontent with his diplomacy of "intelligent compromise," Jimmy Byrnes remained confident of his ability to convince legislators individually and the nation collectively that he had succeeded in his negotiations at Moscow. The necessity to inform or persuade Harry Truman was at this time apparently far from his thoughts. In his haste to return to the United States, Byrnes had not attempted to tell Truman of the adjournment of the Moscow conference, trusting to Averell Harriman's staff at the Moscow embassy to keep the president informed; Truman consequently had heard the news of the close of the conference on a commercial U.S. radio broadcast along with the rest of the nation. Additionally, before Byrnes had departed Moscow, his office had scheduled for him a national radio address in the United States for December 30, the night after his expected arrival back at Washington. This schedule did not allot time for Byrnes to brief Truman personally on the results of the conference. During the London conference the previous fall, Byrnes had acted with almost this same degree of independence, and Truman had expressed no dissatisfaction with his actions. The secretary of state was surprised, therefore, when on stepping down from his Army transport airplane at National Airport shortly after noon on December 29, he was met by Dean Acheson with a message from the president.

The undersecretary of state informed Byrnes that Harry Truman, now returned from Key West and spending the remainder of the Christmas holidays aboard the presidential yacht *Williamsburg*, moored on the Potomac River about fifty miles from Washington at Quantico Bay, wished Byrnes to join him there immediately. Fatigued by nearly sixty hours of uninterrupted airplane travel from Moscow, and perhaps the mounting suspicion that criticisms of his Soviet policy behind his back were having an effect, Byrnes snapped from his usual good humor. Quickly he changed in the winter air from what Dean Acheson had perceived as a munificent Saint Nicholas to what now seemed a spiteful small Irishman with a black temper. "Goddamn it to hell, I can't do that," Byrnes exclaimed to a doubtless startled Acheson. "I've got to work on this speech."

Acheson quickly recovered, however. He both persuaded and mollified the secretary, and less than four hours later, after a brief reunion with his wife and a return to his Shoreham apartment for a few hours' rest, Byrnes was again on an Army transport airplane. This time he was bound for Quantico, Virginia.

Waiting aboard the presidential yacht for Byrnes in addition to Truman were a number of the president's "new men" who frequently accompanied Harry Truman on these no-wives holiday trips and who were all largely unfamiliar to Byrnes. They included such acquaintances of Harry Truman as General Harry Vaughan, Clark Clifford, Charlie Ross, and Matt Connelly. Among the few whom Byrnes knew well among those on board was Admiral Leahy, who had been retained by Truman as the chief of White House staff, and the admiral was no friend to the secretary of state. Leahy had had a bone to pick with Jimmy Byrnes ever since the two had disagreed over the surrender terms with Japan.

Byrnes experienced a reception aboard the *Williamsburg* that was a bit short of hostile. Truman, meeting first privately in his stateroom with Byrnes for more than an hour, complained only mildly to him about not having been kept regularly informed about the Moscow conference. He seemed to accept Byrnes' explanation that delays in sending his reports from the U.S. embassy at Moscow probably had resulted in Truman's learning of the adjournment over commercial radio. Truman may in fact not have cared much about this delay or about his not receiving the daily details of the negotiations, and Byrnes inferred as much. In unpublished notes the secretary kept about this meeting with Truman, Byrnes wrote that "it was my deduction that some of his friends on board the ship had suggested to the president that he should have been advised," and that Truman was objecting to the lack of information from the State Department upon the instigation of these friends.

In any case, Truman was cheerful in bringing Byrnes out his stateroom to rejoin the rest of the ship's company, and he expressed his approval of Byrnes' actions at Moscow in front of the others. Despite Byrnes' obvious exhaustion, the president insisted that his secretary of state stay aboard for dinner. During the meal, only Leahy openly criticized Byrnes' agreements, stating that he did not believe that the Soviets would honor their agreements on Romania or Bulgaria. Byrnes asked Leahy what he would have done had he been at the Moscow conference and, receiving no direct reply, pointedly reminded Leahy that he had been with him at Yalta and Potsdam and had concurred in the attempts there to continue the Soviet alliance. The Moscow agreements, Byrnes told him, were "simply another effort to achieve the objectives of the previous agreements entered into by the heads of government." Byrnes was not about to let Leahy forget that he, too, had supported the Rooseveltian alliance and that its continuation by the Truman administration was still the accepted U.S. policy.

Truman signaled an end to the meal, and broke up what might have become a heated quarrel between Byrnes and Leahy, by calling on his guests to join him in a postdinner game of poker. Once again, Byrnes was the odd man out; despite his convivial habits of drinking and storytelling developed over decades of politicking, Jimmy Byrnes never had been much of a poker player. Citing his exhaustion and desire to return home and work on his radio speech, he departed, but not before Truman had obtained from him a promise to return to the yacht on December 31 and rejoin the president's group for a New Year's Eve party.

Truman in later years claimed that his meeting that night of December 29, 1945, with Byrnes in the stateroom of the *Williamsburg* had been anything *but* the demonstration of presidential support it appeared to Byrnes to be. "Byrnes got the real riot act," Truman later told an interviewer in his retirement. Truman before the end of his second term also produced a handwritten letter that he said he had composed and read aloud to Byrnes a few days after their *Williamsburg* meeting. In this letter, dated January 5, 1946, Truman catalogs what he considers Byrnes' failures as a secretary of state, including disastrous compromises on the governmental organizations of "those two police states" Romania and Bulgaria. "I am not going to agree to the recognition of those two governments unless they are radically changed," the letter states. The close of Truman's letter is blunt: "I'm tired of babying the Soviets."

Byrnes later was emphatic that he did not receive a "riot act" or a verbal rebuke in the stateroom of the presidential yacht and that such a letter was never sent or read to him by Harry Truman. Had the president done either of these things, Byrnes maintained, "I would have resigned immediately." There is no reason to doubt Byrnes' word. Always touchy in regard to his independence and his prerogatives, Byrnes on at least two occasions during the Roosevelt administrations had submitted his resignations as OES or OWMR director when he had felt insulted, only to have Roosevelt refuse to accept them; Jimmy Byrnes would not have been any less quick-tempered in resigning from the service of a president he regarded with less affection than FDR, particularly if upbraided in the manner Truman described for having "babied" the Soviets. Truman, a much more impulsive and decisive man than Roosevelt, would have angrily accepted

Byrnes' resignation had his secretary angrily offered it. Also in support of Byrnes' claim that he never saw this letter or had it read to him is the fact that on at least one other occasion involving a journalist during his presidency, Truman was known to have composed angry letters that he later neither sent nor read to the intended audience, but which he kept in his files.

Jonathan Daniels was not on board the yacht that night, but knowing both Truman and Byrnes, he later stated his belief that Truman exaggerated the terms of his rebuke to Byrnes and that the president wrote the letter at a later date primarily to vent his own anger. Daniels felt certain that Truman did not show or read the letter to his secretary of state on January 5, 1946, or at any other time; but he also believed that Jimmy Byrnes, sublimely confident, plainly disregarded the other, less dramatic but equally clear signs of presidential dissatisfaction that Truman demonstrated to him that night aboard the *Williamsburg*.

Whatever passed between these two men, the secretary the following night in a thirty-minute broadcast on NBC reported to the nation on the Moscow conference in an unapologetic manner. He insisted on the necessity of his diplomacy in recognizing the Soviet sphere of Balkan influence in exchange for anticipated cooperation from Stalin. "It must be recognized that the Soviet government has a very real interest in the character of the government of these states," Byrnes said in regard to Romania and Bulgaria. "These countries are neighbors of the Soviet Union and they were involved in the war against the Soviet Union." Byrnes continued, "It is, therefore, to be expected that the withdrawal of Soviet troops from these countries may depend upon the Soviet government's confidence in the peaceful character of these governments." It must also be remembered in appraising Byrnes' concessions to the Soviet sphere that, whatever the sufferings or heroisms of individual Romanians or Bulgarians under Soviet occupation, the wounds inflicted by the Axis governments upon the Allies were still fresh in late 1945. The fascist and anti-Semitic Iron Guard of Romania, for example, had fought on the German flank during the siege of Stalingrad; and the unsuccessful U.S. air raids on the Ploiesti oil fields in Romania beginning in 1942 had been among the most costly in the European theater in terms of American airplanes lost and airmen killed. The Bulgarian fascist army also had enthusiastically participated with German forces in the invasion of Greece, inflicting atrocities that were savage even by Balkan standards, murdering as many as 70,000 individuals in reprisals for attacks on Axis forces.

The night after this speech, on December 31, Byrnes returned to the *Williamsburg*, as he had promised, to join in the president's New Year's Eve party. In front of the other presidential advisers, Truman once again praised Byrnes' actions at Moscow and stated his support of Byrnes' speech. And despite Truman's strong language about his own intentions of not recognizing the Balkan governments, which the president may or may not have expressed to Byrnes, the United States formally recognized the government of Romania on February 5, 1946.

But there was no denying that Jimmy Byrnes was on the defensive. Throughout the month of January 1946, anonymously credited news stories, probably instigated by Leahy, appeared in *Newsweek* and the *Washington Post* intimating that a fundamental rift between Truman and Byrnes had occurred. It was difficult for Byrnes to counter these stories. He had caught a bad head cold returning from the presidential yacht in the sleet storm of December 29 and was bedridden for several days in early January. By the time he had recovered, later in the second week of the month, he had to travel to London to attend the meeting of the UN Security Council. During Byrnes' absence from Washington, Donald Russell was responsible for maintaining effective political relations for the State Department. Russell in mid-January sent a package to Cassandra Connor, who had accompanied Byrnes to London. "I do not wish to disturb the Justice," Russell wrote, "but I thought you would like to see the attached." The package contained a clipping from *Newsweek* on the latest report of the Truman-Byrnes break. "It considerably expands on the general gossip that was being bruited about town," Russell wrote. Russell also provided Cassandra Connor with a possible warning on the conduct of international relations for her to pass on to Byrnes as a result of Russell's talking with journalists and congressmen around Washington in the winter of 1946. "I must confess," Russell wrote, "that there is apparently more anti-Russian spirit than I thought possible."

The anti-Soviet spirit among the press and the Congress continued after Byrnes' return from London the following week, and it had become painfully evident to Byrnes that his policy of a continued alliance with the Soviet Union based on compromise was failing. In Byrnes' view, Stalin was welshing on his agreements made with the United States, not only at Yalta and Potsdam but also at Moscow. In the Balkans the Soviets failed to abide by their agreement to install even a few nominal opposition ministers in the Communist governments there. Worse, the systematic murder of all non-Communist politicians in Soviet-occupied Poland beginning in late 1945 and early 1946 made Byrnes' statement after Yalta that the differences between the Lubin Poles and the London Poles resembled the differences between the Democratic and the Republican national committees now seem fatally glib. The transcript of his February news conference shows that Byrnes, in selecting questions to be answered for publication, dodged the issue of responsibility for Poland. "OFF THE RECORD: 'One man asks about Poland and so-called war trials. He *would* want to get me in trouble.' "

Truman had continued to support his secretary, at least with presidential silence. It had been widely speculated in newspapers, including the *New*

York Times and the *Washington Post*, that if the president chose to disagree with his secretary of state, he would do so in his State of the Union speech, scheduled a few days after Byrnes' broadcast on December 30. But in this address to Congress on January 3, 1946, Truman made no mention of the Moscow conference or of Byrnes' earlier speech. The president chose instead to talk almost exclusively about domestic matters. Jimmy Byrnes apparently still was the only secretary of state Harry Truman had. But although the president was for the moment keeping his "able and conniving secretary of state," he was beginning to be influenced by new men such as Clark Clifford and George Kennan who were urging him to adopt a more confrontational policy toward the Soviet Union and to assert his authority over Byrnes. Eventually this advice became enshrined in two of the primary documents of the Cold War—Kennan's "Long Telegram" and the Clifford-Elsey report. Both would serve as instruments for Byrnes' removal.

It was time for Jimmy Byrnes to go out into the cold. He had done so once before, risking both his reputation and his job in an attempt almost single-handedly to continue the Rooseveltian alliance with the Soviet Union. That attempt had failed, with results that were not simply disadvantageous to Jimmy Byrnes personally but also calamitous for the peoples of Eastern Europe and the Balkans. It was now plain to Byrnes that both politically and diplomatically he had to go out even farther alone, this time into the different direction of confrontational relations with the Soviet Union. This was a direction that the new men about Truman had been urging but that Byrnes felt that he, as the "ideal pilot," in Halifax's phrase, was uniquely qualified to direct. Eventually the new men prevailed and obtained Byrnes' resignation, in January 1947, but not before James F. Byrnes had successfully managed the first major diplomatic and military confrontation of the postwar world between the United States and the Soviet Union. This confrontation would not come in Eastern Europe or in the Balkans, where Byrnes had risked and lost so much of his prestige and energy. Instead, Byrnes would chose his fight for the local sovereignty of a neighbor of the Soviet Union in an area that continued to be central to Cold War struggles: the oil fields of Iran.

18

Iranian Winter
and a
Cold Warrior

Jimmy Byrnes had kept his eye on
the oil fields of Iran as a critical area of postwar interest to the U.S. State
Department and the U.S. military since the summer of 1943, when he was
named the director of the Office of War Mobilization. Barely fifteen days
into his new OWM position, Byrnes had hosted a meeting at his East Wing
offices at the White House on June 12, 1943, with representatives from the
Departments of State, War, Navy, and the Interior. Their subject was the
alarming rate at which the U.S. domestic oil reserves were being consumed
by this country's military needs and its lend-lease shipments of domestic
oil to the Allies. The oil reserves of the United States would be seriously
depleted by the end of the war unless a greater use was made of the Middle
Eastern oil fields then under control of the British and Soviet governments,
they agreed; in particular, "vigorous negotiations" should begin, as Byrnes
later phrased it in his memorandum reporting to Roosevelt on this OWM
meeting, "for acquisition by the United States government of a third interest in the Iranian oil fields owned by the Anglo-Iranian Company."

In making this recommendation, Byrnes was greatly influenced by Fred
Searls, Jr., a geologist who advised various wartime agencies and whose

opinions Byrnes highly valued. Searls had confirmed to Byrnes that, in his judgment, "it is entirely possible that the overproduction of crude oil within the United States has become a matter of history." Like others in the OWM office, Searls then turned his eyes eastward to a source of petroleum that would enable the United States to continue fighting the war while sparing its domestic reserves for postwar consumption. "The oil reserves in Iran and Saudi Arabia are known to be enormous," Searls wrote to Byrnes in a memorandum that summer of 1943. "Four fields in Iran (under British control) are known to contain in excess of sixteen billion barrels, which is a greater content that the total known reserves within the United States."

Byrnes became in 1943–44 an enthusiastic backer of a plan proposed by Searls and others in the Roosevelt administration to duplicate in the Iranian oil fields the construction of an oil pipeline similar to the Texas "Big Inch" pipeline that Jimmy Byrnes had already successfully supervised at the OWM. This time Byrnes and Searls envisioned the U.S. government building and maintaining ownership of a titanic oil pipeline originating in Kuwait, at the head of the Persian Gulf, and ending at U.S.–controlled ports on the Mediterranean, 850 miles away. A major branch of the pipeline would extend from the oil fields of Iran to U.S. refining centers located near the British Palestinian port of Haifa for shipment of Iranian oil to the United States.

"Its ownership by the United States will give to our government a commanding position in the development of these fields," Byrnes wrote in to Roosevelt in January 1944, urging the construction of the giant pipeline. Searls had been even more frank. He had predicted in his 1943 memorandum to Byrnes that U.S. ownership of the major shipping and refining operations in the Middle East would enable the U.S. government to negotiate for, "say, a third interest in the Anglo-Iranian pools, and be possessed of the facilities to make the production immediately available to the post-war world."

However, the obvious need to station U.S. military in the Middle East after the world war in order to guard the proposed pipeline raised isolationists' opposition in the United States, and the Petroleum Reserves Corporation, the government-financed agency created by Roosevelt to negotiate oil rights, never was able to negotiate successfully either with foreign governments or with privately owned U.S. oil companies. The Petroleum Reserves Corporation also failed to achieve a political consensus even within the Roosevelt administration. According to Jesse Jones, since the members of the corporation, to which Jimmy Byrnes belonged and of which Harold Ickes was chairman, "were using RFC money, I suggested to Mr. Byrnes that I should be on the Board of Directors; but Secretary Ickes would not have it. The President let Harold have his way." Shortly after FDR's death, Byrnes and Searles were forced to shelve their idea for a trans-Iranian pipeline, despite the project's quick approval in 1944 by the Joint Chiefs of Staff.

Byrnes' efforts had won him some political allies. "This war is being fought with oil," the *St. Louis Post Dispatch* declared in 1944 in support of the OWM-endorsed Iranian pipeline. "The nation that runs out of it is whipped. Future wars will be fought with oil."

Now, in the winter months of 1946, following Secretary Byrnes' return from Moscow to his isolated watch at the U.S. State Department, the area where the future war appeared most likely to be fought was Iran. Byrnes apparently had been willing to accept at Moscow the Soviet occupations of Romania, Bulgaria, and Hungary as a fait accompli about which he or the U.S. military could do little; but Jimmy Byrnes was determined upon his return to Washington that the Soviet forces numbering at least thirty thousand soldiers stationed in Iran be withdrawn from that country. Unlike the Balkan states, Iran had never joined the Axis countries in the war with the USSR, and Jimmy Byrnes, always profoundly legalistic, probably was offended personally by the continuing illegality of this Soviet occupation. Of at least equal importance to Byrnes' pragmatic mind in his decision to confront the Soviets over the issue of Iranian independence during the winter of 1946 was the fact that Iran was then the world's fourth-largest producer of crude petroleum.

The ensuing dispute over the independence of Iran and access to its oil fields brought the United States and the Soviet Union in 1946 closer to a direct military confrontation than at any other time in the first half of this century. At the height of the Iranian crisis, Byrnes would argue that country's case before the United Nations for removal of the Soviet troops, having earlier publicly warned the Soviet Union that, in a clear repudiation of the accommodations at Moscow, the United States stood ready with its military force to support the independence of Iran "should the occasion arise."

The Cold War, fueled by the U.S. need for oil reserves in the Middle East, had begun. And out of a strange mixture of idealism and practicality, Jimmy Byrnes in 1946 became the first U.S. secretary of state to be a Cold Warrior. Convinced that he was championing the rule of international law over an unprovoked aggression, Byrnes was willing to confront the Soviet Union militarily on the issue of removing its troops from Iran until all sides could agree to allow the United Nations to adjudicate the issue. At the same time, Byrnes could not afford politically to give Stalin the opportunity to "welsh" on any more territorial agreements; and as the Soviet and U.S. military confronted one another over the Iranian issue in April of 1946, Secretary of the Navy James Forrestal sent Byrnes a memorandum again emphasizing to him the importance to U.S. security of staking out an unimpeded claim to buy Middle Eastern oil.

"If we ever got into another world war," Forrestal wrote Byrnes, "it is quite possible that we would not have access to the reserves held in the Middle East, but in the meantime the use of those reserves would prevent the depletion of our own, a depletion which may be serious within fifteen years."

Jimmy Byrnes pragmatic adroitness during the Iranian crisis of 1946 would have been worthy of Roosevelt himself, had FDR been alive to appreciate it. But another man was president in 1946, and Harry Truman was keenly aware that Jimmy Byrnes in a different sense considered himself the worthy successor to Franklin Roosevelt. The Iranian crisis was Byrnes' finest performance as a diplomat, but after its resolution, Jimmy Byrnes would find himself the last of Roosevelt's prominent advisers to be removed from Truman's cabinet. The new Cold Warrior would not survive politically for another winter.

Jimmy Byrnes had begun his Cold War policies toward Iran with an unlikely ally for a diplomat: Colonel H. Norman Schwarzkopf, Sr. Having been frustrated in 1944 in his plans to advance U.S. construction of the trans-Iranian oil pipeline, Byrnes had acted rapidly in 1945 upon becoming secretary of state to renew the highly classified contract of what was then known in the State Department as the Schwarzkopf mission. Colonel Schwarzkopf, an American expert in training paramilitary state police, had been working in Iran under State Department contract since 1942. His mission, supported by about twenty other U.S. military officers and enlisted men, was to form the Iranian state police into a modernized force capable of quelling troublesome internal dissidents, including in the northern part of that country the increasingly strong Iranian Communist party, the Tudeh, or Democratic party. Schwarzkopf, his salary paid by the U.S. War Department and under instructions to report intelligence to the U.S. State Department, was accepted by the Iranian government as the commander of its country's gendarmerie, a force that under Schwarzkopf's direction was enlarged in 1945 to about 21,000 Iranian policemen and officers.

The Schwarzkopf mission to Iran had been scheduled to end shortly after the surrender of the Axis powers, under the terms specified by Congress in the Second War Powers Act (1942). That act, which authorized the U.S. secretary of state to send military advisers to those friendly nations requesting them, had been written in part by then Supreme Court justice James F. Byrnes. But in the autumn of 1945 Byrnes, himself now the new U.S. secretary of state, wrote to War Secretary Robert Patterson recommending the wisdom of "continuing indefinitely" the Schwarzkopf mission to the Iranian state police, as well as the War Department's funding of a second U.S. military mission to the Iranian army. "Strengthening of Iran's internal security forces by the American Missions contributes to the stabilization of Iran," Byrnes wrote on October 17, 1945, in what was eventually a successful effort to obtain funding from Patterson's department for the Schwarzkopf mission for two more years. "The stabilization of Iran, moreover, will serve to lay a sound foundation for the development of American commercial, petroleum, and aviation interests in the Middle East."

Byrnes had other reasons to be anxious in late 1945 that the State Department continue to maintain an experienced U.S. officer in command of 21,000 paramilitary police in Iran. The Schwarzkopf mission provided a counterforce, if needed, to the 31,000 Soviet troops then occupying northern Iran, which neither the U.S. State Department nor the government of the young Mohammed Reza Pahlavi could seem to dislodge. Soviet and British troops had occupied Iran in 1942 in order to secure the Iranian oil fields from Axis control and to provide security for the American lend-lease supply lines to the Soviet Union. To ensure Iranian cooperation, these two of the Big Three powers signed what was termed the tripartite agreement, which promised that all foreign Allied troops would be removed from Iran within six months of the conclusion of the war with Germany and the other Axis powers. About 80,000 U.S. troops from the Persian Gulf command later moved into the British-secured area to aid in moving war material to the Soviet Union. The Iranian parliament had attempted to secure an honest observance of the tripartite agreement by voting to postpone any discussion of selling postwar oil concessions to the Allied governments until all foreign troops were withdrawn from its soil. The Iranian prime minister also implied that if the tripartite agreement was not honored, he would bring his country's case to the first meeting of the General Assembly of the United Nations, scheduled to convene in London in January 1946.

After German generals signed the unconditional surrender on May 7, 1945, and as the deadline approached, Britain and the United States began to withdraw their troops from the area they controlled in southern Iran; but the 31,000 Soviet troops remained in oil-rich Iran, around the province of Azerbaijan. The Soviet government, its own petroleum industry and refining facilities much more damaged by the war than it admitted, began to insist in late 1945 that the Iranian government agree to an exclusive and highly favorable treaty for importing Iranian oil to the USSR before the Soviets would observe the tripartite agreement. The Soviets also logically argued that with the signing of the armistice with Japan on September 2, 1945, a close reading of the tripartite terms meant that the deadline was now advanced to March 2, 1946. But more disturbing, in a pattern similar to the Soviet creation of military satellite governments in occupied Bulgaria and Romania, the Soviet officers in the northern Iranian provinces began to arm the Kurdish minorities there for a general uprising against the Teheran government. Also under the Soviet sponsorship, a small minority of Tudeh Communist rebels in the Iranian province of Azerbaijan joined by Kurdish rebels began military preparations in 1944 in order to declare Azerbaijan a state separate from Iran.

This was not the rule of senatorial compromise that Jimmy Byrnes had in the early fall of 1945 anticipated in his dealings with the Soviet government. Instead of building cooperative "post offices," the United States and the Soviet Union were by the end of the year arming their surrogates in Iran—Stalin with his Tudeh rebels in the northern provinces and Byrnes with his Schwarzkopf mission operating out of Teheran. And, increasingly, the Soviet refusal to leave Iran was perceived by Byrnes as a clear attempt to deny to the United States postwar access to this major Middle Eastern oil reserve.

Byrnes nevertheless had made a last attempt in 1945 at reaching a compromise on Iran during the artificial conviviality of the Moscow conference. At a brief meeting with Stalin in his Kremlin offices the night before Christmas Eve, Byrnes, accompanied by his translator, Charles "Chip" Bohlen, told Stalin that he wished to talk about Iran. Byrnes was certain, he told the Soviet chairman, that both their countries wanted to keep the "embarrassing position" of the Soviet occupation from becoming the first subject for discussion at the UN General Assembly later the next month. He reminded Stalin of Iranian cooperation in shipping American lend-lease goods to the USSR during the war; and he referred to the tripartite agreement on Iran "to respect the territorial integrity and independence of this small state."

But by this time news of Byrnes' secret renewal in October 1945 of the Schwarzkopf mission for a minimum of two more years had been leaked and so widely publicized that it had become known even in Moscow. Three weeks before the Moscow conference, on the floor of the U.S. House of Representatives, the Republican isolationist congressman Karl Mundt had criticized Byrnes' actions in a December 3 speech reprinted in national and international newspapers. Should the Iranian issue come before the United Nations, "the American State Department does not enter the court of world opinion with clean hands," Mundt said, "while it proposes to continue Colonel Schwarzkopf in command of the Iranian gendarmery for another two years under a contract already signed with the Iranian Government." Mundt elaborated, "This gendarmery as of last September [1944] consisted of a headquarters and 15 regiments, totaling 20,000 men and 1,000 officers, distributed over approximately 600,000 square miles and available for concentrated use at any trouble point. The functions of the *gendarmery* parallel those of the state police in the United States and in addition include quasi military action."

Mundt had noted scornfully of the Schwarzkopf mission approved by Byrnes, "I think many will be surprised to learn that American Army officers on the pay roll of the War Department are assigned by the State Department for such purposes in these times. In my mind, this is backing up a long way from the pious phrases once enunciated in the Atlantic Charter."

Stalin now replied to Byrnes' overture in the early evening of December 23 by remarking that, at least in the Soviet government, "no one had any reason to blush" if the issue of foreign troops operating in Iran was raised in January at the first meeting of the UN General Assembly. Stalin also noted, quite accurately, that the Soviet Union had never asked the United States to remove its combat troops. As to Iranian cooperation with the Soviet Union during the world war, it was true that the Soviet and Iranian governments had worked together to defeat their mutual enemies, Stalin said; but in a possible veiled reference to the pro-Western tilt shown by the Iranian government's postwar continuation of the Schwarzkopf mission, he added that since the end of the war, in regard to Iran "much water has flowed under the bridge."

Iran did file a protest on January 19, 1946, before the UN Security Council. Charging that the Soviet Union "through the medium of its officials and its armed forces" had violated the terms of the tripartite agreement, the Iranian representative asked the Security Council to hold an open hearing on the Soviet refusal to withdraw its troops.

Byrnes had no ethical or legal reason to blush because of this request for an open hearing before the Security Council by the Iranian ambassador; that is, despite suspicions at the time by isolationist politicians and by revisionist historians later, there is no documentary evidence that the Iranian request for a Security Council hearing was a put-up job by Byrnes or that the Iranian ambassador had acted either at the insistence of Byrnes or in collusion with him. In fact, more than two weeks before the Iranian government presented its request before the Security Council, the Iranian ambassador to the United States had asked the State Department on January 2 for "assurance in advance that the United Nations and Great Britain would support the Iranian position. In the absence of such assurance, the Iranian government would hesitate to take a step which would further widen the breach between Iran and the Soviet Union."

Byrnes always had a healthy respect for the political fix, but he always had an even greater respect for the principles of the law, evinced by his earlier insistence upon due process and impartial hearings while he was a Supreme Court justice. Here, before the newly formed and never before tested UN Security Council, Byrnes saw the chance for his respected principle of due process to be applied on a grand scale.

Byrnes therefore promptly responded to the Iranian ambassador's request for assurances of U.S. support: "The American government could not undertake to give advance assurances of the position it would take in any case of this kind to be brought before the UNO. The United States has friendly relations with both the Soviet Union and with Iran, and for us to give advance commitments to either side was not in harmony either

with those friendly relations or with the spirit of the United Nations."
Byrnes pointedly added, "The United States is of the view that *any* member
of the UNO should be entirely free to present its case to that organization"
(emphasis added). Any member presumably could include Great Britain,
the United States, or the USSR, as well as Iran.

Byrnes' legalistic tendency was also evident on the evening after the
Iranian ambassador had asked Byrnes for a prehearing assurance, when
Undersecretary Dean Acheson telephoned Byrnes at his home on January
3. Acheson passed on to Byrnes the information that the British ambassador to the United States had come to see Acheson that afternoon to ask
the United States to join Great Britain in urging Iran not to present its
complaint before the Security Council. The British representative had argued for more time in order to proceed with less public negotiations between Iran and the USSR before bringing the issue to the United Nations.

Byrnes promptly told Acheson, "We could not possibly urge Iran not
to bring the matter up if they wished to do so." The secretary also told
him that during the past week, in the absence of any statement from
Molotov that the Soviet Union was reconsidering any change of its policy,
"there was little hope for Soviet cooperation prior to a Security Council
hearing."

Thus, during the Iranian crisis, if a political fix was in, it probably was
not the U.S. secretary of state who had attempted to put it there. Rather,
one should look to the British. British and U.S. interests, despite all the
wartime talk of a "special relationship" between the two countries, were
not necessarily identical in Iran. Byrnes would certainly have worried on
hearing Acheson's telephoned message that any delay in bringing the Iranian complaint to the UN might allow Great Britain sufficient time to
negotiate a de facto sphere of influence for the Anglo-Iranian Oil Company
in a Soviet-influenced or satellite-state Iran. An acknowledged and permanent Soviet influence in Iran would lead to increased domestic and
international pressure for U.S. troops to be dispatched to protect pro-
Western oil facilities in that Middle Eastern nation. Without prompt UN
action, therefore, the United States might be in late 1946 where British
policy since at least mid-1944 had been trying to place it: that is, in the
position of having its troops guard British-owned refineries and pipelines.

So with the minimal exceptions of Dean Acheson and a few other
advisers at the State Department, and of the Iranian ambassador and the
Soviet ambassador to the United States, Byrnes was walking a finer line
on the Security Council issue than anyone else—perhaps including President Truman—appreciated at the time. On the one hand, Byrnes did not
wish to disrupt the possibility of continued Grand Alliance cooperation
among the United States, Great Britain, and the USSR. On the other
hand, Byrnes was aware of the white paper circulating in the State Department since the preceding September and noting, "There is widespread

feeling among the Iranians that their only hope is U.S. assistance since they fear the British might compromise with the U.S.S.R. on spheres of influence."

Walking that fine line between cooperation and confrontation also meant, at least at first, not unnecessarily antagonizing the Soviets. There is no documentary evidence that, in the weeks before or after Iran presented its complaint to the Security Council, Byrnes intended to give the Soviets any reason to blush—no documentation, that is, that he attempted to establish the United Nations as a Western-sponsored propaganda machine to embarrass the Soviets. Despite the later criticisms by such revisionist historians as Lloyd Gardner of Byrnes' "public diplomacy" or the flat assertion by the historians Joyce and Gabriel Kolko that from November 1945 through January 1946 the Iranian prime minister "was assured that Iran take its dispute with Russia to the UN it could count on United States backing," Secretary Byrnes' public and private actions suggest otherwise. A more accurate appraisal of his motives is that of Daniel Yergin, who finds in the secretary of state's actions at this time a motivation for "an equivocal, rather low key policy on Iran." Yergin asserts that in early 1946 "his own instinct was still to seek a cloakroom compromise."

Evidence of Byrnes' preference for the cloakroom compromises over confrontation with the Soviets is in the memorandum written for staff use on January 24, 1946, by Adlai Stevenson, then a senior adviser to the U.S. delegation in London, after Stevenson's meeting with Byrnes five days after Iran had lodged its complaint before the Security Council:

> In talking with Secretary Byrnes just before he left today about the political issues, he expressed the following views:
>
> When a state files a complaint alleging a "situation or dispute" we must assume that it is filed in good faith and that the complainant is entitled to a hearing and discussion of his complaint in the Security Council.
>
> Applying this principle to the Iranian case, it should be our policy to support the right of Iran to present its case to the Security Council. If the presentation is "reasonable" we should actively support and speak for an investigation.
>
> This policy is, however, *not intended to preclude a recommendation that bilateral negotiations between Russia and Iran be attempted first should the parties be disposed to proceed in that manner and should there be evidence of any reasonable likelihood of success.* In short, if full attempts have not been made for the parties to get together and resolve the question, it would seem proper for them to do so before commending an investigation. In the event of any such bilateral negotiations the Security Council should be kept closely informed of all the developments. [emphasis added]

Byrnes' position was complicated, however, when only one day after Iran filed its complaint with the Security Council, the Iranian prime minister unexpectedly resigned, on January 20, 1946, and the young shah replaced him with Qavam Saltaneh, perceived by the West as friendlier to the Soviets than the prior minister was. Before the Security Council agreed to schedule the Iranian complaint upon its agenda, the Soviet government announced that it would receive the new prime minister in Moscow to negotiate the differences between their two countries.

Byrnes, who had arrived in London to attend the opening UN Assembly after his mixed reception in the United States, was skeptical; although he was in favor, as he had told Stevenson, of private negotiations between Iran and the USSR conducted outside the publicity of UN administration, so long as the Security Council was "closely informed," Byrnes stated in London that the Iranian question "having been brought before the Council should remain there pending settlement." But with the UN's authority to deal with the Iranian question left hanging in the air, the Soviet government dispatched an airplane to bring Prime Minister Qavam to Moscow on February 18.

Byrnes' newfound skepticism toward the Soviet Union was justified in February and March. Back in Washington, he received reports from George Kennan at the U.S. embassy in Moscow that Prime Minister Qavam's reception by Stalin after his arrival at the Moscow airport was said to have been "very rough." The U.S. embassy at Teheran also filled Byrnes in on some of the confidential details available on the meetings between Qavam, Stalin, and Molotov. The two Soviets had presented the Iranian prime minister with a stark ultimatum: either recognition of an independent Communist state of Azerbaijan in northern Iran and creation of a new Russo-Iranian partnership, 51 percent to be controlled by the Soviet government, to develop northern Iranian oil for USSR import, or else the Soviet troops would remain in Iran past the March 2 deadline. At one point in their negotiations, Molotov and Stalin angrily exclaimed to the Iranian prime minister, "We don't care what the U.S. and Britain think, and we are not afraid of them."

Meanwhile, Schwarzkopf was receiving intelligence and passing on to the U.S. State Department reports that the Tudeh Communist party was planning coups in Iranian provinces in addition to Azerbaijan; and as the March 2 deadline passed and the Iranian prime minister refused to accede to the Soviet demands, Byrnes received an urgent telegram on March 6 from Robert Rossow, the U.S. vice counsel in the northern Iranian city of Tabriz, detailing that Soviet reinforcements were pouring across the Iranian border and moving toward Teheran: "On March 3—450 Soviet trucks heavily laden with supplies, mainly ammunition, departed Tabriz toward Tehran," Rossow wired Byrnes. "Last night 20 tanks with 100 trucks departed in same direction."

The night that Rossow's telegram was received at the State Department, two of Byrnes' assistants prepared a blown-up map of Azerbaijan with large arrows to mark the reported Soviet troop movements and took the map upstairs to Byrnes' office. "Once the secretary had familiarized himself with the map, we pointed out the size and direction of each thrust," Edwin Wright, one of the assistants wrote more than twenty years later. "Mr. Byrnes asked the significance of each arrow and noted that they aimed at the Turkish border, [and] the Iraqi border. [A] third was headed due south (possibly indicating a thrust toward the oil fields) and [also possibly indicating] a drive toward the capital at Tehran."

Wright's recollection of the event for an internal State Department history continued, "Mr. Byrnes, having gone over the telegram and verified the place names with the map, remarked that it now seemed clear the USSR was adding military invasion to political subversion in Iran, and, beating one fist into the other hand, he dismissed us with the remark: 'Now we'll give it to them with both barrels.' "

Byrnes' toughness was simplified and claimed as his own six years later by Harry Truman, after he and Byrnes had quarreled. Truman in an off-the-cuff recollection of the Iranian crisis in a news conference in mid-1952 recalled that in his first presidential term he had sent "an ultimatum to the head of the Soviet Union to get out of Persia." Truman added that the Soviets "got out, because we were in a position to meet a situation of that kind." Curious reporters, eager to obtain details about this 1946 ultimatum and unable to obtain any copy, were told by a White House spokesman that "the president was using the term 'ultimatum' in a non-technical sense" and that "the president was referring to the United States leadership in the United Nations, particularly in the Security Council and through diplomatic channels, in the spring of 1946, which was the major force in bringing about Soviet withdrawal from Iran."

Although not named by the White House in this 1952 clarification of Truman's recollections of the events of 1946, there can be no doubt that Jimmy Byrnes, and not Harry Truman, was the preeminent diplomatic strategist of the U.S. position in the resolution of the Iranian crisis, beginning almost at the moment when he read Rossow's cable in his upstairs office. Despite the secretary's bellicose remark and Truman's later recollection, no ultimatum concerning Iran was sent in 1946 by Truman, Byrnes, or anyone else in the U.S. State or War Department; and Byrnes knew as well as the president that the United States in 1946 might not be "in a position" in Iran to back up a threat to the Soviet Union. The Schwarzkopf mission constituted the only credible pro-Western military force in Iran at the time, and it did not possess the heavy armored vehicles that Rossow was reporting the Soviets were then rushing toward Teheran.

In order to achieve the removal of Soviet troops from Iran, Byrnes would have to use his traditional weapons of legality and political maneuver. Byrnes did indeed plan to give the Soviets "both barrels," but he planned a diplomatic offensive, a ballistic one. In the following weeks of March 1946, under Secretary Byrnes' leadership at the State Department, the possible use of the U.S. military was implied at least once to the Soviets, but before the UN Security Council and not on any battlefield.

Acting on his own initiative while Truman "sat on the sidelines," in the words of one historian, Byrnes on March 11 quickly informed Prime Minister Qavam, then safely returned to Teheran from Moscow, that the United States would fully support Iran's demand to have its complaint heard before the next meeting of the Security Council, scheduled for New York City on March 25. Qavam, for his own nationalistic reasons, agreed. But the issues involved were now larger than simply competing interests for oil concessions, Byrnes believed; as he later wrote to Dean Acheson, the United Nations, if it did not at least attempt to impose a legal settlement of the first postwar dispute, would "die in its infancy of inefficiency and ineffectiveness."

In the two weeks between Qavam's agreement in Teheran on March 11 and the opening session in New York City on March 25 of the Security Council, Byrnes tried to prevent Iran from going the way of Soviet occupied Romania, Hungary, and Bulgaria. The prospects did not look good for preserving Iran's territorial integrity until its future hearing at law. "Last night another force consisting of 20 medium tanks, 20 armored cars, and 40 truckloads of infantry departed Tehran-ward," Rossow reported in a second cable from northern Iran to Byrnes. "I cannot overstress the seriousness and magnitude of the current Soviet troop movement here. This is no ordinary reshuffling of troops, but a full scale combat deployment." When Byrnes had George Kennan deliver a note of protest to the Soviet government concerning these reported troop movements, Byrnes on March 15 was told by the Kremlin that such reports simply "did not correspond to reality." Meanwhile, having obtained information from its own Iranian sources, the *New York Times* reported and Byrnes read on March 15 that six Soviet fighter planes had been spotted a few miles from Teheran, "sitting on an apron, ready to take off," and that Soviet troops deployed in Iran had doubled, to an estimated sixty thousand. And in what seemed to be a prelude to declaring a state of war that had in fact already begun, the Soviet Union, having learned of Iran's intent to bring its case to the Security Council, warned the Teheran government on March 16 that it would consider such an appeal "an unfriendly act."

Byrnes responded to these now unveiled Soviet threats by leading a campaign of what was later described as "public diplomacy," a sequence of speeches given by him and planned in personal coordination with Winston Churchill's own "Iron Curtain" speech of March 5. Byrnes in his public remarks made it clear that the United States was not ruling out the use of its military forces to preserve Iranian integrity; and his public comments marked the first official statement of what a year later became known as the "Truman Doctrine" of containment. The first of these two speeches was Byrnes' address to the Overseas Press Club of America on the evening of February 28, 1946. After the food had been cleared from the press club's tables at the dining room of the Waldorf-Astoria Hotel, this secretary of state who only a year earlier had urged a remorselessly "hard" war against Japan by dropping an atomic bomb to forestall death rates as high as those on Okinawa now began his remarks by noting that "it is good to open a newspaper without the fear of finding in the casualty lists the name of one near and dear to us."

But if the world was not at war in the winter of 1946, then neither could the current conditions be called a peace. "I should be lacking in candor if I say to you that world conditions are sound or reassuring," Byrnes cautioned the assembled reporters. Currently the integrity of the United Nations and the rule of international law "that no state has the right to maintain its troops on the territory of another independent state without its consent." Without referring specifically the Soviet Union or the scheduled hearing of the Iranian complaint before the Security Council, Byrnes nevertheless made clear the intention of the United States to enforce the legal finding of the Security Council if the hearing went against the Soviet Union. "Unless the great powers are prepared to act in defense of law, the United Nations cannot prevent war," Byrnes said, adding emphatically, "The Charter [of the UN] forbids aggression, and we cannot allow aggression to be accomplished by coercion or pressure or by subterfuge such as political infiltration."

London newspapers in their morning editions the day after Byrnes' Waldorf-Astoria speech generally praised his "unusually forceful language" and the *Daily Mail* headlined its front-page coverage "Russia Warned: You Have Gone Far Enough." Following his speech Byrnes traveled to Florida to meet with Churchill prior to the latter's "Iron Curtain" speech in Fulton, Missouri, on March 5; and on March 11 Byrnes again met privately with Churchill for over two hours at his office in Washington. These meetings were preparatory to the second major address by Byrnes in regard to the Iranian crisis, on March 16 in the ironic setting of an after-dinner talk in New York City to two thousand members of the Society of the Friendly Sons of Saint Patrick. Although Byrnes did not refer specifically to Churchill's Fulton address, "Mr. Churchill's theme was inherent" throughout the text of Byrnes' March 16 speech, the *New York Times* noted in its report on Byrnes' speech.

Once again, Byrnes did not mention the Soviet occupation of Iran or the Soviet challenge to Iran's right under the UN Charter to appeal its case to the Security Council; but telling his audience that he wished to speak that night on "the military strength of the United States," Byrnes then turned to the question of what purpose the U.S. military strength might soon be put to. "This is a fair question. It deserves a fair answer," Byrnes said.

"The answer is simple. The United States is committed to the support of the charter of the United Nations. Should the occasion arise, our military strength will be used to support the purpose and the principles of the charter."

Byrnes' message to the Soviets regarding the Iranian appeal was clear: the United States was now prepared to use "both barrels" of diplomatic and military force to ensure Iran's legal right to appeal its case to the UN. This was not simply a matter of sending an ultimatum to the Soviets to get out of Iran; Byrnes wanted a hearing on the legality of the tripartite agreement before the Security Council. The strategy of this March 16 speech, which succeeded in delaying further Soviet military advances into Iran, was, like the man himself who delivered the speech to the Friendly Sons of Saint Patrick, both morally unimpeachable and politically devious. Stalin was using legality as a pretense for applying military force; but Jimmy Byrnes, aware that two increasingly besieged military missions were all that the United States had at its disposal at the time in Iran, used the pretense of force in order to apply legality.

Byrnes subsequently announced that he personally would argue the U.S. support of Iran's case when the Security Council convened on March 25. Byrnes also sent a notice to representatives of U.S. oil companies that the State Department in the meanwhile expected a scrupulous respect for the Iranian government's decision to postpone any selling of oil concessions until the terms of the tripartite agreement were fulfilled. Byrnes cabled the same message on March 24 to the U.S. ambassador in Teheran, insisting that the embassy there prevent any premature negotiations between U.S. companies and the Iranian government. "We are most anxious that [an] impression should not be obtained that we have been influenced in our recent actions before the Security Council by any selfish interest in Iranian petroleum," Byrnes wrote. Oil had occasioned this quarrel between the Soviet Union and the United States; but as Byrnes had written to Dean Acheson, he now saw the legal issue of establishing the UN's authority to adjudicate disputes as paramount to this country's obtaining Middle Eastern oil reserves. Jimmy Byrnes did not want any smudge of petroleum upon the brief he intended to present to the Security Council.

Over twenty-five hundred spectators were on hand to cheer Secretary Byrnes when, accompanied by Chip Bohlen and Ben Cohen, he arrived in New York City on March 24 to argue before the Security Council the U.S. case for hearing the Iranian complaint. "No nation has the right to take the law into its own hands," Byrnes announced upon his arrival. "If disputes cannot be settled by friendly negotiation, they must be brought before the Security Council."

Byrnes presented his case on the afternoon of March 26, in the converted gymnasium of Hunter College in the Bronx that was the temporary headquarters of the Security Council of the United Nations. The ad hoc surroundings of the new organization added urgency to Byrnes' point that the decision whether or not to hear the Iranian complaint was a make-or-break decision in determining the permanence of the United Nations. "We must put the matter on the agenda," Byrnes declared that day to the eight other council members. "When a member of the United Nations advises the Council that a situation exists which is likely to threaten the peace and security of the world, we cannot deny to that nation the opportunity to be heard."

Andrei Gromyko, the Soviet ambassador to the UN, plainly furious over the U.S. insistence on a public discussion of the events in Iran, responded by walking out of the gymnasium on March 27 when Byrnes' motion to place the complaint on the council agenda carried by a vote of 7 to 2 (Poland and the USSR voted against). "The Soviet Union took a walk at the United Nations Security Council meeting yesterday," James Reston noted the next day in the *New York Times*. "It will come back to the Council when it feels like it."

With Gromyko's chair now empty, Byrnes still insisted upon the legal supremacy of the Security Council to hear the dispute, and on March 29 he obtained passage of a motion calling on the Soviet Union to report to the council on its intention to withdraw from northern Iran by no later than April 3. That deadline was eventually extended to May 6. During those next five weeks, Jimmy Byrnes and the rest of the non-Soviet world waited to see whether the United Nations would in truth become a world adjudication body or just another group of international well-wishers meeting inside a Bronx school gymnasium.

There was not unanimous domestic support for Byrnes' tough new line with the Soviets, however. Charles "Chip" Bohlen had accompanied Byrnes to New York, and in Bohlen's later recollection, at a dinner party with the Lippmanns in New York City preceding the hearing, "Walter Lippmann was critical of Byrnes' decision to plead the Iranian case, pointing out that any confrontation between the great powers contained the theoretical danger of war. I outlined all the efforts the United States government had made to avoid this issue and said that a war was highly unlikely. In the lively discussion that ensued, Mrs. Lippmann, in support of her husband, interjected to say, 'Well, Chip, all I can say is that in your war I will not be a nurse's aide.' "

The Iranian crisis broke on May 6. On that deadline date, Byrnes received a cable from the U.S. consul Robert Rossow in Tabriz informing him that the Soviets had reversed the direction of their troop movements and were now drawing back into the USSR. The U.S. ambassador to Teheran later confirmed to Byrnes that the Soviets had stopped their advance toward the Iranian capital and were withdrawing their forces from the province of Azerbaijan as well.

There could be little doubt that Byrnes' five-week insistence upon keeping the Iranian complaint on the Security Council agenda, plus his explicit promise on March 16 to use U.S. military forces to support a UN decision to oppose the Soviet occupation, forestalled what was plainly a Soviet-planned coup against the Teheran government. Stalin was reported to Byrnes in the spring of 1946 as being "very bitter," in a conversation with Harriman, the U.S. ambassador to Moscow, over Byrnes' public diplomacy at the UN in regard to the Iranian complaint; but a fait accompli similar to that of the Soviet-dominated governments of Hungary, Romania, and Bulgaria had been avoided for the time being in a Middle Eastern country whose oil reserves were critical to the United States, and a small country's right to a hearing before the great powers of the Security Council had been vindicated.

Toward the end of 1946 the pro-Western stabilization of Iran, which Jimmy Byrnes had hoped to accomplish with his continuation of the Schwarzkopf mission, appeared to have been largely achieved. Colonel Schwarzkopf himself by midsummer was promoted to brigadier general. To encourage the Soviets in their May 6 withdrawal, the Teheran government had promised to consider future Soviet oil concessions and to respect Azerbaijani autonomy. But late in the year, the central Iranian government, both its internal security forces and its military forces strengthened significantly, informed the Soviets that their request for oil concessions was no longer being considered; and in December 1946 the Iranian state police succeeded in reentering the province of Azerbaijan, where the pro-Soviet government had slowly collapsed after the Soviet withdrawal. There the Schwarzkopf-trained gendarmerie took a terrible revenge against the Kurds and other Azerbaijani people who had supported the Tudeh-Democratic government. On December 12 Byrnes received another cable from the U.S. consul in the Azerbaijani town of Tabriz describing the success of their diplomacy.

"At the sight of my car with American flag, people cheered and shouted long live America," the consul wrote. Security forces and Iranian civilians "are armed and engaged in hunting out former Democrats," he wired Byrnes, and at the former headquarters of the Tudeh-Democrat party the empty offices were "littered with bread and eggs and empty cups and cigarette butts, the traces of the last few hours of indecision." The consul continued to drive through Tabriz, Byrnes read, "through milling crowds who cheered when they saw my flag. Shots were fired near us, but I only saw one blood covered spot on main street which looked as though someone had been killed there."

The United States subsequently reiterated its position with the public statement by Ambassador George V. Allen that the U.S. government supported any further effort by Iran in maintaining order within that country's own provinces. By the end of 1946, eight days after Byrnes had received the dispatch from the American consul at Tabriz, the secretary sent the following congratulatory cable to Ambassador Allen:

> You have fulfilled all the expectations I came to have on the basis of your fine work in New York last spring. I like to think of the achievement of Iranian unity not in terms of victory or defeat for any outside nation, but rather as proof of the strength and effectiveness of the United Nations in helping those countries which truly desire independence. I hope that you will continue to impress upon Iranian leaders the great importance of carrying out a program of economic and social reform and of raising the standard of living of the Iranian people, thereby enabling Iran to make a contribution to the community of nations.
>
> Sincere good wishes to you and your family for Christmas and the New Year.

Secretary Byrnes had won the first battle of the Cold War.

The favorable resolution of the Iranian crisis marked the apogee of James F. Byrnes' powers emanating from his upstairs office at the U.S. State Department Building. He was chosen *Time* magazine's Man of the Year for 1946, and both in the popular press and among his traditional base of political support in the U.S. Senate, his new policy of what he now called "firmness and patience" toward the Soviet Union seemed to have won him back his reputation as the most skilled and politically adept administrator in the Truman administration. He also had gained some admirers among the career staff at the State Department. Porter McKeever, a young career diplomat and future biographer of Adlai Stevenson, who had accompanied Byrnes in 1946 on his trip to New York City to argue the U.S. case, later wrote Byrnes, "Your battle with the Soviet Union over Iran in the Security Council marks one of the most successful diplomatic gambits against the Soviets in the entire postwar world. You mobilized world opinion against the Soviets. Moreover, at a time when we didn't in fact have the power to back it up, you successfully convinced the Soviets that we would feel obliged to back up our treaty with Iran by *force* if they didn't get out— *and they got out*" (McKeever's emphasis).

Thus the available documents confirm the opinion of Robert Rossow, Jr., that "the Cold War began on March 4, 1946. On that day fifteen Soviet armored brigades began to pour into the northwestern Iranian province of Azerbaijan." In contrast, the conventional wisdom of later historians is that the beginning of the Cold War officially was articulated by Secretary Byrnes only after more than a year and a half following the Iranian crisis, when in a speech in Stuttgart, Germany, Byrnes announced that the U.S. government refused to accept as permanent the division of occupied Germany and intended to continue to garrison its troops in Germany so long as the armies of other occupying powers, including that of the USSR, remained there. And it is also the accepted wisdom of historians that this confrontational rhetoric of Byrnes was more aggressively institutionalized as U.S. policy by Byrnes' successor as secretary of state, George Marshall, in Marshall's implementation of the Truman Doctrine, or "containment" policy toward perceived Soviet expansion.

But the elements present at the sites of all later Cold War confrontations—including the conflicts in Angola, Nicaragua, and Vietnam during the early 1960s—were anticipated by the events of the Iranian crisis of 1946. These included the proxy combat of Iranian factions armed and in some cases supported militarily by both the United States and the Soviet Union. This internecine Iranian conflict was a result of at least the *perception* by each superpower that its strategic interests were at stake in Iran; and each superpower publicly and privately insisted that the strategic views of the other "did not correspond to reality" or were designed to be an impediment to a market-based and pro-Western "standard of living of the Iranian people." Despite the historical significance later accorded the Stuttgart speech and Secretary Marshall's announcement of the Truman Doctrine, more accurate is the assessment of the historian Gary Hess in the mid-1970s that "the essentials of the 'containment' policy, formally enunciated in the spring of 1947, had certainly crystallized during the Iranian showdown."

Nevertheless, Byrnes was able in 1946 at long last to see the work completed on the minor Axis treaties, as had been agreed at Moscow, at the Paris peace conferences that spring. Throughout the Iranian crisis that winter, Byrnes had refused to discuss with the Soviets any postponement of the spring meeting of the Council of Foreign Ministers, insisting that this negotiation and the resolution of the Iranian crisis were two separate issues. The conference began as scheduled in Paris in mid-June 1946, and it and a subsequent conference ran in almost continuous session until late October, with Byrnes in attendance much of that time. A third conference, in New York City, was required before there was complete agreement, by December 1946 to the treaties that Byrnes had once hopefully described as simply the quick "spade work" to a permanent peace with Germany.

The recognition by the Council of Foreign Ministers' final treaties of the Soviet-sponsored police regimes of Bulgaria, Hungary, and Romania was a bad piece of work. But the secretary could take satisfaction in the fact that no European country not under actual Soviet military occupation at the end of the war had been added to the Soviet sphere. Also over the initial objections of the Soviets, Byrnes was able to obtain the council's final agreement on comparatively moderate reparations for Italy and Finland, thereby increasing the likelihood that both countries would soon recover economically and seek admission to the United Nations. As the Italian prime minister walked past him at the Paris conference, Byrnes impulsively and generously stood up and extended his hand. "It was," observed Harold Nicolson, a man usually unimpressed by American diplomats, "an occasion not unworthy either of the conquerors or the conquered."

And as was so characteristic of Jimmy Byrnes when he was enjoying his powers, he found time, even during the negotiations of the Paris peace conference, to repay old scores in domestic politics, acting forgivingly toward his dead enemies and remorselessly toward his live ones. On July 10, 1946, shortly after Byrnes arrived in Paris, his political nemesis Sidney Hillman died of a heart attack. Hillman's daughter, Philoine, was then in Czechoslovakia, where her husband was a cultural attaché for the U.S. embassy. In that first postwar year, civilian air transport from Europe was difficult at best, and often impossible from the cities of war-damaged Central Europe; but at the arrangement of Byrnes' staff at Paris, the State Department provided an airplane to return Philoine Hillman Fried to New York City in time to attend her father's funeral.

Byrnes was not so charitable toward Henry Wallace, then Truman's secretary of commerce. While still attending the peace conference, Byrnes was infuriated upon reading in the Paris edition of the *Herald Tribune* reports of a speech given by Wallace at Madison Square Garden the night of September 12, to an audience composed largely of CIO-PAC supporters. The man whom Byrnes had sponsored for the vice presidency in 1940 now publicly attacked the "imperialistic" policies of the U.S. secretary of state toward the Soviet Union. Scorning the success of Byrnes' new "get tough" policy with the Soviet Union during the Iranian crisis, Wallace told his audience, "We cannot allow national oil rivalries to force us into another war." Claiming that "the tougher we get, the tougher the Russians will get," Wallace castigated a U.S. diplomatic policy that he described as "purchasing oil in the Near East with the lives of American soldiers."

That stung, both as an untruth and as a near-truth. Jimmy Byrnes had openly distanced himself and his department from any discussions of oil concessions during the Security Council debates, just as he had attempted secretly through his renewal of the Schwarzkopf mission to the Iranian police to distance U.S. soldiers from becoming at least the first casualties of a U.S.–Soviet war over Iranian oil reserves. During the following week, his political watchdog back in Washington, Donald Russell, cabled Byrnes of the wide publicity Wallace's speech was receiving, and of the speculation in the press that the speech signaled a White House disavowal of Byrnes' policies. (Wallace had stated twice during the course of his Madison Square

Garden speech that Truman had read and approved his speech before its delivery, although Truman later issued the ambiguously clarifying statement that he was approving not the *content* of Wallace's remarks but only his right publicly to speak his mind.)

This was not a right that Byrnes proposed to give to Henry Wallace. He was particularly angered by the timing of Wallace's remarks, for they came six days after Byrnes had delivered a major get-tough speech on September 6 in Stuttgart, Germany. In a message directed to the French and Soviet governments and their policies toward occupied Germany, Byrnes announced the intentions of the U.S. and British governments to merge their two zones of occupation economically in order to encourage the reestablishment of a capitalist economy and representative government in whatever German nation emerged after the resolution of the peace treaties among the Allies. And in direct opposition to the policy of U.S. military withdrawal later urged by Wallace, Byrnes stated unequivocally in Stuttgart to an enthusiastic German audience that the United States had no intention of allowing occupied Germany to become totally contained within the Soviet sphere of influence. "As long as there is an occupation army in Germany, American forces will be part of that occupation army," the secretary declared.

Byrnes immediately stopped his participation in the Paris talks until he was more certain of his White House support, and on September 18 he sent his own version of a State Department ultimatum in a cable to the president: "If it is not completely clear in your own mind that Mr. Wallace should be asked to refrain from criticizing the foreign policy of the United States while he is a member of your Cabinet, I must ask you to accept my resignation immediately."

Truman and Byrnes held a transatlantic Teletype conference the night of September 18 after the president received Byrnes' cable. Byrnes typed out that he could not accept a momentary "moratorium from criticism" by the president's simply asking Wallace to refrain from foreign policy speeches during the Paris conference. At his end of the wire back at the Map Room of the White House, Truman had his operator type out the message to Byrnes that "the situation will be made perfectly clear tomorrow. You have done an excellent job. Nobody appreciates it more than I do and I shall continue to support you with everything I have." On the morning of September 19, the White House announced that President Truman the previous night had requested and received the resignation of Henry Wallace.

Jimmy Byrnes went back to work at Paris with a temporarily satisfied mind, and at the close of the third conference of the Council of Foreign Ministers, in New York City on December 12, 1946, he saw the last of the preliminary treaties completed. Yet within seven days of the end of the New York conference, Byrnes himself in a letter to Truman on December

19 submitted his resignation as secretary of state, effective in January 1947. Byrnes' resignation was not a necessary consequence of that cold meeting with Truman aboard the *Williamsburg* a year earlier, although some of the president's new men who were present there had speedily wished it so. But by mid-1946 these new men had been joined by some of Byrnes' older domestic political enemies in a simultaneous effort to force Jimmy Byrnes out of the State Department.

Two days prior to Wallace's delivery of his Madison Square Garden speech, Harry Truman had received a telegram at the White House from a major CIO delegation meeting that week in convention in Chicago informing the president of the unanimous opinion among the labor delegates that "the State Department under Secretary James F. Byrnes has become an instrumentality of domestic and worldwide reaction opposing the rise of democracy and the development of freedom abroad, and has become the champion of our World War II enemies at the expense of our friends and allies, as especially witnessed by his recent Stuttgart pro-enemy speech." The CIO telegram demanded "the removal of Mr. Byrnes from the high office he has proved unqualified for."

Truman's response to the CIO telegram, typed on White House stationery and signed by Truman on September 12, 1946, was, at least initially, very forthright. "As far as the secretary of state is concerned," Truman wrote the CIO, "the president appoints a secretary of state in whom he has confidence and that will continue to be the policy of this administration. Mr. Byrnes stays." But either Truman or his secretary subsequently crossed out in pencil the entire text of this letter, and underneath Truman's signature is the handwritten addition "Did not send."

Byrnes was aware of some of these efforts against him. In the middle of the Iranian crisis, on March 5, 1946, Colonel Lawrence Pinckney, his old political ally in South Carolina, had sent him a copy of an unsigned handbill that had been distributed in large numbers the previous day throughout the city of Charleston. "Our 'Jimmy' Byrnes Is Embarrassed! We Must Help Him Out!" the handbill was headlined. "While Secretary of State Byrnes is trying to teach the Bulgarians democracy, only two out of ten people in his home state take part in elections," the text continued. "No wonder Jimmy Byrnes' face is red!" The handbill called for the end of the poll tax and other forms of official racial discrimination in South Carolina, which it claimed "our famous son" had overlooked while at the U.S. State Department. "We favor, furthermore, equality of economic opportunity," the bill went on; "in particular, we favor the establishment of a permanent Fair Employment Practices Committee." Byrnes acknowledged receipt of the handbill and Pinkney's unsuccessful efforts to determine the authorship with a short note: "Thanks—looks like some of our CIO friends."

But what proved to be the most damaging attacks on Byrnes' position at the State Department came not from the political left but from the political right within the Truman administration. Clark Clifford, Admiral Leahy, and, to a lesser degree, George Kennan, Dean Acheson, and other new men on the president's executive office staff acted in concert to remove Jimmy Byrnes from the cabinet by early 1947. Two days after Henry Wallace was fired, Clifford met with Truman's appointments secretary, Matthew Connelly, and others on the White House staff. "Despite the messy way it had happened, we were all pleased that Wallace was gone," Clifford later recalled, "and we looked forward to the impending departure of Byrnes. We all felt strongly that the sooner Harry Truman replaced his former political rivals with his own men the better." And, despite Byrnes' recent and successful diplomatic maneuvers to remove Soviet troops from Iran, his departure apparently was achieved by these new men by their consistently portraying Jimmy Byrnes to Truman as an appeaser to communism, both abroad and at home.

Despite his innate conservatism, Byrnes had been unexpectedly vulnerable to a political charge of this kind since his assuming the secretariat, not because of any ideological disposition on his part toward communism but because of his firm insistence during his year and a half tenure at the Department of State upon observing the due processes of law. This insistence cost Byrnes dearly, not only providing his political enemies with the means to force him from the cabinet by the winter of 1946–47 but also later making him the first public subject of Senator Joseph McCarthy's wild attacks on supposed subversives in government. These charges against Byrnes originated in the so-called *Amerasia* incident, of June 1945, one month before Byrnes assumed his office at State.

That month the FBI arrested six men, including one State Department employee and also John S. Service, a distinguished Foreign Service officer and at the time one of the most respected authorities on China. All six were charged with wartime espionage. The charges resulted from the FBI's having been alerted to the publication of documents previously classified as "secret" and "top secret" by the State Department and the OSS in *Amerasia*, a left-wing publication often critical of current U.S. policy in China. In a subsequent search of the offices of *Amerasia*, agents found other classified documents and copies of classified documents and received testimony that John Service often had lent such documents to the editor of *Amerasia* for use in preparing articles. But as the FBI began presenting its evidence to a grand jury that summer of 1945, the government's case against the defendants, particularly Service, began to fall apart. Testimony revealed that, although the documents had been classified as "secret" and "top secret," their content actually was common knowledge among China researchers, the documents having been so classified apparently to speed their handling through the State Department offices. Furthermore, testimony revealed that the overnight sharing of government documents with journalists outside the government was routine throughout wartime Washington, in many departments in addition to State. The FBI also was forced to admit that, although it had had the six defendants under constant surveillance for at least a month prior to their arrest, it had no evidence that any of the documents had been shown to any group or individual beyond writers on the *Amerasia* staff. Consequently, the members of the grand jury refused to indict any of the six defendants on the espionage charge, and the editors of *Amerasia* received only a comparatively small fine in the final resolution of the case. Service was neither indicted nor fined, and a subsequent bipartisan congressional investigation of the incident declared that although he had been imprudent in his lending of documents, the loyalty of Service and the other government officials involved in the *Amerasia* case was "above question."

Jimmy Byrnes was under intense political pressure upon taking office in July 1945 to dissociate himself and his new administration at the State Department from the fate of John Service. After all, the *Amerasia* affair was arguably the responsibility of his predecessor, Edward Stettinius, Jr., and his watch at State. Byrnes, however, respected the grand-jury procedure; he refused to make any critical statement about Service while the indictment was being considered, and on August 14, the day the grand jury announced its refusal to support the FBI's case against Service, Byrnes wrote to the now cleared official. The letter was published with Byrnes' approval the following week in the State Department *Bulletin*, under the heading "Vindication of John S. Service."

"My dear Mr. Service," Byrnes wrote, "I am advised that the grand jury, after hearing the testimony of witnesses, has found nothing to warrant an indictment against you. One of the fundamentals of our democratic system is the investigation by a grand jury of criminal charges. By that process you have been cleared." Byrnes was restoring Service to active duty at his prior level of responsibility, he wrote him, continuing, "I congratulate you on this happy termination of your ordeal and predict for you a continuance of the splendid record that I am advised you have maintained since first you entered the Foreign Service. With all good wishes. . . ."

Byrnes had chosen to see the resolution of the charges against Service as a vindication of the U.S. judicial system and its presumption of innocence, but to conservatives both within and outside of the Truman administration, John Service became an early symbol of the tolerance of subversion within the federal government. (In 1951, although Service had been cleared by six prior hearings of the State Department's Loyalty Board and testimony by George Kennan of his anticommunism, Dean Acheson, Byrnes' successor as U.S. secretary of state, fired Service on the basis of a "reasonable doubt" about his loyalty in the *Amerasia* case. Service challenged the constitutionality of his firing in court, and in 1957 the U.S. Supreme Court by a unanimous decision ruled that Service's termination by Acheson had been unconstitutional, and ordered Service reinstated with back pay.)

But shortly before Byrnes left for the Moscow conference in November 1945, the John Service issue was raised again. Patrick J. Hurley, a conservative Republican lawyer who had been serving as ambassador to China, submitted his resignation to Truman in protest, he publicly announced, of the "communistic leanings and actions of a number of assistants in the State Department." John Service was specifically named by Hurley in his public accusations, which the exiting ambassador repeated in late November in testimony before the Senate Foreign Relations Committee.

Asked to testify in rebuttal to Hurley's charges, Byrnes was able to convince his friends on the Senate committee that Service's disagreements with Hurley over the wisdom of an unqualified support for General Chiang Kai-shek were legitimate differences of opinion over policy and not attempts at subversion. Nevertheless, the damaging perception was being advanced by Byrnes' enemies in the White House as early as his first six months in office that he and his personally chosen assistant secretary for administration, Donald Russell, were not sufficiently vigilant in their protection of State Department security or ideological purity. The idea that Byrnes or Donald Russell, both former attorneys specializing in the practice of corporate law in Spartanburg, South Carolina, were intellectually or emotionally susceptible to communism is worse than ridiculous; but Leahy continued to worry this bone of anticommunism in front of Truman at every opportunity. Before leaving for Moscow, Byrnes had met with Truman, General George Marshall, and Admiral Leahy on November 28, 1945, to discuss the "military and diplomatic situation" in China. Leahy that night confided to his diary, and probably had passed on to Truman after Byrnes had left, the opinion that "today for the first time I sense a feeling that Secretary Byrnes is not immune to the communistically-inclined advisers in his department."

The political and administrative pressures on Byrnes intensified with the decision by the White House staff to transfer approximately four thousand former employees of the OSS and other wartime agencies to the State Department for possible permanent employment. Byrnes was opposed to this transfer on ideological grounds, believing in general that the executive branch should be kept small and in particular that the transfer of such a large number of former intelligence and special-operations agents would transform the State Department from an advisory agency into an independent policy-making agency. Also, the personal backgrounds and political affiliations of some of these former agents and operatives might be dubious; to protect both the integrity of the State Department and the reputations of applicants from unsubstantiated charges of disloyalty, Byrnes had by early 1946 therefore set up a three-tiered system of security clearances under the direction of Russell, with the final evaluation of an applicant's background for permanent employment being made in the State Department. Under this system, the FBI had only an advisory role in deciding whether the State Department should continue to employ any of the transfers; the final decision was made after an independent investigation of an applicant's background by the department's security committee, chaired by Russell and overseen by Secretary Byrnes.

Byrnes' system reduced the importance of statements by unnamed informants often present in FBI background reports and showed the former Supreme Court justice's consistent sympathies for the legal rights of an individual during any possible adversarial hearings with the federal government. But the secretary's respect for due process apparently was too substantial for some of his critics. On July 18, 1946, Congressman Bartel Jonkman, a conservative Republican from Michigan, wrote a letter of complaint to Byrnes. Too many temporarily transferred employees were remaining on the State Department rolls, Jonkman complained, when he himself had confidential information that many of the transferred employees were subversive or communistically inclined. In response Byrnes had Russell send Jonkman a letter three days later in which the department's rate of security clearances was defended and in which Russell testily said to the congressman, "Neither you nor the people of this country would countenance the use of 'gestapo' methods or the harassment and persecution of loyal employees who are American citizens on flimsy evidence or dubious hearsay and innuendo supplied by 'confidential informants.' "

Jonkman, however, continued to make private and public statements to other members of the House that "the State Department was honeycombed with communistically inclined employees who had pro-Russian sympathies." And at a July 26 news conference Byrnes reacted unusually strongly when asked about Jonkman's charges: "There are lots of people who are suspected of disloyalty to the government who are just as loyal to the government as you and I," the secretary declared to the assembled reporters. "It is a very serious matter to charge any man with disloyalty to the government," Byrnes continued. "If you do it, if the government does it, you destroy that man for life. You can ruin a man's reputation in a few minutes. Therefore, in any department—and I don't care what department—it must be a matter that is discreetly and wisely done."

Five days after this press conference, Congressman Adolph Sabath of Illinois, a powerful Democrat who was chairman of the Rules Committee, rose to defend Byrnes' security procedures in a speech on the floor of the House. Probably in prearrangement with Byrnes, Sabath introduced into the *Congressional Record* the text of a letter written to him by Byrnes on the day of Byrnes' July 26 news conference and enumerating the cases investigated so far by the State Department's security committee. Of the 3,000 employees whose case histories had been examined to date by Russell's committee, Byrnes wrote, 285 had been evaluated adversely by the committee; of those 285 employees, 79 had been terminated. Hence a total of 206 employees in the State Department either were awaiting being fired or, in the opinion of Russell or Byrnes, were not so adversely evaluated by the security committee as to justify their being fired. With his characteristic respect for individual civil liberties in the face of a government investigation, Byrnes in his letter deliberately did not disclose the names either of the fired employees or of the other 206 employees.

Sabath by his public disclosure of this letter from Byrnes obviously hoped to reduce his and his party's vulnerability to Republican charges of domestic Democratic appeasement to communism during the congressional elections of fall 1946. Already the GOP National Committee had issued a special foreign policy plank for use by its party's candidates in the upcoming elections, resolving that, after the expected GOP victories that fall, "the State Department be so reorganized that it may possess cohesion and unity of purpose; [and] that only those persons who believe in the American way of life and are loyal to the American government shall be employed in the Department." But despite Jimmy Byrnes' efforts that summer of 1946 to defuse the loyalty of State Department employees as a campaign issue, it apparently contributed to the exceptional victories of Republican challengers that fall. The GOP won enough new seats that Truman faced a Republican majority in both chambers when the Eightieth Congress was organized in 1947.

Among the freshman senators in the GOP's "class of 1946" was a young Joseph McCarthy, who had scored an upset victory in the Wisconsin elections. In the spring of 1950 McCarthy demanded yet another congressional rehearing of John S. Service and the *Amerasia* case, a hearing that once again concluded that this incident involved a thoughtless mishandling of low-grade classified documents rather than an organized espionage ring. And on February 9, 1950, McCarthy used the text of Byrnes' letter to Sabath printed four years before in the *Congressional Record* as the basis of his famous Wheeling, West Virginia, speech in which he began his campaign of claiming to possess undisputable evidence of Communist infiltration and subversion within the U.S. government.

"I have here in my hand a list of 205," McCarthy told his West Virginia audience at the Lincoln's Day speech, "a list of names which were made known to the secretary of state as being members of the Communist Party and who nevertheless are still working and shaping policy in the State Department."

McCarthy, of course, had nothing more in his hand than a copy of Byrnes' letter, which the secretary of state had allowed to be made public four years earlier; he did not have the names on the list, because Byrnes had refused to put them there. Byrnes' instinctive conservatism always favored the individual against what he perceived as the growing powers of the state, but by the time of Joseph McCarthy's rise, Jimmy Byrnes had left government service in Washington, his type of political conservatism apparently having gone out of fashion there. The difference between the total of 206 names referred to in Byrnes' letter and the 205 names McCarthy claimed to have in his hand apparently was simply the result of an error in arithmetic on McCarthy's part. McCarthy was inconsistent on this total, varying it up and down, during the next few years.

Clark Clifford, who three months earlier had risen to the position of special counsel to the president, had meanwhile not forgotten his and his associates' resolution to force Jimmy Byrnes from the Truman administration, at a time when the secretary of state's security program was coming under attack by the Republican right-wing congressional challengers of 1946. Four days after his September 22 meeting with other White House staffers at which the "impending departure" of Byrnes was discussed, Clifford handed to Truman a lengthy memorandum on Soviet militarism, espionage, and subversion that Clifford and his protégé George M. Elsey had prepared at Truman's request. The Clifford-Elsey report had been occasioned by the receipt during the height of the Iranian crisis of an 8,000-word telegram sent from Moscow by George Kennan on February 22, 1946. Kennan's "Long Telegram," as it had become known in the State Department, warned that the northern Iranian occupation by Communist subversives and Soviet troops was simply one instance in a worldwide campaign of violence and subversion directed by Moscow at Western interests, and that U.S. diplomatic relations with the Soviet Union "should be approached with the same thoroughness and care as solution of [a] major strategic problem in war."

Kennan's Long Telegram, properly regarded as one of the first documents declaring a Cold War, was addressed to the current U.S. secretary of state, James F. Byrnes. Byrnes' response was to cable Kennan five days later his congratulations on what Byrnes termed a "splendid analysis"; but this message from Moscow was prompted at least in its initial drafts by Kennan's anger toward that current secretary of state. "Perhaps it was the visit of Secretary Byrnes to Moscow [in December 1945] that caused the pot of my impatience to boil over with relation to this area of our diplomacy, as it had boiled over with respect to so many others," Kennan later recalled. "My reaction to this boiling over was, in any case, the usual reaching out of the pen." On trips back to Washington in the spring and summer of 1946, both Kennan and Averell Harriman made clear to their friends in the administration their conviction that Byrnes, despite his toughness over Iran, continued to underestimate the hostility of Soviet policy.

As subsequent scholars of the Cold War have pointed out, with considerable understatement of Byrnes' fluid pursuit of foreign policy, "through the winter of 1945–46, the Department of State was by no means an ideological monolith." Byrnes, ever the erratic statesman, was moving his department's policy rightward, toward an ideology of containment of

Soviet territorial gains. This change in policy was the result not of any intellectual "boiling over," as in the case of Kennan, but of Byrnes' subjective—and often solitary—perceptions of Soviet intentions and of the increased domestic criticism of Byrnes' compromises in 1945 by such conservative Republicans as Senator Arthur Vandenberg. As usual, Byrnes had his critics from both sides. It was the astringent judgment of Walter Lippmann that by late 1946 Byrnes had achieved a diplomatic status between the United States and the USSR in which it was easier for diplomacy to fail than to succeed. But it must be considered that with Byrnes as head of the State Department, successful negotiation with the Soviet Union was at least *possible*. Had Byrnes perceived that it was in his best political interests to change U.S. policy toward an increased cooperation with the Soviet Union after the Iranian crisis, *and* had he convinced himself that he perceived in Soviet actions a justification for such change in policy, he certainly would have steered leftward. But as events happened, after the receipt of the Kennan memorandum of February 22, the Long Telegram became a stick for Byrnes' more ideological enemies in the State Department—including George Kennan—to get Jimmy Byrnes out. The Long Telegram received wide circulation in the administration, and when Truman decided to call for a memorandum specifying the consequences for future U.S. policies implied in Kennan's telegram, he chose Clifford and not Byrnes to prepare the document.

Clifford subsequently met both with Leahy and with Byrnes on July 18 in each man's office during the course of preparing his memorandum for the president. Clifford, impressed "by Leahy's loyalty to the president" during their meeting, the same day also met with Jimmy Byrnes for background information on U.S. relations with the Soviet Union. During their conversation in the secretary of state's office, Clifford got the impression that Byrnes was being defensive and answering with "evident sarcasm" his questions about past diplomatic agreements with the Soviets. It seems more than plausible that Clifford also passed on his contrasting impressions of Byrnes and Leahy to the president when he transmitted the Clifford-Elsey report on September 24, 1946. "He went so far as to claim that he could not even be sure he was aware of 'every agreement' Roosevelt had made with the Russians," Clifford later wrote. "Some might be in Harry Hopkins' private papers, and others might be 'buried' in Franklin Roosevelt's files. I found Byrnes' statements about 'lost agreements' both incredible and offensive. When I discussed them with the normally mild and careful George Elsey that afternoon, he exploded in anger at what he termed 'a complete lie.' "

There was more to Byrnes' edginess than a simple personal dislike of Clark Clifford. Byrnes had been greatly embarrassed politically six months earlier by a public statement by Dean Acheson about the most controversial agreement between Roosevelt and the Soviets, the Yalta accords. Byrnes early in the Truman administration had made much about his being "the man at Yalta," including his presenting Truman with a gilt-lettered, maroon-colored edition of the transcribed shorthand notes Byrnes had taken at Yalta. Byrnes therefore had been distressed when Dean Acheson at a January 22, 1946, press conference had referred to a hitherto "secret" agreement reached at Yalta whereby the Soviets were allowed occupation rights of the Kuril Islands, north of Japan. Acheson further had stated at this press conference that although the undersecretary understood that the Yalta agreements had not guaranteed the Soviets permanent postwar occupation rights, "perhaps he was mistaken."

"Mr. Acheson was indeed 'mistaken,' " the Soviet government quickly declared to the world through the USSR's state radio and press. In effect, the Soviets produced a receipt for the Japanese islands signed by the Big Three. According to the official Soviet announcement, "In the Yalta Agreement of the three powers which were signed on February 11, 1946, by I. V. Stalin on behalf of the Soviet Union, by Mr. Churchill on behalf of Great Britain and by Mr. Roosevelt on behalf of the USA, but [not] published at that time for understandable reasons, it was clearly stipulated that after the victory over Japan the Kuril Islands would be turned over to the Soviet Union and also that the southern part of the island of Sakhalin and all the islands adjacent thereto should be returned to the Soviet Union."

The public uproar in the United States over Acheson's "mistaken" understanding of Roosevelt's negotiations at Yalta and the public outcry following the Soviet confirmation of the "secret" deal with FDR had forced Jimmy Byrnes in February 1946 to declare publicly that he had never read the entire documents of the Yalta accords. In fact, Byrnes declared that he was not able to find the complete documents in the Department of State archives. Byrnes told his press and radio audience that he "had never seen the original agreement" and "had first learned of it after the surrender of Japan." Denying a reporter's question that this Yalta accord about the Kurils was "so phrased that it could be interpreted as an award to the Soviet Union," Byrnes suggested that the complete text of all Yalta agreements might be found in the White House files.

In making these statements Jimmy Byrnes embarrassed not only himself but also the truth. In the autumn of 1945 in denying General Hurley's accusations of communist influence in the State Department, Byrnes had told both the U.S. Congress and the U.S. press that he "remembered well" the Yalta agreements concerning the Kuril Islands. Now talking to Clifford at their July 18, 1946, meeting, the Secretary of State could be forgiven for thinking that perhaps Clifford was going on a fishing expedition to find new documents that could further embarrass the secretary of state who so well remembered the now-unpopular agreements at Yalta.

Even after more than nearly half a century, the Clifford-Elsey report is a shocking document to read. Clifford went beyond Kennan's opinions in the Long Telegram that Soviet expansionism could best be met by an informed diplomatic policy and a healthy U.S. economy and society. Much more bellicose that Kennan's analysis, Clifford's memorandum warned Truman that relations with the Soviet Union were so adversarial and so volatile that in all future U.S.–USSR conflicts "the United States must be prepared to wage atomic and biological warfare, if necessary." Nor did the report neglect the perceived vulnerability of the U.S. economy and government to Communist espionage, such as had recently been claimed to exist in the U.S. State Department. "The Soviet government, by utilizing the membership of the Communist Party in the United States," Clifford and Elsey wrote, "has thousands of invaluable sources of information in various establishments as well as in the departments of the government."

In his 1991 memoirs Clifford regretted having inaccurately warned Truman of the existence of "thousands" of informants operating within the government departments. "In retrospect, this was the most unfortunate section of the Clifford-Elsey Report," he wrote in his memoirs. At the time of the memorandum, however, this false assertion served its purpose, because this statement by Clifford and Elsey, whatever its accuracy, was to Truman one more argument for the effecting the "impending departure" of Byrnes.

Byrnes had seen the Clifford-Elsey report, and he also had seen the handwriting on the wall. As early as the first week of March 1946, the *Army Times* had carried an anonymous story, probably instigated by Leahy or Clifford and later reprinted by the civilian press, including the *Washington Post*, that Truman intended as soon as possible to replace Byrnes as secretary of state with General George C. Marshall. The military *Times* stated that Byrnes had proven "ineffectual in dealing with power politics" and that he should be replaced by Marshall "before the damage done is beyond repair."

The new men had begun to wear down the old political operator in more ways than one. In addition to being increasingly weakened by these intra–White House policy struggles, Byrnes was becoming physically tired. During his 562 days as secretary of state, he was abroad at foreign conferences for 350 days, traveling on military aircraft under conditions that were often grueling. Now, at the age of sixty-four, he was developing health problems.

Byrnes had begun to experience chest pains early in April 1946, during the Iranian crisis. He wrote a letter to Truman on April 16 stating, "The only way I can comply with the advice of the doctor is to resign," and requesting that Truman begin considering a successor as soon as that summer. Byrnes had perhaps hoped at the time of this first letter of resignation that he would complete both the preliminary treaties and the significant work on the major treaties with Germany and Japan before his resignation.

But now increasingly aware of the influence with Truman of such new men as Acheson and Clifford during his absences abroad and of the fact that even the preliminary treaties had taken one year more than he had estimated, Byrnes in a letter of December 19, 1946, reminded Truman of that earlier letter and asked him to consider his resignation to be effective "as soon as my successor is appointed and qualified."

Truman responded with a "my dear Jim" letter of January 7, 1947, accepting Byrnes' resignation. "I realize full well how arduous and complex have been the problems which have fallen to you since you took office in July, 1945. Big events were then pending, and the months that have ensued have presented problems of the utmost moment, with all of which you have dealt with rare tact and judgment and—when necessary—firmness and tenacity of purpose." On January 21 George C. Marshall succeeded Byrnes to become the Truman administration's third secretary of state.

Byrnes' resignation was a major loss for any possible postwar U.S.– USSR cooperation, in the views of General Lucius Clay and later of one of Clay's biographers, the diplomatic historian Jean Edward Smith. "Like Clay, Byrnes, whose attitude in dealing with the Russians was one of pragmatic compromise, genuinely believed that cooperation with the Soviet Union was possible," Smith wrote. Despite the historical inevitability of military conflict with the Soviet Union implied by George Kennan's Long Telegram and stated even more explicitly by the Clifford-Elsey report, Byrnes had shown that it was possible for the United States to obtain agreements favorable to its interests in its diplomatic negotiations with the Soviet Union, as in the repatriation agreements over Italy and Finland. At the same time, his military firmness toward the Soviets over their Iranian invasion clearly showed that the secretary was no appeaser. And his past actions leave little doubt that, had Byrnes remained with the administration, the domestic loyalty program begun in earnest by the Truman administration in 1947 would have been applied more "discreetly and wisely" under the direction of this former Supreme Court justice.

But Clark Clifford, among others, was determined that Jimmy Byrnes' departure from the State Department be interpreted, whatever the actual historical record, as a timely disavowal by the Truman administration of a Byrnes-sponsored policy of appeasement toward the Soviet Union. Clifford in fact revised a major document of the Cold War to support this interpretation. Six weeks after Byrnes' resignation, Truman was presented with the final draft of a message planned for his delivery before a joint session of Congress on March 12, 1947, in which the president would announce the establishment of the "Truman Doctrine" of containment by U.S. military aid to other countries, if needed, to block Soviet-sponsored aggression. The first draft of this announcement prepared by the president's advisers quoted Byrnes' speech to the Overseas Press Club on February 28, 1946, in which the secretary of state at the height of the Iranian crisis had warned the Soviets that the United States would not let "coercion or pressure" on other nations go unchallenged. This preliminary draft identified Byrnes by name, but when it was forwarded to Clifford for his approval, he objected to the inclusion of Byrnes among the early advocates of a doctrine of containment. Maintaining that the president should not quote others in his speeches, Clifford succeeded in having this reference to Byrnes and his statements during the Iranian crisis deleted from the final draft of the 1947 speech announcing the Truman Doctrine. Byrnes thus was dropped from the administration's roll of early anti-Communists.

Jimmy Byrnes' time seemed to have passed. Dean Acheson, always a source of good advice and malicious wit, later remarked that Byrnes reminded him of the mythological character of Tithonus, who having been granted immortality by the gods, forgot to ask for eternal youth. As for the former secretary, he and his wife planned to return to Spartanburg. Byrnes would write his memoirs and practice law part-time at a prestigious Washington law firm; as his political mentor and friend General Lucius Clay remarked, it was time for Byrnes to make "a little money" after close to two decades in public life during which he had voluntarily reduced his private income twice by becoming a U.S. senator and OWM director.

But despite Acheson's gibe about a politically immortal but enfeebled Jimmy Byrnes, this perennially self-made man had enough energy for at least one more significant role in national politics. Byrnes would indeed retire from international diplomacy and return to South Carolina; but on an obscure backwater of the Santee-Cooper impoundment created during one of his earlier political lives as a U.S. senator, there would arise a legal dispute over the rights of black children in South Carolina to have access to the same schools as white children across the water. The dispute would become part of the historic *Brown* v. *Board of Education* case, challenging the system of racially segregated education, and James F. Byrnes, now returned actively to politics and elected the governor of South Carolina, would become both the major opponent of the NAACP in that case and the most politically powerful critic of the Truman administration's domestic policies on race and federal activism. And despite the outwardly cordial parting of Byrnes and Truman in 1947, Governor James Byrnes would in a few years have begun to bring his state and the other states of the Deep South into a seemingly permanent political alignment with the GOP. Before the end of the decade, Harry Truman would scarcely be able to mention the name of Jimmy Byrnes without cursing.

19

A Disquisition
on Government

"**H**e can do as he damn pleases,"
Harry Truman snapped to a group of startled journalists gathered at the
White House on January 19, 1950. The president's tart statement was in
response to a reporter's question at a news conference that day, asking
Truman for his reaction to the announcement that Jimmy Byrnes was
leaving private life in order to run for the governorship of South Carolina.
Little more than three years had passed since former Secretary of State
James F. Byrnes had resigned from Truman's cabinet with a cordial exchange of "Dear Mr. President" and "My dear Jimmy" letters. But during
that time much water had flowed under the bridge, to use one of Joseph
Stalin's favorite expressions; and although Byrnes had continued after leaving the federal government to give strong public support to the administration's Cold War policies, Jimmy Byrnes had by 1950 emerged as the
foremost critic of the Truman administration's domestic policies.

Byrnes at first kept to his plans to retire from public affairs and "make
a little money." Less than three months after Byrnes had resigned from
the State Department, newspapers in the nation's capital and other major
cities carried the announcement in April 1947 that the former secretary of

state had become an associate in practice at the Washington law firm of Hogan and Harrison. The smiling and prosperous Frank Hogan had died in 1944, but his nameplate still occupied the front office door, and before his death Frank "You Can't Beat a Million Dollar Fee" Hogan had built Hogan and Harrison into one of the nation's most lucrative law practices. Byrnes became a well-paid corporate lawyer again, just as he had been in the 1920s, now representing Paramount Pictures Incorporated, among other film studio clients. Throughout the 1940s, Jimmy and Maude Byrnes divided their time between a leisurely semiretirement at their Spartanburg home and Byrnes' occasional—and highly profitable—appearances on behalf of his clients in appellate courts in Washington.

In the first years of his retirement, Byrnes also composed what later proved to be a premature memoir of his government career. The book, ghostwritten with the help of Porter McKeever, was published in 1947 under the title of *Speaking Frankly*. As the first published account by a major American participant at the Yalta and Potsdam conferences, it quickly became a best-seller. Byrnes made $125,000 from his writing that year, independent of his income from his law practice. Once *Speaking Frankly* was published, Byrnes for the first time in his life had both the time and the financial security to reflect upon his accomplishments and perhaps upon what can only be called the essential singularity of his ambitious life: how as the posthumous child of an impoverished Irishman from Charleston he had become the political representative of the Bourbon ruling class of the South with his strongest political allies among that region's Jewish politicians; how as Roosevelt's most consistent political ally among the conservative Democrats he nevertheless had been denied the vice presidency and the White House itself; and how as the former adviser to two presidents on the use of the atomic bomb during World War II, Jimmy Byrnes in the postwar world was becoming rich by representing Hollywood film studios.

Byrnes was never a particularly self-reflective man, however, either in his memoirs or in his private correspondence; and the truth is that by 1950 his most consistently felt emotion was boredom. At age sixty-eight, Jimmy Byrnes was bored by what now seemed to him to have been a premature retirement from politics, just as nine years earlier Senator Byrnes in 1941 had been both bored and vexed by his first retirement from politics to sit on the U.S. Supreme Court. Politics, not money or fame, quickened the heartbeat of this inveterate campaigner. The personal accumulation of money itself meant little to Byrnes, who had no children as heirs and who had boasted throughout the 1930s and 1940s that all he desired from his work was "two tailored suits a year, three meals a day, and a reasonable amount of good liquor." Byrnes had long since been able from his investments guided by Baruch and his federal salaries to provide these and all other material needs for himself and his wife. He and Maude Byrnes decided to donate the entire $125,000 from *Speaking Frankly* to the establishment of a charitable foundation for orphans in South Carolina.

But the political happiness money cannot buy may nevertheless have been found by Byrnes on a trip to South Carolina in 1949. According to that state's political lore, Jimmy Byrnes late one afternoon in the backseat of his Cadillac was sharing a bottle of Jack Daniels bourbon with his old friend and political ally Sol Blatt, the Jewish Speaker of the South Carolina house. Byrnes throughout the long, time-killing chauffeur-driven ride across the Carolina landscape had been complaining of his dissatisfaction at returning to Washington and the practice of corporate law, until finally Blatt, exasperated and expansive with drink, declared, "Well, Jimmy, if you feel that way about it, why don't you come back to South Carolina and run for governor?"

The story is probably apocryphal. Byrnes always preferred drinking Hankey Bannister brand bourbon. But it is true that Byrnes had been looking for encouragement to reenter national politics on a platform larger than simply the relief of his own boredom. Jimmy Byrnes was too much of an old political professional to want to give up the elective game, even at age sixty-eight; but he also was too proud of his major accomplishments as the "assistant president" and the former U.S. secretary of state to want to diminish that record by taking a lesser job, unless he could convince himself that such an action was in the public interest. He did not need a job; he needed an ideological reason to take a job. And since at least the late fall of 1949, when Byrnes had been invited as a speaker to the Southern Governors' Conference in Biloxi, Mississippi, conservative politicians throughout the South such as Sol Blatt had been encouraging him to reenter elective politics as their region's foremost spokesman against the domestic policies of the Truman administration.

By the time of the supposed conversation in the backseat of Byrnes' Cadillac, the long-anticipated division in the Democratic party had become a political fact. As in the earlier, unforgotten quarrels dating from Roosevelt's attempted purge of the party in 1938, many domestic issues separated liberal and conservative Democrats; but as in 1938–39, the sticking point once more was race. Harry Truman surprisingly had become by 1949 the first twentieth-century president strongly in favor of federal activism to eliminate racial discrimination—a conversion that surely would have astonished Franklin Roosevelt, who had in 1944 raised the Missourian as a compromise candidate to conservative southerners. But as Truman and his advisers began to plan for his own run for the presidency in 1948, he was not forgetful, as FDR had not been before him, of the critical importance of black pluralities to the national Democratic ticket. Truman was also genuinely shocked on reading the conclusions of the committee he himself had appointed to investigate racial relations in the postwar United States. The committee's report, published on October 29, 1947, as *To*

Secure These Rights, cataloged a disturbing pattern of violence and discrimination against minorities across both the southern and the northern states, and the far western United States.

Clark Clifford advised the president in a memorandum in late November 1947 that whatever the domestic racial policies of his administration in the next election, "the South can be considered safely Democratic." For both pragmatic and personal reasons, Truman decided shortly thereafter to run for election in 1948 on a strong civil rights program. Citing the findings of *To Secure These Rights*, Truman in a special message to Congress early in 1948 called for passage of a national civil rights program, including the enactment of legislation that Jimmy Byrnes and other southern conservatives had spent much of the 1930s and early 1940s successfully blocking: elimination of the poll tax in the South, federal antilynching laws, and establishment of a permanent FEPC.

Truman's proposed civil rights program and the endorsement by his administration of *To Secure These Rights* touched what one contemporary observer called the "exposed nerve" of southern Democratic conservatives such as Byrnes. Truman's intended federal activism was the surest sign yet to these southern Democrats that the Compromise of 1877, and the one-party system and racial segregation supported by it, had outlived its usefulness to the current leadership of the national Democratic party. When, at the national convention in Philadelphia in 1948, party liberals led by Hubert Humphrey of Minnesota succeeded in having the party adopt a platform plank stating, "We highly commend President Harry Truman for his courageous stand on civil rights," a familiar scene was reenacted: all of the members of the Mississippi delegation and some of the Alabama state delegation promptly walked out of the hall. Cotton Ed Smith was not in Philadelphia that year, having been that summer four years in his grave; but apparently his restless spirit from the 1936 convention in Philadelphia still moved some state delegations.

Disaffected former Democrats met in regional conventions across the states of the old Confederacy after the 1948 convention to form the States' Rights party, its presidential electors competing with or taking the place of the names of electors of the national Democratic ticket on the ballots in many southern states. The States' Rights party, or the Dixiecrats, as they were almost universally known by July 1948, seemed to be fulfilling the prophecy made ten years earlier by the southern members of the congressional conservatives that the Democratic party eventually would split into two regional parties. In its party platform accompanying the fielding of presidential and vice-presidential candidates to oppose the national Democratic party ticket of Harry Truman and Alben Barkley, the Dixiecrats declared their conviction that the proposed civil rights program of the Truman administration "would be utterly destructive of the social, economic, and political life of the Southern people."

But despite this separatist rhetoric, Truman's victory total of 303 electoral college votes in the election that fall marked a substantial win for the national Democrats. Clark Clifford had been at least more than half right about the South. Even in the eleven states of the old Confederacy, the Dixiecrats won no more than 39 electoral college votes, scattered across five southern states. Byrnes and other white southerners had been apprehensive about the Truman administration's increasing commitment to civil rights for the nation's black citizens, but a large majority of white southerners apparently were not yet at the point of abandoning the national Democratic party for a strictly regional, segregationist southern party. Among those most disappointed by this southern reluctance to leave the national party was the States' Rights candidate for president—J. Strom Thurmond, a longtime political acquaintance of Jimmy Byrnes from Ben Tillman's old political base of Edgefield County.

Although he enjoyed a local friendship with Thurmond, Jimmy Byrnes sidestepped the Dixiecrat revolt of 1948. Just as Byrnes had attempted in 1938 to keep out of sight at his Sullivan's Island retreat and to remain on friendly terms with both the late Cotton Ed Smith and Franklin Roosevelt during FDR's attempted purge, Byrnes also kept a low public profile during Truman's presidential campaign of 1948. "In 1948, sincerely wishing to stay out of politics, I had taken no part in the political campaign," Byrnes later wrote. Apparently by this time Byrnes had learned from his late friend Franklin Roosevelt how to mix sincerity with self-contradiction. It was true that Byrnes did not attend the Democratic convention that summer in Philadelphia. (This was the first national Democratic convention Byrnes had missed since the party had nominated Al Smith in 1928.) Nor did Byrnes chose to attend the two "rump" conventions held after Philadelphia by the Dixiecrats in Birmingham, Alabama, and Houston, Texas, where Thurmond eventually was nominated. But Byrnes' self-imposed retirement from the campaign in 1948 had less to do with his sincere desire to avoid politics that year than with his clear-headed appraisal of the dead end of third-party politics.

"Jimmy knew that third parties were never going anywhere," W. F. Prioleau, a political confidant and personal attorney of Byrnes from the low country later recalling about Jimmy Byrnes' carefully distancing himself in 1948 from the Dixiecrats. Having been a participant or an observer in presidential campaigns since the late nineteenth century and the heyday of Pitchfork Ben Tillman, Byrnes personally could remember how the Populist party—at its height in 1896 far stronger and more national in its appeal than the movement of Strom Thurmond and the Dixiecrats—nevertheless had failed to dislodge either of the two established political parties. Thus the hard rules of political realism governing the fate of third parties in the United States determined Jimmy Byrnes' inactivity in 1948, regardless of whatever ideological or personal sympathies Byrnes may have felt toward the young Thurmond. Still maintaining his lifelong ties to the national Democratic party and, for the moment, his cordial relations with Harry Truman, Byrnes sent a congratulatory telegram to Truman the day after the election on November 3. In a choice of words that was almost certainly an unintentional echoing of Hubert Humphrey's phrasing at the Philadelphia convention, Byrnes praised the newly elected Truman for his "courageous victory" over the Republican and Dixiecrat tickets.

But though Jimmy Byrnes in 1948 had a long political memory stretching back to 1896, in 1949 he had his political knives out for the second Truman administration. National health insurance, expanded unemployment benefits, increased deficit spending, and larger federal subsidies for public housing also were part of the Fair Deal that Truman, in addition to his civil rights program, was urging the newly organized Eighty-first Congress to pass in 1949. Byrnes was unquestionably more moderate in his view of racial relations than many of his longtime acquaintances among the single-issue Dixiecrats; but Byrnes' commitment to fiscal conservatism, dating back to the late 1930s when he had opposed many of these same proposals then sponsored by Harry Hopkins, made an ideological quarrel in 1949 with Truman almost inevitable. "Sam, I've decided to break with President Truman," Byrnes told an old friend and fellow conservative, the Speaker of the House, Sam Rayburn, within five months of Truman's second inauguration, when the two politicians chanced to meet over drinks amid the restored grandeur of colonial buildings in Williamsburg, Virginia. "It's official as of this moment," Byrnes confirmed.

The occasion was a reception for Byrnes, Speaker Rayburn, and Senator Harry Byrd of Virginia as distinguished guests after graduation ceremonies at Washington and Lee University on June 18, 1949. Byrnes had delivered the graduation address that afternoon, and in his first major public comment on national and international affairs since his 1947 retirement, he voiced a strong, if generally phrased, criticism of Truman's proposed Fair Deal programs. Without specifically referring to the president's advocacy of a permanent FEPC or other domestic proposals, Byrnes told his university audience, including reporters from the *New York Times* and other national newspapers, "We are going down the road to statism."

He did not mention the Fair Deal or the presidency of Harry Truman by name. But Byrnes was clearly understood to mean the Truman administration's proposals currently before Congress when he declared, "If some of the new programs seriously proposed should be adopted, there is danger that the individual—whether farmer, worker, manufacturer, lawyer, or doctor—will soon be an economic slave pulling an oar in the galley of the State."

"Byrnes Hits Trend to 'Welfare State,' " the *New York Times* headlined its coverage of the speech the next day, and other newspapers across the country also picked up the story of this Democratic former secretary of state criticizing the policies of the Truman administration in phrases that were harsher, in some cases, than those of its Republican critics. Truman was furious on reading these headlines, and he committed his anger to paper in a handwritten postscript to a letter intended for Byrnes' reading. This time Harry Truman mailed the letter. Three days after the speech at Williamsburg, a letter sealed in a White House envelope addressed to Byrnes was received at the law offices of Hogan and Harrison. After some routine and typewritten pleasantries about minor State Department press articles printed since Byrnes' departure, Truman closed his "Dear Jim" letter with the handwritten postscript "Since your Washington & Lee speech, I'm sure I know how Caesar felt when he said, 'Et tu, Brute.' "

As soon as Truman's letter was forwarded to him, Byrnes responded with a two-page letter of his own, written from his Isle of Palms retreat, where he had traveled after giving the Washington and Lee speech. Its tone initially was of puzzled hurt. There was no familiar "Dear Harry" in this response. "Dear Mr. President," Byrnes began, "I am very sorry you added to your personal note of recent date the postscript." The postscript, he added, "is not pleasant and not justified." Byrnes continued at length:

In that speech I spoke approvingly of the foreign policies of your administration. In discussing domestic affairs I spoke very critically of new programs seriously proposed and the danger of giving too much power to the state. I did not mention you. I did not mention any one political party. On the contrary my warning was followed by the statement that "each political party tries to outpromise the other." You may have regarded it as a criticism of you because you have approved certain proposals pending in the Congress. But surely if a personal friend expresses criticism of a proposal pending in the Congress which you approve, or criticizes a proposal submitted by you, you are not going to consider it a betrayal by your friend.

Byrnes closed his letter of July 9, 1949, as follows:

I hope you are not going to think of me as a Brutus, because I am no Brutus.
I hope you are not going to think of yourself as a Caesar, because you are no Caesar.
With best wishes for your health and happiness, I am sincerely yours, James F. Byrnes.

These closing words probably were no more flippant than those of many earlier written or oral exchanges between Jimmy Byrnes and Franklin D. Roosevelt in the late 1930s, when Byrnes as a leader of the conservative coalition in public speeches had frequently disagreed with the domestic policies of the Second New Deal without losing his personal friendship with the president. Senator Byrnes, remember, had criticized in detail the proposed relief spending for the WPA by Harry Hopkins for fiscal 1939 in a speech to the Southern Society of New York City and had lunched the next day with Roosevelt, who had greeted his friend with an impromptu and good-natured singing of "Oh Where, Oh Where, Is My Wandering Boy?" But although 1949 bore many domestic political resemblances to 1939, Harry Truman was no FDR. Harry S. Truman, like Byrnes himself and other self-made men, had built his career over a crushed foundation of real or perceived insults; and the "You're no Caesar" tag was seen by Truman as only the latest provocation in a series of affronts to his authority by Jimmy Byrnes. (Truman was even quicker than Byrnes to perceive a slight where perhaps none had been intended. The previous November when Truman at his Key West vacation residence had received Byrnes' telegram congratulating him on his "courageous victory" in the presidential election, reporters standing near Truman had heard him grumble that Byrnes and his friend Baruch, for all their congratulations, were "disloyal" Democrats.) Truman did not reply to Byrnes' letter of July 9, nor was there ever to be any further correspondence or conversations between the two men for the remainder of their lives. In a manner that at least seemed rueful, Byrnes later was to conclude in his memoirs that his "reference to Caesar had gone deeper than intended."

But whether Jimmy Byrnes sincerely thought that he could disagree with the policies of the Truman administration without personally quarreling with the president, as had been the case between Byrnes and Roosevelt, or whether he was simply a smooth southern disloyalist pretending butter would not melt in his mouth, as Harry Truman liked to think, the two by the end of 1949 had come to a parting of ways. The exact spot of their parting was Biloxi, Mississippi. There, on November 21, Jimmy Byrnes addressed the Southern Governors' Conference in a speech that the *New York Times* the next day on its front page accurately reported as "a vigorous attack on the fiscal and taxation policies of the national administration."

Speaking to an after-dinner audience composed of the region's governors, other influential state office holders, and what the *Times* described as "several prominent leaders of the States-Rights Democrats," Byrnes ridiculed what he termed the Truman administration's "trickle back" system of economics, by which the federal government returned to the states only a small percentage of tax dollars it collected from local economies in order to concentrate spending for unemployment relief, public housing, and other social services in Washington, under the control of the national administration. In anticipation of the "revenue sharing" idea later initiated by the Nixon administrations, Byrnes in his 1949 speech urged the region's governors to "perform a great public service" by "standing together and fighting" for a return to the states of a greater share of federal tax revenues and a greater local role in deciding how that money was to be spent for social programs.

Once again, Byrnes made no specific reference to Truman's proposed civil rights program in his criticism of the growing powers of the federal government; nor did he criticize by name either the Democratic party or any members of the Truman administration. "No party or individual is entitled to a monopoly of the blame, or credit," for the growth of the centralized state, Byrnes told the governors in his Biloxi speech. (Byrnes was surely aware that his audience could remember that as a former war mobilizer and as a New Deal senator he himself had greatly helped pass legislation to create the modern state apparatus.) But despite Byrnes' disclaimers, in what the *Times* described as "an atmosphere heavy with political speculation," his call to "stand together and fight" was understood to be a political challenge specifically to the Truman administration. It was also understood that Jimmy Byrnes was prepared to be the one to lead the southern governors in that challenge. "In recent weeks it has been widely reported in South Carolina, Mr. Byrnes' home state, that he would be a candidate for governor next summer," the *Times* noted in its coverage of the Biloxi speech.

Once more, Byrnes' remarks on the domestic policies of the Fair Deal received national attention, and once more Jimmy Byrnes demonstrated his lifelong knack of acquiring unexpected political allies. In the summer preceding the Biloxi speech, Alfred A. Knopf of the New York City publishing firm of the same name had sent Byrnes a complimentary copy of V. O. Key's classic study *Southern Politics in State and Nation*, published that year by his firm. ("I think you will find Southern Politics, as I have, to be fascinating reading," Knopf had written to Byrnes in August 1949.) Within a week of the Biloxi speech Knopf wrote again to Byrnes to offer the emerging South Carolina critic of the growing centralized power of the government a short note of personal encouragement. "Dear Mr. Byrnes," Knopf wrote on November 28, "As one late convert to another, I can only wish you good luck." Byrnes promptly wrote back, thanking Knopf for the encouraging note and assuring him, "What I stated at Biloxi has always been my philosophy of government."

"What Is Jimmy Byrnes Up To Now?" rhetorically asked a fellow southerner, the Atlanta newspaper publisher Ralph McGill, in the title of an article written for the *Saturday Evening Post* in the months after the Biloxi speech. Other interested individuals across the nation as politically disparate as Harry Truman and Alfred Knopf also were wondering about the answer to that same question. It was clear that Byrnes' political intentions in the year following the Biloxi speech were far more ambitious than the single-issue platform of the segregationist States' Righters. "The canny

Byrnes had given the Dixiecrats no aid or comfort in 1948 and in 1950 he ignored them," McGill noted. In fact, both Jimmy Byrnes' ambitions and his political memory went far beyond the States' Rights campaign of 1948 or the fiscal and racial conditions of the United States in 1950. Jonathan Daniels, the political acquaintance of Byrnes and biographer in 1951 of Harry Truman, spoke more truth than perhaps he realized when he stated that Jimmy Byrnes was running a race in history with John C. Calhoun. For what Jimmy Byrnes was up to in 1950—with a fair chance of succeeding—was nothing less than a fundamental restructuring of America's two political parties, as had first been described in 1850 by John C. Calhoun in his later published study *A Disquisition on Government.*

Byrnes saw the possibility in 1950 of reinventing John C. Calhoun's nineteenth-century theory of the concurrent majority in order to shape the future of twentieth-century American politics. Calhoun's theory, by which a conservative South and a liberal North each could exercise a political veto over the actions of the other and therefore force the other to compromise, had been put into practice by Byrnes intermittently during the 1930s, when he was a leader of the conservative coalition in the U.S. Senate to counterbalance the New Deal northern liberals. Now, in the wake of the Dixiecrats and Truman's proposed Fair Deal, Jimmy Byrnes was returning to the theories of the author of *A Disquisition on Government* with a vengeance.

Byrnes knew that the Dixiecrats had been amateurs. But in attempting to lead the South out of an automatic loyalty to the Democratic party, Strom Thurmond had pointed a way to Jimmy Byrnes to accomplish nationally what he had earlier done in the Senate chamber. Byrnes knew that if the South's 127 electoral college votes had not been diverted by the Dixiecrats in 1948—and if under the direction of a politician much more experienced and prestigious than Thurmond, southern voters had been persuaded to vote as a bloc for the Republican party—then the outcome of the 1948 presidential election would have been quite different. Without the support of the southern electoral bloc, Truman would have received 176 electoral college votes in the 1948 election; Dewey's possible total with the complete support of the southern bloc would have been 316 electoral college votes. In 1948, 266 electoral college votes were required to win.

Jimmy Byrnes intended by winning the governorship of South Carolina in 1950 to become that southern leader who, like John C. Calhoun, could direct his region as a bloc to exercise a political veto over the policies of the Fair Deal. "If we act in concert with other southern states on these questions," Byrnes in 1952 told the South Carolina Democratic party, "and let the leaders of both political parties know we are no longer 'in the bag' of any political party, we will no longer be ignored." To a young historian then studying and writing in the 1950s at Columbia University, Richard

Hofstadter, it was immediately obvious what Jimmy Byrnes and the other southern conservatives were up to: "Here is the concurrent majority *redivivus*," Hofstader wrote.

But it was the candidacy of Jimmy Byrnes redivivus that most angered Harry Truman. Even at age sixty-eight, Jimmy Byrnes sitting in the governor's chair in Columbia, South Carolina, could cause significant national difficulties for the political initiatives of the second Truman administration or, for that matter, Truman's own renomination in 1952, a privilege for which he was then constitutionally eligible. Truman's anger was immediately evident. He interrupted a reporter's question at his weekly press conference on January 19, 1950, to make his feelings plain. " 'Do you have any comment on former Secretary of State James Byrnes' entry into the political'—that was as far as the reporter got," the *New York Times* wrote the next day. Truman cut off the reporter to declare that Jimmy Byrnes was "a free agent and he can do as he damn pleases." A month later, under the banner headline of "Byrnes-Truman Friendship Turned Sour, May Change Course of Solid South's Political System and Nation's Political History," *U.S. News & World Report* analyzed the probable results of a victorious Byrnes' gubernatorial candidacy that fall in South Carolina and the reasons for Truman's anger. Jimmy Byrnes as South Carolina's next governor would, the magazine predicted in February, "become a rallying point for conservatives of the South, including the States' Righters."

"In that way, he could lead a strong delegation into the Democratic convention of 1952," the magazine continued. "There is also speculation that, if he is unsuccessful in the convention, or in moderating President Truman's policies, a deal could be made with the Republicans to nominate a candidate acceptable to the southerners."

Byrnes declared his gubernatorial candidacy for the state of South Carolina on January 14, 1950, at his Spartanburg home. Typically, Byrnes refrained from mentioning either his disagreements with the liberal wing of the Democratic party or his "soured" friendship with Harry Truman as possible reasons for his decision, saying only that "the trend of political events" had influenced his reentering public life. Byrnes added in his announcement that in seeking the South Carolina governor's chair he did not intend to be a presidential candidate "of any party under any circumstances." Byrnes was probably sincere in making this statement; he would be content like John C. Calhoun with merely being the presidential kingmaker, independently brokering his regional personal support and the bloc of southern electoral college votes under his control in 1952 to the Democratic or Republican presidential candidate he judged to be most acceptable to the South.

Jimmy Byrnes' subsequent campaign tour of his state after his gubernatorial announcement was less the traditional palmetto stump than a victory procession. Byrnes ran against Harry Truman rather than against his South Carolina gubernatorial opponents, ignoring local issues and instead giving nationally reported stump speeches in which he insisted that the real issues of the campaign were the excessive costs to state taxpayers of the Truman administration's proposed national health insurance program and the need to reduce what Byrnes termed "the encroachment of the federal government into the rights of sovereign states." Correctly assuming that in the July 11 primary election he would overwhelm his three hapless opponents, who had entered the state Democratic party primary before his announcement, Byrnes made leisurely trips across the state with his wife in a new chauffeur-driven automobile. Dressed in his traditionally dapper double-breasted navy blue suits with starched white shirts, Byrnes waved cheerily to crowds across his state, which by the spring and early summer of 1950 included at least two generations of South Carolina voters who had known him familiarly as Jimmy. He won the Democratic nomination in the primary that summer, an event still tantamount to victory in the fall general election in his state, by a margin of nearly 100,000 votes.

But despite his easy success, Byrnes did not fail to notice in 1950 that, for the first time in his political career, there appeared a sprinkling of black faces among the crowds of South Carolina voters waving back to him. Under the duress of a federal court order issued in 1947 in Charleston by an acquaintance of Byrnes', Judge J. Waties Waring, the previously whites-only South Carolina state Democratic party had grudgingly begun by the summer of 1950 to admit small numbers of black citizens to its membership rolls and to its primary voting rights. Soon after he won the general fall election, Governor-elect Byrnes set about gaining the gratitude of the state's few voting black citizens and demonstrating what he had long declared to both the Roosevelt and the Truman administrations—that white conservatives such as himself could accomplish far more for civil rights locally than federal legislation or fiat could attain. Most noteworthy was Byrnes' immediate action against the Ku Klux Klan. In the years preceding his gubernatorial election, the Ku Klux Klan in South Carolina had enjoyed something of a postwar resurgence. Now declaring that there was "no room" for the Klan in South Carolina, Governor-elect Byrnes announced in late 1950 that he intended, on taking office, to introduce a state bill designed to put the Klan out of business in his state by outlawing the public wearing of masks by adults or the burning of crosses on private property without the owner's consent. The state's self-declared grand dragon of the Ku Klux Klan, Thomas Hamilton, was furious on hearing of Byrnes' intentions. The grand dragon shortly before Christmas 1950 wrote a letter to Byrnes, also sending a copy to the state's outgoing governor, Strom Thurmond, in which the Klansman with possible accuracy stated to Byrnes, "I am satisfied that if you had made that statement before you were elected, you would not be the governor."

(Governor Byrnes with evident enjoyment signed the anti–mask and cross-burning bill in early 1951. By then, the U.S. Senate had for the final time in the Eighty-second Congress failed to overcome a filibuster against legislation establishing a permanent FEPC and abolishing the poll tax. The failure to gain closure on the debate effectively ended any possibility that these bills would pass during Truman's second administration. "Don't you think I could have stopped that filibuster?" Jimmy Byrnes once had asked Franklin Roosevelt in what now seemed another political lifetime.)

Byrnes in his inaugural address on January 16, 1951, made clear that, although he intended to maintain the strict racial segregation of the state's schools and other public facilities as required by state laws passed under Pitchfork Ben Tillman, he also intended to become the first South Carolina governor actually to provide the state's black schoolchildren with equal educational funding. Byrnes announced his intention to obtain the first sales tax in the state's history, with the tax revenues going exclusively to the state's public school system and with the revenues to be divided equally between schools for black children and schools for white children. "It is our duty to provide for the races substantial equality in school facilities," Byrnes told his audience of over 100,000 largely white South Carolinians who had gathered at the state capitol early on the frosty January morning in 1951. "We should do it because it is right," Byrnes added in his address. "For me, that is sufficient reason. If any person wants an additional reason, I say it is wise."

Yet only twenty-five days earlier, on December 22, 1950, a small group of black families in the South Carolina low country, with the advice of the NAACP legal counsel Thurgood Marshall, had filed a lawsuit challenging the constitutionality of the state's racially segregated school system. The challenge originated in conditions at a tiny school district for blacks located in the changed landscape of the basin of the Santee-Cooper power dams created years earlier by the then senator Jimmy Byrnes. Byrnes had not been directly involved with the Santee-Cooper project for nearly a decade, and intending to concentrate on his larger interests in national politics, he had obviously hoped to put the necessity of defending segregation behind him with his announced plan of equal school funding. But as he now commenced the final phase of his government career as a state governor, the case brought by Thurgood Marshall and the black parents from Clarendon County, South Carolina, refused to go away.

"Unfortunate though it may be, our consideration of every question must include consideration of the racial question." Once again, Jimmy Byrnes' words from a private letter written in the 1920s proved unwittingly prophetic of his public career in the 1950s. Byrnes returned to elective politics in 1951 anticipating a public role for himself as a regional elder statesman such as John C. Calhoun in the previous century, independently brokering the electoral votes of the South to effect a national return to fiscal conservatism and a revival of the concurrent majority. Settling a personal score with Harry Truman was also probably part of Byrnes' motivation, although racial prejudice never had been; Jimmy Byrnes was no Dixiecrat. But just as a hundred years earlier the political exigencies of defending his region's "peculiar institution" had led to Calhoun's being remembered not as a political philosopher but as a remorseless defender of slavery, so Byrnes' involvement with the Clarendon County case indelibly linked his governorship with his state government's legal defense of segregation. Court hearings on the school segregation case from the low country occupied much of Byrnes' four years as governor; and when on May 17, 1954, in the last full year, this appealed case from South Carolina was decided, along with three others, in a combined decision by the U.S. Supreme Court, Jimmy Byrnes was forever part of the historic *Brown* v. *Board of Education* decision outlawing school segregation.

The roots of the *Brown* decision in South Carolina and in Jimmy Byrnes' life began to take hold the day in the mid-1940s when the muddy waters of the Santee River were first backed up by one of the new Santee-Cooper dams built at the southern end of Clarendon County. The impoundments of the two giant lakes formed by the hydroelectric project flooded more than just the abandoned mansions of the old Huguenot planters. The dams also backed up many feeder creeks throughout the county, causing them in the rainy seasons of the year to overflow their banks onto the roads that linked some of Clarendon County's most remote black communities. One such community was the tiny settlement of Jordan. In order to attend the nearest segregated elementary school, the children from Jordan at times had to row a boat over a flooded stretch of the road leading to the school. The older children who wished to attend high school then had to walk an additional nine miles to the nearest segregated high school for black students. No one in the state or county government in South Carolina had thought to build them a bridge or provide them a school bus.

When a small group of the black parents had asked the white chairman of the local school board in 1947 for a school bus for their children, they were refused. Three years later, encouraged in part by the Truman administration's publicized commitment to civil rights, forty parents from the Jordan community tried again. This time they sought more than just a school bus. Thurgood Marshall, chief counsel of the NAACP Legal Defense Fund, had traveled to Clarendon County, and after talking with Mr. and Mrs. Harry Briggs, two of the parents there, Marshall agreed to file a class action suit challenging the constitutionality of Clarendon County's operating a racially segregated school system. *Briggs* v. *Elliott*, in which the white school chairman was named as one of the suit's codefendants, was filed by Marshall in federal court in Charleston on December 22, 1950. The suit was composed as a two-part attack on school segregation. Having failed to provide equality between the two races for the use of school buses and other educational facilities, Marshall's suit argued, Clarendon County was in violation of the South Carolina state law requiring public education for both its black and its white children; the county therefore should be required to dissolved the dual school system and integrate its students into one efficient system. In addition, even if the racially segregated schools required by state law were equally funded and supplied, Marshall's suit also argued, segregation was psychologically damaging to those who experienced it and was per se a violation of the "equal protection" clause of the Fourteenth Amendment.

The Clarendon County suit, the first challenge to the constitutionality of school segregation scheduled to be heard in a southern court in the twentieth century, was intended by the NAACP to be the test case for four other actions to be filed by the association later that year challenging the separation of races in public schools. The right of each state legislature legally to require separation of the races in the operation of public facilities within its state borders had been upheld by the U.S. Supreme Court in the *Plessy* v. *Ferguson* decision in 1896 and had remained the law of the land in the more than half century since. A decision in the Clarendon County case overturning the *Plessy* decision would, Marshall knew, open the door legally to eliminating racially segregated schools not only in South Carolina but also in the twenty other states, including Kansas, New Mexico, Arizona, and Wyoming, where racial segregation in public schools was required by state law in 1950. A hearing on the Clarendon County suit was scheduled before a special three-judge federal panel on May 28, 1951, in the federal courthouse in Charleston, located at the Four Corners of Law, where Jimmy Byrnes as an office boy in the nineteenth century had run errands for a local Bourbon law firm.

Jimmy Byrnes, as the state's governor-elect in 1950, had known almost immediately about Thurgood Marshall's filing the Clarendon County suit. There was no event of legal or political significance affecting any of the southern states that Jimmy Byrnes at this stage of his life did not know about. Byrnes knew, for example, that the NAACP was correct in asserting that the Clarendon County public schools for black children were a disgrace. It was not simply a matter of a lack of buses to transport the children to their segregated schools. Running water, electricity, and indoor toilets were absent from most of the county's frame school buildings reserved for black children. All of these basic amenities were available at the stucco and brick school buildings reserved for the county's white children. There were also gross inequities in the curricula available to the children of the two races. Throughout the summer and spring preceding the court hearing in 1951, Byrnes was being kept informed on the conditions of the Clarendon County schools by the Charleston attorney he had hired to represent the school board in its suit. The attorney, Robert Figg, considered to be one of the best trial lawyers in the South, on at least one occasion telephoned a report in to Governor Byrnes on what he had seen that day in a tour of Clarendon County's schools. "I told him that the total equipment in the home-economics class at the black high school was a single sewing machine—and it was broken."

Byrnes was capable of feeling compassion for—and perhaps even identification with—the educationally handicapped lives of the black children from Clarendon County. After all, his own formal schooling had been curtailed at age fourteen because of his family's economic privation, and as an associate justice of the U.S. Supreme Court, Byrnes always had shown a scrupulous regard for the equal protection of civil rights for black citizens in criminal court cases. But to Byrnes' mind, the ethical question of whether to eliminate school segregation could not be separated from the political consequences of that act. Byrnes was convinced that a decision suddenly overruling the state's school segregation laws—whether issued that summer by the Charleston court or by the U.S. Supreme Court on appeal—would result in a return to the racial violence and demagoguery he had spent much of his public life trying to eliminate in the South. And by 1951 there was much political evidence that Jimmy Byrnes was right.

The rapid fall by then in political prestige among white southerners of the Dixiecrat movement and the rise of more moderate leaders such as Byrnes in the Deep South states were the direct results of the "exposed nerve" of southern race relations no longer being perceived as susceptible to the reformist federal pressure of 1948. By 1951 even committed social liberals in the Truman administration were forced to admit that the ambitious civil rights legislation of the Fair Deal was hopelessly deadlocked in Congress by the threats of southern filibuster. Southern white conservatives anticipated further significant concessions on civil rights platforms from both major parties in the presidential election of 1952, when Jimmy Byrnes was expected to effectively broker his region's electoral votes to the candidate most favorable to the southern establishment. As a result, the white supremacists and other single-issue segregationists who had threatened to dominate southern politics in 1948 had lost much of their popular appeal and power by 1951. Not only was Governor Byrnes the winter before the date of the Clarendon County hearing able to pass through his state legislature an anti–mask and cross-burning bill, but also that year, across the Savannah River in Georgia, the newly elected Governor Herman Talmadge, having campaigned on a platform comparatively nonracist for his state, was able to obtain passage of an antimask bill. And in the same year that Byrnes won his state office, Alabama also elected a moderate governor, Gordon Persons, who scarcely discussed race during the campaign there. Although Alabama had been a hotbed of Dixiecrat sentiment in the summer of 1948, Persons easily defeated his most racist opponent in the Alabama primary, Eugene "Bull" Connor, the police commissioner of Birmingham who later would gain international notoriety in 1963 for his use of police dogs and fire hoses against nonviolent civil rights demonstrators. Connor finished sixth in a field of six candidates in the 1950 Alabama primary.

But scratch a Eugene "Bull" Connor and under his skin is a Eugene "Coley" Blease, as an experienced Jimmy Byrnes well knew from his own campaigns and personal loss against Klan-sponsored candidates in the 1920s and 1930s. Byrnes was convinced that any radical change in his state's or region's segregation laws as a result of the Clarendon County court hearing in 1951 would lead to a new generation of white southern demagogues coming to power in the later 1950s and 1960s. Figg agreed that any change by the court in the state's legally fixed racial relations would, in his words, result in "dangerous tensions and unrest." Byrnes as a governor proposed to follow what was to him an honorable middle way. He kept his word to both black and white citizens in his inaugural address that South Carolina should provide equal funding for the state's schools for black children "because it is right." In the state legislative session early in 1951 preceding the Charleston hearing, Byrnes gained passage of a state sales tax financing $75 million of new school construction and buses, with the announced intention that his administration would spend the money in order to bring the state's school facilities for black children into parity with those for white children. Byrnes was probably the only public figure in the South at this time with sufficient prestige and respect to have been able to obtain from a white state legislature passage not only of an anti–Ku Klux Klan bill but also of a financial appropriation of such magnitude intended largely for the education of black schoolchildren. At the same time Jimmy Byrnes, the inveterate campaigner and the only living former Supreme Court justice, planned court strategy with Figg in order to defeat Thurgood Marshall's suit.

Hundreds of black spectators lined Meeting Street in Charleston in front of the federal courthouse, and reporters from the national and international press were in attendance at the second-story courtroom when the three-judge federal panel convened there to hear the Clarendon County suit on the morning of May 28, 1951. A few moments after the judges entered and the court was called to order, Thurgood Marshall's face registered surprise when Figg rose to his feet before any opening arguments could be made. In a strategy prearranged with Byrnes, Figg announced that he had no objection to the court's finding that conditions at the Clarendon County segregated schools for blacks and whites were grossly unequal. Summarizing for the judges the changes and purchases intended by Byrnes' $75 million equalization plan scheduled to begin that July, the state's attorney told the court that all that was being asked on behalf of his clients on the school board was "a reasonable time" in which to make the segregated school facilities truly separate but equal.

Byrnes' court strategy vitiated much of Marshall's planned argument. By openly admitting to the judges as uncontested facts the inequities of the Clarendon County school system, Byrnes and Figg prevented Marshall from being able to bring before the judicial panel a long string of witnesses, each with a dramatic story of a deteriorating school system for black children operating without buses, running water, lunchrooms, or indoor toilets. Marshall, his face described by most of the reporters present in the courtroom as still looking shocked at this unexpected strategy, protested that the state's admission of facts was an attempt to "choke off" his most important witnesses on conditions in Clarendon County. Nevertheless, Marshall was forced by the judges to begin his case with less persuasive testimony from social scientists, who argued that racial segregation was psychologically damaging to the county's black children who were so singled out. Jimmy Byrnes had known from his own experience as a jurist that sociological and psychological considerations were not nearly as likely to affect the judges' ruling as legal precedents or findings of fact; and having cleverly avoided an emotional hearing before the judges on the findings of fact in the Clarendon County schools, Byrnes and Figg had agreed that at the trial the state would call no witnesses of its own to refute the plaintiff's claims. Figg instead emphasized time and time again to the judges that the undeniable precedent of *Plessy* v. *Ferguson* established racial segregation as a "normal and not an abnormal procedure" and that the state intended to remedy the differences between the schools as soon as possible.

Despite Marshall's impassioned plea in his closing arguments that what he was asking for was "rights that must be given now," the decision in the Clarendon County case was almost completely what Jimmy Byrnes had been asking for. The three-judge panel on June 23, 1951, by a 2-to-1 decision refused to overturn *Plessy* v. *Ferguson* on Marshall's arguments, and instead, finding the segregation of Clarendon County's public schools to be legal, instructed the county to report back to the court within a specified time on the progress that had been made in upgrading the schools for black schoolchildren. The dissenter among the three judges in issuing the opinion was Judge J. Waties Waring, a Charleston native of an old Bourbon family and the same federal judge who four years earlier had ruled that South Carolina's blacks were eligible to participate in the state Democratic primaries.

Waring was furious at Byrnes' behind-the-scenes success in undercutting Marshall's argument. (In fact, Waring himself had the previous year acted indirectly and behind the scenes in communicating to Marshall that he would look favorably upon a constitutional challenge to school segregation.) After the end of each side's final presentations in the Clarendon County case and a subsequent hour and a half private conference in chambers with the other two judges, Waring returned to his Meeting Street home and complained bitterly that night to his wife about the other two judges in the case "just throwing aside all the testimony." Waring told his wife that the other judges in conference had tried to persuade him to join with them in writing a unanimous opinion by arguing, in his version of their words, that " 'Jim Byrnes will equalize the schools; just give him time. Jim found this state in an awful condition. He is taxing the people to raise the money and we can't hinder him by interfering with state affairs.' " Besides, Waring was told, in the upcoming presidential election of 1952 " 'a Republican victory was assured,' " and presumably a power broker such as Jimmy Byrnes could negotiate with the judges and Justice Department officials of a new administration for a more moderate and acceptable resolution of civil rights suits than was currently sought by the NAACP or the zealots in the Truman administration. Waring had considered this judicial faith in the good intentions of Byrnes to be a form of moral temporizing. Waring told his wife that "with disgust" he had replied to the two other judges that "Byrnes was no better and even worse than Thurmond."

Jimmy Byrnes was no Strom Thurmond. Unlike some other prominent southern white politicians, Byrnes issued no exultant public statements when the decision in *Briggs* v. *Elliott* was announced, instead giving the local and national press only a terse, and characteristic, "No comment." He had other fish to fry. With the local Clarendon County suit apparently settled beyond hope of a successful appeal by Marshall to the U.S. Supreme Court, Byrnes turned his attention to the larger issue of Harry Truman and the upcoming 1952 presidential election. At the biennial Southern Governors' Conference in Hot Springs, Arkansas, in November 1951, Byrnes came into the open with his opposition to Truman's renomination. Having lined up support from a majority of the other governors for his policy of a unified southern bloc, Byrnes on the last day of the conference announced to reporters he had assembled from the *New York Times* and the *Washington Post* that in the 1952 election the South "would put loyalty to country above loyalty to party."

Byrnes' announcement was a deliberate rebuff to Democratic party regulars such as Speaker of the House Sam Rayburn, who was a personal friend of both Harry Truman and Jimmy Byrnes and who the day before Byrnes' press announcement had traveled to Hot Springs to plead with his fellow southerners, somewhat lamely, to support the Democratic party's nominee in 1952 "no matter who he is." Byrnes now told the assembled reporters that although he was not forming an official movement to defeat Truman's attempts at renomination, he was ready "to advise and counsel with any who see things as I do."

(Byrnes apparently had been startled to learn on the opening day of the Southern Governors' Conference that not all white southerners saw things as he did. As the speaker at the opening day's luncheon of governors, Harry Ashmore, an editor of the area's dominant newspaper, the Little

Rock *Gazette*, had urged the assembled state leaders of the South to accept at least the moral principle behind the idea of the FEPC—that of equal employment opportunity—even if the governors opposed the enactment of a permanent FEPC itself. Ashmore had warned the governors to their faces, including Jimmy Byrnes', "We cannot turn our backs upon injustice simply because a black man is the victim, nor can we find a safe retreat in the sort of legalistic buck passing that recognizes the existence of an evil but insists that it is somebody else's responsibility." In the stunned silence following Ashmore's remarks, not one Democratic governor applauded. The reporter for the *New York Times*, apparently knowing that Ashmore and Byrnes were both from South Carolina, seized the moment to ask Byrnes for his reactions to the speech. All that Jimmy Byrnes could manage was a shocked reaction as though he had just witnessed an appalling breach of table manners from a member of a newer generation: "Why, I believe I know that boy's family!")

Truman, spending the end-of-the-year holidays in Key West, did not respond publicly to Byrnes' announced intention to separate the South in 1952 from its traditional loyalty to the Democratic party, nor did he comment on the rejection of the message of Sam Rayburn, who had traveled to Hot Springs at Truman's request. But the high taxes and inflation of late 1951, which Byrnes had attributed to the Fair Deal's fiscal policies, along with the disaffection for the administration's social policies being engineered among southern voters by Byrnes, were among the reasons for President Harry S. Truman's declaring on March 29, 1952, that he would not be a candidate for renomination for the presidency.

Jimmy Byrnes had done as he pleased, to paraphrase Truman's remark two years earlier. And not only the Fair Deal domestic liberalism of Harry Truman but also the previously Democratic Solid South were the next targets in 1952 of Byrnes' concurrent majority redivivus. "I am interested in the platform as well as the candidate," Byrnes stated when he learned of Truman's withdrawal. "I want a platform pledged to respect the rights of states." Byrnes found much of what he wanted in that year's GOP platform. Although both national parties at their 1952 conventions approved comparatively strong planks on civil rights, the Republican platform passage on civil rights contained a significant disclaimer of federal activism that the Democratic platform lacked: "We believe that it is the primary responsibility of each state to order and control its own domestic institutions," the GOP platform declared, "and this power, reserved to the states, is essential to the maintenance of our federal government." Byrnes attended the 1952 Democratic convention at Philadelphia, but he was noticeably cool to the party's candidate, Adlai Stevenson; and after Dwight Eisenhower received the GOP presidential nomination, Byrnes greeted the former general at the statehouse steps in Columbia in September 1952 in a reception for a Republican presidential candidate that was unprecedentedly enthusiastic for South Carolina. Eisenhower was seated after greeting Byrnes when a band nearby struck up the martial strains of "Dixie." Eisenhower immediately rose from his chair and delighted the local crowd by saying, "I always stand up when they play that song."

Eisenhower's actions were political music to Jimmy Byrnes' ears. Although he was not yet ready officially to leave the Democratic party, Byrnes took the leadership that fall in organizing an Independents for Eisenhower network of disaffected Democrats across the southern states. As a result, Eisenhower in addition to sweeping the general election scored the greatest victories in the Deep South of any Republican candidate since Herbert Hoover in 1928; four of the eleven states of the old Confederacy voted for Eisenhower in the fall of 1952. Interestingly, Byrnes' leadership of the Independents for Eisenhower succeeded in bringing the Dixiecrats surreptitiously back into the fold of one of the national parties, even if Byrnes knew that the former Dixiecrats were not yet ready to call themselves Republicans. In areas of the South where the Dixiecrats had done well in 1948, Eisenhower generally was at his strongest in 1952; and thanks to Byrnes' implicit endorsement of the GOP ticket, the Dixiecrat ticket itself was inconsequential throughout the South in the election of 1952.

Jimmy Byrnes was winning his imaginary race with John C. Calhoun. Within less than two years of his return to elective politics in South Carolina, Byrnes had emerged as his region's foremost spokesman for the concurrent majority theory of the state governments' participation in determining national fiscal policies and social reforms. Byrnes had succeeded as well as a political broker independent of either party in breaking up a Democratic Solid South that had existed since the Compromise of 1877. The apparently local issue of South Carolina's segregated school system no longer figured in Byrnes' mind as an important impediment to his ambitions for a national return to fiscal and social conservatism. Considerably more confident than the day after the Clarendon County decision was first announced, Byrnes now told the *New York Times* that the opinion of the federal judiciary at Charleston in upholding South Carolina's segregation laws was "unanswerable" and that this court's "well-reasoned opinion" demonstrated that the 1896 *Plessy* v. *Ferguson* constitutional doctrine of separate-but-equal facilities was still valid for the United States in the midtwentieth century. And by the late fall of 1952, Byrnes' promise of substantial equality in the education of South Carolina's black children was being fulfilled. The governor's $75 million tax program had resulted in an unprecedented building of schoolhouses, purchase of buses, and increases in teachers' salaries for both races across the state. Byrnes paid particular attention to the improvement of the black schools in Clarendon County, where construction for a new $261,000 high school for black students was under way. Byrnes also used his influence in Washington to speed delivery of building supplies that were in short supply nationally to the Clarendon County building site. And, at last, shiny new yellow buses began to carry black children across the county's roads.

But Thurgood Marshall and the parents from the Jordan community refused to go away. Harry Briggs, whose son's name, Harry Briggs, Jr., had been first listed on the *Briggs* v. *Elliott* suit filed at Charleston, had been fired from his job at a white-owned Clarendon County automobile garage; his wife also had been dismissed from her work as a maid at one of the whites-only motels along the highway to the Santee-Cooper and Myrtle Beach resort areas. Jimmy Byrnes had nothing to do with these actions, and would have found them distasteful had he known of them; but Byrnes, despite his confidence after the Clarendon County decision, was mistaken in thinking that the black people of his state or the nation had voluntarily joined with him or been coerced into accepting the separate-but-equal doctrine as politically or legally "unanswerable." However kind or just Governor Byrnes was to individual black citizens, black people as political entities or simply as individuals with a desire to end the legal system of segregation were still largely "invisible" to him. Jimmy Byrnes throughout his life always had prided himself on his attention to people and political details; but Byrnes apparently had not seen the significance of the hundreds of local black men and women who had stood outside the federal courthouse on Meeting Street for hours on a hot summer day awaiting news of the Clarendon County hearing; nor did he see the significance of the fact that, although Thurgood Marshall had lost his case in the hearing in Charleston, after the last day's arguments dozens of the city's black residents had pressed forward to shake Marshall's hand as he left the courthouse in admiration for his having even dared to challenge the legal system of segregation in the very birthplace of Bourbon conservatism and of the leader of the state's white establishment, Jimmy Byrnes.

Soon after the conclusion of the Charleston hearing, Marshall and the NAACP announced their intention to appeal to the U.S. Supreme Court the decision in *Briggs* v. *Elliott*, as well as proceeding with court hearings and appeals in two other similar court challenges in Virginia and Delaware to the constitutionality of school segregation. President Truman also instructed the Justice Department to assist the NAACP in the hearings before the high court. But as these cases and appeals worked their ways through the lower federal courts by late 1952, the Republican electoral victory that Judge Waring had been told "was assured" took place. Finally, the Court agreed to schedule arguments in a combined hearing on the three school cases for December 1952, nearly a month after the election of the new Republican president, whom Jimmy Byrnes had helped to put into power.

This time Byrnes arranged for South Carolina's segregation laws to be defended not simply by the best lawyer in the South but by perhaps the best appeal lawyer in the United States. In August 1951, one month after Marshall and the NAACP had announced their intention to appeal the

Clarendon County case to the U.S. Supreme Court, Byrnes traveled to see an old friend living in New York State. There, at the established comfort and wealth of a fifteen-acre Tudor estate on Long Island, Byrnes sought out the company of the only attorney in the United States who arguably was more qualified than the South Carolina governor himself to defend his state's laws before the U.S. Supreme Court: John W. Davis.

Seldom has a lawyer been more distinguished or more suited to his potential client than was Davis, a highly educated native of West Virginia. Like Byrnes, the seventy-eight-year-old Davis in 1951 had the reputation of having been denied the presidency in favor of a much less qualified man. Davis in fact had received the Democratic presidential nomination in 1924, having served the Wilson administration as its ambassador to Great Britain, only to lose the election that year to Calvin Coolidge. What either Davis or Byrnes would have done as president is an intriguing and unknowable might-have-been; but both men also had the satisfaction of knowing to a certainty that they had resisted the most overt forms of racism in their public careers, and both had paid a political price for their decisions. The Democratic party in 1924 had been riven by tens of thousands of members who were also participants in the Ku Klux Klan, and contributing to Davis' defeat that year had been his insistence during the campaign in renouncing any Klan support, just as Jimmy Byrnes had in the same year experienced his sole electoral defeat by refusing to accept a Klan endorsement.

Davis and Byrnes had known each other since 1911, when they both were freshmen New Freedom congressmen and considered young liberals by the southern standards of the time. In the intervening years Davis had earned a substantial fortune as a corporate lawyer specializing in appeals for Wall Street firms, and at the time of Jimmy Byrnes' visit, he had personally argued or participated in the writing of more cases before the U.S. Supreme Court—more than 250—than any other attorney of the twentieth century. Both these men had grown distinguished in the practice of law, and as Davis sat reading the court documents Byrnes had brought him at the beautifully attended estate overlooking Long Island Sound, he could find no fault in his friend's actions. Davis listened sympathetically when Byrnes described his efforts to equalize the Clarendon County schools. The issue of the case, Byrnes said, was not the subjugation of the black race but the right of a state's governor and a local school board to arrange a compromise on an issue between two races without the interference of "politicians in Washington." This last appeal struck a sympathetic chord in Davis. Davis was a graduate of Washington and Lee University, where Byrnes two years earlier had delivered his warning against the growing federal "statism" of the twentieth century. "Mr. Davis was a southerner," one of his chief assistants later recalled, and firmly believed that his fellow white southerners such as Jimmy Byrnes knew best how to resolve the racial disputes and tensions of their region without either betraying black interests or giving rise to violent white demagogues. A few days after Byrnes' visit, Davis wrote him that he would accept the case. Davis refused Byrnes' offer of a fee; he was making the arguments in this case directly out of loyalty to his native region, his respect for legal precedent, and his personal friendship for Byrnes.

The Supreme Court scheduled a combined two-day hearing on *Briggs* v. *Elliott* and on similar suits brought by the NAACP against school segregation in Virginia, Delaware, and the District of Columbia, to begin on December 9, 1952. As during the Charleston hearing, there were overflow crowds that day outside the Supreme Court Building. Local black and white residents, as well as the nation's reporters and legal scholars, recognized the significance in their own lives of this first direct challenge to *Plessy* v. *Ferguson* precedent of separate-but-equal public facilities and to the principle that requiring a racially segregated school system was a legitimate right of a state legislature unaffected by the "equal protection" clause of the Fourteenth Amendment. The case was, the *Washington Post* ventured the day of the hearing, "the most fateful in Negro history since the Dred Scott slavery decision of 95 years ago."

Davis' defense of the constitutionality of the segregated South Carolina school system was expected to be the major event of the hearings beginning December 9, but Byrnes and Davis were determined that this argument before the Supreme Court not be popularly perceived simply as an examination of the South's "peculiar institution" of segregation. To them, the issue was the legitimacy of local self-determination. Byrnes, acting literally at the last moment, telephoned the governor of Kansas and succeeded in persuading him to have his state's attorney general also file a brief in defense of Kansas's school segregation laws with the Supreme Court on December 8, in time to be considered at the same hearing with the arguments for the four southern systems. The school board of Topeka also was being sued by the NAACP on behalf of Oliver Brown and other plaintiffs.

Although the attorney general of Kansas was not particularly enthusiastic about defending his state's segregated school system on short notice before the Supreme Court, Byrnes was intent on having the Kansas case brought before the Court at the same time as the other suits and on its being called before the South Carolina case. Byrnes knew that unlike those in the cases from the four southern systems, the plaintiffs named in the Kansas suit never had been shown to have suffered individually from the effects of the segregated schools in the Topeka system, and therefore the legality of the Kansas state legislature's requiring a racially segregated school system was to be presented to the Court with less legal and moral ambiguity than the southern cases could be. Thus, by a twist of precourtroom strategy, when John Davis rose in a hushed chamber on December 9 to defend the constitutionality of the segregated Clarendon

County school system, the struggles of Harry Briggs, Jr., and the other black children from the Jordan community entered most histories of the U.S. Supreme Court not as *Briggs* v. *Elliott* but as *Brown* v. *Board of Education of Topeka.*

Davis defended Byrnes' case that whatever educational evils the governor had inherited in the Clarendon County school system had resulted from local oversight rather than from basic flaws in South Carolina's segregation laws, the constitutionality of which had been upheld in 1896 by the *Plessy* v. *Ferguson* decision, and that the remedy for correcting local ills was local solutions through the acts of locally elected officials, such as Governor Byrnes' passage of the state educational tax bill, a remedy that took precedence over any federal court fiat issued under authority of the Fourteenth Amendment. Interestingly, Davis' argument to the Supreme Court was not an unconditional defense of racial segregation itself. "If conditions have changed *so that segregation is now considered unwise* [emphasis added], it is a matter for the legislature to decide. The Court has no right to read its ideas of sociology into the Constitution." To Marshall's opening argument that the federal guarantee of civil liberties under the Fourteenth Amendment implied the right freely to enter any public school system regardless of one's race, Davis further replied that of the thirty states that had ratified the amendment in 1868, twenty-three had continued to operate separate schools for white and black children. So long as states acted in accordance with the precedents of constitutional law, Davis argued, the rights of the states individually to determine their own solutions to the problems of racial segregation in local school systems must be left undisturbed. "Is it not a fact," he asked the justices, "that the very strength and fiber of our federal system is local self-government in those matters for which local action is competent?"

Byrnes was not in the capacity crowd at the Supreme Court that morning to hear Davis defend the constitutionality of his acts in preserving the segregation of Clarendon County's schools. He had returned to Columbia, having read and approved Davis' brief before the attorney presented his oral arguments to the Court. "I want you to know," Byrnes had written Davis, "that this client is proud of his lawyer." Privately, Byrnes considered the *Brown* v. *Board of Education* case to be as good as settled in his state's favor by an 8-to-1 decision. (Justice William O. Douglas, one of the last of the New Deal's die-hard liberals and the man whom perhaps Roosevelt had most wanted as his vice-presidential candidate in 1944, was considered by Byrnes to be the only Justice sure to vote to overturn the Plessy decision.)

Neither Byrnes nor Davis took with particular forebodings the subsequent agreement among the nine justices of the Court after hearing Davis' and Marshall's first arguments that the justices would not issue a ruling that spring but would carry the Brown case over into the 1953 session. The

Court at that time planned to hear further arguments on the history and intent of the framing of the Fourteenth Amendment. The additional time gave Jimmy Byrnes the opportunity to press his views in person, an activity in which he always excelled. Soon after the Court ordered a rehearing in *Brown*, President Eisenhower wrote to Byrnes on February 14, 1953, inviting Byrnes to join him in a meeting at the White House later that month for "a discussion of problems dealing with Federal-State relations," according to Eisenhower's letter. It was presumably at this February 26, 1953, meeting with the president that Byrnes, as he later recorded in his memoirs, urged upon the president the hope that he "would not feel bound by the position previously taken by the Democratic administration" to have the U.S. attorney general file a supplemental brief in support of the NAACP case. Eisenhower referred Byrnes to his attorney general, who in turn told Jimmy Byrnes that his request to forgo the brief "sounded reasonable" and promised to consider it.

Twenty years earlier the same Jimmy Byrnes as a U.S. Supreme Court justice had boldly stated for the Court in writing the majority opinion in *Edwards* v. *California* that no state "might gain a momentary respite from the pressures of events by the simple expedience of shutting its gates to the outside world." (On the back of Byrnes' final draft of the majority opinion, circulated among his brethren, Justice Frankfurter had written in pencil, "What you say is truly good.")

Now, in the spring and summer of 1953, before the rehearing, Byrnes made the rounds of his former place of employment at the Court trying legally to shut the gates of his native state to the events of the outward world. He lobbied two old friends there, Chief Justice Fred Vinson and Associate Justice Felix Frankfurter. Vinson, a Kentucky native and hardened politician who had followed Byrnes as a director of the OWMR before being appointed chief justice in 1946 by Truman, liked and trusted his fellow southerner governor Byrnes. Vinson was sympathetic to Byrnes' argument that he needed only "a reasonable time" to upgrade the schools for black children in his state without the necessity of the Court's overturning *Plessy*, and that white southerners throughout the South would insist that their state governments eliminate funding for public schools rather than integrate them. Even more important in swinging the Court's opinion in his favor was Byrnes' restatement of these arguments to his friend Justice Frankfurter. During his brief 1941 tenure on the Court, Byrnes had formed what was perhaps his only abiding personal friendship among the other contemporary justices with Felix Frankfurter. The two men shared a deep philosophic distrust of judicial activism, and despite the obvious cultural differences between the urbane, Jewish intellectual from Boston and the self-made politician from Charleston, Byrnes and Frankfurter had continued to delight in each other's company after Byrnes had left the Court. Frankfurter also believed Byrnes' promise that the governor would upgrade the segregated schools, and Frankfurter's opinion could swing other votes.

Frankfurter "had a fear that the whole thing was moving too fast," a former law clerk of his later recalled about those months of the justices' deliberations over segregation laws preceding the 1953 rehearing of *Brown*. "He'd hear that view from Jimmy Byrnes, with whom he had become good friends when Byrnes was on the Court, and he admired Byrnes as an able administrator and a man of action when Byrnes was in the Senate working for the White House. And so the Justice would listen when Byrnes insisted the South was really and finally moving to improve the black schools and that to outlaw segregation might kill the public-school system in the South."

Harry S. Ashmore also had his personal contact describing the deliberations in the Court's chambers while the *Brown* case was being carried over. Ashmore's source used the language of the street rather than that of the memoir to describe how the justices were discussing among themselves that "if and when" *Plessy* were overturned, the effect in the southern states would be that "the guys who talked nigger would be in charge, there would be riots, and the army might have to be called out." Such talk, according to Ashmore's source, "was scaring the shit out of the Justices, especially Frankfurter and Jackson, who didn't know how the Court could enforce a ruling against *Plessy*."

But when John Davis returned to argue his client's case at the Supreme Court chambers on the opening day of the rehearing, December 7, 1953, there had already occurred substantive changes, both in the Court and in the domestic policies of the Eisenhower administration, which all the private persuasiveness of Jimmy Byrnes could not have turned aside. Only three months before the day of the rehearing, Chief Justice Fred Vinson, the former protégé of Byrnes' at the OWMR and the justice most sympathetic to Byrnes' position, had unexpectedly died; his replacement appointed by Eisenhower, the former California governor Earl Warren, had not lived in a southern racially segregated society and was much less friendly toward its continuation. In addition, Thurgood Marshall and the other members of the NAACP legal staff had responded to the Supreme Court's request for additional arguments on the intent of the framers of the Fourteenth Amendment with a 235-page brief, which inclined Frankfurther and other uncommitted justices to admit the amendment's application to the administration of public schools. (Along with the history of the 1868 constitutional amendment, the NAACP brief provided an account of how the Compromise of 1877 frustrated the application of the amendment to the southern states, and of the post–Civil War political rise of "Ben Tillman, the leader of South Carolina.") And, in an undeniable disavowal of Jimmy Byrnes' earlier personal request to Dwight Eisenhower, the NAACP brief also was accompanied by an amicus curiae brief filed in support of Marshall's argument filed by the U.S. Eisenhower's attorney general, Herbert Brownell.

Despite these reversals, however, Davis was so certain that the precedent established in *Plessy* v. *Ferguson* and his arguments to the Court against the reasons for overturning it were secure that Byrnes was correct in his earlier assertion that the decision rendered by the Charleston court in 1951 was "unanswerable." Three weeks after the rehearing in *Brown*, Byrnes received a note from Davis asserting, "Let us hope that the Olympian Nine will take the same point of view—*and I really think they will and must*" (his emphasis).

But the gods of fate, a sense of justice, or simply the political exigencies of the 1950s decided against the case of Jimmy Byrnes. On May 17, 1954, after frequent consultations among the nine justices but particularly between Earl Warren, the new chief justice, and Associate Justice Frankfurter, the Supreme Court in a unanimous decision ruled that racially segregated public school systems—"even though the physical facilities and other 'tangible' factors of white and Negro schools may be equal"—were in violation of the Constitution under the "equal protection" clause of the Fourteenth Amendment. The opinion by the nine Warren Court justices in *Brown* v. *Board of Education* was phrased in words both adamant and unconditional: "Any language in *Plessy* v. *Ferguson* contrary to this finding is rejected." The attorney generals of South Carolina and the other three states involved in the *Brown* suits were ordered by the Supreme Court to respond to it within fifteen months on plans to implement the desegregation of public school facilities.

The Supreme Court's decision in the *Brown* case suddenly and emotionally made old men of both Jimmy Byrnes and John W. Davis. Byrnes, previously notable for the youthfulness of his spirits despite his seventy-two years, became an embittered man. The unanimity of the Court's decision must have been particularly galling to him, since it seemed to set aside as of no account the personal promises he had made to such friends as Vinson and Frankfurter that the separate-but-equal doctrine would be enforced by him with a new fairness. Byrnes and Davis both considered themselves honorable men who had fought for and given their personal prestige to what they considered a high governmental principle; and both Byrnes and Davis had thought that they knew best in regard to the personal interests of black men and women, such as Mr. and Mrs. Harry Briggs, or their children. In defeat, Byrnes and Davis both turned southward. Byrnes gathered his political strength in Columbia to plan a response. The eighty-one-year-old Davis, physically drained by the shock of his unexpected defeat, according to the observations of one member of his law firm, returned to South Carolina to die within the year.

From his governor's mansion Byrnes on the day the Court announced its *Brown* decision passionately declared that "time and time again" prior justices of the U.S. Supreme Court had found the principle of separate-but-equal facilities to be legal and that he was "shocked to learn that the Court has reversed itself." Before the end of May 1954, he met with other southern governors to plan a legal strategy to delay or thwart the implementation of school integration that was now the law of the land.

John W. Davis returned that winter to Charleston, as he had done for decades since his defeat in the 1924 presidential election. Davis avoided the New York winters each year by spending several months at Yeamans Hall, a former plantation outside the city and the site of many prior social gatherings with Jimmy Byrnes, Bernard Baruch, and other members of the Bourbon ruling class of the low country. There, physically exhausted by weakened lungs and emotionally worn, Davis died on March 24, 1955. The day before his death, Davis had been visited and much cheered by Jimmy Byrnes, who was on his way to Washington; as soon as he learned of Davis' death, Byrnes returned to Yeamans Hall. At the former plantation Byrnes found Davis's longtime butler and general manservant crying disconsolately over the attorney's death. Byrnes put his arm around the crying man and, speaking low words of consolation, took him for a long walk down a tree-lined lane, one symbol of a vanished social order comforting and supporting another symbol of that order.

Seven days after the Supreme Court announced its decision in the *Brown v. Board of Education of Topeka* case, a young scholar at Harvard University, Arthur M. Schlesinger, Jr., paused from his research for a biography of Franklin Roosevelt and wrote a letter that he intended to be discussed with Jimmy Byrnes. Not knowing Byrnes personally, Schlesinger sent the letter to his acquaintance Ben Cohen, a New Deal liberal of whom Byrnes was known to be fond and who had worked as Byrnes' assistant at the OWMR and at State.

"Dear Ben," Schlesinger wrote Cohen on May 24, 1954,

> as I read the decision, the segregated states will have an opportunity in the next few months to present scheduled programs for orderly transition to non-segregation. If this is so, it would seem to me that the working out of these plans represent the greatest challenge to constructive statesmanship that we have had in this country. It will be up to responsible southerners to devise programs which, while taking local conditions into account, are still honestly directed toward the abolition of segregation in the schools. It will be up to responsible northerners to understand the difficulties of the southern position and not to insist on abrupt or precipitate changes in customs so deeply rooted in prejudice and emotion.

It is obvious that this presents the greatest opportunity for southern statesmanship since the time of John C. Calhoun. Do you suppose that it is wholly beyond the realm of imagination that Governor
Byrnes might now accept the inevitable and dedicate these last years
to an earnest attempt to work the thing out? First, there is no one
who could better unite the South behind this effort; there is nothing
which would win him a more secure place in American history; and
I do not know of anyone who could put the arguments for this to
him more effectively than yourself.

Cohen thought it worth a try. He sent a copy of the letter to Byrnes
for his reading, with Cohen's own commendation of Schlesinger's proposal.
"You have a rare and precious ability," Cohen wrote Byrnes, "when dealing with contending forces, of finding a middle road on which most men
and women of goodwill despite their differences can march forward together."

A decade earlier, in 1944, in another political lifetime, Jimmy Byrnes
might have heeded this request, had it been made personally and openly
by Franklin Roosevelt; but if Jimmy Byrnes in 1944 might have been willing
to moderate his views and his region's views on racial segregation at the
request of Franklin Roosevelt, Jimmy Byrnes in 1954 was not willing to
do so for Roosevelt's biographer. No written answer to Schlesinger's proposal was later found in Byrnes' papers. The career and historical reputation of Byrnes by the mid-1950s had come in fact to resemble that of
John C. Calhoun's, but in a way that only a few years earlier, before the
Brown decision, neither Jimmy Byrnes nor Arthur M. Schlesinger, Jr.,
could have anticipated. Byrnes became, like Calhoun in the last year of
his life, alienated from both major political parties and angrily prepared
for an impending crisis over the fate of black people in the South.

Rather than advocating an orderly compliance with the *Brown* ruling,
Byrnes in speeches threatened to use his powers as governor to close the
public schools of South Carolina—although he later thought the better of
this extreme action and did not do so. Working instead behind the scenes,
Byrnes met and corresponded with other southern governors, most frequently with Governor Herman Talmadge of Georgia, to plan a strategy
of "massive resistance" to the *Brown* decision, challenging its implementation at every opportunity in local courts and setting up church-sponsored
schools to encourage the withdrawal of white students from the public
systems. (More than a decade earlier, Jimmy Byrnes had known and gotten
along tolerably well with Herman Talmadge's father, who was also a governor of Georgia, the fiercely segregationist Eugene Talmadge. Such was
Byrnes' age that he was now dealing with the sons of men he had known
in his political prime to continue the segregationist policies of their fathers.)
And if the Democratic liberals, northerners and southerners alike, now

thought that Jimmy Byrnes was "no better than Thurmond," Jimmy Byrnes made certain that Strom Thurmond was what the Democratic party got. Byrnes engineered a write-in senatorial campaign for Thurmond in 1954, after state Democrats loyal to the national party and still angry about Thurmond's defection to the Dixiecrats had succeeded in keeping his name off the ballot. Byrnes' efforts that year resulted in Thurmond's first election to the U.S. Senate.

Byrnes' larger ambitions for a revival of the concurrent majority by making the South independent of the Democratic party in presidential elections and by encouraging the growth in his region of the Republican party also were hamstrung by his bitterness over the *Brown* decision. In the presidential election of 1956, Byrnes announced that, although he could not support the Democratic ticket of Adlai Stevenson, because of the latter's commitment to civil rights, Eisenhower had made, in Byrnes' indirect reference to Chief Justice Earl Warren, "unfortunate appointments to the courts." Byrnes announced to friends in 1956 his intention to vote for an independent slate of electors pledged to Senator Harry Byrd of Virginia and Congressman John Bell Williams of Mississippi. Although Eisenhower later wrote a friendly letter to Byrnes assuring him of the White House's intention in regard to southern school integration "to make haste slowly," as Eisenhower quoted a Roman general's phrase, the slowness of a Dwight D. Eisenhower was apparently too hasty for Jimmy Byrnes. Byrnes wanted a civil rights policy so conservative that neither major party could satisfy him; and with that insistence, along with his support for a vice-presidential candidate such as the former Dixiecrat John Williams, Jimmy Byrnes began to drift into a national political irrelevance. The independent slate he backed in the presidential election of 1956 went nowhere; and although the Republican ticket continued to gain in the South, adding Louisiana in 1956 to the four states Eisenhower had carried in 1952, Byrnes had nothing to do with the GOP's gains that year. His retirement from politics seemed certain after the completion in 1955 of his gubernatorial term, which under South Carolina's constitution could not be succeeded by a second term even for this inveterate and still dissatisfied campaigner.

After leaving the governor's mansion in 1955, Byrnes, then seventy-three years old, seemed at last to have entered a true retirement with at least some peace of mind. He and his wife settled into a comfortable house in an upper-class suburb of Columbia. A few days each week he traveled, now chauffeured by a black servant, to a downtown office he maintained, still staffed by his constant secretary over the years, Miss Cassandra Connor. Correspondence both from national historians and local supporters continued to flow into the office at a great rate. As the South entered the turmoil of the civil rights movement in the late 1950s and early 1960s, Byrnes remained unapologetic to all inquisitors for his role in the *Brown* case; and just as he had predicted, demands for immediate changes in the segregated society of the South had resulted instead across the region in a backlash of elections of white politicians skilled in racial demagoguery, replacing the more moderate, older Bourbon southern white leaders such as himself. Byrnes particularly kept his eye on a young former treasurer of the Dixiecrat party, George Wallace, who in 1962 was elected governor of Alabama.

But there also were occasional signs, perhaps equally disturbing to Byrnes, that he had been wrong in assuming that he knew best for both southern blacks and whites, and in assuming that local black citizens since the *Brown* case had been led astray by outside agitators from their true southern conservative benefactors such as himself. One day in 1961 the mail brought to Byrnes' office a strange packet from an old and loyal political supporter of his in Aiken. The supporter, the white owner of several textile mills, told Byrnes how he had purchased and demolished an old farmhouse adjacent to his vacation home in Aiken County. "The house was occupied by George McKie (colored—now deceased), a good citizen in the community, and an employee in the picker room of our Warren Mill until his retirement," the owner wrote Byrnes.

> In tearing down the house, a box of old letters and papers was emptied on the ground, and while supervising some cleaning up work, I happened to be standing near the pile of papers. In glancing down, my eye was attracted to a letter from the "National Association of Colored People." In rummaging through the pile, I found a number of the "NAACP" letters, and this was just a little bit of a surprise to me. Most of them are dated back in 1951, 1952, and 1953, and it is clear that McKie was an active participant, and that an intensive fund raising and membership drive were in progress.

The millowner included the NAACP papers with his letter, suggesting that Byrnes might find some amusement in reading them. But if Byrnes read the enclosed papers, their content would have been anything but amusing to him. "Special Counsel Thurgood Marshall reports by telephone that everything is ready for the Clarendon County case against segregation and high school education to be heard in Charleston May 28th," the state headquarters of the NAACP in 1951 informed local members such as McKie and warned that "Byrnes, in the background, is marshaling every resource of the state." The mood among the state's blacks was exhortatory as Marshall prepared the first legal challenge to segregation and as the state NAACP chapter in Columbia solicited local members in Aiken to increase their membership rolls and organizational funds for Marshall's support: "How is your drive coming? Do you need help? Does your drive lack pep? If so, let us know!!!" As he held these decade-old papers in his hands, Byrnes may have wondered that a black man who was a "good citizen in the community" had kept such a life apart from his white employers and political masters, the secrets being revealed only when the black man's house was torn down after his death for vacation property. But if Byrnes wondered, he kept such doubts to himself; he carefully placed George McKie's papers in his office files without written comment.

When Byrnes was in his seventies and eighties, the black man whom he knew best was his chauffeur, J. William "Willie" Byrd. A dignified-appearing man in his late fifties who was young only in comparison with Jimmy and Maude Byrnes, Byrd lived at their house and drove their black Cadillac on their trips across the state to occasional lunches with Bernard Baruch at his Georgetown property, or he drove Byrnes alone in the backseat on his morning trips to his downtown office. As Byrnes grew even older and appeared to care less for politics, he began to direct Byrd to drive not to the office but out into the Carolina countryside for a day of fishing—or, as Byrnes preferred to put it, an afternoon of the two of them "communing with the bass." Byrnes would have packed a lunch and a fishing rod for his chauffeur, and the two would spend the afternoon talking and fishing, more as companions than as employer and employee.

One afternoon in June 1964, shortly after Byrnes had celebrated his eighty-second birthday and his fifty-eighth wedding anniversary, he rode with Byrd to a high school in rural South Carolina recently named in Byrnes' honor. While Byrnes was visiting the school, at his request Willie Byrd drove the Cadillac to a nearby Phillips Petroleum service station to refill the gasoline tank. While the car was being refilled, Byrd asked if there was a "colored" restroom he could use; directed inside the station building by the white attendant and repeating his request, Byrd was brusquely told by the white owner of the station that there was no restroom there he could use. Byrd immediately told the attendant to stop putting gasoline in the car and, after finding another service station that allowed him to use a restroom, returned to the school to tell Byrnes of his experience.

Byrnes was furious. The next day he wrote a letter of complaint to the Phillips Petroleum corporate headquarters in Missouri, insisting that the service station chain equally provide restrooms for its black customers across the South. In reply, Byrnes a month later received a letter explaining that although the corporation supplied the gasoline to the service stations displaying its brand, each station was operated independently and "we have no control over many of these small out-of-town accounts. Unfortunately, the man who owns the [South Carolina] station tends to be argumentive and generally ornery."

The corporate reply was, to use one of Byrnes' favorite words on the maintenance of segregation, unanswerable. More than a decade earlier, Jimmy Byrnes himself had successfully supported a variation of this same argument in federal court in Charleston—that individual states and local communities, so long as they broke no constitutional laws, should be free of any larger administrative control in treating the two races as they chose. That argument had since been discredited in the operation of public schools, but not yet in the operation of private facilities. There were no federal or South Carolina laws in mid-1964 prohibiting a service station or its supplying interstate corporation from refusing the use of a restroom to Willie Byrd because of his race, or prohibiting an independent service station owner in South Carolina from not even bothering to provide seg-regated restrooms for black customers. Jimmy Byrnes had spent no small part of his public career in preventing such laws from being passed, even as he now objected to the consequences of those actions in the life of a dignified and kind man, Willie Byrd, whom Byrnes correctly considered his close friend.

Byrnes seemed in his eighties to have outlived the usefulness of his political ideas, and at last to have suffered the common fate of all old men—to have lost his power to make things happen. His mind still clear even as his physical strength and his political powers seemed to diminish, Byrnes in the 1960s appeared to be fulfilling Dean Acheson's cruel gibe that, like the mythical lover of Aphrodite, Jimmy Byrnes had asked for immortality while forgetting to ask for eternal youthfulness. As the South entered a period of violent racial change in the 1960s and Byrnes entered his mideighties, there seemed to be no chance for another Jimmy Byrnes redivivus on the political scene.

But then Richard M. Nixon came southward looking for votes.

20

South Carolina Coda

At the grave, just after the coffin was lowered
(it went down so quickly, so quietly, it was astonishing!)
somebody asked him about a speeding ticket.

"My word's good as far as the Savannah River,"
he said. "After that you're in the hands
of Herman Talmadge."

GEORGE GARRETT, "Politician"

Jimmy Byrnes had been sounding out Richard Nixon politically and personally since at least the summer of 1958, when Nixon began to be mentioned frequently in the press, along with Senator John Kennedy of Massachusetts of the Democratic party, as one of the two most likely presidential candidates in 1960. Nixon returned to his vice-presidential office one day in late July 1958 and received a note telling him that, while he was out, "Governor Jimmy Byrnes of South Carolina called," and in the vice president's absence had exchanged pleasantries over the telephone with his secretary. He called, Byrnes had said to the secretary, to do little more than to tell Nixon's office to expect in the mail some page proofs of articles written by Byrnes mentioning the vice president and to wish "good luck" to him and his wife. Yet even on the most prosaic of occasions Byrnes could still turn on the charm after all these years. At the bottom of the message left for his reading, Nixon saw the parenthetical notation his secretary had voluntarily typed after talking with Jimmy Byrnes: "(Nice fellow)."

Byrnes was attempting to get all the nice fellows back once more into a political party sympathetic to the needs of the conservative white South.

And remarkably, he was turning to Richard M. Nixon and the newer generation of national GOP leaders in order to find those nice fellows. Byrnes had planned in 1952 to create a politically independent South not "in the bag" for either major party. Even when most actively trying to break up the traditionally Democratic voting patterns of the Solid South in that year's presidential election, Byrnes had not publicly identified himself with the GOP but instead had organized the Independents for Eisenhower. When the moderation of Dwight Eisenhower in regard to federal enforcement of public school integration had proved just as objectionable to him as the federal activism of Harry Truman, Byrnes in 1956 had carried himself and his state even farther into the political wilderness outside either major party by organizing votes for the peripheral States' Rights ticket.

But now that his attempt to revive the concurrent majority by keeping the South independent of the two major parties had proved to be ineffectual, Byrnes was in the late 1950s again trying to return to the South the voting power it had enjoyed when the Solid South was central to the Democratic party's presidential victories. This time, however, Jimmy Byrnes was trying to create a South that was solidly Republican.

Byrnes intended not to make the South more amendable to the Republican party but to make the Republican party more amendable to the South. The potential was certainly there for Byrnes to reverse the Democratic voting patterns that had existed in the South since the end of the Civil War and Reconstruction. Even in Charleston, the former "holy city" of southern secession, where a Republican candidate for president had not received a majority of the vote since 1876, such was the prestige of Dwight Eisenhower and of Jimmy Byrnes' indirect endorsement of him that the GOP ticket had carried that city with astonishing strength in the presidential election of 1952. Less than one month after the inauguration of the Republican Abraham Lincoln, Charlestonians had gathered at the city park overlooking their harbor to cheer and dance in joy at the bombardment of Fort Sumter and the start of the Civil War; but in November 1952 they had voted for General Eisenhower over the Democratic candidate by a citywide margin of almost two to one. Only in the city's single black ward, where comparatively few residents were allowed by the state government to vote, had the Democratic presidential ticket received a majority.

As the political conventions and the presidential election of 1960 approached, Byrnes' mind was as sharp as ever, and he perceived the Democratic party attempting to defeat the Republicans by putting together again the unique Democratic coalition of northern labor and black urban pluralities. It was a coalition last perfected by Franklin Roosevelt at the convention of 1944 in his successful balancing of the constituencies represented by Sidney Hillman and Walter White against the other traditional Democratic interests. And even the Fair Employment Practices Commission, that bête noire casually left behind for his party by Franklin Roosevelt after the 1944 convention, played in 1960 an important part in binding together the Democratic coalition. Powerful labor leaders such as Walter Reuther of the United Auto Workers agreed with black political leaders that the 1960 Democratic platform should contain an unequivocal pro-FEPC plank.

This was not a coalition in which southern Democrats were particularly needed or wanted, as Byrnes himself had discovered after traveling to Chicago in 1944. Even without the traditionally solid base of Democratic electoral votes in the South, a Democratic presidential candidate still could scrape by with a win so long as the party continued to carry the northern and the industrial midwestern states and limited its southern defections to three or four Deep South states, as had occurred, to Harry S. Truman's great happiness, in 1948. Yet if only somehow the electoral votes of all the eleven formerly Confederate states could be delivered as solidly to the Republican party as they once had been delivered to the Democratic party, Byrnes knew, the winning situation would be reversed.

A solidly Republican South, in combination with the traditionally Republican strongholds in the Midwest and in California, could guarantee victory in presidential elections as regularly as had been enjoyed by the Democratic party during the four terms of Franklin Roosevelt; and southern Republicans would then occupy as important a position in their party as had southern Democrats during the prelabor and black coalition years of the two-thirds rule, as when FDR in 1932 had been forced to rely upon the support of such southern conservatives as Joe Robinson, Pat Harrison, and, of course, Jimmy Byrnes. But in attempting this latest practical application of the theory of the concurrent majority, Byrnes was resisted not only by the political traditions of his region and state but also by his own deeply felt political loyalties over a lifetime as a Democrat.

Jimmy Byrnes had cut his political milk teeth under the tutelage of a former Red Shirt, Pitchfork Ben Tillman, when the violent "redemption" of white rule in the post–Civil War South was still within living memory. Consequently for Byrnes and at least one more following generation of white southerners, the Republican party was inevitably associated across the South with the military rule of 1865–76. The Democratic party of the white Redeemers became "the house of our fathers," in the widely quoted phrase of the nineteenth-century U.S. senator Benjamin H. Hill from Georgia. An unquestioning allegiance to the Democratic party by the white southern voting minority was understood to be the means by which the southern "fathers' house" of economic and social conservatism, including a legal segregation of the races, was to be continued into the twentieth century.

Jimmy Byrnes as much as any other white male coming to voting age in the post–Civil War South had accepted the patriarchal inheritances available to him through his state Democratic party. Byrnes had since 1910 run for public offices, ranging from congressman to governor, eleven times on the Democratic ticket, and such was the dominance in his state and region by the Democratic Party that, having survived the fiercely competitive party primaries, Byrnes had not once faced any Republican opposition. Acceptance by the one-party southern system brought with it for its chosen political heirs such as Byrnes a social identity as well as a party label. There were many worldly mansions prepared for the white southern believers in the house of the state Democratic parties. Although Byrnes had never been particularly interested in the accumulation of personal wealth, loyalty to the traditional, Bourbon values of the Democratic party had provided him, and scores of other southern congressmen and senators born without family money or connections, with a social and economic upward mobility otherwise unavailable to him. Byrnes had first moved into the middle class, for example, when the paternal and aristocratic Judge Aldrich of Aiken had taken upon himself the responsibility for seeing that his promising young assistant Jimmy Byrnes read law and entered a profession. So strong were these political and cultural ties to the Democratic party throughout the South that Byrnes even in 1952 had hesitated to dissociate himself from it personally and had considered himself an independent Democrat despite his voting for Eisenhower.

But since the advent of the labor and black voter coalition, all sorts of people had been let into the Democratic party. Almost twelve months to the day before Byrnes telephoned Richard Nixon in 1958, Senator Richard Russell of Georgia, who had known Byrnes well in the Senate, aired the frustrations of many southern Democrats when he denounced by name such influential men in the Democratic party as Walter Reuther and Hubert Humphrey. Russell knowingly continued the metaphor used by his nineteenth-century predecessor that had a special meaning for his white southern twentieth-century contemporaries: "I'm very frank to say that I'm apprehensive about the growing strength and domination in the party of the extreme left wing group," Russell told the *Atlanta Journal* on July 28, 1957. "They have said the Democratic Party is better off without us."

"If that group ever dominates the party," Russell continued with deliberate emphasis, "we might be driven out of the political house of our fathers. But we would carry with us the ark of the covenant—the Constitution."

Russell, unlike his friend Jimmy Byrnes, never officially left the Democratic party. That political change would be the last act of Byrnes' long public career, a political coda enacted in South Carolina that would be of great significance both for his region and for the Republican party, even in the decades after Byrnes' death in 1972. Byrnes' public renunciation of the Democratic ticket in 1960 and his encouragement of white southerners to vote for the first time as Republicans marked a major beginning step in the direction of a South that by the mid-1960s he saw had become solidly

GOP in presidential elections. Byrnes' actions directly helped bring into being what in 1992 the political scientists Earl Black and Merle Black termed "the vital South"—that bloc of electoral votes, usually solidly Republican, that since 1968 has determined the outcome of all presidential elections and that will continue to do so until at least the next century.

"For all presidential elections through 2000," the Blacks observed in 1992, "sweeping the South will permit the Republicans to win the presidency with slightly more than three-tenths of the northern electoral vote. Conversely, the loss of southern electoral votes means that the Democratic Party must now win a higher percentage of the North's electoral vote (69 percent if no electoral votes are won in the South) than the Republicans once needed when they had to write off the South."

Jimmy Byrnes may not have carried the ark of the covenant with him when he left his fathers' house in 1960, but he certainly carried away with him the means for the Democratic party to win the presidency with any consistency for the next forty years. Of course, Byrnes was not alone in his plans. He needed a Republican candidate whose domestic policies he could persuade his fellow white southerners to support over the traditional Democratic ticket, a candidate with whom he could, in the emphatic phrase of the Blacks, "southernize the modern Republican Party." Byrnes found such a candidate in Richard Nixon.

The Democratic convention of 1960, which nominated John F. Kennedy as the party's presidential candidate, pledged unequivocally in its platform that "the new Democratic administration will support federal legislation establishing a Fair Employment Practices Commission to secure effectively for everyone the right to equal opportunity for employment." Byrnes did not travel that year to the convention in Los Angeles, and after Kennedy received the nomination, he remained silent in South Carolina throughout the summer on any endorsement of the Democratic candidate. Joseph Kennedy, Sr., worried that his family's Roman Catholicism might cost his son the large Protestant vote of the South, telephoned Byrnes and asked on the basis of their long and cordial friendship that Byrnes publicly endorse the Kennedy ticket. The request was plausible. As long ago as his secretary of state years, Byrnes had shown an affectionate interest in the nascent political career of Joseph Kennedy's eldest surviving son. In the summer of 1946 Byrnes had even taken a few moments away from the ongoing negotiations at the Conference of Foreign Ministers to write the senior Kennedy about John Kennedy's first run for elective office and, incidentally, to reveal Jimmy Byrnes' own encyclopedic knowledge about local politics hundreds of miles from his own state. "While in Paris, I was told by some mutual friends that one of your boys was a candidate for Congress," Byrnes had written to Joseph Kennedy in July 1946. "Tell me about it. I hope he is running in the district formerly represented by Peter Tague. As I recall it, that was Monasney Martin's district, where a Democrat was assured of a fair count. Love to you, Jim."

But since that time much water had flowed under the bridge. If Joseph Kennedy himself were on the ticket, Byrnes replied to Joseph Kennedy's telephoned request, he would willingly endorse it; but he added that what he would willingly do for the father, he could not do for the son. With this charmingly cold-blooded compliment, the relationship between these two pragmatic and calculating Irishmen for all practical purposes came to an end in 1960.

(After the presidential election that year, Byrnes wrote to his former Supreme Court clerk, James Doyle, then a well-respected attorney and active Democrat in Wisconsin, cautioning Doyle not to expect any judicial appointment or other forms of patronage from the Kennedy administration's Justice Department, because of Doyle's prior associations with Byrnes and John Kennedy's party rival for the nomination, Adlai Stevenson. "While I do not know the Attorney General," Byrnes wrote, "I knew his father well and know how vindictive he was in his feelings against President Roosevelt because of an utterly unjustified belief that the president had prevent[ed] the awarding of the Congressional Medal of Honor to his son Joe. Evidently Bobby has inherited this trait from his father.")

Earlier that spring before the Republican convention, Byrnes had been spreading among other southern political leaders his opinion that "there is no doubt that Nixon is a much better man than he has been represented to be, and then too, he may have developed." Even so, Byrnes might have been considering a third-party endorsement, as he had made in 1956, until he had a second telephone conversation, this time with Richard Nixon, after the elimination that summer of Nelson Rockefeller as a viable Republican presidential candidate and Nixon's subsequent receipt of his party's nomination to the presidency.

Nixon called to arrange with Byrnes a major campaign visit to South Carolina; the Republican campaign "cannot write off any state," Nixon told Byrnes, and the GOP candidate intended to canvass aggressively for votes across the previously Democratic South. In fact, before telephoning Byrnes, Nixon already had begun his maiden trip on the 1960 presidential trail by speaking that August in Greensboro, North Carolina, with following campaign stops before enthusiastic crowds in Alabama and in Atlanta, Georgia. When he telephoned Byrnes after these southern appearances, Nixon apparently was unaware that Byrnes had reverted to his old habit of keeping verbatim shorthand notes on their conversation, and as they discussed the possibility of Byrnes' appearing at a Nixon campaign stop in South Carolina, Byrnes quickly took down Nixon's responses to his questions in regard to the GOP candidate's position on organized labor and the FEPC.

"I know I am not going to have the support of any major labor leaders," Nixon told Byrnes. "The price is too heavy to pay." The older South Carolina politician, who at the 1944 convention also believed that he had been denied the support of organized labor because of too heavy a price being asked of his party, was then told over the telephone by Richard Nixon what he wanted to hear about civil rights. "As to the FEPC," Nixon said with considerable understatement, "it is a field that is very sensitive." Unlike the Democratic platform, which proposed the establishment of compulsory FEPC hiring programs, Nixon said, the Eisenhower administration instead had relied upon the indirect techniques, which Byrnes could appreciate, of private appeals and avoidance of confrontation in racial hirings. In the administration's awarding of federal contracts for government work, Nixon said, "we have never denied a contract and never revoked a contract" because of race; rather, in his years as the vice president he had worked with federal contractors behind the scenes and "persuaded employment and promotion of Negroes."

If Byrnes and Nixon then also discussed the enforcement of the *Brown* decision, which had proceeded at a snail's pace across the South since 1954, he chose to keep no shorthand record of this part of the conversation. But he had heard enough. Before the end of September 1960, Jimmy Byrnes became one of the first prominent Deep South politicians publicly to endorse the Republican ticket of Nixon and Lodge, and the first South Carolina governor since the withdrawal of federal troops from his state in 1876 to call on South Carolinians and other southerners to vote for the Republican party. Declaring that southerners "should not vote for a party label just because their grandfathers voted that way a century ago," Byrnes in a statement widely published throughout the South announced on September 22 that in the upcoming November presidential election "I shall vote for Richard Nixon and Henry Cabot Lodge."

Byrnes was at pains to dissociate this public leaving of the Democratic party with any motives directly related to race. "If in the Democratic platform there was no mention of civil rights," Byrnes said, "I still would regard it as the most dangerous program ever adopted by a political party." Byrnes had other reasons for leaving the party of Franklin Roosevelt, and his political memories stretched back well before 1954. Among his reasons for not being able to support John Kennedy, Byrnes said, was that "he did not want a president who, before making a decision on important questions, will be forced to say—'Clear it with Reuther.' "

There were other historical antecedents to Byrnes' decision not to support the Democratic ticket in 1960 that this former "assistant president" chose not to mention in his endorsement of Nixon. The South Carolina Progressive party, the same state organization that at the Chicago convention of 1944 had protested the seating of the whites-only state party delegation headed by Byrnes and Maybank, had begun a campaign in South

Carolina for the Kennedy-Johnson ticket a few days before Byrnes' announcement for Nixon. Among the speakers invited by the Progressive Democrats in 1960 to promote the national ticket was the Reverend Marshall Shepard.

Byrnes' drinking companion Walter Brown prepared a press release to accompany Byrnes' endorsement of Nixon by noting that the planned visit to the state by the Reverend Shepard "has caused many old-timers to recall that at the Democratic National Convention in 1936, when the Rev. Shepard was given the important assignment of opening the first session with prayer, Senator 'Cotton Ed' Smith walked out of the convention. Two years later in his campaign for the Senate, Senator 'Cotton Ed' in his picturesque way gave a portrayal of the convention scene and declared that the party had turned its back on the South and the principle of States' Rights." Even after nearly a century, the Red Shirt apparently was still being used to sway South Carolina voters.

Whatever its historical antecedents, this endorsement delighted Nixon and his campaign managers, but Byrnes later outdid himself when he appeared with Nixon at a campaign rally at the South Carolina capitol shortly before the end of the 1960 campaign. Running virtually even with Kennedy in polls taken in most areas of the country, Nixon attempted to make a last-minute sweep of the Carolinas and edge ahead of Kennedy with electoral votes taken from these and other Deep South states previously Democratic strongholds. Four days before the November 7 election, Nixon flew to Columbia, where he was greeted at a flag-draped stage at the statehouse steps by Jimmy Byrnes and the crowd that he and the other local organizers had assembled. Nixon's face appeared to show a genuinely startled expression when he saw the exceptional size of the crowd—approximately 35,000 people, or about three times the number that had turned out the previous week to greet John Kennedy on his visit to the state. The traditional Confederate battle songs, including "Dixie," which had once appeared to arouse Dwight Eisenhower, were again played for Richard Nixon's benefit; and in an implicit rebuke by the rally's local organizers of John Kennedy's Catholicism, before Byrnes introduced Nixon the well-known evangelist Billy Graham appeared on stage and opened the event with a prayer, asking for divine guidance in the next week's presidential election in order "to make a decision pleasing to Almighty God."

"Then up strode James F. Byrnes," wrote the *Washington Post* reporter present there, to introduce Nixon as, in Byrnes' words, "the best qualified man" for the presidency in 1960. To offset the influence of the labor and black voter coalition in the Democratic party, Byrnes urged that "next Tuesday the voters of the South will have the same [type of] coalition with the Republicans."

Nixon in his remarks after Byrnes' introduction continued Jimmy Byrnes' theme to this previously Democratic crowd that, in Nixon's words,

"it is not enough to vote as your fathers and your grandfathers voted."
Warming to the crowd and "interrupted frequently by applause and rebel
yells," according to local press accounts, Nixon rose to a stirring denun-
ciation of the Democratic Party: "I say to you today that the party of
Jackson, Jefferson, and Wilson is at the opposite ends of the poles of
Schlesinger and Galbraith and Reuther and Bowles. And we want no part
of it in the South or any part of the country."

Byrnes and Nixon both were bitterly disappointed by their failure the
following week to obtain the southern electoral bloc for the GOP in 1960.
In part because of the animated campaigning in the South of the Democratic
vice-presidential candidate, Lyndon B. Johnson of Texas, Nixon carried
only three of the eleven states of the former Confederacy—Virginia, Tennessee, and Florida. Had Nixon carried the remaining eight other southern
states, their totals combined with his victories in the midwestern states and
in California would have made him, rather than John Kennedy, the next
president of the United States. However, there were some encouraging
signs for the GOP. Nixon lost the urban areas of the state of Texas by
margins in some cities of only a few dubious thousand votes; and although
Byrnes was not able to deliver his own Deep South state to Nixon, the
popular loyalty to the Democratic party there was razor thin, and South
Carolina showed the greatest percentage increase of any southern state
between the presidential elections of 1952 and 1960 in the number of its
residents voting Republican.

Nevertheless, Nixon lost the presidency, and the losers of any bitterly
fought contest, whether southerners or Quaker-raised Irishmen, tend to
remember better than do the winners those who stood by them. On January
11, 1961, nine days before the inauguration of Kennedy and Johnson,
Richard Nixon wrote to Byrnes, "Before my term of office as vice president
draws to a close, I want to take this opportunity to tell you how deeply
grateful I am for all that you did in my behalf during the recent campaign."

"I shall never forget the magnificent introduction you gave me when I
spoke from the capitol steps in South Carolina," Nixon continued. "As I
told you at the time, I have never had a better introduction in my whole
political career. I know what courage it took for you to come out for me
in the face of the overwhelming opposition of the Democratic Party leaders
not only in South Carolina but throughout the South. For that reason your
support meant far more to me than I can adequately describe in this letter."
At the close of his letter, Nixon wrote, "I agree completely, incidentally,
with the analysis of some of the causes for our defeat which you included
in your letter of November 14."

Byrnes had written Nixon within seven days of the latter's defeat to
emphasize that there was a reason other than Lyndon Johnson for the
GOP's failure to carry the South solidly. As always, it was race. Nixon's
vice-presidential running mate, Henry Cabot Lodge, had badly hurt the

chances for his party's success in the South, Byrnes wrote. Lodge late in the campaign and without prior consultation with the Nixon headquarters had promised in a speech before a Harlem audience that, if the Republican ticket were elected, a cabinet position would be reserved for a black appointee. Lodge repeated this statement in a speech in North Carolina, and both with and without encouragement by Lyndon Johnson's organization, news of this unilateral promise by Lodge was widely publicized among white southerners, with disastrous results that November for the Republican party south of the Mason-Dixon line.

"I feel that Lodge's statement about the Cabinet member did not gain for you in the northern states a sufficient number of Negroes to off-set the losses in states like the Carolinas and Texas," Byrnes wrote to Nixon on November 14, 1960. Byrnes had kept the southern political axiom that every question must include a consideration of the race question always present in his mind for nearly half a century, and he intended that in future years Richard Nixon should remember it too.

In the years following the 1960 election, Byrnes wrote again to Nixon, encouraging him to run for the California governorship, and telling him that after serving as vice president he would probably enjoy the comparatively lighter duties of settling state and local affairs, as Byrnes said he himself had enjoyed the South Carolina governorship after leaving the helm of the State Department. Byrnes also continued to work for a South that would vote solidly Republican in presidential elections. Although surely recognizing that no Republican presidential candidate was likely to win the 1964 election following the politically remorseful year of John Kennedy's assassination, Byrnes appeared with the Republican candidate, Barry Goldwater, on a regionally broadcast television appeal in late fall 1964, asking for southern support of the GOP ticket.

Byrnes' television appearance in 1964 probably was the result of equal parts affection for Goldwater and hatred of Johnson. Like many other southern white politicians of his generation, Jimmy Byrnes loathed Lyndon Johnson with an intensity that was almost familial. Johnson's remarkable management of the passage of the Civil Rights Act of 1964 during his first full year as president certainly added to that animus, but it did not fully account for it. Even during Johnson's years as a U.S. senator from Texas, Byrnes had privately jeered in letters to friends that as Lyndon Johnson's ambitions for the presidency increased, so did the frequency of referring publicly to himself as a "western" rather than a southern senator. As Byrnes had noted in a letter to a friend, "it hurts" when such actions were taken "by a senator from a state whose soldiers fought with South Carolinians in the War Between the States." Johnson was perceived by Byrnes and other southern politicians not only as a political traitor but also as regional one, who had renounced the principles of the southerners "fathers' house" for personal advancement. Nor would it have escaped Jimmy Byrnes' long memory that Senator Lyndon Johnson in the congressional session of 1955–56 had declined to join nineteen other southern U.S. senators—including the other Texas senator—in signing the "Southern Manifesto," urging a massive resistance to the Supreme Court's decision in the *Brown* v. *Board of Education* ruling.

(Jimmy Byrnes, despite a personal commitment to liberalism during his years as New Deal senator that was at least equal in sincerity to Lyndon Johnson's, never achieved the White House, and this disappointment may have sharpened his malice toward Johnson. Byrnes was well aware that he had been supplanted in reputation as the most charmingly guileful and accomplished national politician in the twentieth century to rise in the Democratic party from the provincial South. "You are far more brilliant and impressive than Jimmy Byrnes when you can bring yourself to talk about the true character of your big assignment," Joseph Alsop had written to Lyndon Johnson in 1954 after spending a morning talking with the young senator about the national legislative agenda. "And I can think of no higher praise than that, for I have always regarded Jimmy as the prime teacher of government in the real sense of that much misused word." "I have regarded Jimmy," and "you are far more brilliant and impressive." Both within and outside of their fathers' house, the younger sons since the days of the biblical story of the gift of the coat of many colors have been more praised and rewarded for possessing the same virtues as the older and aging sons. And Jimmy Byrnes knew this fact of human nature as well as did any of the biblical Joseph's malevolent older brothers.)

The Republican party did carry South Carolina and four other southern states in the presidential election of 1964. Byrnes could take little comfort, however, in the fact that even Goldwater could not improve upon the record of carrying only five of the eleven southern states for the GOP, a maximum set by Eisenhower. The South still seemed, for the moment, reasonably solid for the Democratic party. But there was an unexpected, and largely pleasant, political turn of events for Byrnes in the months preceding the election. Although not up for reelection that year, Strom Thurmond, the state's junior U.S. senator and the Democratic former protégé of Byrnes from Edgefield County, decided as a result of regard for Goldwater to change political parties, becoming the first Republican senator from a Deep South state since Reconstruction. Thurmond's conversion promised to encourage the emergence of other Republican candidates throughout his state and region, but he was still uncertain of how his old political mentor Byrnes would react to this sudden and irrevocable change. Accompanied by Harry Dent, the state chairman of the Republican party and later the presidential counsel to Richard Nixon, Thurmond traveled to Byrnes' suburban home in Columbia, where he and Dent with some trepidation planned to break the news privately to Byrnes in order to gauge his reaction before making a public announcement. When they arrived,

Jimmy Byrnes proved that even at eighty-two he was still capable of enjoying the political game for what it was worth.

"Maude! Maude! Bring me a drink!" Byrnes shouted from his study in mock horror when he heard the news of Thurmond's changing into a Republican. Once the bourbon had been produced by his wife and Byrnes had laughed at the effect his feigned shock had upon the startled Thurmond and Dent, he gave his blessing to this unexpected union. It was as if Thurmond and Dent had traveled to Byrnes' suburban home feeling that they were going to see the oldest maiden aunt in a southern family to break the news that one of the youngest members of the family was becoming betrothed to, well, a northern gentleman. But once the shock had subsided and the alcohol been served, the aunt decided that, after all, connections to northern families, with their new ideas and their new money, had their good points. "Why, Strom, that'd be audacious," Byrnes declared in an expansive mood after his drink. "That'd be a bold action, a daring action."

Other suitors considered more persistent than audacious also came to the South in the next presidential election. Richard Nixon was "never our first love" among southern Republicans, in the memorable phrase of Harry Dent, but Nixon had seen the possibilities since he spoke with Jimmy Byrnes in 1960 of building what later was to be termed the southern strategy of a strong GOP electoral base in the South. "In 1968 the South was to be one of the most important regions in terms of winning both the nomination and the election," Richard Nixon wrote in his post-presidential memoirs. Although the Deep South might remain unwinnable for the GOP that year, because of the complication of the third-party campaign of the white supremacist George Wallace, Nixon was determined in the 1968 election not to "concede the Carolinas, Florida, Virginia, or any of the states on the rim of the South. These states became the foundation of my strategy; added to the states that I expected to win in the Midwest, the Great Plains, the Rocky Mountains, and the Far West, they would put me over the top and into the White House."

Southern Republicans were in fact instrumental in Nixon's obtaining the presidential nomination that year over the candidacies of Nelson Rockefeller and Ronald Reagan. (As a result of the exceptional growth of the GOP in the region since Byrnes first endorsed Eisenhower in 1952, southern delegates formed the largest voting bloc at the Miami convention. The southerners were persuaded to back Nixon over Reagan following Nixon's promises to GOP southern state chairmen to protect the region's textile industry and to select a vice-presidential candidate friendly to the South.) Nixon in the fall general election of 1968 set out to avoid the error Jimmy Byrnes had told him eight years earlier had cost him majorities in the Carolinas and other critical southern states. Neither Nixon nor his vice-presidential running mate, Spiro Agnew, had any intention of taking a position on racial matters that was liberally in advance of the Democratic ticket. Speaking in Mississippi, Nixon had in 1960 publicly scorned what he called the "fool's gold" of the Republican party's trying to go after the white supremacist votes in the South, which initially appeared to be supporting Wallace in 1968; but Jimmy Byrnes and other moderate segregationists had shown Nixon the trail to what could be seen as the region's true electoral gold, and Nixon decided to go down it. The accommodation to conservative southerners such as Byrnes of the Republican party's policies on racial issues became the basis of Richard Nixon's southern strategy that year; and the racial issue that was most important to Byrnes and other white southern leaders in 1968 was the same one that had been the most important to them in 1954: the desegregation of public schools ordered by the Supreme Court in *Brown* v. *Board of Education*.

The fourteen years since *Brown* had seen little substantive change in the racial composition of the student bodies at the traditionally white and black public schools in the South. This continuation of de facto racial segregation was largely the result of the Court's decision in its 1955 hearings on compliance with its ruling in *Brown* that the district federal courts in the affected states would be responsible for enforcing the 1954 decision. The southern district courts, in consequence, usually had been satisfied in the first decade after *Brown* to have each school district under the court's authority submit only a "freedom of choice" plan, whereby each student was allowed to transfer to another school in the district, rather than to require from the school districts any extensive plans for fully racially integrating all their schools. Freedom of choice was considered to be enough; as Judge John Parker, one of the three federal district judges in the original court hearing in the Clarendon County case, later decreed in disposing of *Briggs* v. *Elliott* in 1955, "The Constitution, in other words, does not require integration. It merely forbids segregation."

In practice, of course, only a few black students across the South chose to transfer to previously all-white schools in their educational districts; and the white students almost never chose to transfer. Under such terms, the Supreme Court in 1955 had given Jimmy Byrnes and his conservative allies much of what they had asked for in 1954 during the months preceding the *Brown* decision: federal judicial interference in local affairs was kept to a minimum, and the transfer of only one or two occasional black students at any time guaranteed that the change toward a fully racially integrated school system in the South would be extremely gradual. But by the last year of the Great Society, the Department of Health, Education, and Welfare (HEW) had begun to withhold federal funds from southern school districts that did not provide further evidence of more accelerated plans toward integration. The Supreme Court also signaled in a 1968 decision against a previously totally segregated Virginia school district that its patience with freedom of choice plans was being exhausted and that the court-ordered busing of students to achieve desegregation in the Virginia case might be applied throughout the South. And subsequently the Democratic presidential candidate in 1968, Hubert H. Humphrey, publicly endorsed the withholding of HEW funds as a means to encourage more rapid and complete southern compliance with the *Brown* decision.

Nixon now saw his chance to do in the South what Jimmy Byrnes had told him Henry Cabot Lodge had failed to do. Nixon flew to Charlotte, North Carolina, for a two-day stay in mid-September 1968. In a television interview broadcast in the Carolinas and the Upper South only a few days after the opening of public schools throughout the region, Nixon declared himself adamantly opposed to the HEW's withholding of federal funds from school districts not in compliance with HEW desegregation guidelines. "I wouldn't want to see a federal agency punish a local community," Nixon said, adding, "That kind of activity should be very scrupulously examined, and, in many cases I think should be rescinded." He agreed with the 1954 *Brown* decision, Nixon told his television audience, but he had no timetable for nationwide school desegregation; busing students to achieve desegregation accomplished nothing, in his opinion, because the children from the poorer schools "are two or three grades behind and all you do is destroy their ability to compete." He personally favored "freedom of choice plans," provided that the local plans were not just "used to perpetuate segregation."

The South got the message. Byrnes' acquaintance Harry Dent immediately bought a videotape of the Charlotte interview and arranged for it to be rebroadcast and for a printed transcript to be distributed throughout the region. Dent was at first strongly opposed in these actions by the few northeastern Republican liberals working in the national Nixon headquarters in New York City. "They just did not want him [Nixon] saying anything about favoring freedom of choice in public school desegregation and about being against forced busing directly on TV," Dent later recalled. But the candidate Richard Nixon and the man whom Dent called "this sage political wizard"—Jimmy Byrnes—knew what they were doing. In an interview with national newspaper editors on October 7, Nixon repeated his conviction that HEW had been "overzealous" in trying to enforce that department's desegregation guidelines, particularly in its rejection of freedom-of-choice plans. Three days before this interview, Nixon had met and talked briefly with Byrnes at a luncheon for the Republican candidate in Spartanburg. At that luncheon Nixon had promised Byrnes that he would return to South Carolina the following year to pay Jimmy Byrnes yet another visit, and that when he did so, he would be president of the United States.

Richard Nixon kept his word. His victory that November, by 302 electoral college votes to 191 for Hubert Humphrey, confirmed the effectiveness of the southern strategy. As anticipated, the Republican presidential ticket lost that year in New York State and in a tier of other urbanized, northern states; but Nixon carried California and the Midwest, and in a sweep of what later would be called the Sunbelt states he garnered the electoral college votes of the southwestern states and the Upper South. These GOP gains, including the Carolinas, Virginia, and Florida, more than offset the unpopularity of the Republican ticket that year in the Northeast; and for the first time the critical importance was evident in a presidential year of the Democratic party's loss of the Solid South. Of the eleven formerly Confederate states, the Democratic ticket succeeded in carrying only Texas; had the Democratic party retained its traditional bloc of the ten other southern states and carried its previously loyal four border states, Hubert Humphrey with his support in the New York State area would have been elected president.

Senior among the southern Republican leaders, Jimmy Byrnes in partnership with Richard Nixon had been able fully to achieve in only eight years what Republican leaders since Rutherford Hayes in 1876 had desired: the retrenchment of the Republican party from a position on racial issues more liberal than that of the Democrats, and the rebuilding of the South as a solid GOP electoral base. Jimmy Byrnes had been willing to move himself and his region a few degrees toward the national political center by persuading much of the South to abandon racial supremacist third parties and to accept without further overt resistance a highly qualified compliance with the *Brown* decision. In exchange, Nixon was willing to move the Republican party many degrees toward the political right occupied by the white South by forgoing his party's traditional federal activism in enforcing school desegregation. At the time of the 1968 campaign, as the extent of his southern strategy became evident, the *New York Times* observed that Nixon seemed to have traded a very big Republican quid for a very questionable southern quo. But as subsequent presidential elections have demonstrated, in the partnership between Nixon and Byrnes, the Republican president seems to have gotten as good as he gave.

Byrnes and Nixon appear to have effected in 1968 among white southern voters what the political scientist V. O. Key termed a "critical" election, one that results in a significant realignment of voting loyalties to be repeated in subsequent elections. As a result of white majority defections, the Democratic Solid South was in 1968 in the penultimate stage of being transformed into the GOP Solid South. The third-party candidacy of George Wallace in 1968 prevented Nixon from making a sweep of all eleven states of the former Confederacy; but white southern voters, exiting either to the extreme segregationist party of Wallace or to the "southernized" Republican party as defined by Nixon and Byrnes, left the traditional Democratic house of their fathers. A campaign worker for Nixon in 1968 later turned political scientist, Kevin Phillips, was quick to note the magnitude of this change in his 1969 study, *The Emerging Republican Majority*. Pointing out that in some areas of the South the Democratic share of the presidential vote had declined from 90 percent in 1932 to 26 percent in 1968, Phillips correctly observed that throughout the nation's recent political history the abandonment of the Democratic party by white southerners could be matched in its passion and political meaning by "only one other political change—the related Negro trend to the Democrats."

A solidly GOP South—and solidly white southern GOP—in combination with western moderate and conservative Republicans could constitute a powerful electoral college bloc against the labor-black Democratic coalition still present among the declining urban populations of the northeastern states. This new GOP coalition was not one in which there was much room or even need for the black vote. "Substantial Negro support is not necessary to national Republican victory in light of the 1968 election," Phillips concluded. Here was Jimmy Byrnes' concurrent majority redivivus. "The electoral votes being lost by the Northeast are going to the South as well as the West," Phillips wrote after the election. "Expanding on the pattern of Richard Nixon's 1968 victory, the South, Heartland and California together can constitute an effective *national* [his emphasis] victory." Phillips, who grew up in a Bronx Irish family, had been blunter during the 1968 presidential campaign in an interview with the political writer Garry Wills. "The Civil War is over," Phillips declared to Wills as the two sat in Phillips' office at Nixon's campaign headquarters overlooking a busy New York City street. "The [political] parties don't need to compete for the little corner of the nation *we* live in. Who needs Manhattan when we can get the electoral votes of eleven southern states? Put those together with the Farm Belt and the Rocky Mountains, and we don't need the big cities. We don't even want them." Jimmy Byrnes had run his race with John C. Calhoun.

The new president also kept his promise to return to South Carolina in 1969 and visit again with Byrnes. A presidential trip to attend the annual running of the Kentucky Derby had been planned by the White House for late spring; Nixon decided to combine this trip with a stop in Columbia, South Carolina, to see Byrnes and his wife the day after the May 2 date that marked both their anniversary and Jimmy Byrnes' birthday. And so, six months after the presidential election, Nixon and his wife, accompanied by a sizable White House entourage, stopped by the Columbia suburban house of the man once characterized as "the most honest-looking horse thief" in international diplomacy.

It was not planned to be an extended visit to South Carolina. Only ninety miles away from Columbia, the Reverend Ralph David Abernathy of the Southern Christian Leadership Conference (SCLC) had the day before Nixon's visit been temporarily released on bond from the Charleston city jail, after he and the widowed Coretta Scott King had that week led hundreds of civil rights demonstrators into the streets of Charleston. Abernathy and the widow of the recently assassinated Dr. Martin Luther King were leading the demonstrations in protest of the refusal of the state of South Carolina to recognize a union of predominately black menial workers organized at a state-owned hospital in Charleston. "I had heard that the president was coming to South Carolina the next day to pay his respects to a former Supreme Court Justice James Byrnes, a well-known segregationist; and I hoped that perhaps he would speak with us if only to show his impartiality," Abernathy later recalled in 1989. "We made inquiries to see if I could meet with him, but we were told that he would not be available for such a meeting." This was Abernathy's first personal experience with the emerging Republican coalition with southern conservatives, and the declining political importance to GOP leaders of black civil rights leaders after the 1968 presidential election. Twenty years after this incident Abernathy noted, "He was not the last Republican who would disappoint me in this regard."

There was no disappointment that day at the Byrnes home. Nixon and Byrnes had the opportunity to speak privately for a few moments about the course of action the new administration planned to take in the continuing Vietnam War. And then, according to the account published the next day in the *Washington Star*, "Nixon and the other guests in the unpretentious white brick home sang 'Happy Birthday' to 'Jimmy' as the ailing old man managed a big smile." The reporter correctly noted Byrnes' declining health. The years had begun to catch up at last with Jimmy Byrnes by his eighty-seventh birthday, and he had been hospitalized the previous month with heart trouble. "I have kept my promise," Nixon said to Byrnes before the birthday singing. "You couldn't come to us, so we came to you." Nixon's kind remark bespoke his undeniable personal affection for this senior southern strategist; but in a larger, unintentional sense it also expressed the ideological movement of the Republican party toward the political right accomplished the previous year by Nixon and Byrnes.

The presidential group left shortly after the birthday singing on the Byrnes' front porch for their motorcade ride back to *Air Force One* and their travel on to horse races; and Jimmy and Maude Byrnes, both now helped in their walking by Willie Byrd, went back inside their house. This meeting with Nixon on May 3, 1969, was to be Jimmy Byrnes' last major public appearance. Because of his declining health, Byrnes in the preceding months had given up even the pretense of having Byrd chauffeur him to his downtown office. The death, earlier in 1969, of Cassandra Connor, his constant private secretary and companion at all his offices since the 1920s, made him even less inclined to visit an office empty except for himself and the photographs and files accumulated over six decades of political activity.

Byrnes had earlier also been depressed by the death of his friend and prior patron Bernard M. Baruch. The friendship between Byrnes and Baruch had at times been strained. The passion that quickened their friendship throughout the 1930s and the 1940s had been the quest for power, and after each had failed in advancing his own and the other's ambitions, like partners in an unhappy marriage they began silently to reproach each other. Nevertheless, Byrnes had continued to look out for the interests of his older friend, and in one instance in the late 1950s perhaps had saved Baruch from a murder attempt while the elderly financier vacationed at his South Carolina home of Hobcaw Barony. In one of the last instances of the rising spirit of Coley Blease, the South Carolina Law Enforcement Division received a confidential report that the Ku Klux Klan was planning to kill Baruch at his coastal home. The police did not have sufficient evidence to make arrests, but Byrnes arranged to have several South Carolina law enforcement officers pay a visit to the prime suspect, a low-country farmer who the police noted was carrying a pistol in his back pocket. The officers were able to persuade the farmer that it would be unwise for him or any others to harm Baruch; and although the man told the officers that he knew of no Klan plot against Baruch's life, he declared that "it would be a pretty good idea if somebody did kill the old Jew son of a bitch." At Byrnes' insistence, Baruch never knew of this covert police protection. Byrnes privately noted that if Baruch did learn of this possible threat against his life and that he was perhaps not well beloved by the white, lower-class neighbors of his South Carolina barony, the shock would kill him.

Baruch died at his New York City town house in 1965 with Jimmy Byrnes by his side. Byrnes had been making regular trips to Baruch's New York residence when the financier's health began to fade in the summer of that year and he became bedridden. A visibly shaken Byrnes told a reporter the day of Baruch's death that Byrnes had lost a close friend of more than forty years—the loss of friend, that is, who filled a gap in Byrnes' private and public life since the deaths of Woodrow Wilson and of Ben Tillman four and five decades earlier.

In his last years Byrnes whenever capable occupied his energies with the charitable foundation he and his wife had established to pay the college expenses of academically talented orphans in South Carolina. Byrnes enjoyed selecting some of the recipients himself, choosing both white and black high school students for his scholarships with an apparent impartiality. The fund continues to be sustained from sales of his memoirs. In the late 1950s Byrnes again had passed up an opportunity to become wealthy by donating his share of the sales of a second book of reminiscences, *All in One Lifetime*, to the Byrnes foundation. Although he wrote it, with the assistance of the history professor George Curry, primarily to pay college expenses for hundreds of children whose parents he would never meet, Byrnes nevertheless returned briefly in this 1958 memoir to his concern for continuing negotiations with the Soviet Union and for protecting civil liberties in the United States. Apparently some old political wounds still stung this sometime Cold Warrior.

By the time this memoir was being written, more than a decade had passed since Byrnes' resignation from State in 1947, and Senator Joe McCarthy had been in his grave for nearly a year, having died in the spring of 1957, after a declining national political influence and a suspected cirrhosis of the liver. Byrnes nonetheless recalled in *All in One Lifetime* how while at State "at one and the same time I was attacked (by Wallace among others) for being the leader of the 'get tough with Russia' crowd and (by Admiral Leahy among others) for continuing to negotiate and talk with the Russians at all." And Byrnes apparently remained angry over McCarthy's boast in 1951 that "up in West Virginia we read the audience a letter written by Jimmy Byrnes" on which, McCarthy claimed, was a list of the names of 205 State Department employees "that were known to the Secretary of State as being members of the Communist Party."

By the time of the publication of Byrnes' second memoir, Alger Hiss, a medium-ranking State Department employee under Secretary Byrnes and two previous secretaries of state, had been convicted of perjury and served a sentence in a federal prison for having stated under oath that Hiss had not known or passed State Department documents to a member of the Communist party in 1930s. Byrnes now reminded his readers in 1958 that "a real, but less often remarked, element of the tragedy is that suspicion was thrown upon the entire State Department because Hiss had occupied a position of responsibility."

Byrnes' words in *All in One Lifetime* marked more than just a self-serving attempt to improve his historical reputation as a former U.S. secretary of state. He had personally witnessed how the Truman's administration's loyalty program in the State Department harmed reputations other than his own. For instance, the gifted Porter McKeever had written Byrnes in 1951 telling his former employer of finding himself, with little notice or reason, being under investigation by the Loyalty Board concerning whether or not he ever had "any association with Alger Hiss."

McKeever for some time had been considering resigning his UN post as director of information of the U.S. Mission in protest, he wrote Byrnes in the same letter, because of what he considered Secretary of State George Marshall's attempt to reduce this country's membership in the UN from the planned "cornerstone of United States policy" during the last Roosevelt administration to "the size of a pebble" in 1951. "The most annoying part of it all," he wrote, "is that I can't resign now until I get the whole thing cleared up because otherwise I would be listed as resigning under inquiry. Isn't it ironic? Here I've spent six years devoting most of my waking hours to fighting psychological warfare against the Communists and the Soviet Union, and now I'm held up for something like this."

(McKeever did resign in 1952, after passing the Loyalty Board's inspection. "Mr. McKeever is right in asserting that the 'withering away' of the United Nations would be a great victory for the Soviet Union in the Cold War," the *New York Times* editorialized at the time of his resignation.)

But in this second memoir Byrnes chose not to recall how, at a news conference on July 26, 1946, Secretary Byrnes had responded with a simple no to a reporter's question on whether Alger Hiss had received an adverse report from the department's security committee. After Hiss' subsequent trial and conviction, Byrnes more than a decade after this news conference apparently found it embarrassing that neither he nor his friend Assistant Secretary Donald Russell had uncovered sufficient evidence of Alger Hiss' disloyalty to his government to warrant firing him or reporting his activities to a federal attorney. Nor did Byrnes choose to quote from his own unsolicited remarks following the question about Alger Hiss at that 1946 news conference: "It's a very serious matter to charge any man with disloyalty to the government. If you [the press] do it, if the government does it, you destroy that man for life." Instead, in these memoirs Byrnes chose to emphasize how he had used his still considerable legislative influence to help secure passage of the so-called McCarran amendment to a State Department funding bill, which made possible the dismissal by the secretary of any career State employee "for the good of the service." Byrnes apparently did not wish to be remembered in 1958 as the U.S. secretary of state who in 1946 had insisted upon both anonymity and due process for State employees simply *accused* of disloyalty—whether the target of the accusations was the vindicated John S. Service or the tried and convicted Alger Hiss.

(It is surprising that Jimmy Byrnes, as a rule so skillful and adroit at manipulating his future historical image, chose to jump the wrong way in his second book of memoirs by excising so much of his virtuous political past. As a result, his documentable role in defending due process throughout the *Amerasia* incident has been completely ignored by scholars of the period. Byrnes should have known that the historical, political, and literary knives were out for him in any circumstances and that therefore he might as well have claimed his political good deeds for what they were and then braced himself for the inevitable consequences. And, as Jimmy Byrnes would surely have known at age seventy-six, virtue has never turned away a sword's point, but malice has sharpened many a blade.)

On "good" days throughout the late 1960s, when his health permitted it, scores of Byrnes scholarship holders visited the house of the childless elderly couple, whom they were encouraged to call "Mom" and "Pop" Byrnes. Jimmy Byrnes would organize sing-alongs and piano playing for the mixed group of college students, as he had once done for his Supreme Court colleagues. And so long as health permitted, Byrnes maintained social and professional contact with his former Court colleagues, with one singular incident. Justice William O. Douglas recalled that once, while

Justice Douglas was attending a convention of the American Bar Association in Portland, Oregon, a parade organized by the convention came by the hotel where Justice Douglas was staying; there in the parade was Jimmy Byrnes, "in an open limousine, waving his hat, bowing to the ladies," as Justice Douglas later wrote. "There was a break in the parade, so I ran down to the car, put out my hand and said, 'How are you, Jimmy?' He brushed my hand aside as if I were a peddler of cocaine or heroin or some other dangerous drug. That really hurt me, as we had been good friends for so long."

Byrnes simply may not have recognized his old friend extending a hand among the press of people around the limousine; or this act may have revealed some of enmity that Byrnes may have felt for a fellow justice whose ideology was so far to the left of his own, and whose views on marriage and sexuality were diametrically opposed to Byrnes' conservative Episcopalian-Catholic values; or, if this account is accurate, perhaps Byrnes was motivated by his knowledge by this time that Douglas' presence on the 1944 vice-presidential ticket had been much more desired by Roosevelt than had been Jimmy Byrnes'. Douglas chose to believe that Byrnes' ill will toward him had begun as early as 1941, when Douglas had joined a concurring opinion to the majority opinion written by Byrnes in *Edwards* v. *California*. In this case, Byrnes speaking for the majority had decided that no state in the Union could close its borders to U.S. citizens from another state because of a strict-constructionist interpretation of the interstate commerce clause of the Constitution; Justice Douglas had argued on more broadly constitutional grounds for open state borders, on the basis of a right by any U.S. citizen to travel freely within this country as protected by the privileges and immunities clause.

"Years later, at another meeting I was attending at Portland," Justice Douglas continued in his memoir, "I was stopped by a gentleman who was a friend of Jimmy Byrnes from South Carolina. He said that Jimmy was on his deathbed and the only thing he could talk about was me and how he wanted to see me. Since Oregon is a long way from South Carolina, I thought my coming would violate his views on interstate travel." Justice Douglas chose not to make the trip. In his memoir written after Byrnes had died, Douglas at least was judicially impartial enough to note what many would call a mean-spirited decision: "I have regretted that many times."

(Even more regrettable to the accuracy of the history of the U.S. Supreme Court's deliberations is Douglas' representation that Byrnes had written for the majority in *Edwards* only because "Jimmy reasoned that since livestock could pass state lines unless they were diseased, the same would hold true for people." The records available to Douglas when he wrote this statement in 1980 do not justify such a characterization of Byrnes' reasoning. As Douglas was aware from the notes of the Court's conference on *Edwards*, from the drafts of the majority opinion that Byrnes twice circulated among his brethren, or from the collection of Chief Justice Harlan Stone's correspondence available to Douglas at the National Archives, Byrnes in his first draft had been willing to find for the right of citizens to travel freely domestically as a constitutionally guaranteed privilege and immunity. Byrnes had changed the grounds of the majority opinion only after Chief Justice Stone had written to Byrnes on November 13, 1941, that, although he was "greatly pleased" with Byrnes' first draft, in order to sustain a majority agreement on the Court in favor of the right to interstate travel, "we must find them [precedents in constitutional law] principally in the Commerce Clause and the Fourteenth Amendment." Byrnes rewrote his majority opinion as the chief justice asked him. Jimmy Byrnes was no celebrated civil libertarian, but neither was he in his legal reasoning as paleolithic as the late Justice William Douglas in his memoirs would have had us believe.)

The good days of parades and smiling to the ladies were becoming less frequent for Byrnes. Three months after Nixon's visit he was hospitalized again for a heart attack, and he was able to return home only intermittently from stays at hospitals over the next three years. On the afternoon of April 9, 1972, he died peacefully at his home.

He would have appreciated his front-page obituary appearing the next day in the *New York Times*. "A Master of Men" was how the newspaper headline characterized his political career in the three branches of government in an article occupying the news space usually reserved for the announcement of the passing of a former head of state. Earlier, when the news of Byrnes' death had been passed along to Nixon the afternoon of April 9 at his Key West vacation retreat, Nixon had ordered the nation's flag over the White House to be lowered as a sign of respect. "No man in American history has held so many positions of responsibility in all branches of our government with such distinction," Nixon said. "He was a great patriot who always put his country ahead of his party." Nixon's wife traveled to Columbia two days later to represent the White House at the funeral, which was attended by several thousand others.

Even in death, Jimmy Byrnes drew a "strange mixture" of friends and political associates attending his funeral, ranging from retired cotton textile workers to U.S. Supreme Court Justice Warren Burger. A group of the last surviving liberal Brain Trusters turned up, as did Governor Herman Talmadge of Georgia and dozens of other, similarly conservative southern politicians. The body was buried in the churchyard of Trinity Episcopalian Cathedral, within walking distance of the state capitol. Byrnes had chosen his site well; it occupies a pleasant corner of the churchyard, and Maude Byrnes, who attended the funeral in a wheelchair, was buried there beside him in 1976. A flowering white dogwood tree shades both graves.

Worldly power also was the fathers' house in which Jimmy Byrnes had moved, from the day when as an orphan he had entered the offices of a nineteenth-century Bourbon law firm to his death at age ninety as a senior political adviser to the Nixon administration. His pursuit of power, and his achievement of it, tells us as much about the nation and region that produced a Jimmy Byrnes as about the man himself: profoundly pragmatic, far more interested in results than in ideology or party labels, Byrnes represented a transition from an older social and political order, rather than the beginning of a new one. Having benefited himself from the "Horatio Alger" possibilities of nineteenth-century capitalism, Byrnes remained distrustful of any enlargement of the government's supervisory power over its economy or its citizens, even though he himself during the Second World War presided over the most regimented U.S. economy and society in our history. He also carried well into twentieth-century American history the nineteenth century's unshakable faith in the ultimate benefits of technology, remaining untroubled by his endorsement of the atomic bomb as an acceptable weapon in the waging of total war. At the same time, Byrnes valued compromise over confrontation; and instead of "dictating our own terms" at the end of the war, he based his conduct of international diplomacy, at least initially, upon his assumption that the basic rationality and benevolence of American intentions in the postwar world made impossible any irreconcilable differences between the United States and other nations, even including the Soviet Union. His life represents the achievements, the limitations, and the contradictions of a "natural-born" American and southern politician; and the political house of this nation remains profoundly changed for his having moved through it.

BIBLIOGRAPHY

BOOKS

Abernathy, Ralph David. *And the Walls Came Tumbling Down*. New York: Harper & Row, 1989.

Abrahams, Henry J. *Justices and Presidents: A Political History of Appointments to the Supreme Court*. 2d ed. New York: Oxford Univ. Press, 1985.

Acheson, Dean. *Present at the Creation: My Years in the State Department*. New York: W. W. Norton, 1969.

Adams, Henry. *History of the Unites States of America during the First Administration of Thomas Jefferson*. Vol. 1. New York: Charles Scribner's Sons, 1891.

Allen, George E. *Presidents Who Have Known Me*. New York: Simon and Schuster, 1950.

Alperovitz, Gar. *Atomic Diplomacy: Hiroshima and Potsdam: The Use of the Atomic Bomb and the American Confrontation with Soviet Power*. Expanded and updated ed. New York: Penguin Books, 1985.

Alsop, Joseph, and Turner Catledge. *The 168 Days*. Garden City, N.Y.: Doubleday, Doran, 1938.

Ashmore, Harry S. *An Epitaph for Dixie*. New York: W. W. Norton, 1958.

Bibliography

————. *Hearts and Minds: The Anatomy of Racism from Roosevelt to Reagan.* New York: McGraw-Hill, 1982.

Bailey, Charles, and Fletcher Knebel. *No High Ground.* New York: Harper, 1960.

Bartley, Numan V. *The Rise of Massive Resistance: Race and Politics in the South during the 1950's.* Baton Rouge: Louisiana State Univ. Press, 1969.

Baruch, Bernard M. *Baruch: My Own Story.* New York: Henry Holt, 1957.

————. *Baruch: The Public Years.* New York: Holt, Rinehart and Winston, 1960.

Bass, Jack, and Walter DeVries. *The Transformation of Southern Politics: Social Change and Political Consequence since 1945.* New York: Basic Books, 1971.

Bellush, Bernard. *The Failure of the NRA.* New York: W. W. Norton, 1975.

Berman, William C. *The Politics of Civil Rights in the Truman Administration.* Columbus: Ohio State Univ. Press, 1970.

Bernstein, Irving. *Turbulent Years: A History of the American Worker, 1933–1941.* Boston: Houghton Mifflin, 1970.

Biddle, Francis. *In Brief Authority.* Garden City, N.Y.: Doubleday, 1962.

Black, Earl. *Southern Governors and Civil Rights: Racial Segregation as a Campaign Issue in the Second Reconstruction.* Cambridge: Harvard Univ. Press, 1976.

Black, Earl, and Merle Black. *The Vital South: How Presidents Are Elected.* Cambridge: Harvard Univ. Press, 1992.

Blum, John Morton. *V Was for Victory: Politics and American Culture during World War II.* New York: Harcourt Brace Jovanovich, 1976.

Bohlen, Charles E. *Witness to History, 1929–1969.* New York: W. W. Norton, 1973.

Bowles, Chester. *Promises to Keep: My Years in Public Life, 1941–1969.* New York: Harper & Row, 1971.

Burns, James MacGregor. *Roosevelt: The Lion and the Fox.* New York: Harcourt, Brace, 1956.

Burton, Orville. *In My Father's House Are Many Mansions: Family and Community in Edgefield, South Carolina.* Chapel Hill: Univ. of North Carolina Press, 1985.

Byrnes, James F. *All in One Lifetime.* New York: Harper, 1958.

————. *Speaking Frankly.* New York: Harper, 1947.

Calhoun, John C. *A Disquisition on Government and Selections from the* Discourse. Indianapolis: Bobbs-Merrill, 1953.

Carlton, David L. *Mill and Town in South Carolina, 1880–1920.* Baton Rouge: Louisiana State Univ. Press, 1982.

Catledge, Turner. *My Life and* The Times. New York: Harper & Row, 1971.

Catton, Bruce. *The War Lords of Washington.* New York: Harcourt, Brace, 1948.

Clements, Kendrick A., ed. *James F. Byrnes and the Origins of the Cold War.* Durham, N.C.: Carolina Academic Press, 1982.

Clifford, Clark, with Richard Holbrooke. *Counsel to the President: A Memoir.* New York: Random House, 1991.

Coit, Margaret. *Mr. Baruch.* Boston: Houghton Mifflin, 1957.

Connally, Tom. *My Name Is Tom Connally.* New York: Crowell, 1954.

Cooper, William J. *The Conservative Regime: South Carolina, 1877–1890.* Baltimore: Johns Hopkins Press, 1968.

Daniels, Jonathan. *The Man of Independence.* Philadelphia: J. B. Lippincott, 1950.

————. *A Southerner Discovers the South.* New York: Macmillan, 1938.

————. *The Time between the Wars: Armistice to Pearl Harbor.* Garden City, N.Y.: Doubleday, 1966.

Daniels, Josephus. *The Cabinet Diaries of Josephus Daniels, 1913–21.* Edited by E. David Cronon. Lincoln: Univ. of Nebraska Press, 1963.

Dent, Harry S. *The Prodigal Son Returns to Power*. New York: Wiley, 1978.

Drago, Harry Sinclair. *Canal Days in America: The History and Romance of Old Towpaths and Waterways*. New York: C. N. Potter, 1972.

Edgar, Walter B. *History of Santee Cooper, 1934–1984*.

Ellis, John. *Brute Force: Allied Strategy and Tactics in the Second World War*. New York: Viking Press, 1990.

Feis, Herbert. *From Trust to Terror: The Onset of the Cold War, 1945–1950*. New York: W. W. Norton, 1970.

———. *Japan Subdued: The Atomic Bomb and the End of the War in the Pacific*. Princeton: Princeton Univ. Press, 1961.

———. *Seen from E. A.: Three International Episodes*. New York: Alfred A. Knopf, 1947.

Ferrell, Robert H. *Off the Record: The Private Papers of Harry S. Truman*. New York: Harper & Row, 1980.

Fraser, Steven. *Labor Will Rule: Sidney Hillman and the Rise of American Labor*. New York: Free Press, 1991.

Fraser, Walter. *Charleston! Charleston! The History of a Southern City*. Columbia: Univ. of South Carolina Press, 1989.

Freidel, Frank. *Franklin D. Roosevelt*. Vol. 4, *Launching the New Deal*. Boston: Little, Brown, 1973.

———. *Franklin D. Roosevelt: A Rendezvous with Destiny*. Boston: Little, Brown, 1990.

Friedman, Leon, and Fred L. Israel, eds. *The Justices of the United States Supreme Court, 1789–1969: Their Lives and Major Opinions*. Vol. 4. New York: Chelsea House, 1969.

Gaddis, John. *The Long Peace: Inquiries into the History of the Cold War*. New York: Oxford Univ. Press, 1987.

———. *The United States and the Origins of the Cold War*. New York: Columbia Univ. Press, 1972.

Gardner, Lloyd C. *Architects of Illusion: Men and Ideas in American Foreign Policy, 1941–1949*. Chicago: Quadrangle Books, 1970.

Garfinkel, Herbert. *When Negroes March: The March on Washington Movement in the Organizational Politics for FEPC*. Glencoe, Ill.: Free Press, 1959.

Garson, Robert A. *The Democratic Party and the Politics of Sectionalism, 1941–1948*. Baton Rouge: Louisiana State Univ. Press, 1974.

Grant, James. *Bernard M. Baruch: The Adventures of a Wall Street Legend*. New York: Simon and Schuster, 1983.

Grantham, Dewey W. *The Life and Death of the Solid South: A Political History*. Lexington: Univ. of Kentucky Press, 1988.

Grundstein, Nathan D. *Presidential Delegation of Authority in Wartime*. Pittsburgh: Univ. of Pittsburgh Press, 1961.

Hall, Jacquelyn Dowd, et al. *Like a Family: The Making of a Southern Cotton Mill World*. Chapel Hill: Univ. of North Carolina Press, 1987.

Harbaugh, William H. *Lawyer's Lawyer: The Life of John W. Davis*. New York: Oxford Univ. Press, 1973.

Harrett, William H. *Off the Record with F.D.R.* New Brunswick: Rutgers Univ. Press, 1958.

Heard, Alexander. *The Costs of Democracy*. Chapel Hill: Univ. of North Carolina Press, 1960.

Heard, Alexander, and Donald S. Strong. *Southern Primaries and Elections, 1920–1949*. University: Univ. of Alabama Press, 1950.

Highsaw, Robert B., ed. *The Deep South in Transformation: A Symposium*. University: Univ. of Alabama Press, 1964.

Hodges, James A. *The New Deal Labor Policy and the Southern Cotton Textile Industry, 1933–1941*. Knoxville: Univ. of Tennessee Press, 1986.

Hull, Cordell. *The Memoirs of Cordell Hull*. New York: Macmillan, 1948.

Ickes, Harold L. *Back to Work: The Story of PWA*. New York: Macmillan, 1935.

———. *The Secret Diary of Harold L. Ickes*. 3 vols. New York: Simon and Schuster, 1953–54.

Janeway, Eliot. *The Struggle for Survival: A Chronicle of Economic Mobilization in World War II*. New Haven: Yale Univ. Press, 1951.

Jones, Jesse H. *Fifty Billion Dollars: My Thirteen Years with the RFC, 1932–1945*. New York: Viking Press, 1955.

Jones, Joseph M. *The Fifteen Weeks: (February 21–June 5, 1947)*. New York: Viking Press, 1955.

Josephson, Matthew. *Sidney Hillman: Statesman of American Labor*. Garden City, N.Y.: Doubleday, 1952.

Keegan, John. *The Second World War*. New York: Penguin Books, 1989.

Kennan, George F. *Memoirs: 1925–1950*. Boston: Little, Brown, 1967.

Kesselman, Louis Coleridge. *The Social Politics of FEPC: A Study in Reform Pressure Movements*. Chapel Hill: Univ. of North Carolina Press, 1948.

Kirkendall, Richard, ed. *The Truman Period as a Research Field*. Columbia: Univ. of Missouri Press, 1967.

———, ed. *The Truman Period as a Research Field: A Reappraisal, 1972*. Columbia: Univ. of Missouri Press, 1974.

Kluger, Richard. *Simple Justice: The History of* Brown v. Board of Education *and Black America's Struggle for Equality*. New York: Alfred A. Knopf, 1975.

Kolko, Gabriel. *The Politics of War: The World and United States Policy, 1943–1945*. New York: Random House, 1968.

Kolko, Joyce, and Gabriel Kolko. *The Limits of Power: The World and United States Foreign Policy, 1945–1954*. New York: Harper & Row, 1972.

Kuniholm, Bruce Robellet. *The Origins of the Cold War in the Near East: Great Power Conflict and Diplomacy in Iran, Turkey, and Greece*. Princeton: Princeton Univ. Press, 1980.

Lahne, Herbert Jay. *The Cotton Mill Worker*. New York: Farrar & Rinehart, 1944.

Lamis, Alexander P. *The Two-Party South*. 2d ed. New York: Oxford Univ. Press, 1990.

Lanouette, William, with Bela Szilard. *Genius in the Shadows: A Biography of Leo Szilard, the Man behind the Bomb*. New York: Charles Scribner's Sons, 1992.

Leuchtenburg, William E. *The Perils of Prosperity, 1914–1932*. Chicago: Univ. of Chicago Press, 1958.

Link, Arthur S. *Wilson*. Princeton: Princeton Univ. Press, 1947–.

Louchheim, Katie. *The Making of the New Deal: The Insiders Speak*. Cambridge: Harvard Univ. Press, 1983.

Lubell, Samuel. *The Hidden Crisis in American Politics*. New York: W. W. Norton, 1970.

———. *Revolt of the Moderates*. New York: Harper, 1956.

———. *White and Black: Test of a Nation*. New York: Harper & Row, 1964.

McCullough, David. *Truman*. New York: Simon and Schuster, 1992.

MacDonald, Lois. *Southern Mill Hills: A Study of Social and Economic Forces in Certain Textile Mill Villages*. New York: A. L. Hillman, 1928.

Maddox, Robert. *The New Left and the Origins of the Cold War.* Princeton: Princeton Univ. Press, 1973.

Marshall, F. Ray. *Labor in the South.* Cambridge: Harvard Univ. Press, 1967.

Messer, Robert L. *The End of an Alliance: James F. Byrnes, Roosevelt, Truman, and the Origins of the Cold War.* Chapel Hill: Univ. of North Carolina Press, 1982.

Miller, Merle. *Plain Speaking: An Oral Biography of Harry S. Truman.* New York: Berkely, 1974.

Moley, Raymond. *After Seven Years.* New York: Harper, 1939.

————. *The First New Deal.* New York: Harcourt, Brace & World, 1966.

Morgan, Chester. *Redneck Liberal: Theodore G. Bilbo and the New Deal.* Baton Rouge: Louisiana State Univ. Press, 1985.

Morgan, Ted. *FDR: A Biography.* New York: Simon and Schuster, 1985.

Mowry, George E. *Another Look at the Twentieth Century South.* Baton Rouge: Louisiana State Univ. Press, 1973.

Murray, Robert K. *The Politics of Normalcy: Governmental Theory and Practice in the Harding-Coolidge Era.* New York: W. W. Norton, 1973.

Nixon, Richard M. *RN: The Memoirs of Richard Nixon.* New York: Grosset & Dunlap, 1978.

Novick, David, Melvin Anshen, and W. C. Truppner. *Wartime Production Controls.* New York: Columbia Univ. Press, 1949.

Parmet, Herbert S. *Richard Nixon and His America.* Boston: Little, Brown, 1990.

Patterson, James T. *Congressional Conservatism and the New Deal: The Growth of the Conservative Coalition in Congress, 1933–1939.* Lexington: Univ. of Kentucky Press, 1967.

Phillips, Kevin P. *The Emerging Republican Majority.* New Rochelle, N.Y.: Arlington House, 1969.

Polenberg, Richard. *War and Society: The United States, 1941–1945.* New York: Harper Collins, 1990.

Pope, Liston. *Millhands and Preachers: A Study of Gastonia.* New York: Oxford Univ. Press, 1942.

Porcher, Frederick Adolphus. *The History of the Santee Canal.* Charleston: South Carolina Historical Society, 1903.

Potter, David M. *The South and the Concurrent Majority.* Baton Rouge: Louisiana State Univ. Press, 1972.

Pushing Back the Darkness: The Story of Santee Cooper. N.p., n.d.

Quint, Howard H. *Profile in Black and White: A Frank Portrait of South Carolina.* Washington, D.C.: Public Affairs Press, 1958.

Reeves, Thomas C. *The Life and Times of Joe McCarthy: A Biography.* New York: Stein and Day, 1982.

Rhodes, Richard. *The Making of the Atomic Bomb.* New York: Simon and Schuster, 1986.

Roosevelt, Franklin D. *The Public Papers and Addresses of Franklin D. Roosevelt.* New York: Macmillan, 1938–41.

Rosen, Elliot A. *Hoover, Roosevelt, and the Brains Trust: From Depression to New Deal.* New York: Columbia Univ. Press, 1977.

Rosenman, Samuel I. *Working with Roosevelt.* New York: Harper, 1952.

Ruchames, Louis. *Race, Jobs, and Politics: The Story of FEPC.* New York: Columbia Univ. Press, 1953.

Savage, Henry, Jr. *River of the Carolinas: The Santee.* New York: Rinehart, 1956.

Schlesinger, Arthur M., Jr., ed. *History of American Presidential Elections, 1789–1968.* Vol. 4. New York: Chelsea House, 1971.

Schwartz, Bernard. *Swann's Way: The School Busing Case and the Supreme Court.*
    New York: Oxford Univ. Press, 1986.
Schwarz, Jordan A. *The Interregnum of Despair: Hoover, Congress, and the Depres-*
    sion. Urbana: Univ. of Illinois Press, 1970.
————. *The New Dealers: Power Politics in the Age of Roosevelt.* New York:
    Alfred A. Knopf, 1993.
————. *The Speculator: Bernard M. Baruch in Washington, 1917–1965.* Chapel
    Hill: Univ. of North Carolina Press, 1981.
Seabury, Paul. *The Waning of Southern "Internationalism."* Princeton: Princeton
    Univ., Center for International Studies, 1957.
Shannon, Fred A. *The Farmer's Last Frontier: Agriculture, 1860–1897.* New York:
    Farrar & Rinehart, 1945.
Sherwin, Martin. *A World Destroyed: The Atomic Bomb and the Grand Alliance.*
    New York: Alfred A. Knopf, 1975.
Sherwood, Robert E. *Roosevelt and Hopkins: An Intimate History.* New York:
    Harper, 1948.
Simkins, Francis Butler. *A History of the South.* New York: Alfred A. Knopf,
    1953.
————. *Pitchfork Ben Tillman: South Carolinian.* Baton Rouge: Louisiana State
    Univ. Press, 1944.
Smith, Gene. *When the Cheering Stopped: The Last Years of Woodrow Wilson.*
    New York: William Morrow, 1964.
Smith, Jean Edward. *Lucius D. Clay: An American Life.* New York: Henry Holt,
    1990.
Somers, Herman Miles. *Presidential Agency OWMR: The Office of War Mobili-*
    zation and Reconversion. Cambridge: Harvard Univ. Press, 1950.
South Carolina: The WPA Guide to the Palmetto State. New York: Oxford Univ.
    Press, 1941.
Speer, Albert. *Inside the Third Reich: Memoirs.* New York: Macmillan, 1970.
Sullivan, Mark. *Our Times: The Unites States, 1900–1925.* Vol. 6. New York:
    Charles Scribner's Sons, 1937.
Swain, Martha H. *Pat Harrison: The New Deal Years.* Jackson: Univ. Press of
    Mississippi, 1978.
Taylor, Carl C. *The Farmers' Movement, 1620–1920.* New York: American Book
    Co., 1953.
Thomas, Hugh. *Armed Truce: The Beginnings of the Cold War, 1945–46.* New
    York: Atheneum, 1987.
Tillman, Benjamin R. *The Struggles of 1876. How South Carolina Was Delivered*
    from Carpet-Bag and Negro Rule. Speech at the Red-Shirt Reunion at An-
    derson. Personal Reminiscences and Incidents by Senator B. R. Tillman.
    N.p, 1909.
Tindall, George Brown. *The Disruption of the Solid South.* Athens: Univ. of Geor-
    gia Press, 1972.
Truman, Harry S. *Memoirs.* Vol. 1, *Year of Decisions.* Garden City, N.Y.: Dou-
    bleday, 1955.
————. *Off the Record: The Private Papers of Harry S. Truman.* Edited by Robert
    H. Ferrell. New York: Harper & Row, 1980.
Tugwell, Rex. *The Brains Trust.* New York: Viking Press, 1968.
The United States at War: Development and Administration of the War Program by
    the Federal Government. New York: Da Capo Press, 1972.
Unites States Civilian Production Administration. *Industrial Mobilization for War:*

History of the War Production Board and Predecessor Agencies, 1940–1945. Washington, D.C.: Government Printing Office, 1947.

Wallace, David Duncan. *History of South Carolina.* Vol. 4. New York: American Historical Society, 1935.

———. *South Carolina: A Short History.* Columbia: Univ. of South Carolina Press, 1961.

Wallace, Henry A. *The Price of Vision: The Diary of Henry A. Wallace, 1942– 1946.* Edited with an introduction by John Morton Blum. Boston: Houghton Mifflin, 1973.

Ward, Patricia Dawson. *The Threat of Peace: James F. Byrnes and the Council of Foreign Ministers, 1945–1946.* Kent, Ohio: Kent State Univ. Press, 1979.

Weart, Spencer R., and Gertrud Weiss Szilard, eds. *Leo Szilard: His Version of the Facts: Selected Recollections and Correspondence.* Cambridge: MIT Press, 1978.

Wheeler-Bennett, John W., and Anthony Nicholls. *The Semblance of Peace: The Political Settlement after the Second World War.* London: Macmillan, 1972.

White, Walter. *A Man Called White: The Autobiography of Walter White.* New York: Viking Press, 1948.

Williams, Harry T. *Romance and Realism in Southern Politics.* Baton Rouge: Louisiana State Univ. Press, 1961.

Woodward, C. Vann. *Origins of the New South, 1877–1913.* Baton Rouge: Louisiana State Univ. Press, 1951.

———. *Reunion and Reaction: The Compromise of 1877 and the End of Reconstruction.* Boston: Little, Brown, 1966.

Yarbrough, Tinsley A. *A Passion for Justice: J. Waties Waring and Civil Rights.* New York: Oxford Univ. Press, 1987.

Yergin, Daniel. *The Prize: The Epic Quest for Oil, Money, and Power.* New York: Simon and Schuster, 1991.

———. *Shattered Peace: The Origins of the Cold War and the National Security State.* Boston: Houghton Mifflin, 1977.

Zeigler, John A. *Progress Picture Story: Santee-Cooper.* Monks Corner: South Carolina Public Service Authority, 1944.

DISSERTATIONS AND ARTICLES

Alsop, Joseph, and Robert Kintner. "Sly and Able: The Real Leader of the Senate, Jimmy Byrnes." *Saturday Evening Post,* 20 July 1940, 18–19.

Bernstein, Barton J. "Roosevelt, Truman, and the Atomic Bomb, 1941–1945: A Reinterpretation." *Political Science Quarterly* 90 (1975): 23–69.

Burnside, Ronald D. "The Governorship of Coleman Livingston Blease of South Carolina." Ph.D. diss., Univ. of Indiana, 1963.

Byrnes, James F. "Preparations for Peace on the Homefront." *Proceedings of the Academy of Political Science* 21 (1944): 121–28.

Cann, Marvin L. "Burnet Rhett Maybank and the New Deal in South Carolina, 1931–1941." Ph.D. diss., Univ. of North Carolina, 1967.

Cosman, Bernard. "Presidential Republicanism in the South, 1960." *Journal of Politics* 24 (1962): 303–22.

Doenecke, Justus D. "Iran's Role in Cold War Revisionism." *Iranian Studies* 5 (1972): 96–111.

———. "Revisionists, Oil and Cold War Diplomacy." *Iranian Studies* 3 (1970): 23–33.

Dunbar, Leslie. "The Changing Mind of the South: The Exposed Nerve." *Journal of Politics* 26 (1964): 3–21.

Flynt, J. Wayne. "The New Deal and Southern Labor." In *The New Deal and the South*, ed. James C. Cobb and Michael V. Namorato. Jackson: Univ. Press of Mississippi, 1984.

Frazier, Jefferson. "The Southerner as American: A Political Biography of James F. Byrnes." B.A. thesis, Harvard College, 1964.

Hall, Jacquelyn Dowd. "Disorderly Women: Gender and Labor Militancy in the Appalachian South." *Journal of American History* 73 (1986): 354–82.

Hayes, Jack Irby. "South Carolina and the New Deal, 1932–1938." Ph.D. diss., Univ. of South Carolina, 1972.

Hess, Gary. "The Iranian Crisis of 1945–46 and the Cold War." *Political Science Quarterly* 89 (1974): 117–46.

Herken, Gregg F. " 'Stubborn, Obstinate, and They Don't Scare': The Russians, the Bomb, and James F. Byrnes." In *James F. Byrnes and the Origins of the Cold War*, ed. Kendrick A. Clements. Durham, N.C.: Carolina Academic Press, 1982.

Hinchey, Mary Hedge. "The Frustration of the New Deal Revival, 1944–46." Ph.D. diss., Univ. of Missouri, 1965.

Hofstadter, Richard. "From Calhoun to the Dixiecrats." *Social Research* 16 (1949): 135–50.

Hollis, Daniel W. " 'Cotton Ed Smith'—Showman or Statesman." *South Carolina Historical Magazine* 71 (1970): 235–56.

Janeway, Eliot. "Jimmy Byrnes." *Life*, 4 Jan. 1943, 62–64.

Leigh, Michael. "Is There a Revisionist Thesis on the Origins of the Cold War?" *Political Science Quarterly* 89 (1974): 101–16.

Link, Arthur S. "The South and the 'New Freedom': An Interpretation." *American Scholar* 20 (1951): 314–24.

McGill, Ralph. "What Is Jimmy Byrnes Up to Now?" *Saturday Evening Post*, 14 Oct. 1950, 32–33.

Messer, Robert L. "The Making of a Cold Warrior: James F. Byrnes and American-Soviet Relations, 1945–1946." Ph.D. diss., Univ. of California at Berkeley, 1975.

Mills, Anthony Barry. "Palmetto Politician: The Early Political Career of Olin S. Johnson, 1896–1945." Ph.D. diss., Univ. of North Carolina, 1976.

Mixon, Kenneth. "The Senatorial Career of Coleman Livingston Blease, 1925–31." M.A. thesis, Univ. of South Carolina, 1970.

Moore, Winfred B. "New South Statesman: The Political Career of James Francis Byrnes, 1911–1941." Ph.D. diss., Duke Univ., 1976.

———. "James F. Byrnes: The Road to Politics, 1882–1910," *South Carolina Historical Magazine* 84 (1983): 72–88.

Nicolson, Harold. "Peacemaking at Paris: Success, Failure or Farce?" *Foreign Affairs* 25 (1947): 190–203.

Partin, John William. " 'Assistant President' for the Home Front: James F. Byrnes and World War II." Ph.D. diss., Univ. of Florida, 1977.

———. "Roosevelt, Byrnes, and the 1944 Vice-Presidential Nomination," *Historian* 42 (1979): 85–100.

Paterson, Thomas G. "Potsdam, the Atomic Bomb, and the Cold War: A Discussion with James F. Byrnes." *Pacific Historical Review* 41 (1972): 225–30.

Rossow, Robert, Jr. "The Battle of Azerbaijan, 1946." *Middle East Journal* 10 (1956): 17–32.

Shannon, J. B. "Presidential Politics in the South." *Journal of Politics* 10 (1948): 466–89.

———. "Presidential Politics in the South, 1938." *Journal of Politics* 1 (1939): 146–70, 278–300.

Theoharis, Athan. "James F. Byrnes: Unwitting Yalta Myth-maker." *Political Science Quarterly* 81 (1966): 581–92.

Ward, Patricia Dawson. "James F. Byrnes and the Council of Foreign Ministers, 1945–1946." Ph.D. diss., Univ. of Texas at Austin, 1975.

Ward, William Augustus. "A Retrospective Economic Analysis of the Santee Cooper Project." M.A. thesis, Clemson Univ., 1967.

INTERVIEWS CONDUCTED BY THE AUTHOR

Alperovitz, Gar. 1990.
Ashmore, Harry. 1993.
Dent, Harry. 1992.
McKeever, Porter. 1991–92.
Navarro, Elizabeth. 1989.
Prioleau, William F. 1990.
Russell, Donald. 1992.

NOTES

ABBREVIATIONS

BMB Bernard M. Baruch Papers, Mudd Library, Princeton University, Princeton, New Jersey
BRT Benjamin R. Tillman Papers, Cooper Memorial Library, Clemson University, Clemson, South Carolina
CR *Congressional Record*
DAB *Dictionary of American Biography*
FDR Franklin D. Roosevelt Papers, Franklin D. Roosevelt Library, Hyde Park, New York
FRUS U.S. Department of State, *Foreign Relations of the United States* (cited by year, volume, and page)
HST Harry S. Truman Papers, Harry S. Truman Library, Independence, Missouri
JFB James F. Byrnes Papers, Cooper Memorial Library, Clemson University, Clemson, South Carolina
RMN Richard M. Nixon Papers, Richard M. Nixon Library, Yorba Linda, California

INTRODUCTION

"Bourbon Horatio Alger" was the trenchant characterization of James F. Byrnes by Jefferson Frazier, a Harvard undergraduate who traveled to South Carolina in the early 1960s to interview Byrnes for his senior honors thesis. Frazier's thesis, "The Southerner as American: A Political Biography of James F. Byrnes," completed on 27 March 1964, but regrettably still unpublished, is the best monograph on Byrnes' political career. Frazier was perhaps simply fortunate in his success by arriving to interview Byrnes and his political confidants while most of that generation of southern politicians had retired from office but were still in good health and eager for a youthful audience; but Frazier made clear his intentions by dedicating his thesis to Judge J. Waties Waring of Charleston, the former political associate of Byrnes who had split with him over the issue of Byrnes' resistance to public school integration. As a consequence, Frazier viewed Byrnes with an objectivity frequently absent from Winfred B. Moore, Jr., "New South Statesman: The Political Career of James Francis Byrnes, 1911–1941" (Ph.D. diss., Duke Univ., 1976).

Byrnes exemplified his nineteenth-century generation's belief in the Horatio Alger myth by his presuming that the U.S. presidency itself lay well within the realm of his possible achievements. The final frustration of that presidential ambition in 1944, as narrated in the introduction, is described more extensively in chapter 13, on the Democratic National Convention of 1944. Notice should be given here, however, of a valuable primary source, *Roosevelt and Hopkins: An Intimate History* (New York: Harper, 1948), by Robert Sherwood, who documented many of Byrnes' administrative and political activities with a not unsympathetic eye.

1 *"When I grow too old"* to *"devil of a way to spend"*: James F. Byrnes, *All in One Lifetime* (New York: Harper, 1958), 180–82.
3 *"Coal will be mined"*: *NYT*, 3 May 1943, p. 4, cols. 2–5.
4 *cheerfully inaccurate alchemist*: Sherwood, *Roosevelt*, 115, 214.
4 *"Red, Red Robin"*: Byrnes, *Lifetime*, 181.
4 *"That's a nice one"*: JFB, Folder 74(2), Walter Brown's Diary, 12 July 1944.
5 *told by Roosevelt to be "in charge"*: JFB, FDR File, Roosevelt to Byrnes, 11 Nov. 1943.
5 *"called 'The Assistant President' "*: JFB, Folder 637(1), Roosevelt to Byrnes, 10 June 1944.
6 *"Keep the hell out of my business"*: Sherwood, *Roosevelt*, 634.
7 *more than seven hundred delegates*: Byrnes, *Lifetime*, 227.
8 *"You are the best qualified"* to *"If you stay in"*: JFB, Folder 74(1).
8 *Roosevelt now wanted . . . William O. Douglas*: JFB, Folder 43(2).
9 *"Jimmy, that is all wrong"* to *"Jimmy, you're close to me personally"*: JFB, Folder 74(1), "Transcribed note of JFB-FDR telephone conversation [14] July 1944."
11 *"It's a shame some people"*: Quoted in William H. Harrett, *Off the Record with F.D.R.* (New Brunswick: Rutgers Univ. Press, 1958), 329.

1: CAN ANYTHING GOOD COME OUT
OF CHARLESTON?

Byrnes as a political son of Bourbon conservatism in many ways defeated his own presidential ambitions. The best study of both the ideological strengths and the weaknesses of the Bourbon political society in which Byrnes grew to adulthood is William Cooper's *The Conservative Regime: South Carolina, 1877–1890* (Baltimore: Johns Hopkins Press, 1968). During these years of the Bourbon ascendancy, southern state governments and academies produced numerous commercial yearbooks and histories of their states. They are now of little value, except as evidence that the positive accomplishments of Reconstruction, the political unrest of black southerners, and the earliest attempts at unionizing the white southern work force were largely invisible to these Bourbon authors. Hence, the primary sources for the public events and circumstances of Byrnes' childhood in Charleston are taken largely from the Tenth Census of the United States, nonregional newspapers, and the *History of the United States of America during the First Administration of Thomas Jefferson* (New York: Charles Scribner's Sons, 1891), by Henry Adams, an author whom no one in New England or the South has ever accused of an excess of emotion.

Only in 1989 was a comprehensive history of the city of Charleston published with proportionate allotments to discussions of the influences in that city of economic, racial, and social groups other than the Bourbon first families. The first images of Jimmy Byrnes' natal city too frequently are limited to the popular romanticism of figures such as the blockade-running Rhett Butler or, when considering life among the lowly, the quaintness of a Porgy and Bess. The result is such teleological descriptions of Byrnes' life as are found on occasion in Winfred Moore's dissertation, when the young Jimmy Byrnes, a native of the city, is said to have "visited the many historical sites in Charleston." (To a child, all sites are historical, and boring, whether in nineteenth-century Charleston or in the representatively urban housing developments now surrounding the historic district of the city.) It must be remembered that Jimmy Byrnes' Charleston had also been the city of the slave insurrectionist Denmark Vesey and of the Beth Elohim Synagogue, built in 1749, and that by the late nineteenth century it contained a ward composed of economically pinched but politically canny and proudly Catholic Irish immigrants. Walter J. Fraser's well-researched book *Charleston! Charleston! The History of a Southern City* (Columbia: Univ. of South Carolina Press, 1989) helps dispel that fallacy of Charleston defined only by the Old South.

A final excellent primary source on Byrnes' early and middle career is Joseph Alsop and Robert Kintner's article "Sly and Able," in the *Saturday Evening Post* of 20 July 1940, from which this biography partly takes its title. Their article in equal parts irritated and pleased Jimmy Byrnes and his sister, Leonore Fuller, and no more can be asked of the biographer's art.

16 *"not conclude that I have gone crazy"*: JFB, Personal 1930, Byrnes to Claus Busch, 10 April 1930.

17 *house on Calhoun Street mortgage free*: JFB, Folder 1210(1), Leonore Fuller to Walter Brown, 10 April 1940; and JFB, Folders 1275, 1029, and 877(1).

17 *"industrial progress of South Carolina"*: Quoted in Cooper, *Regime*, 117.

18 *"Can anything good"*: Quoted in Marvin Cann, "Burnet Rhett Maybank and the New Deal in South Carolina, 1931–1941" (Ph.D. diss., Univ. of North Carolina, 1967), 1.

18 *"The small society of rice"*: Adams, *History*, 149.

20 *small cities along the route*: Fraser, *Charleston*, 327.
20 *Charleston grew hardly at all*: Census Office, *Statistics of the Population of the United States at the Tenth Census (June 1, 1880)* (Washington, D.C., 1883), table 14, pp. 526–27; table 8, p. 442; table 12, p. xxix.
20 *these Charleston-based Democrats*: Cooper, *Regime*, 17.
21 *attic of the Charleston Orphan House:* Fraser, *Charleston*, 236–37.
21 *"Messrs. Morris, Brown & Company"*: JFB, Folder 476(1), Cassandra Connor to Frank Gervais, 13 Dec. 1946.
21 *"impelled by the ambition"*: Byrnes, *Lifetime*, 13.
22 *"died rather than enter"* to *gentle boy who was his mother's favorite*: Alsop and Kintner, "Sly," 42.
23 *began with a slight deception*: Winfred B. Moore, "James F. Byrnes: The Road to Politics, 1882–1910," *South Carolina Historical Magazine* 84 (1983): 76.
24 *"always 'tomorrow' that counted"*: JFB, Folder 1210(1), Leonore Fuller to Walter Brown, 10 April 1940.
24 *"rude, ignorant, and in some"*: Adams, *History*, 153.
24 *shot and killed his predecessor* to *"damnedest, gamecockingest"*: Alsop and Kintner, "Sly," 42.
24–25 *going home for lunch* to *"I was vain enough to think"*: Byrnes, *Lifetime*, 17.
27 *"He Is a Self Made Man"*: JFB, Scrapbooks.
28 *Byrnes formally converted*: Byrnes, *Lifetime*, 16.
28 *moved over the entire theological landscape*: Robert L. Messer, "The Making of a Cold Warrior: James F. Byrnes and American-Soviet Relations, 1945–1946" (Ph.D. diss., Univ. of California at Berkeley, 1975), 455.
30 *"Progressivism had more of a middle-class"*: T. Harry Williams, *Romance and Realism in Southern Politics* (Baton Rouge: Louisiana State Univ. Press, 1966), 58.
31 *source of this Democratic strength*: Cooper, *Regime*, 34–39, 195–200.
32 *Byrnes and Garris had shared a carriage* to *"Has Anyone Here Seen Kelly"*: Byrnes, *Lifetime*, 20–21.
33 *remained a memory of the neoclassical*: Author's visit to the former post office building at Aiken, S.C., 1986.
33 *"had indeed been good to me"*: Byrnes, *Lifetime*, 21.

2: PITCHFORK BEN TILLMAN

For the generation of southern white men who participated in or witnessed the overthrowing of Reconstructionist state governments, the events of 1876–77 assumed the proportions of a melodrama they carried well into the twentieth century. Later novels, such as Thomas Dixon's *The Clansman* (1905), subsequently adapted by D. W. Griffith for his motion picture *The Birth of a Nation*, added layers of images to the popular image of a virtuous South oppressed by carpetbaggers and duplicitous Negroes. Jimmy Byrnes moved among men who believed in this melodrama; they included not only his first major patron, U.S. Senator Tillman, but also Woodrow Wilson, who commented after viewing a private showing at the White House of *The Birth of a Nation*, "It is like writing history with lightning. And my only regret is that it is all too true."

This book is a biography, not a history, and the correction of that specious historical melodrama of Reconstruction by such recent scholars as Eric Foner is noted here but not discussed in the text; instead, preference is given to such primary documents as Benjamin Tillman's *The Struggles of 1876* in an attempt to present how those participants themselves perceived their actions, and how they explained them to a subsequent generation of white southerners, including Byrnes. As a consequence no black historical voices are to be heard in this chapter; they were "howled down," both physically and politically, by Tillman's political machine.

Among the generation of southerners born after Reconstruction, the historian Francis Butler Simkins, himself a native of Edgefield County, endures as the preeminent biographer of Tillman. Although Simkins has been faulted by later, more quantitative historians, who emphasize landholdings among the agrarians rather than the force of Tillman's personality, Simkins is substantially correct on most points regarding Tillman's career.

Edgefield County, part of Congressman Byrnes' district, is the South even more so, and has attracted over the past two centuries such diverse historians and political writers as Parson Mason Weems, the "cherry tree" biographer of George Washington, and Samuel Lubell, a researcher and writer for both Byrnes and Bernard Baruch. The reader interested in the continuing drama—not melodrama—involving the black and white families living there is encouraged to read Orville Burton's neglected but compellingly written study *In My Father's House Are Many Mansions: Family and Community in Edgefield, South Carolina* (Chapel Hill: Univ. of North Carolina Press, 1985).

Outward signs of the town of Hamburg, S.C., site of Ben Tillman's political killings, effectively disappeared in the decades after a WPA writer in the late 1930s revisited the massacre scene. The town does not appear on modern state maps, and no historical markers are there for either the white or the black men killed in 1876. The area has largely become a bedroom community for Augusta, Ga., located immediately across the Savannah River. This later southern city is historically prominent for its celebrated golf tournament, the Masters.

34 *probably wouldn't hurt it: CR*, 62d Cong., 2d sess., 1911, 2596. See also Byrnes, *Lifetime*, 30.
35 *"daughters of the congressional family"*: "Congress Hall Reminiscences Called Forth," *Christian Science Monitor*, 5 Dec. 1929. I am indebted to the Martin Luther King Memorial Library, District of Columbia, for providing this source.
36 *"enlivening the passing moments"*: "Painless Statesman," *Collier's*, 25 March 1933, 13.
37 *"because they were obligated": George S. Legaré Memorial Addresses* (Washington, D.C.: Joint Committee on Printing, 1914), 77.
38 *"hear about that Pujo business"* to *"such a nice little fellow"*: Alsop and Kintner, "Sly," 44–45.
39 *"the work was done by slaves"*: BRT, Tillman to Byrnes, 15 Nov. 1913.
40 *"nothing has to be explained to me"*: Quoted in Arthur S. Link, *Wilson*, vol. 1, *The Road to the White House* (Princeton: Princeton Univ. Press, 1947), 3.
40 *another young couple sympathetic*: Moore, "Statesman," 25.
41 *"as with hooks of steel"*: John A. Chapman, *History of Edgefield County* (Newberry, S.C.: E. H. Aull, 1897), 20.
41 *"I came to love him"*: BRT, *Benjamin Ryan Tillman Memorial Addresses* (Washington, D.C.: Joint Committee on Printing, 1919), 18.
42 *"breezy visits to the hotel"*: JFB, Folder 1210, Tillman to Byrnes.
42 *thank God for his peculiarities*: BRT, Scrapbook 2, 1883–93.
42 *"sub-tone of appealing melody"*: William Watts Ball, *The State That Forgot:*

South Carolina's Surrender to Democracy (Indianapolis: Bobbs-Merrill, 1932), 226–27.

43 *farmer's poetry of particular*: BRT, handwritten note on stationery of U.S. Senate Committee on Naval Affairs, 22 March 1915.

43 *isolated as "affection and sympathy"*: *Tillman Memorial Addresses*, 18.

44 *"desperate strain" among the male Tillmans*: David Duncan Wallace, *South Carolina: A Short History* (Columbia: Univ. of South Carolina Press, 1961), 615.

45–46 *fruits of her labor* to *"Confederate money was plentiful"*: BRT, "My Childhood Days," undated MS. See also Rev. R. M. Shannanhouse, "Sen. Benjamin R. Tillman's Early Life," Columbia *State*, 14 July 1918.

47 *turkey, fruitcakes, and pig's feet*: BRT, Tillman to Mrs. Smeltz, 13 Jan. 1913; Tillman to Dr. Babcock, 15 Jan. 1914; Tillman to Mrs. Moore, 27 July 1914.

48 *armed intimidation of the black majority*: For a patently "Redemptionist" interpretation of these political murders and the forcible end of Reconstruction, see David Duncan Wallace, *History of South Carolina*, vol. 4 (New York: American Historical Society, 1935), 303–21. For a more balanced narration, see Cooper, *Regime*, 86–92.

49–50 *"provoke a row"* to *he was very hungry*: Benjamin Tillman, *The Struggles of 1876: How South Carolina Was Delivered from Carpet-bag and Negro Rule. Speech at the Red-shirt Reunion at Anderson. Personal Reminiscences and Incidents by Senator B. R. Tillman* (n.p., 1909), 14–26.

51 *negotiations held at Washington*: The definitive account is C. Vann Woodward, *Reunion and Reaction: The Compromise of 1877 and the End of Reconstruction* (Boston: Little, Brown, 1966).

52 *"killed every obnoxious radical in court"*: Tillman, *Struggles*, 38.

54 *populism was spread throughout the South*: Fred A. Shannon, *The Farmer's Last Frontier: Agriculture, 1860–1897* (New York: Farrar & Rinehart, 1945), 76–95. See also Carl C. Taylor, *The Farmers' Movement, 1620–1920* (New York: American Book Co., 1953), 280–86.

54 *Tillman succeeded in most precincts*: Francis Butler Simkins, *A History of the South* (New York: Alfred A. Knopf, 1953), 295–311. See also Cooper, *Regime*, 153–86.

55 *"homeliest man in the state"*: Byrnes, *Lifetime*, 20.

55 *"I'm simply a clop-hopper"*: Quoted in Simkins, *Pitchfork*, 354.

56 *"Why didn't your dog"*: BRT, "Address Delivered by Senator James F. Byrnes on May 1, 1940, at the Unveiling of a Monument to the Late Benjamin R. Tillman," 32.

56 *"expectorate upon the floor"* to *"doesn't rise and set in Charleston"*: Quoted in Simkins, *Pitchfork*, 129–31.

57 *no post-Reconstruction governor*: See C. Vann Woodward, *The Strange Career of Jim Crow* (New York: Oxford Univ. Press, 1961), 34–45.

59 *"crude and ignorant minds"*: Quoted in Link, *Road*, 25.

60–62 *"would not think of endorsing"* to *"the official bottle opener"*: JFB, Folder 1210, Byrnes-Tillman correspondence, May–Oct. 1913.

63 *"wild asses of the desert"*: *NYT*, 11 March 1913.

64 *"we fulfill another campaign pledge"*: Byrnes, *Lifetime*, 32.

65 *"Make it strong"*: JFB, Folder 1210, Byrnes to B. R. Tillman, Jr., 5 May 1917.

65 *"the old man was sick"*: BRT, Byrnes to constituent, 2 May 1917.

65–66 *"sincerely hope that your arm"* to *"bottom of the sore"*: JFB, Folder 1210, Byrnes-Tillman correspondence, May 1917.

66 *sent articles, anonymously*: Simkins, *Pitchfork*, 540.

67 *"young women to fight my battles"* to *"have not lost my mind"*: BRT, March–May 1918.

67 *urbane and scholarly-looking*: The physical description of Lever and the summary of his career are based on photographs in the Lever Papers, Clemson Univ., and on John C. Garlington, *Men of the Time* (Spartanburg, S.C.: Garlington, 1902), 256.

68 *new type of leader in the South*: For a full discussion of the relation between Wilson and the southern agrarians, see Arthur S. Link, "The South and the 'New Freedom': An Interpretation," *American Scholar* 20 (1951): 314.

68–69 *"following his ambitions blindly"* to *"Byrnes is writing this"*: BRT, Tillman to constituents, April 1918.

69 *"I have assurances from Burleson"*: BRT, Tillman to President W. M. Riggs of Clemson College, 9 May 1918.

69 *"wondering what it was about"*: Byrnes, *Lifetime*, 41. Byrnes in this memoir recalls the appointment as occurring in June 1918, but the Wilson papers record no meeting between Wilson and Byrnes that month. The White House Appointment Books, 1915–24, Woodrow Wilson Papers (Library of Congress microfilm) record a May appointment with Byrnes, ser. 1, reel 3. Byrnes' version of the meeting and the direct quotation by Wilson are from Byrnes, *Lifetime*, 41–42. The physical description of Wilson is from Arthur S. Link, *Wilson*, vol. 2, *The New Freedom* (Princeton: Princeton Univ. Press, 1956).

71 *"thank God for Woodrow Wilson"*: Quoted in Simkins, *Pitchfork*, 541.

71 *"My Dear Mr. Lever"*: BRT, Scrapbooks 37, 38.

72 *"My dear Mr. Byrnes"*: Woodrow Wilson Papers (Library of Congress microfilm), ser. 3, reel 156.

74 *gravesite today is marked*: Author's visit to Tillman farm, Edgefield County, S.C., 1986.

74 *"something else in mind"*: Byrnes, *Lifetime*, 44.

3: DEAR MR. BARUCH

Bernard M. Baruch before his death made certain that future researchers of his life should not want for materials, having commissioned the writing of two autobiographies and a biography and bequeathing his public and private papers to Princeton University. The latter papers are cited below as *BMB*. Baruch's two nominal autobiographies, *My Own Story* (New York: Holt, 1957) and *The Public Years* (New York: Holt, Rinehart and Winston, 1960), must be read with an eye cast frequently toward independent corroboration, a caution also warranted in regard to his commissioned biography, *Mr. Baruch* (Boston: Houghton Mifflin, 1957), by Margaret Coit.

More exacting in scholarship is Jordan A. Schwarz's *The Speculator: Bernard M. Baruch in Washington, 1917–1965* (Chapel Hill: Univ. of North Carolina Press, 1981). James Grant's *Bernard M. Baruch: The Adventures of a Wall Street Legend* (New York: Simon and Schuster, 1983) also is a reliable account, particularly for Baruch's early and later years in South Carolina.

Cole Blease has not attracted biographers. (The present author attempted to interview descendants of Blease in South Carolina, but discovered that the hard feelings that Senator Blease's supporters directed toward Jimmy Byrnes and his supporters in the 1924 and 1930 primaries are still very intact.) A commendably evenhanded account of Byrnes' most tenacious political enemy is the unpublished master's thesis completed at the University of South Carolina in 1970 by Kenneth Mixon, "The Senatorial Career of Coleman Livingston Blease, 1925–31."

Although justly deserving her receipt of the Pulitzer Prize for her prior biography of John C. Calhoun, Margaret Coit did not do enduring work when retained by Baruch to write his biography. Nevertheless, although totally dependent for a time upon Baruch's good will and her salary from him, and having completed her literary task under extraordinary financial and personal hardships, Ms. Coit later generously acknowledged the greater scholarship of Jordan Schwarz and gave openly to him the benefits of her research. Professor Schwarz noted his debts to Ms. Coit in the preface and particularly the last chapter of his book.

76 *"had more sense in a minute"*: Byrnes, *Lifetime*, 14. See also JFB, uncataloged Byrnes-Fuller genealogical chart.
77 *"Mother isn't much better"*: JFB, Personal 1930, Leonore Fuller to Byrnes, undated.
78 *Roosevelt had been less than grateful*: Ted Morgan, *FDR: A Biography* (New York: Simon and Schuster, 1985), 216–17.
79 *"dining tables of London"* to *it had been a good war*: Moore, "Statesman," 48, 60.
80 *Wilson traveled over eight thousand miles*: Gene Smith, *When the Cheering Stopped: The Last Years of Woodrow Wilson* (New York: William Morrow, 1964), 60.
80 *"Some men may have forgotten"*: JFB, Folder 1210(1), news clipping.
81 *repellent to many Wilsonian progressives*: Jonathan Daniels, *The Time between the Wars: Armistice to Pearl Harbor* (Garden City, N.Y.: Doubleday, 1966), 81. See also William E. Leuchtenburg, *The Perils of Prosperity, 1914–32* (Chicago: Univ. of Chicago Press, 1958), 66, 77–79.
83 *"I guess I better not try it"*: Quoted in Smith, *Cheering*, 186.
84 *"Onward, Christian Soldiers"*: Byrnes, *Lifetime*, 47–48.
84–85 *"little Jimmy Byrnes"* to *Battling Byrnes*: JFB, Scrapbooks, 1921–22.
85 *"Real Dusky Hue"*: JFB, Folder 22, news clipping.
85 *most violent racial riots*: Mark Sullivan, *Our Times: The United States, 1900 –1925*, vol. 6 (New York: Charles Scribner's Sons, 1937), 178.
86 *they could go elsewhere*: Quoted in Moore, "Statesman," 52–53.
86 *Byrnes always claimed later*: Byrnes, *Lifetime*, 38–39.
86 *"Unfortunate though it may be"*: Quoted in Moore, "Statesman," 54.
88 *"to steal my mule"*: Quoted in Eliot Janeway, "Jimmy Byrnes," *Life*, 4 Jan. 1943, 66.
88 *"To hell with the Constitution"*: Quoted in "Palmetto's Hero," *Outlook and Independent* 156, no. 2 (10 Sept. 1930): 57.
88 *"Roll up yer sleeves"*: Quoted in O. L. Warr, "Mr. Blease of South Carolina," *American Mercury* 16 (1929): 29.
89 *"felt so good when I came downtown"*: Quoted in Ronald D. Burnside, "The Governorship of Coleman Livingston Blease of South Carolina" (Ph.D. diss., Univ. of Indiana, 1963), 184–86.
89 *"by some obscure rule"*: C. Vann Woodward, *Origins of the New South 1877– 1913* (Baton Rouge: Louisiana State Univ. Press 1951), 392.
89 *"probably was a psychopath"*: Frazier, "Southerner," 21.
89 *number of textile workers*: Mixon, "Blease," 84.
90–91 *"liable to drift down South"* to *treated "justly and rightly"*: Quoted in Frazier, "Southerner," 25, 66.
91 *"give Mr. Byrnes the flowers"*: JFB, Scrapbooks, 1924.

92　*"Trade with Klansmen"*: Daniels, *Time*, 121–22; Leuchtenburg, *Perils*, 209–13; Arnold S. Rice, *The Ku Klux Klan in American Politics* (Washington, D.C.: Public Affairs Press, 1962), 58–61, 74–83. Daniels and Leuchtenburg inaccurately imply that Byrnes approved of the Klan.

92　*turned down the grand kleagle's offer*: JFB, Folder 14, Byrnes to Frank Hogan, 13 Oct. 1937.

93　*"who served on the altar"*: JFB, Folder 18, copy of newspaper endorsement.

94　*a bed sheet hung*: Bruce Littlejohn, *Littlejohn's Political Memoirs (1934–1988)* (Spartanburg, S.C.: Littlejohn, 1989), 123–24.

95　*"can't convict a million dollars"*: Sullivan, *Times*, 346.

96　*"rich man what am scared"*: Byrnes, *Lifetime*, 51.

97　*he hired Cassandra Connor*: JFB, Folder 1190.

98　*"Your election is the only comfort"*: JFB, Folder 25, Byrnes to Roosevelt, 12 Nov. 1928.

99–100　*Big Thursday* to *"urge me to be a candidate"*: Byrnes, *Lifetime*, 54–55.

100　*careful not to overestimate his virtues*: Moore, "Statesman," 85–86.

102　*"What say you, sire"*: Cartoon reproduced in Schwarz, *Speculator*, 446.

103　*"an advisor to persons of wealth"*: Alexander Heard, *The Costs of Democracy* (Chapel Hill: Univ. of North Carolina Press, 1960), 272–77.

103　*"would appreciate your help"*: JFB, Folder 21, Byrnes to Baruch, 8 Oct. 1938.

103　*politics below the Mason-Dixon line*: Louise Overacker, *Money in Elections* (New York: Macmillan, 1932), 246.

103　*Baruch's Old Masters*: Quoted in Chester Morgan, *Redneck Liberal: Theodore G. Bilbo and the New Deal* (Baton Rouge: Louisiana State Univ. Press, 1985), 70–71.

104　*"his old political alter ego"*: Quoted in Matthew Josephson, *Sidney Hillman: Statesman of American Labor* Garden City, N.Y.: Doubleday, 1952), 614.

105　*"every princess and every wealthy man"*: Quoted in Yousuf Karsh, *Faces of Destiny* (Chicago: Ziff-Davis, 1946), 22.

105　*Baruch had become a millionaire*: Grant, *Baruch*, 1–22, 104–6.

107　*"Hebrew Wall Street speculator"*: Quoted in Schwarz, *Speculator*, 58–59.

108　*Daniels' objection was elsewhere*: Josephus Daniels, *The Cabinet Diaries of Josephus Daniels, 1913–21*, ed. E. Cronon (Lincoln: Univ. of Nebraska Press, 1963), 131. According to Daniels' version of the meeting, Wilson had replied, "Did you ever see a Jew who was not?"

109　*"elevated human sentiment"*: JFB, Folder 1037, Baruch to Byrnes, 7 June 1962.

109　*followed that gift with a check*: Grant, *Baruch*, 221, 223.

110　*"pleasures of duck-shooting"*: Baruch, *Public Years*, 209.

110　*"Mr. Baruch became Bernie"*: to *"system of barter and sale"*: Schwarz, *Speculator*, 184, 186.

110　*payable to the election expenses*: Grant, *Baruch*, 232.

111　*two-story, neo-Georgian mansion*: This description is based upon the author's visit to Hobcaw Barony in the summer of 1989, prior to the destruction by Hurricane Hugo at Waccamaw Point.

111　*"effectively bought for himself"*: Schwarz, *Speculator*, 188.

111　*Hobcaw Barony as a commercial club*: BMB, Baruch to Christie Benet, 18 Aug. 1927.

111　*"a big reservation, like Barney Baruch"*: CR, 70th Cong., 1st sess. 1928, 6699.

112　*Brother to Cole*: JFB, Folder 21, and Miscellaneous 1937, "The Baruch Case." During this decade of the 1930s, Byrnes also became a close political associate and personal friend of Solomon Blatt, Sr., a Jewish attorney from Barnwell,

S.C., who eventually became speaker of the South Carolina house. So closely identified were the political interests of these three men that they were referred to by other contemporary South Carolina politicians simply as "the three Bs"—Baruch, Byrnes, and Blatt. For a further reference, see Eli N. Evans, *The Provincials: A Personal History of Jews in the South* (New York: Atheneum, 1974), 146.

113 *"nigger and liquor" campaign*: Mixon, "Blease," 128–31.
115 *"situation is very encouraging"*: JFB, Miscellaneous 1930 and prior, Byrnes to Baruch, 21 July 1930.
116 *"outside money pouring into the state"*: Frazier, "Southerner," 33.
117 *"poor devil with a half bale"*: JFB, Miscellaneous 1930 and prior, "Radio Speech," 8 Sept. 1930.
117 *"God Almighty and his son Jesus Christ"*: Quoted in Frazier, "Southerner," 111.
118 *"only human nature is vile"*: JFB, Personal 1934, Baruch to Byrnes.

4: FIXER FROM THE PALMETTO STATE

Nearly half a century after the death of its founder, the New Deal continues to reinvent and to reintroduce itself into American life and politics. Biographers and other interpreters of this era therefore must, in Franklin Roosevelt's favorite political phrase, "adjust to changing conditions." Foremost among reinterpretive scholars succeeding to the earlier works of Arthur M. Schlesinger, Jr., and Frank Friedel is Jordan A. Schwarz in *The New Dealers: Power Politics in the Age of Roosevelt* (New York: Alfred A. Knopf, 1993). The massive transfer of public wealth into the infrastructure of the southern and southwestern states, Schwarz argues, is the enduring elegancy of the New Deal, rather than the social reforms attempted by Harry Hopkins, Henry Wallace, and others. Although Jimmy Byrnes is not discussed in this book, the senator's championing of federal funds for his region and his sponsorship of the Santee-Cooper project for his state are case studies for Schwarz's thesis.

Winfred Moore's previously cited dissertation, "New South Statesman," does not discuss New Deal macroeconomics, the General Textile Strike of 1934, or the Santee-Cooper project, but it is a workmanlike, scholarly, sound chronicle of Byrnes' voting record and speeches throughout the 1930s.

121 *"with us B.C."*: Quoted in Jim Bishop, *FDR's Last Year: April 1944–April 1945* (New York: William Morrow, 1974), 85.
122 *"delighted to have you both"*: JFB, Folder 25, Roosevelt to Byrnes, 14 Jan. 1932.
122 *he had first checked*: JFB, Byrnes Miscellaneous, telegram, James M. Baker to Byrnes, 19 Jan. 1932.
123 *two-thirds of the delegates*: For a succinct history of the two-thirds rule, see *Washington Post*, 22 June 1936, p. 2, col. 5.
124 *Byrnes was well positioned*: Rex Tugwell, *The Brains Trust* (New York: Viking Press, 1968), 196–97.
124 *armed with automatic shotguns*: NYT, 1 Dec. 1931, p. 1, col. 7.
125 *"When do we eat"*: *Time*, 16 Jan. 1933, 11.
126 *Harrison hosted a dinner*: Martha H. Swain, *Pat Harrison: The New Deal Years* (Jackson: Univ. Press of Mississippi, 1978), 249.
126 *"most influential southern member"*: George E. Mowry, *Another Look at the*

Twentieth-Century South (Baton Rouge: Louisiana State Univ. Press, 1973), 55.

126 *Byrnes' accelerated rise*: For an appreciation of the "caste system" during Byrnes' terms in the Senate, see Donald R. Matthews, *U.S. Senators and Their World* (Chapel Hill: Univ. of North Carolina Press, 1960), 148–59.

127 *"con the pants off anyone"* to *"a certain caginess"*: Turner Catledge, *My Life and The Times* (New York: Harper & Row, 1971), 71. For the physical appearance and biography of Harrison, see *DAB*, suppl. 2, p. 560. On his indebtedness to Baruch, see Swain, *Harrison*, 132, 281.

128 *"like the old rooster"*: Quoted in James T. Patterson, *Congressional Conservatism and the New Deal: The Growth of the Conservative Coalition in Congress, 1933–1939* (Lexington: Univ. of Kentucky Press, 1967), 18. For the physical appearance and biography of Glass, see *DAB*, suppl. 4, p. 330.

130 *"cut down his best friend"*: Catledge, *Life*, 72.

132 *dignified IOU*: Marvin L. Cann, "Burnett Rhett Maybank and the New Deal in South Carolina, 1931–1941" (Ph.D. diss., Univ. of North Carolina, 1967), 54.

132 *joining with Hoover's floor leaders*: Jordan A. Schwarz, *The Interregnum of Despair: Hoover, Congress, and the Depression* (Urbana: Univ. of Illinois Press, 1970), 99, 241–43; *CR*, 72d Cong., 1st sess., 1932, 3911–14.

133 *"should not assume responsibility"*: JFB, Folder 25, Byrnes to Robinson, 31 Oct. 1931.

134 *"I wish much"*: Ibid., Roosevelt to Byrnes, 11 March 1932.

134 *"made quite a favorable impression"*: Ibid., Byrnes to Roosevelt, 11 March 1932.

135 *"strong disposition not to instruct"*: Ibid., Byrnes to Roosevelt, 12 June 1932.

136 *"friends and neighbors"*: V. O. Key, Jr., *Southern Politics in State and Nation* (New York: Alfred A. Knopf, 1949), 131–32.

136 *anti-Roosevelt delegates*: Jack Irby Hayes, Jr., "South Carolina and the New Deal, 1932–1938" (Ph.D. diss., Univ. of South Carolina, 1972), 23–24.

137 *"it would be idiotic"*: *NYT*, 27 June 1932, p. 1, col. 1.

139 *an angry apparent majority*: Elliot A. Rosen, *Hoover, Roosevelt, and the Brains Trust: From Depression to New Deal* (New York: Columbia Univ. Press, 1977), 256–57.

139 *Pat Harrison was asleep*: There are as many versions in contemporaneous memoirs of Byrnes's frantic taxicab ride, and Harrison's semiconsciousness, as of Paul Revere's ride. The most reliable summary is in Swain, *Harrison*, 28–29.

140 *Baruch's suite at Chicago's Blackstone*: Rosen, *Hoover*, 246–54.

141 *"tall, lean figure"*: Tugwell, *Trust*, 273.

141 *"the Roosevelt political family"*: JFB, Folder 25, Byrnes to Roosevelt, 12 July 1932.

141 *"delegated to us by Baruch"* to *"the most generous angel"*: Tugwell, *Trust*, 455–57.

142 *"I gave two hundred thousand"* to *Byrnes' "sharp mentality"*: Raymond Moley, *The First New Deal* (New York: Harcourt, Brace & World, 1966), 388, 366.

142 *"pudgy, overdressed loudmouth"* to *elders were former New Freedom*: Tugwell, *Trust*, 309, 231.

143 *staying in a spare bedroom*: Raymond Moley, *After Seven Years* (New York: Harper, 1939), 61.

143 *"You're the one who's cheap"* to *"get the hell out"*: Quoted in Frank Freidel,

Franklin D. Roosevelt, vol. 4, *Launching the New Deal* (Boston: Little, Brown, 1973), 76.

144 *"Look Homeward, Angel"*: Moley, *Seven Years*, 61.

145 *"economic champion in Congress"*: Quoted in Frazier, "Southerner," 45.

146 *Bourbon Horatio Alger*: Quoted in Messer, "Making," introd.

146 *"I owe $12,000 to banks"*: JFB, Byrnes Personal, Byrnes to T. H. Gooding, 10 March 1933.

147 *drafting major New Deal legislation*: JFB, Folder 25, Byrnes to Roosevelt, 28 Dec. 1932; Roosevelt to Byrnes, 6 Nov. and 19 Oct. 1933.

148 *"carries on a whispered conversation"*: JFB, Byrnes Scrapbook 1934, *Today*, 17 Jan. 1934, unnumbered.

148 *"I don't want to talk to him"*: Quoted in Frazier, "Southerner," 45.

149 *"This was a new way"*: Quoted in Katie Louchheim, *The Making of the New Deal: The Insiders Speak*, (Cambridge: Harvard Univ. Press, 1983), 200–201.

149 *up the patronage tree*: JFB, Miscellaneous 1933–34, Byrnes to W. D. Workman, 22 Dec. 1934; Byrnes to Winchester Smith, 28 May 1934.

149 *"constant messenger from the White House"*: Tom Connally, *My Name Is Tom Connally* (New York: Crowell, 1954), 188.

151 *writing the administration's economy legislation*: James E. Sargent, "Roosevelt's Economy Act: Fiscal Conservatism and the Early New Deal," *Congressional Studies* 7, no. 2 (Winter 1980): 37–40, 43, 47, 51; Robert R. Browder and Thomas G. Smith, *Independent: A Biography of Lewis W. Douglas* (New York: Alfred A. Knopf, 1986), 80–82.

152 *"wild men" in the Senate*: Byrnes, *Lifetime*, 76–79.

153 *"I'm a Democrat like you"*: Quoted in Patterson, *Conservatism*, 74.

153 *sweating over a hot wood stove*: Interview with Dorothea Jackson, South Carolina journalist.

154 *"being scandalously wasted"*: JFB, Miscellaneous 1935 and prior, Wade Stackhouse to Byrnes, 20 Feb. 1933.

154 *"ardent advocate of states' rights"*: JFB, Scrapbook, *Textile Bulletin*, 1933, undated.

155 *"When the emergency passes"*: Byrnes' speech is printed in *CR*, 73d Cong. 2d sess., 1934, 67–70.

5: THE GENERAL TEXTILE STRIKE OF 1934

The story of the General Textile Strike of 1934 was largely untold for nearly thirty years, until the completion, in 1963, of James Hodges' dissertation at Vanderbilt University, "The New Deal Labor Policy and the Southern Cotton Textile Industry, 1933–1941." Hodges found space in one chapter of this academic work for the voices that had been preserved by newspapers or collected correspondence of various participants in the great strike of 1934. Although, in Hodges' own words, his finished dissertation "lay abandoned" by him for many years, primarily because he "discovered the miserable failure of the cotton textile unionists," his subsequent determination that the story of the textile unionists not be forgotten changed his resolve not to publish his dissertation. His revised research appeared under the original title: *The New Deal Labor Policy and the Southern Cotton Textile Industry, 1933–1941* (Knoxville: Univ. of Tennessee Press, 1986). All references below are to this published version.

Of earlier works, only Herbert J. Lahne's *The Cotton Mill Worker* (New York: Farrar & Rinehart, 1944) discussed the textile strike of 1934 in any detail. Later scholarly works that are tangentially or directly useful include Bernard Bellush, *The Failure of the NRA* (New York: W. W. Norton, 1975), F. Ray Marshall, *Labor in the South* (Cambridge: Harvard Univ. Press, 1967), David L. Carlton, *Mill and Town in South Carolina, 1880–1920* (Baton Rouge: Louisiana State Univ. Press, 1982), Irving Bernstein, *Turbulent Years: A History of the American Worker, 1933–1941* (Boston: Houghton Mifflin, 1970), and Jacquelyn Dowd Hall et al., *Like a Family: The Making of a Southern Cotton Mill Worker* (Chapel Hill: Univ. of North Carolina Press, 1987), which contains a collection of interviews.

Given the limits of the above research, sources published at the time of the 1934 textile strike therefore remain the most authoritative accounts. Two books researched during the 1930s but published in the early 1940s must be considered of near-contemporaneous value and essential to understanding the events of that decade. Liston Pope, *Millhands and Preachers: A Study of Gastonia* (New York: Oxford Univ. Press, 1942), and *South Carolina: The WPA Guide to the Palmetto State* (New York: Oxford Univ. Press, 1941) provide invaluable primary information.

Jonathan Daniels wrote of his participation in the 1934 strike in *A Southerner Discovers the South* (New York: Macmillan, 1938). Six years before the 1934 general strike, the remarkable scholar Lois MacDonald traveled from Columbia University to the industrialized Appalachian cotton mill villages and collected information not only relevant to the textile strikes of the 1920s but also anticipatory of the events of general strike of 1934, in her *Southern Mill Hills: A Study of Social and Economic Forces in Certain Textile Mill Villages* (New York: A. L. Hillman, 1928).

Also essential to understanding the general strike of 1934 is a survey of local and national newspapers published throughout the mid-1930s, of the partisan magazines of the 1930s, and of subsequent academic journals. Specifically cited below, these sources include a survey throughout the year 1934 of the *New York Times*, the *Washington Post*, the Washington *Star*, the *Nation*, the *Textile Bulletin*, the *Charlotte (N.C.) Observer*, and the Columbia (S.C.) *State* newspaper. Both the *State* newspaper and the Associated Press were remarkably nonpartisan in their coverage of the strike events of 1934, unlike many southern newspapers, such as the *Charlotte Observer*, which took an unfailing and predictable probusiness stance. Particularly commendable and reliable is the reporting of Ashley Halsey of the Associated Press, who in 1934 at considerable personal risk covered such events as the murders at Chiquola Mill and other strike sites.

157 *employed more American workers*: Bellush, *Failure*, 41. An example of the slighting attention that historians previously gave to the great strike of 1934 is the one-paragraph summation of it found in Arthur M. Schlesinger, Jr., *The Age of Roosevelt*, vol. 2, *The Coming of the New Deal* (Boston: Little, Brown, 1959), 294. The great strike received a more proportionate attention in 1994 in the nationally broadcast PBS documentary prepared by Professor George Stoney of New York University's Tisch School of the Arts, entitled "The Uprising of '34."

158 *Five "faithful employees"*: Pope, *Millhands*, 293–94.

159 *National Textile Workers Union*: Lahne, *Worker*, 216–17.

159 *like fires seen at night*: For a discussion of the significance of women workers as participants and organizers in the Appalachian textile strikes of the 1920s, see Jacquelyn Dowd Hall, "Disorderly Women: Gender and Labor Militancy in the Appalachian South," *Journal of American History* 73 (1986): 354–82. For a contemporary discussion of this nontraditional aggressiveness by women textile workers, see MacDonald, *Mill Hills*, 34.

159 *"a place to acquire melancholia"*: Quoted in Bernstein, *Years*, 299.

159 *a girl's school frock*: Advertisement, Columbia *State*, 26 Aug. 1934, 5–6.

159 *Baruch's worst nightmares*: See the economic analysis of the cotton textile industry, in the description of the cause of the Loray strike, in Pope, *Millhands*, 220–21.

160 *fractional profit margin: FDR*, OF 407b, "Winant Report." See also Hall et al., *Family*, 195–96.

160 *high-speed Draper looms*: Hodges, *Labor Policy*, 14. See also *JFB*, Miscellaneous, Minnie King to Byrnes, 25 March 1935.

160 *"the stretch-out"*: Lahne, *Worker*, 154. See also J. W., "The Textile Strike," *Nation*, 5 Sept. 1934, 273.

160 *"constant cry"*: Quoted in Hodges, *Labor Policy*, 65. See also Bernstein, *Years*, 299–300.

161 *"How many men are carrying"*: Pope, *Millhands*, 234.

161 *women workers also were humiliated*: Ibid., 229. For a contemporary reference to the sexual harassment by foremen and second hands of those women working in the mills who were classified as "Other," see J. W., "Textile Strike."

161 *"Second Hand Row"*: Hall et al., *Family*, 51, 96–97.

162 *"Old Man Sargent"*: Quoted in Hayes, *New Deal*, 324.

162 *percentage increase of married women*: Lahne, *Worker*, table 6, p. 290.

162 *the "high lonesome"*: Quoted in Hall et al., *Family*, 124.

162 *"startling red earth"*: "Ella May's Songs," *Nation*, 9 Oct. 1929, 382–83.

164 *famous Section 7(a)*: Leon Keyserling interview, in Louchheim, *Making*, 196–97. See also Bellush, *Failure*, 26, and J. Wayne Flynt, "The New Deal and Southern Labor," in *The New Deal and the South*, ed. James C. Cobb and Michael V. Namorato (Jackson: Univ. Press of Mississippi, 1984), 65.

164 *Byrnes immediately protested*: Byrnes later summarized his public and behind-the-scenes efforts during the 1933 NRA hearings to outlaw the stretch-out to a labor organizer in Union, S.C. *JFB*, Miscellaneous 1932–33, Byrnes to F. L. Dodd, 19 Sept. 1934.

164 *constructed under Johnson's administration*: Hayes, *New Deal*, 326–28. See also Bernstein, *Years*, 300–301, and, for the pro-industry bias of the Bruere Board, Bellush, *Failure*, 44–45.

165 *"You men have done"*: Quoted in Hodges, *Labor Policy*, 53. For a trenchant analysis of the flawed administrative structure of the Bruere Board, see ibid., 62–69, 92.

165 *"just can't help thinking"*: Columbia *State*, 19 July 1934, 1.

165 *series of public hearings*: As a representative example of the conditions imposed by the stretch-out in textile mills and of Byrnes' sincere but laconic compassion for the southern working class, consider the following exchange from the 13 July 1933 transcript of the NRA Official Hearing of the Stretch-Out System between Senator Byrnes and P. W. Cooper, described in the transcript as a mill worker and part-time schoolteacher:

> BYRNES: When you worked in Union [the Union Mill of Union, S.C.] in 1930, how many looms did you operate?
> COOPER: Twenty to twenty-four.
> BYRNES: How many do you operate now?
> COOPER: From 54 to 72.
> BYRNES: What wages do you get for your work now?
> COOPER: Around twelve to fourteen dollars a week.

BYRNES: What did you get back in 1930?
COOPER: Fifteen.
BYRNES: That was when you operated twenty-four looms?
COOPER: Yes, sir.
BYRNES: [*as his final question*] You are going to teach school again?
COOPER: Yes, sir.

JFB, Miscellaneous, 1933–34. For the national attention that the press and radio gave these hearings scheduled by Byrnes at Spartanburg and Greenville, S.C., see Hodges, *Labor Policy*, 64, 67.

165 *Board could take no action*: Bellush, *Failure*, 44.
166 *reclassified as "learners"*: Hayes, *New Deal*, 343.
166 *UTWA claimed to have three hundred locals*: For estimates of UTWA membership nationwide, see Hodges, *Labor Policy*, 61, and Bellush, *Failure*, 93.
166 For a contemporary analysis of the political significance of the movement to organize the textile industry, see the remarks to a pre–Labor Day rally in Providence, R.I., of Representative Frances Condon, that the efforts of the UTWA were "a fight to vindicate President Roosevelt and Congress for writing 7(a) into the Recovery Act." *NYT*, 4 Sept. 1934, p. 3, col. 1.
167 *Picker Stick Clubs*: Hall et al., *Family*, 337. I am indebted to Mr. Archie Todd, a former supervisor during the 1960s at the Chiquola Mills in Honea Path, S.C., for informing me in conversations from 1991 to 1993 about such textile tools as picker sticks and for explaining to me the hierarchy of skilled labor in the operation of a representative cotton textile mill of the 1930s. These positions were, in rising order of skill and salary, (1) bobbin boy, a beginner, (2) spinner (usually held exclusively by women workers in the 1930s), (3) doffer, and (4) card room operator. (The last job and that of weaving were the most dangerous ones in the mill, as the fabric was "carded" or combed in the 1930s by machinery that frequently had exposed moving belts. ["I sure love it," one textile worker said of his loom to a WPA writer touring South Carolina mills in the 1930s. "This same one has belonged to me for 25 years or more. But I'm scared of it just the same—it'll bite me if I don't watch out." *WPA Palmetto State*, 347–48.])
167 *upstate town of Gaffney*: Hayes, *New Deal*, 344–47, 398–400. See also the description in 1940 of the preference for violent amusement among residents of Gaffney, in the *WPA Palmetto State*, 349. For Gaffney's deserved reputation among labor organizers in the 1930s, see the description of the stoning at Gaffney of the Congregational minister and labor organizer Dr. Witherspoon Dodge, Flynt, "Southern Labor," 84.
167 *catch Hamrick's eye*: Haynes, *New Deal*, 346, 398–400.
168 *"system of espionage"*: JFB, Miscellaneous, 1933–34, John Peel to Brynes, 14 Nov. 1933.
168 *the 3,920 complaints*: Hodges, *Labor Policy*, 92.
168 *"in a general way"*: JFB, Miscellaneous 1933–34, Byrnes to John Peel, 15 Nov. 1933.
169 *a rock and picker stick battle*: Hall et al., *Family*, 336.
169 *UTWA officials agreed to accept*: Lahne, *Worker*, 225.
169 *spoiling for a fight*: Flynt, "Southern Labor," 82–83. See also Bernstein, *Years*, 305–6, and Alexander Kendrick, "Alabama Goes on Strike," *Nation*, 29 Aug. 1934, 233–34. For General Hugh Johnson's opinion of the illegality of the Alabama textile strikes, see *FDR*, OF 407b, Johnson to Marvin McIntyre, 18 Aug. 1934.

170   *"We will tell General Johnson"*: See *NYT*, 15 Aug. 1934, p. 31, col. 1; 16 Aug. 1934, p. 6, col. 2; 26 Aug. 1934, p. 25, col. 4. Particularly ominous was the statement by a UTWA organizer, in North Carolina prior to the deadline to prevent the textile strike, quoted in the *NYT*, 27 Aug. 1934, p. 3, col. 3: "If it takes violence to win, I believe we can produce the goods."

170   *one million workers nationwide: NYT*, 1 Sept. 1934, p. 1, col. 8.

170   *under no circumstance negotiate*: Columbia *State*, 30 Aug. 1934, p. 1, col. 2.

170   *"sealed orders"*: Quoted in Bernstein, *Years*, 308.

171   *"passive resistance"*: Columbia *State*, 3 Sept. 1934, p. 1, col. 3.

171   *Religion was more important*: Pope, *Millhands*, 232.

172   *"We fight for the Lord"*: Columbia *State*, 4 Sept. 1934, p. 11, col. 5. See also the opening prayer by T. Pou Taylor, quoted ibid.

172   *"Thou canst smile upon"*: Columbia *State*, 4 Sept. 1934, p. 1, col. 7.

172   *By midweek*: See the Associated Press estimates, front page, Columbia *State*, 5 Sept. 1934.

172   *"Buddies, why don't you"*: Columbia *State*, 6 Sept. 1934, p. 12, col. 6.

173   *"doors broken open"*: Columbia *State*, 5 Sept. 1934, p. 1, col. 8.

173   *"lines of cars"*: Daniels, *Southerner*, 26.

173   *Sweepers had not been regarded*: Bellush, *Failure*, 43. For a contemporary discussion of the NRA as the "Negro Removal Act," see the quotation found in Flynt, "Southern Labor," 85.

173   *"Dig McClellan up"*: Daniels, *Southerner*, 27.

174   *"Beauty is no advantage"*: Ibid., 26.

174   *"Blows from oak clubs"*: Columbia *State*, 6 Sept. 1934, p. 1, col. 6.

174   *"constables without compensation"*: Hayes, *New Deal*, 356.

174   *The state militia*: See photographs in *NYT*, 2 Sept. 1934, p. 10, cols. 2–4.

175   *"taunting the soldiers"*: Daniels, *Southerner*, 26.

175   *as many as 325,000*: Columbia *State*, 6 Sept. 1934, p. 1, col. 8.

176   *"If you are going to be forced"*: JFB, Miscellaneous 1933–34, Byrnes to Roosevelt, 4 Sept. 1934.

176   *"feed the strike"*: Columbia *State*, 5 Sept. 1934, p. 7, col. 3. See also Bernstein, *Years*, 308.

176   *"I believe that you could"*: JFB, Byrnes Miscellaneous, Minnie King to Byrnes, 25 March 1935.

177   *yet another advisory board: FDR*, OF 407b, draft of Executive Order, 1 Sept. 1934. See also Columbia *State*, 6 Sept. 1934.

177   *Chiquola Mill*: Hall et al., *Family*, 338–40. See also *WPA Palmetto State*, 420.

178   *"Textile War Zone": Washington Post*, 7 Sept. 1934, p. 1, col. 8.

178   *"They died for the rights"*: Columbia *State*, 9 Sept. 1934, p. 1, col. 4.

178   *"I know who fired it"*: Columbia *State*, 10 Sept. 1934, p. 1, col. 4.

178   *reopening for production*: See front page, Columbia *State*, 7 Sept. 1934.

178   *Peel of the UTWA had countermanded*: *State*, 11 Sept. 1934, p. 1, col. 8. The textile strikers having been told by UTWA organizers and sympathizers, "We have a friend in the White House" (*NYT*, 4 Sept. 1934, p. 1, col. 7), many evicted southern textile workers wrote directly to Franklin Roosevelt asking for his personal help in finding new shelter. See as a representative example the telegram by the evicted textile worker Paul Hawkins of Forest City, N.C., to Franklin D. Roosevelt, in *FDR*, OF 407b, Box 8.

179   *"beg that food be given them"*: JFB, Miscellaneous 1933–34, telegram, Byrnes to Hopkins, 7 Sept. 1934. See also telegrams from UTWA locals to Byrnes, 7 through 9 Sept. 1934, ibid., and J. W., "Textile Strike."

179   *Byrnes began mailing checks*: JFB, Miscellaneous 1933–34, Byrnes to E. W. Reynolds, Chairman, Relief Committee, UTWA, 18 Sept. 1934.

179   *"farmers, soda-jerks"*: Columbia *State*, 11 Sept. 1934, p. 1.

179   *violence spread to the New England States*: Columbia *State*, 14 Sept. 1934, p. 1, cols. 2–3.

180   *"barbed-wire concentration camp"*: *NYT*, 20 Sept. 1934, p. 1, col. 1. Professor Hodges is of the opinion that the harshness of the Georgia incarceration was exaggerated and that the *Times* erred in describing the involuntarily detained strikers at Fort McPherson as prisoners of a "concentration camp." See Hodges, *Labor Policy*, 110.

180   *"professional strike-breakers"*: JFB, Folder 1, Byrnes to John Peel, 2 March 1935, in regard to the Bergoff organization of New York City providing armed strikebreakers for rental to southern textile millowners.

180   *Byrnes wrote to U.S. Attorney General*: JFB, Miscellaneous 1933–34, Byrnes to Homer S. Cummings, 13 Sept. 1934.

180   *"a great deal of interest"*: JFB, Miscellaneous 1933–34, Homer Cummings to Brynes, 19 Sept. 1934.

181   *"The board feels that"*: The text of the Winant report is quoted in *NYT*, 21 Sept. 1934, p. 18, col. 5.

181   *"my heart weeps"*: *NYT*, 15 Sept. 1934, p. 2, cols. 2–5. For a summary of conservative and liberal public reactions to General Johnson's speech, including Norman Thomas' declaration that there was now "open warfare between labor leaders and Johnson," see *FDR*, OF 407b, telegram of Stephen Early to Roosevelt, 16 Sept. 1934. Johnson himself sent a telegram to Marvin McIntyre to pass on to the president Johnson's opinion that newspaper accounts of his New York speech were "absurd" and that, given sufficient authority, he (Johnson) could restore public order in Rhode Island "within twenty-four hours." See OF 407b, telegram General Hugh Johnson to Marvin McIntyre, 13 Sept. 1934. (Johnson gave his Carnegie Hall speech the evening of 14 Sept. 1934, but as he had made no other speeches that month in New York State, the telegraphic copy, on being received by Roosevelt's White House staff, apparently was misdated by one day in the official files.)

182   *"one of the greatest in labor history"*: *NYT*, 23 Sept. 1934, p. 1, col. 1.

182   *"nothing to say"*: Ibid., p. 29, col. 1.

182   *"force and hunger"*: *NYT*, 20 Sept. 1934, p. 1, col. 1.

183   *"fine spirit"*: JFB, Miscellaneous 1933–34, Byrnes to Gorman, 4 Oct. 1934.

183   *refusing to rehire strikers*: JFB, Miscellaneous 1933–34, Gorman to Byrnes, 1 Nov. 1934.

183   *"sold out" the UTWA locals*: Hodges, *Labor Policy*, 117–18.

184   *Hillman directed the operation*: *DAB*, suppl. 4, pp. 374–76.

185   *"Christ Is Out"*: Hayes, *New Deal*, 398.

185   *the rival Congress of Industrial Organizations*: For a succinct history of the rise of Sidney Hillman and the use of the Committee for Industrial Organizations (CIO) to subsume the UTWA and to break away from the AFL to form the Congress of Industrial Organizations (CIO), see ibid., 138–50. See also Lahne, *Worker*, 263, and Hayes, *New Deal*, 404.

185   *"the statesman of labor"*: *DAB*, suppl. 4, pp. 374–78. For more on Sidney Hillman's leadership of the "Operation Dixie" to unionize southern textile mills, see the authoritative biography by Steven Fraser, *Labor Will Rule: Sidney Hillman and the Rise of American Labor* (New York: Free Press, 1991), 305–7.

6: THE PHILADELPHIA STORY

The antics of Senator E. D. Smith at the Philadelphia convention of 1936 justly deserve no more bibliographical permanence than the fading clippings of national and regional newspapers, which are the most frequently cited sources below. However, a remarkably skilled historian and social critic emerged from this journalistic turmoil. Harry S. Ashmore learned his writing craft in the 1930s by reporting the activities of Senator Smith for the *Greenville (S.C.) News*. Ashmore, a native South Carolinian with two Confederate grandfathers, very likely drew on his personal experiences in the 1930s with the social malignities of Cotton Ed Smith's political racism; two decades later, he won a Pulitzer Prize for his courageous stand for school integration while editor of the Little Rock, Ark., *Gazette* in 1958. Ashmore's subsequent books, including *Epitaph for Dixie* (New York: W. W. Norton, 1958), *Hearts and Minds: The Anatomy of Racism from Roosevelt to Reagan* (New York: McGraw-Hill, 1982), and *The Man in the Middle* (Columbia: Univ. of Missouri Press, 1966), are essential for understanding the importance from the 1930s to the 1960s of the southern "politics of color."

186   *"You are responsible"*: JFB, uncataloged presidential file, telegram, Byrnes to Roosevelt, 6 Nov. 1934.
187   *only he could persuade Carter Glass*: Moore, "Statesman," 161–63.
187   *"personally objectionable"*: Frazier, "Southerner," 54.
188   *two most dangerous men*: Roosevelt quoted in Frank Freidel, *Franklin D. Roosevelt*, vol. 3, *The Triumph* (Boston: Little, Brown, 1956), 331.
188   *"The Lord has invited us"*: Columbia *State*, 24 March 1935, p. 1, cols. 4–5.
189   *stenographer paid by Byrnes*: JFB, Miscellaneous 1935, Byrnes to B. M. Edwards, 21 March 1935. Edwards, president of South Carolina Bank, which Byrnes had helped save during the Bank Holiday of 1933, received the following request from Byrnes: "Dear Bill, I would appreciate it if you would have a stenographer take Senator Huey Long's speech at Columbia. I will telephone you Saturday evening to get substance of same. Sincerely. . . ."
189   *Byrnes continued his control*: Moore, "Statesman," 175–76.
189   *"my old friend Cole Blease"*: JFB, Miscellaneous 1936, Byrnes to Baruch, 4 June 1936.
190   *"Ellison Durant and he sure do"*: Swain, *Harrison*, 42.
190   *large, walrus-like man*: See the written description of Smith in Patterson, *Conservatism*, 42, and the photograph of him in *Time*, 29 Aug. 1938, 11, as well as the photograph of a perplexed E. D. Smith headlined "Constitutional? Let me think!" on the front page of the *Charleston News and Courier*, 26 Jan. 1938.
191   *"Senator Smith was getting quite old"*: Quoted in Patterson, *Conservatism*, 43.
191   *Cotton Head Smith*: JFB, Folder 14, Robert Allen to Byrnes ("Please *don't* remember me to 'Cotton Head' Smith"), 16 Nov. 1936. For a summary of Smith's antagonism toward Rexford Tugwell, see Daniel W. Hollis, " 'Cotton Ed Smith'—Showman or Statesman," *South Carolina Historical Magazine* 71 (1970): 249.
191   *"purge" Smith from the Democratic party*: Ashmore, *Epitaph*, 99.
192   *"smell the clover"*: NYT, 24 June 1936, p. 1, cols. 3–4.
193   *"Roosevelt in 1936 chose a Negro"*: Harvard Sitkoff, *A New Deal for Blacks* (New York: Oxford Univ. Press, 1978), 93, 351. See also the obituary for the Reverend Shepard, in *NYT*, 22 Feb. 1967, p. 29, col. 3.

194 *"You did right, Ed"*: Ibid., 100–101.
194 Thomas Wolfe, *The Web and the Rock* (Garden City, N.Y.: Sun Dial Press, 1940), 240–41. The author of the present biography, growing up in Alabama in the early 1950s, one generation later than Wolfe's first readers, can personally recall hearing variations of this story in the barbershops and courthouses of his youth.
196 *"Hell, Ed, tell us"*: Ashmore, *Epitaph*, 100.
196 *"Where was Senator Byrnes"*: See press clippings from the state's newspapers found in *JFB*, Miscellaneous 1936, "Negroes."
196 *"Your opponents will undertake"*: JFB, Miscellaneous 1936, Lever to Byrnes, 28 June 1936.
197 *"I wish every Negro in the country"*: NYT, 3 July 1936, p. 5, col. 8. Byrnes, according to this news story, had just come from a meeting with Roosevelt at the White House where the two discussed plans for the national Democratic campaign.
197 *"the writer was white, black, or blue"*: JFB, Miscellaneous 1935, Byrnes to O. D. Busbee, 19 Aug. 1935.
198 *"dirty, evil-smelling Negroes"*: JFB, Byrnes Scrapbook, 1936–40.
198 *a Christian forbearance*: NYT, 26 June 1936, p. 15, col. 5.
198 *"no Negro could pray for E. D. Smith"*: JFB, Miscellaneous 1936, Lever to Byrnes, 28 June 1936.
199 *"In your heart and mine"*: Quoted in Moore, "Statesman," 208.
199 *"the bad language you so often employ"*: JFB, Miscellaneous 1936, Glass to Byrnes, 13 Aug. 1936.
201 *Democratic candidate for president*: JFB, Miscellaneous 1936, Joseph Kennedy, Sr., to Byrnes, 30 Oct. 1936.

7: A VAST EMPIRE NEARBY

The Santee Cooper project is evaluated so variously in the public and private papers of Franklin Roosevelt, Jimmy Byrnes, Harold Ickes, the South Carolina Public Service Authority, and the U.S. Army Corps of Engineers that a reader may well think that five separate hydroelectric projects are under discussion. All these sources must be read with caution, particularly the private observations in *The Secret Diary of Harold L. Ickes*, 3 vols. (New York: Simon and Schuster, 1953–54), and the interior secretary's book *Back to Work: The Story of PWA* (New York: Macmillan, 1935).

The least tendentious account of the twentieth-century construction at Santee Cooper is William Augustus Ward, "A Retrospective Economic Analysis of the Santee Cooper Project" (M.A. thesis, Clemson Univ., 1967). *River of the Carolinas: The Santee* (New York: Rinehart, 1956), by Henry Savage, Jr., is thoroughly critical of the project, whereas *History of Santee Cooper, 1934–1984* (Columbia, S.C.: R. L. Ryan, 1984), written by Walter B. Edgar with the encouragement of the South Carolina Public Service Authority, is thoroughly favorable to the project. Although obviously partisan, the brief for the South Carolina Public Service Authority filed on 20 January 1938, in the U.S. Fourth Circuit Court of Appeals in defense of the Santee-Cooper project against suits brought by several private power companies contains many useful summaries of litigation. This document is cited below as *Brief for Appellees*.

Accounts of the construction of the Santee Canal throughout the eighteenth and nineteenth centuries are on safer scholarly ground. Invaluable is *The History of the Santee Canal* (Charleston: South Carolina Historical Society, 1903), by Frederick Adolphus Porcher, who as a child at his family's plantation had witnessed the drying out and abandonment of the original canal. An interesting account of the enthusiasm for canal-building in the early-nineteenth-century United States is Harry Sinclair Drago, *Canal Days in America: The History and Romance of Old Towpaths and Waterways* (New York: C. N. Potter, 1972).

202 *"He has a very pleasant way"*: Ickes, *Diary*, 7: 489–90.
202 *"Byrnes went along"*: Ibid., 2:63.
203 *"it was Santee-Cooper again"*: Ibid., 1:490.
203 *"Honest Harold"*: See the brief biographical summary of Ickes in Otis L. Graham, Jr., and Meghan Robinson, eds., *Franklin D. Roosevelt: His Life and Times* (Boston: G. K. Hall, 1985), 199.
204 *"a vast empire nearby"*: *Brief for Appellees*, 17.
205 *natural highway of the Santee*: Porcher, *Canal*, 1.
205 *a group of prominent merchants*: Ibid., appendix, pp. 13–14. See also Edgar, *History*, 3.
206 *"I should be very happy"*: George Washington's letter is quoted in *Brief for Appellees*, 8–10, and in the *Charleston News and Courier*, 20 Jan. 1936, 1.
206 *"governed by an inordinate vanity"*: Porcher, *Canal*, 4.
207 *plat book of imaginary riches*: Savage, *River*, 246, the plans of Ralph Izard for Izardville. See also Porcher, *Canal*, 4.
207 *The great killer was malarial fever*: Porcher, *Canal*, 7.
207 *"the hardship of these slaves"*: Drago, *Canal Days*, 293.
208 *$40,000 a mile*: Porcher, *Canal*, 5.
208 *took the place of his dead overseers*: Savage, *River*, 245.
208 *greatest engineering feat*: Edgar, *History*, 4; Porcher, *Canal*, 8; Savage, *River*, 247.
209 *"they were utterly deceived"*: Porcher, *Canal*, 4, 11.
209 *charter was revoked by the state*: Edgar, *History*, 4.
210 *the pot of gold*: James C. Derieux, "He Changed the Map of a State," *American Magazine*, July 1932, 53.
210 *preliminary license*: JFB, Miscellaneous 1933–34, pp. 1–2. See also *Greenville News*, 3 Sept. 1939, p. 3, col. 3; Cann, "Maybank," 141–42; *Charleston News and Courier*, 29 Sept. 1932, p. 1, cols. 6–7.
210 *power license was amended and renewed*: *Charleston News and Courier*, 29 Sept. 1932, p. 1, col. 6. See also *Greenville News*, 3 Sept. 1939, p. 3, col. 7.
210 *its parent corporation*: Cann, "Maybank," 144.
210 *sensing the possibility of new money*: JFB, Miscellaneous 1934, "Review of Application of Columbia Railway and Navigation Company to the Federal Public Works Administration for a Loan of $34,000,000."
210 *"vision of an industrial empire"*: Quoted in Edgar, *History*, 5. See also Cann, *Maybank*, 149.
211 *"no chance on earth"*: See also "Chinaman's Chance," *Charleston News and Courier*, 19 April 1935, p. 1, col. 7.
211 *funding only public institutions*: Cann, "Maybank," 147.
211 *news was not all bad*: JFB, Folder 49(2). Byrnes' first-person, undated account entitled "Santee-Cooper" was an unpublished narrative, probably for his private use, of his political involvement with this power project. See p. 2 of this document.
211 *more than 160,000 acres*: Savage, *River*, 357.
212 *It was an economic curiosity*: Ward, "Analysis," 32–33.

212 *The private power companies: Charleston News and Courier*, 11 Oct. 1935, p. 1, col. 4.

213 *Residents of the Santee delta*: Ibid., 19 Dec. 1935, p. 14, col. 2.

213 *despoil the federal bird sanctuary: Bird Lore*, Nov. 1935, 443.

213 *"a muddy lake and a big powerhouse"*: Archibald Rutledge, "What Price Power?" *Nature Magazine*, March 1936, 174.

213 *honorary title of laureate*: See "South Carolina vs. Rutledge," *Nature Magazine*, July 1936, 42.

213 *Jimmy Byrnes persisted*: JFB, Miscellaneous 1938, "Santee Cooper 1903–1934," Byrnes to Ickes, 14 Dec. 1934.

215 *Hell Hole Swamp: WPA Palmetto State*, 294–96.

215 *"blaze that, never quenched"*: Ibid., 294.

215 *called the French Santee*: For a description of the cultural, economic, and aesthetic uniqueness of the Huguenot settlement along the Santee River in the eighteenth and early nineteenth centuries, see Savage, *River*, 108–9.

216 *empty tombs of weathered cypress*: JFB, "A Survey of the Early Buildings in the Region of the Proposed Santee and Pinopolis Reservoir," U.S. Department of the Interior, 1939, pp. 2–3, and photographs, pp. 34 and 38.

216 *264 deaths from malaria*: Census Bureau, *Vital Statistics of the United States, 1937*, pt. 1 (Washington, D.C., 1939), table 17, p. 363.

216 *Army hear testimony from him*: JFB, Miscellaneous 1933–34, Byrnes to General Lytle Brown, 23 Nov. 1933.

216 *worst possible timing*: U.S. Corps of Engineers, *Improvements of Santee River, N.C. and S.C.*, 69th Cong., 1st sess., 1933, House Doc. 308, 2.

217 *going to be a hard sell*: JFB, Miscellaneous 1933–34, General Brown to Byrnes, 1 Dec. 1933.

217 *"open to the most severe criticism"*: Ibid., Nicholas Roosevelt to Byrnes, 5 Jan. 1934.

218 *"Roosevelt will grant any request"*: Ibid., L. H. Harvin of Carolina Power and Light to Byrnes, 19 May 1934.

218 *FDR busied himself during the meeting: Charleston News and Courier*, 19 April 1935, p. 1, col. 8. Byrnes' unpublished narrative of his political activities in 1934–35 with the Santee Cooper project found in *JFB*, 49(2), p. 4, flatly contradicts the newspaper reports of his presence at the 19 April 1935 meeting with Roosevelt: "Those members of the [S.C.] Commission and others interested frequently requested me to see the president with reference to the project. I declined to do so on the ground that there was nothing upon which the president could act and that unless the emergency division [of the PWA] should find the project to be practical from an engineering standpoint, the President would never be called upon to pass upon the project."

218 *Byrnes immediately informed the president*: JFB, Folder 49(2), pp. 4–9.

219 *"not very anxious to engage in partnership"*: Ibid., 6.

219 *high diplomatic post*: Byrnes, *Lifetime*, 85.

220 *first obtained agreement from Hopkins*: JFB, Miscellaneous 1933–34, memorandum by Byrnes to Hopkins, undated.

220 *Byrnes ghostwrote for FDR*: The text of Roosevelt's 15 July 1935 letter, later published in FDR's official correspondence, is also found in *JFB*, Folder 49(2), p. 7.

220 *only "65 percent correct"*: Columbia *State*, 31 July 1935, p. 1, col. 6.

220 *"an unusual thing"*: Ibid., 8.

221 *"Plan Called Big Bluff"*: Quoted ibid., 9. See also *Charleston News and Courier*, 12 Aug. 1935, p. 1, col. 6.

222 *delegated that daily task*: There are well over one hundred letters in the Frank
      Lever papers located at the Strom Thurmond Institute, Clemson, S.C., in
      regard to applications to Lever for employment at the Santee-Cooper site.
223 *"it would never do to proceed"*: JFB, Miscellaneous 1938, Byrnes to Maybank,
      19 Aug. 1935. See also FDR's refusal to Byrnes' request to revoke the special
      engineering board requested by Ickes. Engineers assigned to the project,
      Roosevelt assures Byrnes, "are technically qualified for this work and whose
      openmindedness is above suspicion," *JFB*, Folder 14, Roosevelt to Byrnes,
      26 Sept. 1935.
223 *"I want your help"*: JFB, Miscellaneous 1938, "Santee-Cooper 1935," Byrnes
      to Hopkins, 18 Sept. 1935.
224 *"our friends expect us to go through"*: Ibid., Byrnes to Roosevelt, 12 Oct.
      1935.
224 *"sly and active one"*: Ickes, *Diaries*, 2:64.
224 *"The president is for the project"*: Ibid., Byrnes to Geer, 23 Dec. 1935.
225 *declared the project to be "feasible"*: Columbia *State*, 19 Dec. 1935, p. 15,
      cols. 2–3.
225 *Roosevelt, there was no telling*: "At his [Dec. 17] press conference, the pres-
      ident nodded his head approvingly but said nothing when asked about the
      report, submitted to him by Ickes. It was presented by a special board of
      engineers named by the PWA administration after an initial allotment of
      $500,000 had been approved for the project." Columbia *State*, 18 Dec. 1935,
      p. 11, col. 6.
225 *"would be taken care of"*: Charleston *News and Courier*, 20 Dec. 1935, p. 1,
      col. 8.
226 *adjust to changing conditions*: Ickes, *Diary*, 1:488.
226 *"I would not pay excessive prices"*: Ibid., 490.
226 *bureaucratically to wash his hands*: Ibid., 498. See also ibid. for Roosevelt's
      statement to Ickes regarding "so many of his rich friends."
227 *must have occurred to Byrnes*: Charleston *News and Courier*, 22 Dec. 1935,
      p. 1, col. 4.
228 *"big job that will pour millions"*: Charlotte *Observer*, 19 Dec. 1935, p. 1,
      col. 6.
228 *barring Harry Hopkins*: Charleston *News and Courier*, 24 Dec. 1935, p. 1,
      cols. 7–8. See also "Threat Serious, Byrnes Admits," ibid., 25 Dec. 1935,
      p. 1, col. 1.

8: THEY WERE UTTERLY DECEIVED

Since even before the first turbines began to turn and generate electricity at the
Pinopolis station, the Santee-Cooper project has not wanted for impressively
printed publications extolling the project's virtues, many of them published and
distributed by the South Carolina Public Service Authority itself. These publications
include the previously cited *History of the Santee Cooper*, by Walter Edgar; John
A. Zeigler, *Progress Picture Story: Santee-Cooper* (Moncks Corner: South Carolina
Public Service Authority, 1944); and *Pushing Back the Darkness: The Story of
Santee Cooper* (n.p., n.d.), published by the corporate communications office of
the Santee Cooper Authority and later distributed in video medium to most of the
state's libraries with assistance from the South Carolina Educational Television
Network; and the annual reports issued by the South Carolina Public Service

Authority. The print version of *Pushing Back the Darkness* is hereafter cited as *Pushing Back*.

Counterbalancing these corporately connected publications are the primary sources, most of them highly critical of the Santee-Cooper project, contained in the PWA records at the National Archives in Washington, D.C., and the Department of the Interior records at the FDR presidential library. The most detailed account of the building of the Santee-Cooper project from the perspective of South Carolina politics is in the chapter about the power project in Marvin Cann's dissertation, "Burnet Rhett Maybank and the New Deal in South Carolina."

Yet the most authoritative sources on the history of the Santee-Cooper project are certainly the photographs, letters, news stories, and personal experiences of those who were there during the 1940s. These witnesses include the FSA photographer Jack Delano and the journalist Harry Ashmore. The latter, although employed in the early 1940s by a conservative South Carolina newspaper, reported the destruction of the Santee basin with a dispassionate thoroughness. Nevertheless, Ashmore provided in a 1993 conversation with this author a necessary corrective to judging the events of the Santee-Cooper project during the 1930s and 1940s by the standards of the 1990s: "Of course, it was a boondoggle. But what you have to remember is how God-awful isolated were the people there at that time. Any available work was good work."

229 *"pretensive, illusory, and inconsequential"*: *Brief for Appellees*, 2.
230 *"source of cheap electrical energy"*: Ibid., 4, 14, 17.
230 *George Washington and Franklin Roosevelt*: Ibid., appendix, pp. 8–11.
230 *advised seeking a postponement*: JFB, Folder 49(2), "Santee Cooper," 13, 16.
230 *"a great deal of telephoning"*: Ickes, *Diaries*, 2:92.
231 *what the Supreme Court would do*: Cann, "Maybank," 165.
231 *Ickes argued, and Roosevelt agreed*: FDR, PPF 2816, memorandum, Byrnes to Roosevelt, 15 March 1937.
232 *had been "earmarked"*: JFB, Folder 49(2), "Santee Cooper," 14–15. See also *NYT*, 3 Sept. 1937, p. 7, col. 1.
232 *both sides agreed was "voluminous"*: *Greenville News*, 3 Sept. 1939, p. 1, col. 1.
232 *"one matter of legal importance"*: *NYT*, 3 Sept. 1937, p. 7, col. 1; Hayes, *New Deal*, 305.
232 *this appeal would be denied*: See the news clippings written by Byrnes' associate Walter Brown, "Santee-Cooper Victory Looms," 25 Jan. 1938, *JFB*, Scrapbook.
232 *A friendly journalist tipped*: JFB, Miscellaneous 1938, Byrnes to D. C. Roper, 23 Dec. 1936. See also *JFB*, Folder 49(2), "Santee Cooper," 13.
233 *inundations were considered useful*: Ward, "Analysis," 79.
233 *"not justified at this time"*: FDR, OF 284, Acting Secretary of War Johnson to Roosevelt, 19 March 1938.
233 *Byrnes' turn to fall into a perfect snit*: Ibid., Roosevelt to Acting Secretary of War Johnson, 21 March 1938.
234 *"Byrnes fully expects us to go ahead"*: Ibid., Roosevelt to Ickes, 25 April 1938.
234 *second week of May 1938*: Ibid., Missy LeHand to Marvin McIntyre, 10 May 1938.
234 a *single word—"denied"*: *Charleston News and Courier*, 24 May 1938, p. 1, col. 8.

234 *dinner guests of the Roosevelts*: Ibid., p. 2, col. 2.
235 *graves would remain "lost"*: Members of a local DAR chapter searching the
     basins before the final flooding found the gravestones of three individuals
     shattered into nineteen pieces on the ground, "having been placed there by
     a Santee-Cooper workman." This same group also compiled in one day a list
     from one parish record of eight individuals buried in the Santee basin during
     the eighteenth and nineteenth centuries whose burial sites remained listed in
     1942 as "unidentified" by the Santee-Cooper Authority. See JFB, Martha
     Carson, *Records from the Area to be Flooded by the Santee-Cooper Project
     in South Carolina* (Chester, S.C.: Privately printed, 1942), 40–41.
235 *"only sentimental or historical associations"*: Thomas Waterman, *A Survey
     of the Early Buildings of the Region of the Proposed Santee and Pinopolis
     Reservoirs in South Carolina* (n.p.: U.S. Department of the Interior, National
     Park Service, 1939), 38.
235 *average of over twelve dollars*: Edgar, *History*, 49.
235 *gave each resettled farmer*: Ibid., 64.
236 *the greatest beneficiaries*: Columbia *State*, 14 April 1939, p. 4B, col. 4. Private
     corporations in Brooklyn and Chicago were the largest landowners, together
     holding 60,000 acres of land bought at premium prices. *Greenville News*, 17
     Sept. 1939, p. 1, col. 5.
236 *"project was conceived in sin"*: Columbia *State*, 21 April 1939, p. 5B, cols.
     1–2.
237 *largest earth-moving project: Pushing Back*, 10.
237 *far above the original $37.5 million*: Ward, "Analysis," 96.
237 *"no new cases": Greenville News*, 24 Sept. 1934, p. 1, col. 2. Harry Ashmore
     characterized the swamps in the Santee basin in 1930 as "some of the world's
     finest malaria country."
237 *declined significantly from the 1933–34 levels*: Census Bureau, *Statistical Ab-
     stract of the United States, 1940* (Washington, D.C., 1941), tables 375–76, p.
     338; Census Bureau, *Sixteenth Census of the United States, 1940: Population*,
     vol. 1, *Number of Inhabitants* (Washington, D.C., 1942), table 3, p. 977, and
     vol. 3, *The Labor Force*, pt. 5, tables 24–26, pp. 278–84. See also Cann,
     "Maybank," 232–33, and *Statistical Abstract of the United States, 1939*, table
     373, p. 333.
237 *payrolls in manufacturing industries*: See *Statistical Abstract, 1940*, table 375,
     p. 338.
238 *"located at the edge of swamps"*: JFB, Miscellaneous 1941, Pinckney to How-
     ard Hunter, Acting Commissioner of WPA, 11 April 1941; Pinckney to Major
     E. H. Leavy, Acting Commissioner of WPA, 14 Sept. 1940.
238 *the problem with snakes*: William Bartram, *The Travels of William Bartram*
     (New York: Dover, 1947), 224–27; Archibald H. Rutledge, *Santee Paradise*
     (Indianapolis, Bobbs-Merrill, 1956), 136, 150–51; Ward, "Analysis," 48.
239 *"necessary for the national defense"*: Zeigler, *Progress Picture Story*, 230;
     JFB, Folder 49(2), "Santee Cooper," 18.
239 *euphemistically called deferred clearing*: Ward, "Analysis," 41–43.
240 *never reached its goal*: Cann, "Maybank," 174.
240 *an office building misplaced*: "Project Dimensions," Zeigler, *Progress Picture
     Story*, 231.
240 *"just people in trouble"*: Columbia *State*, 30 Sept. 1990, p. 5E, col. 1.
241 *"how they treating us folks"*: Quoted in *New Deal Art in South Carolina*,
     museum catalog, 16 June–14 Oct. 1990, pp. 75–81. That there was also
     considerable concern among white South Carolinians about the forced dis-

placement of black residents is evidenced by Harry Ashmore's long article "Worse Than Yankee Troops, Some Claim/Negro Tenants Are Bewildered," *Greenville News*, 17 Sept. 1939, p. 7, col. 2.

241 *"Bit of South Is Doomed"*: *NYT*, 19 March 1939, sec. 12, p. 5, col. 4.

241 *"golden flow of wealth"*: Zeigler, *Progress Picture Story*, 4.

241 *Heavy deposits of silt*: U.S. Corps of Engineers, *Shoaling in Charleston Harbor* (Charleston: n.p., 1966), unpaginated "Syllabus."

242 *dredging had risen to $302,897*: Ibid., 9.

242 *to redivert much of the Santee*: Ibid., "Syllabus"; South Carolina Public Service Authority, *31st Annual Report*, 1966.

243 *new dam and power station*: Santee Cooper Annual Report, 1987, 15.

243 *total of four in 1950*: U.S. Public Health Service, *Vital Statistics of the United States, 1950*, vol. 3, *Mortality Data* (Washington, D.C., 1953), table 55, p. 235.

244 *motels and restaurants do not require*: Ward, "Analysis," 96–98.

244 *below the national poverty line*: Census Bureau, *1980 Census of Population*, vol. 1, *General Social and Economic Characteristics*, pt. 42, *South Carolina* (Washington, D.C., 1983), table 57, pp. 14–16; table 178, pp. 336–40.

244 *work camps that once housed*: *Greenville News*, 10 Sept. 1939, p. 1, cols. 1–2.

244 *lines of commercial barges*: Savage, *River*, 362; Ward, "Analysis," 61–66.

245 *people whose graves were removed*: Zeigler, *Progress Picture Story*, 4.

9: JUMPING THE TRACES

Preeminent among the studies of ideological opposition in Congress to the liberal policies of the first six years of the Roosevelt administration is James T. Patterson's *Congressional Conservatism and the New Deal*. The study of southern congressional recidivists is carried from the 1930s to the 1960s in David M. Potter, *The South and the Concurrent Majority* (Baton Rouge: Louisiana State Univ. Press, 1972). Also useful in understanding the continuation of the congressional conservative coalition into the midtwentieth century and its persistence under different party labels are George E. Mowry, *Another Look at the Twentieth-Century South*, and Dewey W. Grantham, *The Life and Death of the Solid South: A Political History* (Lexington: Univ. of Kentucky Press, 1988).

The 168 Days (Garden City, N.Y.: Doubleday, Doran, 1938), by Joseph Alsop and Turner Catledge, published shortly after the resolution of the Supreme Court controversy of 1937, offers an extraordinary example of writing about a historic incident while it is still fresh; this book remains the definitive account of that controversy nearly sixty years after its first publication. Catledge's subsequent memoir, *My Life and The Times*, also is a valuable source from an acute observer of domestic politics from the 1930s to the 1960s. Finally, there is that work from the nineteenth century that intellectually anticipated so many of Senator Jimmy Byrnes' political motivations throughout the middle and later 1930s—*A Disquisition on Government*, written by Senator John C. Calhoun of South Carolina and published in 1853.

246 *proposed that the Constitution*: Moley, *Seven Years*, 307 n.

247 *"the John C. Calhoun"*: Quoted in Moore, "Statesman," 228.

247 *"Conservative Manifesto"*: Patterson, *Conservatism*, 203.

247 *impromptu singing*: Byrnes, *Lifetime*, 87.

247 *"move to hold back"*: *NYT*, 25 Dec. 1938, E3.
248 *"The emergency has passed"*: Byrnes' radio address is quoted in Moore, "Statesman," 228, and Patterson, *Conservatism*, 141.
248 *"pauper's oath"*: Patterson, *Conservatism*, 142–43.
248 *Byrnes asked Hopkins*: Quoted in Moore, "Statesman," 230.
250 *"face the new Reconstruction"*: Quoted in Grantham, *Solid South*, 111.
250 *"Republican president"*: Mowry, *Look*, 89.
250 *"concurrent majorities"*: Calhoun, *Disquisition*, 19–23.
251 *Old Masters*: Jay Franklin's contemporary description in the Washington *Star* is quoted in Swain, *Harrison*, 283.
252 *"The southerners"*: Catledge, *Life*, 67–68.
252 *promise to Byrnes*: Alsop and Catledge, *Days*, 130.
252 *"How could a man"*: Frazier, "Southerner," 72.
254 *"flushed mahogany"*: Alsop and Catledge, *Days*, 66.
254 *"Boys," he said*: Ibid., 67.
254 *"to rape the Supreme Court"*: Quoted ibid., 115.
254 *"If you're going to pack"*: Quoted ibid., 159.
255 *"stronger for the plan"*: *NYT*, 14 Feb. 1937, p. 1, col. 8.
255 *KKK*: JFB, Miscellaneous 1937, undated handbill.
256 *"The President laughed"*: Alsop and Catledge, *Days*, 78.
257 *"some of our friends"*: JFB, Miscellaneous 1937, Byrnes to Garner, 9 July 1937.
258 *"greatest effort of the C.I.O."*: *NYT*, 19 March 1937, p. 3, col. 1.
258 *"We Shall Not Be Moved"*: Hayes, *New Deal*, 393.
258 *"It is the sense"*: *CR*, 75th Cong., 1st sess., 1937, 3017–24, 2079–88.
258 An interesting contemporary account of the increasing occurrence in the late 1930s of sit-down strikes is found in the article "Harvard Professor Defends Sit Downs," *NYT*, 31 March 1939, p. 9, col. 5.
259 *began to abuse each other*: Alsop and Catledge, *Days*, 131–33.
259 *"We trusted you to be our friend"*: JFB, Byrnes Legislative 1933–41, M. E. Alverson, Secretary UTWA, to Byrnes, 5 April 1937.
259 *"hawked and spit in the face"*: Ibid., G. F. Wright to James Byrnes, 5 April 1937.
259 *wrote to Colonel Lawrence Pinckney*: Ibid.
259 *"disinclined to give the president"*: Alsop and Cartledge, *Days*, 132.
260 *"I know not what effect"*: Quoted in Moore, 221. See also Alsop and Catledge, *Days*, 135–40.
260 *"Why run for a train"*: Quoted in Patterson, *Conservatism*, 120.
261 *"Joe is too old"*: Robert Allen, "The New Deal Fights for Its Life," *Nation*, 10 July 1937, 35–37.
261 *"harmony conference"*: *NYT*, 26 June 1937, p. 4, col. 1.
262 *"not kill any more senators"*: Quoted in Schwarz, *Speculator*, 319.
262 *"worked himself to death"*: Alsop and Catledge, *Days*, 255–67.
263 *"In your case, Joe"*: Quoted in Patterson, *Conservatism*, 65.
264 *"anyone we've overlooked"*: Catledge, *Life*, 96–97.
264 *Roosevelt appeared agreeable*: Byrnes, *Lifetime*, 99.
264 *"Dear Alben"*: Quoted in Patterson, *Conservatism*, 146.
265 *got Harry Hopkins to do the job*: Swain, *Harrison*, 159. An expression of Roosevelt's distrust of Harrison's fidelity to New Deal tax policy in a conversation with Jim Farley is also quoted ibid., 155.
265 *"laughing, more than maliciously"*: Alsop and Catledge, *Days*, 282–83.
265 *"carload of patronage"*: Connally, *My Name*, 193.

265 *Byrnes had confidently*: Swain, *Harrison*, 160.

266 *"had double-crossed Pat"*: Alsop and Catledge, *Days*, 282.

266 *"White House errand boy"*: Patterson, *Conservatism*, 148. See also Byrnes' own description of the meeting in his office (*Lifetime*, 100). For a more candid description of his possible plans for behind-the-scenes revenge against the defectors, see JFB, Folder 14, Byrnes to Senator Bankhead, 22 July 1937.

10: THE PURGE OF 1938

The 1967 study by James Patterson of the conservative coalition remains the starting point for anyone interested in Roosevelt's attempted purge of the Democratic party. Marvin Cann's 1967 dissertation examines the political consequences of Roosevelt's actions not only in South Carolina but also in the southern states at large. The most authoritative source for the political purge of 1938 remains J. B. Shannon's two-part article "Presidential Politics in the South: 1938," *Journal of Politics*, vol. 1 (1939). A background study of the economic forces underlying the schism of the Democratic party is discussed in detail in the paper "The Recession of 1937–38," presented before the Econometric Society in Chicago, 27–30 Dec. 1947.

267 *"Democratic Party may split"*: Ickes, *Diaries*, 2:153.

267 *Hopkins was thinking the same:* Time, 12 Sept. 1938, 22.

268 *"in terms of 1938, 1948, and 1958"*: NYT, 30 Aug. 1938, p. 1, col. 1.

269 *"so many copperheads"*: "Fireside Chat," 24 June 1938, in *The Public Papers and Addresses of Franklin D. Roosevelt: 1938 Volume* (New York: Macmillan, 1941), 391–400.

270 *"mixing medicine"*: JFB, Folder 30, Baruch to Byrnes, 30 April 1938.

270 *"most will appreciate your help"*: JFB, Folder 21, Byrnes to Baruch, 28 Sept. 1938.

270 *"it was folly"*: Byrnes, *Lifetime*, 100–101.

271 *thousand-dollar contribution*: Schwarz, *Speculator*, 323–24.

272 *"team of Byrnes & Maybank"*: Time, 9 Aug. 1938, 11. See also the *Charleston News and Courier*'s editorial analysis of Byrnes' political motives, 1 Sept. 1938, p. 4, cols. 3–4.

272 *"That is human nature"*: JFB, Folder 30, Byrnes to Baruch, 5 May 1938.

273 *sent a long telegram*: JFB, Folder 637(2), Byrnes to Hopkins, 9 Aug. 1938.

273 *"Lewis was bringing pressure"*: JFB, Folder 21, Byrnes to Baruch, 16 Aug. 1938.

274 *"a man can live on fifty cents":* Time, 9 Aug. 1937, 4.

274 *"There's the old pirate"*: Quoted in Hollis, "Smith," 253.

274 *"We can all agree about fishing"*: Byrnes, *Lifetime*, 103.

274 *"Before I stop"*: Greenville News, 12 Aug. 1938, p. 1, col. 8.

275 *"All the fighting Irish blood"*: FDR's bodyguard is quoted in Moore, "Statesman," 277.

275 *"called for substantial help"*: JFB, Folder 21, Byrnes to M. A. Boyle, confidential secretary to Baruch, 17 Aug. 1938.

275 *a day off with pay*: FDR, OF 300, South Carolina 1933–45, memorandum from Early to McIntyre, 21 Aug. 1938.

276 *Red Shirts once again appeared:* NYT, 30 Aug. 1938, p. 1, col. 1.

277 *"We fought with bullets then"*: Quoted in Hollis, "Smith," 254. See also "Midnight in Columbia," *Time*, 12 Sept. 1938, 26.

277 *"Well, you beat me"*: Byrnes, *Lifetime*, 104.

278   *"gleaming red petticoats"*: *Washington Post*, 18 Dec. 1938, p. 1, cols. 2–3.

278   *"little Sherman"*: JFB, Miscellaneous 1938, Byrnes to Garner, 29 Sept. 1938.

278   *took a sweet revenge*: Patterson, *Conservatism*, 296–97.

278   *"My Wandering Boy"*: Byrnes, *Lifetime*, 87.

279   *"We'll forget it"*: Ibid., 104.

281   *"wholesale transfer of Negro voters"*: *NYT*, 28 Aug. 1938, p. E7, cols. 1–4.

282   *"bill to arouse ill-feeling"*: *CR*, 75th Cong., 3d sess., 1938, 305.

283   *70 percent of the American people . . . 4672 murders*: *CR*, 76th Cong., 3d sess., 1940, 156, 168, 174. See also Daniel T. Williams, ed., *The Lynching Records at Tuskegee Institute* (Tuskegee: Tuskegee Institute, 1969). For a history of white southern resistance to lynching, see Jacquelyn Dowd Hall, *Revolt against Chivalry: Jessie Daniel Ames and the Women's Campaign against Lynching* (New York: Columbia Univ. Press, 1979), 256.

284   *"soul of the South"*: *CR*, 75th Cong., 3d sess., 1938, p. 310.

286   *"the battle must go on"*: *CR*, 76th Cong., 1st sess., 1939, 558.

286   *"glad to get you off their necks"*: Poppy Cannon, *A Gentle Knight: My Husband, Walter White* (New York: Rinehart, 1956), 219–20.

286   *"minor" committee chairmanship*: See the press release in JFB, dated 2 June 1938, written by Byrnes' longtime journalist friend and "bullbat time" companion Walter Brown: "Senator Byrnes held a hearing on the lynching resolution, but because the arguments for the expenditure of money for such an investigation did not impress him and his colleague on the committee, Senator Nathan Bachman of Tennessee, and the other members being absent, the Van Nuys resolution has not been reported to the Senate."

11: JUSTICE BYRNES AND
THE COMING OF WAR

The events deserving documentation during Justice Byrnes' sole term on the U.S. Supreme Court are more political than juristical, but it is significant that their political importance persisted for the next two decades. It was, for instance, during this October 1941 term of the Court that Byrnes formed his close friendship with Justice Felix Frankfurter, an event that later directly affected the speed of the Court's deliberations from 1952 to 1954 in *Brown* v. *Board of Education*.

A number of letters and memoranda exchanged between Byrnes and Chief Justice Harland Stone are contained in Justice Stone's papers at the National Archives, but this correspondence is of a social nature or concerns the more pedestrian business of the Court. The most important source for Byrnes' Court years is Leon Friedman and Fred L. Israel, eds., *The Justices of the United States Supreme Court, 1789–1969: Their Lives and Major Opinions*, vol. 4, (New York: Chelsea House). The brief biographical sketch prepared for this volume by Walter Murphy is the best-written short life of Byrnes. Murphy ends his sketch by shrewdly noting that had Byrnes "been born in Massachusetts rather than in South Carolina, his playing the role of pragmatic broker-politician would have been more obvious— and his ambitions probably more completely filled."

Also useful are Henry J. Abraham's *Justices and Presidents: A Political History of Appointments to the Supreme Court*, 2d ed. (New York: Oxford Univ. Press, 1985), and the various memoirs and articles cited below.

288   *rumors had reached Harold L. Ickes*: Ickes, *Diary*, 2:63–64. Ickes also recorded being told by Harry Hopkins' liberal ally Thomas Corcoran that "per-

haps Byrnes was trying to create a nuisance value for himself" by delaying passage through the Senate of New Deal social programs until Roosevelt would appoint Byrnes to the Supreme Court.

289 *"do not say anything"*: JFB, Folder 21, Byrnes to Baruch, 7 Dec. 1939.

290 *out of loyalty to Roosevelt*: For instances of Byrnes' persistent behind-the-scenes maneuvering to achieve passage of the president's reorganization bill in 1938, see Ickes, *Diaries*, 2:311.

291 *"I should be considered for the nomination"*: JFB, Folder 72(1), Byrnes to John Crewes, 15 Feb. 1940.

292 *"except in case of attack"*: Byrnes, *Lifetime*, 122.

292 *let anyone out of the restroom*: Moore, "Statesman," 326.

292 *"sitting on his veranda"*: JFB, Scrapbooks 1940, unidentified South Carolina newspaper clipping.

293 *"That's all right with me"*: Cordell Hull, *The Memoirs of Cordell Hull*, vol. 1 (New York: Macmillan, 1948), 859–62.

293 *"go down the line"*: Samuel I. Rosenman, *Working with Roosevelt* (New York: Harper, 1952), 215.

294 *"For God's sake"*: Quoted in Moore, "Statesman," 333.

295 *"all possible aid short of war"*: Byrnes, *Lifetime*, 113.

295 *memories of English aid*: Alexander DeConde, "The South and Isolationism," *Journal of Southern History* 24 (1958): 340–45. For further discussion of southern Anglophilism, including the bellicose support of Great Britain by such influential southern politicians as Hull and Glass and for H. L. Mencken's scornful view of their loyalty, see Paul Seabury, *The Waning of Southern "Internationalism"* (Princeton: Princeton Univ., Center for International Studies, (1957), 3, 7, 16, 18.

295 *"ancient quarrel with Congress"*: Quoted in Byrnes, *Lifetime*, 111.

295 *"Hitler wants to go places"*: Quoted in Moore, "Statesman," 245.

296 *"unfortunate Jews of Germany"*: FDR, OF 3186, telegram, Byrnes to Roosevelt, 16 Nov. 1938.

296 *"grand telegram of November"*: Ibid., Roosevelt to Byrnes, 18 Nov. 1938.

297 *"not lose more than a dozen Democrats"*: FDR, PPF 2816, "Memorandum for the President," E. H. Watson to Roosevelt, 18 Jan. 1941.

297 *"able management of Byrnes"*: Quoted in Moore, "Statesman," 351.

297 *"Of course, I will appoint him"*: Quoted in Abraham, *Justices*, 215. See also Byrnes, *Lifetime*, 130.

299 *"We beg of you"*: FDR, OF 41a, telegram, Walter White to Roosevelt, 16 March 1941.

300 *"terribly embarrassed"*: Byrnes, *Lifetime*, 132.

300 *"called the Senate to order"*: Washington *Star*, 8 July 1941, p. 7, cols. 2–3.

301 *"Even Homer nods"*: Richard Funston, "Great Presidents, Great Justices?" *Presidential Studies Quarterly* 7 (1977): 195.

301 *almost–brushing by*: JFB, Folder 1226, Philip Graham to Byrnes, undated. See also Richard M. Nixon, *RN: The Memoirs of Richard Nixon* (New York: Grosset & Dunlap, 1978), 25.

302 *"shutting its gates"*: Quoted in Friedman and Israel, eds., *Lives*, 2539.

302 *"an ignorant Negro"*: Justice Byrnes' personal text and notes regarding this decision, including his notation of the "sweet-talked" quotation, are found in JFB, Folder 1248, which also contains the printed decision of this case, no. 974, U.S. Supreme Court, Oct. 1941 term.

303 *Byrnes was a "misfit"*: William O. Douglas, *The Court Years: The Autobiography of William O. Douglas* (New York: Random House, 1980), 26.

303 *He wrote no dissenting opinions*: For a friendly review of Byrnes' performance during the Oct. 1941 term, see William Pettie, "Justice Byrnes and the United States Supreme Court," *South Carolina Law Quarterly* 6 (1954): 423–28. For a chronology of Justice Black's dissents, see Friedman and Israel, eds., *Lives*, 2522–23. The reader should keep in mind that the above appraisal of Justice Byrnes in the *South Carolina Law Quarterly* was published one month after the U.S. Supreme Court's decision in May 1954 in the combined cases in *Brown* v. *Board of Education*, a decision in which Byrnes was intimately involved, along with other members of the almost whites-only South Carolina bar association.

303 *wrote "I approve"*: Friedman and Israel, eds., *Lives*, 2530.

304 *"The result was usually horrible"*: Douglas, *Years*, 27.

305 *"depressed by Pat's death"*: JFB, Personal 1941, Byrnes to Mrs. John Gardner, 23 June 1941.

306 *"shoot-on-sight" orders*: Frank Freidel, *Franklin D. Roosevelt: A Rendezvous with Destiny* (Boston: Little, Brown, 1990), 392–94.

306 *Hillman had been named: The Public Papers and Addresses of Franklin D. Roosevelt: 1940 Volume*, 684. On the day that Roosevelt had witnessed the swearing-in of Justice Byrnes to his presumably lifetime appointment, the *Washington Post* also noted that, after the Byrnes party had left, "OPMer Sidney Hillman, followed by labor's Phil Murray, polished off [FDR's] morning" of White House visitors.

307 *"The great cure for discord"*: Henry A. Wallace, *The Price of Vision: The Diary of Henry A. Wallace, 1942–1946*, ed. John Morton Blum (Boston: Houghton Mifflin, 1973), 565.

307 *"I get so damn lonely here"*: Catledge, *Life*, 71.

12: THE ASSISTANT PRESIDENT

It is true that the real war never gets into books, not even the economic war. The economic changes implemented by Byrnes as the nation's wartime "assistant president" continue to affect the lives of Americans in ways unnoticed and unrecorded, just as no one questions who first decreed that men's trousers be made without cuffs in order to save fabric or that annual federal income taxes be withheld from paychecks. Byrnes' decrees and activities as director of the OES and OWMR were part of a larger and permanent restructuring of postwar U.S. society for which there is yet no comprehensive history. Nevertheless a few individual works of history serve to place his political activities in a larger context. These are John M. Blum's excellent *V Was for Victory: Politics and American Culture during World War II* (New York: Harcourt Brace Jovanovich, 1976) and Richard Polenberg's *War and Society: The United States, 1941–1945* (New York: HarperCollins, 1990). Two other books, although appearing not to be directly relevant to the life of the economic czar of World War II, are also greatly useful in understanding the background of Byrnes' public decisions and their consequences today: John Costello, *Virtue under Fire: How World War II Changed Our Social and Sexual Attitudes* (Boston: Little, Brown, 1985), and Paul Fussell, *Wartime: Understanding and Behavior in the Second World War* (New York: Oxford Univ. Press, 1989). After all, Jimmy Byrnes needs to be remembered as the originator of the "Byrne out"—the wartime order determining the degree of illumination available in nightclubs, amusement parks, and hotel rooms.

Two much more specialized academic studies essential to understanding Byrnes' work as a member of the executive branch are John William Partin, " 'Assistant President' for the Home Front: James F. Byrnes and World War II" (Ph.D. diss., Univ. of Florida, 1977), and Herman M. Somers, *Presidential Agency OWMR: The Office of War Mobilization and Reconversion* (Cambridge: Harvard Univ. Press, 1950). The latter, though obviously a history of the "superagency" OWMR, contains very useful information on pre-1941 defense planning and the subsequent creation of the OES. *The United States at War: Development and Administration of the War Program by the Federal Government* (New York: Da Capo Press, 1972), originally published in 1947 by the War Records Section of the Bureau of the Budget, provides much useful data, but must be read with the caution necessary when one approaches any official history. (The book owes much of its lasting value to the historian V. O. Key, Jr., who contributed to writing some of its chapters.) David Novick, Melvin Anshen, and W. C. Truppner, *Wartime Production Controls* (New York: Columbia Univ. Press, 1949), is an independent scholarly history of wartime agencies and officers. Another excellent and independent scholarly study of this period is Nathan D. Grundstein's *Presidential Delegation of Authority in Wartime* (Pittsburgh: Univ. of Pittsburgh Press, 1961). Finally, an unjustly neglected memoir, *The War Lords of Washington* (New York: Harcourt, Brace, 1948), by Bruce Catton, is a first-person and spirited defense of the administrative defeats of Catton's boss, Donald Nelson, at the hands of Jimmy Byrnes, Bernard Baruch, Jesse Jones, and other Roosevelt administration conservatives. Catton's book is written with the absence of gentlemanly restraint that so characterized Nelson as a private individual and that so marred his own record of the war years, *Arsenal for Democracy: The Story of American War Production* (New York: Harcourt, Brace, 1946).

311 *"he was more nervous"*: Byrnes, *Lifetime*, 147.
312 *"who takes care of it"*: JFB, Folder 637(4), Biddle to Roosevelt, 9 Jan. 1942.
312 *assembled in a haphazard manner*: See, for example, the Escher-like chart of twenty-three major defense offices and commissions in 1941 prepared by the Bureau of the Budget and illustrated in *U.S. at War* (p. 39). According to the chart, five offices reported directly to the Office of Productions Management (OPM), two reported separately both to the OPM and to the Office of Price Administration, and the OPM itself shared an equal and uneasy overlapping of authority with the War Manpower Commission.
313 *"for convenience call him Hopkins"*: JFB, Folder 1249, "Memorandum for Mr. Hopkins," and narrative by Byrnes, both undated.
314 *created through executive order*: Executive Order No. 9024, *Federal Register*, 16 Jan. 1942, pg. 329.
315 *"Could we not appoint"*: Biddle, 192–93.
317 *approximately 20 percent higher*: *U.S. at War*, 253.
317 *to manufacture without the interruptions*: Sherwood, *Roosevelt*, 479.
317 *followed immediately by a postwar deflation*: The U.S. cost of living in 1920 was 104.5 percent higher than in 1914, and in 1919 over 20 million Americans were unemployed. See Robert Murray, *The Politics of Normalcy: Governmental Theory and Practice in the Harding-Coolidge Era* (New York: W. W. Norton, 1973), 3.
317 *the price in power*: See the editorial page in the *Washington Post*, 5 Oct. 1942: "It cannot be said that the best interests of the Court were served by making what has now proved to be a temporary appointment to that tribunal." During Jan. 1942, an accompanying column on the same page noted, the "inflationary gap is daily increasing as government expenditures rise and the

amount of civilian goods shrinks in volume." Like most people, Franklin D. Roosevelt probably did not like to see his debts, political and fiscal, discussed in print.

318   *fig leaf's cover of constitutionality*: See the discussion in Grundstein, *Delegation*, p. 50, of how the establishment of the Office of Emergency Management by the reorganization act of 1939 became the statutory precedent for the later establishments of the Office of Economic Stabilization and the Office of War Mobilization. As to Roosevelt's threat "to act unilaterally by executive order under his government reorganization authority and the war power acts," see Title I of the First War Powers Act, partly written by Byrnes: "The President is hereby authorized to make such redistribution of functions among executive agencies as he may deem necessary, including any functions, duties, and powers hitherto by law conferred upon any executive department. . . ."

318   *Roosevelt liked the political cunning*: Freidel, *Rendezvous*, 438.

319   *"I suggested James F. Byrnes"*: Baruch, *Public Years*, 308–9.

319   *"control of civilian purchasing power"*: A copy of the complete text EO 9250 is contained in JFB, OES, OWMR Packet 1-2, 1942–43.

320   *"housewifery on a continental scale"*: *Life*, 4 Jan. 1943, 664–68.

320   *news ticker machine*: Byrnes, *Lifetime*, 161.

320   *"Your decision is my decision"*: Ibid., 155.

321   *"Keep the hell out of my business"*: Sherwood, *Roosevelt*, 634. Sherwood added that it was "improbable that Hopkins was entirely faithful" to Byrnes' request.

321   *"You and I can make a lot of money"*: Morgan, *FDR*, 544.

321   *"I don't know how he stood it"*: HST, Oral History Interview with Judge Marvin Jones, p. 116.

322   *"typical bit of Washington overlaying"*: Catton, *War Lords*, 203.

322   *urged that the WPB be merged*: JFB, Folder 61, Byrnes to Roosevelt, 26 Jan. 1944.

322   *"You have been called"*: Quoted in Byrnes, *Lifetime*, 213.

323   *to control rising food prices*: JFB, Folder 91, Secretary of Agriculture Claude Wickard to Byrnes, 19 Oct. 1942; JFB, OES-OWM Packet 3, "Miscellaneous," Roosevelt to Byrnes, 27 Oct. 1942. See also Partin, "Assistant President," 121–23, 266; Byrnes, *Lifetime*, 166–67.

324   *RFC spent over $1.5 billion* and *spent with its left hand*: Jesse H. Jones, *Fifty Billion Dollars: My Thirteen Years with the RFC, 1932–1945* (New York: Viking Press, 1955), 372–74.

324   *"agree that two and two makes five"*: Catton, *War Lords*, 203.

324   *in a burst of patriotic fever*: Polenberg, *War*, 159.

325   *economy to "hold the line"*: Partin, "Assistant President," 82–86.

325   *Murray shouted in Byrnes' face*: Byrnes, *Lifetime*, pp. 176–77. Byrnes' interview with Jefferson Frazier about this incident is quoted in Frazier, "Southerner," 92, with more detail than is found in Byrnes' autobiography.

325   *"it held much better"*: Byrnes, *Frankly*, 19.

326   *"help you instead of hurting you"*: JFB, Folder 24, Byrnes to Roosevelt, 14 May 1943.

326   *The letter had spoiled his weekend*: Byrnes, *Lifetime*, 184.

327   *"Byrnes' authority was exceeded"*: *Washington Post*, 29 May 1943, p. 4, cols. 6–8.

328   *Within this twelve-month period*: JFB, "Crude Oil Pipeline," OES, OWMR, 1942–43.

328 *"little Joe was recommended"*: JFB, Folder 69(5), memorandum Byrnes to Roosevelt, 20 March 1944.

328 *soldiers' voting act* and *"bring Jimmy Byrnes into the picture"*: JFB, memorandum Biddle to Roosevelt, 4 Sept. 1943, and memorandum, Roosevelt to Byrnes, 8 Sept. 1943.

328 *Jones would physically assault*: Byrnes, *Lifetime*, 192; Wallace, 220–21. After this confrontation, Robert Sherwood later wrote, "Roosevelt dissolved the Board of Economic Warfare, of which Wallace was chairman, and put its functions and various others connected with foreign economic matters, which had been in Jones' department, under the authority of Byrnes." Sherwood, *Roosevelt*, 740–41.

330 *"beginning to think about it seriously"*: Byrnes, *Lifetime*, 220–21.

13: THE CONVENTION OF 1944

All historians who since 1979 have written about the events of the Democratic convention of 1944 owe an incalculable scholarly debt to John Partin, previously noted for his dissertation on the economic histories of the OES-OWMR. Partin's article "Roosevelt, Byrnes, and the 1944 Vice-Presidential Nomination," *Historian* 42 (1979): 85–100, is central to understanding the larger strategies of the convention as well as the defeated ambitions of Jimmy Byrnes. Prior to Partin's work, the best summary of the 1944 Democratic convention was written some eighteen hundred years earlier by the Roman historian Tacitus. Describing a struggle in imperial Rome for Caesarian power, Tacitus wrote in his *Annals*: "There occurred, too, a thick succession of portents, which meant nothing."

The thick succession of letters, telephone calls, and promises emanating from Franklin Roosevelt in the White House in 1944 had been interpreted by historians before Partin's article appeared either as portending nothing or as marking inchoate and unsuccessful efforts by a dying president to determine the outcome of his party's convention. The fact that Roosevelt was seriously ill and that his poor health was openly discussed in 1944 is documented by citations to contemporary newspapers, speeches, and conversations below; and that Roosevelt after the convention did nothing to prepare Harry Truman adequately for possible succession to the presidency has been established amply by historians and by the account of Truman himself. But it was Partin's article that most fully demonstrated that Franklin Roosevelt, despite his deteriorating physical health and his absence from Chicago, was in masterful control of the 1944 Democratic convention's nomination of his running mate.

It was Roosevelt's covert strategy, as revealed by Partin, to preserve the "urban coalition" of organized labor, enfranchised blacks, and urban political machines by the sacrifice of Jimmy Byrnes' vice-presidential ambitions. The foremost leader of this urban coalition in 1944 was Byrnes' old political nemesis from the General Textile Strike, Sidney Hillman of the CIO-PAC and sit-downs of the 1930s. Hillman has been the subject of two biographies, Matthew Josephson's adulatory *Sidney Hillman: Statesman of American Labor* and Steven Fraser's more balanced *Labor Will Rule: Sidney Hillman and the Rise of American Labor*, probably the definitive work. This coalition and its collision with southern political interests is well described in Robert A. Garson, *The Democratic Party and the Politics of Sectionalism, 1941–1948* (Baton Rouge: Louisiana State Univ. Press, 1974).

However, the critical and central importance in 1944 of enfranchised black Americans to the Democratic urban coalition has been largely neglected by most scholars. The most dramatic collision of this part of the urban coalition with the southern sectionalists, over the once controversial Fair Employment Practice Commission, appears to have been forgotten completely. The three most important books on the FEPC are out of print: Herbert Garfinkel, *When Negroes March: The March on Washington Movement in the Organizational Politics for FEPC* (Glencoe, Ill.: Free Press, 1959), Louis Coleridge Kesselman, *The Social Politics of FEPC: A Study in Reform Pressure Movements* (Chapel Hill: Univ. of North Carolina Press, 1948), and Louis Ruchames, *Race, Jobs, and Politics: The Story of FEPC* (New York: Columbia Univ. Press, 1953). The weekly editorial columns written for the Negro newspaper *The Defender* by Walter White throughout July 1944 also are a neglected source for an evaluation of the black vote in that year's presidential election.

It is the thesis of this writer that Roosevelt forgot nothing necessary for his political survival during the summer of 1944 and that foremost in his mind was the emerging political importance of black voters in "doubtful" states with large numbers of electoral college votes and histories of slim Democratic majorities. The quantitative reality and significance of this black vote to the Democratic party in the presidential election of 1944 is supported in detail by the demographic tables and election returns collected by J. B. Shannon in "Presidential Politics in the South," *Journal of Politics* 10 (1948): 464–89. Although this article was published four years after the election of 1944 and three years after Roosevelt's death, the data presented by Shannon were published in national newspapers, including the *New York Times*, the Washington *Star*, and the *Washington Post*, at the time of the 1944 convention, and were therefore available for Roosevelt's reading or for that of his most confidential advisers.

Byrnes himself never seemed fully to appreciate the importance of the issue of civil rights for black Americans as the motive in the machinations against him at the Chicago convention; as late as 1966 Byrnes wrote to a fellow former senator about the 1944 Democratic convention that not until recently had he known that "David Niles was taking such an active part in 1944" (JFB, Folder 1163). David Niles enjoyed considerable access to Roosevelt, with a special responsibility for informing the president on minorities; since both Niles and Philleo Nash continued to work as civil rights advisers during the Truman administration, their papers at the Harry S. Truman Library are a rich source of material for the 1944 convention, particularly those of Philleo Nash. Other primary sources and the resulting published scholarship available at the Truman Library relevant to the black vote in the 1944 election include numerous transcripts of oral history interviews as cited below; out-of-print memoirs, such as Ed Flynn's *You're the Boss* (New York: Viking Press, 1947), George E. Allen's *Presidents Who Have Known Me* (New York: Simon and Schuster, 1950); Jonathan Daniels' *Man of Independence* (Philadelphia: J. B. Lippincott, 1950); and Edwin Pauley's remarkably self-serving first-person memorandum, in which the California author implies he alone achieved Truman's nomination.

Other items concerned primarily with the Truman administration but of some use in understanding the racial reason for the defeat of Jimmy Byrnes' ambitions at the 1944 convention include William C. Berman's *The Politics of Civil Rights in the Truman Administration* (Columbus: Ohio State Univ. Press, 1970); *The Truman Period as a Research Field* (Columbia: Univ. of Missouri Press, 1967) and *The Truman Period as a Research Field: A Reappraisal, 1972* (Columbia: Univ. of Missouri Press, 1974), both edited by Richard Kirkendall. Also useful in regard to Byrnes is the dissertation, regrettably still unpublished, completed under Professor Kirkendall by Mary Hedge Hinchey, "The Frustration of the New Deal Revival, 1944–46" (Univ. of Missouri, 1965).

333 *"to uphold due process"*: Quoted in Arthur M. Schlesinger, Jr., ed., *History of American Presidential Elections*, vol. 4 (New York: Chelsea House, 1971), 2956.
333 *"available and competent Negro workers"*: Quoted in Ruchames, *FEPC*, 15–16.
333 *declined to only 2.5 percent*: Garson, *Sectionalism*, 19.
333 *nation's Negroes to march*: Garfinkel, *March*, 38, 56–57, 60.
334 *"people will* really *march"*: Walter White, *A Man Called White: The Autobiography of Walter White* (New York: Viking Press, 1948), 192.
334 *Executive Order 8802*: The text of this EO is quoted in full in HST, Nash, "Important Dates in FEPC History: President's Committee on Fair Employment Practice, Division of Review and Analysis, Division of Review and Analysis, April 8, 1944," p. 1.
335 *stepchild of the federal government*: For a useful summary of the administrative chronology of the FEPC, see ibid., 1–3.
335 *liaison officer*: *NYT*, 12 June 1943, p. 28, col. 1. Byrnes replaced William H. McReynolds.
336 *"one of the sorest places"*: FDR, OF 4245g, memorandum, Daniels to McIntyre, 26 Jan. 1943.
336 *abruptly canceled the hearings*: Ruchames, *FEPC*, 51.
337 *"A bunch of crackpots"*: *CR*, 78th Cong., 1st sess., 1943, 10294–95.
337 *"Let me know what you think"*: FDR, OF 4245g, memorandum, FDR to JFB and Rosenman, 11 March 1943.
338 *"Negroes now want the committee"*: FDR, OF 4245g, memorandum, Byrnes to FDR, 15 March 1943.
339 *One of the worst beaten*: *NYT*, 13 June 1943, p. 34, cols. 3–6.
339 *suits did not meet wartime specifications*: For an example of the government-mandated simplicity of civilian clothing, see the WPA-enforced standards for work clothing publicized in the Washington *Star*, 5 Oct. 1942, p. 9, cols. 6–7.
339 *"race prejudice should not be ignored"*: *NYT*, 13 June 1943, p. 30, col. 3.
340 *"no useful purpose"*: This correspondence is reprinted in *CR*, 78th Cong., 2d sess., 1944, 6027–28.
340 *"directive" of the president's wishes*: *NYT*, 28 Oct. 1943, p. 25, col. 1.
340 *"what will be the reaction of the Negro"*: Quoted in Ruchames, *FEPC*, 65–66.
341 *"aids Hitler propaganda"*: Quoted in *NYT*, 30 Oct. 1943, p. 17, col. 5.
341 *"These provisions are mandatory"*: Associated Press news story carried in newspapers including the *Kansas City Star*, 7 Nov. 1943.
341 *"clears it up once and for all"*: *NYT*, 7 Nov. 1943, p. 21, col. 1.
342 *similar revolts against Roosevelt*: Garson, *Sectionalism*, 94–112.
343 *"The trouble in Texas"*: FDR, PSF 175, Byrnes to Roosevelt, 1 June 1944. Byrnes' memorandum is accompanied by unidentified press clippings, presumably from southern newspapers intended by Byrnes for Roosevelt's reading of what are described as unruly and violent conventions held in South Carolina by the largely black Progressive Democrats. This memorandum has an interesting archival provenance. Now available at the FDR presidential library from the President's Secretary File, the Byrnes memorandum carries an original notation of "File Personal" and apparently was kept during Roo-

sevelt's years in the White House in the president's more restricted file. No complete copy or draft of this memorandum is to be found in the collection of Byrnes' papers that Byrnes deposited in Clemson, S.C. I am indebted to Partin, "Nomination," for calling my attention to the existence of this letter in the FDR presidential library. The statement by Byrnes to Roosevelt that an increase in oil prices was not necessary for the Roosevelt ticket to carry Texas refers to the administration-sponsored subsidy of "stripper," or marginal, oil wells, by which on the basis of militarily necessitated oil consumption Texas wells producing only a few barrels a day were federally guaranteed a high market price. Jones, *Dollars*, 377.

343   *would call "reverse discrimination"*: CR, 78th Cong., 2d sess., 1944, 5040.

344   *"Oh! This is the beginning"*: Ibid., 5054.

344   *Truman did not take advantage*: For Truman's absence and his failure to record his opinion on the Buck amendment to exempt the FEPC from dependence upon an annual congressional appropriation, an amendment greatly desired by congressional friends of the FEPC, see Ibid., 3061–62. Also of note is the news clipping from the *St. Louis Star Times* in which Chester Stovall, editor of the Negro newspaper the *Saint Louis Call*, was reported as asking the city's ministers to gather petitions protesting discrimination against Negroes in local defense industries: "Since the Truman committee whitewashed the situation here," Stovall was quoted as saying, "we intend to send the petitions directly to the President's Fair Labor Practices Board." The day after the story appeared, a major St. Louis manufacturer wrote a letter to Senator Truman urging the senator and his committee to stand firm against the FEPC and offering to "hop to it" if he could be of use politically to Truman. Truman's foremost secretary, Harry Vaughan, wrote back to the manufacturer by the end of the month thanking him for the letter to Senator Truman and stating, "Mr. Stovall is one of the particular class of humans to which I am allergic—an Ethiopian graduate of Harvard." HST, Truman Senatorial, "Negroes," Walter Hilliker to Harry Truman, 24 Oct. 1941; H. H. Vaughan to Walter Hilliker, 31 Oct. 1941.

344   *"We pledge the establishment"*: Quoted in Schlesinger, ed., *Elections*, 3050.

345   *"straighten out their policies"*: Quoted in Garson, *Sectionalism*, 97.

345   *"A Message to the Republican"*: NYT, 24 June 1944, p. 8, cols. 4–8.

345   *"equal wages for equal work"*: Quoted in Garson, *Sectionalism*, 121.

346   *"it will split the party open"*: Quoted in Freidel, *Rendezvous*, 531.

347   *Byrnes, she answered*: JFB, folder 74(2), "Walter Brown's Diary," July 1944.

348   *gave him a light*: NYT, 12 July 1944, p. 1, col. 1.

351   *"the green light to run"*: JFB, Folder 74(2), "Walter Brown's Diary," July 1944. Of interest as a possible instance of Jimmy Byrnes' exercising historical revisionism on a small scale is that in the margin of Walter Brown's diary recounting the episode on 11 July 1941 when Byrnes is described as sending word to Roosevelt that "it would mean something" if Byrnes supported the FEPC, the word "wrong" is added in pencil. (The entries in Brown's diary concerning the events of the 1944 convention are accurate both in their direct quotations and in their summaries, whenever verifiable by independent sources. However, Brown is frequently mistaken in chronology and days of the week in his diary for July 1944, and there is no other recorded source for this statement by Byrnes in regard to the FEPC.) The handwriting of the word "wrong" is unidentifiable. Before a transcript of a selected portion of Brown's diary was deposited with the Byrnes papers, Jimmy Byrnes asked and received from his former employee Brown permission to review the diary.

See also JFB, Folder 74(1), "The Vice Presidency, 1944," 6; and HST, Oral History Interview with George E. Allen, "Appendix B," undated, Edwin W. Pauley Memorandum, pp. 3–4 (hereafter cited as HST, Pauley Memorandum).

351 *Frank "I Am the Law" Hague*: FDR, PSF 175, summary of telegram by Grace Tully from Hague to Roosevelt, 11 July 1944.

352 *Truman forthrightly voted*: David McCullough, *Truman* (New York: Simon and Schuster, 1992), 243. Truman also was more acceptable to organized labor than was Byrnes, the enforcer of the "hold the line" policy on wages. See JFB, Folder 65, JFB to FDR: "The non-operating railroad employees pressed their fight for legislation granting them the straight eight cents an hour increase. Truman introduced the legislation." 16 Dec. 1943.

352 *"fill the places"*: NYT, 5 July 1944, p. 18, col. 1.

354 *"in the bag for Jimmy:"* Quoted in Byrnes, *Lifetime*, 226–27.

355 *"kiss Negro vote goodbye"*: ER, Box 1751, text of White's speech to the National Wartime Conference of the NAACP, 16 July 1944, p. 8. See also ibid., White to Roosevelt, 19 July 1944.

355 *Roosevelt had won Illinois*: Shannon, "Politics," 469–70. Shannon's demographics are based in part on the tables in the *Sixteenth Census, 1940*, vol. 2, pt. 2, 484–85, and pt. 5, pp. 22–23.

355 *southern Illinois, the "Egypt" area*: Robert Sutton et al., *The Heartland: Pages from Illinois History* (Lake Forest, Ill.: Deerpath, 1975), 107. In 1818, as many as 2,000 slaves worked in the territory-owned salt mines within present-day Illinois.

356 *"He cannot be my candidate"*: Quoted in Doris E. Saunders, "The Day Dawson Saved America from a Racist President," *Ebony*, July 1972, 49. For a physical description of Dawson, including the wounds he sustained in combat during World War I, see *CR*, 78th Cong., 2d sess., 1944, 5059.

356 *he was "OK"*: JFB, Folder 74(2), "Walter Brown's Diary," 16 July 1944.

356 *also indicated conservative victories*: NYT, 17 July 1944.

356 *recite for him the speech*: JFB, Folder 74(2) "Walter Brown's Diary," 17 July 1944.

357 *choice of the words*: Partin, "Nomination," 99–100.

357 *Byrnes had declined to meet with Hillman*: Steven Fraser, the most recent biographer of Hillman, described in 1991 (*Labor*, 530) as accepted fact the "personal scarring" Hillman had received administratively with the orchestrated demise of the OPM "at the hands of Byrnes and his warlord allies in 1942." The unacknowledged source for this "scarring" adjective is Eliot Janeway's *The Struggle for Survival: A Chronicle of Economic Mobilization in World War II* (New Haven: Yale Univ. Press, 1951), 348. Fraser also identifies Janeway with Bernard Baruch as being among the political "friends" and boosters of Byrnes for the vice presidency, but Ed Pauley explicitly identifies Janeway, then a writer at *Time* magazine, as an organizer at the 1944 Democratic convention for the vice-presidential candidacy of William Douglas. HST, Pauley Memorandum, p. 6.

Robert Messer in his 1975 dissertation ("Making," 102) correctly wrote that "Roosevelt in 1944 used both Ed Flynn and Sidney Hillman as his surrogates in blocking Byrnes' nomination." But Professor Messer in the next sentence curiously adds, "Hillman, Secretary of the C.I.O.'s Political Action Committee, was a stranger to Byrnes." Messer in his subsequent book (*Alliance*, p. 28), refers to Roosevelt's having in July "secretly met alone with Hillman on the 12th," although Messer's source for this statement is Byrnes' second memoir, *All in One Lifetime*, where it is stated that Hillman's meetings with FDR on either July 12 or July 13 were known to Byrnes when Byrnes recognized Hillman walking into the Oval Office on July 13, 1944.

357   *not oppose the selection of Byrnes*: Byrnes, *Lifetime*, 228.

357   *if he were a delegate to the convention*: NYT, 13 July 1944, p. 1, col. 1. See also "Would Back Wallace, FDR States in Letter, Stock of Byrnes Rises," *Greenville News*, 18 July 1944, p. 1, cols. 7–8, and Wallace, *Diary*, 362.

357   *placards printed reading "Roosevelt and Byrnes"*: JFB, Folder 74(2), "Walter Brown's Diary," 17 July 1944.

357   *"veiled reference to James F. Byrnes"*: NYT, 18 July 1944, p. 9, col. 6.

358   *"It's all over. It's Byrnes"*: Hannegan's remark to Flynn is quoted in Allen, *Presidents*, 131.

358   *"cut him to the quick"*: JFB, Folder 74(2), "Walter Brown's Diary," 17 July 1944.

359   *"not seen anyone since I left home"*: JFB, Folder 74(1) "Memorandum of Telephone Conversation with FDR on Tuesday, July 18, 1944."

360   *"Always sincerely, Franklin Roosevelt"*: The complete text of FDR's note to Hannegan is reproduced in HST, Pauley Memorandum, p. 6. A partial text of this note also is reproduced in Schlesinger, ed., *Elections*, 3061, but the editor of this volume chose to omit the valedictory "Always Sincerely," so characteristic of Franklin Roosevelt.

360   *"at liberty" to show Byrnes the letter*: JFB, Folder 74(2), "Walter Brown's Diary," 18 July 1944.

360   *"Hannegan with great earnestness"*: JFB, Folder 74(1), notes dated 18 July 1944.

360   *"men were so many tools"*: JFB, Folder 1163, Byrnes to Wheeler, 6 April 1966.

361   *"in deference to the wishes of the president"*: JFB, Folder 532. See also *NYT*, 25 July 1944, p. 18, col. 5.

361   *Then to revenge*: NYT, 25 July 1944, p. 18, col. 5. Krock in this article states that Hillman was at the White House on 12 July, a statement that supports Messer's description of a "secret" meeting between Roosevelt and Hillman that day and explains Byrnes' observing Hillman entering the Oval Office the following day, 13 July 1944, from "the colonnade used by occupants of the White House residence." Catledge in his memoir (*Life*, 148) writes that this story was run under Krock's byline rather than under Catledge's because Catledge's friendship with Byrnes and Chicago's mayor, Ed Kelly, "was well known." Hence, either Byrnes or Kelly almost certainly was the source provided to Catledge for the statements used in Krock's article.

361   *"Communists have registered"*: Quoted and tabulated in Schlesinger, ed., *Elections*, 3034. For further examples of scholarly overestimation of the CIO-PAC, see the statements in Fraser, *Rule*, that because of the rise and influence of the CIO-PAC, "the Supreme Court ruled against the whites-only primary in 1943," (p. 500) and that in 1944 "Cotton 'Ed' Smith of South Carolina" was among those Democrats losing in primaries "to PAC-endorsed candidates" (p. 514). The Supreme Court's precedent-making *Smith* decision, ruling that blacks could not be excluded from the primaries of the Democratic party of Texas, was announced in April 1944. The ruling was 8 to 1, the sole dissenter being Justice Owen Roberts of Philadelphia, who in the 1939 majority decision in *Hague* v. *CIO* had voted in favor of the CIO.

In South Carolina, Cotton Ed Smith did indeed lose the 1944 primary to Olin Johnson, but it must be remembered that *both* candidates were ardent racists in comparison to Byrnes and that the CIO-PAC failed to support the South Carolina Progressive Democratic candidate, who campaigned on the CIO-PAC program of *both* unionism and racial equality. For a thorough discussion of the disavowal of the principle of racial equality by the CIO-endorsed candidate Olin Johnson in the South Carolina senatorial primary of 1944, see Anthony Barry Mills, "Palmetto Politician: The Early Political Career of Olin S. Johnson, 1896–1945" (Ph.D. diss., University of North Carolina, 1976), 448–50.

362 *"president and I were as disturbed"*: ER, Box 1751, Eleanor Roosevelt to White, 19 July 1944.

363 *"just dropped into the slot"*: Ed Flynn is quoted in Schlesinger, ed., *Elections*, 3025.

363 *inside his coat pocket*: Turner Catledge, "Portrait of a Realist," *NYT Magazine*, 8 July 1945, 37.

363 *neither Byrnes nor his wife rose*: HST, Oral History Interview with Jonathan Daniels, pp. 61–62.

363 *exquisitely malicious sense*: JFB, 74(1) telegram with penciled notation, 17 July 1944.

364 *the constituency of urban Negroes: NYT*, 13 July 1944, p. 1, col. 1.

364 *"I invented the FEPC"*: Quoted in Kesselman, *FEPC*, 209.

364 *filibuster led by southern senators*: For a detailed and authoritative account of the congressional destruction of the FEPC during the late Roosevelt and early Truman administration, see Will Maslow, "FEPC—A Case History in Parliamentary Maneuver," *University of Chicago Law Review* 13 (1946): 411–44. See also Hinchey, "Frustration," 112–202.

364 *The coalition thus held*: Schlesinger, ed., *Elections*, 3096.

364 *"For a tired, quarrelsome"*: FDR, PPF 2816, telegram, Byrnes to Roosevelt, 8 Nov. 1944.

14: ROOSEVELT'S LAST GIFT

Any reader of the literature of logistical supply and the macroeconomics of the Second World War is apt, on concluding that study, to agree with Albert Speer, who ironically expressed relief when Allied aircraft bombed the Ministry of Armaments building in Berlin on 22 Nov. 1943, destroying much of the paperwork in Speer's office: "Although we have been fortunate in that large parts of the current files of the Ministry have been burned and so relieved us for a time of useless ballast, we cannot really expect that such events will continually introduce the necessary fresh air into our works."

There are nevertheless among the wide tedium of primary documents and officially sanctioned histories the occasional spots of insightful research and honest writing worth saving. Among the latter, available in reprint, is the official history prepared by the War Records Section, Bureau of the Budget, *The United States at War*. The tables of organization of the various war agencies found on pp. 386 and 398 of this volume are particularly useful for any student of Byrnes' wartime administration and assumption of authority. A cautious reader will remember, however, that Director of the Budget Harold D. Smith clashed frequently with Jimmy Byrnes at the OES and OWM/OWMR over questions of authority (Somers, *OWMR*, 66–70) and that Byrnes is frequently slighted by omission in the budget's text.

Other useful studies, cited in chapter 12, are David Novick, Melvin Anshen, and W. C. Truppner's *Wartime Production Controls* and Eliot Janeway's *The Struggle for Survival*. By no means the most tedious of the studies is the history prepared by the Civilian Production Administration, *Industrial Mobilization for War*. This book is quite well written in stretches, but, to paraphrase Dr. Johnson, since it contains 1,010 pages, no man or woman ever wished it longer.

It is regrettable that the two dissertations that discuss Byrnes' wartime administration most professionally do not compare it at greater length to that of his Third Reich counterpart, Albert Speer. John Partin's " 'Assistant President' for the Home Front" does not mention Speer at all. Robert Messer's "The Making of a Cold Warrior" limits its comparison of Byrnes and Speer to half a sentence. Such omissions are all the more glaring since the English-language translation *Inside the Third Reich: Memoirs of Albert Speer* (New York: Macmillan, 1970) has long been available and since at the same time in early 1942 that Jimmy Byrnes was urging Roosevelt to appoint an armaments czar ("For convenience's sake, call him Hopkins") Speer was advancing the same argument with Hitler ("There must be one man to make all decisions. Industry does not care who it was.")

The charge of an increasing authoritarianism imposed upon the U.S. economy, a development that Speer in chapter 15 of his memoirs ascribes to his American counterparts Byrnes and General Clay, is vigorously answered in the negative in Jean Edward Smith's masterly biography, *Lucius D. Clay: An American Life* (New York: Henry Holt, 1990). This work is rich in statements by Clay about his personal friend and longtime political mentor. The result of nearly twenty years' research and numerous interviews with General Clay, Smith's book is likely to remain the definitive account of the life of Byrnes' deputy at the OWMR.

All factual references to the weapons and battles of the Second World War in this chapter are, unless otherwise noted, to John Keegan's *The Second World War* (New York: Penguin, 1989), which within but a few years of its initial publication appears to have been accepted by the historians and readers of the United States and the United Kingdom as the best one-volume military history of that conflict. The British historian John Ellis' *Brute Force: Allied Strategy and Tactics in the Second World War* (New York: Viking Press, 1990) cannot be praised highly enough. Extrapolating a covert Allied strategy from logistics tables and the unnecessary suffering of Axis and Allied soldiers and civilians alike, Ellis has simply done the most significant research on the Second World War since the end of that conflict. At the same time, Ellis does not forget that, for all the postwar academic analysis of strategy and military technology, the Second World War "was in reality a war of desperate attrition, and victory in the end hinged upon human death" (p. 526).

365   *Don't be a sorehead*: HST, Oral History Interview with Judge Marvin Jones, p. 119.
366   *"they are free to think"*: JFB, Folder 74(1), Frankfurter to Byrnes, 27 July 1944.
367   *"Harry S. Truman, U.S.S."*: Ibid., telegram, Truman to Byrnes, 27 July 1944.
367   *"Better ask Jimmy Byrnes"*: *Complete Presidential Press Conferences of Franklin D. Roosevelt*, vol. 23 (New York: Da Capo Press, 1972), 216.
367   *"He had a way"*: HST, Jones Interview, p. 124.
367   *"almost to hero worship"*: *NYT*, 28 Nov. 1944, p. 22, col. 5.
368   *"traditional southern internationalist"*: Lloyd C. Gardner, *Architects of Illusion: Men and Ideas in Foreign Policy, 1941–1949* (Chicago: Quadrangle Books, 1970). For a closer study of the tradition of internationalism among

the South's politicians and its displacement by a Cold War chauvinism, see Seabury, *Waning*.

368 *"carried the torch for Woodrow Wilson"*: *NYT*, 31 Oct. 1944, p. 15, col. 7.

369 *a Wehrmarcht division*: Keegan, *War*, 439.

369 *tax deducted in advance*: Partin, "Assistant President," 69, 72.

369 *suffer 400,000 casualties*: For the reaction of a pro-reconversion publication to Byrnes' estimate, see "Byrnes 'Tip' on Casualties Gives OWL Headache," *PM*, 28 Dec. 1943, p. 6, col. 1.

370 *"work or fight"*: Somers, *OWMR*, 164–67.

370 *Betting at horse racetracks*: Blum, *Victory*, 96–97.

371 *"it now vanished utterly"*: Catton, *War Lords*, 292.

371 *"devoted entirely to storage"*: Quoted in Polenberg, *War*, 173.

371 *suffered a "Byrne-out"*: This colloqualism is quoted in William Manchester, *The Glory and the Dream: A Narrative History of America, 1932–1972* (Boston: Little, Brown, 1973), 274.

372 *a de facto civilian draft*: Somers, *OWMR*, 169.

372 *Byrnes politely replied*: Byrnes, *Lifetime*, 251.

372 *"privileged one hundred companies"*: Blum, *Victory*, 123.

372 *ever consider changing*: Somers, *OWMR*, 117.

373 *"an inner circle conflict"*: Wallace, *Diary*, 287.

374 *"Nazis have at Cassino"*: James F. Byrnes, "Preparations for Peace on the Homefront," *Proceedings of the Academy of Political Science*, 21 (1944): 121–28.

374 *"coming together of the corporations"*: C. Wright Mills, *The Power Elite* (New York: Oxford Univ. Press, 1956), 212. But the sole source that Mills cites in support of his assertion is Catton's *War Lords*, which was admittedly annecdotal rather than analytic and an apologia for Donald Nelson.

374 *interpreted his duties as war mobilizer*: Somers, *OWMR*, 83–84.

374 *tells the story: Industrial Mobilization for War*, 761–62.

374 *simply had run out of shells*: Quoted in Ellis, *Brute Force*, xvii.

375 *nicknamed . . . "the Ronson"*: Elizabeth-Anne Wheal, Stephen Pope, and James Taylor, *A Dictionary of the Second World War* (New York: Peter Bedrick Books, 1990), 432; Keegan, *War*, 399, 401.

375 *ballistically and technologically inferior*: Thomas Parrish et al., eds., *Encyclopedia of World War II* (New York: Simon and Schuster, 1978), 224.

375 *"an authoritarian stiffening"*: Speer, *Inside*, 211.

376 *"worse than the Germans"*: Fussell, *Wartime*, 268.

376 *"winter of 1864–65 all over again"*: Catton, *War Lords*, 293–94.

377 *"victory goes to the side"*: Quoted in Ellis, *Brute Force*, 275.

377 *Biddle notified the two companies*: Blum, *Victory*, 136–38.

378 *"engaged in the S-1 project"*: JFB, Folder 637(3), memorandum, Byrnes to Roosevelt, 13 Sept. 1944.

379 *"That's exactly it"*: Quoted in Messer, *Alliance*, 35.

379 *"interested in that cause in 1919"*: FDR, PSF 121, Byrnes to Roosevelt, 13 Sept. 1944.

380 *"go with me on this trip"*: Byrnes, *Lifetime*, 252.

380 *"much to be said"*: HST, Daniels Interview, pp. 55–56.

380–82 *Byrnes later was warned* to *"Father Flynn will say Mass"*: Byrnes, *Lifetime*, 252–55.

383 *"did not come along for the ride"*: HST, Daniels Interview, pp. 55–56.

383 *reminded Byrnes of "new corn"*: FDR, Stephen Early Papers, box 1, "Press

and Radio Conference #9 Held by War Mobilizer Director James F. Byrnes, 13 February 1945," p. 1 (hereafter cited as FDR, Early).

383 *"most honest-looking horse thief"*: Quoted in Wallace, *Diary*, 475.

384 *use of a concealed microphone*: R. J. C. Butlow, "The FDR Tapes," *American Heritage* Feb.–March 1984, 8–23.

385 *"funeral parlor with Hollywood parentage"*: FDR, Early, 1. In confirmation of Byrnes' description of this White House theater, known among employees there as the Hat Box, see William Seale, *The President's House: A History* (Washington, D.C.: National Geographic Society, 1986), 978–79, 982–83.

386 *"made to the president"* to *"weather, and that sort of thing"*: FDR, Early, 6, 10–11, 25.

386 *"your press conferences have been grand"*: FDR, PSF 121, memorandum, Roosevelt to Byrnes, 26 Feb. 1945.

387 *"V-E Day is far off"*: FDR, PPF 2816, Byrnes to Roosevelt, 24 March 1945.

387 *"knocked off my feet"*: JFB, Folder 70(2), Roosevelt to Byrnes, 25 March 1945.

387 *"hate to have you go"*: Reprinted in *F.D.R.: His Personal Letters*, ed. Elliott Roosevelt, vol. 4 (New York: Duell, Sloan, and Pearce, 1950), p. 1579.

387 *"It is not pleasant"*: FDR, PPF 2816, Roosevelt to Byrnes, 31 March 1945.

387 *"some people are so prima-donnish"*: Quoted in Harrett, *Off the Record*, 329.

388 *"find Jimmy Byrnes for me"*: HST, Daniels Interview, p. 120.

388 *"balance things up"*: Harry S. Truman, *Memoirs*, vol. 1, *Year of Decisions* (Garden City, N.Y.: Doubleday, 1955), 34–35.

389 *"He'd been to Yalta"*: Quoted in Merle Miller, *Plain Speaking: An Oral Biography of Harry S. Truman* (New York: Berkley, 1974), 49.

389 *"smart boys in the State Department"*: Harry S. Truman, *Off the Record: The Private Papers of Harry S. Truman*, ed. Robert H. Ferrell (New York: Harper & Row, 1980), 49.

15: POLITICS AND THE BOMB

Any general reader approaching the dark woods of radical historical revisionism of the atomic bomb should keep at hand the works of two scholars. Although described as a "New Left" historian by some writers associated with the Harry S. Truman Library, Barton S. Bernstein provides a nonideological and comprehensive discussion of the motivations behind the bombing of Hiroshima and Nagasaki in "Roosevelt, Truman, and the Atomic Bomb, 1941–1945: A Reinterpretation," *Political Science Quarterly* 90 (1975): 23–69. Bernstein concludes, after surveying the revisionist arguments, that military considerations were primary. A more centralist scholar, Robert Maddox, criticizes radical revisionist scholarship in more detail in *The New Left and the Origins of the Cold War* (Princeton: Princeton Univ. Press, 1973). Although not citing the omission of Byrnes' letter of 3 May 1945, to Benjamin Cohen, included in chapter 16's discussion of the scholarship of Gar Alperovitz, Maddox details many similar instances of disregarded or truncated primary sources in revisionist scholarship.

Alperovitz in *Atomic Diplomacy: Hiroshima and Potsdam: The Use of the Atomic Bomb and the American Confrontation with Soviet Power* (New York: Penguin Books, 1985) quotes frequently and approvingly from Robert Messer's previously cited dissertation, "The Making of a Cold Warrior," in defense of his thesis. The reader is cautioned, however, as is illustrated in the notes below, to compare Alperovitz's elliptical use of quotes to the full text cited in Messer. Alperovitz does not discuss in his book the article Messer published subsequent to his dissertation: "Paths Not Taken: The United States Department of State and Alternatives to Containment, 1945–1946," *Diplomatic History* 1 (1977): 297–319. Messer here details how the Clifford-Elsey report preempted a more accommodationist policy toward the Soviet Union being proposed by Byrnes' closest adviser at State, Freeman Matthews.

In defense of Alperovitz's characterization of Secretary Byrnes as "exceedingly complex, secretive, and devious," it should be noted that in 1962, while researching the first edition of *Atomic Diplomacy*, Alperovitz wrote to Byrnes asking permission to see the 1945–46 papers in his files. Miss Cassandra Connor replied, denying the request, explaining that Byrnes "only had duplicates of a few memoranda and letters of a personal nature for that period" (JFB, Folder 1063).

Currently available archival materials both within and outside the Byrnes files support the thesis of the following two chapters: that the atomic bomb was used against Japan as the consequence of the Allied strategy of "brute force" and the domestic political exigencies faced by Byrnes and Truman.

390   *"If I can be of service"*: HST, OF237, telegram, Byrnes to Truman, 13 April 1945.
392   *"secrecy attached to 'Manhattan' "*: JFB, Folder 615(2), Byrnes to Stimson, 11 Sept. 1943.
393   *"definite assurance yet of production"*: JFB, Folder 596(2), 3 March 1943.
398   *"Byrnes made short work"* to *"Mr. Byrnes expressed a fear"*: Richard Rhodes, *The Making of the Atomic Bomb* (New York: Simon and Schuster, 1986), 634, 646. See also Martin J. Sherwin, *A World Destroyed: The Atomic Bomb and the Grand Alliance* (New York: Alfred A. Knopf, 1975), appendix L, for minutes of the Interim Committee meeting.
398   *politically untenable in Congress*: Polenberg, *War*, 241.
400–404   *"there was trouble ahead"* to *"communicate with Byrnes"*: Spencer R. Weart and Gertrud Weiss Szilard, eds., *Leo Szilard: His Version of the Facts: Selected Recollections and Correspondence* (Cambridge: MIT Press, 1978), 181, 183–85.
404   *"As the Einstein letter"*: Byrnes, *Lifetime*, 284.
405   *"bonus" of using the atomic bomb*: Barton J. Bernstein, "Roosevelt, Truman, and the Atomic Bomb, 1941–1945: A Reinterpretation," *Political Science Quarterly* 90 (1975): 60.
408   *LeMay personally contributed to writing*: Curtis LeMay, *Mission with LeMay: My Story* (Garden City, N.Y.: Doubleday, 1965), 375.
411   *"only way to find out"*: Bard's memorandum is quoted in its entirety in Sherwin, *World*, appendix O.
413   *"it is not clear whether Byrnes"*: Ibid., 194.
413   *"even more magnanimous policy"*: Messer, "Making," 279.

16:   THE STREET TO HIROSHIMA

415   *"It isn't a matter of whether"*: *Washington Post*, 3 July 1945, p. 1, col. 7.
415   *these peace feelers existed: FRUS*, 1945 6:487–95. See particularly "Memorandum of Acting Director of the Office of Strategic Services (Magruder) to the Secretary of State," 9 Aug. 1945: "Mr. [Allen] Dulles comments that there is no direct evidence that these suggestions from the Japanese group in Switzerland are based on instructions from Tokyo. Mr. Dulles has again

cautioned Jacobsson [Per Jacobsson, a Swedish banker contacted by a Japanese private citizen] that the only question is whether the Japanese are ready to accept unconditional surrender as set forth in the Potsdam and other previous declarations" (p. 495). See also *FRUS, The Conference of Berlin (The Potsdam Conference)*, 1945, 2:1589–90, and, for a determination of the knowledge of these peace feelers among the U.S. delegation at Potsdam, ibid., 1:878.

416 *Byrnes therefore approved the actions*: FRUS, Potsdam, 1945, 1:902–3.

417 *confirming Senator Capehart's assertions*: "Concerning Japanese Peace Offers: Statement by Acting Secretary Grew" (reprint of press release issued by U.S. Department of State on 19 July 1945), *Department of State Bulletin* 13 (15 July 1945): 84–85.

418 *"equivalent of unconditional surrender"*: FRUS, Potsdam, 1945, 1:888–92.

418 *"terrible political repercussions"*: See ibid., 2:1267, for the text of Hull's confidential cable of 16 July 1945 to Byrnes. See also ibid., 1268, for the memorandum regarding the telephone conversation between Grew and Hull, cabled to Byrnes on 17 July 1945: "Mr. Hull stated that he had thought that point over carefully—the political side—and he appreciated the other side as well. He thought, however, that we would have a very difficult time there, and that was the reason he suggested that we wait for other developments, to see if something wouldn't happen." See also Martin J. Sherwin, *A World Destroyed: The Atomic Bomb and the Grand Alliance* (New York, Alfred A. Knopf, 1975), 229: "This debate—which bore closely on the question of whether or not to modify the demand for unconditional surrender—was temporarily settled by Byrnes, who sided with Acheson and MacLeish on the advice of the ailing former Secretary of State, Cordell Hull."

419–20 *"we are at the psychological moment"* to *"so I pressed it no further"*: FRUS, Potsdam, 1945, 2:1265–67.

420 *"in so much on the kill"*: JFB, Folder 54(1), "W.B.'s Notes," 24 July 1945.

421 *"Jimmy Byrnes played his cards"*: W. Averell Harriman and Elie Abel, *Special Envoy to Churchill and Stalin, 1941–1946* (New York: Random House, 1975), 488.

421 *"do not at this present time"*: FRUS, Potsdam, 1945, 2:276.

421 *Soviet Union would "keep its word"*: Ibid., 1582–87.

422 *"it would take a large army"*: Forrestal in his diary noted only that Byrnes was eager to end the war before the Soviet Union's entry: James Forrestal, *The Forrestal Diaries*, ed. Walter Millis (New York: Viking Press, 1951). In subsequent interviews with Herbert Feis, however, Feis noted Byrnes as telling him that at his meeting with Forrestal, Byrnes had also been briefed on the size of the Soviet forces along the Manchurian border and had agreed with Forrestal's opinion that there was little the United States could do to prevent their deployment into China. JFB, Folder 297, H[erbert] F[eis] memo on Byrnes, undated.

422 *"inevitable that Russia come in"*: Quoted in Thomas G. Paterson, "Potsdam, the Atomic Bomb, and the Cold War: A Discussion with James F. Byrnes," *Pacific Historical Review* 41 (1972): 228.

423 *"answer of course will be negative"*: FRUS, Potsdam, 1945, 2:460.

423 *initial publication, in 1949, of Leo Szilard's memoirs*: Leo Szilard, "A Personal History of the Atomic Bomb" (University of Chicago Round Table radio discussion, 25 Sept. 1949), 14–16.

424 *"with the ease of a professional"*: Frazier, "Southerner," 120.

424 *"come with me into Macedonia"*: Byrnes, *Lifetime*, 10–11. For the 1946 Yugoslav confrontation, see *NYT*, 12 Aug. 1946, p. 1, col. 4.

425 *"could not have remembered much"*: Robert H. Ferrell, "Truman Foreign Policy: A Traditionalist View," in Kirkendall, ed., *Research Field: A Reappraisal*, 12–14, 24–30, 45.

425 *imputes in a primary way*: Michael Leigh, "Is There a Revisionist Thesis on the Origins of the Cold War?" *Political Science Quarterly* 89 (1974): 101–16.

425 *termed the "radical" revisionists*: Jerald A. Combs, *American Diplomatic History: Two Centuries of Changing Interpretations* (Berkeley: Univ. of California Press, 1983), 255–56.

425–26 *"exceedingly complex, secretive, and devious"* to *"experienced moral difficulties with killing"*: Gar Alperovitz, *Atomic Diplomacy: Hiroshima and Potsdam: The Use of the Atomic Bomb and the American Confrontation with Soviet Power*, expanded and updated ed. (New York: Penguin Books, 1985), 38, 46, 48, 54.

426 *comparatively inconsequential mistake*: Ibid., 40.

426 *"Byrnes supported the Dixiecrat"*: Gabriel Kolko, *The Politics of War: The World and United States Policy, 1943–1945* (New York: Random House, 1968), 554.

427 *disregard for the verifiable facts*: Although Paterson's article concerning the entry from Senator Austin's diary is cited in the "Bibliography of Important Sources" to *Atomic Diplomacy* (p. 382), this diary entry is nowhere discussed in the text of the 1965 or the 1985 edition. The closest Alperovitz's comes to referring to Byrnes' confidential conversation with Senator Austin is his general statement "We know that the politicians involved often told people want they wanted to hear, and they very often did not tell them of other related, confidential matters. In some cases there is reason to believe the Secretary of State may have been currying favor with individuals who subsequently recorded their conversations, and that what was said was far different from what Byrnes believed" (p. 36). The sole source cited by Alperovitz for this assertion is his reference "See Messer, 'The Making of a Cold Warrior' (Ph.D. dissertation), for a discussion of this problem [with Byrnes] in general" (p. 389). Messer does discuss this primary document in his dissertation (pp. 301–2). His interpretation is that "this political use of the bomb is an early manifestation of Byrnes' practice of atomic diplomacy." Austin's diary is not discussed in Messer's subsequent *Alliance*.

427 *"bourbon and branch water"*: Messer, "Making," 470.

427 *seriously questioned by the editor*: Author's interview with Harry S. Ashmore, 1993.

427 *many of the obvious misstatements*: Messer, "Making," 455.

428 *"to say nothing of the atomic bomb"*: Alperovitz, *Diplomacy*, 40.

428 *"so secret he would not mention it"*: JFB, Folder 189, Personal, Byrnes to Cohen, 3 May 1945.

428 *"provision of information"*: Alperovitz, *Diplomacy*, x. Messer in his 1975 dissertation is more judicious, noting only that Walter Brown, as determined by entries in his diary from March to July 1945, was unaware of Byrnes' meetings with the Interim Committee. In the bibliography to his 1985 introduction to *Diplomacy* (p. 385), Alperovitz quotes in part the approving footnotes by Messer in his dissertation that "the fundamental argument of the bomb's influence on United States diplomacy at Potsdam put forth by Gar Alperovitz in *Atomic Diplomacy* . . . is persuasively supported by contemporary evidence . . . ." (ellipses by Alperovitz). The full citation, found on p.

491 of Messer's dissertation, reads, "The fundamental influence on United States diplomacy at Potsdam put forth by Gar Alperovitz in *Atomic Diplomacy: Hiroshima and Nagasaki* (New York, 1965), echoing the early, more speculative insights of P. M. S. Blackett, in *Fear, War, and the Bomb* (New York, 1948), is persuasively supported by contemporary evidence, most especially the diaries kept by Walter Brown, Joseph Davies, and Henry Stimson. However, Alperovitz's narrow chronological focus and his selective use of Byrnes' retrospective accounts leads [*sic*] him to overstate his case in respect to the Secretary of State's thinking."

428   *guilty as hell*: Quoted in Gregg F. Herken, " 'Stubborn, Obstinate, and They Don't Scare': The Russians, the Bomb, and James F. Byrnes," in *James F. Byrnes and the Origins of the Cold War*, ed. Kendrick A. Clements (Durham, N.C.: Carolina Academic Press, 1982), 49. See also James F. Byrnes Transcript, Dulles Oral History Project, Dulles MSS, Princeton, N.J.

429   *Alperovitz repeats three times to "war without an invasion"*: Alperovitz, *Diplomacy*, 55, 154, 282, 386.

430   *"fought the* Wehrmacht*"*: *Washington Post*, 2 June 1945, p. 1, col. 5.

430   *"proposals could be made through Russia"*: Ibid, 26 May 1945, p. 2, col. 2.

430   *approximately 2,675 kamikaze airplanes*: Herbert Feis, "The Atomic Bomb and the End of World War II," in *The Atomic Bomb: Critical Issues*, ed. Barton J. Bernstein (Boston: Little, Brown, 1976), 152.

431   *"under any circumstances whatsoever"*: JFB, Folder 571, Togo to Sato, 21 July 1945.

432   *depressed him greatly*: JFB, Folder 297, "H[erbert] F[eis] memo on Byrnes ms." undated.

433   *Stalin had been caught "asleep"*: Paterson, "Byrnes," 229. For a discussion of the likelihood that Professor Klaus Fuchs or Dr. Alan May provided details of Anglo-American atomic research to the USSR, see John W. Wheeler-Bennett and Anthony Nicholls, *The Semblance of Peace: the Political Settlement after the Second World War* (London: Macmillan, 1971), 372–73.

433   *at least 78,000 people*: Keegan, *War*, 584.

433   *twenty-three American prisoners*: For a discussion of the deaths of Allied POWs as a result of the U.S. atomic bombings, and the subsequent indifference of the U.S. military, see Sherwin, *World*, 269. For the report of two U.S. captives tied up and stoned to death by their Japanese guards at Hiroshima immediately after that city's bombing, see Gordon Thomas and Max Morgan-Witts, *Ruin from the Air: The Enola Gay's Atomic Mission to Hiroshima* (London: H. Hamilton, 1977), 336.

434   *"prerogatives of His Majesty"*: FRUS, 1945, 6:627.

434–35   *Byrnes protested angrily to "crucifixion of the president"*: JFB, Folder 602, "W.B.'s book," 4–5. See also Herbert Feis, *Japan Subdued: The Atomic Bomb and the End of the War in the Pacific* (Princeton: Princeton Univ. Press, 1961).

436   *"they were free-will telegrams"*: Wallace, *Diary*, 473–74.

436   *"Our position is as follows"*: FRUS, 1945, 6:631–32.

437   *withholding from its people*: Ibid.

17: ROCKING THE BOAT WITH TRUMAN

Two dissertations, and the books based on them, are central to understanding James F. Byrnes' actions at the U.S. State Department. The first is Patricia Dawson

Ward, "James F. Byrnes and the Council of Foreign Ministers, 1945–1946" (Univ. of Texas at Austin, 1975), published as *The Threat of Peace: James F. Byrnes and the Council of Foreign Ministers, 1945–1946* (Kent, Ohio: Kent State Univ. Press, 1979). The second is Robert Messer's previously cited "The Making of a Cold Warrior," published as *The End of an Alliance.*

Professors Ward, Messer, and other scholars of Byrnes such Gregg F. Herken participated in a symposium on Byrnes' diplomacy at the University of South Carolina at Columbia during the first week of Nov. 1979. Papers read and comments made at this symposium were recorded on tapes now available from the James F. Byrnes collection at Clemson, S.C. Some of the articles and comments also were transcribed under the editorship of Kendrick A. Clements and published as *James F. Byrnes and the Origins of the Cold War* (Durham, N.C.: Carolina Academic Press, 1982). It is unfortunate that neither Porter McKeever, an accomplished author and former delegate to the UN who was an unstinting admirer of Byrnes, nor any of the prominent revisionist critics of Byrnes such as Gar Alperovitz or Gabriel Kolko attended or spoke at this symposium. Thus an opportunity was missed for a full intellectual engagement among the admirers and critics of Byrnes' career. With the outstanding exception of the original and well-cited research of Herken, most of the monographs presented at this symposium by such scholars as Clements and Robert Ferrell lean toward the midwestern "Kirkendall school" of historical interpretation, relying overmuch upon the sources at the Harry S. Truman Library, in Independence, Missouri. These sources in regard to Byrnes frequently are incomplete; and in the case of many papers deposited at the library during Truman's lifetime by former political adversaries of Byrnes in the Truman administration, the documents often are post hoc attempts to please a former boss.

The records of this symposium are useful, however, thanks to the remarkable gathering there of a coterie of Byrnes' contemporaries and confidants during his years at the State Department and afterward. These persons included Walter Brown, George Curry, and U.S. Appellate Judge Donald S. Russell. Mr. Brown's remarks were not recorded; but Judge Russell, who has the reputation with this author and many other authors of equaling his late mentor Jimmy Byrnes in remaining pleasantly enigmatic during interviews, unburdened himself on this occasion of his strongly held opinions regarding the public service of Henry Wallace, Byrnes, and Truman, and of his evaluation of the general quality of Byrnes scholarship as of 1979. Judge Russell's lengthy remarks were recorded on tape but, unfortunately, not published in Clement's edited text.

Other first-person narratives by his contemporaries useful in appraising Byrnes' public career are Charles Bohlen's favorable *Witness to History, 1929–1969* (New York: W. W. Norton, 1973), George F. Kennan's *Memoirs: 1925–1950* (Boston: Little, Brown, 1967), Dean Acheson's *Present at the Creation: My Years in the State Department* (New York: W. W. Norton, 1969), and Clark Clifford's *Counsel to the President: A Memoir* (New York: Random House, 1991). The last three are uniformly hostile to Byrnes' reputation; of the three, Clifford's book is the most objectively honest. When discussing past political disputes in which he emerged as the unqualified winner and when all other participants in the dispute are dead, Clifford is frank in recounting his motives and tactics.

However, historical reputations particularly among diplomats are highly volatile as state papers are released and the temperaments change among succeeding generations of scholars. A case in point is the posthumous tumble of Byrnes' occasional ideological opponent, John McCloy, whom scholars of the last ten years seem to have successfully deconstructed as being unworthy of inclusion among the six "wise men" of U.S. postwar diplomacy. Nevertheless, two scholarly studies largely disapproving of Byrnes' diplomacy are likely to remain useful to future readers: Gabriel Kolko's *The Politics of War* and the more balanced and objectively researched *The United States and the Origins of the Cold War, 1941–1947* (New York: Columbia Univ. Press, 1972), by John Lewis Gaddis.

A final primary source of unique historical and literary value has been curiously neglected by subsequent scholars. This is Harold Nicolson's article "Peacemaking at Paris: Success, Failure or Farce?" *Foreign Affairs* 25 (1947): 190–203. Ward makes some use of this article, written soon after Nicolson had returned from Paris after reporting on the conference for the BBC, in her dissertation and book; it is nowhere cited in Messer's *Alliance*. Nicolson, a former diplomat, created a historical and literary gem of post-apocalyptic melancholy in this article. Never an admirer of Americans in general or of their diplomacy in particular, Nicolson wrote with great insight and surprising charity his opinion of Byrnes, not only in this article but also in his private letters and diary, now published in the UK. All lives, public or private, are filled with strange encounters; but perhaps none is stranger in Byrnes' life than that this biographer of the diplomat Lord Curzon and the political writer Benjamin Constant, the husband of Vita Sackwell-West, and the Bloomsbury companion of Virginia Woolf, should observe the U.S. secretary of state, Jimmy Byrnes from Charleston, S.C., enter the Palace of the Luxembourg in 1946 and feel some sympathy and kinship with him.

441   *"Don't look that way to me"*: JFB, Folder 73(1), Script of Gridiron Club Dinner.
443   *"treated me like a human being"*: JFB, Vault File I, "Audio Tape, 9 November 1979."
443   *"able and conniving"*: Truman, *Off the Record*, 49.
443   *near-unanimous confidence*: For favorable and often slighted appraisals of Byrnes' performance as Secretary of State, see the chapter "Byrnes, the Underrated Secretary," in Bohlen, *Witness*, 243–57, and Chester Bowles, *Promises to Keep: My Years in Public Life, 1941–1969* (New York: Harper & Row, 1971), 58–60.
443   *quickly recruited Benjamin Cohen*: Byrnes, *Life*, 288.
443   *quickly fired Nelson A. Rockefeller*: Graham A. Stuart, *The Department of State: A History of Its Organization, Procedure, and Personnel* (New York: Macmillan, 1949), 425–27, 432–33, and the unpaginated chart "Organization of the Department of State."
444   *"spade work" would be completed*: JFB, Folder 557, "Transcript of Press Conference," 8 Feb. 1946, p. 11.
445   *"he differs markedly from Mr. Truman"*: James L. Gormly, "Secretary of State James F. Byrnes: An Initial British Evaluation," *South Carolina Historical Magazine* 79 (1978): 198–205.
445   *"Harry," rather than as "Mr. President"*: Quoted in Walter Isaacson and Evan Thomas, *The Wise Men: Six Friends and the World They Made* (New York: Simon and Schuster, 1986), 372.
445   *"running a race with John C. Calhoun"*: HST, Daniels Interview, pp. 119–205.
445   *Ivy League educated*: Godfrey Hodgson, *The Colonel: The Life and Wars of Henry Stimson, 1867–1950* (New York: Alfred A. Knopf, 1990), 172, 374, 386.
446   *"those little bastards"*: Quoted in Messer, *Alliance*, 126.
446   *"I know how to deal with the Russians"*: Quoted in Herken, "Russians," 53.
447   *"We've pushed these babies"*: Quoted in Messer, *Alliance*, 132.

447 *"typical senatorial fashion"*: JFB, Folder 602, "W.B.'s Book," entry for 13 Sept. 1945.
447 *followed Byrnes into the bathroom*: Ward, *Threat*, 42–43.
448 *"It took considerable courage"*: Bohlen, *Witness*, 257.
448 *"Russians are welshing"*: Quoted in Ward, *Threat*, 46.
449 *"situation was pretty bad"*: FRUS, 1945, 2:59–61.
449 *Byrnes argued against such publicity*: H. Bradford Westerfield, *Foreign Policy and Party Politics* (New York: Octagon Books, 1972), 199.
450 *"come to terms with the Chinese communists"*: Wallace, *Diary*, 521.
450 *"mixing various policies"*: Gardner, *Architects*, 98.
450 *Byrnes on his own initiative*: Byrnes, *Frankly*, 109.
451 *"put in my place and I stayed there"*: Bohlen, *Witness*, 250.
451 *larger* conference *of foreign ministers*: Ward, *Threat*, 61–63; Messer, *Alliance*, 153.
452 *"this was unexpected news"* to *"And so, on Christmas morning"*: Byrnes, *Frankly*, 115.
454 *"wants an agreement for its political effect"*: Kennan, *Memoirs*, 287–88.
454 *not attempted to tell Truman*: Truman, *Memoirs*, 548–49.
455 *"Goddamn it to hell"*: Quoted in Messer, *Alliance*, 156–57.
456 *"tired of babying the Soviets"*: Truman, *Off the Record*, 80.
457 *he kept in his files*: See the discussion of Truman's self-described "long hand spasms" in David McCullough, *Truman* (New York: Simon and Schuster, 1992), 480, 499–501.
457 *recognizing the Soviet sphere: NYT*, 31 Dec. 1945, p. 4, cols. 3–4.
458 *"more anti-Russian spirit"*: JFB, Folder 569(1), Donald Russell to Cassandra Connor, (undated) Jan. 1946.

18: Iranian Winter and a Cold Warrior

The events occurring in Iran during 1946, which occupied most of the first full year of Secretary Byrnes' tenure at the U.S. State Department, are the seeds from which have arisen crops of mutually warring academic historians. For the convenience of the common, educated reader, these historians can be grouped into at least four main bibliographical areas: (1) the revisionists who maintain that the Soviet military threat to the Iranian province of Azerbaijan in 1946 was willfully exaggerated by reports from right-wing Western journalists, State Department employees, and royalist Iranians; (2) revisionists who also interpret the U.S. diplomacy during this period, particularly the actions of Byrnes, as primarily motivated by a desire to obtain exclusive oil franchises for U.S. corporations rather than, as Byrnes claimed, to establish the legitimacy of the UN to mediate disputes between large nations and small ones; (3) revisionists as well as more establishmentarian historians who maintain that the 1946 crisis between Iran and the Soviet Union was peacefully resolved because the Iranian and Soviet leaders acting on their own initiatives and interests *agreed* to resolve it peacefully, and that the efforts of Byrnes and other Western diplomats at the UN were peripheral or, at worst, inimical to Iranian-Soviet peace; and (4) historians who maintain that there was no Iranian crisis of 1946 at all. Thus, interpretations of events in Iran vary from Truman's statement to W. Averell Harriman in the spring of 1946 that within a few weeks "we may be at war with the Soviet Union over Iran" (quoted in Herbert Feis, *From Trust to Terror: The Onset of the Cold War* [New York: W. W. Norton, 1970], 82–83) to Robert Messer's 524-page dissertation on Byrnes and Soviet diplomacy in which there is a one-page, three-paragraph mention (p. 439) of the events in 1946 in Iran. (At a 1979 symposium on "James F. Byrnes and the Origins of the Cold War," U.S. Appellate Judge Donald Russell, who in 1946 was Byrnes' assistant secretary at the State Department, began his remarks with a memorably sharp-tongued rebuke to Professor Messer, who was also present, concerning Messer's paper read that day in which Messer had made no mention whatever of U.S.-Iranian diplomacy in 1946. The reader will note that this symposium was held during the 1979–81 Iran–U.S. embassy crisis. See JFB, Vault File 1, "Audio Tape, 9 November 1979.")

The question of whether the Soviet military presence in Iran had been exaggerated has been raised by the revisionists John Gaddis in *The United States and the Origins of the Cold War*, Gabriel Kolko in *The Politics of War*, and Joyce and Gabriel Kolko, in *The Limits of Power: The World and United States Foreign Policy, 1945–1954*, (New York: Harper & Row, 1972), which describes the reports received by the U.S. government from its representatives in Azerbaijan as "rumors of a massive Soviet troop build-up," (p. 239). (Actually, the reports—or rumors—were of a massive armor buildup, much more worrisome to the West because Soviet tanks and their crews were at that time technologically and tactically superior to any other armored forces in the world, including those of the United States.) Although this rumors-or-report question cannot be answered in detail until Western historians have unimpeded access to military archives from the former Soviet Union, the Western historian Bruce R. Kuniholm in *The Origins of the Cold War in the Near East* (Princeton: Princeton Univ. Press, 1980), credibly demonstrates on pp. 317–24 from several independent sources that the Soviet armored buildup in Azerbaijan was massive and was intended for an offensive campaign. The reports to Secretary Byrnes by Robert Rossow, Jr., who from Dec. 1945 to June 1946 was the American consul at Tabriz, and which Rossow subsequently described in his article "The Battle of Azerbaijan, 1946," *Middle East Journal* 10 (1956): 17–32, therefore received an independent substantiation by scholars of the 1970s and 1980s.

The third question of oil as the primary motivation for U.S. actions toward Iran in the spring of 1946 is argued with great zeal by Gaddis, the Kolkos, and, with the most popular success, Daniel Yergin in *Shattered Peace: The Origins of the Cold War and the National Security State* (Boston: Houghton Mifflin, 1977), and the commercial best-seller, *The Prize: The Epic Quest for Oil, Money, and Power*. In the former Yergin states that acquisition of oil rights "was very much at the heart of the Iranian crisis, although American officials almost routinely denied it." He acknowledges the existence of the memorandum written by Byrnes and sent to the U.S. embassy at Teheran, quoted in this chapter, in which Byrnes orders in no uncertain terms that oil concessions not be discussed while the Iranian case is on the Security Council agenda; but Yergin deals with this documentary counterexample provided by Byrnes by writing that "though such a statement was accurate in a narrow sense, it was in a larger sense an exercise in mystification, an effort to disguise the American interest in order to avoid legitimizing the Russian one" (p. 181). Yergin insists upon interpreting Jimmy Byrnes as simply sly, and as oil slick.

This revisionist argument is credibly countered by two well-documented articles by Justus D. Doenecke: "Revisionists, Oil and Cold War Diplomacy," *Iranian Studies: A Bulletin of the Society for Iranian Cultural Social Studies* 3 (1970): 23–33, and "Iran's Role in Cold War Revisionism," *Iranian Studies* 5 (1972): 96–111. An account written at the time of the Iranian crisis by Herbert Feis, an economic adviser to the State Department, *Seen from the E. A.: Three International Episodes* (New York: Alfred A. Knopf, 1947), is very useful if read with caution, because Feis personally knew and professionally reported to Byrnes and usually wrote very sympathetically of him. It should also be noted that Feis was one of the proponents of the creation of the Petroleum Reserve Corporation in 1943.

Whether the Iranian crisis was any crisis at all, and whether Byrnes deserves praise, much less of sympathy, is answered in the negative so far as Jimmy Byrnes is concerned by Stephen L. McFarland, "A Peripheral View of the Origins of the Cold War: The Crisis in Iran, 1941–47," *Diplomatic History* 4 (1980): 333–51. Even the historian Joseph M. Jones, whose book *The Fifteen Weeks*: (*February 21–June 5, 1947*) (New York: Viking Press, 1955) is generally favorable to Byrnes as a successful secretary in dealing with the Soviets, concludes that his actions had limited immediate effect on the Soviet withdrawal from Iran and that the Kremlin decided that "it could probably achieve its ends [which Jones argues were the satellitization of Iran] over a somewhat longer period by promising to withdraw its troops, removing the case from the Security Council, and exerting continued, steady, but somewhat more reasonable pressure on Qavan" (p. 53).

That there *was* in fact a military and diplomatic crisis of international significance in Iran in 1946 is amply demonstrated by the excellent summaries found in Peter Avery, *Modern Iran* (New York: Praeger, 1965), 396–97, and in Barry M. Rubin, *Paved with Good Intentions: Iran and the American Experience* (New York: Oxford Univ. Press, 1980), 29–37, and by the detailed chronology of political and military events in Iran during early 1946 in Gary Hess, "The Iranian Crisis of 1945–46 and the Cold War," *Political Science Quarterly* 89 (1974): 117–46.

The domestic actions of Secretary Byrnes before and after the Iranian crisis in attempting to ameliorate the early excesses of the Truman administration's loyalty program—eventually to be legitimized, after Byrnes left, by Executive Order 9835—have not yet been fully appreciated, in part because the secretary himself after his retirement from the U.S. State Department and his assumption of the governorship of South Carolina found it politically embarrassing to be remembered as ever having been such a civil libertarian. Nevertheless, the *State Department Bulletin* issues from the years 1946–47 and transcripts of Byrnes' frequent press conferences as cited below offer evidence that due process, free speech, and the right to privacy were well protected among State Department employees and Foreign Service officers during 1945–46 by those two political conservatives—Secretary James F. Byrnes and Assistant Secretary Donald Russell.

460   *Byrnes had hosted a meeting*: Kuniholm, *Origins*, 182.
460   *"Anglo-Iranian Company"*: JFB, Folder 61, memorandum, Byrnes to Roosevelt, 4 Oct. 1943.
461   *"our government a commanding position"*: JFB, Folder 12(1), memorandum, Byrnes to Roosevelt, 25 Jan. 1944.
461   *pipeline raised isolationists' opposition*: Feis, *Seen from E. A.*, 146–55.
462   *"nation that runs out of it is whipped"*: JFB, Folder 1167(1), undated 1944 news clippings.
462   *a fait accompli*: See the statements by George Kennan regarding Byrnes' views of the irrevocability of Soviet-occupied territories, quoted in Ward, *Threat*, 65–66, 77. See also the statement by Mark Ethridge on the opinion he expressed to Secretary Byrnes, in the Ethridge report, that the Soviets were "hell-bent on holding on" to the East European countries occupied in 1945–46 by Soviet troops. HST, Oral History Interview with Mark F. Ethridge, p. 13.
462   *"got into another world war"*: Quoted in Yergin, *Prize*, 407.
463   *"continuing indefinitely" the Schwarzkopf mission*: FRUS, 1945, 3:534–36.
464   *oil-rich Iran*: Feis, *Seen from E. A.*, 176.

466   *"much water has flowed under the bridge"*: FRUS, 1945, 2:751–52.
466   *violated the terms of the tripartite agreement*: FRUS, 1946, 7:304.
466   *"advance commitments to either side"*: Ibid., 292–93.
467   *Byrnes promptly told Acheson*: Ibid., 293–94.
467   *troops guard British-owned refineries*: Feis, *Seen from E. A.*, 156–69. See also Doenecke, "Revisionists," 27–28: "When the British arrived that month [April 1944], for talks with the U.S. Petroleum Reserves Corporation [of which Byrnes was a member], they told the Americans that any United States proposal must provide for British, commercial, and military welfare."
468   *"count on United States backing"*: Kolko and Kolko, *Limits Power*, 238.
468   *"cloakroom compromise"*: Yergin, *Shattered*, 183. See also Doenecke, "Iran's Role," 100–101.
468   *written . . . by Adlai Stevenson*: FRUS, 1946, 7:309.
469   *said to have been "very rough"*: Ibid., 337.
469   *Schwarzkopf was receiving intelligence*: Ibid., 439.
469   *"Last night 20 tanks"*: Ibid., 340.
470   *"give it to them with both barrels"*: Ibid., 347.
470   *"to get out of Persia"*: Ibid., 348–49.
471   *"die in its infancy of inefficiency"*: Ibid., 389.
471   *"force consisting of 20 medium tanks"*: Ibid., 340.
471   *"I cannot overstress the seriousness"*: Ibid., 344.
471   *note of protest to the Soviet government*: Ibid., 340–41, reprinted as "U.S. Position on Soviet Troops in Iran," *Department of State Bulletin* 14 (17 March 1946): 435–36.
472   *"United Nations cannot prevent war"*: NYT, 1 March 1946, p. 1, col. 8. For British reaction, see ibid., p. 10, col. 1.
473   *"our military strength will be used"*: NYT, 16 March 1946, p. 1, col. 3.
473   *did not want any smudge of petroleum*: JFB, Folder 548, telegram, Byrnes to U.S. Embassy at Teheran, 8 April 1946. The "Top Secret" classification of this document at least suggests that Yergin is inaccurate in characterizing these instructions by Byrnes as an attempt to create a public "disguise."
474   *"We must put the matter"*: NYT, 27 March 1946, p. 1, col. 8.
474   *"will not be a nurse's aide"*: Bohlen, *Witness*, 252.
475   *promoted to brigadier general*: FRUS, 1946, 7:439.
475   *"empty cups and cigarette butts"*: Ibid., 561–62.
476   *"Sincere good wishes"*: Ibid., 563.
476   *"most successful diplomatic gambits"*: JFB, Folder 1465, McKeever to Byrnes, 28 March 1951.
476   *"Cold war began on March 4, 1946"*: Rossow, "Battle," 17.
477   *"crystallized during the Iranian showdown"*: Hess, "Crisis," 145.
477   *not under actual Soviet occupation*: Jones, *Fifteen*, 105.
478   *"not unworthy either of the conquerors"*: Wheeler-Bennett and Nicholls, *Semblance*, 188.
478   *State Department provided an airplane*: Fraser, *Labor*, 573.
478   *"national oil rivalries to force"*: See NYT, 13 Sept. 1946, p. 1, col. 1, and p. 2, cols. 6–7.
479   *"accept my resignation immediately"*: JBF, Folder 619(2), Byrnes to Russell, 18 Sept. 1946.
480   *"his recent Stuttgart pro-enemy speech"*: HST, PSF, telegram, CIO Executive Board to Truman, 10 Sept. 1946; unsent letter, Truman to Grant Oakes, CIO, 12 Sept. 1946.

480 *"some of our CIO friends"*: JFB, Folder 532, Pickney to Byrnes, 25 Oct. 1946, including attached handbill; Byrnes to Pickney, 8 March 1946.

481 *"messy way it had happened"*: Clifford, *Counsel*, 127.

481 *FBI arrested six men*: "Arrest of State Department Employee and Foreign Service Officer," *Department of State Bulletin* 12 (10 June 1945): 1088.

482 *"My dear Mr. Service"*: "Vindication of John S. Service: Letter from the Secretary of State," *Department of State Bulletin* 13 (26 Aug. 1945): 295.

483 *Service reinstated with back pay*: See the biographical entry on Service in Eleanora Schoenebaum, ed., *Political Profiles*, vol. 3 *The Truman Years* (New York: Facts on file, 1978), 498–99. See also "House Group Sifting Documents Clears Officers," *NYT*, 25 Oct. 1946, p. 10, cols. 4–5.

484 *subversive or communistically inclined*: CR, 79th Cong., 2d sess., A4891.

484 *"the use of 'gestapo' methods"*: JFB, Folder 575(2), Russell to Bartel Jonkman, 29 July 1946.

484 *"You can ruin a man's reputation"*: JFB, Folder 562, transcript of press conference, 26 July 1946, p. 14.

485 *did not disclose the names*: CR, 79th Cong., 2d sess., A4892.

485 *"only those persons who believe"*: Ibid., A4891.

485 *McCarthy used the text of Byrnes' letter*: Thomas C. Reeves, *The Life and Times of Joe McCarthy*, (Stein and Day, 1982), 225–27. See also Cabell Phillips, *The Truman Presidency: The History of a Triumphant Succession* (New York: Macmillan, 1966), 378–79.

486 *Iranian occupation by Communist subversives*: FRUS, 1946, 6:696–709.

486 *Byrnes termed a "splendid analysis"*: Quoted in Deborah Larson, *Origins of Containment: A Psychological Explanation* (Princeton: Princeton Univ. Press, 1985), 256.

486 *"usual reaching out of the pen"*: Kennan, *Memoirs*, 290.

486 *"an ideological monolith"*: Robert L. Messer, "Paths Not Taken: The United States Department of State and Alternatives to Containment, 1945–1946," *Diplomatic History* 1 (1977): 301.

487 *Byrnes was being defensive*: Clifford, *Counsel*, 112.

488 *"perhaps he was mistaken"*: FRUS, 1946, 6:683. This incident is also discussed in detail in Athan Theoharis, "James F. Byrnes: Unwitting Yalta Mythmaker," *Political Science Quarterly* 81 (1966): 581–92. The summary of Byrnes' press conference is found in "Agreement at Yalta on the Kuriles and Sakhalin," *Department of State Bulletin* 14 (10 Feb. 1946): 189.

489 *"membership of the Communist Party"*: The complete text of the Clifford-Elsey report is reproduced in Arthur Krock, *Memoirs: Sixty Years on the Firing Line* (New York: Funk & Wagnalls, 1968), 419–82. The reference to biological warfare is on p. 478.

489 *"most unfortunate section"*: Clifford, *Counsel*, 177.

489 *carried an anonymous story: Washington Post*, 8 March 1946, p. 7, col. 3.

489 *Byrnes . . . was abroad at foreign conferences*: Jones, *Fifteen*, 105.

490 *"as soon as my successor is appointed"*: HST, PPF, Byrnes to Truman, 19 Dec. 1946.

490 *"I realize full well"*: HST, PPF, Truman to Byrnes, 7 Jan. 1947.

490 *Byrnes had shown that it was possible*: Smith, *Clay*, 295.

491 *Byrnes thus was dropped*: Jones, *Fifteen*, 54, 153–54.

491 *forgot to ask for eternal youth*: Cited in Messer, *Alliance*, 215–16.

491 *"a little money"*: Quoted in Smith, *Clay*, 191.

19:   A DISQUISITION ON GOVERNMENT

Any discussion of post–World War II race relations in the South must begin with the masterly and comprehensive study of the then existing white political establishment, Numan Bartley's *The Rise of Massive Resistance: Race and Politics in the South during the 1950's* (Baton Rouge: Louisiana State Univ. Press, 1969). Also useful are William Berman's previously cited *Politics of Civil Rights in the Truman Administration*, Earl Black's *Southern Governors and Civil Rights: Racial Segregation as a Campaign Issue in the Second Reconstruction* (Cambridge: Harvard Univ. Press, 1976), and George Brown Tindall's *The Disruption of the Solid South* (Athens: Univ. of Georgia Press, 1972).

The impending crisis of the Clarendon Country, S.C., school suit, initially resolved in 1954 by the U.S. Supreme Court's first ruling in the *Brown* v. *Board of Education* case, is vividly anticipated in Robert Garson's *The Democratic Party and the Politics of Sectionalism, 1941–1948* (Baton Rouge: Louisiana State Univ. Press, 1974). Richard Kluger's *Simple Justice: The History of* Brown v. Board of Education *and Black America's Struggle for Equality* (New York: Alfred A. Knopf, 1975) is universally accepted as the authoritative history of that decision. Howard H. Quint's *Profile in Black and White: A Frank Portrait of South Carolina* (Washington, D.C.: Public Affairs Press, 1958) was written at great professional and possible physical risk to its author, formerly a South Carolina educator who left the left the state after his book's publication. The animus that his book provoked among the majority of its white readers in South Carolina had been matched only by the reactions of the majority of white southerners to the economic indictment of slavery in Hinton Helper's *The Impending Crisis of the South*. Helper, a North Carolina journalist, also found it professionally and physically in his interests to move to a northern state after his book's 1857 publication. The outraged reactions by most white southerners to the facts contained in both books reflect the closed societies each author found it necessary to leave.

By the time the Clarendon County suit had reached the Supreme Court, Harry S. Ashmore, the young journalist who a decade earlier had reported so honestly for the *Greenville News* of the destruction of homes along the Santee River, had returned to his native South from World War II and had begun to hit his intellectual and professional stride. While working as the editorial page editor for the Little Rock *Gazette*, Ashmore had several unique encounters with Byrnes during the late 1940s and early 1950s, and he won a Pulitzer Prize in 1958 for his editorials in support of President Eisenhower's decision in 1957 to use federal troops to enforce legal integration at Little Rock's Central High School. His subsequent book *Hearts and Minds* is indispensable for understanding what had become the central issue of southern and national domestic politics during those decades; it is also a mine of anecdotes concerning Jimmy Byrnes. In a two-hour telephone conversation from his California home with this author in 1993, Ashmore provided several other richly characterizing anecdotes concerning Jimmy Byrnes and the late politician's surviving friends, which for certain prudent reasons will not be repeated here in print.

Among particularly useful documents regarding Byrnes' political activities is an essay by Leslie Dunbar, of the Southern Regional Council, "The Changing Mind of the South: The Exposed Nerve," *Journal of Politics* 26 (1964): 3–21. Ralph McGill's "What Is Jimmy Byrnes Up to Now?" *Saturday Evening Post*, 14 Oct. 1950, a lively portrait of Byrnes caught in political midaction. Richard Hofstadter provides a scholarly analysis of the same political activities in his "From Calhoun to the Dixiecrats," *Social Research* 16 (1949): 135–50. Also among Governor Byrnes' contemporaries, W. F. Prioleau, for many years a political confidant and personal attorney of Byrnes, candidly and cogently expressed the ideology of Byrnes in an interview with the author in 1990. The lives of two other of Byrnes' contemporaries—one an intimate friend, John W. Davis, and the other a former political ally of Byrnes who split with Byrnes over the issue of race, Judge J. Waties Waring of Charleston—are well documented in William H. Harbaugh's *Lawyer's Lawyer: The Life of John W. Davis* (New York: Oxford Univ. Press, 1973) and Tinsley E. Yarbrough's *A Passion for Justice: J. Waties Waring and Civil Rights* (New York: Oxford Univ. Press, 1987).

The most significant of all historical documents, in its effect upon the daily lives of black and white southerners, is the brief first heard before the U.S. Supreme Court for the Oct. 1952 term by Thurgood Marshall on behalf of the young schoolboy Harry Briggs and others in the case of *Briggs* v. *Elliott* eventually combined with three other challenges to racially segregated schools, including *Brown* v. *Board of Education*.

493 *Byrnes made $125,000*: McGill, "What," 187.
495 *"the south can be"*: Clifford, *Counsel*, 192.
495 *"exposed nerve"*: Dunbar, "Mind," 3.
495 *"We highly commend"*: Quoted in Schlesinger, ed., *Elections*, 3182.
495 *"would be utterly"*: Quoted ibid., 3172.
496 *"In 1948, sincerely"*: *Lifetime*, 398.
496 *"Jimmy knew that"*: W. F. Prioleau interview, 1990.
497 *"It's official"*: Conversation quoted in Messer, *Alliance*, 223.
497 *"Byrnes Hits Trend"*: *NYT*, 19 June 1949, p. 2, col. 2.
498 *"Since your Washington & Lee Speech"*: HST, PSF, Box 159, Truman to Byrnes, 21 June 1949.
498 *"you are no Caesar"*: Ibid., Byrnes to Truman, 9 July 1949.
499 *"courageous victory"*: HST OF, Box 200, Byrnes to Truman, 20 Jan. 1949.
499 *"disloyal" Democrats*: Quoted in Messer, *Alliance*, 271.
499 *"deeper than intended"*: *Lifetime*, 400.
499 *"a vigorous attack"*: *NYT*, 22 Nov. 1949, p. 1, col. 1.
500 *"I think you"*: JFB, Folder 1349, Knopf to Byrnes, 26 Aug. 1949.
500 *"Dear Mr. Byrnes"*: Ibid., Knopf to Byrnes, 28 Nov. 1949.
500 *"What I stated"*: Ibid., Byrnes to Knopf, 3 Dec. 1949.
501 *"If we act"*: Quoted in Bartley, *Rise*, 50.
502 *"Here is the"*: Hofstadter, "Dixiecrats," 146.
502 *"Do you have"*: *NYT*, 19 Jan. 1950, sec. 4, p. 7, col. 1.
502 *"Byrnes-Truman Friendship"*: *U.S. News & World Report*, 3 Feb. 1950, 38–39.
502 *"trend of political events"*: *NYT*, 15 Jan. 1950, p. 1, col. 4.
503 *"the encroachment"*: McGill, "What," 184.
503 *Under the duress*: Garson, *Sectionalism*, 185.
503 *"no room"*: *NYT*, 18 Nov. 1950, p. 9, col. 3.
503 *"I am satisfied"*: *NYT*, 20 Nov. 1950, p. 18, col. 2.
504 *"It is our duty"*: Columbia *State*, 17 Jan. 1951, 5B.
504 *twenty-five days earlier*: Quint, *Profile*, 12–13.
505 *muddy waters of the Santee*: Kluger, *Justice*, 17–18.
506 *the first challenge*: Ibid., 380.
507 *"I told him that"*: Quoted ibid., 434.
507 *"Bull" Connor*: Black, *Governors*, 29–34.
508 *Byrnes gained passage*: Kluger, *Justice*, 420.
508 *"a reasonable time"*: Quoted ibid., 435–38.

509 *"choke off"*: quoted in Yarbrough, *Passion*, 181.
509 *"normal and not"*: Ibid., 187.
509 *three-judge panel*: Ibid., 192–96.
510 *"just throwing"*: Mrs. Waring quoted ibid., 189.
510 *"would put loyalty"*: *NYT*, 13 Nov. 1951, p. 3, col. 1.
511 *"know that boy's family"*: Ashmore, *Hearts*, 172–73.
511 *"We believe that"*: Quoted in Schlesinger, ed., *Elections*, 3291.
512 *"I always stand"*: Quoted in Tindall, *Disruption*, 51.
512 *four of the eleven*: Schlesinger, ed., *Elections*, 3337.
512 *"unanswerable"*: Quoted in Yarbrough, *Passion*, 197.
514 *Ku Klux Klan*: Kluger, *Justice*, 667, 669.
514 *"Mr. Davis was"*: Quoted in Harbaugh, *Lawyer*, 484.
515 *"the most fateful"*: *Washington Post*, 10 Dec. 1952, p. 1, col. 7.
515 *attorney general of Kansas*: Harbaugh, *Lawyer*, 503–4.
516 *"If conditions"*: Columbia *State*, 11 Dec. 1952, 7C.
517 *"not feel bound"*: Byrnes, *Lifetime*, 418. See also JFB, Folder 1470, Eisenhower to Byrnes, 14 Feb. 1953.
517 *"is truly good"*: JFB, Folder 1218, undated *Edwards* drafts.
518 *"had a fear"*: Quoted in Kluger, *Justice*, 760.
518 *"was scaring the shit"*: Ashmore, *Hearts*, 188.
518 *"Ben Tillman"*: *Brown* brief, p. 59.
519 *Davis was so certain*: Davis' remarks are quoted in a letter, JFB, Folder 1499, C. C. Wyche to Byrnes, 31 Dec. 1953.
519 *ruled that racially*: The entire text of the Court's decision is reprinted in Kluger, *Justice*, 983–93.
520 *"shocked to learn"*: *Charleston News and Courier*, 25 March 1955, p. 1, cols. 7–8.
520 *Byrnes put his arm*: JFB, Folder 1125, Byrnes to Professor William Harbaugh, 20 July 1965.
520 *"Dear Ben"*: JFB, Folder 1474, Schlesinger to Cohen, 24 May 1954.
521 *"You have a rare"*: Ibid., Cohen to Byrnes, 27 May 1954.
522 *"to make haste slowly"*: JFB, Folder 893, Eisenhower to Byrnes, 23 July 1957.
523 *"The house was"*: JFB, Folder 1055(2), S. Swint to Byrnes, 6 Jan. 1961, including undated NAACP material.
524 *"communing with the bass"*: JFB, undated interview, *Charlotte Observer*, 1963.
524 *The next day*: JFB, Folder 1105, Byrnes to Phillips Petroleum Co., 8 June 1964.
524 *"we have no"*: Ibid., W. David Smith of Phillips Petroleum Co. to Byrnes, 9 July 1964.

20: SOUTH CAROLINA CODA

Three books constitute a virtual how-to for anyone wishing to take control of a national political party's state apparatus and that state's government, control of the ideology of the national party itself, and control of the office of the presidency of the United States. The public life and career of Jimmy Byrnes are central to the text of each of these three. The books are Kevin Phillips' *The Emerging Republican Majority* (New Rochelle, N.Y.: Arlington House, 1969), Harry Dent's *The Prodigal South Returns to Power* (New York: Wiley, 1978), and Earl Black and Merle Black's *The Vital South: How Presidents Are Elected* (Cambridge: Harvard Univ. Press, 1992). Dent's book deserves to be more widely known. Dent, a former special counsel to Richard Nixon during his presidency, provides a vivid account of how the author and a few other Republicans in South Carolina turned their state, with the approval of Jimmy Byrnes, into a GOP electoral stronghold. Since its publication, *The Prodigal South* has been read by comparatively few students of southern and national politics, with the notable exception of the late Lee Atwater, Dent's fellow South Carolinian. Atwater, himself something of a prodigal son, frequently noted during his tenure as George Bush's presidential campaign director that among Atwater's favorite books for rereading were Harry Dent's book and the biography of Huey Long written by Harry T. Williams. The consequences of Atwater's reading habits for the outcome of the 1988 presidential election are obvious.

(It also should be of compelling interest to any reader concerned with the future of political debate that Phillips' *The Politics of Rich and Poor: Wealth and the American Electorate in the Reagan Aftermath* [New York: Random House, 1990] predicts a populist revival in reaction to the emergent majority. Phillips' book was intellectually anticipated on a regional level by Harry Williams' study of neo-Bourbon and populist conflict, *Romance and Realism in Southern Politics* [Baton Rouge: Louisiana State Univ. Press, 1961]. *If* scholars such as Williams, Phillips, the Black brothers, and Jordan Schwartz are correct, the American electorate soon will be highly receptive to a presidential candidate in either major party or a new third party who will be as sly and able as Jimmy Byrnes; as persistent and durable as Richard Nixon; as economically populist and racially divisive as Pitchfork Ben Tillman; and as eloquently charming and unhesitatingly brutal as Huey P. Long. And *if* these scholars are right, that future presidential candidate—man or woman—will come from the South or the Southwest.)

Byrnes unquestionably foresaw many of the electoral consequences for the South and the nation of the political actions he took in the years immediately before his death. Characteristically, Byrnes chose to express these opinions indirectly, as an unacknowledged primary source in publications by one of his former employees at the OWMR, Samuel Lubell. "Has Truman Lost the South?" which Lubell wrote for *Look* magazine (24 October 1954) featured on its front page a smiling Jimmy Byrnes identified as the primary politician who "now symbolizes the anti-Truman tide in the South." Lubell continued with Byrnes' unacknowledged assistance to chronicle the rise of the GOP in the South and, to Lubell's distress, the rise of race as a major factor in national campaigns. The books by Lubell that are very useful for indirectly approaching Jimmy Byrnes' political thoughts in the last years of his life include *Revolt of the Moderates* (New York: Harper, 1956), *White and Black: Test of a Nation* (New York: Harper & Row, 1964), and *The Hidden Crisis in American Politics* (New York: W. W. Norton, 1970).

Other books that shed light on Byrnes' political actions or that use incidents from his public career as examples of an appeal to a changing electorate are the previously cited Dewey Grantham, *The Life and Death of the Solid South*, George Mowry, *Another Look at the Twentieth-Century South*, and George Brown Tindall, *The Disruption of the Solid South*; Robert B. Highsaw, ed., *The Deep South in Transformation: A Symposium* (University: Univ. of Alabama Press, 1964); Jack Bass and Walter DeVries, *The Transformation of Southern Politics: Social Change and Political Consequence since 1945* (New York: Basic Books, 1971); and Alexander P. Lamis, *The Two-Party South*, 2d ed. (New York: Oxford Univ. Press, 1990). The last book is particularly useful in appreciating Byrnes' political accomplishment in reversing the voting trends of white southerners; it quotes J. Strom Thurmond, Byrnes' fellow U.S. senator from South Carolina, as musing in 1978 that, "especially among the less-enlightened" class of people in South Carolina, "there's still that stigma against the Republicans." The reason for the hatred of the GOP, Senator Thurmond patiently explained, "goes back to the military rule of 1866 to 1876." The reader should remember that Jimmy Byrnes was born only six years after Pitchfork Ben Tillman and other Red Shirts had violently overthrown the radical-Republican-sponsored state government in South Carolina that had allowed representation of black citizens, and that the GOP had ever since the Compromise of 1877 been trying to regain its electoral strength in the South. Hence, Jimmy Byrnes' endorsements of Richard Nixon and the Republican platforms in 1960 and 1968 were even more remarkable.

Nixon's memoirs, *RN*, offer another valuable source for Byrnes' political activities during his last years. The papers of Richard M. Nixon available to the public at the Nixon library and museum, at Yorba Linda, Calif., contain many items of correspondence about and with Byrnes that are not found in the papers that Jimmy Byrnes chose to make available to the public in the collection of *his* papers deposited in Clemson, S.C. It should be remembered that Byrnes also at least once chose to make a shorthand transcript of a telephone conversation with Richard Nixon regarding the upcoming 1960 presidential election, and that this record apparently was made without Nixon's knowledge. The bibliographical irony an author could make of the secrecy and the desire to manipulate history inherent in these two archival collections is too facile for discussion; more important, the bibliographical evidence reveals a genuine sympathy between these two "black Irish" politicians despite their habitual political caution and distrust of strangers.

There was reason for that caution and distrust of strangers. Accounts unfriendly to both Byrnes and Nixon during the years of the southern strategy, but useful for a comprehensive view, are the late Ralph David Abernathy's autobiography, *And the Walls Came Tumbling Down* (New York: Harper & Row, 1989), and Bernard Schwartz's extended case study of court-ordered busing, *Swann's Way* (New York: Oxford Univ. Press, 1986). Justice William O. Douglas' previously cited *Court Years* also treats Byrnes unkindly. A masterly and comprehensive social history of the events of the last decades of Byrnes' life, Herbert S. Parmet's *Richard Nixon and His America* (Boston: Little, Brown, 1990), is much more balanced.

Jimmy Byrnes and Richard Nixon both experienced galling defeats in their presidential ambitions, and neither politician ever found it easy to forget; it is for the reader of this biography to decide from the evidence whether Jimmy Byrnes ever chose to forgive.

526   *"Nice fellow"*: RMN, memorandum from vice president's secretary to Nixon, 24 July 1958.
527   *make the South more amendable*: For the change in voting loyalties in Byrnes' home city, see Bernard Cosman, "Presidential Republicanism in the South, 1960," *Journal of Politics* 24 (1962): 310, table 4.
528   *unequivocal pro-FEPC plank*: Schlesinger, ed., *Elections*, 3509.
528   *"house of our fathers"*: Quoted in Woodward, *Origins*, 1–3.
529   *"we might be driven out of the political house"*: Quoted in Bartley, *Rise*, 155.
530   *"For all presidential elections"*: Black and Black, *Vital South*, 56.
530   *"one of your boys was a candidate"*: JFB, Folder 339, Byrnes to Joseph Kennedy, Sr., 17 July 1946.
531   *pragmatic and calculating Irishmen*: JFB, Folder 92(2), Byrnes to Doyle, 16 Sept. 1963.
531   *"Nixon is a much better man"*: JFB, Folder 1011(1), Byrnes to Henry Cauthen, 10 May 1960.

532 *"price is too heavy"*: JFB, Folder 1027, "Tele-call Nixon to JFB," transcript of Byrnes' shorthand notes. Internal evidence suggests that these notes were taken by Byrnes in late summer 1960. However, the transcript is undated, and at least one page of the transcript apparently was removed before this document was placed by Byrnes in his collection of public papers.

532 *"I shall vote for Richard Nixon"*: RMN, statement by James S. [*sic*] Byrnes, 22 Sept. 1960.

533 *"up strode James F. Byrnes"*: *Washington Post*, 4 Nov. 1960, p. 12, cols. 4–8.

534 *loyalty to the Democratic party*: Cosman, "Republicanism," 313.

534 *"how deeply grateful I am"*: RMN, Nixon to Byrnes, 11 Jan. 1961.

535 *"sufficient number of Negroes"*: RMN, Nixon to Byrnes, 14 Nov. 1960.

535 *Johnson's ambitions for the presidency*: JFB, Folder 1023, Byrnes to John Long, 16 Sept. 1960.

536 *"far more brilliant"*: Quoted in Robert Dallek, *Lone Star Rising: Lyndon Johnson and His Times, 1908–1960* (New York: Oxford Univ. Press, 1991), 451.

537 *"Bring me a drink"*: Dent, *Prodigal*, 66.

537 *"never our first love"*: Ibid., 76.

537 *"foundation of my strategy"*: Nixon, *RN*, 316.

537 *southerners were persuaded to back Nixon*: Parmet, *Nixon*, 515–16.

538 *the "fool's gold"*: Quoted in Bass and DeVries, *Transformation*, 29.

538 *"It merely forbids segregation"*: Quoted in Schwartz, *Swann's*, 51–55.

539 *"That kind of activity"*: "Nixon Raps HEW on Schools, Favors 'Freedom of Choice,' " *Charlotte Observer*, 13 Sept. 1968, p. 1, cols. 2–4.

539 *videotape of the Charlotte interview*: Dent, *Prodigal*, 112–13.

541 *"Negro support is not necessary"*: Phillips, *Majority*, 289, 467–68.

541 *"don't even want them"*: Quoted in Garry Wills, *Nixon Agonistes: The Crisis of the Self-Made Man* (Boston: Houghton Mifflin, 1969), 265.

542 *"he would not be available"*: Abernathy, *Walls*, 551–52.

542 *"we came to you"*: Washington *Star*, 10 April 1972.

542 *death . . . of Cassandra Connor*: Columbia *State*, 11 Jan. 1969, p. 1, col. 1.

543 *shock would kill him*: Grant, *Baruch*, 329.

543 *a visibly shaken Byrnes*: NYT, 21 June 1965, p. 1, cols. 7–6.

544 *"I was attacked"*: Byrnes, *Lifetime*, 390.

544 *"up in West Virginia"*: Quoted in Reeves, *McCarthy*, 225–26.

544 *"real, but less often remarked"*: Byrnes, *Lifetime*, 324.

544 *"Isn't it ironic"*: JFB, Folder 1465, McKeever to Byrnes, 28 March 1951.

544 *"Mr. McKeever is right"*: Quoted in Porter McKeever obituary, *NYT*, 4 March 1992, p. 21, col. 1.

545 *has been completely ignored*: See, for example, the absence of any mention of Byrnes in William C. Berman's discussion of the *Amerasia* incident, or at any other point in Berman's essay "Civil Rights and Civil Liberties," in Kirkendall, ed., *Field*, 200–201.

545 *"Mom" and "Pop" Byrnes*: JFB, Folder 1167(1), news clipping "Jim Byrnes Finds Fountain of Youth," Associated Press, 3 Jan. 1967; also letter to the author, from James F. Byrnes Foundation, 26 March 1991.

546 *"peddler of cocaine"*: Douglas, *Years*, 27.

546 *Even more regrettable*: See the drafts of *Edwards* and the responding memorandum by Chief Justice Stone in JFB, Folder 1218. Chief Justice Stone's

memorandum of 13 Nov. 1941 also is filed in the National Archives, the Papers of Harland Fisk Stone, Container 74. These papers have been available at the National Archives to Justice Douglas or to any other members of the public since 1957.

547 *"Master of Men": NYT*, 10 April 1972, p. 1, col. 2.

ACKNOWLEDGMENTS

A book that has been eight years in the making is a labor of love, although not necessarily on the part of the author. Numerous acts of generosity and kindness, performed over nearly a decade by friends from New York State to Alabama from 1985 to 1993 have made possible my completion of this biography.

Foremost among those whose personal kindness must be acknowledged are the members of the Rash family of the Carolinas, who for generations have provided their neighbors across the southern Appalachian Mountains with their gifts of religious faith, their talents at storytelling, at literature, and at the visual arts, and with their willingness to provide a bed and a place at their supper table to literary friends in need. Particularly, I wish to thank Ron and Ann Rash of Pendleton, South Carolina, and Tom and Susan Rash of Buncombe County, North Carolina.

Others to whom I am personally indebted include Professor Harvey Strum of the Sage Colleges of Albany and Troy, New York. During the two years when I was completing research for this book at the FDR Library at Hyde Park, New York, and when I felt like a stranger in a strange land, Harvey provided me with both friendship and intellectual challenge.

It was my great privilege during this book's preparation to talk several times with the late Porter McKeever, a former member of the U.S. Mission to the United Nations, a biographer of Adlai E. Stevenson, and a loyal friend of James F. Byrnes. Mr. McKeever never intimated to me during our telephone conversations the trials of a fatal illness he was then facing; he instead chose to talk encouragingly to me of this biography, to which he contributed substantial insights. Mr. McKeever invited me to dine with him at the Asia Society when I next returned to New York City, an invitation I was unable to accept because of his untimely death in 1992. His cheerfulness, generosity, and diplomatic integrity will be remembered. Grace is strength.

I also wish to thank many friends and members of my family who as well took time from the demands of their own lives to aid me in the preparation of this book. They include Jeanne Bross, Mary Eberhart, Professor Patricia VanDecar, Terry Thomason, USMC, my brother Brian Sellers, and my parents, Jack and Rosemary Sellers. Dallas Ball, Charles Deal, and James Williams, each a South Carolina attorney with a compelling narrative gift and considerable legal knowledge, aided me in informal discussions of southern politics and U.S. constitutional law. Also below the Mason-Dixon line, the noted scholar of southern humor and the foremost biographer of Hank Williams Sr., Professor William Koon of Clemson University, encouraged my literary efforts by providing occasional beefsteak and bourbon. Jack and Jill Rubin, and Jane and Calvin Reeves, both of Clemson, South Carolina, extended me personal credit at their respective businesses far beyond reasonable expectations of literary rewards. A fellowship in nonfiction writing from the Mary Roberts Rinehart Foundation also provided financial and personal freedom in the summer of 1987.

Beyond mere manners and politeness are the debts of personal gratitude I owe to my agent, John Ware, who is surely the most compassionate man on his side of Central Park. I must also express my professional respect and personal gratitude to my outstanding editor at W. W. Norton and Company, Gerald Howard. More than once, Gerry has recalled to my mind the lines of James Dickey's poem "The Bee," written in honor of the football coaches of Clemson College in 1942. They

urge and urge. They want you better
Than you are.

DAVID ROBERTSON
Pendleton, South Carolina
August 1993

INDEX